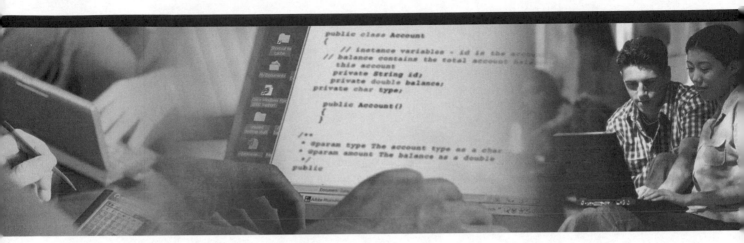

Cisco Networking Academy Program

Fundamentals of Java Programming Companion Guide

Cisco Networking Academy Program
Fundamentals of Java Programming Companion Guide

Cisco Systems, Inc.

Cisco Networking Academy Program

Course Sponsored by Sun Microsystems

Copyright © 2004 Cisco Systems, Inc.

Published by:
Cisco Press
201 West 103rd Street
Indianapolis, IN 46290 USA

Printed in the United States of America   1 2 3 4 5 6 7 8 9 0

First Printing   July 2003

Library of Congress Cataloging-in-Publication Number: 2002104923

ISBN: 1-58713-089-0

Trademark Acknowledgments

Warning and Disclaimer

Feedback Information

At Cisco Press, our goal is to create in-depth technical books of the highest quality and value. Each book is crafted with care and precision, undergoing rigorous development that involves the unique expertise of members from the professional technical community.

Readers' feedback is a natural continuation of this process. If you have any comments regarding how we could improve the quality of this book, or otherwise alter it to better suit your needs, you can contact us through e-mail at networkingacademy@ ciscopress.com. Please make sure to include the book title and ISBN in your message.

We greatly appreciate your assistance.

Publisher	*John Wait*
Editor-in-Chief	*John Kane*
Executive Editor	*Carl Lindholm*
Cisco Representative	*Anthony Wolfenden*
Cisco Press Program Manager	*Sonia Torres Chavez*
Manager, Marketing Communications, Cisco Systems	*Scott Miller*
Cisco Marketing Program Manager	*Edie Quiroz*
Production Manager	*Patrick Kanouse*
Development Editor	*Deb Doorley*
Project Editor	*San Dee Phillips*
Copy Editor	*Krista Hansing*
Technical Editors	*Callum Kateen*
	Wayne Brookes
Assistant Editor	*Sarah Kimberly*
Cover Designer	*Louisa Adair*
Team Coordinator	*Tammi Ross*
Compositor	*Octal Publishing, Inc.*
Indexer	*Brad Herriman*

CISCO SYSTEMS

Corporate Headquarters
Cisco Systems, Inc.
170 West Tasman Drive
San Jose, CA 95134-1706
USA
www.cisco.com
Tel: 408 526-4000
800 553-NETS (6387)
Fax: 408 526-4100

European Headquarters
Cisco Systems International BV
Haarlerbergpark
Haarlerbergweg 13-19
1101 CH Amsterdam
The Netherlands
www-europe.cisco.com
Tel: 31 0 20 357 1000
Fax: 31 0 20 357 1100

Americas Headquarters
Cisco Systems, Inc.
170 West Tasman Drive
San Jose, CA 95134-1706
USA
www.cisco.com
Tel: 408 526-7660
Fax: 408 527-0883

Asia Pacific Headquarters
Cisco Systems, Inc.
Capital Tower
168 Robinson Road
#22-01 to #29-01
Singapore 068912
www.cisco.com
Tel: +65 6317 7777
Fax: +65 6317 7799

Cisco Systems has more than 200 offices in the following countries and regions. Addresses, phone numbers, and fax numbers are listed on the
Cisco.com Web site at www.cisco.com/go/offices.

Argentina • Australia • Austria • Belgium • Brazil • Bulgaria • Canada • Chile • China PRC • Colombia • Costa Rica • Croatia • Czech Republic
Denmark • Dubai, UAE • Finland • France • Germany • Greece • Hong Kong SAR • Hungary • India • Indonesia • Ireland • Israel • Italy
Japan • Korea • Luxembourg • Malaysia • Mexico • The Netherlands • New Zealand • Norway • Peru • Philippines • Poland • Portugal
Puerto Rico • Romania • Russia • Saudi Arabia • Scotland • Singapore • Slovakia • Slovenia • South Africa • Spain • Sweden
Switzerland • Taiwan • Thailand • Turkey • Ukraine • United Kingdom • United States • Venezuela • Vietnam • Zimbabwe

Overview

Table of Contents

Chapter 2   Object-Oriented Programming 73

Chapter 3   Java Language Elements 173

Introduction

Cisco Networking Academy Program Fundamentals of Java Programming Companion Guide provides a conceptual understanding of object-oriented programming. The course also teaches students how to use the Java language's object-oriented technologies to solve business problems. Students will learn how to create classes, objects, and applications using the language. Topics also include language fundamentals and the Java language application programming interface (API). Additionally, the course addresses the demand for training and preparation for the Sun Certified Programmer for Java2 Platform.

As with all programming language topics, students find that their studies are best complemented by hands-on lab exercises. To that end, Cisco Press offers the *Cisco Networking Academy Program Fundamentals of Java Programming Lab Companion*, which includes comprehensive lab exercises that can be completed individually or in small groups. The *Cisco Networking Academy Program Fundamentals of Java Programming Engineering Journal and Workbook* provides additional information, exercises, and review questions that reinforce what the student has learned.

The Audience for This Book

This book's audience includes students interested in learning basic and advanced Java programming skills and preparing for the Sun Certified Programmer for Java 2 Platform. In particular, this book is targeted at students in the Cisco Networking Academy Program, which is offered in schools around the world. In the classroom, this book can serve as a supplement to the online curriculum.

Another audience for this book includes Java programmers presently working in the industry and individuals striving to become Java certified. This book has a broad appeal and is useful both as a reference and as an introductory text on Java programming.

How This Book Is Organized

This book is divided into 15 chapters and five appendixes:

Chapter 1, "What Is Java?," introduces Java as an object-oriented programming language.

Chapter 2, "Object-Oriented Programming," describes the fundamentals of object-oriented design.

Chapter 3, "Java Language Elements," includes topics such as data types, syntax rules, and keywords that constitute the Java language.

Chapter 4, "Java Language Operators and Control Structures," illustrates expressions for manipulating object data as well as logic control structures.

Chapter 5, "Basics of Defining and Using Classes," introduces object design methodology and syntax rules for creating Java classes.

Chapter 6, "`System`, `String`, `StringBuffer`, `Math`, and Wrapper Classes," illustrates the flexibility and efficiency of using the predefined classes included in the Java API.

Chapter 7, "Arrays," describes management of a group of objects as a collection.

Chapter 8, "Classes and Inheritance," introduces inheritance and code reuse as fundamental principles of object-oriented programming.

Chapter 9, "Understanding Packages," demonstrates how the student can create packages of Java classes and access the rich library of packages in the Java API.

Chapter 10, "Creating GUIs Using AWT," explores the java.awt package of classes specifically designed to create graphical applications.

Chapter 11, "Applets and Graphics," describes Java's implementation on the Internet through applets.

Chapter 12, "Exceptions," explains the methodology for managing program errors and creating robust applications.

Chapter 13, "Files, Streams, Input, and Output," describes the Java classes used to send and receive data from a Java program.

Chapter 14, "Collections," introduces the java.util package and the collections framework that provide powerful tools for managing multiple objects.

Chapter 15, "Threads," explores concurrent processing of code for increased efficiency in Java programming.

This Book's Features

This book contains several elements that help you learn about Java programming:

- **Figures, examples, and tables**—This book contains figures, examples, and tables that help to explain concepts, commands, and syntax structure. Figures illustrate Java programming features, and examples provide students with sample Java syntax. In addition, tables provide syntax summaries and comparisons of features and characteristics.

- **Notes, warnings, and tech notes**—These sidebars highlight important information about a subject. This book also includes tech notes, which offer background information on related topics and real-world implementation issues.

- **Chapter summaries**—At the end of each chapter is a summary of the concepts covered in the chapter, which provides a synopsis of the chapter and can serve as a study aid.

- **Review questions**—After the chapter summaries in each chapter are ten review questions that serve as an end-of-chapter assessment. The questions are designed to reinforce the concepts introduced in the chapter and to help students evaluate their understanding before moving on.

The conventions used to present command syntax in this book are as follows:

- **Boldface** indicates commands and keywords that are entered literally as shown. In examples (not syntax), boldface indicates user input (for example, a **javac** command).

- *Italics* indicates arguments for which you supply values.

- Square brackets ([ ]) indicate optional elements.

- Vertical bars (|) separate alternative, mutually exclusive elements.

- Braces and vertical bars within square brackets—for example, [x {y | z}]—indicate a required choice within an optional element. You do not need to enter what is in the brackets, but if you do, you have some required choices in the braces.

About the CD-ROM

A CD-ROM accompanies this book to further enhance your learning experience. The CD-ROM contains a test engine with Java practice exam questions, interactive e-Lab Activities, BlueJ tutorials, Java 1.4 SDK versions, and documents of Java code examples. These materials support self-directed study by allowing you to engage in learning and skill-building exercises outside the classroom. The CD-ROM also provides the following:

- An easy-to-use graphical user interface
- Information and activities not found online
- Accurate and concise feedback on practice exam questions
- Learner-directed practice and study
- Flexibility for learners of all levels

Finally, these learning tools emphasize not only conceptual material, but also the importance of practicing what you have learned. The CD-ROM helps you understand and use the Java programming language, and make the connection between theory and practice.

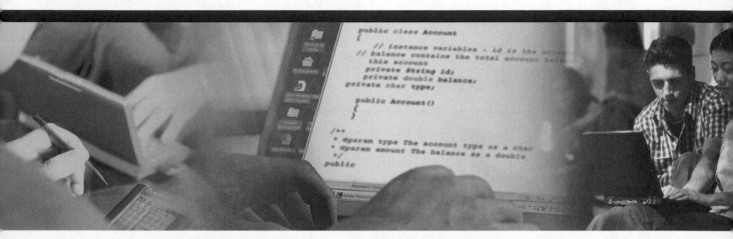

Upon completion of this chapter, you will be able to

- Understand computer basics
- Describe a programming language
- Describe Java
- Understand the Java environment basics
- Understand a Java program
- Enter data at runtime for the Java program
- Identify programming error messages
- Understand integrated development environments (IDEs)
- Understand the banking application case study

Chapter 1

What Is Java?

This chapter is an introduction to the Java programming language. It explains how a computer operates, discusses the different programming techniques, and reviews the history of Java and why it is such a popular programming language. Additionally, it covers the elements of a Java program and teaches how to create and run a Java program. Students can use this knowledge to create and run their own Java program.

Java is a very dynamic and popular computer programming language. The use of Java has increased over the past five years and, by all accounts, will continue to do so. This course teaches the Java programming techniques needed to create powerful applications and web-enabled programs. In this course, students create a virtual bank (the JBANK) and its banking program.

Computer Basics

The computer might seem to be a recent phenomenon. However, the Babylonians invented the early abacus (or abaci), a simple mechanical adding machine (counting board), more than 5000 years ago. An article about the history of the abacus can be found at www.ee.ryerson.ca:8080/~elf/abacus/history.html. In addition, mechanical computers first appeared in Western Europe at the beginning of the 17th century.

In 1623, a German philosopher named Wilhelm Schickard (1592–1635) invented the first digital calculating machine called a "calculating clock." As shown in Figure 1-1, it was a six-digit machine that could add, subtract, and indicate overflow by ringing a bell. Mounted on the machine was a set of Napier's Rods (or Bones), a memory aid that facilitated multiplication. In 1960, the machine was reconstructed from the original plans and was found to be proficient at adding and subtracting numbers. From these early beginnings, computers have grown more sophisticated and powerful, and have become an integral part of society.

Today, computers are smaller, faster, and cheaper. They can also be linked to form networks. The largest network is the Internet, which is composed of many smaller networks and allows those who have access to it to send, receive, and share information.

For this course, a rudimentary understanding of terms such as *hardware, software, operating systems, applications, programs,* and *computer languages* is essential. The meaning of these terms is explored over the course of this chapter.

Figure 1-1 Calculating Clock

This section consists of the following topics:

- Brief history of computers
- Brief future sketch of computers
- Pervasive nature of computers and computing in today's society
- Types of computing
- Hardware
- Software
- Applications
- Operating systems
- Abaci

Brief History of Computers

Before beginning a discussion of the Java language, a brief introduction into the history of the computer is relevant. This section briefly describes four major products within the computer field.

This section consists of the following topics:

- Abacus
- Mainframes
- PCs
- Hand-held computers

Abacus

The abacus is a mechanical aid used in the past by merchants for counting items of merchandise. These appear to have originated about 500 B.C. as stone or wooden boards with lines on them; coins or tokens were placed between the lines to aid in counting. The earliest surviving board is the Salamis tablet, used by the Babylonians around 300 B.C.

The modern abacus consists of a wooden frame with beads on wires, again used for counting. The different wires are used for the 0 place, the 10s place, the 100s place, and the 1000s place in our counting system.

The earliest such abaci appeared in Mesoamerica (Aztec) about 900–1000 A.D. and consisted of maize kernels set on strings on a wooden frame. Similar versions were used in China about 1200 A.D., this time consisting of beads on strings on a wooden frame.

More Information
See www.ee.ryerson.ca:8080/~elf/abacus/history.html.

Mainframes

IBM has been the dominant company in the mainframe arena. The paradigm in the mainframe arena is different from that in the PC arena (described later): It consists of massive centralized computing power with dumb terminals used to access the centralized computer. Until the PC revolution, mainframes were the dominant computer life form.

Mainframe computers were not born overnight. A number of earlier products were tested and improved upon before resulting in today's modern mainframe computers. The following list documents some of those major steps in the development of the mainframe computer:

- Charles Babbage invented his difference engine (1822) and analytical engine (1833), two mechanical calculators.

- Harvard University's Howard Aiken worked with IBM on the Mark I Automatic Sequence Controlled Calculator from 1941–1944. Using electromechanical relays for switches, the calculator could perform four arithmetic operations, logarithmic functions, and trig functions.

- In 1946, J. Presper Eckert and John W. Mauchly, at the University of Pennsylvania, created the Electronic Numerical Integrator and Computer (ENIAC), which could handle 50 division problems or 350 multiplication problems per second. The machine was 18×80 feet in size.

- Eckert and Mauchly then worked with Remington Rand to create the Universal Automatic Computer (UNIVAC). This was sold to the U.S. Census Bureau in 1951. By using memory, UNIVAC could store programs, allowing software reconfiguring of the machine for different programs.

- In 1953, IBM developed its first large commercial computer, the IBM 701. The computer used vacuum tubes as switches and executed 17,000 instructions per second.

- Between 1954–1959, the FORTRAN language was created and issued. The COBOL, LISP, and ALGOL computer languages were created between 1955 and 1960.

- In 1957, IBM released the IBM 305 Random Access Method of Accounting and Control (RAMAC) computer storage disk system.

- In 1959, IBM replaced the vacuum tubes in IBM 701 with transistors. IBM 7090 was a fully transistorized mainframe capable of 229,000 calculations per second.

- In 1964, IBM introduced the System/360 with a choice of 5 processors and 19 combinations of speed, memory, and power. In 1971, IBM released floppy disk storage. In 1975, the first IBM portable computer, IBM 5100 (50 lb), was introduced.

- Since then, IBM has introduced variations on the 360-series computers and has moved into PCs, hand-helds, and supercomputers. In 1997, IBM Deep Blue, a 32-node IBM RS/6000 SP computer that can assess 200 million chess moves per second, played and defeated world chess champion Garry Kasparov. Such computers have practical applications for real-world applications such as weather forecasting and modeling.

- As we move into the future, the world computer markets appear to divide into a couple of major niches: smaller personal-type computers and larger mainframes/supercomputers. Applications for these two kinds of computers will be different.

More Information
See these resources:
www-1.ibm.com/ibm/history/
www.digidome.nl/ibm1.htm
icarus.brainerd.net/~kuck/history/mainfram.html
www.chac.org/chhistpg.html#HistPg_CompHist
www.llcc.cc.il.us/dbeverid/histintr.htm

PCs

Just as the mainframe took time to develop, the advent of the personal computer (PC) didn't occur quickly either. This section documents the products that were built upon to create what is today known as the PC:

- In 1947, William Shockley, Walter Brattain, and John Bardeen invented the point-contact transistor amplifier.
- In 1958, Jack Kilby built the first integrated circuit at Texas Instruments. In 1960, Digital Equipment brought to market the first minicomputer, PDP-1. Then in 1962, Douglas Engelbart invented the computer mouse; he patented it the following year. In 1964, John Kemeny and Thomas Kurtz developed BASIC at Dartmouth College. IBM created the first floppy disk in 1967. In 1968, Robert Noyce and Gordon Moore founded Intel Corporation, and Engelbart demonstrated the keyboard, keypad, mouse, and windows at the Joint Computer Conference. In 1969, Honeywell introduced the first home computer, the H316, priced at about $10,000, and IBM created SCAMP, the first personal computer.
- In 1970, Xerox created the Palo Alto Research Center (PARC), which ultimately invented many of the PC concepts used today. Intel laid out circuitry for the 4004 microprocessor. Bell labs created the UNIX language. 1971 brought the first working 4004 microprocessors from Intel. Texas created the first microcomputer on a chip. Wang Laboratories created the Wang 1200 word-processor system, a killer application that popularized the use of computers. In 1972, Intel introduced the 200-KHz 8008 chip, with 3500 transistors. Kernighan and Ritchie developed the C programming language. Wang Laboratories introduced the 2200 series of small business computers.
- In 1972, Intel introduced the 8080 microprocessor 8-bit, 2 KHz chip. RCA introduced one of the first RISC chips, the 1802 processor. Motorola released the 6800 chip, an 8-bit microprocessor. Popular Electronics published an article announcing the Altair 8800 computer in kit form, using a 2-MHz Intel 8080 processor and

256 bytes of RAM. Bill Gates and Paul Allen wrote BASIC for the 8080 processor. In 1975, Digital Equipment introduced the LSI-11 microcomputer, which used a 16-bit architecture. IBM introduced the IBM 5100 portable computer, which sold for about $10,000.

- In 1976, Steve Wozniak and Steve Jobs created the Apple I computer, formed the Apple Computer Company, sold their first computers, and went on to develop Apple II. Intel released the 5-MHz 8085 processor. IBM created the Inkjet printer.

- Since then, the personal computer revolution has taken society by storm, creating hundreds of thousands of jobs, increasing productivity, and creating wealth across the world. Current desktop machines feature 2.2-GHz microprocessors with RAM of 512 KB to 1 MB, along with 100-GB hard drives, DVD-ROM drives, CD-writable drives, and 17- to 19-inch monitors.

More Information
See the following resource:
www.islandnet.com/~kpolsson/comphist/

Hand-Held Computers

With personal computing becoming smaller and increasingly less cumbersome, it was only a matter of time before computers could be held in the hand. The next few paragraphs document how the rise in hand-held computers began:

- In 1972, Hewlett-Packard introduced the first scientific hand-held calculator (HP-35).

- In 1980, Radio Shack introduced the TRS-80 pocket computer with 1.9 KB of memory. In 1982, Sharp, Radio Shack, HP, NEC, Sanyo, and Toshiba all introduced hand-held computers, the best of which used a 4-MHz microprocessor, 48 KB of ROM, 16 KB of RAM, and a 40×2–character LCD screen. In 1983, Commodore Business Machines, Radio Shack, Casio, Canon, National, Texas Instruments, and Sharp all had pocket computer entries to the market. The best display was an 8-line $\times$ 32–character LCD. In 1984, Seiko introduced the first wristwatch calculator. In 1989, Poqet Computer introduced Poqet PC computer, with 512 KB of RAM, 640 KB of ROM, a 7-MHz Intel 80C88 microprocessor, and an 80×25 text screen, for the cost of approximately $2000.

- In 1992, the term "personal digital assistant" was coined by Apple chairman John Sculley. Eo introduced a hand-held, pen-based microcomputer, the Personal Communicator 880, with a 30-MHz processor, 4 MB of RAM, and a 480×640 screen; it was $13 \times 9 \times 1$ inches in size, a bit on the large side. In 1993, Amstrad,

Apple, and Casio had hand-held entries to market. The best used 20-MHz processors, 1 MB of RAM, 4 MB of ROM, and a 2.8 × 4–inch LCD screen. In 1994, Apple Computer introduced the Newton MessagePad 110, with a 20-MHz processor and 1 MB of RAM. In 1996, 3Com introduced the Palm Pilot and sold about 350,000 units for the year. And so it went through 1997–1999.

In 2000, Compaq Computer introduced the iPAQ pocket PC with a 206 Intel StrongARM processor, 32 MB of RAM, and a 2.2 × 3–inch color screen. Sony Computer Entertainment introduced Sony PlayStation 2. Handspring introduced the Visor Platinum PDA with a Motorola 33-MHz processor, a 3.1-inch screen, dimensions of 4.8 × 3.0 × 0.7 inches, and a weight of 5.8 ounces. Since then, hand-held processor speeds have continued to increase, as have the available memory and software capabilities.

More Information
See the following resources:
www.islandnet.com/~kpolsson/handheld/
www.islandnet.com/~kpolsson/handheld/hand1997.htm

Brief Future Sketch of Computers

No one really knows for certain what the future of computers holds. The next section documents a couple of the more innovative changes that could impact the computer industry in the coming years.

This section consists of the following topics:

- Wearable computers
- Pervasive computers

Wearable Computers

As we move into the future, computers will become smaller, more intelligent, and more specialized. One area in which we expect to see more computing occur is in the arena of wearable computers. A small wearable computer (the size of a wallet or wristwatch) wirelessly connected to the Internet, with speech recognition and intelligent sunglasses, will combine these technologies to create some powerful life-enhancements.

With computer-connected sunglasses, virtual images and information can be overlaid atop the real world. For example, a tourist visiting another city could get details such as street signs, historic images of a site or building as it was centuries ago, directions to the nearest restaurant or public restroom, consumer guide ratings of taxicab companies, and so forth. A firefighter could determine locations of gas and water mains, get information on whether power has been turned off to a building, determine the chemical composition of fumes from a burning building, and so forth. A construction engineer could see overlays of buried pipelines or geological faults. A soldier on a battlefield could get the latest information on the locations of snipers, identify friend or foe by color coding within the virtual overlay, and so on.

More Information
See the following resources:
www.cnn.com/2002/TECH/ptech/05/13/augmented.reality.ap/index.html
www.media.mit.edu/wearables/
http://iswc.tinmith.net/
www.2.cs.cmu.edu/afs/cs.cmu.edu/project/vuman/www/home.html
www.via-pc.com/

Pervasive Computing

The idea behind pervasive computing is for small intelligent devices (personal digital assistants, mobile phones, home and office PCs, and home entertainment systems) to be wirelessly networked so that they can seamlessly access national, global, financial, and personal information, while still maintaining the highest levels of security for confidential information.

As computers and devices become more intelligent, this vision will become more of a reality. Ultimately, if necessary, your refrigerator, toaster, microwave, telephone, lamp, security system, and pool pump can all be networked, giving you access (with security) no matter where you happen to be at that moment.

At this time, such computing is present in a limited fashion, in somewhat crude form. However, in the future, we expect common standards to be developed and intelligent devices to be produced, enabling this to happen seamlessly.

More Information
See the following resources:
www.research.ibm.com/journal/sj38-4.html
www-3.ibm.com/pvc/pervasive.shtml
www-3.ibm.com/pvc/index.shtml
www.pervasive2002.org/

Pervasive Nature of Computers and Computing in Today's Society

To address the pervasive nature of computers and computing in today's society, we need to look at various technologies in use. Some of those things, such as PCs, wireless devices, intelligent networks, intelligent cars, intelligent highway systems, GPS, intelligent clothing, and virtual reality, are good starting points. All of these are addressed in the following sections.

PCs

Approximately 50 percent of U.S. homes now have personal computers used for a variety of purposes: e-mail, word processing, personal finances, databasing information, Internet news access, music, chat rooms, bulletin boards, social groups, and research for student homework.

Wireless Devices

A variety of wireless devices are appearing on the market: cell phones, wireless PDAs, wireless game platforms, and others.

Intelligent Networks

Internet hardware, such as routers, is increasing in intelligence, to better manage flow of the increasing Internet traffic.

Intelligent Cars

As microcontroller and microprocessor intelligence has increased and costs have dropped, increasing numbers of such chips are being incorporated into cars. Fuel efficiency has increased through use of intelligence to control fuel injection. Airbag deployment, GPS systems in cars, automatic suspension adjustment depending on the kind of road surface, travel directions, passenger matching of seat adjustment and mirror adjustment—all are examples of utilizing the intelligence of microcontrollers and microprocessors in cars today.

Intelligent Transportation Systems

Traffic signals and highways that sense the flow of traffic—how heavy the traffic is, how fast it is going, the presence of an accident—can perform functions such as automatically calling the police or ambulances to an accident scene or rerouting traffic around a congested area. These systems are in development. Some day in the future, there could be a system that enables a driver to drive a car onto the highway and then relinquish control of the car to the highway, which then drives the car (and its adjacent cars) in an optimal fashion to maximize traffic flow and minimize accidents.

GPS

Global positioning systems (GPS) indicate where you are—or where your car is—at any given time. They can be used for traffic-navigation systems for cars (in a city or in the countryside), for planes and ships, on battlefields, and so on.

Intelligent Clothing

This clothing senses the outside temperature and your temperature, and then adjusts its permeability accordingly, using smart pads that act as input to a wearable computer.

Virtual Reality

Virtual reality integrates 3D models of reality with goggles and 3D screens for an observer using hand-control devices that mimic the roughness, texture, and feel of a surface. Applications include placing the observer inside a movie as one of the actors or using chairs and floor surfaces to mimic the vibration and feel of a vehicle, for instance. Currently being developed in universities and labs, virtual reality has some applications for gaming. The future will see increasing realism in this arena.

Types of Computing and the Role of Computer Languages in These Areas

With the shift toward more personal computers, three types of computing are generally recognized. These three types are discussed next:

- Personal
- Distributed
- Client/server

Personal

This is a paradigm shift from mainframe computing—in which one massive central computer sits in a room, with many dumb terminals connected it to it—to personal computing. In mainframe computing, the users had to go to the computer. In personal computing, the computers have come to the user: They are smaller, cheaper, and more portable, so they fit on each user's desktop. The next step is for computers to go *with* the user; the computers will become so small and light that they can travel everywhere with the user, just as wallets and purses do now.

Distributed

In this model of computing, the computers (and computing power) are distributed to the users. Computers sit on desktops, and each individual uses a different computer.

Client/Server

In an improved model of computing, one computer acts as a server (for centralized information), and other computers (with their users) act as clients, asking the server-computer for access to information. The server then responds to the client request and sends the information to the client.

Information that need not be centralized continues to reside on the client.

Hardware

Computer *hardware* is the physical equipment that is needed to execute a set of computer instructions. Computers can take a wide variety of forms, ranging from a desktop computer to a personal digital assistant (PDA), or from a cell phone to a watch. In general, the physical parts of the computer are collectively referred to as hardware. Figure 1-2 shows examples of computer hardware: the monitor, keyboard, mouse, printers, hard drives, network cards, CD-ROM drives, removable disk drives, and modem. Disks, CDs, and printer paper are not computer hardware.

All computers consist of three basic parts: a central processing unit (CPU), memory, and electronic components and subassemblies. All of these are described in the sections that follow.

Central Processing Unit

This is the brain of the computer. The CPU receives, interprets, and executes instructions that are contained in software programs. The CPU controls the actions of all the other hardware in a computer. Based on his observations of the computer industry, Gordon Moore, the chairman of Intel, developed a general rule for expressing the rate at which computing power increases with each generation of new computers. He found that computer processing power doubles every 18 to 24 months. In general, this means that a computer purchased today is 32 times faster than a computer purchased 5 years ago. Because the growth in computer engineering has been ongoing since 1980, it is easy to understand why computers are always getting smaller, faster, and cheaper. An article about Moore's beliefs can be found at www.cs.ucsd.edu/~carter/260/bellprize.pdf.

Memory

Memory stores the data that is being processed or the instructions to be used. A computer has two types of memory. The first is persistent memory, such as hard drives, CDs, and disks. Persistent memory retains its stored information when the power is terminated from the computer. Java programs are stored on the hard drive. Dynamic memory, on the other hand, retains only the information stored in the memory chip while there is electricity powering the computer. Dynamic memory is sometimes referred to as random-access memory (RAM). When Java programs are executed, they are usually stored in RAM.

Electronic Components and Subassemblies

These are needed to accept data from a keyboard or a mouse (input devices) and to send data out through a monitor or a printer (output devices).

Figure 1-2 Computer Hardware

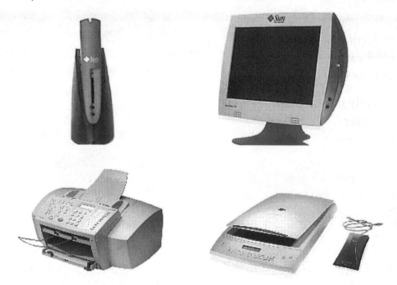

Software

The functions of the software and operating systems control what the hardware does and how it does it.

Hardware cannot perform any meaningful tasks by itself. Hardware needs software to make it operate. Software is a collection of instructions that tell the hardware how to behave. For example, software tells the CD-ROM drive (hardware) in a stereo system (hardware) to play the music. Software provides the CPU with the individual steps that are needed to accomplish a task and describes them in great detail. Imagine that the steps being programmed are similar to drinking from a cup. Although this seems simple enough, it involves many steps, as outlined here:

Step 1   Look at the cup.

Step 2   Extend your hand.

Step 3   Open your hand.

Step 4   Grasp the cup in your hand.

Step 5   Close your hand.

Step 6   Lift the cup to your mouth.

Step 7   Tilt the cup.

Step 8   Sip . . . and so on.

Software can be classified as either an operating system or an application. The distinction between the operating system and an application is based on the types of actions these programs perform. This is discussed later in this section. Both of these terms refer to a collection of computer programs that contain a series of instructions that make the hardware perform specific tasks. These programs are stored in the computer memory, and the instructions are executed one at a time by the CPU.

Software is rarely owned. Instead, a software license is usually purchased. A software license gives a user the right to use the software, but not the right to copy it, share it, or sell it to another person. For example, if a company wants to purchase an e-mail program, it must acquire a license to use the software from the company that created the program. When people talk about buying software, they really mean buying a software license.

As shown in Figure 1-3, there are three ways to obtain software:

1. Buy software that is already written. Software can be obtained easily and inexpensively this way. For example, the word-processing program used to create this document was purchased from a software company. That is, a license to use the software was purchased. However, if the software does not have all the necessary features, or if it is not compatible with the hardware, the user cannot change how the software operates.

2. Modify existing software (if the license permits). A growing trend in the software community is called "open source." This allows anyone to obtain not only the rights to use software, but also the right to modify the programs that are included in the software. Typically, to modify the software, users have to agree to give their modifications at no cost to anyone else who wants to use or modify the software.

3. Write individual software. With proper design and testing, this software does exactly what the user wants it to do. It might be expensive and time-consuming to create individual software. However, with the advent of languages such as Java and related development tools to assist the programmer, program creation time has been greatly reduced.

Figure 1-3 Buy or Create a Program

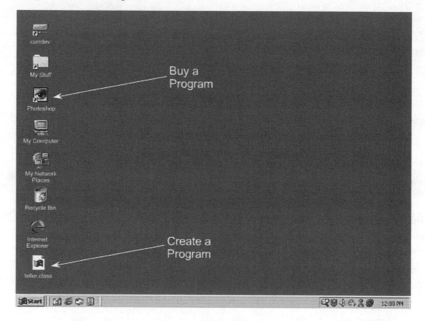

From Command Line to GUI

In command-line computing, the user communicates with the computer through a keyboard-monitor combination using esoteric text commands. This is how things used to be done in the early days of computing (**cd**, **ls**, and **grep** were some of the commands). No pretty graphical user interfaces for computer geeks in those days—this was the case for mainframe computers, minicomputers, and DOS-based personal computers.

Apple Computer, Inc. (and Xerox PARC scientists) revolutionized this field by creating and commercializing graphical user interfaces (GUIs) that are more intuitive for humans to use. The current versions of these GUIs include Windows (from Microsoft), MacOS versions, and UNIX GUIs. A GUI refers to the techniques involved in using graphics, along with a keyboard and a mouse, to provide an easy-to-use interface for a program.

Applications

Applications are collections of computer programs. Word processors, Internet browsers, and computer games are all examples of computer applications. Inside each of these applications are many computer programs that perform tasks. For example, there is usually a spell-checking program inside a word processor that checks the spelling of documents. Another program saves documents to the computer hard disk.

A computer can also process data into meaningful information. Data is raw facts and figures. Applications contain programs that instruct a computer on what data to use and how to process it into meaningful information. The raw facts and figures can include last name, first name, and year of birth. The program processes these facts as data to produce the name and age of an individual, a meaningful line of information.

Most computer users purchase applications for their own computer. Many companies also create software applications that are proprietary. These applications are very specialized and perform critical tasks needed by the business. At the end of this course, students will be able to write and create their own applications, or offer to sell them to other computer users.

How does a user tell an application what to do? For example, to check the spelling in a document, users click a Spell Check button or select Check Spelling from a pull-down menu. Clicking a button or selecting a menu item sends a message to the application stating that the user wants the application to perform a task. When the application finishes checking the spelling in the document, it lets the user know that it is finished. Therefore, applications must have the capability to receive messages from the user when the user wants to perform some task. Likewise, applications must be capable of sending messages to the user with the results of performing that task. The concept of sending messages from one program to another inside the computer is important. How messages are sent from one Java program to another is discussed later in this chapter.

Operating Systems

The operating system in a computer is the collection of programs that directly control the hardware. Why are operating systems necessary when an application handles all the tasks for the computer to perform? One of the basic principles of engineering—and, specifically computer science—is to divide a complex problem into smaller, manageable problems. This engineering principle is similar to the concept of dividing a job into areas of special expertise. For example, when building a house, an architect creates the design, a bricklayer builds the outside walls, a carpenter builds the inside walls, an electrician installs the electrical wires, and a plumber installs the water pipes. Each person has expertise in one aspect of building the house. As a group, they are able to build a complete house. No individual has to master all of these skills to build a house. Instead, they break up the problem of building into a set of smaller problems, such as building walls, installing electrical fixtures, installing plumbing, and so on.

All computers have some combination of floppy drives, hard disks, CD-ROM drives, memory, keyboards, and monitors. Computer scientists looked at the problem of building a computer application and divided it into a number of easier problems to solve. How will the computer read and write data from the hard drive? How will the computer receive data from the keyboard? How will the computer display messages and documents on the monitor? As programs for each of these problems were written, it became apparent that if each application solved these problems independently, each application would have to master not only all the aspects of interacting with the hardware (such as reading and writing data to the hard drive), but also the functions specific to that application (such as creating documents in a word processor). Operating systems were developed to separate the tasks of controlling the hardware from the tasks specifically associated with the application. The operating system controls the hardware, and the application does the rest.

Some computer scientists became experts in controlling hardware. They created operating systems that other computer scientists used as building blocks for their applications. This division of labor had some important side effects that were not originally foreseen by the early pioneers of computer science.

The concept of sending messages between computer programs became critical to the development of operating systems. With the advent of operating systems, applications had to send messages to the operating system to request the use of some piece of hardware, such as reading or writing data to the hard drive. This required the development of interfaces between computer programs. Interfaces are well-documented methods by which computer programs can talk to each other. The Java API is a collection of classes distributed with the Java Development Kit that any programmer can use to build a custom application. Computer interfaces are discussed further in the Java Application Program Interface (Java API). An API can be defined as the specification of how a programmer writing an application accesses the behavior and state of classes and objects.

Different and incompatible operating systems were created. Application developers were now faced with the problem of making their applications compatible with all the different operating systems that users can choose to run on their computer hardware. Re-creating an application for each operating system became a very expensive and time-consuming process for the application developers. To reduce the cost and time needed to develop applications for different operating systems, application developers began to look for ways to make their applications more portable across different operating systems. The Java language is considered a highly portable language, as explained in the next chapter.

When the first operating systems were introduced, there were no windows on the computer monitor and the computer mouse had not been invented. The keyboard was used to enter commands into the computer, and the monitor display was black with white letters and a blinking cursor. The cursor told the user that the computer was still running and waiting for input. Shown in Figure 1-4, the string of characters preceding the blinking cursor is referred to as the command prompt. The empty space after the blinking cursor became known as the command line for the operating system because commands were typed in that space. As operating systems became more complex, the number of commands increased and the names of the commands became harder to understand and remember. The Microsoft DOS operating system and the original versions of UNIX are well-known operating systems that use only a command-line interface.

Figure 1-4 DOS Command Line

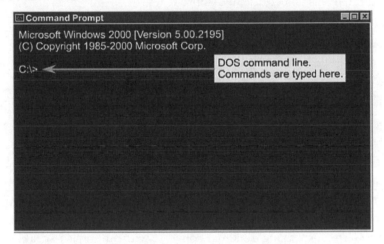

As computers became more popular, it became necessary to find a better way for users to communicate with the operating system. Windowing operating systems were developed to simplify the way in which people interact with a computer. Xerox developed the first commercial windowing operating system, called Star. Before that, they created the first noncommercial windowing operating system, called Smalltalk. Apple then built upon the Star concept and developed the Mac OS. Microsoft followed with Windows. (Of course, there are many other operating systems.) Windows-based operating systems became popular because of their ease of use. Programmers then began developing windowing applications that could run on many of the traditional operating systems that, until recently, provided only a command line—these include Solaris, Linux, and UNIX.

What Is a Programming Language?

To operate computer hardware, programming languages were designed to make the computer perform tasks. The next sections discuss the history of programming languages and point out key differences among the languages. This section covers the following topics:

- The definition of a programming language
- Switches, ones, and zeros
- Early programming languages
- High-level languages
- Object-oriented programming
- Procedural versus object-oriented approaches
- Basic language elements
- Differences among languages

Definition of a Programming Language

Computer hardware needs software to make it operate. Software is a collection of programs that contain the detailed instructions to operate the computer hardware. A programming language is the language used to write computer programs. Just as there are many spoken languages, such as French, German, and English, there are many computer languages. Typically, a program written in one language cannot communicate with a program written in another language. However, there are ways to "translate" messages from one programming language to another, just as there are human translators to help a German-speaking diplomat converse with an English-speaking diplomat at the United Nations.

Choosing which computer language to use for a particular program depends on many factors:

- The programmer's knowledge of that language
- The tools available to develop the program in a particular language
- The characteristics of the computer hardware
- The type of problem that the programmer must solve

The benefits of programming in Java include the following:

- Java is an easy language to learn.
- Many powerful tools help programmers develop complex applications quickly and efficiently.
- Java programs can run on almost any computer hardware.
- Almost any complex business or scientific problem can be solved using programs written in Java.

This section discusses the basic elements of a programming language and the evolution of programming languages from simple switches on the front of the early computers to the most advanced languages such as Java. It also investigates the details of a simple Java program.

Switches, Ones, and Zeros

Program instructions must be in a language that the computer understands. At the hardware level, the computer is nothing more than thousands of switches quickly flipping on and off. As shown in Figure 1-5, a switch can have only two states: on or off. The state of a switch can be numerically represented as 1 for on and 0 for off. The binary system uses these two numbers (0 and 1) to represent the flipping of the switches. During the early years of computer programming, a panel of switches was the only way to enter instructions into a computer. The operator created a plan for instructions by representing the position of each switch as a 0 or a 1. These representations were the early forms of a programming language, and the code was called binary code.

The spoken language is too ambiguous for the computer. Although the human brain can decipher sentences intuitively, a computer understands only the states of switches, represented as 0s and 1s. Because early computers held only data, not programs, programmers had to write code to manipulate the data and calculate results. The only method available at the time was to write instructions in the binary code of 0s and 1s.

Figure 1-5 Switching and Binary Representation

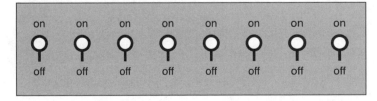

Early Programming Languages

Writing instructions in binary was very tedious, so programming languages were created as a bridge between the binary language of the computer and the written word. Using the highly specific syntax found in a computer programming language, people can instruct the computer to perform complex tasks. As shown in Figure 1-6, these early programming languages used simple, short words to represent a set of binary instructions that the computer could understand. For example, the word *ADD* represents a set of binary instructions that tell the computer what steps to take to add two numbers. These short words are called mnemonics because they use one or more symbols to represent a set of binary instructions in the computer. These early languages were called machine language or assembler language, and are now referred to as low-level languages.

Now that computers could be programmed with groups of letters instead of switches, a keyboard was added to the computer as the main input device. In addition, a special software program was needed to translate the assembly language programs into the binary language of the computer. These translation programs became known as assemblers.

When the assembler programming language became available, more companies began using computers. As computer usage became more widespread, so did the need for more complex software applications. Low-level languages did not provide the quick turnaround needed for business applications. Assembler languages were also complex and difficult to learn. They forced the programmer to think like a computer and to separate each task into a long list of very simple instructions. As applications became more complex, the effort to create and maintain the applications also increased. Application programmers needed high-level languages to quickly and efficiently write computer programs to solve real-world problems.

Figure 1-6 Mnemonic Communications

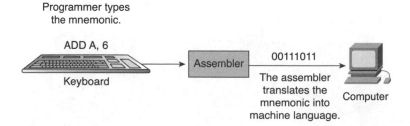

High-Level Languages

High-level languages were developed to help the programmer worry less about the details of each step that the computer must take to execute the program. Programmers then could concentrate on the overall design and construction of the application. These high-level languages included words or abbreviations that were recognizable by English-speakers, so reading and writing the language was easier. Two of the earliest high-level languages were FORmula TRANslator (FORTRAN) and the COmmon Business Oriented Language (COBOL).

As shown in Figure 1-7, high-level languages added one more layers between the computer and the programmer. Therefore, new translator programs had to be created to translate these new languages into the binary language of the computer. Translator programs converted the high-level instructions into binary instructions that the computer understood. These translators were tools provided by the developers of the language.

Languages such as FORTRAN and COBOL use a linear (a single point of entry and exit) approach to solve a particular problem, called *procedural programming*. With this approach, the program defines all the data required by the programming sequence and all the instructions to process the data. The instructions are performed in the sequence described in the program. This methodology requires a great deal of maintenance work by the programmer. Any changes to the data in size, type, or location require changes to many programs. Any changes in business procedures and tasks require significant maintenance work to modify and change programs.

As the applications became more complex, programmers realized that they were repeatedly recreating the same functions in each application. Functions such as writing files to hard disks, sending messages to other computers, and calculating basic mathematical functions began to appear in special libraries that programmers could reuse in each new application. Reusing these functions reduced the amount of time needed to build applications and the cost of maintaining these programs. These libraries became known as application programming interfaces (APIs).

These high-level languages still forced the programmer to think like a computer. The programmer still had to separate the problem into many sequential steps that the computer could perform. Then, the programmer had to describe the problem in terms of how a computer would solve the problem.

Figure 1-7 Evolution of Programming Languages

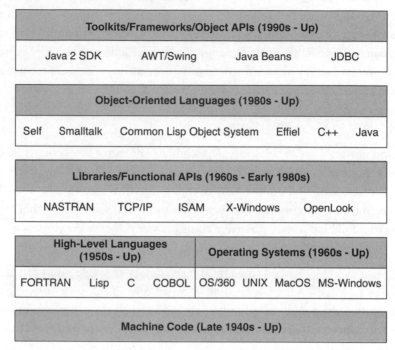

Object-Oriented Programming

Object-oriented programming assembles different components, or objects, into an application. Object-oriented programming breaks the problem into parts. These parts are defined as objects, which perform specific functions. The objects interact by sending and receiving messages. The programmer is focused on how the actions of each of these objects are coordinated and how they communicate with each other. The programmer does not have to know how a particular object performs its function.

The programmer also creates new objects that can be reused in other applications. Most business problems are multifaceted and do not lend themselves well to linear solutions such as procedural programming. As students work through the JBANK case study included in this course, the benefits of code reuse and the ways in which the objects interact with each other will become clearer.

Where do these objects come from? To review, there are three ways to obtain programs: to buy them, modify existing ones, or create them. The same is true of objects—programmers can buy them, modify existing ones, or create them. After all, objects are just parts of programs. Whether programmers buy an object library or build their own object depends on the budget and time. Although creating an object can be expensive, the Java language provides many opportunities for reducing the cost and time needed to create custom objects. For starters, Sun Microsystems provides a rich library of tested and working objects and programs that can be easily reused. Additionally, the Java development community has many websites that provide resources for programmers with both free and fee-based pretested objects and programs.

Because object-oriented programming methods more closely reflect the problem-solving approach used by people, object-oriented programming languages such as Java have become popular in the software industry. This methodology has brought advances in software reuse and maintainability, and improvements in programmer productivity. Procedural programming languages do not allow programmers to easily reuse parts of their code. Therefore, the same code can exist in multiple programs in the same application. This would require maintenance on multiple programs to adjust one piece of code. In object-oriented methodology, only one copy of the code would exist, so only one copy must be updated if a change is required. This is considered a "best practice" in the industry.

The next chapter focuses on how programmers create different objects. Throughout the labs in this course, students will create many different Java objects as they learn more about this exciting new evolution in computer programming.

Procedural Versus Object-Oriented

Within the programming community, individual programmers debate which type of programming language, object-oriented or procedural, is more useful. The next couple sections clarify the arguments for why object-oriented should be utilized. The following topics are discussed:

- The philosophy of an object-oriented (OO) approach
- How OO matches what we experience in the world
- How procedures match some of what we experience in the world

Philosophy of OO

An object-oriented approach divides a problem into small interacting subproblems, divides a task into small interacting subtasks, and divides the world into small interacting classes. Under this philosophy, each class, subtask, or subproblem is developed one at a time, and then these classes interact with one another to solve the problem (or task) at hand. Each class can be a black box—that is, users do not need to know what is in the box as long as they know how this box behaves and what it does.

OO Matches What We Experience in the World

The world is full of black boxes: We don't really understand how they work, yet we use them to accomplish things because we know the *behavior* of these black boxes and what they do. Examples include cars (for many of us), computers, watches, refrigerators, our bodies, our heart, our eyes, biological cells, proteins, and so on.

Procedures Match Some of What We Experience in the World

A procedure is a list of instructions that tell the computer what to do in sequence. We experience such "procedures" in real life when we follow a recipe to bake a cake or obtain directions to drive to a party at a friend's house.

Basic Language Elements

All programming languages have five common elements: vocabulary, punctuation, identifiers, operators, and syntax. Each programming language has a unique set of these elements. Learning a particular programming language requires thoroughly learning all of the following elements:

- **Vocabulary**—The keywords used by a particular programming language
- **Punctuation**—The symbols used by a computer language
- **Identifiers**—The names used to reference data stored in the memory of the computer
- **Operators**—The symbols or commands used to process data
- **Syntax**—Rules of a computer language that the programmer must follow to code properly

As shown in Example 1-1, all computer programs are now written using some form of a text editor, similar to a word processor. The programmer types the program in the editor much like an author types a manuscript for a book.

Example 1-1 *Program That Uses Software Objects*

```
1 /**
2  * JavaProgram: TaxPayer.java
3  *
4  * @author Cisco Teacher
5  * @version 2002
6  */
7 public class TaxPayer
```

Example 1-1 *Program That Uses Software Objects (Continued)*

```
 8 {
 9     int ssn;
10     double grossIncome;
11
12 /**
13  * @param ssnum A 9 digit social security number as an int
14  * @param gross The gross income as an int
15  */
16     TaxPayer (int ssnum, int gross)
17     {
18         ssn = ssnum;
19         grossIncome = gross;
20     }
21
22 /**
23  * @return The social security number as an int
24  */
25     public int getSSN()
26     {
27         return ssn;
28     }
29
30 /**
31  * @return The gross income as a double
32  */
33     public double getGrossIncome()
34     {
35         return grossIncome;
36     }
37 }
```

The program is saved on the hard disk in a file called the source file of the program. The source file contains the *source code* of the program. The source code consists of the programming statements that are created by a programmer with a text editor or integrated development environment (IDE) and then saved in a file. Just as a manuscript of a book must follow all the rules of syntax, punctuation, and spelling for the language of the book, the program source code must follow all the rules of spelling, syntax, and punctuation of the programming language. Some text editors understand the rules of syntax, punctuation, and spelling for different computer languages, so they can automatically correct the source code just as some word processors have spelling and grammar checkers.

Differences Among Languages

Beyond the differences in syntax, operators, identifiers, punctuation, and vocabulary, programming languages are characterized by the way a computer understands the language. Some languages are compiled, and others are interpreted. Java is both a compiled and an interpreted language.

Before a program is ready for execution, the translation of the program's source code into the computer's binary language is required. How the program's source code is translated determines whether it is compiled or interpreted by the computer. The creators of the language, and the creators of the program that does the translation, determine how the program is translated.

Compiled Languages

A *compiler* is a special-purpose program that converts the entire source-code file into the binary language of a particular computer. The binary language is called native code or processor code. The resulting translation is a file that contains the native code for that computer, as shown in Figure 1-8. The file containing the compiled code is also known as an executable file. Typically, the compiler names the new file with the same name as the original and adds a suffix of .com, .exe, or .bin. Each compiler is specifically designed to translate source code to meet the native language specifications of a particular computer. Programmers need to understand the rules of the compiler for each and every machine on which they want to run a program.

The programmer then runs the file with the compiled code, and the computer performs the functions defined in the source file by the programmer. Each time the program is run or executed, the computer reads the compiled code file to find the native code instructions that are needed to run the program. The source code has to be compiled only once, and the compiled program can be executed many times.

Figure 1-8 Compiled Code of a Java Program

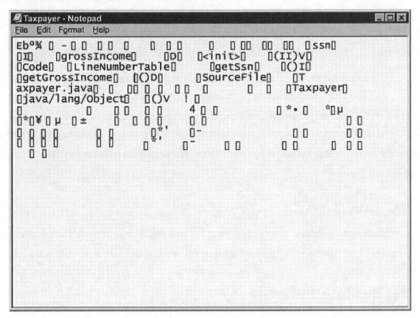

The program will run only after every instruction has been compiled correctly. Typically, the first time a programmer writes a program, there are errors in the source file. The compiler detects these errors and informs the programmer of the errors. The programmer goes through a process of understanding the compiler errors, editing the source file, and compiling the source file before the program will compile successfully. As programmers become more experienced with a particular programming language, this process is usually shortened. Students will have a chance to work with compiler errors in a lab activity later in this chapter.

Interpreted Languages

When a language is interpreted, the computer analyzes each instruction in the source-code file as the program runs (or is executed) on the computer. Another program, the language *interpreter*, converts each instruction in the source file to native code for that computer and executes that instruction.

With an interpreted language, the computer analyzes each instruction in the source file as the program executes. Each time a program is run, it must go through this interpretation process. Therefore, one disadvantage of an interpreted language is that if a program or programmer repeats an instruction, the interpreter must reanalyze and convert that instruction into native code before executing it. Compiled languages thus typically execute faster than interpreted languages. One advantage of interpreted languages is that the programmer can enter one instruction at a time on the keyboard without writing a source-code file. This makes interpreted languages very popular for short programs that accomplish a limited number of related tasks.

Examples of interpreted languages include JavaScript, VBScript, and HTML. JavaScript and HTML are languages that have become popular for developing web pages for the Internet, and VBScript is popular for developing business applications on computers that use the Microsoft Windows operating system. Note that JavaScript is not related to the Java programming language, except for some similarities in syntax.

What Is Java?

This section provides a general overview of Java—what it is, the history of the language, some background information, and why it's such an important language.

Historical Background of Java

The *Java programming language* was developed at Sun Microsystems in 1991, when a team of Sun engineers, led by Patrick Naughton and James Gosling, set out to design a special-purpose computer language. This new language would be used to program consumer electronic devices such as cable TV switch boxes. To work with all the different consumer electronic devices, the language had to be portable—that is, it had to be capable of running on many different processors. The language had to create programs that were small and efficient because of the limited resources in a consumer electronic device. It also had to be easy to program. Although the Java programming language for consumer devices did not become a huge commercial success, Java is used today to program many different hand-held devices, such as cell phones and personal digital assistants (PDAs).

With the dramatic increase in the use of the Internet, it soon became apparent that the benefits that Java could deliver were ideally suited to programming web pages. Small and efficient Java programs called applets could be downloaded quickly from the Internet. These applets gave the web programmer much more programming flexibility and many more graphical elements than simple HTML. The portability of the language enabled the development of business solutions using Java for different types of computers connected to the Internet. The earliest break for the language came with the release of the Netscape browser in 1996. This version of the Netscape browser and all subsequent versions, as well as the Microsoft Internet Explorer browser, are Java-enabled.

As programmers created larger and more complex Java applets, the time required to download these applets increased substantially. Java applets were quickly replaced with other programming languages such as JavaScript and Flash. These were easier to use by nonprogrammers such as graphic artists.

Although Java applets have been largely replaced and consumer devices use other languages, Java did not die out as a programming language. In fact, it has become the most popular language for creating business applications. Java is now widely used to create large-scale distributed applications such as those for running and accessing data on many different networked computers.

Java is a dynamic and evolving language. The number of prewritten programs that come from the Java API has doubled with each new version. Table 1-1 provides a history of the versions of the Java language and a summary of the new features introduced in each version. The authors of Java, James Gosling and Patrick Naughton, best described these unique features in their definition of the Java language as "a simple, object-oriented, network-savvy, interpreted, robust, secure, architecture-neutral, portable, high-performance, multithreaded, dynamic language."

Table 1-1 Java Version History

Version	When and New Features
Java 1.2 or 2	1998
	Security enhancements
	Swing (JFC)
	Java 2D (JFC)
	Accessibility (JFC)
	Drag and Drop (JFC)
	Collections
	Java Extensions
	JavaBeans enhancements
	Input method framework
	Package version
	Identification
	RMI enhancements
	Serialization enhancements

continues

Table 1-1 Java Version History (Continued)

Version	When and New Features
Java 1.2 or 2 (Continued)	Reference objects
	Audio enhancements
	Java IDL
	JAR enhancements
	JNI enhancements
	JVMDI
	JDBC enhancements
Java 1.1	1997
	Abstract windowing toolkit (for developing GUIs), .jar files
	Internationalization, signed applets, and digital signatures
	Remote method invocation
	Object serialization
	ReflectionInner classes
	New Java native interface
	Byte Short and Void classes
	Deprecated methods
	Networking enhancements
	I/O enhancements
Java 1.0	1995

NOTE

Why was the name Java chosen for the language? The original name was Green-Talk. When the developers did not accept this name easily, the name Oak was chosen. When it was discovered that another language named Oak existed, however, the name Java was chosen.

The next section discusses a few types of applications that have been created with the Java language.

History of Java: Timeline

The Java programming language has had an interesting history. Some of the major points on that timeline are summarized as follows:

- In 1991, project Green was initiated by a Sun group. Its task was to develop operating software for consumer electronic devices such as set-top boxes. Gosling realized that C++ was not adequate for this and started developing a new language named Oak, which was later named Java.

- In 1994, the web browser WebRunner, later renamed HotJava, was written in Java.

- In 1995, the alpha version of Java and HotJava was released. Netscape licensed Java and used it to build Netscape 2.0. Beta JDK then appeared. SGI, IBM, Adobe, and Microsoft licensed Java.

More Information
See the following resources: www.npac.syr.edu/users/gcf/javatutorial98.1/foilsepimagedir/018IMAGE.html#buttons java.sun.com/people/jag/

History of Java: Key People

Project Green, which led to the creation of Java, started at the end of 1990 and ended September 3, 1992. The members of the team were Mike Sheridan, Patrick Naughton, James Gosling, Ed Frank, Craig Forrest, Al Frazier, Jon Payne, Chris Warth, David Lavallee, Cindy Long, Joe Palrang, Don Jackson, Chuck Clanton, Bob Weisblatt, and Sheueling Chang.

More Information
See the following resources: java.sun.com/people/jag/Presentations/TheStoryOfJava/img8.htm java.sun.com/people/jag/green/index.html

Use of Java as a Programming Language

Java is now used to create standalone programs that run on computers of any size. (See Figure 1-9.)

These can take the form of a personal assistant, a cellular phone, or a special program embedded in a piece of jewelry. These can also include a major banking application that manages millions of transactions for banks. One such example lies in the use of e-commerce applications. E-commerce applications use Java programs to enable the buying and selling of goods and services across the Internet. These programs use Enterprise Java Beans, Java Beans, and Remote Method Invocation (RMI) libraries to support these business applications. These aspects of programming in Java are discussed later in this course. Other examples of modern Java programs are shown in Figure 1-10.

Figure 1-9 Types of Hardware That Java Runs On

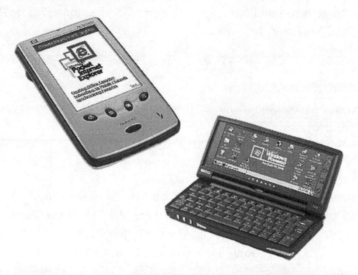

Figure 1-10 Types of Java Applications

Automotive Customer Data Retrieval Avionics
Inventory Control Systems **Sprinkler Systems** VCR Imaging
TV Customer Transactions PDAs **Flight Control Systems**
Instrumentation **Transaction Processing** Navigation Medical Records
Information Retrieval Therapeutic Equipment Banking
Custom Personal Applications **Test and Diagnosis** **Business Automation**
Telephones Medical Microwaves Prosthetics
Load Balancing Accounting Communication **Personal Communications**
DVD **Entertainment** **Training** **Flight Safety** **Factory Control Systems**
Web Site Development Accounting Systems **Phones** Dryers
Emergency Notification Cellular Business-to-Business Transactions
Infrastructure Entertainment **Custom Business Applications**
Lighting Home Appliances **Power Controls** Internet
Measurement Systems **Communications** Safety **ATMs**
Engine Control Environmental Controls Audio Systems

A programmer must also be familiar with the common terms listed in Table 1-2. Programming terms describe what a programmer can accomplish with Java. As more of the details of the Java language are explored in this chapter, the meanings of these terms will become clearer.

Table 1-2 Common Programming Terms

Common Terms	Descriptions
Simple	Java syntax and the Java API (application programming interface, a library of Java code) are simple and designed to be easy to learn and use.
Object-oriented	The idea behind objects is quite simple. Instead of designing a long and complex set of instructions, or routines, to perform one or more tasks, the programmer can break these into various parts. Each part can perform one or more discreet tasks, and contains all the data needed to perform the task. This is an object. Java files define an object or a class of objects.
Distributed	The Java language provides a library of program routines to open and access objects across the Net via URLs, with the same ease as when accessing a local file system. Data can easily be sent across the Net with Java programs.
Robust	The design of the Java platform ensures that the programs run correctly and do not break when the unexpected happens.
Secure	Java programs can be downloaded from a location on the network. Such downloaded Java programs cannot access files on your computer or destroy programs on your computer.
Architecture-neutral and portable	Java-language programs can be written on one machine and run on a machine with a different type of CPU.
Interpreted	Java source code is translated to a bytecode that is interpreted one instruction at a time by the Java Virtual Machine.
Multithreaded	More than one Java program can run simultaneously and share data and instructions. Multithreading provides the capability to view animation or a video clip, or listen to music in a browser while reading or searching for some other information on the World Wide Web.

continues

Table 1-2 Common Programming Terms (Continued)

Common Terms	Descriptions
Dynamic	Dynamic has several meanings as it applies to the Java language. For example, the language has special capabilities that enable the program to call upon resources as needed dynamically when the program is running in memory. Such a resource can be another Java routine. The software-development process is dynamic. Java enables a programmer to approach a solution to a problem in incremental steps. At each step of the solution, a small number of routines can be built with newer routines using the work of already defined routines. This fosters reuse of code.

The Internet contains a wealth of information on Java, its functions, and its use. Table 1-3 provides a list of websites that programmers might find useful.

Table 1-3 Helpful Websites Listing

Website Address	Website Description
www.bluej.org/	IDE tools, books, tips, training
www-4.ibm.com/software/ad/vajava/	IDE tools, information, support, news, education
java.sun.com/	Source for Java technology, events, standards, Java information
softwaredev.earthweb.com/java	Training, certification, jobs, events, software development
javaboutique.internet.com/	Application source code, tools, jobs, tutorials, news, events
www.apple.com/java/	Java for Apple and Mac products
www.javaworld.com/	News, tips, general information, Q&A, training
www.blackdown.org	Java for Linux
www.javacoffeebreak.com/	Java training, books, newsletter, FAQs, product information
www.ibm.com/developerworks/java/	Tools, products, education, FAQs, events, developer information

Table 1-3 Helpful Websites Listing (Continued)

Website Address	Website Description
www.sys-con.com/java/	Magazine, events, articles, news, commentary, buyers guide, jobs
www.java-pro.com/	Information, events, newsletters, related fields and products
javareport.com/	Code, events, jobs, buyers guide, information
javascript.internet.com/	JavaScript information, code exchange, jobs, certification sample tests
www.javaarchives.com/	Java web information, news, links, development, chat rooms
www.java-zone.com	General information, related products, source code, tips, database, jobs
www.java-scripts.net/	Free scripts, tools, tutorials, forums
www.javagrande.org/	Events, workshops, conferences
developer.java.sun.com/	Sun's developers site, early access, downloads, news, Q&A
freewarejava.com/	Free code, news, tutorials, books
www.cgi-java.com/	CGI Java information, forums, tutorials
www.javaranch.com/index.jsp	Beginners information, Q&A, forums, explanation and examples

Java and the World Wide Web

One of the key arenas in which Java is used extensively is the World Wide Web. The next sections discuss the role of Java on the Internet.

Java's Role in the Internet and the World Wide Web

Java has the benefits of portability across a wide variety of hardware and software devices. This benefit is key for applications on the Internet and the World Wide Web. For instance, recently, many industry innovators have adopted PersonalJava technology as a standard, to enable a new class of Java-based networked devices. This will permit consumer devices, such as hand-held computers or games, to communicate with each other or with the global network. Devices such as set-top boxes, web-connected TVs, and smart phones are expected to soon have Java as their internal DNA.

More Information
See java.sun.com/pr/1997/july/pr970723-06.html

Future of the Internet (Semantic Net)

The Internet is likely to evolve into what is called the Semantic Net in the future. The basic idea behind this is to code information on the web with tags that help browsers understand the context and meaning of terms on web pages. This will enable context-related inferences and links (more along the lines of what humans do in communicating with one another). A specific word in a civil engineering context can lead to civil engineering–related, linked web content. That same word used in a medical context can lead to medical-related, linked web content. For instance, right now a search for the word "dislocation" on an Internet search engine brings up web pages in completely unrelated fields (such as defects in materials, and fractures and dislocations of human arms and legs). In the semantic web, depending on the context-related tags used, the web will look up only medical dislocations in a medical context, and material defects in a materials-engineering context.

> **NOTE**
>
> Java is one of the few computer languages that makes it easy to use international character and symbols. This will be key in the future, as the Internet continues to become truly international.

More Information
See the following resources:
www.w3.org/2001/sw/
www.w3.org/DesignIssues/Semantic.html (semantic web roadmap)

Why Learn Java?

As a programming language, Java is become increasingly popular and is becoming the object-oriented programming language of choice throughout the country. In the next sections, we discuss where Java currently is used and provide a brief overview of future uses.

Where Java Is Used Currently

Java is used in web browsers for increased interactivity with users and to enable customized queries to database servers. It also is used for building schematic viewing applications, for use in online banking, for analyzing weather data, for U.S. postal service smart forms that provide automatic postage calculation and navigational prompts for bulk mail customers, for web-based healthcare benefits administration, for tracking sales service and warranty information for car customers, and for online catalogs, among a myriad of other business applications.

For more information, refer to java.sun.com/nav/used/.

Brief Overview of Future Java

Java is likely to have expanded use (because of its portability and network compatibility) for a variety of mobile devices, cell phones, personal digital assistants, and similar small devices. Java is also likely to see increased use in wireless networked devices such as those that use Bluetooth technologies to create small-range, small-appliance networks.

Java Environment Basics

When the developers of Java were creating programs to control hand-held devices, they had to take into consideration the power and memory limitations of such small devices. In addition, the language could not be limited to one type of central processing unit (CPU) because manufacturers might choose different CPUs. This led to the design of a portable language that could run on any platform. The language was capable of doing this by generating intermediate code for a hypothetical computer called a virtual machine.

Virtual machines are software programs that handle the communication between the applications written for the hand-held device and the underlying hardware and operating system. The programmer is required to write programs that are understood by the virtual machine. This code then is translated by the virtual machine into code that the specific hardware and operating system in the hand-held device understand. The concept of virtual machines has been expanded to include many different types of computers, not just hand-held devices. Today, there are Java Virtual Machines for most popular operating systems, including Solaris, Windows, Linux, and MacOS.

Before the introduction of virtual machines, a programmer had to rewrite a program for each specific type of CPU. For example, a program written in Basic or C++ had to be rewritten and recompiled to run on a Macintosh. This required a lot of programmer time. The programmer had to not only rewrite the code, but also maintain code for different computers and for different versions of computer hardware and operating systems. As companies changed computers and acquired newer types of computers, a significant amount of money had to be spent on re-creating critical programs for these new computers.

The virtual machine changed all that. Programmers now can write a program in the language of the virtual machine and run it on any computer that has a virtual machine. The program is read and interpreted by this virtual machine, which translates the code into the language of the particular computer hardware. Therefore, the program that was created and tested on an Apple computer can now be loaded and run on a UNIX machine or an Intel machine using Windows software. As shown in Figure 1-11, all of these machines have a virtual machine that can understand the application written by the programmer and translate its instructions into the language of the target computer CPU.

Figure 1-11 Java Development and Runtime Environment

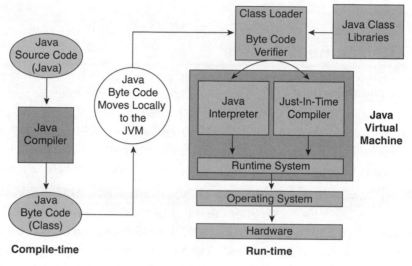

Understanding the Java Virtual Machine

The *Java Virtual Machine (JVM)* is a program that runs on all computers. The JVM creates a software simulation of a CPU and memory, and handles all communication between the Java program and the underlying operating system and hardware. In other words, the Java program thinks that the computer it is running on is the JVM. The burden of understanding and writing code to specific hardware platforms is shifted from the application programmer to the JVM (more specifically, to the programmers of the JVM).

Figure 1-12 graphically illustrates how a Java programmer writes a source-code file of Java code and compiles the code using a Java compiler.

Figure 1-12 Javac Converts to JVM Code

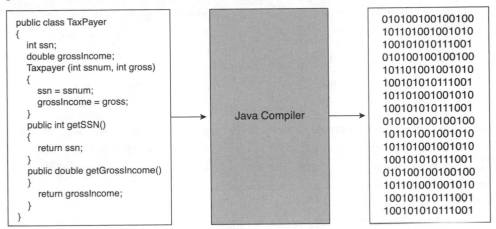

As shown in Figure 1-13, the Java compiler translates the program into *bytecode*, machine-independent code generated by the Java compiler and executed by the Java interpreter. It is the bytecode that will be understood by the JVM, not native code that is understood by a specific computer. The JVM translates the bytecode into binary code (native code or processor code) for the specific CPU that is used to run the program. The JVM is an interpreter for the bytecode, not a compiler for the bytecode. As previously mentioned, Java is both a compiled language (source code compiled into bytecode) and an interpreted language (bytecode interpreted by the JVM into native code).

Figure 1-13 Bytecode to Machine Code

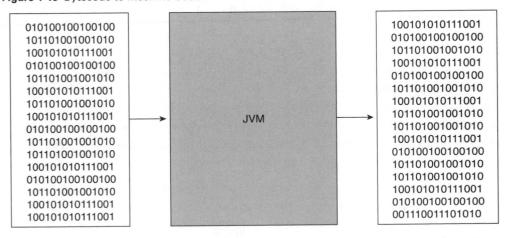

How Java Programs Work on the Computer

To execute a Java program on a computer, the user/programmer must perform three steps:

Step 1   Create a source file.

Step 2   Compile the source file.

Step 3   Run the program.

First, a source file must be created that contains the instructions for the program in the Java language. This file must always have .java as the suffix of the filename. The suffix of a filename is called a file extension, and it is found after the period in the filename. Example 1-2 shows the code for the source file named FirstProgram.java.

Example 1-2 *Java Source Code*

```
 1 /**
 2  * JavaProgram: FirstProgram.java
 3  *
 4  * @author Cisco Teacher
 5  * @version 2002
 6  */
 7 public class FirstProgram
 8 {
 9     public static void main(String[] args)
10     {
11         System.out.println("Hello Students");
12     }
13 }
```

For example, suppose that a student is writing a program that creates and maintains a directory of all the students in a Java class. To call the program StudentDirectory, the file containing the source code must be called StudentDirectory.java. Many Java developers use coding conventions to write their code. In this example, the name of the file is a compound noun (Student and Directory), and the first letter of each word in the name of the file is capitalized. These conventions will continue to appear as the chapter discusses the Java language more.

The second step is to compile the source code into bytecode for the JVM. The Java compiler (called *javac*) is a program that performs this translation from source code to bytecode. The Java compiler creates a file with the same name as the source file, but with a suffix or file extension of .class, as shown in Figure 1-14.

Figure 1-14 Bytecode

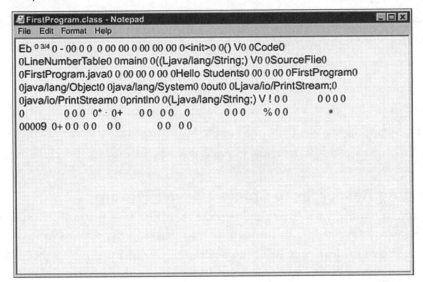

NOTE

The filename in
the window title is
`FirstProgram.class`.

Provided that there are no compiler errors, the third step is to start the JVM and
instruct it to run the program. The JVM is a program called `java`, and it executes the
program on the computer. Figure 1-15 shows the flow of activity from creating a
source file to running a Java program. The JVM interprets the bytecode of the class file
to the specific machine's language. The programmer has to compile the source file only
once and then can run it many times on different computers.

Figure 1-15 JVM and the Runtime Environment

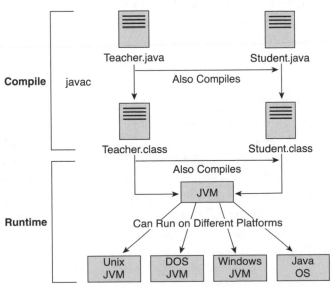

Java Program

This section discusses some basic *Java syntax* and vocabulary. It also outlines the steps of creating a simple Java program.

This section covers the following topics:

- Organizing resources to create a Java program
- Understanding the Java 2 Software Development Kit (J2SDK)
- Understanding the elements of a simple Java program
- Following three steps to create and execute a Java program

Organizing Resources to Create a Java Program

In this section, students will write and execute their first Java program. Students will be writing many Java programs throughout this course. If the reasons behind some of the steps seem unclear, they will become clearer as students progress through the course. The purpose of this section is to introduce the tools used to develop Java programs and to outline the entire process of writing, debugging, and executing a simple Java program.

Selection of the tools to be used to create, edit, and compile the program should be made before creating a Java program. The first selection should be an editor to create the Java source code for the program. The choice of an editor can be a program as simple as the Notepad program or an *integrated development environment (IDE)* software program such as *BlueJ*. An IDE is a programming environment that has been packaged as an application program, typically consisting of a code editor, a compiler, a debugger, and a graphical user interface (GUI) builder. The IDE can be a standalone application or can be included as part of one or more existing and compatible applications. The IDE utilized in this course is the BlueJ IDE. This can help with Java syntax, punctuation, and vocabulary. A Java program in this exercise will be written using Notepad.

The other tools needed to run the Java program are a compiler and a JVM. As discussed previously, Java source code is first compiled into bytecode, which the JVM then interprets and converts into native code. Sun Microsystems provides Java programmers with a rich set of tools for developing and running Java programs, including a compiler and JVM. These Java programs and libraries form the Java Development Toolkit (JDK). The JDK has evolved with each release of the JVM. The current toolkit is formally referred to as J2SDK, or the *Java 2 Software Development Kit*. However, JDK often is used to refer to the toolkit. The *J2SDK* can be downloaded for free from the Sun Microsystems website (java.sun.com).

All the tools in the J2SDK are accessed from a command line. The command line is where the programmer interacts with the computer operating system. The command line on a computer running the Microsoft Windows operating system can be accessed by opening a DOS prompt window—for a UNIX machine, by opening the console or terminal window. When the command **java** is typed at the command prompt, the help screen for the command appears. In a UNIX environment, a terminal or console window displaying the shell prompt is the command line. If an error message appears after typing in the command **java**, the J2SDK has not been installed properly. You must reinstall the J2SDK before continuing with this lesson if an error message appears.

Understanding the Java 2 Software Development Kit

The J2SDK provides all the tools (such as programs) needed to develop a Java program. All of the tools supplied in the J2SDK run only in a command-line window. These tools can be accessed by opening an MS-DOS window, as shown in Figure 1-16, on a PC or a command-line window (such as the console or terminal window on an Apple or UNIX machine).

Figure 1-16 Console Window and Accessing

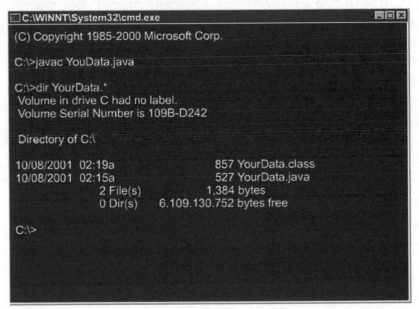

The two tools to become familiar with are javac, the Java compiler, and java, the JVM. As students progress through this course, they will become familiar with each of these tools. Table 1-4 illustrates some of the programs and libraries that make up the Java2 toolkit.

Table 1-4 Java Development Toolkit

Version	When to Use	What It Does
javac	Each time you compile your source code	The command line for javac supplies the name of the source tile containing the Java code. It converts source code to bytecode. Source code is a file with the suffix: .java. The bytecode created by javac is a file with the same name but a different suffix: .class.
java	To run programs on a Java Virtual Machine (JVM)	The Java tool is an interpreter. The command line for Java supplies the name of the file that contains the bytecode. This file has the suffix .class. The command line supplies the name of the file without the suffix.
appletviewer	To run applets	A utility that runs applets outside of a web browser. Applets are HTML documents that contain references to a Java class file.

Understanding the Elements of a Simple Java Program

This course shows students how to use the Java language to do both simple and complex tasks. Before doing this, however, students need to understand the elements of a Java program. The Java program SayHello will be used to explore a few of the elements of the language.

Recall that all programming languages have five basic elements: vocabulary, identifiers, punctuation, operators, and syntax. Because this is the first time students have seen a Java program, much of the vocabulary, syntax, and punctuation will be new to them. All of the language elements are explained in detail in later chapters. At this point, students should get a feel for how to compile and run a Java program. The details of the language will become clearer as they progress through the course.

The sample program shown in Example 1-3 describes an object named SayHello. This object contains some data (a name, a number, and a message) and knows how to print this data to the command line (not the printer).

Example 1-3 *SayHello Object*

```
1 /**
2  * Java Program: SayHello.java
3  * @author Cisco Teacher
4  * @version 2002
```

Example 1-3 *SayHello Object (Continued)*

```
 5  */
 6  //  This program will say "Hello"
 7
 8  /*
 9      Cisco Network Academy
10      Java course: Chapter 1
11      Java program file  SayHello.java
12  */
13
14  public class  SayHello
15  {
16      public static void  main(String[] args)
17      {
18          String name = "Student";
19          int number = 1;
20
21          System.out.println ("Hello ");
22          System.out.println (name);
23          System.out.println ("Your Lucky Number is " + number);
24      }
25  }
```

For Example 1-3, you can view the text associated with the numbered buttons by accessing the full, interactive graphic for this figure on the book's accompanying CD-ROM. The title of the activity is "SayHello Object" and it can be found under the heading of e-Lab Activities.

Several key points should be noted in this example:

- Comments are a critical part of every program. Programmers use comments to help clarify what the program is supposed to do. Students will learn more about comments in Chapter 3: Java Language Elements.

- Every Java source-code file starts by defining one class (or more). Classes and objects are discussed in greater detail in the next chapter, but think of a class as the blueprint for an object. Each class has a unique name, and the source code for a particular class must be stored in a source file that has the same name as the class. This example has defined a class named SayHello. It is saved in a file named

SayHello.java. By convention, the name of a class begins with a capital letter. There are three class names in the SayHello program: String, System, and SayHello.

- Classes contain both data and methods. Data can be numbers, pieces of text, or other objects. Methods are pieces of code that tell the object what to do with the data in the object. Students will learn more details about data and methods in the following chapters.

The SayHello class has one method named main. The main method in a Java program has a unique definition. It is the point where the JVM starts to read and execute the program. As students start to write their own classes and methods, they will see that there are many different ways to write a method. The method signature is not really how the method is written, but how the method is identified—namely, the unique combination of method name and types and numbers of arguments. The main method must have a specific method signature so that the JVM can find it. As shown in Example 1-4, there are only two ways to write the method signature for the main method.

Example 1-4 *Main Method Signature*

```
1 public static void main (String[] args)
2 //or
3 public static void main (String args[])
```

NOTE

The braces ([]) are in a different place in the two method signatures. Either way is correct. Students are likely to see it both ways, so they should be aware of both. Students will learn more about the main method, and ways to write other methods, in the following chapters.

The symbol for a period (.) has a very special meaning in the Java language: It is called the *dot operator*. It lets the programmer access methods or objects in other objects. In the SayHello program, the two periods in the expression System.out.println tell the Java compiler that there is a need to use the println method in the out object found in the System class. The dot operator is explained in more detail in later chapters.

Three Steps to Creating and Executing a Java Program

Recall that it takes only three steps to create and run a Java program:

Step 1   Create the source code using an editor. The source code is stored in a .java file. Because the Java program SayHello has been created, Step 1 is complete.

Step 2   Compile the source code to create the bytecode using the program javac. The bytecode is stored in a .class file

- Enter the command **javac** SayHello.java. javac is the name of the compiler program for Java. This program will create a bytecode file with the same name as the source-code file, but with the suffix of

.class. Remember that Java is a case-sensitive program. When compiling the program **javac** sayhello.java, the SayHello.java file will not be compiled.

- Verify that the .class file has been created by entering the command **dir** SayHello.*. The SayHello.class file is present.

Step 3 Run the program. The output from running the program is shown in Figure 1-17.

Figure 1-17 JVM and the Runtime Environment

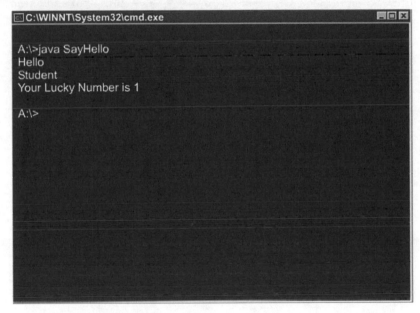

```
C:\WINNT\System32\cmd.exe

A:\>java SayHello
Hello
Student
Your Lucky Number is 1

A:\>
```

- To execute the program SayHello, type the command **java** SayHello.
- The results of the program are displayed.

Entering Data at Runtime for the Java Program

The Java language also allows users to enter input that will dictate what the Java program will do next. This feature can be quite useful. Often user data, such as a user's address or age, is important for the program to operate properly.

Modifying the HelloStudent Program to Accept Input at Runtime

In this section, the SayHello program will be modified to read data from the command line. First, it will accept input at *runtime*.

The most common function of a program is to receive input data from some source such as the command line, a file, or another program. The program then performs calculations or decisions based on that data and sends the result somewhere, such as to the console, to a file, or to another program. The console window used to compile and run the programs is a program running on the computer. The command line accepts text as an input message, as shown in Figure 1-18, and can pass that message to other programs—in particular, to the next Java program.

Figure 1-18 Modifying Input at Runtime

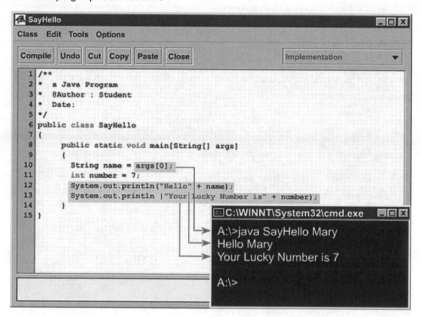

The console program takes all the text on the command line, and interprets the first word as the name of a program and the rest of the words as input parameters for that program. When **java** `SayHelloSayHello "Fred Smith"` is typed at the command line, the console program tells the operating system to execute a program called `java` with the input parameter `SayHelloSayHello "Fred Smith"`. The `java` program—in this case, the JVM—tries to execute the program `SayHelloSayHello` with the input parameter `"Fred Smith"`.

To understand how the `java` program will receive the message that contains `"Fred Smith"`, students must understand a little more about the syntax of the `main` method. Students will learn more about methods in later chapters, but here is a preview to help with this lab activity.

The method signature for the `main` method is described as listed here:

```
public static void main (String[] args)
```

The key to sending a message to the `main` method is the `String[]` args inside the parentheses. There are several key points to know for this lab exercise:

- All methods receive data as input in the form of an argument list. The argument list is the text inside the parentheses after the name of the method. For the `main` method, the argument list is `String[]` args.

- The argument list for a method is a list of word pairs. The first word identifies what type of data the argument must be. The second word is the identifier, or name, of the argument. In the `main` method, the identifier for the input data is "args" and the class type is "`String array`".

- An array is a list of elements, all of the same type. A `String` array is a list of objects, which are all `Strings`. A `String` object contains text, such as "`Sam Smith`" or "`123-34-1234`". The brackets "`[]`" are the operators that denote an array in Java. They can follow the identifier of the array, or they can follow the name of the type of elements in the array. In this example, `String[]` args or `String` args`[]` both mean an array of `String` objects. Now it is clear why there are two ways to write the `main` method.

- Because an array is a list of elements, there must be a way to tell the program to look at the first, or fifth, or hundredth element in the list. You can access any element in the array by using an index. An index is a number that corresponds to the element's position in the array. The numbering for arrays starts at 0, not 1. This can cause confusion for new programmers. The first element in the `String` array called args is args[0], not args[1]. The reference args[1] refers to the second element in the array. The 37th element in the array is referenced with args[36], not args[37]. When students study arrays in more detail in Chapter 7, "Arrays," they will learn why array indices start at 0.

To complete the example from the command line, **java** SayHelloSayHello "Fred Smith", the input parameter for SayHello is converted by the JVM into a `String` array with one element, "Fred Smith".

If there had been more text on the command line, each word separated by a space would become an element in the array args. For example, suppose that **java** SayHello "Fred Smith" "John MacKenzie" "Peter Bull" was written on the command line. The `String` array in the program would resemble the following:

- args[0] would contain Fred Smith.
- args[1] would contain John MacKenzie.
- args[2] would contain Peter Bull.

Now, it is the student's turn to modify the HelloStudent1 program from the previous lab to receive messages from the command line.

Understanding Programming Error Messages

Whenever a program is written, no matter what the language is, a programmer can expect to receive errors. This section introduces the types of errors that can occur in programs and illustrates how to edit a Java program for compiler and runtime errors.

Types of Errors in Programs

Three types of programming errors exist: compiler errors, runtime errors, and logic errors. Each type is described in the following sections.

Compiler Errors

Compiler errors are detected by the compiler and prevent the compiler from creating the class file from the source code.

Runtime Errors

Runtime errors occur when the program is executed, after all the compiler errors have been corrected.

Logic Errors

Logic errors are not detected by the compiler. The program functions but does not produce the intended result. For example, if a program is designed to add two numbers, but the programmer unintentionally uses a – symbol instead of the + symbol, a logic error is created.

Compiler errors are discussed, and then students will have a chance to experiment with a sample program that has some compiler errors (as shown in Figure 1-19). The detailed discussion of runtime errors is presented in Chapter 12, "Exceptions."

Figure 1-19 Compile Errors

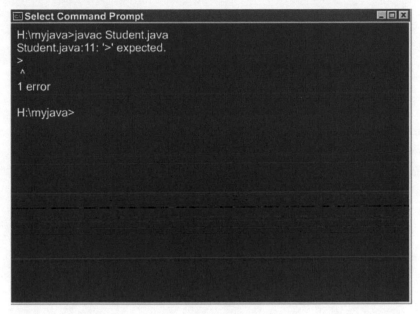

Editing a Java Program for Compiler Errors

All programmers encounter some common errors in the code they have created:

- Java keywords or class names spelled incorrectly
- Inconsistent references for identifiers
- Braces ({}), brackets ([]), or parentheses (( )) that have not been closed
- Missing dot operators (.)
- Missing semicolons (;)

Most of these errors are caused by not following the syntax rules of the language. The compiler javac identifies these errors and displays diagnostic messages to help programmers find and correct them. Becoming familiar with compiler error messages is a required skill for all programmers (see Figure 1-20).

Figure 1-20 Compiling Errors

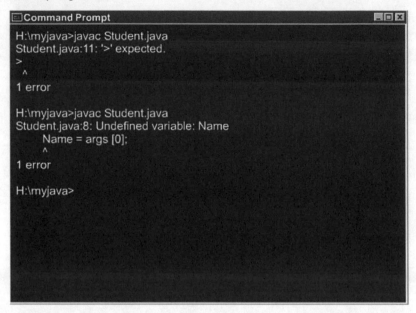

The best way to reduce the number and frequency of these errors is to carefully learn the five elements of a programming language that were previously discussed. These elements are defined in the sections that follow.

Vocabulary

Vocabulary is the set of keywords used within the language.

Punctuation

Punctuation refers to the symbols used by the language.

Identifiers

Identifiers are the names used to reference the data stored in the memory of the computer.

Operators

Operators are commands or symbols used to process data. Examples of symbols for arithmetic activity, or testing of data, are as follows: +, *, %, and, or, not, !, > , <.

Syntax

Syntax refers to grammar or rules of usage for the previous elements.

Other techniques can help reduce the number of compiler errors in the program:

- Use an integrated development environment (IDE) to write the Java code. Most IDEs color-code the different elements of the language so that programmers can spot errors quickly. They also warn programmers before they make simple syntax errors, such as omitting parentheses, brackets, or braces. BlueJ is an IDE that is included with this course; it is discussed later in this chapter.
- Check the spelling of all keywords.
- Indent the source code a few spaces (two to four) with each brace. Indenting the code makes the braces easier to find and makes the code more readable, as shown in Example 1-5.

Example 1-5 *Indenting Source Code*

```
1 public static void main (String[] args)
2 {
3     //start the first line here with
4     //2-4 spaces of indentation
5
6     // more code here . . . . .
7 } //end main method
```

The first brace also can be put on the same line as the method declaration, as shown in Example 1-6.

Example 1-6 *Brace Placement*

```
1 public static void main (String[] args){
2     //start the first line here with
3     //2-4 spaces of indentation
4     // more code here . . . . .
5 } //end main method
```

Because the brace does not have its own line, more lines can be seen in an editor window at one time:

- Note the closing comment after the closing brace in the previous example. Adding a closing comment like this after the closing brace for each method also makes it easier to find and check the braces in the source code.

- Coding style has been the subject of much debate among programmers. You can read more about the coding style that has been adopted for the Java language here. As students progress through this course, some of the more common coding conventions or styles are outlined.

- Check for closing brackets and parentheses. Remember that the arguments for every method are enclosed in parentheses.

- Check the spelling and capitalization of the identifiers, method names, and class names in the program. Java is a case-sensitive language. Thus, referencing a class called `String` is not the same as referencing a class named `string` or `STRING` or `StrinG`. Because the `main` method has a special meaning in Java, if programmers write `public static void MAIN (String[] args)`, the compiler will not create the `main` method that the JVM needs to run the program. It will create the class with a method called `MAIN`, but the JVM will not recognize it. This error will actually create a runtime error, not a compiler error.

- Proofread the code before compiling it.

- Read the compiler error messages carefully.

- Fix the compiler errors in the order that they appear. Start with the first error and fix it before fixing the second error, and so on. Many times, the first compiler error will cause other compiler errors. For example, if a brace has been forgotten, the compiler does not know where one method stops and another one begins. One missing brace can cause many compiler errors. If students start to find compiler errors that do not make a lot of sense, they should recompile the code with the fixes in place from the previous errors. This might clear up many of the compiler errors.

- Do not forget to save the source code after making changes. If there are exactly the same compiler errors as in the previous compilation, it's important to make sure that changes made to the source code were actually saved to the source-code file. The Java compiler reads the source-code file, not what is displayed in the editor's window.

Remember that the compiler will not create the `.class` file (bytecode) for the JVM until all the compiler errors are fixed. Students might have to compile the source code, fix compiler errors, and then recompile the source code several times before the compiler will produce a functioning `.class` file. After all the errors have been fixed, the program will run correctly, as shown in Figure 1-21.

Figure 1-21 Corrected Program

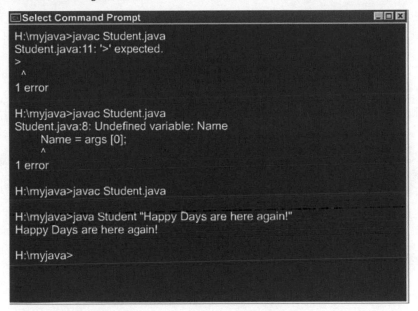

Editing a Java Program for Runtime Errors

After a program has compiled successfully, the programmer might still encounter errors when the program is executed. These errors are called runtime errors. In the Java language, runtime errors are also called exceptions because they create an exception to the normal flow of the program (see Figure 1-22).

The JVM monitors each Java program for exceptions and displays messages when they occur. Typically, a program that encounters an exception will be terminated. Some of these errors can be anticipated and avoided so that the program can run to completion. A programmer can write code to handle exceptions as they occur. One of the benefits of using the Java language is the set of tools built into the language for handling exceptions. Exceptions and exception handling are discussed later in Chapter 12, "Exceptions."

A program still might not return the expected result, even though the program compiled successfully and the JVM has not displayed any exception messages. This is often the result of logic errors in the program. Simply stated, the sequence of instructions is not yielding the expected result. This requires analyzing what the instructions are doing. This process of "walking through the code" is a part of debugging the program.

Figure 1-22 Runtime Error

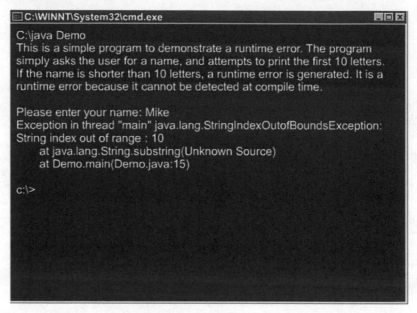

Several techniques can be used for debugging the logic of the code. The most common is to look at the values of intermediate results in the code to make sure they are as expected.

Understanding Integrated Development Environments

After enough experience is gathered, programmers often utilize an *integrated development environment (IDE)* for their programming tasks. The IDE is a graphical interface that can easily replicate tasks and sometimes indicate errors as they occur. IDEs also utilize some type of coloring scheme to better indicate to the programmer the major points of their program. This section covers the following topics:

- What an IDE is
- Examples of IDEs
- Basic editing with the BlueJ IDE
- The BlueJ tutorial

What Is an IDE?

Many Java applications have hundreds of Java objects and, hence, hundreds of Java source files. Creating, editing, and managing Java source code and class files for such a project can be overwhelming. Organizing these files helps programmers understand the function of all the classes, their relationship to each other, and which ones can be reused. Many software tools exist just for the purpose of assisting the programmers in managing, maintaining, and creating Java source code. These are known as integrated development environments (IDEs), as shown in Example 1-7. IDEs might integrate a text editor, a Software Development Kit (SDK), a window to display results, and even tools to create graphical user interfaces (GUIs). Many of them provide drag-and-drop capabilities and GUI symbols to design the Java classes. Some collect class definition information and create a source file, generating the necessary Java language code. All that the programmer needs to do is add any details or modifications.

Example 1-7 *BlueJ IDE*

```
1 /**
2  * Java Program: SayHello.java
3  * @author Cisco Teacher
4  * @version 2002
5  */
6 public class SayHello
7 {
8      public static void main(String[] args)
9      {
10         String name = "Student";
11         int number =7;
12         System.out.println("Hello ");
13         System.out.println(name);
14         System.out.println("Your Lucky Number is " + number);
15     }
16 }
```

Many IDEs enable the programmer to plan the application using simple symbols that can be dragged and dropped onto a GUI. These symbols can be interconnected to show not only the relationship between the classes, but also how they communicate with each other. The IDE creates the source files for each of the symbols from a set of templates. All the programmer has to do is fill in the details of each object's function and add extensive comments so that the next programmer can understand the function of the object. There is also a special language of symbols that has developed around object-oriented programming: the Unified Modeling Language (UML). The IDE used in this course uses UML, which is discussed in greater detail in Chapter 2, "Object-Oriented Programming."

Examples of IDEs

Some of the more popular IDEs that are available are discussed next. This section consists of the following topics:

- BlueJ
- Forte
- JBuilder
- JDeveloper
- VisualAge for Java
- Symantec Visual Café
- NetBeans

Blue J

BlueJ is an integrated Java environment that is particularly useful for Java beginners. The software is free (at this time) and is available at www.bluej.org/index.html. BlueJ has a graphical class structure display, graphical and text editing capabilities, and a built-in editor, compiler and debugger. Its interface is easy to use.

More Information
See www.bluej.org/what/what.html.

Forte

Forte is an integrated development environment (IDE) for Java developers, manufactured by Sun. Its focus on building and deploying web services across multiple hardware and software platforms. It is a modular, extensible IDE. At this time, there is an enterprise edition and a free community edition. The community edition can be used to create standalone applications, applets, and JavaBeans components, or to build database-aware web applications.

For more information, see: www.sun.com/software/Developer-products/ffj/.

JBuilder

JBuilder is a comprehensive visual development environment from Borland Software for building applications, applets, JSP/Servlets, JavaBeans, Enterprise JavaBeans, and distributed J2EE applications for the Java 2 Platform.

For more information, see www.borland.com/jbuilder/.

JDeveloper

Oracle 9i JDeveloper is a Java development IDE from Oracle Corporation. It includes dynamic feedback on coding in progress and has a first-class debugger. At this time (2003), this IDE is available for free but needs to be licensed for commercial use.

More Information
See the following resources:
www.eweek.com/article/0,3658,apn=3&s=708&a=21152&app=1&ap=2,00.asp
www.eweek.com/article/0,3658,s=708&a=21152,00.asp

VisualAge for Java

VisualAge for Java, from IBM, is a comprehensive tool for creating applications that target IBM's WebSphere software platform for e-business. This is an IDE, with Servlet and JavaServer Pages development and testing, a WebSphere Testing Environment, and the Tool Integrator API.

For more information, see www-3.ibm.com/software/ad/vajava/about/index.html.

Symantec Visual Café

Visual Café is an IDE with a built-in editor, compiler, and interpreter. It provides a customizable, easy-to-use environment for creating and deploying Java applications. This is a visual environment, so GUIs can be developed using drag-and-drop technology.

For more information, see www.irt.org/software/sw019/.

NetBeans

NetBeans is a modular IDE written in Java. This IDE is an open source project, with contributions from numerous programmers.

For more information, see www.netbeans.org/.

Basic Editing with the BlueJ IDE

This course introduces an IDE using a simple shareware tool named BlueJ. The following lab activity teaches students how to create, edit, save, compile, and run a simple Java program using BlueJ, shown in Example 1-8.

Example 1-8 *BlueJ IDE II*

```
 1 /**
 2 * a Java Program
 3 * @Author : Student
 4 */
 5 //   Date:
 6
 7 /*
 8 Cisco Network Academy
 9 Java course: Chapter 1
10 Java program file  SayHello.java
11 */
12
13 public class SayHello
14 {
15
16
17  public static void main(String[] args)
18 {
19   String name = "Student";
```

It is important to understand that the BlueJ program makes the process of editing, compiling, and running programs easier and faster than using the command line and Notepad. BlueJ automates several of the tasks for the programmer.

For Example 1-8, you can view how BlueJ handles the task of cutting and pasting by accessing the full, interactive graphic for this example on the book's accompanying CD-ROM. The title of the activity is "The BlueJ IDE" and can be found under the heading of e-Lab Activities.

To compile a Java program, BlueJ still uses the javac program, just as students did when compiling the HelloStudent program. BlueJ also uses the same JVM (java) that has been used when it is told to run a program.

BlueJ Tutorial

BlueJ has an online tutorial, shown in Figure 1-23, that is simple to follow and well written. However, students might encounter some terms that are specific to Java. Some of these terms have not been covered because the tutorial assumes that the reader is an accomplished Java programmer. Do not worry about these terms for now; they will become familiar as the course proceeds.

Figure 1-23 BlueJ Tutorial

In this lab activity, students explore the many other features of BlueJ. Students need to become familiar with these features because they will be used as students learn more about the Java language and develop more sophisticated Java programs later in the course.

Case Study: JBANK, a Banking Application

This course provides students with an opportunity to use the Java language in a real-world application. Figures 1-24 and 1-25 display what the JBANK application might look like at the end of the course. This case study involves a banking application.

Figure 1-24 JBANK Application

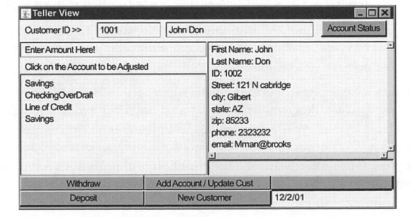

Figure 1-25 JBANK Application II

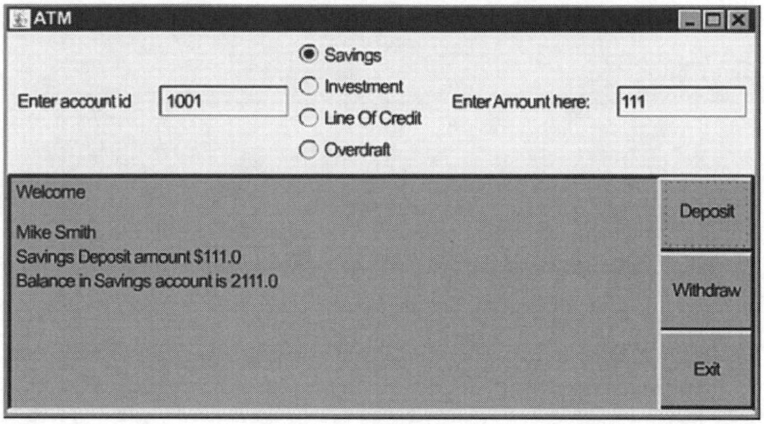

This chapter creates one of the programs (objects) needed for the banking application, the `Teller` object. In the following labs, students will create a simple `Teller` program that displays a message using the BlueJ IDE. One lab creates the `Teller` program to display a message on the console, and the second lab accepts input at runtime and displays the message.

Summary

Programming provides a set of logical instructions for a computer to perform tasks. The languages used to program a computer can be described as either procedural or object-oriented. Procedural programming languages are coded with linear logic, and the executable files are created using compilers. FORTRAN and COBOL are both examples of procedural languages. Object-oriented languages such as Java break the program into objects, each of which performs a specific function within the program.

Some languages are compiled, while others are interpreted. Java is both compiled and interpreted. The **javac** command is used to compile the code. The **java** command then is used to interpret and execute the code.

A Java program can be created using a simple editor such as Notepad, or by using an IDE tool such as BlueJ. Programmers use tools that help them produce programs quickly. BlueJ is an effective IDE for creating Java programs and learning the Java language, which consists of vocabulary, punctuation, identifiers, operators, and syntax. The Java programming language includes a rich library of programs known as classes. These form the Java language application program interface (API).

Correcting errors is part of the programmer's job. One type of error is a compiler error, which the compiler identifies for the programmer. Compiler errors prevent the code from being compiled. Runtime errors are caused by exceptions that occur in the normal flow of the program. They also occur if the program does not accomplish what it was designed to accomplish.

Syntax Summary

Throughout this chapter, you might not have been familiar with some syntax used. This section briefly summarizes the important syntax:

- `main`—This is the special keyword of a method used by the Java interpreter to start a program.
- `{`—The opening brace tells the compiler the start of the method definition.
- `}`—The closing brace informs the compiler of the end of the method definition.
- `.`—The dot operator enables the programmer to access methods or objects in other objects.
- `.java`—This is the suffix ending for compiling the source code in the command line.
- **`javac`**—This command is used for compiling the source code.
- `.class`—The bytecode is stored with this suffix ending.
- **`java`**—This command is used with the class name to execute the program in the command line.
- `String[] args`—This is used in the `main` method for sending a message. `String` is the class type and `args` is the identifier for the input data.

Resources

This book is not meant to be a comprehensive manual for everything Java. To include everything relevant to Java would take volumes. As such, many resources are available on the web. The next sections documents a couple of those resources.

Websites for Material

Sun Java website: java.sun.com/

Sun Developer site: developer.java.sun.com/developer/

Tutorials on the Web

Sun Java tutorial: java.sun.com/docs/books/tutorial/

Java tutorial and frequently asked questions: java.sun.com/docs/books/tutorial/information/FAQ.html

Java code samples: developer.java.sun.com/developer/codesamples/

How to run your first program in Java: java.sun.com/docs/books/tutorial/getStarted/cupojava/index.html

Introduction to the Sun Website and Java API

Sun Java website: java.sun.com/

Sun Java products and APIs: java.sun.com/products/

How to Download and Install Java

Java 2 platform (standard edition) download: java.sun.com/j2se/1.4/download.html

Java installation instructions: java.sun.com/j2se/1.4/install-windows.html

How to Download and Install BlueJ

What BlueJ is: www.bluej.org/what/what.html

Why BlueJ is useful: www.bluej.org/why/why.html

Blue J download: www.bluej.org/download/download.html

BlueJ documentation: www.bluej.org/doc/documentation.html

BlueJ frequently asked questions: www.bluej.org/help/faq.html

Links to BlueJ Tutorial

BlueJ tutorial: www.bluej.org/tutorial/tutorial.pdf

BlueJ documentation: www.bluej.org/doc/documentation.html

Key Terms

BlueJ Integrated Java environment specifically designed for introductory teaching.

bytecode Computer object code that is processed by a program, usually referred to as a virtual machine, instead of by the "real" computer machine, the hardware processor. The virtual machine converts each generalized machine instruction into a specific machine instruction or instructions that this computer's processor will understand. A bytecode is the result of compiling source code written in a language that supports this approach.

compiler Program to translate source code into code to be executed by a computer. The Java compiler translates source code written in the Java programming language into bytecode for the Java Virtual Machine.

hardware Physical aspect of computers, telecommunications, and other information technology devices.

integrated development environment (IDE) Programming environment that has been packaged as an application program, typically consisting of a code editor, a compiler, a debugger, and a graphical user interface (GUI) build.

interpreter Module that alternately decodes and executes every statement in some body of code. The Java interpreter decodes and executes bytecode for the Java Virtual Machine.

Java 2 Software Development Toolkit (Java 2 SDK) Software Developer's Kit (SDK) is a set of programs used by a computer programmer to write application programs.

Java programming language Object-oriented programming language developed at Sun Microsystems, Inc.

Java Virtual Machine (JVM) Software "execution engine" that safely and compatibly executes the bytecode in Java class files on a microprocessor (whether in a computer or in another electronic device).

javac Command used in the Java language to compile a program.

object-oriented programming languages Object-oriented programming is a method of programming based on a hierarchy of classes and well-defined and cooperating objects.

procedural programming languages Procedural program is written as a list of instructions, telling the computer step by step what to do: Open a file, read a number, multiply by 4, display something. Program units include the main or program block, subroutines, functions, procedures; file scoping; includes/modules; and libraries.

runtime The process of executing the `.class` byte code. The runtime system includes all the code necessary to load programs written in the Java programming language, dynamically link native methods, manage memory, handle exceptions, and implement the Java Virtual Machine.

software, programs, applications General terms for the various kinds of programs used to operate computers and related devices.

source code Programming statements that are created by a programmer with a text editor or an IDE and then saved in a file.

Check Your Understanding

1. The three basic components of a computer are

   A. Keyboard, mouse, and printer

   B. CPU, memory, and subassemblies

   C. CPU, RAM, and hard drive

   D. RAM, hard drive, and subassemblies

2. Which of the following are not examples of computer hardware?

   A. Keyboard, mouse, hard drives

   B. Monitor, CD-ROM drives, printer

   C. Floppy disk, CDs, printer paper

   D. Removable disk drives, modem

3. Which of the following is false?

   A. Persistent memory retains stored information when the power is terminated.

   B. Java program usually is stored in persistent memory when it is executed.

   C. Dynamic memory does not retain stored information when the power is terminated.

   D. A Java program is stored in dynamic memory when it is executed.

4. What is a computer operating system?

   A. A computer program, such as a spell checker, that is included in an application

   B. A computer application that directly controls the software installed on a computer

   C. A collection of programs that directly control computer hardware

   D. A set of programs that work together, such as a web browser, word processor, and computer game

5. Which of the following is not true about the Java programming language?

   A. Java is an easy language to learn.

   B. There are many powerful tools to help programmers develop complex applications quickly and efficiently.

   C. Java programs are compatible with a small number of hardware devices.

   D. Almost any complex business or scientific problem can be solved using programs written in Java.

6. COBOL and FORTRAN are examples of

   A. Machine languages

   B. Assembler languages

   C. Object-oriented languages

   D. High-level languages

7. Why has object-oriented programming become a popular model for problem solving?

   A. The object-oriented approach more closely resembles the process used by people.

   B. A software object is created once and reused in many different programs.

   C. Object-oriented programs are easier to maintain and more efficient to produce.

   D. All of the above.

8. In computer programming, what is a procedure?

   A. A black box that behaves in a predetermined way to accomplish a task

   B. A set of instructions executed sequentially by the computer

   C. A software object that interacts with other objects to complete a task

   D. A piece of data, such as a number or a date

9. What is the function of a compiler?

   A. A compiler executes the source code of a program.

   B. A compiler converts source code into native code.

   C. A compiler executes the native code of a program.

   D. A compiler converts native code into source code.

10. Why has Java become a popular language for the Internet and the World Wide Web?

    A. Java supports an international character set for a globally connected Internet.

    B. Java is portable and can be used on a variety of hardware, such as computers and cellular phones.

    C. Java can be used on multiple computing platforms.

    D. All of the above.

11. Which type of code is interpreted by the Java Virtual Machine into native code?

    A. Source code

    B. Bytecode

    C. Processor code

    D. Bit code

12. A Java class contains

    A. Data only

    B. Methods only

    C. Neither data nor methods

    D. Both data and methods

13. Which of the following is the file containing Java source code for a class named JavaDemo?

    A. JavaDemo.class

    B. JAVADEMO.java

    C. JavaDemo.java

    D. JavaDemo.exe

14. Which of the following is the file containing Java bytecode for a class named JavaDemo?

    A. JavaDemo.class

    B. JAVADEMO.java

    C. JavaDemo.java

    D. JavaDemo.exe

15. The correct syntax for the `main` method is

A. public void main(String[] args)

B. public static void main (String args)

C. public static void Main (String[] args)

D. public static void main (String[] args)

16. Which type of error has occurred if a program functions but does not produce the desired result?

A. Default error

B. Logic error

C. Runtime error

D. Compiler error

17. The grammar and usage rules of a programming language are referred to as

A. Syntax

B. Vocabulary

C. Identifiers

D. Operations

18. In which case will the Java compiler successfully create a class file from the source file?

A. The source file contains code that results in compiler errors and runtime errors.

B. The source file contains code that results in compiler errors and logic errors.

C. The source file contains code that results in runtime errors and logic errors.

D. The source file contains code that results in compiler errors, runtime errors, and logic errors.

19. BlueJ, Forte for Java, JDeveloper, and JBuilder are examples of

A. Java Virtual Machines

B. Integrated development environments

C. Java compilers

D. Java web browsers

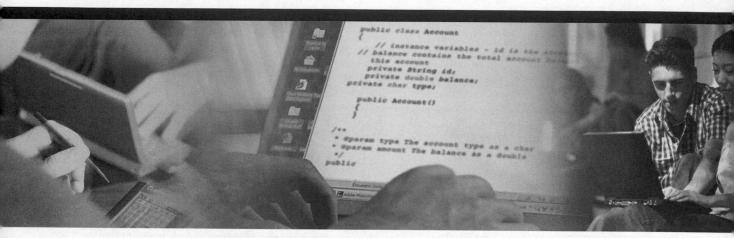

Upon completion of this chapter, you will be able to

- Understand object-oriented programming
- Define and describe objects
- Use the terminology applied to a Java program
- Understand the `java.lang.System` class
- Apply the Java language concepts that you have learned in this chapter to the JBANK case study
- Visualize how an object-oriented language, like Java, is structured using the `JavaZoo` application

Chapter 2

Object-Oriented Programming

Object-oriented programming is fundamentally different than procedural programming. In this chapter, students learn about objects and classes. To create Java programs, students need to understand how objects and classes work, how they are created, and how they are used. Students also learn to use the Unified Modeling Language (UML), an industry-standard technique for describing objects.

Overview of Object-Oriented Programming

This section highlights the key differences between procedural and object-oriented programming methodologies, and it introduces the basic Java terminology that will be used throughout this course.

Procedural Versus Object-Oriented Languages

Chapter 1, "What Is Java?", introduced students to two types of programming methodologies: procedural and object-oriented.

A procedural language creates a program in which the tasks performed by the computer are described in a logical sequence. When the program executes, the instructions are followed in the sequence defined in the program. In Chapter 1, the simple process of drinking from a cup was broken down into the following eight sequential steps:

Step 1   Look at the cup.

Step 2   Extend your hand.

Step 3   Open your hand.

Step 4   Grasp the cup in your hand.

Step 5   Close your hand.

Step 6   Lift the cup to your mouth.

Step 7   Tilt the cup.

Step 8   Sip.

Additionally, all of the data to be processed by the program is described within the program. The idea behind this is that there will be only one approach to solving a particular problem. Thus, procedural languages require modifying the program if the data that is to be processed changes. If a large number of programs are accessed to complete complex tasks, these changes also would have to be included in each of these programs. Because these changes often are costly and time-consuming, object-oriented programming (OOP) has become popular, particularly for business applications.

OOP languages describe tasks to be performed on objects. These objects are created first and are stored in the memory of the computer. They contain the data and instructions to perform tasks specific to that object. When a program runs, the computer system loads these objects and performs operations on these objects when instructed. Therefore, the program is viewed as a collection of interacting objects.

OOP is popular for several reasons. Because each object is relatively small and self-contained, software written with OOP languages can run on small devices. Some software objects that already have been defined, tested, and used can be reused for other purposes. Such reuse makes designing new solutions relatively inexpensive and quick. Productivity also is improved because required changes need to be made only once.

NOTE

The following sections address the procedural approach and the objected-oriented approach separately.

Procedural Approach

The procedural approach generally can be described by the following:

- Data structures can be represented as a network of associated structures referring to one another.
- Procedures can be represented as a network of routines that call one another, as in a "call tree."

Object-Oriented Approach

The object-oriented approach generally can be described by the following:

- It is a collection of discrete objects that incorporate data structures and behavior.
- Each data structure has procedures that apply to that data structure.
- This approach contrasts with conventional programming, in which data structures and behavior are only loosely connected.
- These entities, called objects, can be associated with one another in one network rather than two.

Object-oriented design (OOD) programmers can usually work with procedural programming just fine; however, the opposite is usually not true. In fact, when procedural programmers start using a language that is object-oriented, they usually try to program the old way, which results in object code that has to be thrown away and rewritten. It takes months (or sometimes years) for procedural programmers to really "get it" and think in terms of objects.

More Information
More discussion on procedural versus object-oriented programming can be found at http://javaboutique.internet.com/articles/ITJ/qanda/q20.html.

In this course, students learn to create a business application, relevant to the banking industry, using Java. This application provides students experience in designing solutions that use object-oriented programming models. This consists of many software objects that are defined with the Java language. Students use existing objects from the application programming interface (API) library and also reuse their own objects for different tasks. Additionally, students also experience the use of procedural programming techniques that are implemented in methods of an object.

Basic Java Terminology

The Java concepts and terms listed in Table 2-1 are used throughout this course. Several of them are described in the sections that follow.

Table 2-1 Java Concepts and Terms

Object-Speak		
accessors	information hiding	mutators
attributes	instance	object
class	member data	object relationships
constructors	member methods	object speak
data	message sending	polymorphism
encapsulation	methods	reuse
generalization/specialization	modeling	UML

The following sections name and describe the most commonly used Java terminology.

Object

An *object* contains data and instructions for processing the data. An object is a representation of something.

Class

A *class* is a blueprint for an object. A class contains the attributes and behaviors of the object it defines.

Attribute

Attributes describe the state of objects. Attributes are also called *data*.

Data Type

A *data type* describes what kind of information a certain attribute is.

Behavior

Behaviors describe what objects can do. Behaviors are also called methods.

Method

A *method* is a set of instructions that are executed by an object.

Inheritance

Some objects derive attributes and behaviors from other objects. This is called *inheritance*.

Encapsulation

Encapsulation is the process of combining data and methods together in one class.

What Are Objects?

Objects are the principal building blocks of object-oriented languages, such as Java. Each object is a programming unit consisting of data and functionality. Understanding how to define and implement objects is key to becoming a successful object-oriented programmer.

This section covers the following topics:

- Introduction to objects
- Classification of objects
- Identification of objects
- Definition of object classes
- Creation of objects
- Operation on objects
- Encapsulation
- Object relationships
- Inheritance
- Object mutability and destruction

Introduction to Objects

Almost anything and everything that is tangible is an object. A person, organization, machine, or event can be regarded as an object. The following lists some object definitions from experts in the field:

- A tangible and/or visible thing, something that can be understood intellectually, or something toward which thought or action is directed. An individual, identifiable item, unit or entity, either real or abstract, with a well-defined role in a problem domain. Anything with a crisply defined boundary.
- Anything that can be distinctly identified. At the appropriate level of abstraction, almost anything can be considered to be an object. Thus, a specific person, organization, machine, or event can be regarded as an object.
- A person or thing through which action, thought, or feeling is directed. Anything visible or tangible; a maternal product or substance.

The following list illustrates some general characteristics of objects:

- An object is anything real or abstract that has importance for the tasks the computer should perform. Data and instructions to manipulate data are stored in the object.
- Objects have certain attributes, which is data, and can exhibit certain behaviors. An object "knows things" and "knows how to do things." Objects do not know things or know how to do things the way people do. Instead, objects contain data (how it knows things) and instructions or procedures to process the data (how it knows how to do things).

- Similar objects can be classified under common definitions of attributes and behavior. That is, object definitions can be generalized to a class from which more specific objects can be derived.

- Objects interact with or operate on each other. This means that one object might perform an instruction that manipulates the data of another object.

- The specific way in which an object functions does not have to be understood in order to interact with it. An object can be thought of as a black box; the inside workings of the black box are not visible to the user. The user must trust the object to consistently perform the tasks for which it is designed.

- Objects that exist in one system can be reused and included in another system. *Reuse* occurs when a user creates a specific object that derives its features from another general object. The specific object is said to extend from the general object, and it can interact with or have relationships with many other objects.

All objects have attributes and exhibit behaviors. Figure 2-1 shows some specific examples of objects that a programmer can model in an object-oriented program. Attributes describe an object, such as its size, color, or shape. A dog, for example, can be large or small; black, brown, or white; and skinny or fat. Behaviors, on the other hand, describe what objects do. A dog, for instance, runs, eats, and sleeps. Attributes are also known as data, while behavior is referred to as methods. As students begin to use the Java language for describing and interacting with objects, the terms *data* and *methods* will be more commonly used than *attributes* and *behaviors*.

Figure 2-1 Introduction to Objects

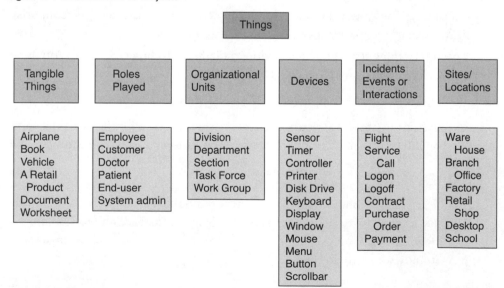

The activity in Figure 2-2 helps the student understand the difference between attributes and behaviors of objects. The cup and hand objects can be used to create an object-oriented alternative. Which of the labels shown at the bottom of the figure correctly describes what each object knows and knows how to do?

Figure 2-2 Introduction to Objects

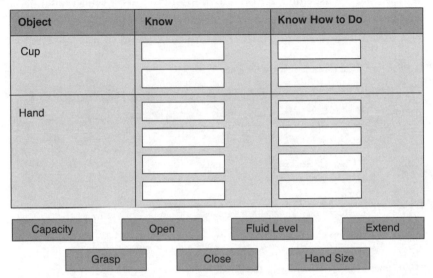

You can check your answers using an interactive graphic on the book's accompanying CD-ROM. The title of the activity is "Introduction to Objects," and it can be found under the e-Lab Activities.

Classification of Objects

From a programmer's point of view, objects in a computer have different classifications, such as those listed here:

- User interface objects
- Operating environment objects
- Task-related objects
  - Documents
  - Multimedia
  - Problem domain

The following sections provide descriptions and examples for these object classifications.

NOTE

Object-oriented meth-
odology permeates
modern computer sys-
tems and languages. A
familiar example to
computer users is a
GUI (Windows, X
Window System, or
Macintosh) applica-
tion. The application
has actions on the
menu bar; these are
called methods (New,
Open, Save, Quit).
The application also
has attributes; these
are called properties
(size, color, name).
When you open a
document via the
application (File,
Open), you call or
invoke a method via
an event handler
responding to a
mouse click.

User Interface Objects

These objects appear on a screen and often are called widgets (for "window gadgets"). End users interact directly with them. Buttons, scrollbars, text boxes, drop-down lists, check boxes, and radio buttons are all examples of user interface objects. To create GUIs, users create software objects that know how to render the image of the widget. They can also hold the user-interaction data and interact with objects that can process the input of the user. For example, a scrollbar knows how to scroll, and a button knows how to be pushed. Figure 2-3 illustrates the implementation of user interface objects.

Figure 2-3 Program That Uses Software Objects

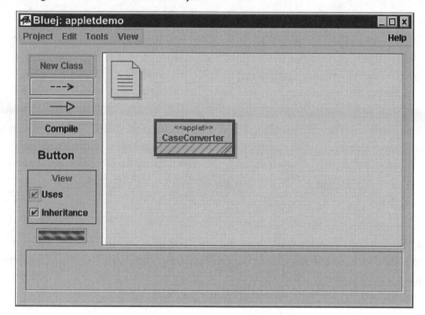

Operating Environment Objects

Operating environment objects describe aspects of the computer they exist on, the network it connects to, or other computers on that network and the services they provide. For example, a server is an object that provides services for other objects, such as software objects.

Task-Related Objects

Task-related objects are used to complete work and typically are divided into subgroups. Here's one good way of dividing task-related objects into groups:

- Documents

- Multimedia
- Problem domain

The following sections provide descriptions and examples for theses three subgroups of task-related objects.

Documents
Documents include objects created by an application. The World Wide Web is a collection of document objects.

Multimedia
Multimedia such as sound clips, images, animation, and video are objects. Users can interact with some of these objects.

Problem Domain
A problem domain object is a special object created by the programmer to meet the needs of the end user. Customers, products, orders, employees, invoices, stock, inventory, items, and reports are examples of problem domain objects. For example, a customer object holds data about customers. The attributes and behaviors of a customer object are based on what the bank needs to know about the customer and what it needs to do based on that information. In the banking application that students will be working on as part of the course project, there are definitions for an account object, a customer object, and a bank object. These are the requirements of the end users, the personnel at JBANK who will use the application.

Identification of Objects
To build any application using an OOP approach, objects first must be identified. Object-speak is the unique vocabulary that is used to describe objects and object features in programming. Object-think is a thinking process that can help users in defining and identifying objects.

To identify objects, or object-think, a programmer must assess the needs of the end users. Most programmers refer to this as the requirements-gathering phase of a project. This generally provides a list of potential problem domain or task-related objects. To meet the end user's needs, programmers also might need to define specialized objects that support the problem domain objects. For example, to provide a way for the user to input data, a programmer might create user interface objects such as windows, buttons, scrollbars, and text boxes. To provide users access to data in files, a programmer might create operating environment objects such as files, input/output, clients, and a server. To store the data in a relatively permanent location, a programmer might create objects that write to files or databases. All of these objects interacting with each other result in an OOP application.

When designing objects, it helps to ask these questions:

1. What are the attributes of the object?
2. What are the behaviors of the object?

Apply these questions to the user interface object of a button. Your list of attributes and behaviors for the button might look like the following:

- I know what window I am attached to.
- I know my position in a window.
- I know my height and width.
- I know my background color.
- I know what the label that appears on me says.
- I know what to do when pushed.

Next, apply these questions to the problem domain object named Account. Your list of attributes and behaviors for an account might look like the following:

- I know the balance.
- I know the ID of the customer who owns this account.
- I know how to withdraw—that is, deduct an amount from the balance.
- I know how to deposit—that is, add an amount to the balance.
- I know how to provide the balance.

Definition of Object Classes

Objects can be classified into categories, as shown in Table 2-2.

Table 2-2 Object Classifications

Classes of Objects	
Object reference	How does a programmer use a class or an object?
Object relationships	How do objects interact with or relate to each other?
Object class operations	How do objects operate? What procedures do they know?
Class inheritance	Are there derived behaviors and attributes that are derived from another class? How can class definitions be reused?

For instance, trucks, vans, and cars are classified as vehicles. A class is a general type of thing. Objects fall within a class. A car, for example, is an object of the class vehicle. Objects are *instances of classes*. Therefore, a car is an instance of the class vehicle. In general terms, a class is a general category and an object is a specific instance.

Consider the example in Figure 2-4 of three buttons. Each button is an object. Together they make up a class. Each button is also a specific instance of the class Button.

Figure 2-4 Objects of the Class Button

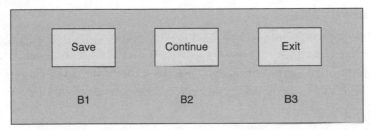

A class of customers, for example, defines all the common features of the customers. It defines a specific type of customer for a particular problem domain. When used for a hotel registration system, the definition of the class—named, in this case, HotelCustomer—might include attributes for name, address, credit card, and room preferences. The definition of a VideoStoreCustomer class might include attributes for name, address, credit card, video rental limits, and an expiration date of membership. The definition of an InstantMessengerCustomer class might include attributes for name, e-mail address, and screen name.

The objects that will be used by the application are specific instances of the appropriate customer class. Each customer who reserves a room at the hotel is represented as an instance of the HotelCustomer class that is an object of the type HotelCustomer. Each customer who rents a video from the video store is represented as an instance of the VideoStoreCustomer class—that is, an object of the type VideoStoreCustomer. The programmer creates the definition for these specific customer classes based on the data and methods in each scenario.

The name of the class is called an *identifier*. An identifier is a series of characters that the programmer uses to name classes, objects, variables, and so on. The identifier is used in the Java program to call the class, object, or variable that is stored elsewhere on the computer when it is needed.

In addition to a class, objects have an *object reference* that identifies where it is stored in memory. The object references B1, B2, and B3 in Figure 2-4 are the locations where the button objects are stored in memory. The actual memory location of these variables and the objects is invisible to the programmer. This is one of the major strengths of the Java language, in that the programmer is relieved of the responsibility of knowing and handling in detail memory allocation and specific storage and addressing of variables and data. The programmer can use the object reference to access a button object. When the programmer refers to B2, the program knows exactly where to locate the Continue button.

Creation of Objects

To create an object, a special method is used. Methods are the functional components of a Java class. A *constructor method* is a method that defines procedures for how to create an object. The constructor method has the same name as the class. The request to create an object is made by using the keyword **new**. An example of a constructor is shown in Example 2-1.

Example 2-1 *Creating Objects: Object Construction*

```
1 /**
2 * Java Program: Customer.java
3 * @author Cisco Teacher
4 * @version 2002
5 */
6 public class Customer
7 {
8     public static String name;
9     public static String screenName;
10
11 /**
12 * @param nm The customer's name as a String
13 * @param sn The customer's screen name as a String
14 */
15     public Customer(String nm, String sn)
16     {
17         name = nm;
18         screenName = sn;
19     }
20
```

Example 2-1 *Creating Objects: Object Construction (Continued)*

```
21      public static void main(String[] args)
22      {
23          Customer c1 = new Customer("John Doe", "JohnDeer");
24          System.out.println(name);
25          System.out.println(screenName);
26      }
27 }
```

Operation on Objects

Object-oriented languages are powerful because they define what objects do. This is known as object behavior, operations, or methods. An object can have many methods. Under some circumstances, different methods can have the same name (this is object-speak for overloaded methods). Think of a method as a step-by-step procedure for accomplishing a task. Therefore, a method sometimes is referred to as a procedure. Procedures describe object behaviors using procedural programming rules. Although a distinction was made between procedural programming and OOP at the beginning of this chapter, OOP programmers write procedural code in the methods of a Java class.

Methods are based on the end user's needs. For example, the video store Hollywood Best might have different rules for renting videos than the video store VideosRYou. Although both have a need for objects to handle the rental process, the methods defined in a class of these objects could be different for each store.

Objects interact with each other by sending messages (*message sending*) and performing operations or procedures. These actions occur in methods. For one object to interact with another object, it must know the identifier (the name given by the programmer) or object reference (the location in memory). The request for that method is a message. The message is sent to an object using the *method signature*. The method signature identifies the name of the method and provides the method with the data defined in the method signature. A method signature provides the method name and the data it needs to complete the procedure. A method definition must include a return type. Example 2-2 provides sample code that highlights the method name, data required, and results returned for the method chargeRent(). When one object needs to send a message to another object, it uses the identifier or object reference, the name of the method, and the message for that method.

Example 2-2 *Methods*

```
1      /**
2       * Java Program: VideoRented.java
3       * @author Cisco teacher
4       * @version 2002
5       /*
6  public class VideoRented
7  {
8      public static int numberOfDays = 2;
9      public static double rent;
10
11     /**
12      *  @param days The number of days, as an integer,
13      *                  for which the video was rented
14      */
15     static double chargeRent(int days)
16     {
17      return days * 3.00;
18      }
19
20     public static void main(String[] args)
21     {
22             rent = chargeRent(numberOfDays);
23             System.out.println(rent);
24      }
25 }
```

You can find the full, interactive graphic for this example on the book's accompanying CD-ROM. The title of the activity is "Methods" and can be found under the e-Lab Activities.

The VideoRented class has a chargeRent method that calculates the charge for renting a video based on the number of days it has been rented. The method returns the result of the calculation in the chargeRent method.

- Name: chargeRent
- Data required: numberOfDays
- Result: Calculates a charge and returns the result of the calculation

Methods that change or manipulate data values for an object also are referred to as *mutators*. These methods generally are named using the format setObjectData. Methods that access data from an object are referred to as *accessors*. These methods generally are named using the format getObjectData. ObjectData is the identifier for the specific value of both the mutator and accessor methods. This identifier is defined as an attribute for the object.

For example, in creating classes for a video store application, the VideoRented class might have the attributes DateRented and DateDue. The class also has accessor methods (to retrieve the data), mutator methods (to change the data), and other custom methods. Three of these methods include these:

- setDateRented (mutator method), which assigns the date that the video was rented to the dateRented attribute
- getDateRented (accessor method), which retrieves the date
- calculateDueDate (custom method), which calculates the date on which the rental is due from the date rented and sets the value of dateDue

Figure 2-5 demonstrates how a Customer object operating on a VideoRented object can use the mutator method setDateRented to set the dateRented attribute to January 1, 2002.

Figure 2-5 How Methods Function

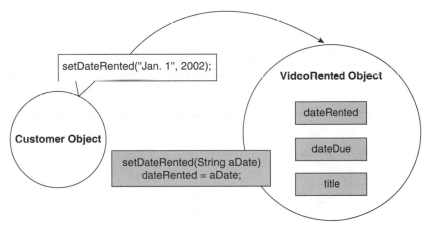

You can find the full, interactive graphic for this figure on the book's accompanying CD-ROM. The title of the activity is "How Methods Function," and it can be found under e-Lab Activities.

Figure 2-6 demonstrates how a `Customer` object operating on a `VideoRented` object can use the custom method `calculateDueDate` to set the `dueDate` attribute of the `VideoRented` object.

Figure 2-6 How Methods Function

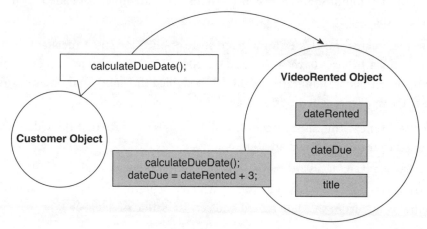

You can find the full, interactive graphic for this figure on the book's accompanying CD-ROM. The title of the activity is "How Methods Function," and it can be found under the e-Lab Activities.

Encapsulation

Encapsulation hides details (*information hiding*) of an object. It makes objects robust by protecting data from being accessed and changed by other objects. Users know the name of the methods within the object, but not how the methods work. In most cases, there is no need for others to know how it works. For example, most people do not care how the gas gauge of a car knows that the gas tank is almost empty. However, they do know that when the needle of the gas gauge hovers near the "E," it is time to fill up.

Encapsulation also means "to package together." An object always has its data and methods packaged together. For example, a `Customer` object cannot access the `DateDue` attribute of the `VideoRented` object and set its value. The Customer object must call the `VideoRented` object's `calculateDateDue` method.

Object-oriented languages implement encapsulation through special keywords that a programmer can use in defining classes. For example, the Java language uses keywords **private**, **public**, and **protected** to identify different levels of encapsulation of an object. These identifiers often are described as access modifiers. Access modifiers define the level of access to the class, data, or method. According to best practices, a properly encapsulated object has most of its member data declared as **private** and most of the accessors and mutators declared as **public**.

Use the activity shown in Figure 2-7 to identify the level of access allowed by each access modifier. Choose an appropriate access modifier from the following list:

- private
- protected
- public

Figure 2-7 Encapsulation

Any other object can access the data or the method.	
Only methods defined within the class can access.	
Only objects in the same named package (that is directory) can access.	

You can check your answers using an interactive graphic on the book's accompanying CD-ROM. The title of the activity is "Encapsulation," and it can be found under the e-Lab Activities.

> **More Information**
>
> Consider a real-world object such as a bicycle. The URL java.sun.com/docs/books/tutorial/java/ concepts/object.html provides an example of OO concepts as they relate to a bicycle.

The beauty of objects is that you can use them even if you don't know how they work inside. Objects are "little black boxes of functionality." The following box sample is one answer to the question "What is a black box?" and includes a detailed description.

> A black box is an engineering term that works like this. First, you drop something into a black box. Then, you wait while this thing is "magically transformed" inside the black box. Finally, you receive a new, transformed thing back from the black box. The beauty of a black box is that all you need to know is how to drop something into it and what to expect on the other side. You do not need to understand the magic inside.

Examples of Black Boxes in the Real World

Your television, your car, your VCR, your refrigerator . . .. You can turn your television on and off, change channels, and set the volume by using elements of the television's interface—turn dials, use the remote control, plug in the power—without understanding anything about how the thing actually works. The same goes for a VCR, although if stories about how hard people find it to set the time on a VCR are true, maybe the VCR violates the simple interface rule.

Object Relationships

All programs include the definitions of classes. When defining classes, a programmer can design them to be related to other classes. These can be association relationships, whole-part relationships, or inheritance relationships.

Association Relationships

One relationship between objects is based on the association of objects in a context. Association means that an object "knows" about another object. In the video store application, a `VideoStoreCustomer` object "knows" about the `VideoRented` object. It knows information about the rented videos such as the date of rental, the date due, the date returned, the amount due, and so on. The `VideoRented` object "knows" about the `VideoItem` object and might know about many `VideoItem` objects, as many as those currently rented by the customer. Chapter 7, "Arrays," discusses collections of references to objects. The `VideoItem` object itself "knows" about a title, a type, a copy number, and a unique ID for inventory and licensing purposes. It might even hold data about ratings and other data that represents information about the real-world object, the video. As shown in Figure 2-8, when one object has a reference to another object, it demonstrates an association relationship.

Whole-Part Relationships

Whole-part relationships suggest a stronger relationship between objects. Not only does one object know about another object, but the second object cannot exist without the existence of the first object. As illustrated in Figure 2-9, a `VideoRented` object cannot exist unless a `VideoStoreCustomer` object exists. In real-world terms, data for video renting does not exist until a customer rents a video. Both association and whole-part relationships are containment relationships. These differ from inheritance relationships in that they do not inherit attributes or behaviors from other classes.

TIP

The *"has a" relationship* means that one type of object contains another or is composed of another. Some examples are a car "has an" engine, a bicycle "has a" wheel, and a coffee cup "has a" coffee.

The *"is a" relationship* means that one type of object is a more specific version of a general type. Some examples are a car "is a" vehicle, a bicycle "is a" vehicle, and a coffee cup "is a" cup.

Figure 2-8 Association Relationship

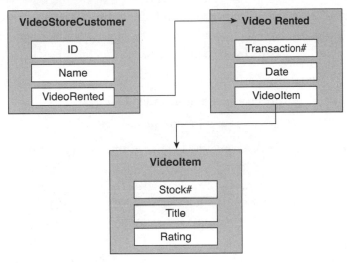

Figure 2-9 Whole-Part Relationship

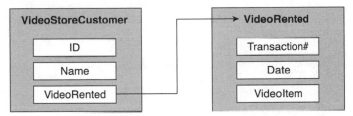

Inheritance Relationships

The programmer defines a class as a parent class (superclass). Other classes are defined as subclasses that derive behaviors and attributes from the superclass. Inheritance provides for the reuse of class definitions and the enforcement of certain methods and behaviors, to ensure that the business application performs in dependable and predictable ways.

Inheritance

Inheritance embodies the principle of reuse in OOP languages. Inheritance also defines the relationship of classes to each other in much the same way that living objects inherit some attributes and behaviors from their ancestors:

- Deriving behaviors and attributes
- Adapting these features to each unique individual
- Being both the same and different from their ancestors

For example, in Figure 2-10, a dog named Rover is an instance or object of the class GoldenRetriever. Rover inherits attributes common to all Golden Retrievers. Golden Retrievers inherit from the class Dog. Rover inherits the behaviors of all dogs and behaviors specific to Golden Retrievers.

Figure 2-10 Inheritance

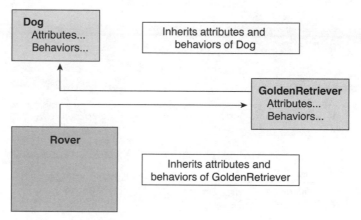

This hierarchy of relationships between classes of animals extends to the world of programming through the use of OOP. Java provides this sharing of behaviors (methods) and attributes (data) between classes of objects by allowing inheritance.

As described earlier, in an inheritance relationship, the programmer can define a class as a parent class (superclass). Other classes are defined as subclasses that derive behaviors and attributes from the superclass. Inheritance provides for the reuse of class definitions and the enforcement of certain methods and behaviors, to ensure that the business application performs in dependable and predictable ways. An instance of a subclass (object) that is derived from another class (inheritance) has access to the data and methods of the superclass, or parent class. Figure 2-11 shows attributes that are inherited by the Teacher object and Student object, from the Person object.

Figure 2-11 Inheritance Concepts

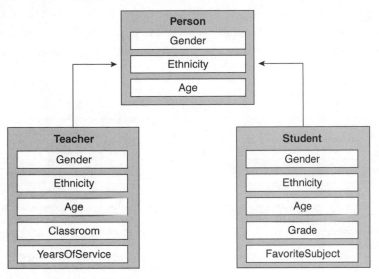

More Information
Consider a real-world object such as a chair. The URL http://tuts.cit.nih.gov/java_evans/prelims/oom_chair.htm provides an example of OO concepts as they relate to a chair.

In Phase II of the Banking application, students will define an inheritance model for checking accounts in the following manner: The Account class is a parent class. The Checking class derives attributes from this class, and the two classes OverdraftProtection and CreditLimit derive attributes from the Checking class. Thus, at each level of class definition, students define only attributes and behaviors that are specific for that class. The classes Checking, OverDraftProtection, and LineOfCredit would all derive the attribute Balance from Account. In addition, LineOfCredit would have an attribute for credit limit and, possibly, an attribute for interest. A single keyword, **extends**, defines the inheritance. The class LineOfCredit **extends** the class Checking. The UML diagram for the Banking application shows the inheritance between these classes.

Inheritance properties of a class also are referred to as "is a" relationships. In the earlier Rover example, Rover "is a" Golden Retriever. A Golden Retriever "is a" dog. Note that this works only in one direction. A dog is not a Golden Retriever, and a Golden Retriever is not a Rover. The same is true when working with objects and classes in Java. A class dependent on another class has an "is a" relationship, but the reverse is not true.

Association and whole-part relationships are containment relationships between objects and are referred to as "has a" relationships. The object of the class Student has a reference to an object of the type Teacher, as shown in Figure 2-12. But both Student and Teacher inherit from the class Person, so they have an "is a" relationship with the class Person.

Figure 2-12 Inheritance Concepts

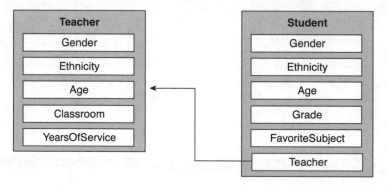

Object Mutability and Destruction

Sometimes, data held by an object must never be changed after the object is created. In the video rental example, the DateRented attribute and the reference to the VideoItem object should not change after a VideoRented object is created for a customer. When a customer rents a video, the video information and date do not change. To ensure this, a class definition can include specifications for the mutability (or changeability) of object data. The Java language uses the keyword **final** to define this feature of a class, which is to define immutability of an object attribute after it is created.

Objects are created in memory. As large and complex applications are created, many objects might be needed, but not necessarily all at the same time. What happens when the object is no longer needed and it is occupying memory that might be needed for another object? Some OOP languages require that the programmer address all of these memory-management issues. When a programmer forgets to destroy the objects that are no longer needed, or destroys objects too soon, bugs and memory leaks occur. These cause programs to fail, and end users become frustrated.

Tools such as the JVM manage memory. To free up resources, the Java Virtual Machine can do the following:

- Identify an object for destruction by the garbage collector.
- Request that the garbage collector do its work.

- Define specific cleanup procedures that must be completed before the object is destroyed. These definitions include changing the object reference to **null** (having no address), calling the gc method of a Java language class the Object class, and defining a method named finalize for the class. The finalize method contains the instructions for cleanup before an object is destroyed.

The programmer needs only to notify the JVM of the objects that are no longer needed. The programmer does not need to destroy the object or manage the memory needed for objects. The JVM implements a garbage-collector program that manages the allocation and reallocation of memory for objects. To ensure that only the necessary objects are retained and the memory of the computer is used efficiently, a programmer can define methods or operations to identify objects for destruction. The programmer does not have control over the schedule of the garbage collector. The garbage-collector program of the JVM runs on its own schedule. This program runs only when it runs out of memory. In small programs, it might never need to run because there might be ample memory for all the objects needed.

Describing Objects

Many complex concepts and terms form the body of OOP. The successful use of such a methodology requires the presence of a uniform system of symbols and terms to communicate the design of classes and applications. This section describes one such system, the Unified Modeling Language (UML). This section covers the following topics:

- Modeling languages and symbols
- Basic class symbols
- Additional types of UML diagrams

Modeling Languages and Symbols

Current OOP designing methods use UML to define OOP constructs and models. UML is a result of efforts to standardize the terminology and diagramming of object models. Many software products provide graphical tools to create UML diagrams. Industry-leading products, such as Rational Rose and Visio, are used for the development of large and complex applications. BlueJ, the IDE for this course, provides the object diagrams with a look and feel that is similar to UML, as shown in Figure 2-13.

Figure 2-13 Modeling Languages and Symbols

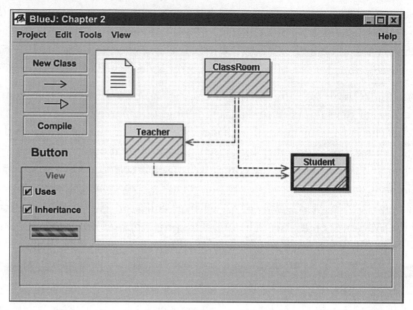

What exactly is UML? The *Unified Modeling Language (UML)* is a collection of symbols and patterns of symbols. It is used to describe objects, the relationship between objects, the use of objects, and the state of objects.

UML has many different types of diagrams that can be used to describe object models. Among those that will be used in this course are the following:

- Use-case diagram—A use-case diagram describes how users will use the objects in the system, as shown in Figure 2-14.

Figure 2-14 Use-Case Diagram for a Banking Application

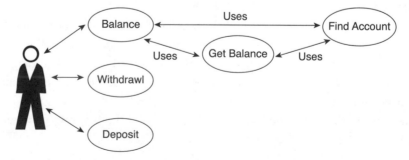

- Class diagram—A class diagram, shown in Table 2-3, describes the attributes of objects in the system.

Table 2-3 Class Diagram

Name		VideoRented
Attributes		title rentDate charge dueDate
Operations or Methods		videoRented getRentDate setDueDate chargeRent getDueDate

■ Statechart diagram—A statechart diagram describes the stages or life cycle of objects, as shown in Figure 2-15.

Figure 2-15 Statechart Diagram

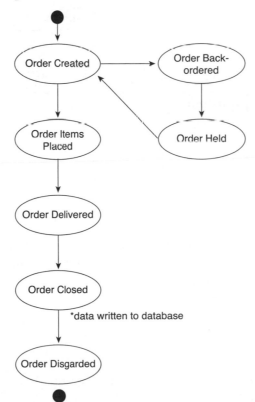

UML is a broad and comprehensive language. The purpose of introducing this language is to provide a very elementary understanding and familiarity with the class diagram. This diagramming technique helps to simply communicate to a programmer the definitions of a class and its relationships to other classes in ways that are easy to understand.

Basic Class Symbol

Several symbols are associated with a class diagram. These are listed and described here, and are shown in Figure 2-16.

- Rectangles describe classes.
- Lines describe relationships.
- Special symbols describe accessibility and strength of relationships.

Figure 2-16 UML Symbols

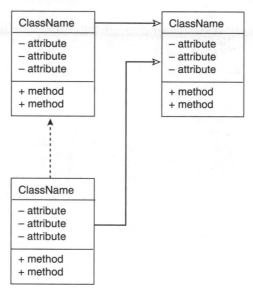

A rectangle represents a class of objects. It is divided into three compartments: the name compartment, the attribute compartment, and the operation or method compartment, as shown in Table 2-4.

Table 2-4 Use-Class Diagram

Name		VideoRented
Attributes		title
		rentDate
		charge
		dueDate
Operations or Methods		videoRented
		getRentDate
		setDueDate
		chargeRent
		getDueDate

Class diagram symbols are used to indicate accessibility. The UML symbols for access modifiers are as follows:

- +: **public**.
- -: **private**.
- #: **protected**.
- No symbol indicates default access.

Implementation of these access modifiers in a class diagram is shown in Table 2-5.

Table 2-5 Class Diagram Symbols

VideoRented
- title
- rentDate
- charge
- dueDate
+ videoRented
+ getRentDate
+ setDueDate
+ chargeRent
+ getDueDate

Review the symbol chart in Figure 2-17 to become familiar with some of the more commonly used case diagramming symbols.

NOTE

UML's object-oriented system of notation has evolved from the work of Grady Booch, James Rumbaugh, Ivar Jacobson, and the Rational Software Corporation. These renowned computer scientists fused their respective technologies into a single, standardized model. Today, UML is accepted by the Object Management Group (OMG) as the standard for modeling object-oriented programs.

Figure 2-17 Class Diagram Symbols

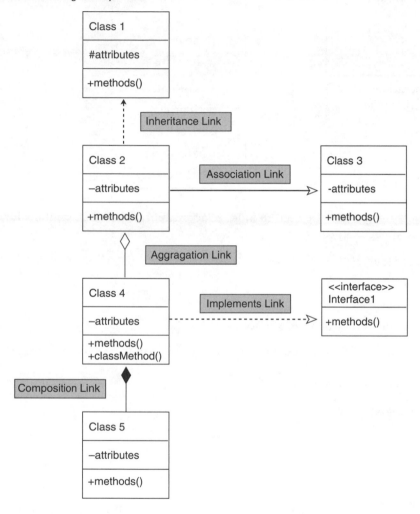

Additional Types of UML Diagrams

You were introduced to the three types of UML diagrams that are used in this course:

- Class
- Use case
- Statechart

This section expands on these and introduces the following additional UML diagrams:

- Package
- Object
- Sequence
- Collaboration
- Activity
- Component
- Deployment

Class Diagrams

Class diagrams are the backbone of almost every object-oriented method, including UML. They describe the static structure of a system, as shown in Figure 2-18).

Figure 2-18 UML Diagram

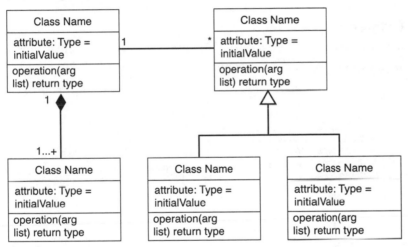

Package Diagrams

Package diagrams are a subset of class diagrams, but developers sometimes treat them as a separate technique. Package diagrams organize elements of a system into related groups to minimize dependencies between packages, as shown in Figure 2-19.

Figure 2-19 Package Diagrams

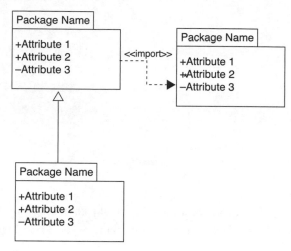

Object Diagrams

Object diagrams describe the static structure of a system at a particular time. They can be used to test class diagrams for accuracy, as shown in Figure 2-20.

Figure 2-20 Object Diagrams

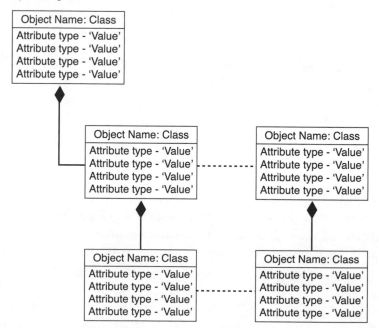

Use-Case Diagrams

Use-case diagrams model the functionality of systems using actors and use cases (see Figure 2-21).

Figure 2-21 Use Case

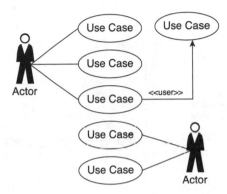

Sequence Diagrams

Sequence diagrams describe interactions among classes in terms of an exchange of messages over time, as shown in Figure 2-22.

Figure 2-22 Sequence Diagrams

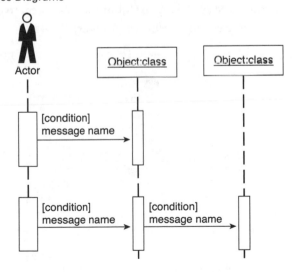

Collaboration Diagrams

Collaboration diagrams represent interactions between objects as a series of sequenced messages. Collaboration diagrams describe both the static structure and the dynamic behavior of a system (see Figure 2-23).

Figure 2-23 Collaboration Diagrams

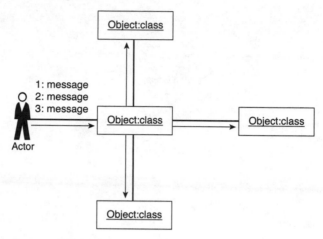

Statechart Diagrams

Statechart diagrams describe the dynamic behavior of a system in response to external stimuli. Statechart diagrams are especially useful in modeling reactive objects whose states are triggered by specific events, as shown in Figure 2-24.

Figure 2-24 Statechart Diagrams

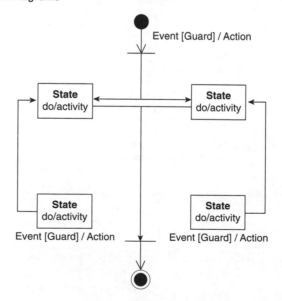

Activity Diagrams

Activity diagrams illustrate the dynamic nature of a system by modeling the flow of control from activity to activity. An activity represents an operation on some class in the system that results in a change in the state of the system. Typically, activity diagrams are used to model workflow or business processes and internal operations (see Figure 2-25).

Figure 2-25 Activity Diagrams

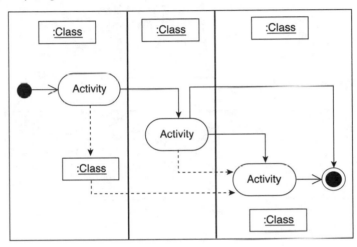

Component Diagrams

Component diagrams describe the organization of physical software components, including source code, run-time (binary) code, and executables (see Figure 2-26).

Figure 2-26 Component Diagrams

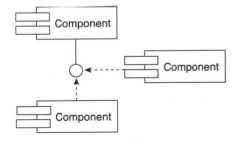

Deployment Diagrams

Deployment diagrams depict the physical resources in a system, including nodes, components, and connections, as shown in Figure 2-27.

Figure 2-27 Deployment Diagrams

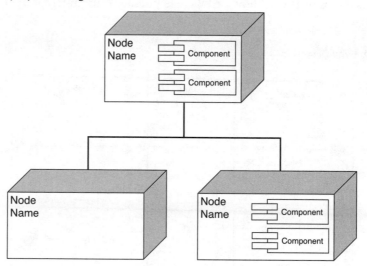

Object Terminology Applied to a Java Program

This section demonstrates how a Java programmer defines a class, including its attributes and methods, and then creates an object of the class. The following topics are addressed:

- Class definition
- Object methods

Class Definition

Example 2-3 illustrates the *class definition* of the class Person.

Example 2-3 *Class Definition*

```
 1  /**
 2   * Java Program: Person.java
 3   * @author Cisco Teacher
 4   * @version 2002
```

Example 2-3 *Class Definition (Continued)*

```
 5  */
 6  public class Person
 7  {
 8      private String name;
 9      private String dateOfBirth;
10      private int id;
11
12      public Person (String  aName, String aDate, int aID)
13      {
14          name = aName;
15          dateOfBirth = aDate;
16          id = aID;
17      }
18  }
```

The first line of the program (**public class** Person) is the class definition. It includes the word **class** and a name for the class—in this example, Person.

The definition of the class attributes and methods follows this first line and is enclosed by a matching pair of braces, as shown here:

```
public class Person
{
}
```

The keyword **public** allows another class to use it. Classes that are **public** must be defined in separate files.

Creating Objects

Class definitions can include methods that specify the data values that an object will store upon creation. These methods are called constructors.

In Java, a constructor has the same name as the class and no return type. In the sample class definition shown in Example 2-3, a single constructor has been defined.

This constructor will be executed once for every object created. In the example, the constructor Person requires that the user of the Person class provide data for the name, the date of birth, and an identification number. The terms *String* and *int* refer to Java data types, where String is a series of characters and **int** is an integer. (Java data types are discussed in Chapter 3, "Java Language Elements.") The constructor procedure creates an instance of Person and assigns the data provided as values to the member variables of the object. Figure 2-28 is a graphic illustration of this process, showing the data in the constructor being assigned to the member variables of the object.

Figure 2-28 Objects for an Object-Oriented Program

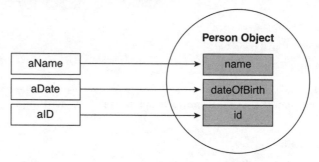

You can find the full, interactive graphic for this figure on the book's accompanying CD-ROM. The title of the activity is "Objects for an Object-Oriented Program," and it can be found under the e-Lab Activities.

Specific instances of objects contain different data values. Data that is part of each instance of a class, or each object of a class, is referred to as member data or member attributes. Lines 8, 9, and 10 in Example 2-3 define member data or member attributes.

Understanding Variables and Data

The data for each object is stored in memory. All programming languages use the concept of variables to reference data in memory. A variable is a storage location in memory that a programmer can use to store data. A variable has five facets, as shown in Figure 2-29, which illustrates these facets for the member attribute id of the Person class.

Figure 2-29 Variables: Storage Locations for Data

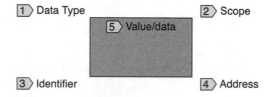

You can find the full, interactive graphic for this figure on the book's accompanying CD-ROM. The title of the activity is "Variables—Storage Locations for Data," and it can be found under the e-Lab Activities.

The following list illustrates each of these facets for the member attribute `id` of the `Person` class:

- Data type: **int**
- Identifier: `id`
- Scope: As long as a `Person` object is used.
- Address: Address in memory. This is not visible to the programmer.
- Value/data: The value is assigned upon creation of a `Person` object.

For example, the `Person` class shown in Example 2-3 defines three variables: `name`, `dateOfBirth`, and `id`.

Java includes several keywords to implement the OOP principle of encapsulation. In this example, the keyword **private** is applied to member data to make this data inaccessible to other objects. This data is accessible to methods within the class. Other objects need to use an accessor method to retrieve the data that is stored or referenced by the variables `name`, `dateOfBirth`, and `id`.

Object Methods

The program defines several procedures that an object of the class `Person` does. These are the methods of the object. The class definition includes standard methods (accessor and mutator) but does not have any custom methods. Method instructions are shared among objects of a class. Only one copy of the method is in memory. All methods except the constructor have a return type. If no data is returned, the return type is **void**. The following sections cover mutator and accessor methods, method arguments, and return values for methods.

Mutator Method

The mutator method changes object data. Assume, for example, that there is a `Person` object named `JohnDoe`. `ObjectA` might provide new data to `JohnDoe` and, thus, change the data in `JohnDoe`. If the data for `JohnDoe` is encapsulated (hidden), the only way `ObjectA` can change the data in `JohnDoe` is by sending messages to `JohnDoe` and specifying a method name from the `Person` class. Example 2-4 shows two mutator methods for the `Person` class.

Example 2-4 *Mutator Method*

```
1 public void setName(String aName)
2 {
3     name = aName;
```

continues

Example 2-4 *Mutator Method (Continued)*

```
4 }
5 public void setDateOfBirth(String adate)
6 {
7      dateOfBirth = adate;
8 }
```

Accessor Method

The accessor method retrieves object data. ObjectA can retrieve data from JohnDoe (again, an object of the class Person) by sending a message. The data returned needs to be stored in ObjectA. Example 2-5 shows two accessor methods for the Person class.

Example 2-5 *Accessor Method*

```
1 public String getName()
2 {
3      return name;
4 }
5 public String getDateOfBirth()
6 {
7      return dateOfBirth;
8 }
```

Method Arguments

Methods with no arguments are methods that require no data when used. Methods that require one or more arguments are generally methods that change the data of an object and require the user of the object to provide the new data to be used. The method can request one or more data items. These methods in the class Person require data when called. Figures 2-30 and 2-31 illustrate how ObjectA operates on a Person object by using the **public** method setName to change the value of the name attribute.

Figure 2-30 Methods with One or More Arguments

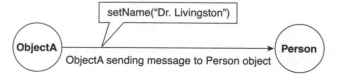

Figure 2-31 Methods with One or More Arguments

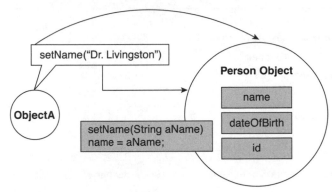

Return Values for Methods

One object can interact with another object to retrieve data from the second object. A message to an object to use a method that will provide data can include arguments. Figure 2-32 illustrates how `ObjectA` operates on a `Person` object by using the **public** method `getName` to receive the value of the `name` attribute.

Figure 2-32 Methods with Return Values

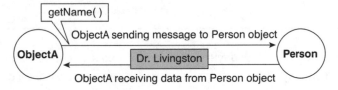

Introduction to `java.lang.System` **Class**

The `System` class represents an example of a predefined class that has been tested and compiled for use by any other class. This section introduces the student to the `out` object of the `System` class, which can be used to send data for display to the console.

System Class

Chapter 1 introduced the Java program `SayHello`, shown in Example 2-6. This section revisits the `SayHello` source code to review the `System.out` object and its methods.

Example 2-6 SayHello *Source Code*

```
1 /**
2 * Java Program: SayHello.java
3 * @author Cisco Teacher
4 * @version 2002
5 */
6 public class SayHello
7 {
8     /*
9         @param args your name; your lucky number
10     */
11    public static void main(String[] args)
12    {
13      String name = "Student";
14      int number = 1;
15      System.out.println("Hello");
16      System.out.println(name);
17      System.out.println ("Your Lucky Number is " + number);
18    }
19 }
```

In the class definition, the class SayHello does not hold any member data. SayHello objects do not store any object data. The main method, however, uses data it receives to print information. Data stored in an object is referred to as member data. Data stored by an object's methods is referred to as local or temporary data. When the method has been completed, this data is no longer in memory.

The main method of the SayHello object uses methods in another object (System.out) to get its work done. This syntax of calling another object and its methods is what students will be defining in almost all of their classes.

Analyze the use of the System.out object. One of the most useful objects is the out object referenced in the System class. The out object sends data for display to the console. While large applications almost never use this object to display data to end users, programmers use this object frequently to verify data values in objects and to test their programs.

Predefined classes, such as the System class, form the extensive library of prebuilt classes that is available with the Java Language Toolkit (J2SDK). This library of classes is also known as the application programming interface (API). Students will learn how to locate and use the documentation for the API in this course.

More Information

This small Java program uses the System class (twice), first to retrieve the current user's name, and then to display it:

```
class UserNameTest {
    public static void main(String args[]) {
        String name;
        name = System.getProperty("user.name");
        System.out.println(name);
    }
}
```

The program never instantiated a System object; it just referenced the getProperty() method and the out variable directly from the class. You will learn in later chapters how to use methods and data that do not require the creation of any objects. These methods and data are part of a class and are shared by objects of the same class or accessed by methods in other classes and objects. These are also known as static methods and data.

Case Study: JBANK Application

The JBANK application introduced in Chapter 1 provides students with an opportunity to apply the Java language concepts learned throughout this course. In the labs for Chapter 2, students will begin defining and modeling the classes for Phase I of the banking application.

Defining and Modeling the JBANK Application

Before beginning the labs for the JBANK application, students should review the provided case study documents. Figure 2-33 displays what the JBANK application might look like at the end of the course. In the labs, students will begin defining and modeling the classes for Phase I of the banking application JBANK. These labs provide descriptions of the class as defined by the end users. Using these descriptions, students will identify the class data and methods. Students will also create the UML diagrams in these labs. Subsequent labs will use these UML diagrams to create classes. A UML test tool is also provided, which can be used to verify that the created classes match the UML diagram defined.

Figure 2-33 The JBANK Application

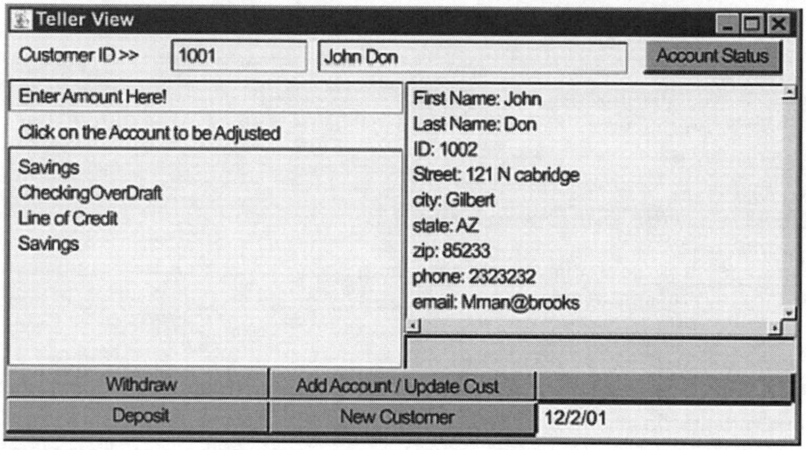

The JavaZOO

The JavaZOO expands on Java concepts and terminology discussed in this chapter. These JavaZOO sections are particularly important to those students who have no programming experience.

Overview of the JavaZOO

The JavaZOO sections provide background information for students to visualize how an OOP language, such as Java, is structured. It underscores the basic concepts of objects, classes, attributes, behaviors, data types, constructors, and methods.

Imagine that a programmer's assignment is to create a virtual zoo on a computer. How does the programmer start this task? The programmer first determines what kind of objects would be in a real zoo. Because there are zookeepers, cages, and animals in a real zoo, the virtual zoo would also have them.

Then the programmer thinks about each of these objects. What are their characteristics? What do they do? What is done to them? Animals, for example, are kept in cages. They are of a certain type (species), color, and size, and have names given by the zookeepers.

The following sections address the three types of objects found in the JavaZOO: zookeepers, cages, and animals.

Zookeepers

The zookeepers are responsible for taking care of the animals. They feed them when they are hungry and clean the cages when they get dirty. In the next JavaZoo section, these objects are defined.

Cages

Cages have different dimensions, depending on the size of the animal. They can also be covered to protect the animals from the weather. The cages become dirty, and zookeepers need to clean the cages.

Animals

Animals in the JavaZoo have a name, type, color, and age and are either hungry or not hungry.

Objects

The first section of the JavaZoo described three types of objects found in the zoo: zookeepers, cages, and animals. Now the programmer must define the animal and cage objects.

For animal objects, every animal has a name. It is also necessary to know what type of animal it is. The color and age of the animal should be included in the definition as well. It is important to know whether an animal is hungry. When an animal is hungry, a zookeeper can feed it. These requirements are the definition for every animal that will be in this zoo:

- Every ZooAnimal has a name.
- Every ZooAnimal is of a certain type.
- Every ZooAnimal has a color.
- Every ZooAnimal has an age.
- Every ZooAnimal is hungry or is not hungry.

So, the definition of a ZooAnimal looks like this:

```
ZooAnimal
name is ?
type is ?
color is ?
age is ?
isHungry is?
```

Now that a `ZooAnimal` has been defined, it must be housed in a cage. To design the definition of a cage, its attributes must be determined. Every cage in this zoo has a certain length, width, and height. Also, a cage will be either covered or uncovered by a tarp. Sometimes a cage becomes dirty. If a cage is dirty, a zookeeper should clean the cage.

So, the definition of a cage looks like this:

```
Cage
length is ?
width is ?
height is ?
IsCovered ?
IsDirty ?
```

Before continuing, a closer look at the types of information stored in these definitions is in order. The three types of information are words, numbers, and a value that is either true or false. For example, when a `ZooAnimal` is created, its `name` will be a word such as `Maurice` or `Sophia`. For a `Cage`, its `length` will be a number such as `20` or `57`. But what about the characteristic `isCovered`? A `Cage` is either covered or it is not. The characteristic `isCovered` is not a word or a number. Think of `isCovered` as a question with an answer of true or false. Using these three types of information, the definitions created previously for `ZooAnimal` and `Cage` are defined more clearly by including the type of information that each characteristic should be:

```
ZooAnimal
name is a word
type is a word
color is a word
age is a number
isHungry is true or false

Cage
length is a number
width is a number
height is a number
IsCovered is true or false
IsDirty is true or false
```

In the activity in Table 2-6, how would you complete the definition for a ZooKeeper by using either word, number, or true or false? The two completed definitions, with actual information, can be used as a reference.

Table 2-6 JavaZOO Definitions

Definitions
In this zoo,
Every ZooKeeper has a name.
Every ZooKeeper has a title (Mrs., Mr., Dr.).
Every ZooKeeper has a payRate.
Every ZooKeeper either has a zoology degree (hasDegree) or does not have a zoology degree.
Definitions Activity
ZooKeeper
name is a _____
title is a _____
payRate is a _____
hasDegree is a _____

Definitions Examples	
ZooKeeper myFirstZooKeeper	ZooKeeper myOtherZooKeeper
name is Jesper Reed	name is Sally Johnstead
title is Mr.	title is Dr.
payRate is 14	payRate is 35
hasDegree is **false**	hasDegree is **true**

You can check your answers using an interactive graphic on the book's accompanying CD-ROM. The title of the activity is "JavaZOO Definitions," and it can be found under the e-Lab Activities.

The basic instructions for each ZooAnimal and Cage object have been created. Although each ZooAnimal created with this definition might have different names and be of different types, all will be ZooAnimal objects. Additionally, the cages might be of different sizes because a ZooAnimal of type elephant would require a very large cage, whereas a ZooAnimal of type mouse requires only a small cage. Regardless of whether the cage is for an elephant or a mouse, it is still a Cage object.

Now specific `ZooAnimal` and `Cage` objects can be created. This is done in two steps:

Step 1   First, the `ZooAnimal` and `Cage` objects each need a reference name. This is not to be confused with the `name` attribute in the `ZooAnimal`. The name for the entire object is a way to refer to it. For example, if there are many `ZooAnimal`s created in the `JavaZOO`, this name serves as a means for telling them apart. This name can be any word or multiple words joined without spaces, but it is always a good idea to use something descriptive. The reference names chosen here are `myFirstZooAnimal` and `myFirstCage`.

Step 2   When the `ZooAnimal` and `Cage` objects have reference names, look at the definitions and replace the types of information with actual information to describe the `ZooAnimal` and `Cage` objects, such as `Pecanzo`, `elephant`, and gray. Be sure to provide words, numbers, and either a **true** or **false** for each attribute:

```
ZooAnimal myFirstZooAnimal
name is Pecanzo
type is elephant
color is gray
age is 15
isHungry is false

Cage myFirstCage
length is 100
width is 240
height is 12
isCovered is false
```

In this example, `myFirstZooAnimal` is a gray elephant named Pecanzo. It is 15 years old and is not hungry. Also, `myFirstCage` is an uncovered cage with dimensions of 100 m × 240 m × 12 m.

This section of the `JavaZOO` created definitions for the `ZooAnimal` and `Cage` objects. Then the characteristics, such as `name`, `length`, and `isHungry`, that describe each object were added. Next, each characteristic will be assigned a type of information. The three types of information, or data types, in this example are word, number, and true or false (`isHungry`). Actual information then replaces these data types so that specific `ZooAnimal` and `Cage` objects are created. A reference name is also assigned to distinguish each individual object.

Data Types

Data type is an important concept in programming. A data type describes what kind of information a certain attribute is. Data types are essential because they let the computer know how to process the attributes they describe. For example, if the data type is a number, the computer can use the attribute to do multiplication, subtraction, and many other mathematical functions. If the data type is a word, the computer can display the value of the attribute as text or can format it by capitalizing the first letter or all of the letters. Capitalization does not make sense to perform on a number, so the computer does this function only if it knows that the data type of an attribute is a word. Similarly, division does not make sense if performed on words, so the computer does this function only if it knows that the data type is a number.

The data type also determines the size of the storage space reserved for the value of the attribute. The storage locations in a computer's memory are known as variables. The data type of the attribute determines the size of the variables. For instance, the size of a variable to store an integer is smaller than the size of a variable to store a word.

Data types describe attributes, and attributes describe the state of objects. Many data types exist in the Java language. In this section, three kinds of data types have been explored so far: words, numbers, and true or false. In Java, there are specific names for each of these data types. If an attribute is a word, its data type in Java is String. A String gets its name because a word is a string of characters. Although the Java language contains many different data types for numbers, this section focuses only on the type called **int**. The data type **int** is short for "integer." Integers are whole numbers, such as 1, 2, and 3. Integers can also be 0 or negative whole numbers. A special data type exists for a value that can be only true or false. It is called a **boolean** value. Among the other Java data types that programmers use are **char** for single characters (a, A, or &, for example) and **double** or **float** types for numbers with decimal places.

The data type is placed in front of the attribute, as in the following example:

```
ZooAnimal
String name
String type
String color
int age
boolean isHungry
```

In the activity in Table 2-7, what is the appropriate Java data type for each attribute listed? Possible answers include String, **int**, and **boolean**.

Table 2-7 JavaZoo Data Types

ZooAnimal	ZooAnimal
name is a word.	_____ name
type is a word.	_____ type
color is a word.	_____ color
age is a number.	_____ age
isHungry is true or false.	_____ isHungry
Cage	**Cage**
length is a number.	_____ length
width is a number.	_____ width
height is a number.	_____ height
isCovered is true or false.	_____ isCovered
isDirty is true or false.	_____ isDirty
ZooKeeper	**ZooKeeper**
name is a word.	_____ name
title is a word.	_____ title
payRate is a number.	_____ payRate
hasDegree is true or false.	_____ hasDegree

You can check your answers using an interactive graphic on the book's accompanying CD-ROM. The title of the activity is "JavaZoo Data Types," and it can be found under the e-Lab Activities.

The main Method

The main method pulls together all of the classes to create a Java program. Students will see how to write a main method for the JavaZoo class.

Thus far, the process of creating Java classes with attributes, methods, and a constructor method has not yielded a program for the JavaZoo. But all of these classes will be used to create objects that interact to accomplish the task of behaving like a zoo.

The environment in which these objects will be created and interact with one another is a main method. This method is just like other methods. It is declared **public**, has curly braces, and contains many statements. The main method is the one the JVM looks for to run a program. Therefore, the main method must be contained in a Java class. None of the JavaZOO classes have a main method; this is why they are classes and not considered programs.

The code that actually creates ZooAnimal objects and Cage objects will be included in another class separate from these classes. This class will not have a constructor, and an instance of this class will not be created. Its sole purpose will be to act as an interface for the objects, a place where all of the objects can interact to accomplish the task. In this case, the class will include only the main method.

The syntax for every main method in Java is shown in line 9 of Example 2-7.

Example 2-7 JavaZOO *with a* main *Method*

```
 1 /**
 2  * The JavaZOO class has the main method.  It will be used as the
 3  * environment for the objects of the JavaZOO to interact.
 4  *
 5  */
 6
 7 public class JavaZOO
 8 {
 9      public static void main(String args [])
10      {
11            ZooAnimal myFirstAnimal  = new ZooAnimal();
12            ZooKeeper myFirstKeeper = new ZooKeeper();
13            Cage myFirstCage = new Cage();
14      } //end main
15 } // end JavaZoo
```

Some components of the syntax should look familiar. The name of the method is main, and it is declared **public**. Additionally, the return type is **void**. It has the parentheses and curly braces as well. This method is different from other methods that have been introduced, in that it contains the word ***static*** and the parentheses are not empty. The full meaning and implications of this are discussed in a later section. For now, accept this as the syntax of every main method used in Java.

The JavaZOO is now a working program. It includes several classes and a main method. The main method instantiates three objects, and method calls provide activity within the program.

Instantiation

A Java class is the definition of an object. It is the blueprint that describes the attributes and behaviors of a given object. In the JavaZOO, the definition for ZooAnimal is actually a class, and myFirstZooAnimal is an object created from that class. This section focuses on the concepts of creating objects from Java classes and creating an actual Java program.

Creating an object is known as instantiating an object. From the same class, numerous objects can be created. Each object is called an instance of the class.

In Java, the class definition includes a process for constructing an object. The process is contained in a special method called a constructor method. A constructor method is included in every class. Even if the programmer does not explicitly type a constructor method in the class definition, the JVM provides one. The constructor is the only way to create an object from the definition. Here is a constructor method that could be included in the ZooAnimal class:

```
public ZooAnimal()
{
}
```

The constructor method looks quite similar to any other method. It has parentheses and the curly braces. It includes the keyword **public**, which means that other objects can access it. Two important features make a constructor unique. First, every constructor has the same name as the class it is in. Because this constructor is in the ZooAnimal class, its name is also ZooAnimal. Second, no return type is included. Constructor methods do not return a value, but they cannot contain the keyword **void**. A constructor is identified easily because of these two characteristics.

This constructor is known as a null constructor. Notice that there are no Java statements in the braces. A null constructor creates an object but does not assign values to any of the attributes. If a null constructor is used to create an object, the attributes must be assigned in a later process.

Compare the previous null constructor to this constructor for a ZooAnimal:

```
public ZooAnimal()
{
    name = "Pecanzo";
    type = "elephant";
    age = 15;
    color = "gray";
    isHungry = false;
}
```

This constructor is quite the opposite from a null constructor. It contains several Java statements, known as assignment statements. An assignment statement uses the equals sign (=) to assign the value on the right to the attribute on the left. This constructor assigns values to every attribute of a ZooAnimal object.

A constructor method can assign default values to none, all, or any number of the attributes of an object. Every object created from the constructor has these default values. Although the values can be changed, it is a good idea to assign default values only to attributes that all instances will share. For example, in the ZooAnimal class, a constructor that assigns a default value only to isHungry and age might be most appropriate. Many instances of the ZooAnimal class have different names, types, and colors, so these values can be assigned later.

Earlier in the JavaZOO, an actual ZooAnimal was created and assigned a reference name. The following Java statement creates a ZooAnimal object by using a reference name and the constructor method:

```
ZooAnimal myFirstZooAnimal = new ZooAnimal();
```

ZooAnimal signifies the type of object being created. It is the name of the class from which the object comes.

myFirstZooAnimal is the reference name. This is the name that will be used to refer to the object in code. A reference name can be any combination of letters and numbers, as long as it starts with a letter.

The equals, or equal to, symbol (=) is the assignment operator. In this case, it assigns the new ZooAnimal object to myFirstZooAnimal.

new is a keyword that must be used when creating an object. A constructor method must immediately follow it.

ZooAnimal(); is the constructor method. This is the method that creates the object.

This statement with these five necessary components can be used to instantiate an object. Notice that the line ends with a semicolon because it is a Java statement.

In Table 2-8, design constructor methods for the ZooAnimal, ZooKeeper, and Cage classes that satisfy the following conditions:

- ZooAnimal—Every ZooAnimal starts out in the JavaZOO as not hungry and at age 0.
- ZooKeeper—Every ZooKeeper starts out in the JavaZOO with a payRate of 14.
- Cage—Every Cage starts out in the JavaZOO as clean.

All other attributes for these objects can be assigned later.

How would you complete the constructors for the Java classes by adding one of the following lines of code?

- isHungry = false;
- isDirty = false;
- payRate = 14;

Table 2-8 JavaZOO Constructors

Satisfy These Conditions	Constructor

ZooAnimal: Every ZooAnimal starts out in the JavaZOO as not hungry and at age 0.	```public ZooAnimal()```
	```{```
	``` age = 0;```
	``` ??????????```
	```}```

ZooKeeper: Every ZooKeeper starts out in the JavaZOO with a payRate of 14.	```public ZooKeeper()```
	```{```
	``` ??????????```
	```}```

Cage: Every Cage starts out in the JavaZOO as clean	```public Cage()```
	```{```
	``` ??????????```
	```}```

You can check your answers using an interactive graphic on the book's accompanying CD-ROM. The title of the activity is "JavaZOO Constructors," and it can be found under the e-Lab Activities.

Methods

So far, this chapter has focused on describing an object in terms of its attributes, or data. OOP involves the interaction of objects to accomplish a task by sending and receiving messages. To interact, an object must be capable of doing something. What an object does is known as behavior. In the JavaZOO, ZooAnimals eat when they are hungry. ZooKeepers must feed the animals and clean cages. So eating, feeding, and cleaning are examples of behaviors.

Behaviors in Java are represented by methods. A method is a set of instructions to do a certain task. Any time an object should perform a certain task, it uses a method. The tasks that an object can do are included as part of the object definition. The attributes describe information about the object, and the methods describe what an object can do.

Methods, like attributes, have names. A name for a method is provided to refer to the method in the program. If a definition has several methods, which is usually the case, the name enables the programmer to tell them apart. If an object needs to do several tasks, a method is added to the definition for each task. For example, for a ZooKeeper to feed animals or clean cages, two methods should be added to the definition: one to feed and one to clean.

So far, only attributes, or data, have been included in the definitions of the ZooAnimal and Cage. Now methods will be added to these definitions.

One of the requirements of the ZooAnimal is the ability to eat. So, the definition should include a method for that behavior. The ZooAnimal will simulate the task of eating by displaying a message that says, "The ZooAnimal is eating." The definition of the eat() method would be written as shown in line 12 of Example 2-8.

Example 2-8 ZooAnimal *Code Snippet*

```
 1 /*
 2 The characteristics of a ZooAnimal are:
 3     String name
 4     String title
 5     String color
 6     int age
 7     boolean isHungry
 8 */
 9 /*
10 Two methods for the ZooAnimal are:
11 */
12 void eat()
13 {
14     System.out.println("The ZooAnimal is eating.");
15 }
16 void sleep()
17 {
18     System.out.println("The ZooAnimal is sleeping.");
19 }
```

You can view the explanatory text by accessing the full, interactive graphic for this example on the book's accompanying CD-ROM. The title of the activity is "ZooAnimal Code Snippet," and it can be found under the e-Lab Activities.

 JavaZOO Activity   In this activity, the programmer adds methods to the JavaZOO classes.

Add a method called sleep() to the ZooAnimal definition, as shown in Example 2-8. This method will simulate the behavior of sleeping by displaying this message: "The ZooAnimal is sleeping." Use the word **void** before the method name. Also, include the parentheses and curly braces.

Add a method called feedAnimals() to the ZooKeeper definition, as shown in Example 2-9. This method will simulate the behavior of feeding the animals by displaying this message: "The ZooKeeper is feeding the ZooAnimals." Use the word **void** before the method name. Also, include the parentheses and curly braces.

You can view the explanatory text by accessing the full, interactive graphic for this example on the book's accompanying CD-ROM. The title of the activity is "ZooKeeper Code Snippet," and it can be found under the e-Lab Activities.

Add a method called cleanCage() to the ZooKeeper definition, as shown in Example 2-9. This method will simulate the behavior of cleaning a cage by displaying this message: "The ZooKeeper is cleaning a cage." Use the word **void** before the method name. Also, include the parentheses and curly braces.

Add a method called cageInfo() to the Cage definition, as shown in Example 2-10. This method will simply display a message: "This Cage is part of the JavaZOO." Use the word **void** before the method name, and include parentheses and curly braces. As the definition of the Cage is developed further, this method will display additional information.

You can view the explanatory text by accessing the full, interactive graphic for this example on the book's accompanying CD-ROM. The title of the activity is "Methods in a Class," and it can be found under the e-Lab Activities.

Example 2-9 ZooKeeper *Code Snippet*

```
1 /*
2 The characteristics of a ZooKeeper are:
3      String name
4      String title
5      int payRate
6      boolean hasDegree
7 */
8
9 /*
10 Two methods for the ZooKeeper are:
11 */
12 void feedAnimals()
13 {
14     System.out.println("The ZooKeeper is feeding the ZooAnimals.");
15 }
16 void cleanCage()
17 {
18     System.out.println("The ZooKeeper is cleaning the Cage.");
19 }
```

Example 2-10 *Methods in a Class*

```
1 /*
2 The characteristics of a Cage are:
3      int length
4      int width
5      int height
6      boolean isCovered
7      boolean isDirty
8 */
9 /*
10 One method for the Cage is:
11 */
12 void cageInfo()
13 {
14     System.out.println("This Cage is part of the JavaZOO.");
15 }
```

Syntax rules must be followed when writing Java code. Common syntax errors shown in Example 2-11 include the following:

- In line 1, **public** should not be capitalized;
- **ZooAnimal** should be one word.
- No parentheses are included in a class definition.
- In line 3, a semicolon is needed, not a colon.
- In line 4, **String** is capitalized.
- Double quotes are needed around Java.
- In line 5, no quotes should be included around **true**.
- In line 7, no semicolon should be used.
- In line 8, a curly brace is needed, not a square bracket.
- In line 9, **System** is capitalized.
- In line 10, a curly brace is needed, not a square bracket.

Example 2-11 *Methods in a Class—Syntax Errors*

```
 1 Public class Zoo Animal()
 2 {
 3       int aNumber = 5:
 4       string aWord = :Java';
 5       boolean aBoolean = "true";
 6
 7 public void myMethod( );
 8 [
 9    system.out.println("Hello");
10 ]
11
12 }
```

You can view the text associated with the highlighted code by accessing the full, interactive graphic for this example on the book's accompanying CD-ROM. The title of the activity is "Methods in a Class—Syntax Errors," and it can be found under the e-Lab Activities.

Encapsulation

At this point, the JavaZoo objects contain data to describe the object and methods that give each object its behaviors. The process of putting data and methods together in one structure is called encapsulation. Encapsulation means "packaged together." In OOP, an object, such as a `ZooAnimal`, is a package of information (data) and operations (methods).

Encapsulation is implemented in Java through access modifiers. An access modifier is what a programmer uses to choose which parts of the object are accessible to other objects and which parts remain hidden. Access modifiers are words used in Java code to describe what level of access the attributes and methods will have. Two access modifiers used most often in Java are **public** and **private**. If an attribute is declared **private**, access is restricted to the class where it is defined. If it is declared **public**, then even other objects can access it.

All attributes and all methods of an object should have an access modifier. The programmer must choose carefully which modifier each should be assigned. As a general rule, attributes are declared **private**, as shown in Example 2-12.

Example 2-12 *Encapsulation of Data and Methods*

```
1 private String name;
2 private int age;
3 private boolean isHungry;
4
5 public void eat()
6 {
7     System.out.println("The ZooAnimal is eating.");
8 }
```

By declaring these attributes as **private**, only the `ZooAnimal` class has access to them. This means that they are hidden from other objects and cannot be changed directly by another object.

On the other hand, methods are generally declared as **public**, as shown in Example 2-12. Methods are the means through which objects interact, so they must not be hidden from other objects.

Objects can change the state of another object only through use of a **public** method. An object should have **public** methods that other objects use to alter its **private** attributes. These **public** methods provide a predefined, specific way to change an object's state.

As with methods, most Java classes must be declared with a **public** access modifier. When a class is declared **public**, it can be accessed by other classes.

```
public class JavaZOO{}
```

Examples 2-13, 2-14, and 2-15 show class definitions for the ZooAnimal, Cage, and ZooKeeper, including single-line comments, multiline comments, and Javadoc comments to document the class and each method.

Example 2-13 *The* ZooKeeper *Class*

```
1  /**
2   ZooKeeper - This class defines a ZooKeeper object.  A ZooKeeper has
3      the responsibilities of taking care of ZooAnimals and Cages in
4      the JavaZOO.
5  */
6  class ZooKeeper {
7      /*
8          These are the attributes of a ZooKeeper.  Each ZooKeeper has
9          a name, title, payRate, and either has or does not have a
10         degree in zoology.
11     */
12     String name;
13     String title;
14     int payRate;
15     boolean hasDegree;
16
17     /**
18     feedAnimals - This method is one of the responsibilities of a
19         ZooKeeper. A message is printed to simulate feeding the
20         ZooAnimals.
21     */
22     void feedAnimals()
23     {
24        System.out.println("The ZooKeeper is feeding the Animals.");
25     }//end feedAnimals()
26
27  /**
28     cleanCage - This method is one of the responsibilities of a
29         ZooKeeper. A message is printed to simulate cleaning the cage.
```

Example 2-13 *The* ZooKeeper *Class (Continued)*

```
30      */
31      void cleanCage()
32      {
33          System.out.println("The ZooKeeper is cleaning the Cage.");
34      }//end cleanCage()
35
36 }//end ZooKeeper
```

Example 2-14 *The* ZooAnimal *Class*

```
1 /**
2   ZooAnimal - This class defines a ZooAnimal object.  A ZooAnimal has
3     the responsibilities of acting like a zoo animal in the JavaZOO.
4 */
5 class ZooAnimal {
6     /*
7         These are the attributes of a ZooAnimal.  Each ZooAnimal has a
8         name, type, color, age, and either is or is not hungry.
9     */
10    String name;
11    String type;
12    String color;
13    int age;
14    boolean isHungry;
15
16    /**
17    eat - This method is one of the behaviors of a ZooAnimal.
18        A message is printed to simulate the ZooAnimal eating.
19    */
20    void eat()
21    {
22        System.out.println("The ZooAnimal is eating.");
23    }//end eat()
24    /**
25    sleep - This method is one of the behaviors of a ZooAnimal.
26        A message is printed to simulate the ZooAnimal sleeping.
```

continues

Example 2-14 *The* ZooAnimal *Class (Continued)*

```
27    */
28    void sleep()
29    {
30        System.out.println("The ZooAnimal is sleeping.");
31    }//end sleep()
32
33 }//end ZooAnimal
```

Example 2-15 *The* Cage *Class*

```
1 /**
2   Cage - This class defines a Cage object.  A Cage will
3     contain a ZooAnimal in the JavaZOO.
4 */
5 class Cage {
6     /*
7         These are the attributes of a Cage object.  Every Cage has
8         a length and width.  Also, every Cage is either covered or
9         not covered and is either dirty or not dirty.
10    */
11    int length;
12    int width;
13    boolean isCovered;
14    boolean isDirty;
15
16    /**
17     cageInfo - This method displays a message information about the Cage
18                      object.
19    */
20    void cageInfo()
21    {
22        System.out.println("This cage is part of the JavaZOO.");
23    }//end cageInfo()
24 }//end Cage
```

Examples 2-16, 2-17, and 2-18 show the addition of access modifiers (**public** and **private**) to the attributes and methods of the JavaZOO classes. Also, the eat() and sleep() methods of the ZooAnimal class have been modified to include a change in state, using the following information:

- When a ZooAnimal eats, it is no longer hungry.
- A ZooAnimal becomes hungry when it sleeps.

Example 2-16 *The* ZooKeeper *Class with Access Modifiers*

```
1 /**
2   ZooKeeper - This class defines a ZooKeeper object.  A ZooKeeper has the
3     responsibilities of taking care of ZooAnimals and Cages in the JavaZOO.
4 */
5 public class ZooKeeper {
6     /*
7         These are the attributes of a ZooKeeper.  Each ZooKeeper has a
8         name, title, payRate, and either has or does not have a degree
9         in zoology.
10    */
11    private String name;
12    private String title;
13    private int payRate;
14    private boolean hasDegree;
15
16    /**
17    feedAnimals - This method is one of the responsibilities of
18                  a ZooKeeper.
19       A message is printed to simulate feeding the ZooAnimals.
20    */
21    public void feedAnimals()
22    {
23       System.out.println("The ZooKeeper is feeding the Animals.");
24    }//end feedAnimals()
25
26 /**
27    cleanCage - This method is one of the responsibilities of a ZooKeeper.
28       A message is printed to simulate cleaning the cage.
```

continues

Example 2-16 *The* ZooKeeper *Class with Access Modifiers (Continued)*

```
29      */
30      public void cleanCage()
31      {
32          System.out.println("The ZooKeeper is cleaning the Cage.");
33      }//end cleanCage()
34
35 }//end ZooKeeper
```

Example 2-17 *The* ZooAnimal *Class with Access Modifiers*

```
 1 /**
 2   ZooAnimal - This class defines a ZooAnimal object.  A ZooAnimal has the
 3     responsibilities of acting like a zoo animal in the JavaZOO.
 4 */
 5 public class ZooAnimal {
 6     /*
 7         These are the attributes of a ZooAnimal.  Each ZooAnimal has
 8         a name, type, color, age, and either is or is not hungry.
 9     */
10     private String name;
11     private String type;
12     private String color;
13     private int age;
14     private boolean isHungry;
15
16     /**
17     eat - This method is one of the behaviors of a ZooAnimal.
18         A message is printed to simulate the ZooAnimal eating.
19     */
20     public void eat()
21     {
22         isHungry = false;
23         System.out.println("The ZooAnimal is eating.");
24     }//end eat()
25     /**
26     sleep - This method is one of the behaviors of a ZooAnimal.
27         A message is printed to simulate the ZooAnimal sleeping.
```

Example 2-17 *The* ZooAnimal *Class with Access Modifiers (Continued)*

```
28      */
29      public void sleep()
30      {
31          isHungry = true;
32          System.out.println("The ZooAnimal is sleeping.");
33      }//end sleep()
34
35 }//end ZooAnimal
```

Example 2-18 *The* Cage *Class with Access Modifiers*

```
1 /**
2   Cage - This class defines a Cage object.  A Cage will
3      contain a ZooAnimal in the JavaZOO.
4 */
5 public class Cage {
6     /*
7         These are the attributes of a Cage object.  Every Cage has
8         a length and width.  Also, every Cage is covered or not covered
9         and is dirty or not dirty.
10    */
11    private int length;
12    private int width;
13    private boolean isCovered;
14    private boolean isDirty;
15
16    /**
17     cageInfo - This method displays a message information about the Cage.
18    */
19    public void cageInfo()
20    {
21        System.out.println("This cage is part of the JavaZOO.");
22    }//end cageInfo()
23 }//end Cage
```

The Dot Operator

The dot operator accesses methods from the main method.

At this point in the program, the JavaZOO has a main method and three objects instantiated. Each of these objects has some methods associated with it. The methods are used to make the objects perform some activity. To access these methods, the dot operator is used.

The dot operator is used to access both attributes and methods by an object:

```
object.method();
object.attribute;
```

If an attribute is **private**, though, the object.attribute; syntax can be used only in the class that defines the object. The dot operator is most widely used by other classes to access the **public** methods of an object from another class.

JavaZOOActivity Include method calls in the JavaZOO class after the object instantiation statements that would produce the output in Figure 2-34.

Use the reference name, the dot operator, and the method name to construct valid statements. The method calls that need to be inserted are shown in Example 2-19.

Figure 2-34 JavaZOO

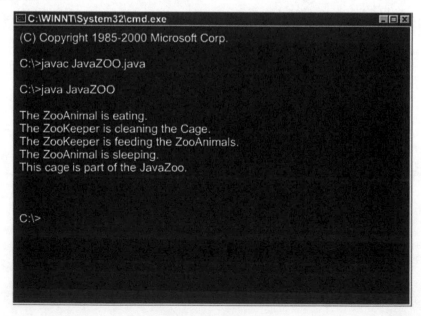

Example 2-19 *Method Calls*

```
1  /**
2   * The JavaZOO class has the main method.  It will be used as the
3   * environment for the objects of the JavaZOO to interact.
4   *
5   */
6  public class JavaZOO
7  {
8      public static void main(String args [])
9      {
10         //instantiate the objects
11         ZooAnimal myFirstAnimal = new ZooAnimal();
12         ZooKeeper myFirstKeeper = new ZooKeeper();
13         Cage myFirstCage = new Cage();
14
15         //call the eat method.
16         myFirstAnimal.eat();
17         myFirstKeeper.cleanCage();
18         myFirstKeeper.feedAnimals();
19         myFirstAnimal.sleep();
20         myFirstCage.cageInfo();
21
22     }//end main
23 }//end JavaZOO
```

Get Methods

Get methods are used to get information from an object. This section of the JavaZOO explains why get methods are needed and how to write get methods.

At this point, the JavaZOO is a very basic program. The objects each perform some action, but they are not interacting in the true sense of OOP. This section introduces advanced method structure and other concepts that allow for interaction between objects.

The methods used thus far are all **void** methods with empty parentheses. When objects interact, they sometimes request information from another object. For example, a ZooKeeper might want to know whether a ZooAnimal is hungry. It would request this information by asking for the value of the isHungry attribute. This information is acquired with a value-returning method. Therefore, the ZooAnimal class should have a value-returning method that returns the information in the isHungry attribute.

Value-Returning Methods

A value-returning method executes a statement or statements and returns information to the place in the program from where it was called. The syntax for a value-returning method is shown in Example 2-20.

Example 2-20 *Value-Returning Method*

```
 1 /*
 2      This is the general syntax for a value returning method.
 3
 4      accessModifier returntype methodName()
 5      {
 6          statements;
 7          return someValue;
 8      }
 9
10 */
11      //This is an example of a value returning method.
12      public int returnInt()
13      {
14          int myNumber = 5;
15          return myNumber;
16      }
```

Every value-returning method must include a return statement as the last statement in the method. After the return statement is called, the method ends. The return type can be any valid data type, such as **int**, String, or **boolean**. The value in the return statement must be of the same data type as the return type.

After a value-returning method is executed, the result is a piece of information with the data type declared as the return type. Therefore, the program must have the means of handling this data upon completion of the method. Usually, this is done with a Java assignment statement.

Accessing information about the state of an object is an important part of object interaction. **public** methods must be provided to access the **private** attributes. Access methods are used to retrieve the value of an object's attributes. Most programmers use get methods to retrieve information about the state of an object. The method name includes the word get combined with the name of the attribute. This is a convention that is widely used among Java programmers.

JavaZOO Activity   Design get methods for the   JavaZOO classes.

These methods will be value-returning methods. Use the name of the attribute in the method name. There should be a get method for each attribute in the ZooAnimal, ZooKeeper, and Cage classes, as shown in Examples 2-21, 2-22, and 2-23.

Example 2-21 *A* ZooKeeper *Class Snippet*

```
1    /**
2    getName - This method returns the value of the name.
3    */
4    public String getName()
5    {
6        return name;
7    }//end getName()
8    /**
9    getTitle - This method returns the value of title.
10   */
11   public String getTitle()
12   {
13       return title;
14   }//end getTitle()
15   /**
16   getPayRate - This method returns the value of payRate.
17   */
18   public int getPayRate()
19   {
20       return payRate;
21   }//end getPayRate()
22   /**
23   getHasDegree - This method returns the value of HasDegree
24   */
25   public boolean getHasDegree()
26   {
27       return hasDegree;
28   }//end getHasDegree()
```

Example 2-22 *A* ZooAnimal *Class Snippet*

```
1      /**
2       getName - This method returns the value of the name.
3       */
4       public String getName()
5       {
6           return name;
7       }//end getName()
8      /**
9       getType - This method returns the value of type.
10      */
11      public String getType()
12      {
13          return type;
14      }//end getType()
15     /**
16      getColor - This method returns the value of color.
17      */
18      public String getColor()
19      {
20          return color;
21      }//end getColor()
22     /**
23      getAge - This method returns the value of age
24      */
25      public int getAge()
26      {
27          return age;
28      }//end getAge()
29     /**
30      getIsHungry - This method returns the value of isHungry
31      */
32      public boolean getIsHungry()
33      {
34          return isHungry;
35      }//end getIsHungry()
```

Example 2-23 Cage *Class Snippet*

```
1    /**
2     getLength - This method returns the value of length
3     */
4     public int getLength()
5     {
6         return length;
7     }//end getLength()
8     /**
9     getWidth - This method returns the value of width
10    */
11    public int getWidth()
12    {
13        return width;
14    }//end getWidth()
15    /**
16    getIsCovered - This method returns the value of isCovered
17    */
18    public boolean getIsCovered()
19    {
20        return isCovered;
21    }//end getIsCovered()
22    /**
23    getIsDirty - This method returns the value of isDirty
24    */
25    public boolean getIsDirty()
26    {
27        return isDirty;
28    }//end getIsDirty()
```

Parameters

Parameters supply methods with information needed to execute tasks within those methods. The JavaZOO uses parameters to change or assign the value of an attribute.

So far, this chapter has examined only methods with empty parentheses. The parentheses in a method are used to contain information known as parameters. Parameters are pieces of information that the method needs to execute its task. The methods used in the JavaZoo and other examples have not required any additional information to fulfill their functionality, so the parentheses have been left empty.

Parameters often are used to change the value of an attribute. The syntax for method parameters is shown in Example 2-24.

Example 2-24 *Method Parameters*

```
1     /*
2     This is the general syntax for a method with parameters.
3
4     methodName(datatype parameter, datatype parameter, ...)
5     {
6         statements;
7     }
8     */
9
10    //This is an example of a constructor method with parameters
11    public Person(String name, int age, boolean mood)
12    {
13        theAge = age;
14        theName = name;
15        isHappy = mood;
16    }
17
18    //these are all valid constructor calls for a Person object.
19    String myName = "Tammy";
20    boolean bool4 = true;
21
22    Person person1 = new Person("Tom", 6, true);
23    Person person2 = new Person(myName, 6, false);
24    Person person3 = new Person(myName, 8, bool4);
```

A method can have any number of parameters in any combination of data types.

In a method that requires parameters of different data types, the order is extremely important. When the constructor in Example 2-24 is called, the variables must be passed in the order of String, **int, boolean**. Otherwise, an error will be generated.

Finally, parameters can be literals. A literal is an actual value, not a variable. For example, in the following statement, 5 is the literal and number is the variable:

```
int number = 5;
```

When String literals are passed, the literal must be contained in double quotes. Note that when a literal value is passed as an **int** parameter, or when the reserved words **true** or **false** are passed as a **boolean** parameter, they are not contained in quotes.

Example 2-24 shows three valid uses of the Person constructor method. The parameters passed to the constructor can be variables, literal values, or a combination of both.

Set Methods

Previously, get methods were designed for the attributes in each class. This allowed objects to access another object's information. But what if an object not only needs access, but also must change the value of another object's information? In this case, **private** attributes should have a **public** method to change its value. The convention of using a set method has been developed and is widely used. A set method takes a parameter and assigns the value of the parameter to the attribute.

Now several methods can be used to create a certain object with a certain state. The constructor is used to initialize some, all, or none of the attributes. The set methods are standard methods that are used to alter the values of individual attributes. This is rather inefficient. In the JavaZOO, every animal will have a name, type, and color. So, each time a ZooAnimal object is created, there must be four methods: the constructor, setName, setType, and setColor.

 JavaZOO Activity   Design set methods for the   JavaZOO classes.

These methods will all be **void** methods requiring one parameter. Use the name of the attribute in the method name. There should be a set method for each attribute in the ZooAnimal, ZooKeeper, and Cage classes, as shown in Examples 2-25, 2-26, and 2-27.

Example 2-25 *A ZooKeeper Class Snippet*

```
1    /**
2     setName - This method sets the value of the name.
3     */
4     public void setName(String newName)
5     {
6         name = newName;
```

continues

Example 2-25 *A* ZooKeeper *Class Snippet (Continued)*

```
7     }//end setName()
8     /**
9     setTitle - This method sets the value of title.
10    */
11    public void setTitle(String newTitle)
12    {
13        title = newTitle;
14    }//end setTitle()
15    /**
16    setPayRate - This method sets the value of payRate.
17    */
18    public void setPayRate(int newPayRate)
19    {
20        payRate = newPayRate;
21    }//end setPayRate()
22    /**
23    setHasDegree - This method sets the value of HasDegree
24    */
25    public void setHasDegree(boolean newHasDegree)
26    {
27        hasDegree = newHasDegree;
28    }//end setHasDegree()
```

Example 2-26 *A* ZooAnimal *Class Snippet*

```
1     /**
2     setName - This method sets the value of the name.
3     */
4     public void setName(String newName)
5     {
6         name = newName;
7     }//end setName()
8     /**
9     setType - This method sets the value of type.
10    */
11    public void setType(String newType)
```

Example 2-26 *A* ZooAnimal *Class Snippet (Continued)*

```
12    {
13        type = newType;
14    }//end setType()
15    /**
16    setColor - This method sets the value of color.
17    */
18    public void setColor(String newColor)
19    {
20        color = newColor;
21    }//end setColor()
22    /**
23    setAge - This method sets the value of age
24    */
25    public void setAge(int newAge)
26    {
27        age = newAge;
28    }//end setAge()
29    /**
30    setIsHungry - This method sets the value of isHungry
31    */
32    public void setIsHungry(boolean newIsHungry)
33    {
34        isHungry = newIsHungry;
35    }//end setIsHungry()
```

Example 2-27 *A Cage Class Snippet*

```
1    /**
2    setLength - This method sets the value of length
3    */
4    public void setLength(int newLength)
5    {
6        length = newLength;
7    }//end setLength()
8    /**
9    setWidth - This method sets the value of width
```

continues

Example 2-27 *A Cage Class Snippet (Continued)*

```
10      */
11      public void setWidth(int newWidth)
12      {
13          width = newWidth;
14      }//end setWidth()
15      /**
16      setIsCovered - This method sets the value of isCovered
17      */
18      public void setIsCovered(boolean newIsCovered)
19      {
20          isCovered = newIsCovered;
21      }//end setIsCovered()
22      /**
23      setIsDirty - This method sets the value of isDirty
24      */
25      public void setIsDirty(boolean newIsDirty)
26      {
27          isDirty = newIsDirty;
28      }//end setIsDirty()
```

Overloaded Methods

Java allows programmers to use the same methods for multiple types of input. These methods are called overloaded methods. Overloaded methods will be used in the JavaZoo to increase the flexibility of the methods.

It is possible to design a constructor that takes parameters. Instead of calling the set methods to individually assign values, a constructor can assign the values of the parameters to the attributes of a ZooAnimal object. The constructor method would have five parameters, one for each attribute. The concept of having multiple methods with the same name is called polymorphism. A method is overloaded if it appears multiple times within a class.

Before discussing the process of overloading a method, another concept must be thoroughly understood. Each method in Java has a unique method signature. The signature of a method is composed of the method name and the parameters. Two methods with the same name have different method signatures when the data types of the parameters are different, in either number or order. The Java language supports any method as long as it has a unique signature. Each of the methods shown in Example 2-28 has a unique signature, even though both have the same name.

Example 2-28 *Overloaded Methods*

```
1 public void aNewMethod(){}
2
3 public void aNewMethod(int age, int height, String name){}
4
5 public void aNewMethod(String name, int height, int age){}
6
7 public void aNewMethod(int age, String name, int height){}
8
9 public void aNewMethod(int height, int age){}
```

A method's signature does not depend on the access modifier, the return type, or the names of the parameters. For example, each pair of methods in Example 2-29 has the same signature and will generate a compile error if written within the same class.

Example 2-29 *Overloaded Method Errors*

```
1 public void aNewMethod(int age){}
2
3 private void aNewMethod(int height){}
4
5 public int aNewMethod(int age){}
6
7 public void aNewMethod(int height){}
8
9 public void aNewMethod(int age, String Name, int height){}
10
11 public void aNewMethod(int height, String Name, int age){}
```

To overload a constructor or any method, provide a method header with the same name but a different list of parameters. Having overloaded methods in a class increases its functionality. In the case of a constructor, allowing several ways to instantiate an object is a functionality that adds to the flexibility of the class.

JavaZOOActivity   In the JavaZOO class, write the necessary statements to fulfill the following requirements.

This activity requires the use of literals. Remember that String literals are enclosed in double quotes.

- Create a ZooAnimal (ZooAnimal2) named Chip. Chip is a brown monkey that is five years old. He is not hungry.
- Create a ZooKeeper(ZooKeeper2) named Mr. Jackson Rock. He has no degree and is paid $14 an hour.
- Create a covered Cage (Cage2) that has a length of 15 and a width of 20. This cage is not clean.

Your code should be similar to that shown in Example 2-30.

Example 2-30 JavaZOO *Overloaded Methods*

```
1 /**
2 * The JavaZOO class has the main method.  It will be used as the
3 * environment for the objects of the JavaZOO to interact.
4 *
5 */
6 public class JavaZOO
7 {
8     public static void main(String args [])
9     {
10        ZooAnimal ZooAnimal2 = new ZooAnimal();
11        ZooAnimal2.setName("Chip");
12        ZooAnimal2.setColor("Brown");
13        ZooAnimal2.setType("Monkey");
14        ZooAnimal2.setAge(5);
15
16        ZooKeeper ZooKeeper2 = new ZooKeeper();
17        ZooKeeper2.setName("Jackson Rock");
18        ZooKeeper2.setTitle("Mr.");
19        ZooKeeper2.setHasDegree(false);
20
21        Cage Cage2 = new Cage();
22        Cage2.setIsCovered(true);
```

Example 2-30 JavaZOO *Overloaded Methods (Continued)*

```
23          Cage2.setLength(15);

24          Cage2.setIsDirty(true);

25

26

27      }//end main

28  }//end JavaZOO
```

Modifying Classes

Many opportunities exist for modifying the JavaZOO classes to add advanced behavior, increased functionality, and object interaction. Eight optional activities modify the classes in the JavaZOO program. These eight activities show students how to overload methods, instantiate objects, create a new class, create a counter, and display results. The figures and examples illustrate possible answers for each optional activity.

JavaZOO Activity 1   Modify the   ZooKeeper class, as shown in Example 2-31.

- Overload the constructor method. The class should include an additional constructor that has four parameters.

- The ZooKeeper will now be capable of feeding a specific ZooAnimal a certain type of food. Change the feedAnimals() method to feedAnimal(). The method will have a ZooAnimal as one parameter and a String as the second parameter to represent the type of food. The method will then call the eats() method of the ZooAnimal. This method should now display a customized message, such as, "Jesper Reed is feeding a ZooAnimal."

- How would you display the message "Jesper Reed is feeding Pecanzo."? (Hint: Get methods retrieve information from other objects.)

- The JavaZOO will now pay a ZooKeeper. Add a method to the ZooKeeper called payMe(). This method will take an **int** as a parameter to represent the number of hours the ZooKeeper has worked. The method will multiply the payRate by the number of hours and return the total amount as an **int**.

Example 2-31 *Modifying the* JavaZOO *Classes*

```
1    /**
2    ZooKeeper constructor - This method is a constructor
3    for a ZooKeeper.
4    It has parameters for each attribute.
5    */
6    public ZooKeeper(String newName, String newTitle,
7    int newPayRate, boolean newHasDegree)
8    {
9        name = newName;
10       title = newTitle;
11       payRate = newPayRate;
12       hasDegree = newHasDegree;
13   }
14   /**
15   feedAnimal - This method is one of the
16   responsibilities of a ZooKeeper.
17   A message is printed to simulate feeding the ZooAnimals.
18   */
19   public void feedAnimal(ZooAnimal theAnimal, String food)
20   {
21       theAnimal.eat(food);
22       String AnimalName = theAnimal.getName();
23       System.out.println(name + " is feeding " + AnimalName);
24   }//end feedAnimals()
25   /**
26   payMe - This method is one of the responsibilities
27   of a ZooKeeper. This method requires a parameter of
28   number of hours worked, and
29   returns the total amount to pay.
30   */
31   public int payMe(int hours)
32   {
33       int money = hours * payRate;
34       return money;
35   }//end payMe()
```

JavaZOO Activity 2   Modify the `ZooAnimal` class, as shown in Example 2-32.

- Overload the constructor method. The class should include an additional constructor that has five parameters, one for each attribute of a `ZooAnimal`.

- `ZooAnimal`s will now have the capability to eat a specific type of food. Modify the `eats()` method. Add a `String` parameter to the method header to represent the type of `food`. The method should now display a customized message, such as, `"Pecanzo is eating peanuts."`, where `Pecanzo` is the name of the `ZooAnimal` and `peanuts` is the type of `food`.

- `ZooAnimal`s will sleep for a specified amount of time. Modify the `sleep()` method. Add an **int** parameter to the method header to represent the number of hours the animal has slept. Display a customized message, such as, `"Pecanzo has slept for 9 hours."`, where `Pecanzo` is the name of the `ZooAnimal` and `9` is the number of hours.

Example 2-32 *Modifying the* JavaZOO *Classes*

```
1    /**
2    ZooAnimal constructor - This method is a constructor for a ZooAnimal.
3        It takes parameters for each attribute.
4    */
5    public ZooAnimal(String newName, String newType, String newColor,
6                     int newAge, boolean newIsHungry)
7    {
8        name = newName;
9        type = newType;
10       color = newColor;
11       age = newAge;
12       isHungry = newIsHungry;
13   }
14   /**
15   eat - This method is one of the behaviors of a ZooAnimal.
16       A message is printed to simulate the ZooAnimal eating.
17   */
18   public void eat(String food)
19   {
20       isHungry = false;
21       System.out.println(name + " is eating " + food);
22   }//end eat()
```

continues

Example 2-32 *Modifying the* JavaZOO *Classes (Continued)*

```
23      /**
24      sleep - This method is one of the behaviors of a ZooAnimal.
25         A message is printed to simulate the ZooAnimal sleeping.
26      */
27      public void sleep(int hours)
28      {
29          isHungry = true;
30          System.out.println(name + " has slept for " + hours + " hours.");
31      }//end sleep()
```

TIP

Declare two String
variables within the
method to store the
type of animal and
name of the animal.

JavaZOO Activity 3   Modify the   Cage class, as shown in Example 2-33.

- Overload the constructor method. Include an additional constructor with all of the necessary parameters for each attribute.

- It would be a good idea in the JavaZOO to include a ZooAnimal as an attribute in the Cage class. Because a cage is built for the purpose of containing an animal, this would increase its functionality and realism. Declare a **private** ZooAnimal attribute. Additionally, write a setAnimal() method that takes a ZooAnimal object as a parameter. It is a **void** method quite similar to the other set methods. Write a getAnimal method that returns a ZooAnimal object.

- Modify the cageInfo method to display a message, such as, "This cage has an elephant named Pecanzo."

Example 2-33 *Modifying the* JavaZOO *Classes*

```
1       /*
2       These are the attributes of a Cage object.  Every Cage has
3       a length and width.  Also, every Cage is covered or not covered
4       and is dirty or not dirty.
5       */
6       private int length;
7       private int width;
8       private boolean isCovered;
9       private boolean isDirty;
10      private ZooAnimal animal;
```

Example 2-33 *Modifying the* JavaZOO *Classes (Continued)*

```
11    /**
12    Cage constructor - This method is a constructor for a Cage.
13         It has parameters for each attribute.
14    */
15    public Cage(int newLength, int newWidth,boolean
16    newIsCovered, boolean newIsDirty)
17    {
18        length = newLength;
19        width = newWidth;
20        isCovered = newIsCovered;
21        isDirty = newIsDirty;
22    }
23    /**
24     cageInfo - This method displays a message
25     information about the Cage object.
26    */
27    public void cageInfo()
28    {
29      String type = animal.getType();
30      String name = animal.getName();
31      System.out.println("This cage is part of the JavaZOO.");
32      System.out.println("This cage has a " + type + " named " + name);
33    }//end cageInfo()
34    /** setAnimal method - assigns a ZooAnimal to a Cage*/
35    public void setAnimal(ZooAnimal newAnimal)
36    {
37        animal = newAnimal;
38    }
39    /** getAnimal method - retrieves the ZooAnimal from the Cage*/
40    public ZooAnimal getAnimal()
41    {
42        return animal;
43    }
```

JavaZOO Activity 4   Modify the JavaZOO class, as shown in Example 2-34.

- Delete all existing statements from inside the main method.
- Instantiate a ZooAnimal object, a ZooKeeper object, and a Cage object using the constructors that require all parameters.
- Add the ZooAnimal object that you created to the Cage using the method setAnimal(). The setAnimal method requires a ZooAnimal as a parameter, so the reference name of the ZooAnimal should be passed to this method.
- Write a statement to display information about the Cage, including what kind of animal is in it.
- Write a statement so that the ZooKeeper feeds the ZooAnimal ZooFOOD, which is a String literal.
- Use a declaration statement to declare a variable called money of type **int**. Use an assignment statement to assign the amount of money paid to the ZooKeeper who works five hours. Then write a statement to display the following message: "The ZooKeeper was paid XXX dollars", where XXX is the total amount paid to the ZooKeeper. (Hint: use the System.out.println() method along with the + to build the message)
- Write a statement to make the ZooAnimal sleep for four hours.

Example 2-34 *Modifying the* JavaZOO *Classes*

```
1 /**
2 * The JavaZOO class has the main method.  It will be used as the
3 * environment for the objects of the JavaZOO to interact.
4 *
5 */
6 public class JavaZOO
7 {
8     public static void main(String args [])
9     {
10        //instantiate the objects
11        ZooAnimal myZooAnimal = new ZooAnimal(
12        "George", "Giraffe", "Brown", 3, true);
13        ZooKeeper myZooKeeper = new ZooKeeper(
14        "Rocco Marque", "Dr.", 15, true);
15        Cage cage01 = new Cage(100, 200, false, false);
```

Example 2-34 *Modifying the* JavaZOO *Classes (Continued)*

```
16
17          //Add the ZooAnimal to the Cage
18          cage01.setAnimal(myZooAnimal);
19          cage01.cageInfo();
20
21          //the ZooKeeper feeds the ZooAnimal
22          myZooKeeper.feedAnimal(myZooAnimal, "ZooFOOD");
23
24          //pay the ZooKeeper
25          int money;
26          money = myZooKeeper.payMe(5);
27          System.out.println("The ZooKeeper was paid " + money + " dollars.");
28
29          //ZooAnimal sleeps
30          myZooAnimal.sleep(4);
31
32      }//end main
33 }//end JavaZOO
```

JavaZOO Activity 5   Create a Dolphin class, as shown in Example 2-35.

- Write a Java Class called Dolphin. This class is a subclass of ZooAnimal. Dolphin has all of the characteristics and behaviors of a ZooAnimal, and it should have a String attribute called trick. Finally, the Dolphin class must have a performTrick() method. The method should print a message that says, "Peter is performing a flip.", where Peter is the name of the Dolphin and flip is the value of the trick attribute.

- Override the eats() method in the Dolphin class. The method will set the value of isHungry to **false**. Also, the method should display the following output on the screen, where Freddy is the name of the Dolphin and mackerel is the parameter passed into the eats() method:

```
Dolphins eat lots of fish.
Freddy is eating mackerel.
```

- Remember the effects of access modifiers. **private** attributes from the superclass must be accessed through the **public** methods.

Example 2-35 *Modifying the* JavaZOO *Classes*

```
1  /**
2   * The Dolphin class is a subclass of the ZooAnimal
3   */
4  public class Dolphin extends ZooAnimal
5  {
6      //an additional attribute
7      private String trick;
8      /**
9       * Constructor for objects of class Dolphin
10      */
11     public Dolphin(String name, String type, String color,
12                    int age, boolean isHungry, String newTrick)
13     {
14         super(name, type, color, age, isHungry);
15         trick = newTrick;
16     }//end constructor
17
18     /** perfromTrick method */
19     public void performTrick()
20     {
21         String name = this.getName();
22         System.out.println(name + " is performing a " + trick);
23     }//end performTrick()
24     /** eat method - this method is overridden*/
25     public void eat(String food)
26     {
27         setIsHungry(false);
28         String name = getName();
29         System.out.println("Dolphins love to eat fish.");
30         System.out.println(name + " is eating " + food);
31     }//end eat()
32 }
```

JavaZOO Activity 6   Modify the JavaZOO class to include the   Dolphin class, as
shown in Examaple 2-36.

- Delete the statements from main.

- Instantiate two objects, a ZooAnimal and a Dolphin, by providing all of
  the parameters to the constructor.

- Call the eat() method for both objects. The ZooAnimal should eat
  zooFOOD and the Dolphin should eat zooFISH.

- Call the performTrick() method.

Figure 2-35 shows the output for the modified JavaZOO class.

Example 2-36 *Modifying the JavaZOO Classes Code View*

```
 1  /**
 2   * The JavaZOO class has the main method.  It will be used as the
 3   * environment for the objects of the JavaZOO to interact.
 4   *
 5   */
 6  public class JavaZOO
 7  {
 8      public static void main(String args [])
 9      {
10          //instantiate the objects
11          ZooAnimal myZooAnimal = new ZooAnimal(
12          "George", "Giraffe", "Brown", 3, true);
13
14          Dolphin myDolphin = new Dolphin(
15          "Harry", "bottlenose", "grey", 7, false, "triple flip");
16
17          ZooAnimal myOtherZooAnimal = new ZooAnimal();
18
19          //call the eat method.
20          myZooAnimal.eat("zooFOOD");
```

continues

Example 2-36 *Modifying the* JavaZoo *Classes—Code View (Continued)*

```
21          myDolphin.eat("zooFISH");

22

23          //call the perfromTrick() method.

24          myDolphin.performTrick();

25

26

27     }//end main

28 }//end JavaZOO
```

Figure 2-35 Modifying the JavaZOO Classes—Output View

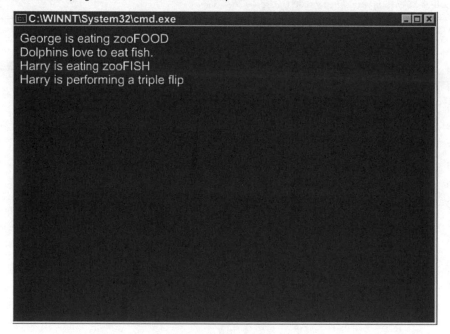

JavaZOO Activity 7   Modify the `ZooAnimal` class by adding an animal counter variable, as shown in Example 2-37.

Do the following:

> **Step 1**   Add a static variable called `animalCounter`. Assign the value of 0 to it. This variable will store the total number of animals created. It should be incremented by 1 each time an object is created. Include a statement in the `ZooAnimal` constructors to increment `animalCounter`.
>
> Add a static method to retrieve the value of `animalCounter`. This method is a value-returning method and returns an **int**.

The **static** modifier for variables and methods is covered in more detail in Chapter 3, "Java Language Elements."

Example 2-37 *Modifying the* JavaZOO *Classes*

```
1    /*
2        These are the attributes of a ZooAnimal.
3        Each ZooAnimal has a name,
4        type, color, age, and either is or is not hungry.
5    */
6    private String name;
7    private String type;
8    private String color;
9    private int age;
10   private boolean isHungry;
11   private static int animalCounter = 0;
12
13   /** getAnimalCounter - a static method */
14   public static int getAnimalCounter()
15   {
16      return animalCounter;
17   }
18   /**
19   ZooAnimal constructor - This method is a constructor for a ZooAnimal.
20      It sets the age to 0 and isHungry to false.
```

continues

Example 2-37 *Modifying the* JavaZOO *Classes (Continued)*

```
21
22    */
23    public ZooAnimal()
24    {
25       age = 0;
26       isHungry = false;
27       animalCounter = animalCounter + 1;
28    }
29 /**
30    ZooAnimal constructor - This method is a constructor for a ZooAnimal.
31    It takes parameters for each attribute.
32    */
33    public ZooAnimal(String newName, String newType, String newColor,
34    int newAge, boolean newIsHungry)
35    {
36       name = newName;
37       type = newType;
38       color = newColor;
39       age = newAge;
40       isHungry = newIsHungry;
41       animalCounter = animalCounter + 1;
42    }
```

 JavaZOOActivity8   Modifythe JavaZOOclasstodisplaythenumberofanimals in the JavaZOO, as shown in Example 2-38.

- Instantiate several ZooAnimal objects.
- Write a statement that displays this message: "There are X animals in the JavaZOO.", where X is the value of animalCounter.

Figure 2-36 shows the output for the modified JavaZOO class.

Example 2-38 *Modifying the* JavaZOO *Classes—Code View*

```
1 /**
2  * The JavaZOO class has the main method.  It will be used as the
3  * environment for the objects of the JavaZOO to interact.
4  *
5  */
6 public class JavaZOO
7 {
8    public static void main(String args [])
9    {
10      //instantiate the objects
11      ZooAnimal myZooAnimal = new ZooAnimal
12      ("George", "Giraffe", "Brown", 3, true);
13      Dolphin myDolphin = new Dolphin("Harry", "bottlenose", "grey",
14            7, false, "triple flip");
15
16      ZooAnimal myOtherZooAnimal = new ZooAnimal();
17
18      //call the eat method.
19      MyZooAnimal.eat("zooFOOD");
20      myDolphin.eat("zooFISH");
21
22      //call the perfromTrick() method.
23      MyDolphin.performTriok();
24
25      //call to a static method in ZooAnimal Class
26      int number = ZooAnimal.getAnimalCounter();
27      System.out.println("There are " + number +
28      " animals in the JavaZOO");
29   }//end main
30 }//end JavaZOO
```

Figure 2-36 Modifying the JavaZOO Classes—Output View

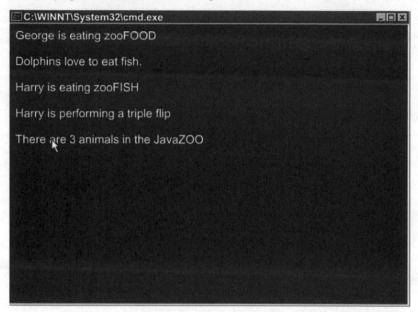

Summary

This chapter introduced the concepts related to OOP, including objects and classes. Objects are members of a class and are also known as instances of classes. Objects can hold data and manipulate that data. Each object has attributes (data) and behaviors (methods). Objects interact with each other through methods. A programmer defines interaction between objects by defining methods in an object and by using objects to send messages from one object to another.

Classes, on the other hand, are "blueprints" for making objects. Classes contain methods, which are sets of instructions for performing tasks. Some methods are used to access information (known as accessors), while other methods are used to change, or manipulate, data (known as mutators). Classes have relationships with other classes. Inheritance is one such relationship in which classes inherit attributes and behaviors from other classes. Class definitions and relationships can be modeled using the UML, a system of symbols that provides a uniform means of communication among and between end users and programmers.

Syntax Summary

`new`   A keyword to request the creation of an object

`public class`   Usually the words used in the first line of a Java program to define the class

`( )`   Empty for an accessor method because data is being retrieved. In a mutator method, the changing object data is placed in the parentheses.

Resources

This book is not meant to be a comprehensive manual for everything Java. To include everything relevant to Java would take volumes. As such, many resources are available to the student, including books and the web. The next sections document a couple of those resources.

Web Resources

www.javaworld.com

www.jguru.com

http://javaboutique.internet.com/tutorials/

Books

Deitel, Deitel, *Java™ How to Program*, Fourth Edition, "Introducing Object-Oriented Design with the UML and Design Patterns"

The following provides a suggested list of books on Unified Modeling Language (UML):

The Unified Modeling Language User Guide—A comprehensive tutorial on UML modeling, from the original developers of the language

Applying UML and Patterns—Some case studies and examples of UML, and a good introduction to applied modeling concepts

Business Modeling with UML: Business Patterns at Work—A guide to applying UML to business systems

Sams Teach Yourself UML in 24 Hours—A concise, nontechnical book on every aspect of UML, with diagrams and practical examples

UML in a Nutshell: A Desktop Quick Reference—In the tradition of other O'Reilly books, a concise but comprehensive overview of this complex topic

UML Distilled: A Brief Guide to the Standard Object Modeling Language—An informative and comprehensive book on how to integrate UML into object-oriented software development

Key Terms

accessor methods   Are methods to retrieve data for an object.

access modifiers   Defines the level of access to the class, data, or method.

attributes or data of a class   Describe the state of objects. Attributes are also called data.

behaviors or operations or methods of a class   Describe what objects can do. Behaviors are also called operations or methods.

class   A blueprint for an object. A class contains the attributes and behaviors of the object it defines.

constructor method   Is a method that defines procedures for how to create an object. It possesses the same name as the class.

custom methods   Are user-defined methods for performing a particular task.

data type   Describes what kind of information a certain attribute is.

encapsulation   The process of combining data and methods together in one class.

information hiding   Is achieved by instituting the keyword `private` to enable limited access to data or methods.

inheritance   Is when some objects derive attributes and behaviors from other objects.

instance of a class   An object of a particular class. The object is a specific instance of a general class.

message sending   Objects interact with each other by sending messages. These actions occur in methods. A message is sent to an object using the method signature, which identifies the name of the method and the data defined in the method.

method   A set of instructions that are executed by an object.

method arguments   Is the information that a method requires to perform its task.

method signature   Identifies the name of the method and provides the method with the data.

mutator methods   Are methods that change or manipulate data for an object.

object   Contains data and instructions for processing the data. An object is a representation of something.

object destruction   The JVM implements the garbage collector program, which cleans up objects destroyed by the programmer.

object mutability   Is whether the object data can be changed. The keyword **final** makes data unchangeable.

object relationships and associations   Is based on the associations of objects in a context. An object knows about another object.

return values for methods   Value required by the method's definition to be sent back to any method that calls that particular method.

reuse   Or overloading methods, is the reuse of the same method name (in the same program) to handle multiple types of input.

Unified Modeling Language (UML)   A uniform system of symbols and terms to communicate the design of classes and applications and their relationships.

Check Your Understanding

1. What is encapsulation?

   A. The process of deriving attributes and behaviors from other objects

   B. The process of combining attributes and behaviors into one class

   C. The process of placing attributes in one class and behaviors in another class

   D. The process of storing data in an attribute

2. What is another term for attributes?

   A. Behaviors

   B. Methods

   C. Data

   D. Objects

3. Which Java keyword is used to create an object?

   A. public

   B. main

   C. create

   D. new

4. Which of the following is not needed when on object sends a message to another object?

   A. The object type

   B. The object reference

   C. The name of the method

   D. The message for the method

5. Which of the following is a false statement about encapsulation?

   A. Encapsulation abstracts, or hides, information about the object.

   B. Encapsulation protects information from illegal access.

   C. Encapsulation is implemented in Java with keywords such as `public` and `private`.

   D. A properly encapsulated object has `public` data and `private` methods.

6. Which of the following is a true statement about inheritance?

   A. A superclass inherits data and methods from the subclass.

   B. A superclass has access to the methods and data of the subclass.

   C. A subclass has access to the methods and data of the superclass.

   D. An inheritance relationship is equivalent to an association relationship.

7. Which tool does the Java Virtual Machine use to manage memory?

   A. Memory manager

   B. Garbage collector

   C. Finalizer

   D. Object destructor

8. The collection of symbols and patterns of symbols used to describe objects, the relationship between objects, the use of objects, and the state of objects is what?

   A. JVM

   B. HTML

   C. XML

   D. UML

9. Which symbol in UML is used to describe a class?

   A. Circle

   B. Rectangle

   C. Triangle

   D. Oval

10. Which is not part of the UML class symbol?

   A. The object compartment

   B. The attribute compartment

   C. The name compartment

   D. The method compartment

11. Which UML diagram can be used to test the accuracy of a class diagram?

   A. Package diagram

   B. Use-case diagram

   C. Object diagram

   D. Sequence diagram

12. Which type of method has the same name as the class with no return type?

   A. Constructor method

   B. Mutator method

   C. Accessor method

   D. `main` method

13. Which of the following is not a valid Java data type?

   A. `int`

   B. `decimal`

   C. `boolean`

   D. `double`

14. Which of the following are allowed as values for a **boolean** data type?

   A. Positive integers

   B. 1 or 0

   C. yes or no

   D. **true** or **false**

15. Which of the following Java statements correctly instantiates an object of the class Person?

    A. `Person myPerson = Person();`

    B. `Person myPerson = static Person();`

    C. `Person myPerson = new Person`

    D. `Person myPerson = new Person();`

16. Which symbols are used to enclose the body of a method?

    A. []

    B. {}

    C. ()

    D. <>

17. What is the dot operator (.) used for in Java?

    A. Every Java statement must end with the dot operator.

    B. The dot operator is used only to access methods of an object or class.

    C. The dot operator is used only to access attributes of an object or class.

    D. The dot operator is used to access both attributes and methods of an object or class.

18. Which of the following is a correct method header for a value-returning method?

    A. `public getAge()`

    B. `public void getAge;`

    C. `public int getAge()`

    D. `public int getAge();`

19. Which of the following is not a true statement about parameters?

    A. Parameters often are used to change the value of an attribute within a method.

    B. The order in which parameters are passed to a method is unimportant.

    C. Parameters provide information to a method needed for task execution.

    D. If a method requires parameters, they are contained inside the parentheses of the method call.

20. A method signature is dependent upon what?

A. The access modifier

B. The return type

C. The names of the parameters

D. The method name

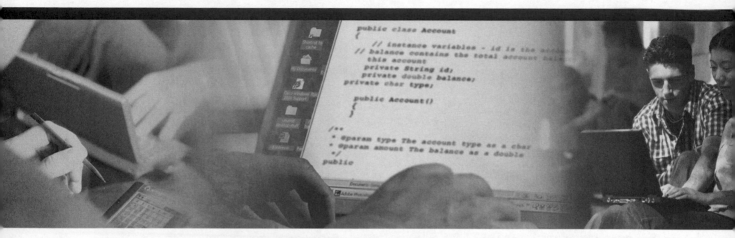

Upon completion of this chapter, you will be able to

- Implement documentation
- Identify the Java language elements
- Explain the where and when of data storage
- Understand the concept of data types
- Define syntax
- Understand object creation, mutability, and destruction
- Apply the Java language concepts that you have learned in this chapter to the JBANK case study

Chapter 3

Java Language Elements

Using Java requires a firm understanding of the keywords of the language and the rules of syntax for defining classes, constructors, methods, and interactions between objects. This chapter presents the fundamental elements of Java and documentation techniques. It presents the use of the Java API, its documentation, and javadoc to generate documentation for classes. This is similar to the documentation provided by the Java API. The Java toolkit includes the program javadoc. To generate documentation, a Java programmer must become familiar with the specific syntax of the tool, known as tags. This chapter introduces the javadoc tags and the guidelines for embedding them in source code.

One primary reason for using object-oriented languages is to reuse program code frequently. To reuse code, a programmer needs to know several things, including the names of classes, what they "know" (attributes), what they "know how to do" (methods), and their association and inheritance relationships with other objects. For proper use of the class, the designer must document this information.

This chapter introduces important ideas about program *data storage*, definition of classes, and methods. Data and storage requirements differ for each type of data. A Java programmer must learn the proper syntax for defining the attributes and methods of the class.

It is an essential programming practice to include remarks or comments in Java programs that document the program features and their use. These comments are designed for the programmer as well as others who need access to the source code of a class. Documenting allows others to read why the coding was done in a particular manner or structure. This greatly helps when troubleshooting a problem with a program.

Documentation

Proper documentation is a critical requirement for the successful Java programmer. This section covers the following Java documentation topics:

- Purpose of the documentation
- An overview of pseudocoding
- Guidelines for documenting classes
- Historical origins of the three kinds of comments used in Java
- The javadoc parameters
- Javadoc automatic generation of comments
- Java language API online documentation
- Generation of API docs for classes using the javadoc tool
- List of javadoc options
- What the javadoc tool options do
- Case study: JBANK banking application

Purpose of Documentation

Program documentation includes charts and diagrams that can be referenced by other programmers. These can include UML diagrams, specific instructions to end users of an application, and documentation in the source code. When developing complex applications with numerous classes, documentation becomes critical. Documentation can affect the success or failure of the project.

Documentation serves two purposes. First, the comments embedded in the source code can assist a programmer in modifying and maintaining the class definition and in tracing errors. Some programmers use comments as the first step in designing a class. In this case, the comments form the skeleton or general plan for the class. This technique is a modified form of pseudocoding, or creating a sketch of the program. The second purpose of documentation is to communicate with other programmers who use the class. The comments help other programmers understand the logic and reasons behind a particular feature, as shown in Figure 3-1.

The Java development community utilizes several documentation features in documenting classes. Documentation in the form of web-based documents or HTML documents also can be generated using the javadoc tool, which interprets embedded special symbols. These can be tags and parameters or text that has been embedded in the source-code file. This generates HTML documents similar to those of the Java *API documentation*.

Figure 3-1 API Documentation

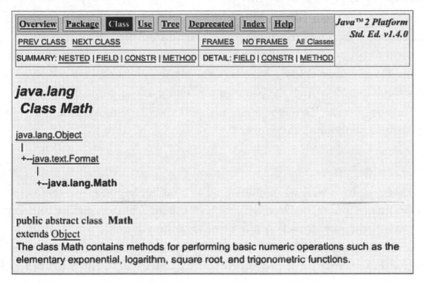

Why Documentation Is Important

Comments make software code more maintainable. In most business environments, the person who maintains the code is rarely the person who wrote the code. Therefore, it is important that later readers of the programs can understand the thought process and algorithms used by the program developers. Comments are very beneficial for communicating this information to later readers and maintainers of the code.

How Much of Maintenance Costs Are a Function of Readable Code?

An easily readable program or code can improve productivity of maintenance personnel significantly. It can take many times the effort to decipher and modify poorly written software compared to well-written, clearly commented software.

How Much of the Program Costs Are in Maintenance?

Depending on the business environment, the initial development of a program can be as little as 25 percent of the time spent on the program, in terms of expanding it and tuning it as the needs of the organization change and evolve. Modifications are made to the program as organizational needs change and as users require improved efficiency or effectiveness.

For more information, see *Java*™ *Rules*, by Douglas Dunn: Section 1.3, "Comments."

An Overview of Pseudocoding

When a problem is presented to a programmer, the first steps are to understand the problem, come up with a plan (or algorithm) to address the problem, reduce the plan to some form of pseudocode, and then reduce the pseudocode to programming language code. Pseudo code is like a sketch of the algorithm using Java-like syntax (but excluding some detail), which the programmer can use as a guide in developing the complete program code. Refinement can occur at the planning stage and also at the pseudocode and program-code stages.

Pseudocoding Types

Pseudocode typically is written in quasi-English that corresponds not to any particular software language, but rather to a reduction of the algorithm to actionable steps. The actual syntax of the pseudocode is more free than that of any current programming language, allowing the programmer to sketch out the logic and control flow for the algorithm without worrying about the compiler's strict syntax rules and other checks. For instance, if you want to give the variable X the value 10, you can write this in any of the following forms:

```
Set X to 10
Assign X the value 10
X := 10
X = 10
X -> 10
```

For intelligibility, the key is to stick with one form. If you decide to use X = 0, consistently use this form.

Most Commonly Used Pseudocoding

It does not appear to matter, except that in a production environment, with many programmers working together, it is beneficial for the individuals on the team to all use the same form.

Guidelines for Documenting Classes

A class should include comments and remarks that become part of the public documentation for the class. Public documentation in HTML is available for other programmers who use the class. These comments describe the features of the class. It is imperative that the designer of the class be diligent in verifying the accuracy of such comments. Although these comments are suitable for other programmers, they are not meant to communicate instructions or messages to end users. Messages to end users become part of the code of the class.

Two types of comments can be included in a Java source file that defines a Java class. Comments or remarks can be single-line or multiline in length. Comments do not cause the computer to perform any tasks—that is, they are not executed when a program runs.

When the comment is a single-line comment, the comment is preceded with the symbols //, as shown in Example 3-1.

Example 3-1 *Purpose of Documentation*

```
 1 // class definition starts here
 2 public class DemoClass
 3 {
 4      //declares a variable to hold the name
 5      //assigns the value 'Student' to the name variable
 6      String name =  "Student";
 7
 8      // defines the getName accessor method
 9      public String getName() {return name;}
10 }
```

When the comment is on multiple lines, the comments are referred to as block comments. The symbol /* precedes the first line or is the first character on the first line; the comment ends with */ on the last line or after the last line, as shown in Example 3-2.

Example 3-2 *Block Comments*

```
 1 /* this method will return data as a String
 2 The method receives a number in the form of a java data type integer */
 3 public String sampleMethod(int aNumber)
 4 {
 5      return "The number is " + aNumber;
 6 }
 7
 8 /*
 9 this method will return data as a String
10 The method receives a number in the form of a java data type integer
11 */
12 public String sampleMethod1(int aNumber)
```

continues

Example 3-2 *Block Comments (Continued)*

```
13 {
14     return "The number is " + aNumber;
15 }
```

Comments also can be used as the first step in creating a class by creating a logical plan for the class definition, as shown in Example 3-3.

Example 3-3 *Purpose of Documentation*

```
1 //Create a Student Object
2
3
4 /*Display information about a student-
5 the name and the grade*/
6
7
8  //Create a Teacher Object
9
```

Because the compiler ignores comments, they are sometimes useful during program development. If a portion of code is causing problems, put comment syntax around it (known as "commenting it out"); the entire section will be ignored by the compiler. When the problem is identified, remove the commenting syntax and recompile the project.

Historical Origins of the Three Kinds of Comments Used in Java

Traditional commenting has been around for many languages. It consists of using /* to start a comment block and then using */ to close the comment block after several lines of comment.

The C language introduced the concept of the partial single-line comment, where using // after a line of code introduced the rest of the line as being a single-line comment.

Java then introduced the next innovation in commenting, with what Java terms *java-doc comments*. These start with /** on one line and, after several lines of comments, terminate with */. These comments are designed to be extracted automatically by a program called javadoc, to create HTML (web page–like) documentation for the program. This is an excellent innovation that really speeds up the documentation process for Java projects.

Javadoc Parameters

Javadoc comments are used specifically for creating the HTML documents for the class and are enclosed within the symbols /** and */. As with the traditional block comments (/* to start a comment block, followed by */ to close the comment block), these comments also are known as block comments because they can span more than one line. These comments are used to explain the purpose of the class, what methods do, what the arguments represent, and so on. As with other comments, the compiler ignores these comments. Although general comments can be placed anywhere in a source file, comments that generate HTML documents using the javadoc utility have specific guidelines and symbols, as shown in Table 3-1.

Table 3-1 Javadoc Parameters

Javadoc Guideline	Javadoc Positioning	Example

Doc comments must be placed before declarations	Doc comments
	
	Declaration
		```/** Purpose of this class```
		```is to store data about a Student```
		```*/```
		```public class Student```
		```{```

Can place doc comments before the declaration but not inside a method	Doc comments
	
	Declaration
		```/** Changes student name and```
		```gradeMethod variables are:String```
		```name and String grd```
		```*/```
		```public void setStudentData(String```
		```name, String grd)```
		```{```
		```// method executable code```
		```herestudentName = name;```
		```grade = grd;```
		```}```

continues

Table 3-1 Javadoc Parameters (Continued)

Javadoc Guideline	Javadoc Positioning	Example
	Unacceptable Declaration Doc comments	```public void setStudentData(String name, String grd) { /** Changes student name and grade Method variables are:String name and String grd */ studentName = name; grade =grd; }```
Generally start the doc comments with a one-sentence summary	One sentence	```/** Changes student name and gradeMethod variables are:String name and String grd */```

Single-line comments can be nested within block comments. Example 3-4, shows the use of nested single-line comments. The single-line comments nested inside javadoc comments (/** */) are incorporated into the HTML documents.

Example 3-4 *Nested Single Line Comments*

```
/**
    The class definition begins here. Objects
    of this class can be stored in a file (serializable)
    Objects of this class type can be cloned (cloneable)
//   Serializable is a marker interface
*/
```

HTML tags can also be inserted within comments. In the sample code of Example 3-5, the HTML tags <tt> and </tt> are used to display the text between the tags in a monospaced font. HTML has many tags, including those to format the text, display tabular data, and call another program. Some HTML tags cause conflicts when the javadoc utility creates HTML documents. Tags that cause conflicts usually include the tags that set up the structure of the document, such as headers, footers, and frames. Use these infrequently. Tags that work well include those that set the font or color or that identify the title text.

Example 3-5 *HTML Tags in Javadoc Comments*

```
/**

    Stores dates and perform date arithmetic.


    This is another date class, but more convenient than

    <tt>java.util.Date</tt> or <tt>java.util.Calendar</tt>


    @version 1.3 October 2001

    @author Cisco Teacher

*/
```

The `javadoc` utility also looks for special tags such as those shown in Example 3-6. These tags are used to call out information of special interest to the reader, such as parameters and return types. Javadoc handles this information specially. The javadoc tags also include others that are not shown here. Launch the tool reference documentation to review these. The tool reference documentation (javadoc.html) generally is installed in the tooldocs folder where the Java Development Kit is stored.

Example 3-6 *Javadoc Tags*

```
1 /**
2      * StringToInt - This method is used to convert a String to an int.
3      *
4      * @author Java Programmer
5      * @version Version 1
6      * @param  number    The number value as a String
7      * @return           The int value of number
8      * @exception        NumberFormatException
9      * @throws           Exception
10     * @see              "The Java Programming Language"
11     */
12     public int StringToInt(String number)throws NumberFormatException
13     {
14        return Integer.parseInt(number);
15     }
```

For Example 3-6, you can view the explanatory text by accessing the full, interactive graphic for this example on the book's accompanying CD-ROM. The title of the activity is "Javadoc Tags" in the e-Lab Activities.

The Start > Find/Search tool in Windows can be used to help find the location of the javadoc.html file, as shown in Figure 3-2.

Figure 3-2 The Find/Search Tool

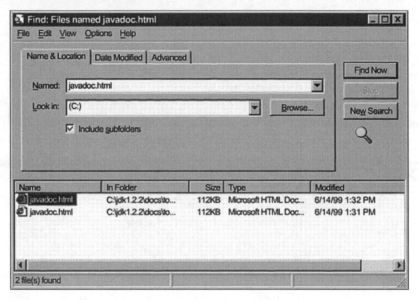

Hours of time can be spent on documentation after a program is written. Using java-doc helps automate a lot of this, reducing both program development and maintenance costs.

For more information, see *Java*™ Rules, by Douglas Dunn: Section 1.3, "Comments."

Java Language API Online Documentation

This section reviews the Core API, which is the set of classes that form the Java platform, and the documentation provided for these. The website http://java.sun.com/docs provides the link to download the documentation for the Java language, as shown in Figure 3-3.

The HTML files that form this extensive documentation should be installed in the jdk#.#.#/docs directory (where the #.#.# represents the latest version, as in jdk1.2.2). Many HTML files form the documentation for the language. The index.html file leads to the screen displayed in Figure 3-4.

Figure 3-3 Java Language API Online Documentation

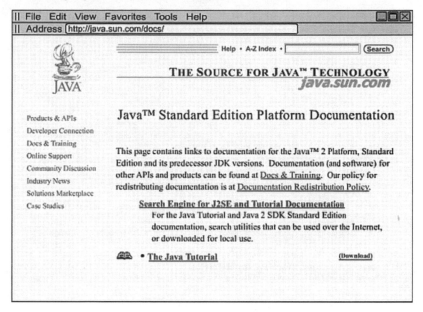

Figure 3-4 Java Language API Online Documentation

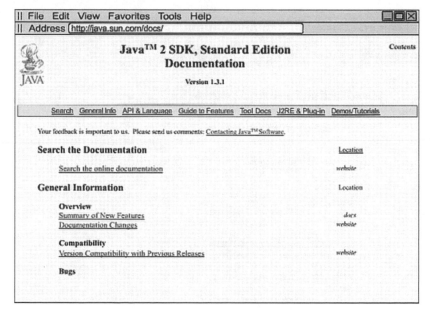

Take time to explore all the features. For example, to learn more about the java and javac tools, select the titles shown in Figure 3-5.

Figure 3-5 Java Language API Online Documentation

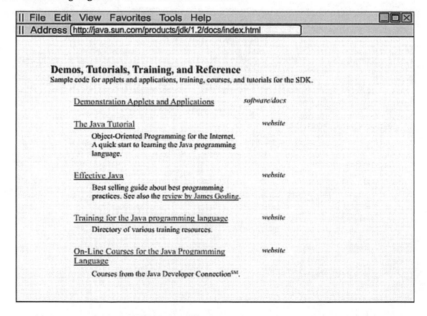

To use the tutorial, select the title shown in Figure 3-6.

Figure 3-6 Java Language API Online Documentation

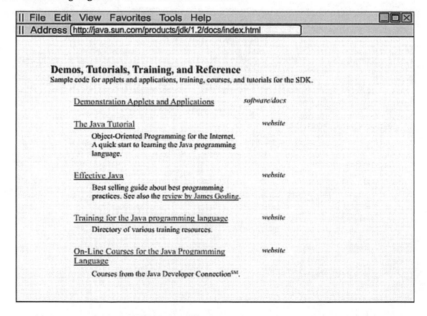

The core classes help to create applications that meet and solve simple and complex problems. In the previous chapters, the System class was used to print or display information on the screen. You can find out more about this class and others by selecting API and Language from the index screen, as illustrated in Figure 3-7.

Figure 3-7 Java Language API Online Documentation

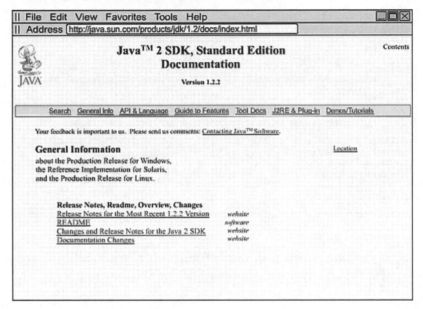

Students can also get to the documentation for the core classes by locating the file jdk#.#.#/docs/api/index.html. The screen that appears when the API documentation is launched is shown in Figure 3-8. This screen shows an overview of the API. Note the links to FRAMES and NOFRAMES in the upper part of the web page. These links change the view of the documents. In a FRAME view, students can navigate among three areas or frames on the screen.

Figure 3-8 Java Language API Online Documentation

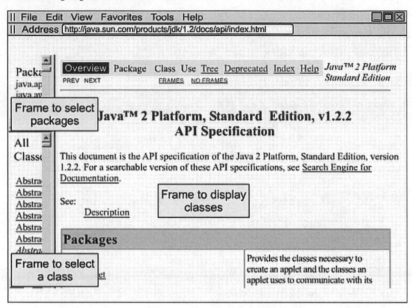

Choose a class such as System, as shown in Figure 3-9, to learn the syntax of this particular class. The information for the System class includes the following:

- The actual class definition statement. In this case, the class definition statement is **public final class** System **extends** Object.

- Links to the description of any word or phrase that is underlined.

- Version and author information.

- A description that includes information on the proper use of the class and restrictions. It provides a section for locating sample code.

- A field summary describing the types of data that the object stores.

- The constructors that are the specific methods for constructing objects. Classes that do not describe constructors use a "null" constructor. These are also known as default constructors.

- A method summary that displays the method signature and the return value for the method.

For Figure 3-9, you can view the explanatory text by accessing the full, interactive graphic for this figure on the book's accompanying CD-ROM. The title of the activity is "Java Language API Online Documentation" in the e-Lab Activities.

Figure 3-9 Java Language API Online Documentation

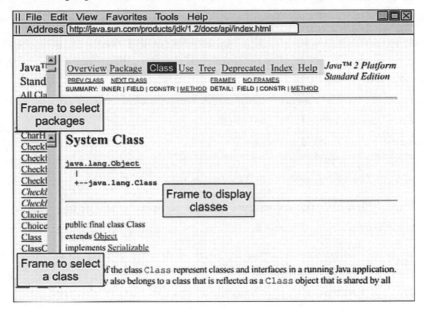

API Defined

The *application programming interface (API)* provides a common set of tools, utilities, and methods that software developers can use to help them develop software. For instance, the Java API provides tools that can be used to develop Java-based software.

Examples of Javadoc Tags

The following list documents some examples of javadoc tags:

- @author
- @version
- @param
- @return
- @exception
- @see
- @since
- @serial
- @deprecated

What the Javadoc Tags Do

The following list provides a description and example for each of the javadoc tags:

- @author—When you include this tag, together with your name, javadoc extracts your name and presents it as the author of the class. Example: @author David Theodore.

- @version—Provides the version number for your class or software section. Example: @version "1.28, 04/15/02".

- @param—Lists the parameters that are to be provided when you invoke the method. Example:

  @param ch the character to be tested; @param int1 the integer.

- @return—Describes the return type and the permissible range of values. Example:

  @return double, 0.0-1000000.0, balance in checking account.

- @exception—Mentions whether the method or class throws an exception of any particular kind. Example:

  @exception IOException If an input or output exception occurred.

- @see—Adds a "see also" heading with a link or text entry that points to a reference. Example:

  @see "Java Language Specification"; @see <a href="URL">label</a>.

- @since—Specifies whether a method or class was added to a specific version of Java. It is not available with earlier editions of Java. Example: @since 1.2. Indicates that this method was added to Java 2 Platform, Standard Edition, API Specification at version 1.2).

- @deprecated—Tells the user whether this API is deprecated and what class or method to use instead. Example:

  @deprecated As of JDK version 1.1, replaced by DateFormat.format(Date date).

For more information, see http://java.sun.com/j2se/javadoc/.

Generating API Docs for Classes Using the Javadoc Tool

After comments and javadoc tags have been inserted in class definitions, the javadoc tool can be used to generate the documentation. To do this, open a DOS or console window and enter **javadoc** at the prompt. Figure 3-10 shows use of the **javadoc** command to generate documentation for the class Teacher.java.

Figure 3-10 Generating Javadoc from the Command Prompt

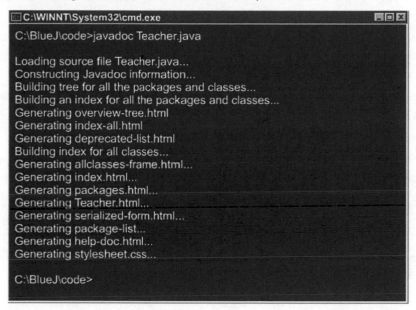

The source file is loaded, and HTML files are generated in the same directory unless the programmer specifies a different one. Version and author information is included in specific javadoc tags within the javadoc comments. To generate the version and author information for `Teacher.java`, a command such as the following would be used:

`C:\BlueJ\code>`**`javadoc`**` -version -author Teacher.java`

The `javadoc` tool has several options that can be requested, such as the following:

- -author—Tells javadoc to utilize @author tags when preparing documentation. Javadoc otherwise ignores these tags.
- -classpath—Tells javadoc where to look for classes that have been referenced in the current class definition.
- -d directory_name—Tells javadoc in what directory to place the HTML files that result from running javadoc.
- -nodeprecated—Excludes classes marked by the @deprecated tag.
- -noindex—Tells javadoc to skip the HTML index page that it usually creates.
- -notree—Tells javadoc to skip outputting the class hierarchy page.

- -overview path\filename—Provides filename and path for any overview documentation that you want to add.

- -package—Tells javadoc to prepare documentation for all members and classes except those with private access. (Packages are discussed in detail in Chapter 9, "Understanding Packages.")

- -private—Tells javadoc to prepare documentation for all members and classes, including those with private access.

- -protected—Tells javadoc to prepare documentation for public as well as protected members and classes.

- -public—Tells javadoc to prepare documentation for only public members, interfaces, and classes.

- -sourcepath path1;path2;path3;...—Provides javadoc search paths for packages for which documentation is to be created.

- -version—Tells javadoc to utilize @version tags when preparing documentation. Javadoc usually ignores these tags.

Case Study: JBANK Application

In general, programmers must get into the practice of embedding documentation in all of their code. Although single-line and block comments are useful when reviewing personal source files, they are not visible to other programmers who have access only to the class files. For a program to be useful, it must be well documented, which includes javadoc comments.

With applications that can include thousands of classes, the need for documentation becomes critical. Many large-scale projects are doomed to fail because of poor documentation. Because the banking application used in this course has multiple classes, it is important that students document each class.

The importance of documentation is emphasized here by including specific instructions for documenting the classes in each phase of the banking application. Every time students change the code of a class, they should rerun the javadoc utility to generate updated HTML documents.

The JBANK labs for Chapter 3 provide the opportunity to insert specific documentation tags in the Customer and Account class of the JBANK project, as shown in Figures 3-11 and 3-12. The javadoc utility will be used to generate the documentation.

Figure 3-11 JBANK Application

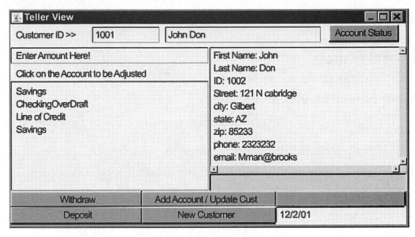

Figure 3-12 JBANK Application

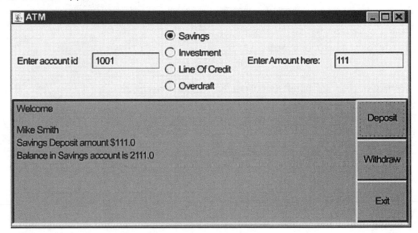

Java Language Elements

Every programming language has elements that make up the language. Almost all languages have keywords, special symbols, names for data or operations, and syntax rules for their use. Some languages use similar elements. Learning one language often makes learning another programming language quite simple. This section addresses the following topics:

- Review of symbols
- Keywords

■ Identifiers

■ Use of braces, semicolons, commas, and whitespace

Review of Symbols

Before Java language elements are explored, a review of the symbols that are used to communicate rules and syntax is necessary.

In general, the following guidelines apply when learning to read *Java syntax rules*:

■ [ ] or < > indicate that enclosed information is optional.

■ ( ), ; {} indicate symbols required in the location specified.

■ Italicized words indicate data provided by the programmer.

■ Bold words or symbols indicate keywords that must be typed exactly as shown.

■ Ellipses represent information that can be repeated.

■ Example 3-7 illustrates the implementation of a number of these Java syntax rules.

Example 3-7 *Java Symbols*

```
 1 public class JavaOperators
 2 {
 3     public void printData(String name, int age)
 4     {
 5         System.out.println("Your name is " + name);
 6         System.out.println("You are " + age + " years old.");
 7     }
 8
 9     public static void main(String[] args)
10     {
11         printData("Joe", 17);
12     }
13 }
```

For Example 3-7, you can view the explanatory text by accessing the full, interactive graphic for this example on the book's accompanying CD-ROM. The title of the activity is "Java Symbols" in the e-Lab Activities.

Examples to Demonstrate Guidelines

Additional examples of the Java syntax rules include the following:

- `[] <>`

  Example: `methodName([arg1]);`

  Indicates that the method is overloaded. For example, the method could be used as `methodName()` or as `methodName(arg1)`. Overloaded methods are covered in detail in Chapter 5, "Basics of Defining and Using Classes."

- `(),; {}`

  Example: `aSpecificMethod(arg1);`

  Indicates that the `(arg1)` is required in the method call.

- Italicized words

  Example: `aSpecificMethod(2,3,4);`

  The italicizing of the `2,3,4` indicates that this is data provided by the programmer.

- Bold words or symbols

  Example: `int x;`

  Indicates that the keyword `int` must be typed exactly as shown.

- Ellipses

  Example: `. . .`

  Indicates that the information can be repeated.

Keywords

Many *keywords* form the vocabulary of the Java language. With a few exceptions, all the java reserved words were selected when the language was first created. Because the Java compiler is case-sensitive, all keywords must be entered in lowercase. (Nonkeywords, such as identifiers, can be all uppercase, all lowercase, or a combination of both. Regardless of the choice, the format should be consistent.) The Java language includes an extensive library of predefined classes. The libraries are evolving and dynamic.

The character sequences shown in Table 3-2, formed from ASCII letters, are reserved for use as keywords and cannot be used as identifiers. ASCII is the acronym for the American Standard Code for Information Interchange. The ASCII code sets the specific bit pattern that represents any letter, number, or punctuation symbol used in the English language, as well as invisible control characters. The code uses 7 or 8 bits of computer storage to represent the symbol or character.

Table 3-2 Keywords

abstract	default	if	private	this
boolean	do	implements	protected	throw
break	double	import	public	throws
byte	else	instanceof	return	transient
case	extends	int	short	try
catch	final	interface	static	void
char	finally	long	strictfp	volatile
class	float	native	super	while
const	for	new	switch	
continue	goto	package	synchronized	

Some keywords are special exceptions. The keywords **const** and **goto** are reserved, even though they are not currently used. They allow a Java compiler to produce better error messages if these C++ keywords incorrectly appear in programs. The Java Language Specification (JLS) can be downloaded from the java.sun.com website. JLS provides additional explanation to the use of **const** and **goto** in the Java language. Although these keywords are not encouraged or applied in the programs created in this course, students interested in writing "native" methods (that is, methods that call programs written in other languages such as C or C++) should explore the JLS.

While true and false might appear to be keywords, they are technically Boolean literals. A literal is an "actual value." For example, in this statement, 1 is an integer literal:

```
int myInt = 1;
```

Similarly, although **null** might appear to be a keyword, it is technically the null literal. When null is assigned to a variable, it does not mean the variable does not have a value, but that the value of the variable is null. Null does not mean absence of a value.

Value is the actual meaning that is associated with the data that is stored and manipulated by the program. The symbol 9 represents a numeric value of nine, for example, and the symbols 45 represent the numeric value of forty-five. The actual value of the data is known only within the program or when the program is executing. Some values are harder to describe using symbols such as characters or numbers. Therefore, in the Java language, the value of data that represents the meaning true or false is represented using the reserved words **true** or **false**.

Example 3-8 presents a sample Java program highlighting the usage of both keywords and nonkeywords. For Example 3-8, you can view the explanatory text by accessing the full, interactive graphic for this example on the book's accompanying CD-ROM. The title of the activity is "Keywords" in the e-Lab Activities. This graphic allows the student to move the mouse over the program to recognize the usage of keywords and nonkeywords, and to identify which of the highlighted words are not keywords.

Example 3-8 *Keywords*

```
 1 // definition of the class Person
 2 public class Person
 3 {
 4      private String name;
 5      private String dateOfBirth;
 6      private int id;
 7
 8      public Person (String  aName, String aDate, int aID)
 9      {
10          name = aName;
11          dateOfBirth = aDate;
12          id = aID;
13      }
14      public void setName(String aName)
15      {
16      name = aName;
17      }
18      public String getName()
19      {
20      return name;
21      }
22      public void setDateOfBirth(String adate)
23      {
24          dateOfBirth = adate;
25      }
26      public String getDateOfBirth()
27      {
28          return dateOfBirth;
29      }
30 }
```

List of Reserved Words

A parallel exists between Java keywords and English parts of speech. Table 3-3 high-lights these parallels for the student.

Table 3-3 Parallels Between Java Keywords and English Parts of Speech

Keyword Category	Keyword	English Part of Speech
Primitive Types and **void**	`byte`	noun
	`short`	noun
	`int`	noun
	`long`	noun
	`char`	noun
	`float`	noun
	`double`	noun
	`boolean`	noun
	`void`	noun
Flow Control Statements	`if`	verb (implicit)
	`else`	verb (implicit)
	`do`	verb
	`while`	verb (implicit)
	`for`	verb (implicit)
	`break`	verb
	`continue`	verb
	`return`	verb
	`case`	verb (implicit)
	`switch`	verb
	`default`	verb

Table 3-3 Parallels Between Java Keywords and English Parts of Speech (Continued)

Keyword Category	Keyword	English Part of Speech
Modifiers	`public`	adjective
	`protected`	adjective
	`private`	adjective
	`abstract`	adjective
	`static`	adjective
	`final`	adjective
	`synchronized`	adjective
	`native`	adjective
	`transient`	adjective
	`volatile`	adjective
Exception Handling	`throws`	verb
	`try`	verb
	`throw`	verb
	`catch`	verb
	`finally`	verb (implicit)
Class or Interface Declarations	`class`	noun
	`interface`	noun
	`extends`	verb
	`implements`	verb
`this` and `super`	`this`	adjective
	`super`	adjective
`package` and `import`	`package`	noun
	`import`	verb
Object Creation	`new`	verb (implicit)
Type Testing	`instanceof`	query

Identifiers

Identifiers are labels that programmers assign to data or storage addresses. Because the compiler and the JVM handle all the details of allocating memory, the Java programmer needs only to provide a label or "handle" for accessing data in storage. Identifiers are also labels that a programmer assigns to class names and to method names.

Java imposes some rules on creating identifiers:

Any character from any alphabet can be used. Although characters used in the English language are represented using the ASCII code, the Java language provides internationalization of code and data by using an extended set of coded symbols known as Unicode. Unicode includes representations for the characters of almost every written language in the world. For example, characters from the Kanji (Japanese alphabet), Arabic, and Greek alphabets can be used in identifiers.

- The first character must be a letter. The subsequent characters can be any alphanumeric character or punctuation.
- Identifiers cannot contain the symbols % (percent) or # (number symbol). They can contain $ (dollar sign) and an underscore.
- Generally, it is recommended that you not use special symbols such as $ and &.
- Identifiers cannot contain spaces.
- Identifiers are case-sensitive.
- Identifiers cannot use certain keywords, known as reserved words.

Using Table 3-4, identify the correct and incorrect identifiers.

Table 3-4 Correct and Incorrect Identifiers

Which Identifiers Are Correct?	
First Name	public
CheckNumber1234	class
firstName	Employee 7
7Employee	case
Amt$cents	Student_7
$charge	Inv7123
7123	pay&bonus

For Table 3-4, you can check your answers by accessing the full, interactive graphic for this table on the book's accompanying CD-ROM. The title of the activity is "Identifiers" in the e-Lab Activities.

Use the sample code in Example 3-9 to identify the Java elements:

- Operator
- Identifier
- Keyword
- Symbol

Example 3-9 *Identifying Code*

```
1 /**
2 * Java Program: SayHello.java
3 * @author : Student
4 * Date:
5 */
6 public class SayHello
7 {
8     public static void main(String[] args)
9     {
10      String name  = "Student";
11      int number = 1;
12      System.out.println("Hello");
13      System.out.println(name);
14      System.out.println ("Your Lucky Number is " + number);
15    } // end of main method
16 }// end of class definition
```

For Example 3-9, you can check your answers by accessing the full, interactive graphic for this example on the book's accompanying CD-ROM. The title of the activity is "Identifying Code" in the e-Lab Activities.

Brief Discussion of Why $ and Underscore Are Used in Identifiers

It is recommended that programmers not use $ in their identifiers. This sign is permitted in Java for reasons of compatibility with legacy systems with code written in the past. It is also used with compiler-generated class and interface names.

In comparison, the underscore is often very useful in clarifying the meaning of identifiers made up of multiple words, such as savings_Account_Balance.

For more information, see *Java*™ *Rules*, by Douglas Dunn: Section 1.4, "Identifiers."

Use of Braces, Semicolons, Commas, and Whitespace

Symbols are necessary for proper Java code compilation.

The following are the most commonly used symbols in Java.

Braces

A *block* is a collection of statements bounded by braces ({ }). These include braces to bound class definitions, method definitions, and other statements that should be executed in a group, as shown in Examples 3-10 and 3-11. Braces that are used to define a class or a method generally should be placed below the definition statement. Placing braces in the alignment of opening and closing braces makes it easier to find errors and debug programs. Some editors, such as BlueJ, include search features to search for matching braces.

Example 3-10 *Use of Braces*

```
{
    Total = a + b + c + d + e;

    System.out.println(" The grade for student " + name + " is: " + grade);
}
```

Example 3-11 *Use of Braces*

```
public class Student
{
    // class definition statements
}
```

Semicolons

A *statement* consists of one or more lines of code that are terminated, or ended, by a semicolon, as shown in Example 3-12. Omitting semicolons is a common compiler error. Before compiling a program, always check that every statement ends with a semicolon.

Example 3-12 *Use of Semicolons*

```
{

    Total = a + b + c + d + e;


    System.out.println(" The grade for student " + name + " is: " + grade);

}
```

Commas

Commas serve as separators or delimiters of data. Methods that require a list of values require that each value be separated by a comma. The method declaration defines values required for a method as one or more list pairs of data type and variable. In general, if the syntax of a language identifies a comma in the description, the programmer also must use the comma. Methods with more than one parameter are used as shown in Example 3-13.

Example 3-13 *Use of Braces, Semicolons, Commas, and White Space*

```
1       /*
2       Method signature:
3       setName(String lname, String fname)
4       */
5
6       //Method use:
7       Student.setName("Disney", "Walt");
```

Whitespace

Whitespace separates keywords and identifiers. You should include whitespace when printing or displaying information.

When Java code is being compiled, Java ignores whitespace, such as spaces, tabs, and carriage returns. Whitespace, particularly in the form of tabs, is used primarily to make programs more readable for programmers.

The following characters are interpreted as whitespace in Java:

- \t—Horizontal tab
- \n—Line feed
- \f—Form feed
- \r—Carriage return
- Space

For more information, see: *Java*™ *Rules*, by Douglas Dunn: Section 1.2, "White Space" and Section 1.7, "Separators."

The Where and When of Data Storage

Any program running on a computer, including Java, must be stored in memory. This section consists of the following topics:

- Data storage introduction
- Stack, heap, static, and constant storage
- Variables and storage locations for data

Data Storage Introduction

A detailed understanding of how a computer stores data electronically is not required to create usable Java classes. Some knowledge of how memory is allocated and used while a program is running is useful, however; it will help with the proper creation of and references to Java data types.

The match game in Figure 3-13 tests the student's knowledge of data storage. Match the terms at the bottom of the figure to the correct definition. For Figure 3-13, you can check your answers by accessing the full, interactive graphic for this figure on the book's accompanying CD-ROM. The title of the activity is "Data Storage Introduction" in the e-Lab Activities.

There are six different places to store data:

- Registers—Memory space in the CPU
- The *stack*—Methods and variables in *random access memory (RAM)*
- The *heap*—Objects in RAM
- *Static* storage—A shared method or variable in RAM
- *Constant* storage—Unchanging variables in RAM
- Non-RAM storage—Disk space (hard drive, floppy drive)

Registers are the memory spaces in the CPU that provide the fastest access. The stack, heap, static, and constant storage locations are all spaces in RAM, and they vary in speed of access. The compiler allocates the storage location for these, and the JVM manages all storage issues. Non-RAM storage uses more permanent spaces such as disks.

Figure 3-13 Data Storage Introduction

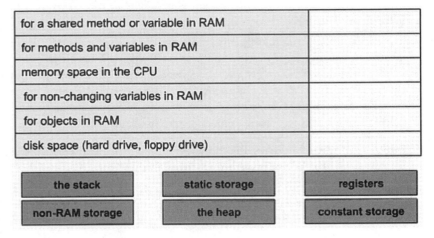

for a shared method or variable in RAM	
for methods and variables in RAM	
memory space in the CPU	
for non-changing variables in RAM	
for objects in RAM	
disk space (hard drive, floppy drive)	

the stack	static storage	registers
non-RAM storage	the heap	constant storage

Stack, Heap, Static, and Constant Storage

Computers are described in terms of memory, in megabytes (MB) and gigabytes (GB), and the speed with which the CPU can process instructions, in megahertz (MHz) and gigahertz (GHz). As a programmer, you should know that the class definitions impact the allocation and usage of RAM. The primary areas of exploration are the storage spaces stack, heap, static, and constant. Programming defines classes that will store data in one or all of these spaces. How the compiler uses these helps to determine the proper creation and destruction of objects and object data, as outlined in Table 3-5.

Table 3-5 Stack, Heap, Static, and Constant Storage

Storage Space	Description
The stack	This exists in the random-access memory (RAM). The stack is very dynamic and is the second-fastest storage space. The compiler must know the storage requirements when creating a program—that is, how much (size) data will be referenced and for how long the data referenced will be needed (life time or scope of data). This reduces the flexibility in use of this storage. Data required or referenced by methods is created in the stack. The stack increases or decreases depending on the methods being used at any given time. Methods are shared among objects. The sequence of methods currently being used store their data in a program stack.

continues

Table 3-5 Stack, Heap, Static, and Constant Storage (Continued)

Storage Space	Description
The heap	Also in the RAM, this is a general-purpose pool of memory. All objects are stored in the heap. The compiler does not need to know how much memory is needed, nor how long the objects need to stay on the heap. Object storage is allocated when you use the keyword or Java operator **new**. Creating heap storage takes longer and is considered expensive.
Static storage	"Static" here means "in a fixed location." Data that is needed for the entire program is stored in this space. For example, the compiler will allocate space here to a programmer defining class data or class methods as static. As long as the program is running, this data will be available to all objects and all methods.
Constant storage	Constants are values that never change. These are placed in a separate area and can exist outside the control of the program. Here "constant" means "fixed"—that is, the data remains unchanged.

What Stack Memory Means

A stack is a single-ended data structure in memory. Data is placed there and needs to be accessed in a last in, first out order. If data element X is placed there after element Y, then X has to be taken off the stack before Y can be accessed. The operating system implements a stack for each running program.

The term stack is also used for the following reason. Think of a stack of books. Let's say that you place books on the stack in the following order: A, followed by B, followed by C, followed by D. Now, if you need to access book C, you can't just pull book C out of the stack. You have to remove ("pop") book D first, after which you have access to book C. Only after you have removed ("popped") book C will you then have access to book B. Stack memories behave like this stack of books. The last piece of data stored on the stack is accessed before previously stored data.

For more information, see www.biglal.net/Memory.html#The_STACK_Segment.

What Heap Memory Means

The heap is nonstack memory. Any data that has to exist after a function call return (or method returns) is placed on the heap. Simply stated, the stack is where method calls and temporary variables go; the heap is where objects go. For more information, see www.biglal.net/Memory.html#The_HEAP_Segment.

The term heap was chosen to be different from stack. Heap memory consists of computer memory that is not stack memory.

The term heap is also used for the following reason. Think of a heap of books. Let's say that you place books on the heap in the following order: A, followed by B, followed by C, followed by D. Now, if you need to access book C, you can just pull book C out of the heap. You don't have to remove ("pop") book D first before you can access book C (as you had to do with the stack). Heap memories behave like this heap of books. The last piece of data stored on the stack does not have to be accessed before previously stored data.

Difference Between RAM and ROM

In addition to RAM, there is read-only memory (ROM). Their differences include the following:

- RAM—Random-access memory. When a program is being run on a computer, it is loaded into the random-access memory. Data in this memory can be accessed at random, not necessarily sequentially. This data can be changed during operation of the computer.
- ROM—Read-only memory. Basic instructions necessary to boot up the computer are placed in this memory area. This memory is hard wired—that is, the data is burned in and cannot be changed during operation of the computer.

Brief Description of Types of RAM

Many different types of RAM exist, designed for different applications.

A number of these types of RAM are described briefly here:

- DRAM—Dynamic RAM. Uses a coupled transistor-capacitor pair to store data. The capacitor acts like a storage tank, and the transistor acts like a gate (faucet) to the storage tank.
- SRAM—Static RAM. This is faster than DRAM but typically has been more expensive. SRAM uses four to six transistors, without a capacitor, to store memory data.
- FPM DRAM—Fast page DRAM. Locates the requested data by row and column and then reads the data bit from that memory location.
- EDO DRAM—Extended data-out DRAM. Speeds up memory access by not waiting for the first data bit to be accessed before beginning processing for the next data bit.

- SDRAM—Synchronous DRAM. Speeds up data access by staying on a single row and reading data bits along the column bits in that same row. This works because most of the time, the CPU requests data in a serial fashion.
- RDRAM—Rambus DRAM. This memory unit uses a high-speed data bus working in parallel to reach very high data speeds.
- FlashRAM—This is a small amount of memory that typically stores information needed to boot up a computer (such as the number and configuration of hard drives on a computer).
- VRAM—This is also called multiport dynamic RAM, and it typically is used for video and 3D graphics accelerators. This memory is multiport because it has both serial access and random-access memory.

For more information, see www.howstuffworks.com/ram4.htm.

Evolution of Storage Technologies

This section provides a brief overview of the evolution of storage technology in the past, present, and future.

Storage in the past:

- Punch cards—Stored data in holes punched on cards. A hole represented 1; no hole represented 0.
- Magnetic tape—Stored data in small magnetized regions on plastic tape coated with iron oxide that could be magnetized locally. A magnetized region represented 1; a nonmagnetized region represented 0.

Storage in the present:

- Magnetic—Stores data in small magnetized regions on disks coated with iron oxide that can be magnetized locally. A magnetized region represents 1; a nonmagnetized region represents 0. Improvements in magnetic materials and read heads have enabled these magnetized regions to become smaller.
- Optical—Stores data in disks coated with aluminum, organic-dye, or phase-change alloy. Small changes in reflectivity are used to store bits. A laser is shined on the surface of the disk. Changes in the power of the reflected beam are read as 1s or 0s in data.
- Solid-state—Uses specially designed transistor cells to store 1s and 0s.

Future varieties of storage:

- Optical—Storage densities will increase as shorter-wavelength, solid-state lasers are improved.

- Holographic—Splitting laser beams and shining them into the storage material can enable storage of data in the volume of the storage material rather than just on the surface of the material. This will increase storage capabilities many fold.

For more information, see these resources:

www.howstuffworks.com/removable-storage.htm

www.howstuffworks.com/holographic-memory.htm

Variables and Storage Locations for Data

The data for each object is stored in memory. All programming languages use the concept of *variables* to reference data in memory. A variable is a storage location in memory that a programmer can use to store data. A variable has five facets. Data types are declared when a variable is created. The data or value in a variable can be a primitive or can be a reference data type.

As shown in Figure 3-14, the five facets of a variable include the following:

- Identifier
- Scope or life of a variable
- Address of the variable
- Data type
- Value

Figure 3-14 Variable and Storage Locations for Data

Each of these facets is described here:

- Identifiers are labels that a programmer uses to refer to storage locations.
- Scope or life of a variable represents the availability of the data while the program executes. The scope of a variable is determined to be within the code block in which it was defined. Variables that store data of an object (attributes of the class) are available for use as long as the object can be referenced. The scope of these variables is for the life of the object. Variables defined in a method are available for use only within the method. Here the variable is further limited in scope if it is nested within the logic of the method. When the method has stopped executing, the variable is said to be out of scope. Variables are considered in scope if they are still in memory and can be referenced.
- The address of the variable is the actual location of the variable and data in memory. Java programmers do not need to be concerned with the exact location of data; they should care only about the identifier for the data that is the variable name because this is used to access data. In fact, the Java programmer has no means of finding out the exact location of data. The capability to access the data by simply using the variable name is a major strength of the language.
- Data types define the storage and proper use of the data. Java language data types are discussed later in this chapter.
- The value of a variable is the contents, or the actual data that is stored in the variable. Some important concepts are related to the value of a variable. If a variable is part of an object, then when the object is created, the variable is assigned default values. The default value depends on the data type of the variable. If the variable is a method variable, then default values are not assigned. The programmer must therefore be diligent in assigning values to these variables in the code for the method in which it will be used.

These storage locations are called *variable* because the data can change during processing. However, these concepts apply to constants (data that does not change) and static (global or class-based data) data also. The main difference among constants, variables, and static data is in the scope and changeability.

Concept of Data Types

As previously presented, data type is one of the five facets of a variable. This section examines the role of data type in the Java language and covers the following topics:

- Java language types
- Java primitives and storage requirements

- Java references
- Object data (instance)
- Class data (static)
- Method data (local)
- Constants

Java Language Types

A *data type* of Java is a classification of a particular form of information. It tells the computer how to interpret and store the data. Although a person can tell whether data is in the form of numbers or text just by looking at it, a computer must use special codes to keep track of the different types of data it processes. Data types are declared by using keywords in a language that inform the computer about the data type. Unlike other programming languages that require data to be identified by type and amount of storage required, Java requires only that the type be declared.

Java is a strongly typed language. This means that the compiler knows the data type of each and every field (attribute) and variable everywhere it is used in the program. With primitive data types, this means that each variable has a defined amount of storage allocated. The compiler knows exactly how much memory is needed for each of these variables. Data can be copied from the storage of one data type to another under specific conditions. This is referred to as type conversion. Figure 3-15 shows a hierarchy of the Java language types.

Figure 3-15 Java Language Types

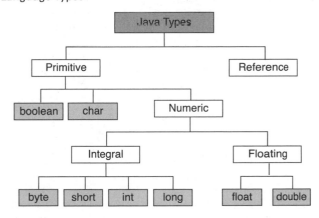

Examples of Type Conversion

The sample code in Example 3-14 illustrates type conversion from one data type to another.

Example 3-14 *Examples of Type Conversion*

```
int aInt = (int) aFloat; // this casts a floating point number into an integer


int aInt = (int) aDouble; // this casts a double precision number into an integer


float aFloat = (float) aDouble; // this casts a double precision number into a
    float
```

Java Primitives and Storage Requirements

Java *primitives* are data types that are used to store simple kinds of data. The other data type is called *reference*. Eight types of Java primitives exist: **boolean, char, byte, short, int, long, float,** and **double.** All of these are listed in Table 3-6. The **boolean** data type stores a representation of the values **true** or **false.** The **char** data type stores any Unicode character.

The remaining six types of primitives are used for numbers.

Table 3-6 Value of Data Types

Primitive Type	Storage Size	Values

boolean	1 bit	Logical value of true or false. The reserved words **true** and **false** can be used to assigned values to a boolean variable:
		 boolean paid = true;
		 boolean paid = false;

char	16 bits	Stores any of 65,436 single characters of the UNICODE set.
byte	8 bits	Signed whole numbers –128 to +127.
short	16 bits	Signed whole numbers –32,768 to +32,767.
int	32 bits	Signed whole numbers -2^{31} to $2^{31} - 1$.
long	64 bits	Signed whole numbers $-9 * 10^{18}$ to $+9 * 10^{18} - 1$.
float	32 bits	Decimal values up to six or seven decimal places.
double	64 bits	Decimal values up to 14 or 15 decimal places.

Use Figure 3-16 to identify possible data types to represent a value.

Figure 3-16 Values of Data Types

Protocol	boolean	char	byte	short	int	long	float	double
4								
2.5								
-3.6111156511876								
-40000								
'a'								
0								
A Bank Account Balance								
Number of Students In Classroom								
A 15-Digit ID number								

Check Answers	Reset	Show Me

What data types can be used for each of the following scenerios? Place a checkmark under the proper types that could be used for each example.

For Figure 3-16, you can check your answers by accessing the full, interactive graphic for this figure on the book's accompanying CD-ROM. The title of the activity is "Values of Data Types" in the e-Lab Activities.

Storage Size

Storage size is defined as the number of *bits* that are required to store a representation of the number, character symbol, or Boolean status. Memory is measured in *bytes*, and there are 8 bits in 1 byte. Each bit can be represented as a place value in the binary number system—that is, a number system using two digits: 1 or 0. An 8-bit storage location can be understood as follows:

Each bit can either be on or off. This is represented as either a 1 (on) or a 0 (off). The actual position of the bit represents a specific value of 2. For example, the first bit represents that value of 2 to the power of 0, which is 0 or 1. (Note: Any number raised to the power of 0 is 1, and the number of units of that power represents the number of 1s. In decimals systems, the rightmost digit of a number is referred to as the "1s" unit). The second bit represents the value of 2 to the power of 1, which is equal to 2. The third bit represents the value of 2 to the power of 2, which is equal to 4. When a bit is turned on, it represents the specific value of 2 assigned to that bit position. A decimal number can be represented in bits by converting the number to units of 2. Adding the value of 2 represented by each bit that has been turned on gives the single decimal value for that set of bits. The eighth bit is used to represent the sign of the number. A 0 is for positive numbers, and a 1 is for negative numbers.

The bit storage shown in Table 3-7 represents the value +60. A 0 in the eighth bit indicates the number as a positive number. To convert from binary to decimal equivalent, only 7 bits are used; the Java languages stores all numeric values as signed.

Table 3-7 Binary Representation: Example 1

Bit 8	Bit 7	Bit 6	Bit 5	Bit 4	Bit 3	Bit 2	Bit 1
0	0	1	1	1	1	0	0
2^7	2^6	2^5	2^4	2^3	2^2	2^1	2^0
0	0	32	16	8	4	0	0
(4 + 8 + 16 + 32 = 60)							

The bit storage shown in Table 3-8 represents the value –60. A 1 in the eighth bit indicates the number as a negative number.

Table 3-8 Binary Representation: Example 2

Bit 8	Bit 7	Bit 6	Bit 5	Bit 4	Bit 3	Bit 2	Bit 1
1	0	1	1	1	1	0	0
2^7	2^6	2^5	2^4	2^3	2^2	2^1	2^0
—	0	32	16	8	4	0	0
(4 + 8 + 16 + 32 and the – from bit 8 = –60)							

You can practice identifying the binary representation of several integer values by accessing an interactive graphic on the book's accompanying CD-ROM. The title of the activity is "Binary Representation" and is under the heading of e-Lab Activities. The historical origin of the words *bit* and *byte* include:

- Bit—Stands for "binary digit." Its oldest usage appears about 1948 in an article by C.E. Shannon in the *Bell Systems Technical Journal*.
- Byte—Appears to have originated as a play on the word *bit*. The word stands for 8 bits and, so, might have originated from BInary digiT Eight or from BinarY Term. It seems to have originated about 1964, possibly coined by W. Buchholz at IBM.

Why are bytes 8 bits and not 10 bits? It appears to be because 8 bits were all the bits historically necessary to express the characters necessary for computing. Eight bits permits a representation of 256 characters.

This section covered the binary number system and the resulting decimal value. Table 3-9 illustrates the octal and hexadecimal number systems and provides the corresponding decimal value.

For more information, see www.wordorigins.org/wordorb.htm.

Table 3-9 Demonstration of Place-Power System for Numbers

Number System	Value	Calculation	Decimal Value
Decimal	123	$(1 * 10^2) + (2 * 10^1) + (3 * 10^0)$	123
Octal	123	$(1 * 8^2) + (2 * 8^1) + (3 * 8^0)$	83
Hexadecimal	123	$(1 * 16^2) + (2 * 16^1) + (3 * 16^0)$	301
Binary	101	$(1 * 2^2) + (0 * 2^1) + (1 * 2^0)$	5

Wrapper Classes

Java primitive data types are not objects. Each primitive type, however, has a class defined in the core classes. These classes can be explored in the Java API documentation. They are referred to as *wrapper classes* and are listed in Table 3-10. Wrapper classes wrap object features and capabilities around a single primitive data type value. This enables a programmer to operate on these types of data as objects. Consider the wrapper class of an object with one attribute, the primitive data type.

Table 3-10 Wrapper Classes

Primitive	Wrapper Class
boolean	Boolean
float	Float
byte	Byte
int	Integer
double	Double
char	Character
long	Long
short	Short

These wrapper classes contain many methods that are ready for use. As an example, the following list highlights some of the methods associated with the Integer class:

- byteValue()—Returns the value of this Integer as a **byte**
- compareTo(Integer anotherInteger)—Compares two Integers numerically
- compareTo(Object o)—Compares this Integer to another object
- decode(String nm)—Decodes a String into an Integer
- doubleValue()—Returns the value of this Integer as a **double**
- equals(Object o)—Compares this object to the specified object
- floatValue()—Returns the value of this Integer as a **float**
- getInteger(String nm)—Determines the integer value of the system property with the specified name
- intValue()—Returns the value of this Integer as an **int**
- longValue()—Returns the value of this Integer as a **long**
- parseInt(String s)—Parses the String argument as a signed decimal integer, and returns an **int**
- toBinaryString(int I)—Returns a String representation of the integer argument as an unsigned integer in Base 2
- toString()—Returns a String object representing this Integer object's value
- toString(int I)—Returns a new String object representing the specified integer
- valueOf(String s)—Returns a new Integer object initialized to the value of the specified String

For more information, see java.sun.com/j2se/1.4.1/docs/api/java/lang/Integer.html.

Java References

All objects are created in heap memory. To access the data in an object or to operate on an object, a variable that can store a reference to the object address is needed on the stack. Variables that store references to object addresses are considered to hold reference data types. In Figure 3-17, variable s holds a reference to the Student object.

The variables studentName and grade, in Figure 3-18, are references to objects of the class type String. String is one of the core classes and is discussed more in Chapter 6, "System, String, StringBuffer, Math, and Wrapper Classes."

Figure 3-17 Java References

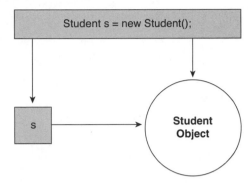

Figure 3-18 Java References

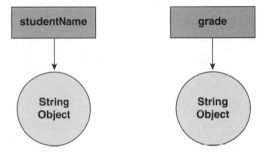

Some programmers think of String objects as one of the basic Java types. This is because so much of the manipulated data is text or "string" data, which is a string of characters, as illustrated in Example 3-15.

Note that String is a class, whereas **char** is a primitive. Sometimes students confuse String with an array of **char**. An array of **char** is manipulated as an array of primitives, whereas String is a class and, when instantiated, an object with specific class properties that differ from those of an array of primitives.

Example 3-15 *Java References*

```
1 /** Student Class establishes the student id, name and grade
2  *  @author Cisco Teacher
3  *  @version 2002
4  */
```

continues

NOTE

The full version of the abbreviated code shown in this example can be viewed using the book's accompanying CD-ROM.

Example 3-15 *Java References (Continued)*

```
 5 public class Student
 6 {
 7     private final String studentName;
 8     private String grade;
 9     private int studentID;
10     public static final int courseNumber = 12345;
11
12     // null constructor
13     public Student( )
14     {
15         studentName = "";
16     }
17
18     // constructor with 2 arguments
19     /**
20      * @param name The student's name as a String
```

Object Data (Instance)

Each object is an *instance of a class*. Objects store the data defined in the class definition. Data stored in the object also is referred to as member data, instance data, or fields. Member data can be primitive or reference types. When a programmer defines a class, the programmer expects each instance to store data separately. When an object is constructed, object data is assigned memory storage based on the data type. Objects that include references to other objects demonstrate the association or containment concept of object relationships.

Objects are created at runtime by a call to the *constructors* of the class. In the code shown in Example 3-16, the constructors are highlighted. The concept of constructors is covered in greater detail later in this chapter.

Example 3-16 *Object Data (Instance)*

NOTE

The full version of the abbreviated code shown in this example can be viewed using the book's accompanying CD-ROM.

```
1 /** Student Class establishes the student id, name and grade
2  *   @author Cisco Teacher
3  *   @version 2002
4  */
5 public class Student
6 {
```

Example 3-16 *Object Data (Instance) (Continued)*

```
 7      private final String studentName;
 8      private String grade;
 9      private int studentID;
10      public static final int courseNumber = 12345;
11
12      // null constructor
13      public Student( )
14      {
15          studentName = "";
16      }
17
18      // constructor with 2 arguments
19      /**
20       * @param name The student's name as a String
21       * @param grd The student's grade as a String
22       */
23      public Student(String name, String grd)
24      {
25          studentName = name;
26          grade = grd;
27          studentID = 99999;
28      }
```

Figure 3-19 shows the two Student objects s1 and s2 in memory. Both objects were created in heap memory by using this constructor:

```
public Student() {}
```

Each Student object is referenced through a reference variable, s1 and s2. Examine the instance and member data or fields for each object. Note that each object stores its own data. Any changes to the object referenced by s1 will not affect the object referenced by s2. What is the value stored in each field? When created, these objects will store certain default values in their fields, determined by the data type. All numeric integrals have a default of 0. All numeric floating-point data has a default of 0.0; **boolean** defaults to **false**, and **char** defaults to Unicode \u0000.

Figure 3-19 Object Data (Instance)

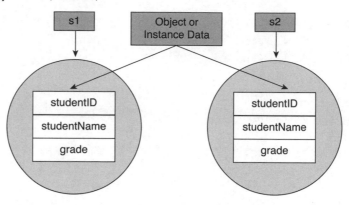

As previously mentioned, an object can also store references to other objects. The default value for the reference data type is **null**. That is, the object that it references has not been created in memory yet, so no address is known. In Figure 3-20, the value for each String field will be **null**. That is, a String object has not yet been created for the Student object to reference.

Figure 3-20 Object Data (Instance)

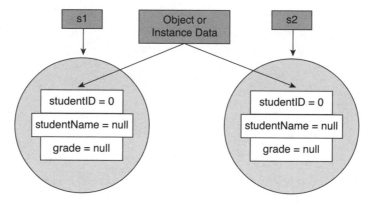

Brief Explanation of Generalization-Specialization Relationship Between Objects

When one object is a specialized form of another, having some specialized features in addition to the more general features of the other, these can be expressed as an "is a" relationship or an "is a kind of" relationship.

Examples of generalization-specialization include the following:

- Lizard/reptile
- Cow/mammal
- Car/vehicle
- Toaster/household appliance
- Telephone/communication device

Brief Explanation of Aggregation Relationship Between Objects

An aggregation relationship between objects occurs when one object "is a part of" another object rather than "being a kind of" the other object.

Examples of aggregation include the following:

- Skeleton/lizard
- Udder/cow
- Engine/car
- Heating element/toaster
- Handset/telephone

Brief Explanation of Container Relationship Between Objects

A container relationship between objects is a specific form of aggregation relationship when one object "is contained by" another object.

Examples of containment include the following:

- Sheep/flock
- Lion/pride
- Goose/gaggle
- Ship/fleet
- Fighter plane/squadron

Brief Explanation of Association Relationship Between Objects

An association relationship between objects occurs where one object "has a" other object, without the second object being necessarily "a kind of" or "contained by" by the first object.

Examples of association are

- Government/city
- President/country

- Armed forces/nation
- Owner/car
- Actor/play

Class Data (static)

Often, objects of a class need to share a single data value. All customers of a bank, for example, share the same information about the bank, such as bank address and bank name. All students in a class might share the same information about a teacher or about the maximum score possible on a test. When data is to be shared among all objects of a class, the data is declared **static** and is the same for all instances of the class. It is shared by all instances. The keyword **static** is used to define data or methods as static. The attributes of the Bank class will be defined as **static**. Static members and methods of the Math class and the System class will also be used.

Examine the Student class shown in Example 3-17. The Student class could define a variable that holds the data for the course, such as a course number. This data does not need to be stored in each Student object. The course number can be declared as **static**. When the class definition is read for the first time, the static variable is created in static memory. All objects can then use this data.

Example 3-17   *Class Data (Static)*

```
1 /** Student Class establishes the student id, name and grade
2  *  @author Cisco Teacher
3  *  @version 2002
4  */
5 public class Student
6 {
7     private final String studentName;
8     private String grade;
9     private int studentID;
10    public static final int courseNumber = 12345;
11
12    // null constructor
13    public Student( )
14    {
15        studentName = "";
16    }
17
```

Example 3-17 *Class Data (Static) (Continued)*

```
18      // constructor with 2 arguments
19      /**
20       * @param name The student's name as a String
21       * @param grd The student's grade as a String
22       */
23      public Student(String name, String grd)
24      {
25          studentName = name;
26          grade = grd;
27          studentID = 99999;
28      }
29
30      // constructor with 3 arguments
31      /**
32       * @param name The student's name as a String
33       * @param grd The student's grade as a String
34       * @param id The student's id as an int
35       */
36      public Student(String name, String grd, int id)
37      {
38          studentName = name;
39          grade = grd;
40          studentID = id;
41      }
42
43      // Print student name and grade
44      public void printData()
45      {
46          System.out.println("Student name is: " + studentName + " Grade is: "
47              + grade);
48      }
49
50      // set student's grade
51      /**
52       * @param newGrade The student's new grade as a String
53       */
```

continues

Example 3-17 *Class Data (Static) (Continued)*

```
54      public void setGrade(String newGrade)
55      {
56          grade = newGrade;
57      }
58
59      // Main method
60      public static void main(String[] args)
61      {
62          Student s1, s2, s3, s4;
63          s1 = new Student();
64          s2 = new Student();
65          s3 = new Student("Mary Jane", "A");
66          s4 = new Student("Mary Martin", "B", 12345);
67      }
68
69 }// End of Student class
```

Static data or methods are loaded in memory before any objects of the class are created. Static data is used in applications such as numbering invoices and setting initial starting values, such as maximums and minimums. It can also be used with interest rates and in setting maximum points for a test, values that must exist before objects that use them are created. The scope of static variables is for the entire execution of the program that uses the class to define these variables. As illustrated in Figure 3-21, class data, or static data, is available to all instances of the Student class.

Method Data (Local)

Whereas objects store data, the operations on the data are performed by methods of the object. Some variables store data for use in a method; this is referred to as method data. For example, to change the student's name, the object must receive new data—that is, receive a new name. The new name is stored in a method variable before it is used to replace the data in the object. These variables are passed to a method as parameters. Additionally, a method might need other variables to perform calculations. The variables defined in a method are known as local and always are created on the stack memory. The stack memory is the second fastest memory location. The compiler allocates and de-allocates stack memory based on the current methods being called. Data that is created in stack memory is available to the method only while it is running. After a method has completed its instructions, this data no longer is available.

Figure 3-21 Static Data in Memory

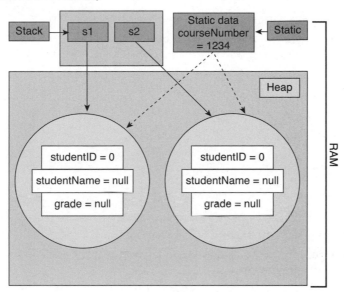

Method data also are called local, or temporary, variables. A local variable is available only to that method, not to any other method. Method data is defined in the body of a method. Method variables include the variables declared in the method signature—that is, the arguments. In Example 3-18, those variables highlighted are local variables; they are used only in the methods in which they were declared, and cannot be used in other methods. Furthermore, variables defined within control structures, such as if or while statements, are used only within the control statements; they are not available to the rest of the method. Many run-time errors of logic are a result of improperly referenced variables.

Example 3-18 *Method Data (Local)*

```
1 /** Student Class establishes the student id, name and grade
2  *   @author Cisco Teacher
3  *   @version 2002
4  */
5 public class Student
6 {
7     private final String studentName;
8     private String grade;
```

continues

Example 3-18 *Method Data (Local) (Continued)*

```
 9     private int studentID;
10     public static final int courseNumber = 12345;
11
12     // null constructor
13     public Student( )
14     {
15         studentName = "";
16     }
17
18     // constructor with 2 arguments
19     /**
20      * @param name The student's name as a String
21      * @param grd The student's grade as a String
22      */
23     public Student(String name, String grd)
24     {
25         studentName = name;
26         grade = grd;
27         studentID = 99999;
28     }
29
30     // constructor with 3 arguments
31     /**
32      * @param name The student's name as a String
33      * @param grd The student's grade as a String
34      * @param id The student's id as an int
35      */
36     public Student(String name, String grd, int id)
37     {
38         studentName = name;
39         grade = grd;
40         studentID = id;
41     }
42
43     // Print student name and grade
44     public void printData()
```

Example 3-18 *Method Data (Local) (Continued)*

```
45    {
46        System.out.println("Student name is: " + studentName + " Grade is: "
47            + grade);
48    }
49
50    // set student's grade
51    /**
52     * @param newGrade The student's new grade as a String
53     */
54    public void setGrade(String newGrade)
55    {
56        grade = newGrade;
57    }
58
59    // Main method
60    public static void main(String[] args)
61    {
62        Student s1, s2, s3, s4;
63        s1 = new Student();
64        s2 = new Student();
65        s3 = new Student("Mary Jane", "A");
66        s4 = new Student("Mary Martin", "B", 12345);
67    }
68
69 }// End of Student class
```

Method variables are created on the stack and must be initialized before use. The Java compiler will not compile the class if the student tries to reference a local variable that has not been initialized and does not have a value. For example, the local variable new-Grade, in the setGrade method, is initiated when the method is called. It then can be used to assign a value to the variable grade. Remember that the value of newGrade is not accessible by any other method. As illustrated in Figure 3-22, the local variable newGrade is accessible only to the setGrade() method.

Figure 3-22 Method Data in Memory

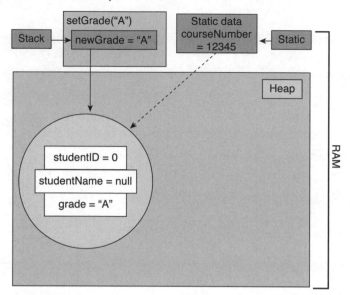

Constants

A constant is also a storage location in memory. Constants have the same five facets as variables: identifiers, scope, address, data type, and value. However, the data in a constant does not change during processing. In Java, the keyword **final** defines a storage location as constant. Both member or instance data and static or class data can be declared as constants using the keyword **final**.

In the Student class, the courseNumber and the studentName can be declared as **final**, as shown in Example 3-19. This also means that when an instance of a Student object is created, the studentName cannot be changed. After the class is loaded in memory for the first time, no object method can be used to change the courseNumber. This allows each object of the Student class to use the same number. The keyword **final** is used to enforce data integrity. Additionally, **final** or constants are more efficient to use. Use these as often as reasonable in class definitions.

Example 3-19 *Constants*

```
private final String studentName;
private static final int courseNumber = 12345;
```

Why **final** Constants Are More Efficient to Use

The **final** constants are more efficient to use because they can be inlined. That is, when a program is compiled, each time the identifier for the final constant appears, it can be replaced immediately with the actual value. This improves efficiency because the virtual machine needs to make one memory access fewer.

Syntax

Syntax refers to the rules for usage of the symbols and keywords in a language.

This section consists of the following topics:

- Variables
- Class
- Method
- Constructors
- Modifiers (**public**, **private**, **protected**, default, **static**, **final**)

Variables

When a variable is declared, the allocation of storage for a variable is being requested. If the variable is defined as part of the object data, default values are assigned to the variable when the object is created. If the variable is a local or method variable, its values must be assigned by the programmer as part of the method definition.

Example 3-20 and Table 3-11 highlight this syntax for the Student class.

Example 3-20 *Syntax in the* Student *Class*

```
 1 /** Student Class establishes the student id, name and grade
 2  *   @author Cisco Teacher
 3  *   @version 2002
 4  */
 5 public class Student
 6 {
 7     private final String studentName;
 8     private String grade;
 9     private int studentID;
10     public static final int courseNumber = 12345;
11
```

continues

Example 3-20 *Syntax in the* Student *Class (Continued)*

```
12      // null constructor
13      public Student( )
14      {
15          studentName = "";
16      }
17
18      // constructor with 2 arguments
19      /**
20       * @param name The student's name as a String
21       * @param grd The student's grade as a String
22       */
23      public Student(String name, String grd)
24      {
25          studentName = name;
26          grade = grd;
27          studentID = 99999;
28      }
29
30      // constructor with 3 arguments
31      /**
32       * @param name The student's name as a String
33       * @param grd The student's grade as a String
34       * @param id The student's id as an int
35       */
36      public Student(String name, String grd, int id)
37      {
38          studentName = name;
39          grade = grd;
40          studentID = id;
41      }
42
43      // Print student name and grade
44      public void printData()
45      {
46          System.out.println("Student name is: " + studentName + " Grade is: "
47              + grade);
48      }
```

Example 3-20 *Syntax in the* Student *Class (Continued)*

```
49
50     // set student's grade
51     /**
52      * @param newGrade The student's new grade as a String
53      */
54     public void setGrade(String newGrade)
55     {
56         grade = newGrade;
57     }
58
59     // Main method
60     public static void main(String[] args)
61     {
62         Student s1, s2, s3, s4;
63         s1 = new Student();
64         s2 = new Student();
65         s3 = new Student("Mary Jane", "A");
66         s4 = new Student("Mary Martin", "B", 12345);
67     }
68
69 }// End of Student class
```

Table 3-11 Syntax for Variables and Methods

Statement	Purpose
`<modifiers> datatype identifier;`	This is the syntax for declaring variables.
`private final String studentname;`	Modifiers: **private**, **final** Data type: Reference to an object of the class String Variable: name Object data default value: **null**

continues

Table 3-11 Syntax for Variables and Methods (Continued)

Statement	Purpose
`private String grade;`	Modifiers: **private** Data type: Reference to an object of the class `String` Variable: grade Object data default value: **null**
`private int studentID;`	Modifier: **public**, **static**, **final** Data type: **int** Variable: studentID Object data default value: **0**
`public static final int courseNumber;`	Modifier: **public**, **static**, **final** Data type: **int** Variable: courseNumber Object data default value: **12345**

`public void setGrade(String newGrade) {`
`// method instructions`
`}`
	Modifier: **public**
	
	Data type: String
	
	Argument Variable: newGrade (String data type)
	
	Return Type: **void**

`public void printData() {`
`// method instructions`
`}`
	Modifier: **public**
	
	Data type: none
	
	Argument Variable: none
	
	Return Type: **void**

Class

The syntax for a class definition is shown in Example 3-21.

Example 3-21 *Class Definition Syntax*

```
1       /*
2          class classname
3          {
4               // definition
5          }
```

Example 3-21 *Class Definition Syntax (Continued)*

```
6        */
7
8        //An example
9        public class Student
10       {
11            //default
12       }
```

Some of the rules pertaining to class definition include the following:

- A **public** class must have a class name that matches the name of the file. The file name and the class name must be the same. Java is case-sensitive. A class name of Student and a file name of Student.java, therefore, are not the same.
- A source file (.java file) can have only one **public** class definition.
- A source file can have more than one class definition, but only one of these can be declared as **public**.
- The accepted convention in naming classes is to begin all class names with an uppercase letter and use a mixed case, where the first letter of each word is capitalized. For example, a class StudentGrade, or Teacher, or StringBuffer uses the first letter as uppercase, and with multiple words, a mixed case with each word starting with an uppercase.

Table 3-12 Class Syntax

Class Definition	Complete the Statement
public class Student	File name Student._____. Accessible to all. Class name is _____. Class file created by the compiler will be Student._____.
class Student2	File name Student2.java Accessible to other classes in the same _____. Class name is Student2 Class file created by the compiler will be _____.class.

Use the exercise in Table 3-12 to practice the syntax. For Table 3-12, you can check your answers by accessing the full, interactive graphic for this table on the book's accompanying CD-ROM. The title of the activity is "Class Syntax" in the e-Lab Activities.

Examples of Class Names

Examples of class names depend on the application. Some examples of class names might be Animal, Dog, Cat, Bank, BankAccount, SavingsAccount, CheckingAccount, Student, Teacher, Class, University, Department, DepartmentHead, Manager, OperationsManager.

Method

When defining methods for a class, consider two types of methods: standard methods for setting and retrieving data of an object, and custom methods, used to implement business rules.

Standard Methods

Standard methods set, retrieve, or change the data of an object. Methods that are standard ways of setting data values for an object also are referred to as mutators. In object-speak, they change or mutate the value of the data. These methods generally are named *setObjectData,* as in setAccountBalance. Methods that use standard ways of retrieving data from an object are referred to as accessors. In object-speak, they access the data from the object. These methods generally are named *getObjectData*, like getAccountBalance. The *ObjectData* is the identifier for the specific value or data that the method will change or return. This identifier is defined as an attribute for the object.

Custom Methods

Custom methods implement business rules, such as a whenButtonPressed method for a button class or a calculateDueDate method for a VideoRented class.

Frequently, mutator, accessor, and custom methods all are used within a single class. For example, in creating classes for a video store application, the VideoRented class might have the attributes dateRented and dateDue. The class also has accessor methods to retrieve the data, mutator methods to change the data, and custom methods:

- setDateRented—Mutator method that assigns the date the video was rented to the dateRented attribute
- getDateRented—Accessor method that retrieves the dateRented
- calculateDueDate—Custom method that calculates the date the rental is due from the date rented and sets the value of dateDue

A Customer object operating on a VideoRented object can, therefore, use the mutator method setDateRented to set the date as the current date or "today's" date. The custom method calculateDueDate can be used to set the dateDue attribute of the Video-Rented object.

The syntax for *method declaration* is shown here:

Method syntax:

```
<modifiers> returntype methodname
(<datatype identifier>, <datatype identifier>, …)
{
   // method instructions
}
```

Primitive return types:

```
public double getSalary()
private int getAge()
char getGrade()
```

Class reference return types:

```
public String getStudentName()
public Day getBirthDate()
```

Method with no return value:

```
public void setSalary(double amt)
public void setGrade(char aGrade)
```

This syntax terminology outlined includes the following:

- returntype—Every method (except constructor methods) must declare a return-type. This can be any primitive data type, such as **boolean**, **char**, **byte**, **short**, **int**, **long**, **float**, or **double**. This can also be a reference to an object. When the return type is a reference to an object, the object class is used as the return type, not a reference variable for a specific instance of the object. If the method does not return any value, the keyword **void** must be used, as shown in Table 3-13.

- methodname—This is the identifier for the method. The convention for naming methods is as follows:

  — Begin method names with a lowercase letter.

  — Include the word *set* for mutator methods and *get* for accessor methods.

  — In mutator and accessor methods, include the name of the object data that is to be changed, as shown in Example 3-22.

Example 3-22 *Method Naming Conventions*

```
public double getSalary(…)        accessor method

public void setSalary(double amt)    mutator method

public String formatPhoneNumber()    custom method
```

- `Modifier datatype identifier`—This represents the arguments for the method. Methods can be declared to have one, many, or no arguments. Arguments are placeholders; they are also known as formal parameters. They provide a formal definition of the type of data to be received by the method. They can also include a modifier **final** to ensure that the value provided cannot be changed. When this method is called by another object or another method in the same class, the syntax to sending a message will include the name of the method and the values for the arguments, as illustrated in Table 3-13.

Table 3-13 Method Arguments

Method Declaration	Explanation	Use in Another Class or Another Method
`public double getSalary()`	No arguments.	`getSalary();`
`public String formatPhoneNumber (Phone ph)`	One argument. Data type for argument is Phone, that is, a reference to a Phone object. Identifier variable named ph.	`Phone ph1 = new Phone(555771234); String newPhone = formatPhoneNumber (ph1);`

`public void setName (String lname, String fname)`	Two arguments.
	
	Data type for first and second argument is String, that is, a reference to a String object.
	
	Identifier variables are lname and fname.
	
	The method takes the first value provided and assigns it the variable lname, and takes the second value provided and assigns it to fname.
		`setName("Disney","Walt");`
		
		`Or String lastName = "Walt"; String firstName ="Disney"; setName(lastName, firstName);`
		
		(Here a reference to the String object lastName and a reference to the String object firstName are sent as the message to the setName method.)
		`setName ("Walt", "Disney");`
		
		(This sets the lastname as Walt and the first name as Disney.)

Table 3-13 Method Arguments (Continued)

Method Declaration	Explanation	Use in Another Class or Another Method
`public void setSalary (int weeks, double amt, char salaryGrade)`	Three arguments. Data types: **int, double,** and **char.** When using this method, the order of data provided must match the order declared here.	`setSalary(26, 400.00, 'E');` (weeks will be assigned 26, amt will be assigned `400.00`, and salaryGrade will be assigned E.)

You can practice identifying the syntax for the method declarations in the Student class by accessing an interactive graphic on the book's accompanying CD-ROM. The title of the activity is "Identifying Code" in the e-Lab Activities. Remember to include the main method in the analysis.

Constructors

All class definitions include a special method that is used to construct objects. The creation of an object requires such a method be defined.

The syntax for a constructor is shown in Example 3-23.

Example 3-23 *Constructor Syntax*

```
 1 /*
 2 The syntax for a constructor is as follows:
 3 //<modifier> Classname( <datatype identifier>, <datatype identifier>, ...)
 4 */
 5
 6 //an example
 7 public Student(String name, String grd)
 8 {
 9     //statements
10 }
```

A constructor is a very special type of method that does not have any return values. The name of the method must be the name of the class. More than one constructor method can be defined in a class. If the programmer has not explicitly defined a constructor method, the compiler will insert one in the class definition during the compilation of the source code.

Two basic types of constructors exist: constructors with no arguments, sometimes referred to as the null constructor, and constructors with arguments.

Example 3-24 shows the `Student` class with three different constructors.

Example 3-24 *Constructor*

```
 1 /**
 2 * Java Program: Student.java
 3 * @author Cisco Teacher
 4 * @version 2002
 5 */
 6 public class Student
 7 {
 8    private final String studentName;
 9    private String grade;
10    private int studentID;
11    public static final int courseNumber = 12345;
12
13    // null constructor
14    public Student( )
15    {
16       studentName = "";
17    }
18
19    // constructor with 2 arguments
20    public Student(String name, String grd)
21    {
22       studentName = name;
23       grade = grd;
24     studentID = 99999;
25    }
26
27    // constructor with 3 arguments
28    public Student(String name, String grd, int id)
29    {
```

Example 3-24 *Constructor (Continued)*

```
30        studentName = name;

31        grade = grd;

32        studentID = id;

33    }

34

35    //more statements...

36 }//end Student Class
```

For Example 3-24, you can view the explanatory text by accessing the full, interactive graphic for this example on the book's accompanying CD-ROM. The title of the activity is "Constructor" in the e-Lab Activities.

Modifiers (`public`, `private`, `protected`, `default`, `static`, `final`)

A class, method, or variable definition can include modifiers. Two categories of *modifiers* exist: access specifiers, *accessors* and *qualifiers*, as shown in Table 3-14.

Table 3-14 Modifiers

Modifier	Explanation
`private`	Access specifier. Allows only methods within the class to access the data or method. This is class-level access only.
`public`	Access specifier. All other classes and objects can reference.
`protected`	Access specifier. Methods within the class and other classes that are stored in the same directory or package can reference.
default (no access specifier)	Access specifier. Methods within the class and other classes that are stored in the same directory and or package can reference.

continues

Table 3-14 Modifiers (Continued)

Modifier	Explanation

`static`	Qualifier. Qualifies the data or method at the class level. No object is needed to use this method or variable. A static variable or method is accessed by identifying the `classname.method()` or `classname.attribute`.
	
	Example for the `Student` class:
	
	`public static void setDate( )`
	
	Accessed as `Student.setDate( )`
	
	`public static courseID`
	
	Accessed as `Student.courseID`
	
	(Note the use of periods or dots in these examples)

`final`	Qualifier. Qualifies the data as fixed, or not changeable.

Access specifiers define the level of access to the method, variable, or class. The keywords are **private**, **public**, and **protected**. If the access specifier is left blank, the access is defined to be default.

Brief Definitions of **private**, **public**, **protected**, and default

The following list briefly describes each of the four access specifiers:

- **private**—A Java keyword. Indicates that a variable or method can be accessed only by methods of its class.
- **public**—A Java keyword. Indicates that a variable or method can be accessed by methods from any other classes.
- **protected**—A Java keyword. Indicates that a variable or method can be accessed by methods from its class, child classes, and other classes in the same package as its class.
- default—Indicates that a variable or method can be accessed by methods from its class and any other classes that are stored in the same directory or package.

Qualifiers define the state of the object, variable, or method. The keywords are **static**, **final**, **native**, and **transient**.

Brief Definitions of `static`, `final`, `native`, and `transient`

The following list briefly describes each of the four qualifiers:

- **`static`**—A Java keyword. When applied to a variable, it indicates that only one copy of that variable will be maintained per class. This copy is shared by all objects instantiated from that class. When applied to a method, it indicates that the method is a class method that operates only on class variables, not on instance variables.

- **`final`**—A Java keyword. It indicates a Java entity that cannot be changed (in the case of a variable), that is inherited from (in the case of a class), or that is overridden (in the case of a method).

- **`native`**—A Java keyword. It indicates that a method is in another source file (than the current class) and is in another programming language.

- **`transient`**—A Java keyword. It indicates that a field is not written to persistent storage when the parent object is stored.

Object Creation, Mutability, and Destruction

The life of an object includes its creation, changes made to the object during its lifetime (*mutability*), and finally the destruction of the object. This section covers the following topics:

- Object creation (constructors)
- Object creation by another class
- Mutability
- Garbage collection
- Finalizers

Object Creation: Constructors

The creation of an object consists of five steps:

Step 1   A reference variable is declared for the object, which initiates a request for storage and the resulting allocation of RAM.

Step 2   Default initialization sets the default values of the object based on the data type.

Step 3   Values are explicitly initialized.

Step 4   The constructor is executed.

Step 5   An object address reference is assigned to the reference variable.

In the Student class shown in Example 3-25, the main method was used to create Student objects.

Example 3-25 *Object Creation in the* main *Method*

```
1 /** Student Class establishes the student id, name and grade
2  *   @author Cisco Teacher
3  *   @version 2002
4  */
5 public class Student
6 {
7      private final String studentName;
8      private String grade;
9      private int studentID;
10     public static final int courseNumber = 12345;
11
12     // null constructor
13     public Student( )
14     {
15         studentName = "";
16     }
17
18     // constructor with 2 arguments
19     /**
20      * @param name The student's name as a String
21      * @param grd The student's grade as a String
22      */
23     public Student(String name, String grd)
24     {
25         studentName = name;
26         grade = grd;
27         studentID = 99999;
28     }
29
30     // constructor with 3 arguments
31     /**
32      * @param name The student's name as a String
33      * @param grd The student's grade as a String
```

Example 3-25 *Object Creation in the* main *Method (Continued)*

```
34        * @param id The student's id as an int
35        */
36       public Student(String name, String grd, int id)
37       {
38           studentName = name;
39           grade = grd;
40           studentID = id;
41       }
42
43       // Print student name and grade
44       public void printData()
45       {
46           System.out.println("Student name is: " + studentName + " Grade is: "
47                + grade);
48       }
49
50       // set student's grade
51       /**
52        * @param newGrade The student's new grade as a String
53        */
54       public void setGrade(String newGrade)
55       {
56           grade = newGrade;
57       }
58
59       // Main method
60       public static void main(String[] args)
61       {
62           Student s1, s2, s3, s4;
63           s1 = new Student();
64           s2 = new Student();
65           s3 = new Student("Mary Jane", "A");
66           s4 = new Student("Mary Martin", "B", 12345);
67       }
68
69 }// End of Student class
```

Object Creation by Another Class

In general, object creation by another class occurs when another class will use the Student class. For example, a teacher usually manages student data. Examine a Teacher class that creates Student objects. Notice that the Student class shown in Example 3-26 no longer has a main method to create Student objects.

Example 3-26 *The Student Class with No* main *Method*

```
1 /** Student Class establishes the student id, name and grade
2  *  @author Cisco Teacher
3  *  @version 2002
4  */
5 public class Student
6 {
7      private final String studentName;
8      private String grade;
9      private int studentID;
10     public static final int courseNumber = 12345;
11
12     // null constructor
13     public Student( )
14     {
15         studentName = "";
16     }
17
18     // constructor with 2 arguments
19     /**
20      * @param name The student's name as a String
21      * @param grd The student's grade as a String
22      */
23     public Student(String name, String grd)
24     {
25         studentName = name;
26         grade = grd;
27         studentID = 99999;
28     }
29
```

Example 3-26 *The Student Class with No* main *Method (Continued)*

```
30      // constructor with 3 arguments
31      /**
32       * @param name The student's name as a String
33       * @param grd The student's grade as a String
34       * @param id The student's id as an int
35       */
36      public Student(String name, String grd, int id)
37      {
38          studentName = name;
39          grade = grd;
40          studentID = id;
41      }
42
43      // Print student name and grade
44      public void printData()
45      {
46          System.out.println("Student name is: " + studentName + " Grade is: "
47              + grade);
48      }
49
50      // set student's grade
51      /**
52       * @param newGrade The student's new grade as a String
53       */
54      public void setGrade(String newGrade)
55      {
56          grade = newGrade;
57      }
58
59 }// End of Student class
```

The Teacher class now creates these objects (see Example 3-27).

Example 3-27 *Object Creation by Another Class*

```
1 /** Teacher Class creates students
2  *  @author Cisco Teacher
3  *  @version 2002
4  */
5
6 public class Teacher
7 {
8     // Main method
9     public static void main(String[] args)
10    {
11        Student s1, s2, s3, s4;
12        s1 = new Student();
13        s2 = new Student();
14        s3 = new Student("Mary Jane", "A");
15        s4 = new Student("Mary Martin", "B", 12345);
16    }
17
18 }// End of Teacher class
```

Mutability

The use of the keyword **final** declares a method, an attribute, or an object to be immutable, which means that it cannot be changed. In the Student class shown in Example 3-28, the studentName is declared **final**.

Example 3-28 *Mutability*

NOTE

The full version of the abbreviated code shown in this example can be viewed using the book's accompanying CD-ROM.

```
1 /** Student Class establishes the student id, name and grade
2  *  @author Cisco Teacher
3  *  @version 2002
4  */
5 public class Student
6 {
7     private final String studentName;
8     private String grade;
9     private int studentID;
```

Example 3-28 *Mutability (Continued)*

```
10    public static final int courseNumber = 12345;

11

12    // null constructor
13    public Student( )
14    {
15        studentName = "";
16    }

17

18    // constructor with 2 arguments
19    /**
20     * @param name The student's name as a String
```

After a Student object is created, the value of studentName cannot be changed. For the object referenced by s1, the name cannot be changed. The String object representing the name does not exist. The objects referenced by s3 and s4 are set at the student-Names of Mary Jane and Mary Martin. These values also cannot be changed. The attribute studentName is considered immutable. For nonstatic attributes declared as **final,** the value for the attribute must be assigned in the constructor.

The pros and cons of the **final** qualifier as it applies to the String class are further explored in Chapter 6.

Garbage Collection

Objects are created in heap memory. Computer memory is finite; only so much is available at any given moment. When running applications with many objects, all objects cannot occupy the heap memory, nor do they need to. The JVM runs a program referred to as the *garbage collector*. The programmer cannot control this program; the garbage collector uses an algorithm to clear memory. Objects that no longer are used and no longer have any references or reference variables storing the addresses are marked for destruction. When the JVM needs memory for new objects, the garbage collector releases the marked objects and cleans them out of memory. Garbage collection algorithms in Java have evolved beyond simple mark-and-sweep algorithms. Some vendors of Java applications have redesigned the garbage collection algorithms to take advantage of specific hardware and operating system capabilities.

A programmer cannot control the schedule of the garbage collector, but it is possible to assign the value of a reference variable to **null**, which identifies the object previously referenced by the variable as ready for the garbage collector. The programmer can also call the method gc from the System class. This is a static method. The call to the gc method is System.gc().

Example 3-29 illustrates the use of the gc method in the main method of the Student class.

Example 3-29 *Garbage Collection*

```
1      // Main method
2      public static void main(String[] args)
3      {
4          Student s1, s2, s3, s4;
5          s1 = new Student();
6          s2 = new Student();
7          s3 = new Student("Mary Jane", "A");
8          s4 = new Student("Mary Martin", "B", 12345);
9
10         /*
11         Object reference set to null.  The object with no name is
12         not being used.  The garbage collector can mark this object
13         for destruction.
14         */
15         s1 = null;
16         /*
17         Request the gc method ( or that the garbage collection
18         method schedule a mark and sweep operation)
19         */
20         System.gc();
21     }
```

Note that inserting System.gc() causes garbage collection to run not immediately, but rather when the operating system runs out of memory. When the programmer includes System.gc() in a program, this does not mean that the garbage collector will immediately run; the command merely informs the operating system that this particular object is ready for garbage collection. The operating system then schedules garbage collection at its convenience, typically when memory is running low enough that it is beginning to impact computational performance.

Finalizers

Every object inherits attributes from a base class named `Object`. This is one of the core classes. Go to the API docs and review the `Object` class documentation, as shown in Figure 3-23.

Figure 3-23 Finalizers and the `Object` Class

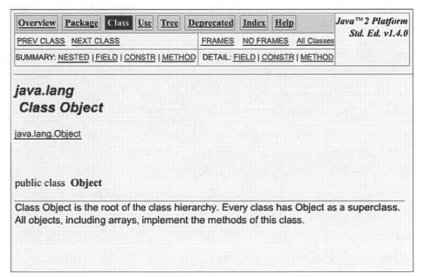

One of the methods inherited in the `Object` class is the *finalize method*. A programmer can insert a custom definition of the `finalize` method, to provide a mechanism for cleanup activities, such as closing files or saving certain data to a file, to occur before the relevant object is garbage-collected. However, the `finalize` method is not guaranteed to run.

Case Study: JBANK Application

The JBANK application introduced in Chapter 1, "What Is Java?", will provide students with an opportunity to apply the Java language concepts learned throughout this course. In the JBANK labs for Chapter 3, students will finish the creation of all four classes of the JBANK Phase1 application, while demonstrating the creation and reuse of objects. Students also will implement several constructors, access static fields of other classes, and print the resulting contents using class accessor methods.

JBANK Application

The banking application is developed in phases. Phase 1 of the banking application will be completed in the following labs. Phase 1 of the banking application creates all the basic classes needed: the Customer, Bank, Account, and Teller classes.

Students already should be familiar with the Teller class. In these labs, students will begin to use the Teller class as the main entry point for the banking application. This will be the class that creates Customer and Account objects.

The Customer class is a "data-filled" class. Although the code is lengthy, it will give students practice in managing classes that hold lots of data; this is not uncommon in real-world applications. The Customer class goes through additional modifications in later chapters. Here, its primary use is to store customer information.

The Account class is a simple class that holds account balance information. This class includes methods for depositing and withdrawing from the account. This is a class that will also be modified further in later chapters.

In Phase 1, the application is in its simplest form and consists of a bank with customers who have only one account. Later phases will introduce additional types of accounts for each customer.

The Bank class provides for the use of **static** qualifiers. This is particularly appropriate because the information pertinent to a bank is shared by all customers. Therefore, if a user needs to display information about the bank and an account for a specific customer, he can obtain the bank information from the Bank class and obtain the customer and account information from the Customer and Account objects. This important concept states that no objects of the Bank class need to be created to use the data in the class. This class will be loaded into memory as soon as a reference is made to this class.

Before beginning the lab, review the UML diagram for Phase 1 and the case study description for the banking application. Figures 3-24 and 3-25 display what the JBANK application might look like at the end of the course.

Figure 3-24 The JBANK Application

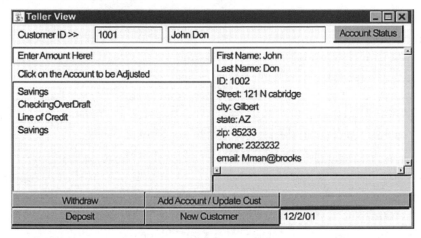

Figure 3-25 The JBANK Application

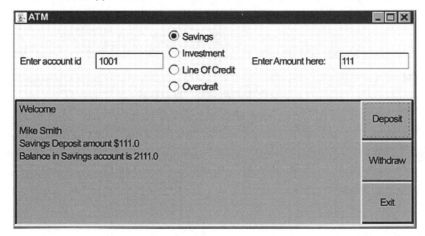

In this lab, the UML test tool will be used by the students to verify the accuracy of their class against the UML provided. This UML test tool is written in Java and generates a UML diagram of the class, which students can compare with the one that is provided with the course.

Summary

This chapter is the first formal introduction to the elements of the Java language. The success of the programs depends on the proper use of language rules and the documentation of the program's features. Code reuse is the cornerstone principle of the Java language and is greatly aided by the strong support for documentation of public features of the programs.

A proficient Java programmer must therefore make a diligent effort to document programs. Documentation benefits the programmer and other users of the class. The javadoc utility interprets specific tags that are inserted into the source code to create HTML documents. These types of comments are enclosed in /** */ documentation. The core API is available in HTML format. This serves as a reference for using this large set of classes that form the Java language platform.

As with any programming language, Java has a rich set of keywords and symbols. The keyword **new** requests storage for an object; this is also known as the new operator. The keywords **public**, **private**, **protected**, **static**, and **final** are modifiers of a class, data, or method. The keyword **static** is a qualifier of data or methods and also is said to be class-based. The keyword **final** is also a qualifier of data or methods but is known as a constant. Reserved words are used to define certain types of values, such as **true**, **false**, and **null**. Identifiers are labels that programmers assign to data or storage locations. Identifiers are also labels that a programmer assigns to class names and to method names. The use of braces, semicolons, commas, and whitespace is common and frequent throughout programmer code; usage must adhere to the Java syntax rules, however.

Java is known as a "strongly typed" language. This references the discipline that is enforced knowing the exact type of data to be stored. In the case of primitives, there is a close link between data type and amount of storage. Data can be stored in six different places: the CPU registers, random-access memory (RAM), and non-RAM storage, such as disk space on the hard drive. RAM memory is divided further into stack, heap, static storage, and constant storage. Storage size is defined as the number of bits required to store a representation of a number, character symbol, or Boolean status.

The Java data types are as follows:

- Primitive
  - **boolean**
  - **char**
  - Numeric
    - Integrals
      byte
      short
      int
      long

- Floating point

    float

    double

■ Reference

Primitive data types are not objects. Classes that create objects that store a single primitive value are known as wrapper classes. These wrapper classes wrap object features and capabilities around a single primitive data type value.

All languages have rules for punctuation, grammar, and proper use of vocabulary. In programming languages, this is referred to as the syntax of the language. Syntax refers to the rules for usage of the symbols and keywords in a language.

The garbage collector is a special program that the JVM runs to free up memory. A programmer can identify an object as ready for destruction by setting the reference to the object as **null**. The finalize method can be customized to perform cleanup activities, such as closing files or saving certain data to a file.

Syntax Summary

There are specific syntax rules for the following:

■ *Variable declaration*:

```
<modifiers> datatype identifier;
```

Example variable declarations:

```
int x = 0;
double y = 0.0;
boolean b = true;
```

■ *Class declaration:*

```
<modifiers> class Classname
{
// definition
}
```

Example class declaration:

```
public class Animal {
   // code here providing details of Animal class
}
```

■ Method declaration (note the inclusion of a return type):

```
<modifiers> return-type methodname (<modifier data-type identifier>, <modifier
data-type identifier>, …)
{
// method instructions
}
```

Example method declaration:

```
public getAccountBalance {
  // code here providing details of AccountBalance
  return accountBalance;
}
```

- *Constructor declaration* (special method that defines how to construct an object):

```
<modifiers> Classname (<modifier data-type identifier>, <modifier data-type
identifier>, …)
{
// constructor instructions
}
```

Example constructor declaration:

```
public Animal() {
  // code here which initializes all objects of class Animal
}
```

- Modifiers include accessors (**public**, **private**, **protected**, and default), and qualifiers (**static** and **final**).

Resources

This book is not meant to be a comprehensive manual for everything Java. To include everything relevant to Java would take volumes. As such, many resources are available on the web:

- Sun Java website: http://java.sun.com/
- Sun Developer site: http://developer.java.sun.com/developer/
- Sun Java tutorial: http://java.sun.com/docs/books/tutorial/
- Java tutorial and frequently asked questions: http://java.sun.com/docs/books/tutorial/information/FAQ.html
- Java code samples: http://developer.java.sun.com/developer/codesamples/
- How to run your first program in Java: http://java.sun.com/docs/books/tutorial/getStarted/cupojava/index.html
- Java API: http://java.sun.com/j2se/1.3/docs/api/

Key Terms

API Documentation (Application Programming Interface)   The specification of how a programmer writing an application accesses the behavior and state of classes and objects.

Declarations:

Variable:

```
<modifiers> datatype identifier;
```

Class:

```
<modifiers> class Classname
{
// definition
}
```

Method:

```
<modifiers> return-type methodname (<modifier data-type
identifier>, <modifier data-type identifier>, …)
{
// method instructions
}
```

Constructor:

```
<modifiers> Classname (<modifier data-type identifier>,
<modifier data-type identifier>, …)
{
// constructor instructions
}
```

`finalize` *Method*   A programmer can insert a custom definition of the `finalize` method to provide a mechanism for cleanup activities, such as closing files or saving certain data to a file, to occur before the relevant object is garbage-collected.

Garbage Collection   The JVM uses an algorithm to clear memory. Objects that no longer are used and no longer have any references or reference variables storing the addresses are marked for destruction. When the JVM needs memory for new objects, the garbage collector releases the marked objects and cleans them out of memory.

Identifiers   Labels assigned to data or storage addresses about an object.

Instance of a Class   An object of a particular class. In programs written in the Java programming language, an instance of a class is created using the new operator followed by the class name.

Java Data Types   A data type of Java is a classification of a particular form of information. It tells the computer how to interpret and store the data:

Primitive   Data types used to store simple data. Eight types of Java primitives exist: `boolean`, `char`, `byte`, `short`, `int`, `long`, `float`, and `double`. With primitive data types, this means that each variable has a defined amount of storage allocated.

Reference   The complex data types that are not primitive. Variables that store references to object addresses are considered to hold reference data types.

Java Syntax Rules   Programming rules established to allow a program to execute properly.

javadoc comments   Start with `/**` on one line and, after several lines of comments, terminate with `*/`. These comments are designed to be extracted automatically by a program called `javadoc`, to create HTML (web page–like) documentation for the program. This is an excellent innovation that speeds up the documentation process for Java projects.

Keywords and Symbols   Elements of a language that represents data and operations of that language. Symbols are used to communicate rules and syntax.

Modifiers   A class, method, or variable definition can include modifiers. Two categories of modifiers exist:

Accessors   Access specifiers define the level of access to the method, variable, or class. The keywords are `private`, `public`, and `protected`. If the access specifier is left blank, the access is defined to be default.

Qualifiers   Qualifiers define the state of the object, variable, or method. The keywords are `static`, `final`, `native`, and `transient`.

Mutability   Determines whether an object can or cannot be changed during its lifetime.

RAM (random-access memory)   A computer's main or primary memory.

Stack   Storage location in RAM for methods and variables.

Heap   Storage location in RAM for objects.

Static   Storage location in RAM for shared methods or variables.

Constant   Storage location in RAM for nonchanging variables.

Storage Size   Defined as the number of bits that are required to store a representation of the number, character symbol, or Boolean status:

> *Bit*   Each bit can be represented as a place value in the binary number system—that is, a number system using two digits: 1 or 0.

> *Byte*   Eight (8) bits equals one (1) byte.

Variables   A variable is a storage location in memory that a programmer can use to store data. A variable has five facets. Data types are declared when a variable is created. The data or value in a variable can be a primitive or can be a reference data type.

Wrapper Classes   Each primitive type has a wrapper class defined in the core classes. Wrapper classes wrap object features and capabilities around a single primitive data type value. This enables a programmer to operate on these types of data as objects.

Check Your Understanding

1. Which type of comments are used to create HTML documentation for a Java class?

    A. Single-line comments.

    B. Javadoc comments.

    C. Multiline comments.

    D. All types of comments are used to create HTML documentation.

2. Which javadoc parameter is used to describe the parameters required by a method?

    A. `@return`

    B. `@parameter`

    C. `@param`

    D. `@deprecated`

3. Which command will generate javadoc documentation for the class `Student`?

    A. **javac** `Student.java`

    B. **java** `Student.java`

    C. **javadoc** `Student.java`

    D. **javadoc** `Student.exe`

4. Which Java keyword is a reserved word but is not currently used?

   A. `transient`

   B. `goto`

   C. `protected`

   D. `instanceof`

5. Which of the following is not a Java keyword?

   A. `return`

   B. `instance`

   C. `public`

   D. `try`

6. Which of the following is a true statement about Java identifiers?

   A. An identifier can contain `%` as long as it is not the first character.

   B. The first character can be a number or a letter.

   C. Identifiers are not case sensitive.

   D. Identifiers cannot contain spaces.

7. Which symbol must be included at the end of each Java statement?

   A. Period

   B. Colon

   C. Comma

   D. Semicolon

8. Which character is used to insert a horizontal tab?

   A. `t`

   B. `/t`

   C. `\t`

   D. `\TAB`

9. Which of these types of memory space is located in the CPU?

   A. Registers

   B. Stack

   C. Heap

   D. RAM

10. What is the default value for a **boolean** variable?

    A. 0

    B. true

    C. false

    D. null

11. How many bits are in 1 byte?

    A. 2

    B. 8

    C. 16

    D. 32

12. What is the correct range of values for a variable of type **byte**?

    A. −128 to 127

    B. −32,768 to 32,767

    C. −128 to 128

    D. −128 to 127

13. Which of the following Java primitive types can store the largest number?

    A. float

    B. byte

    C. long

    D. double

14. Which of the following is not a Java wrapper class?

    A. Integer

    B. Char

    C. Double

    D. Boolean

15. Which Java keyword is used to identify class data?

    A. public

    B. class

    C. static

    D. shared

16. When is static data loaded into memory?

    A. Static data is loaded into memory before an object is instantiated.

    B. Static data is loaded into memory at the same time an object is instantiated.

    C. Static data is loaded into memory after an object is instantiated.

    D. Static data is not loaded into memory—it is stored on the hard drive.

17. In which type of memory are method variables created?

    A. The heap

    B. The registers

    C. Static storage

    D. The stack

18. What is the convention for naming Java classes?

    A. The name of the class should be in all lowercase letters.

    B. The first letter of the class name should be in uppercase.

    C. The name of the class should be in all uppercase letters.

    D. The name of the class should be fewer than seven letters.

19. Which of the following is not an access specifier?

    A. `final`

    B. `public`

    C. `private`

    D. `protected`

20. Which Java statement is used to inform the system that an object is ready for garbage collection?

    A. `Java.garbage();`

    B. `System.collect();`

    C. `Garbage.collect();`

    D. `System.gc();`

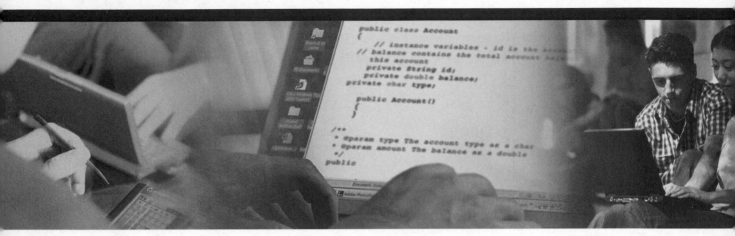

Upon completion of this chapter, you will be able to

- Understand object operations
- Understand numeric data and operations
- Apply concepts of casting and conversion
- Work with character and string data
- Understand control structures
- Use the `java.lang.System` class member `in` and `out`
- Dissect sample code

Chapter 4

Java Language Operators and Control Structures

In this chapter, students will learn to create expressions for manipulating object and method data. These expressions use object access, arithmetic, and logical operators. Students also will identify and apply these operators while adhering to the order and association properties of operators.

Students are introduced to the concept of using control structures to alter the flow of the sequence of instructions in a method. Control structures fall into two major categories: looping control structures, which repeat a sequence of instructions, and decision control structures, which include the `switch`, `if`, and conditional operators that are utilized to perform complex operations on data.

The Operator Precedence Chart, located in Appendix D, is a reference guide for the precedence of operators in the Java language.

Object Operations

Manipulation of data in any language is performed through *operators*. A combination of data and operators used to obtain a result is also known as a formula or an expression. In Java, expressions are parts of statements in which the values of object and class members (fields) are being accessed. Object members also can be assigned data, where data is to be manipulated. Expressions describe other operations on object data, such as arithmetic operations, comparison operations, and conversion operations. The data or values used in an expression are referred to as operands.

This section covers object operations.

Object Operators

Two important symbols or operators (*object operators*) are used with objects: the ***new operator*** and the dot operator.

new Operator

The **new** operator is used to create an object. In each of the examples shown in Example 4-1, the **new** operator results in the constructor for the class being loaded and executed. It uses the instructions in the constructor for the class to allocate storage and then create the object. The reference to the address of the object created in memory is stored in the variable to the left of the = (assignment) symbol.

Example 4-1 *Object Operators*

```
1 Student s1 = new Student( );

2

3 String name = new String ("Mary Martin");

4

5 Customer c1;    // declare a reference variable

6 c1 = new Customer ("Martin", "Mary");
```

Dot Operator

As shown in Example 4-2, the *dot operator* is used to access methods or member data of an object. In this example, the dot operator is used with objects of the Student class, shown in Example 4-3.

Example 4-2 *Object Operators—Dot Operator*

```
//The syntax for the dot operator is ObjectReference.member:
s1.printData();
s1.grade;
s1.studentName.length();
System.out.println("The name " + s1.studentName + " contains " +
s1.studentName.length() + " characters.");
```

To access the **public** printData method of the Student class, using the reference s1 to a Student object, the dot operator can be used. The dot operator can also be used to access nonprivate data from the Student object referenced by s1.

Example 4-3 *Object Operators*

```
1 /** Student Class establishes the student id, name and grade
2  *  @author Cisco Teacher
3  *  @version 2002
4  */
5 public class Student
6 {
7      private final String studentName;
8      private String grade;
9      private int studentID;
10     public static final int courseNumber = 12345;
11
12     // null constructor
13     public Student( )
14     {
15         studentName = "";
16     }
17
18     // constructor with 2 arguments
19     /**
20      * @param name The student's name as a String
```

NOTE

The full version of the abbreviated code shown in this example can be viewed using the book's accompanying CD-ROM.

The dot operator can be chained to more than one method or member data. For example, the studentName attribute of the Student class is a String object. The String class also has a method named length that returns a String object's length. (Research this by using Java API Online Documentation mentioned in Chapter 3, "Java Language Elements.") To determine the length of a student name, the displayed code can be written using the dot operator notation.

The dot operator operates from left to right. The Student object referenced by s1 first accesses the Student class's studentName attribute by using the dot operator and returns a String object. This returned String object accesses the String class's length( ) method using the dot operator and returns an integer.

The statement to display the student name and its length might resemble the one shown in Example 4-2. In this case, the parentheses take precedence. The Student object referenced by s1 first accesses the Student class's studentName attribute using the dot operator and the String class's length( ) method, returning a String object inside the parentheses. The System.out.println method uses this returned String object as its argument.

Within the definition of a method, there is no need to use the dot notation for accessing object data. In Example 4-3, the `printData` method of the `Student` class does not use the dot operator to access the `grade` attribute. However, accessing nonprivate methods or data through interaction between objects, such as the `Teacher` class in Example 4-4, requires the use of the dot operator.

Example 4-4 *Object Operators*

```
 1 /** Teacher Class creates students
 2  *  @author Cisco Teacher
 3  *  @version 2002
 4  */
 5 public class Teacher
 6 {
 7    // Main method
 8    public static void main(String[] args)
 9    {
10       Student s1, s2, s3, s4;
11       s1 = new Student();
12       s2 = new Student();
13       s3 = new Student("Mary Jane", "A");
14       s4 = new Student("Mary Martin", "B", 12345);
15
16       s3.setGrade("A");    //accessing non-private method
17
18       // s3.grade = "A"; this would not be permissible. Grade is private
19    }
20
21 }// End of Teacher class
```

Numeric Data and Operations

As indicated, Java expressions use arithmetic and logical operators. For these expressions to produce the desired results, students must identify and apply these operators while adhering to the order of precedence and association properties of operators. This section consists of the following topics:

- Assignment operators
- Arithmetic operations

- Precedence of operators
- Associative properties of operators
- Arithmetic calculations
- Boolean data
- Comparison and logical operators
- Conditional operators
- Bitwise operators

Assignment Operators

The *assignment operator* takes the form of the equals sign (=). When using the assignment operators, a few rules must be followed. First, all numbers must be signed. Second, the **boolean** data type can be either **true** or **false**. Finally, the right operand must be assignment-compatible with the left operand.

Java works only with signed numbers, which indicate whether they are positive or negative. Each signed number contains a sign bit indicating whether it is a positive or a negative number. The eighth bit of a byte (which contains 8 bits) is used to represent the sign of the number. The sign bit is 1 for negative numbers and 0 for positive numbers. If the number is 0, the sign bit is 0. The code shown in Example 4-5 illustrates how to declare and assign values to variables of the primitive data types.

Example 4-5 *Assignment Operators*

```
1 public class assignData{
2     public static void main (String args []) {
3         // declare integer variables
4         int x, y;
5         // declare and assign floating point
6         float z = 3.414f;
7         // declare and assign double
8         double w = 3.1415;
9         // declare and assign boolean
10        boolean truth = true;
11        // declare character variable
12        char c;
13        // declare String variable
14        String str;
15        // declare and assign String variable
```

NOTE

The full version of the abbreviated code shown in this example can be viewed using the book's accompanying CD-ROM.

continues

Example 4-5 *Assignment Operators (Continued)*

```
16          String str1 = "bye";
17          // assign value to char variable
18          c = 'A';
19          // assign value to String variable
20          str = "Hi out there!";
```

A **boolean** variable must be assigned the keyword **true** or **false**. Unlike in C++, 1 and 0 cannot be used to indicate **true** or **false**. The code shown in Example 4-6 illustrates this as well as a few other common errors of assignment.

Example 4-6 *Assignment Operators Syntax Errors*

```
1 int  w = 175,000; // The comma symbol (,) cannot appear;
2
3 boolean truth = 1;
4 // this is a common mistake made by C / C++ programmers; a
5 // boolean must be true or false.
```

As shown in Example 4-7, when using assignment operators, the right operand (the value to the right of the assignment operator [=]) must be assignment-compatible with the left operand.

Example 4-7 *Assignment Compatibility*

```
1 int x  =1;
2 boolean b;
3 b = x ;    // this is not assignment-compatible
4
5
6 int x =2
7 double d;
8 d = x ;  // this is assignment compatible.
9
10
11 String s = "A";
12 char c ;
13 c = s;
14 // this is not assignment compatible. c is
15 // a primitive. s is a reference to a String object.
```

Arithmetic Operators

Values stored in the computer might need to be manipulated arithmetically through addition, subtraction, multiplication, and division. As shown in Table 4-1, Java provides the use of *arithmetic operator* symbols similar to regular algebraic symbols.

Table 4-1 Arithmetic Operators

Operator	Description	Example	Result
+	Addition	20 + 3	23
–	Subtraction	20 – 3	17
*	Multiplication	20 * 3	60
/	Division with integers	20 / 3	6 (the remainder is lost)
/	Division with floating-point numbers (decimal numbers)	20.0 / 3	6.6666667 for **float** (32 bits of storage), 6.6666666666666667 for **double** (64-bit storage)
%	Modular division returns remainder of division operation	20 % 3	2

Division (/) of integers (variable or constant) results in an integer value. Any fraction or remainder is lost, as shown in Example 4-8. The modulus operator (%) is used to obtain the remainder in integer division. A modulus also can be used to identify whether a number is odd or even. In addition, a modulus can calculate hours and minutes, given a total number of minutes. Modulus (%) is used only with integral numbers, not decimals.

Example 4-8 *Use of Arithmetic Operators*

```
35 / 2 will result in 17  not 17.5
35 % 2 will result in 1
45 % 2 will result in 1 (odd number)
44 % 2 will result in 0 (even number)
200 minutes
200 / 60 = 3
200 % 60 = 20 minutes
200 minutes is 3 hours and 20 minutes
```

Sample code using arithmetic operators is shown in Example 4-9.

Example 4-9 *Arithmetic Operators*

NOTE

The full version of the abbreviated code shown in this example can be viewed using the book's accompanying CD-ROM.

```
1 /**
2  * Simple arithmetic operators
3  * @author Cisco Teacher
4  * @version 2002
5  */
6 // Class definition
7
8 public class DoArithmeticWithTime
9 {
10     // class does not have any member data, and does not use any other class
11
12     // main method entry point of program
13     public static void main(String[] args)
14     {
15         // method  or local variables
16         int aTime = 700;  // time in minutes
17         int bTime = 1200;  // time in minutes
18         int totalTime = aTime +bTime;
19         int differenceInTime = bTime - aTime;
```

Use the expressions in Table 4-2 to practice using the Java arithmetic operators.

Table 4-2 Exercise—Arithmetic Operators

Expression	Result
4 + 6 * 3	
18 / 2 + 14 / 2	
16 / 2	
2.3 * 1.2	
5.67 – 2	
25.0 / 5.0	
17.35 % 3.2	
7 % 3	

You can check your answers by accessing the full, interactive graphic for this table on the book's accompanying CD-ROM. The title of the activity is "Interactive Exercises" in e-Lab Activities.

Unary Operators

In addition to the standard algebraic symbols, Java includes unary operators. *Unary operators* require only one operand, unlike the previous operators, which required two operands (hence, called binary operators). The unary operators are increment, decrement, unary plus, unary minus, bitwise inversion, **boolean** complement, and the cast operator. Some common Java unary and assignment operators are displayed in Table 4-3.

NOTE

Remember, an Operator Precedence Chart is available for reference in Appendix D.

Table 4-3 Unary and Assignment Operators

Operator	Description	Example	Result
++ and --	Act as increment and decrement operators. These operators increase or decrease a value by 1.	`int x = 4;` `int y = 0;` `y = ++x;`	x is 4. y is 0. y is 5 and x is 5.
Prefix ++, -- Postfix ++, --	Can operate on the value as prefix or postfix operators. Prefix changes the value before use. Postfix changes the value after use.	`int x = 4;` `int y = 0;` `y = x++;`	x is 4. y is 0. y is 4 and x is 5.
=	Assigns the value of the right operand of the expression to the left operand of the expression.	`x = 45;`	x is 45.
*=	Multiplies the operand on the right with the operand on the left of the =, and assigns the value to this operand.	`x =45;` `x *= 2;`	x is 45. x is 45 * 2, 90.

NOTE

Beware of the "gotcha" when using the += assignment operator.

This statement increases total by 2:

`int total = 5;`
`total += 2;`

This is commonly miscoded as follows:

`int total = 5;`
`total =+ 2;`

This does compile but simply assigns 2 to total.

continues

Table 4-3 Unary and Assignment Operators (Continued)

Operator	Description	Example	Result
/=	Divides the operand on the left with the operand on the right of the =, and assigns the value to the left operand.	x = 70; x /= 5;	x is 70. x is 70 / 5, 14.
%=	Modulus on the left operand.	x = 90; x %= 8;	x is 90. x is remainder of 90 / 8, 2.

Precedence of Operators

Java performs operations in a specific order based on *operator precedence*. Precedence is a set of rules that Java imposes in the use of all operators. To understand operator precedence better, consider this expression:

```
number = 8 + 170 * 3;
```

Table 4-4 shows the two different results that could be obtained, depending on which operators take precedence. To avoid such confusion, Java assigns precedence to each operator that determines the order in which it performs operations. Each operator is assigned to a precedence group. All operators in a given group have precedence (or priority) over operators in the group below it. Because of this, Java performs operations in a consistent manner.

Table 4-4 Precedence of Operators

number = 8 + 170 * 3;	
Result Calculating from Left to Right Operating on a Pair of Operands	**Result Calculating from Right to Left Operating on a Pair of Operands**
$= 8 + 170 \times 3$ $= 178 \times 3$ $= 534$	$= 8 + 170 \times 3$ $= 8 + 510$ $= 518$

You can access the full, interactive graphic for this table on the book's accompanying CD-ROM. The title of the activity is "Precedence of Operators" in e-Lab Activities.

In a complex expression that uses many operations, a programmer can change the order by using parentheses and unary operators. Expressions that do not contain parentheses are hard to read. To avoid confusion and errors, or bugs in the programs, clarify the order of operations by using parentheses.

Associative Properties of Operators

When several operators belonging to the same group have equal precedence, the operators are performed from right to left or left to right. These are the *associative properties* of a group of operators:

- Arithmetic expressions or calculations are left-associative (evaluated from left to right).
- Assignment operators are right-associative (right to left), so the value must be determined before it can be assigned.

Use Table 4-5 to become familiar with the order of precedence and the use of parentheses to manage these rules of precedence. Calculate the result of each expression in the table following the Java rules of precedence.

Table 4-5 Java Precedence

Expression	Result
4 + 6 * 3	
18 + 6 / 2 + 4	
(18 + 6 / 2) + 4	
(15 − 5) / 2 * 5 + 12	
Where x = 16 + 2; ++x + 12	
Where x = 16 + 2; x++ + 12	
6 * 5 - 8 / 2	
100 % 15 - 2 * 3	

You can check your answers for this table by accessing the full, interactive graphic for this table on the book's accompanying CD-ROM. The title of the activity is "Java Precedence" in e-Lab Activities.

Arithmetic Calculations

The Java programmer needs to have a rudimentary understanding of how the Java language provides for storage of numbers. Numeric data types are divided into integers and real numbers. These are mathematical terms with very precise meanings and complex definitions.

Integers are sometimes described as counting numbers. Subsets of integers include whole numbers {0,1,2,3,4...} and natural numbers {1,2,3,4...}. The four integral data types defined by the Java language are **byte**, **short**, **int**, and **long**.

The mathematical definition of real numbers is beyond the scope of this course. A more common term for real numbers is decimal numbers. Real numbers are used to represent fractions. Any digits to the right of the decimal point are the fractional part of the number.

Floating-point and Integral numbers differ in how one visualizes the number line. In integral types, zero is a dividing point between negative and positive numbers. In a floating-point type, any number can be positive or negative, including zero and Infinity. The set of real numbers is instead divided by one, which, in the context of binary numbers, is expressed as 2^0. Everything to the left of 2^0 is a fraction. And everything to the right of 2^0 is a whole number.

Another important concept to consider when working with numeric data types is the precision of numbers. All primitive numeric data types have fixed-length precision. This means that an **int** or **float** has only four bytes of storage to work with (32 bits), and **long** or **double** have eight bytes. There is a limit to how large or how small a number you can store using a fixed amount of storage. If you exceed the limit in integral types, this is said to overflow or underflow. If you exceed that limit in a floating-point type, you reach zero or infinity.

There are some general guidelines to consider when creating arithmetic expressions:

- Use parentheses to avoid ambiguity.
- Consider the size of resulting values. Integral and floating-point data types have a range of values that they can store. The range of values for integral types were introduced in Chapter 3, "Java Language Elements." The minimum and maximum values for each of the integral data types are as follows:
  - **byte**   –128 and 127
  - **short**   –32768 and 32767
  - **int**   –2147483648 and 2147483647
  - **long** –9223372036854775808L and 9223372036854775807L

For example, the following calculations would result in a number larger than the maximum value allowed in a byte. This would result in numeric overflow at runtime:

byte x = 127, y = 127, z;

z = x + y ;

However, changing the variable z to an int variable:

byte x = 127, y = 127;

int z = x + y ;

would enable the variable z to hold the result of the expression.

- Consider the possible loss of precision. When deciding to use floating-point types, consider three things:

  — Are exact results required? Here, the programmer is concerned more often with expecting results consistent with arithmetic taught in grade school.

  — Are exponential expressions involved? This is a more frequent consideration among scientists, astronomers, and engineers, and infrequent among main-stream business application programmers.

  — What is the required precision? Precision comes in three sizes: single precision (**float**), double precision (**double**), and arbitrary precision (`BigDecimal`). Precision is to the floating-point types what range is to integral types. Just as range is a deciding factor when deciding on which integral data type to use, the precision of a floating-point number can be understood as the significant digits measurement of precision to be an exact number. The term significant digits just means the number of digits in a numeric literal. It does not matter how many digits are before or after the decimal point. Trailing zeros do not count (leading zeros indicate octals, to which this discussion does not apply). The number 123.50 has four significant digits (1235); the number 12345678, 12345.678, and .12345678 all have 8 significant digits. Thus, the precision of floating-point literals is fixed. For example, a **float** is precise up to 8 significant digits, a **double** is precise up to 16 significant digits, and beyond, you use BigDecimal. The precision of values (positive or negative) for a **float** data type (8 significant digits) are 12345678, 12345.678, .12345678 and for a **double** data type (16 significant digits) are 1234567890123456, 1234567890.123456, and .1234567890123456.

- Use parentheses to avoid ambiguity.
- Consider the size of resulting values and the possible loss of precision or accuracy to the desired number of decimal places.

- Multiply first before dividing.
- When using negative numbers with modulus calculation, drop the negative signs from either operand and calculate the result. The sign of the left operand is the sign of the result.
- The + operator can be used to add numbers and concatenate `String` objects.
- Whereas most arithmetic operators have left-to-right association, unary operators (excluding postfix increment and postfix decrement) are evaluated right to left.

  Example: x + y or "Mary" + "Martin"

Use Table 4-6 to determine the results of the various code statements presented.

Table 4-6 Overflow Exercise

Code Fragment	Result

``java
public static void main(String[] args) {
    int x;
    int a = 6;
    int b = 7;
    x = a++;
    x = ++b;
    b += ++a;
    x = a++ + b++;
    int y =0;
    y += x;
    --y;
    a = --x;
}
``
	Value of x is 0.
	Value of a is 6.
	Value of b is 7.
	Value of x is ____; a is ____.
	Value of x is ____; b is ____.
	Value of a is ____; b is ____.
	Value of x is ____; a is ____;
	b is ____.
	Value of y is ____.
	Value of x is ____; y is ____.
	Value of y is ____.
	Value of x is ____; a is ____.

``java
public static void main(String[] args) {
    int a = 4567, b = 1237,
        c, d;
    c = a * b / b;
    d = a / b * b;
}
``
	Value of c is ____.
	Value of d is ____.

You can check your answers for this table by accessing the full, interactive graphic for this table on the book's accompanying CD-ROM. The title of the activity is "Overflow Exercise" in e-Lab Activities.

The example in Example 4-10 illustrates that a programmer needs to pay careful attention to data type and order of operations to ensure that correct values are stored in an object.

Example 4-10 *A Sample Program*

```
1 /**
2  * Demonstrates Arithmetic Calculations
3  * @author Cisco Teacher
4  * @version 2002
5  */
6 public class Example
7 {
8      public static void main (String[] args)
9      {
10         // initialize instance variables
11         int a = 4567, b = 1237, c, d;
12
13         c = a * b / b;
14         d = a / b * b;
15         System.out.println();
16         System.out.println(a + " * " + b + " / " + b + " = " + c);
17         System.out.println(a + " / " + b + " * " + b + " = " + d);
18
19         // reverse the variable's values
20         a = 1237; b = 4567;
```

NOTE

The full version of the abbreviated code shown in this example can be viewed using the book's accompanying CD-ROM.

The output from this code is shown in Figure 4-1.

Using Table 4-7, complete the sentences describing operator guidelines. Use one of the following terms to complete each sentence:

- precision
- String
- parentheses
- negative

You can check your answers by accessing the full, interactive graphic for this table on the book's accompanying CD-ROM. The title of the activity is "Arithmetic Operator Guidelines" in e-Lab Activities.

Figure 4-1 Program Output

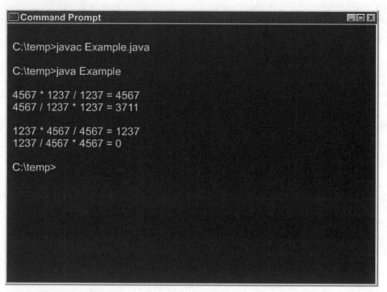

```
C:\temp>javac Example.java

C:\temp>java Example

4567 * 1237 / 1237 = 4567
4567 / 1237 * 1237 = 3711

1237 * 4567 / 4567 = 1237
1237 / 4567 * 4567 = 0

C:\temp>
```

Table 4-7 Arithmetic Operator Guidelines

Arithmetic Operator Guideline
To make your intentions less ambiguous, use _____ to force the order of operations.
Try to predict the size of resulting values for calculations and use an appropriate data type to avoid loss of _____.
When negative numbers are used in a modulus calculation, the negative signs from both operands should be removed. If the left operand is negative, the result will be _____.
The + operator is an overloaded operator. It can be used to add two numbers or combine two _____ objects.

Boolean Data

Boolean logic is based on true or false comparisons. Like numeric data types, a *boolean data type* can hold different values at different times. However, **boolean** variables can hold only two literal values: **true** or **false**. The code shown in Example 4-11 is an example of the declaration and initialization of a **boolean** data type variable.

Example 4-11 *Boolean Data*

```
 1 // The following statements assign data to boolean variables
 2 /*
 3 this statement declares the variable 'truth' as boolean and
 4 assigns it the value true
 5 */
 6 boolean truth = true;
 7
 8 // isNew is a boolean variable
 9 boolean  isNew;  // declares the variable
10 isNew = false;  // assign the value false
11
12 //The following two statements are INCORRECT
13 isNew = 0;  //error 0 is not a boolean value
14 isNew = 1;  //  error 1 is not a boolean value
```

Comparison and Logical Operators

The Java language supports six *comparison operators*. Use Table 4-8 to identify whether the expressions in Columns 2 and 3 are **true** or **false**.

Table 4-8 Comparison and Logical Operators

Operator	Expression 1	Expression 2
< (less than)	3 < 8 _____	8 > 3 _____
> (greater than)	2 > 4 _____	4 > 2 _____
== (equal to)	7 == 8 _____	7 == 7 _____
<= (less than or equal to)	5 <= 5 _____	8 <= 6 _____
>= (greater than or equal to)	7 >= 3 _____	1 >= 2 _____
!= (not equal)	5 != 5 _____	4 != 3 _____

You can check your answers by accessing the full, interactive graphic for this table on the book's accompanying CD-ROM. The title of the activity is "Comparison and Logical Operators" in e-Lab Activities.

Values can be assigned to **boolean** variables based on the results of comparisons. These examples show the use of such assignments. When using any of these operators that have two symbols (==, >=, <=, !=), no whitespace can exist between the symbols.

Expressions using arithmetic operators result in numbers, and expressions using comparison operators result in the **boolean** value of **true** or **false**. Table 4-9 presents several comparison expressions. Evaluate each to its **boolean** result of either **true** or **false**.

Table 4-9 Comparison and Logical Operators

Expression	Result
4 > 1	
43 >= 43	
2 == 3	
2 + 5 == 7	
3 + 8 <= 10	
4 > 1	
3 != 9	
13 != 13	
-4 != 4	
2 + 5 * 3 == 21	

You can check your answers by accessing the full, interactive graphic for this table on the book's accompanying CD-ROM. The title of the activity is "Comparison and Logical Operators" in e-Lab Activities.

Comparison and logical operators return a **boolean** result that is **true** or **false**. They commonly are used to form conditions. Testing conditions and using the **boolean** result of the test to decide on the next step or next instruction can alter the execution sequence of instructions in a method. Comparison operators and logical operators are used in **if**, **for**, and **while** statements. These are further explored in the section on logic.

Three types of comparisons exist, as shown in Table 4-10.

Table 4-10 Comparison and Logical Operators

Type	Symbols	Examples
Ordinal. Tests the relative values of two numeric operands.	< (less than) > (greater than) >= (greater than or equal to) <= (less than or equal to)	x=10, y=20, a=10, b=20. x < y results in the **boolean true**. x > y results in the **boolean false**. x >= a and y >= b results in **boolean true**. a >= b or y >= x results in **boolean true** a <= b results in **boolean true**. y <= a results in **boolean false**.
Equality.	== != (not equal)	a == x results in **boolean true**. a == y results in **boolean false**. a != b results in **boolean true**. a != x results in **boolean false**.
Object-type.	**instanceof** keyword determines whether the run-time type of an object is of a particular class or subclass. *Note:* Object comparisons can also be made by using specialized methods in the object, named the equals method.	Student s1 = new Student(); if(s1 instanceof Student) results in **boolean true.**

The **boolean** data or **boolean** results of multiple comparisons can be evaluated further using logical operators (***boolean** logical operators*). The logical operators provided for operations on **boolean** are *& AND* operation, *| OR* operation, *^ exclusive XOR* operation, short-circuit operator *&& (logical AND)*, short-circuit operator *|| (logical OR)*, and the not operator !, as shown in Table 4-11.

Table 4-11 Comparison and Logical Operators

Operator	Boolean Operations	Examples

& (AND)	op1 & op2 = result
	true & **true** = **true**
	false & **true** = **false**
	true & **false** = **false**
	false & **false** = **false**
	op1 and op2 are operands.
		int x = 10, y = 20,
		        a = 10, b = 30;
		if ((x < y) & (x > b))
		x < y **true**, x > b **false**;
		Result is **false**.
		Each condition test is an operand for the & operation.

l (OR)	op1 l op2 = result
	true l **true** = **true**
	false l **true** = **true**
	true l **false** = **true**
	false l **false** = **false**
	op1 and op2 are operands.
		int x = 10, y = 20,
		        a = 10, b = 30;
		if ((x < y) l (x > b))
		x < y **true**, x > b **false**
		Result is **true**.
		Each condition test is an operand for the l operation.

^ (XOR)	op1 ^ op2 = result
	true ^ **true** = **false**
	false ^ **true** = **true**
	true ^ **false** = **true**
	false ^ **false** = **false**
		int x = 10, y = 20,
		        a = 10, b = 30;
		if ((x < y) ^ (x > b))
		x < y **true**, x > b **false**
		Result is **true**.
		Each condition test is an operand for the ^ operation.

&& (short-circuit AND)	op1 && op2 = result If op1 is **false**, the result is **false** without regard for op2.	
ll (short-circuit OR)	op1 ll op2 = result If op1 is **true**, the result is **true** without regard for op2.	
!	!op1 = result If op1 is **true**, the result is **false**. If op1 is **false**, the result is **true**.	

The operators && (defined as AND) and || (defined as OR) perform short-circuit logical expressions, as shown in Example 4-12. The ^ operator, also known as the exclusive or (XOR) operator, results in **true** when either operand is **true**, but results in **false** when both operands are **true** or both operands are **false**.

Example 4-12 *Comparison and Logical Operators*

```
Student  s1;
if ((s1 != null) && (s1.grade > 90))
{
    // set lettergrade to A
    s1.letterGrade("A");
}
```

The **boolean** expression that forms the argument to the **if**() statement is legal and entirely safe. This is because the second subexpression is skipped when the first subexpression is **false**. The entire expression is always **false** when the first subexpression is **false**, regardless of how the second subexpression evaluates.

Similarly, if the || operator is used and the first expression returns **true**, the second expression is not evaluated because the whole expression already is known to be **true**.

The && and || operators accept **boolean** operands and evaluate the right operand if the outcome is not certain based solely on the left operand. This is determined using the identities shown in Example 4-13.

Example 4-13 *Comparison and Logical Operators*

```
false AND X = false
true OR X = true
where X is a boolean that can be either true or false.
```

In Table 4-12, each pair of comparison expressions is operated on using a logical operator. Assess the **boolean** result of the entire expression as either **true** or **false**.

You can check your answers by accessing the full, interactive graphic for this table on the book's accompanying CD-ROM. The title of the activity is "Comparison and Logical Operators" in e-Lab Activities.

Table 4-12 Comparison and Logical Operators

Expression	Result
Assume that a variable z has been assigned the value 12. What would be the result of these statements?	
z > 3 && z > 6	
z > 3 && z < 20	
z > 3 && z < 0	
Assume that the variable z has been assigned the value 2.	
z > 3 && z > 6	
z > 0 && z > 1	
z < 7 && z == 2	
Assume that the variable z has been assigned the value 5.	
z > 6 ‖ z == 5	
z < 3 ‖ z > 4	
z >= 0 ‖ z < 2	

Conditional Operator

Consider the assignments shown in Example 4-14.

Example 4-14 *Conditional Operator*

```
int score = 20;
char scorelevel;
scorelevel = score >20?'A':'B';
```

The assignment of a value to scorelevel is conditional on whether score is greater than 20. If score is greater than 20, "A" is stored in scorelevel. If score is not greater than 20, "B" is stored in scorelevel. The example shows that different values can be assigned to the same variable by using a conditional operator. The syntax for the *conditional operator* is shown in Example 4-15.

Example 4-15 *Conditional Operator*

The syntax for the conditional operator ?: is

    condition?true value:else value

    condition?—A **boolean** expression or value

    true value—The value to be assigned if the **boolean**
    expression results in **true**

    else value—The value to be assigned if the **boolean**
    expression results in **false**

The conditional operator ?: is also known as a ternary operator. Most operators use only two operands. Ternary uses three operands.

The three operands are condition, true value, and else value.

The following are guidelines for using the conditional operator:

- Syntax is a = x ? b : c;.
- The data type value of x must be **boolean,** or x must be an expression that results in a **boolean** value.
- The data type value for b and c must be compatible with a.
- An **if** statement can do the same task as a conditional operator.
- The value of a will be the value of b if the condition is **true,** but will be c if the condition is **false.**

Evaluate the code shown in Example 4-16.

Example 4-16 *Conditional Operator*

```
double y;
int  x=4;
y = x > 4 ? 99.99 : 9 ;
```
The value of x is _____

The value of y is _____
```
y = x++ > 4 ? 99.99 : 9;
```
The value of x is _____

The value of y is _____

You can check your answers by accessing the full, interactive graphic for this example on the book's accompanying CD-ROM. The title of the activity is "Conditional Operators" in e-Lab Activities.

Bitwise Operators

Bitwise operators are also referred to as bitwise shift operators and bitwise logical operators. The *bitwise shift operators* perform bit shifts of the binary representation of the left operand.

The operands should be integral types that are generally **int** or **long**.

Consider the 32-bit representation of an **int** value 10540 shown in the following example:

```
number is 10540
0 0 0 0 0 0 0 0 0 0 0 0 0 0 0 0 0 0 1 0 1 0 0 1 0 0 1 0 1 1 0 0
0 0 0 0 0 0 0 0 0 0 0 0 0 0 0 0 1 0 1 0 0 0 0 1 0 1 1 0 0 0 0
number is 10540
0 0 0 0 0 0 0 0 0 0 0 0 0 0 0 0 0 0 1 0 1 0 0 1 0 0 1 0 1 1 0 0
0 0 0 0 0 0 0 0 0 0 0 0 0 0 0 0 0 0 0 1 0 1 0 0 1 0 0 1 0 1 1
number is 10540
0 0 0 0 0 0 0 0 0 0 0 0 0 0 0 0 0 0 1 0 1 0 0 1 0 0 1 0 1 1 0 0
0 0 0 0 0 0 0 0 0 0 0 0 0 0 0 0 0 0 0 1 0 1 0 0 1 0 0 1 0 1 1
```

What is the number represented by each of the shifts shown in Table 4-13? Note that the sign of the number is retained in each of these shift operations.

Table 4-13 Bitwise Operations

Bitwise Shift	Result
10540 << 2	
-10540 << 2	
10540 >> 5	
-10540 >> 5	

TIP

To see how bitwise manipulations are useful for managing a set of **boolean** flags, refer to http://java.sun.com/docs/books/tutorial/java/nutsandbolts/bitwise.html.

You can check your answers by accessing the full, interactive graphic for this example on the book's accompanying CD-ROM. The title of the activity is "Bitwise Operations" in e-Lab Activities.

Collections of bits sometimes are used to save storage space where several **boolean** values are needed, or to represent the states of a collection of binary input from physical devices. For example, the results of a survey whose answers to the questions are yes or no could be saved as **boolean** values and operated on with bitwise logical operators.

The *bitwise logical operators* are shown in Table 4-14.

Table 4-14 Bitwise Operations

Operator	Explanation	Bit Operation
| & (AND) | 1 and 1 produces 1; all others produce 0. | ```
  00110011
& 11110000
  00110000
``` |
| \| (OR) | 0 and 0 produces 0; all others produce 1. | ```
  00110011
| 11110000
  11110011
``` |
| ^ (XOR) | 1 XOR 0 produces 1, as does 0 XOR 1. All others produce 0. | ```
  00110011
^ 11110000
  11000011
``` |

In the following example, determine the results of each bitwise operation on the **int** variable y (where int y = 10540;).

ntify the I's and 0's for the shaded areas to reflect the results the bitwise operators, and calculate the resulting value.																																						
	0	0	0	0	0	0	0	0	0	0	0	0	0	0	0	0	0	0	1	0	1	0	0	1	0	0	1	0	1	1	0	0					10540
1	0	0	0	0	0	0	0	0	0	0	0	0	0	0	0	0	0	0																			
1	0	0	0	0	0	0	0	0	0	0	0	0	0	0	0	0	0	0																			
>4	0	0	0	0	0	0	0	0	0	0	0	0	0	0	0	0	0	0	0	0	0	0															

You can check your answers by accessing the full, interactive graphic for this example on the book's accompanying CD-ROM. The title of the activity is "Bitwise Operations" in e-Lab Activities.

Concepts of Casting and Conversion

As a programmer, you might need to assign (or cast) the value of one primitive data type to a variable of another primitive data type. This section covers casting and conversion.

Casting and Conversion

Casting operations with primitive data types consists of assigning a value of one type (such as an **int** or a **double**) to a variable of another type (such as a **long** or a **short**). If the two types are compatible, Java performs the conversion automatically. For
```

example, an **int** value can always be assigned to a **long** variable. When information would be lost in an assignment, the compiler requires that the user confirm the assignment with a typecast. This can be done, for example, when "squeezing" a **long** value into an **int** variable. This is called explicit casting. Explicit casting is shown in Example 4-17, where the 64-bit representation of the **long** variable bigValue is cast into the 32-bit representation of the **short** variable c.

Example 4-17 *Casting and Conversion*

```
long bigValue = 99L;
int squashed = ((int)bigValue);
```

The desired target type is placed in parentheses and used as a prefix to the expression that must be modified. Although it might not be necessary, it is advisable to enclose the entire expression to be cast inside parentheses. Otherwise, the precedence of the cast operation can cause problems.

As shown in Example 4-18, variables can be promoted automatically to a longer form (such as **int** to **long**) when there would be no loss of information.

Example 4-18 *Casting and Conversion*

```
long bigval = 6;    // 6 is an int type, OK
int smallval = 99L;// 99L is a long, illegal
double z = 12.414F;// 12.414F is float, OK
float z1 = 12.414; // 12.414 is double, illegal.  Floating
                         point numbers (like 12.414) by
                         default, are stored as a double.
int y = 3.1415926; // 3.1415926 is not an int;  It requires
                         casting and the decimal portion will
                         be truncated.
float z = 3.14156; // Can't assign a double into a float;
                         This requires casting. Floating point
                         numbers (like 3.14156) by default, are
                         stored as a double.
```

In general, an expression can be thought of as being assignment-compatible if the variable receiving the assignment has a data type that is at least as large (the number of bits) as the expression type.

For binary operators such as the + operator, when the two operands are of primitive numeric types, the result of the operation is promoted to either the wider type of the operands or an **int**. This is determined by which one is the wider type.

This might result in overflow or loss of precision, as shown in the code fragment in Example 4-19.

Example 4-19 *Casting and Conversion*

```
short a, b, c;
a = 1;
b = 2;
c = a + b;
```

The code in Example 4-19 causes an error because it raises a and b to **int** before operating on them. It then tries to assign the resulting **int** value to c, a **short**, which results in loss of precision. However, if c is declared as an **int**, or if a typecast is done as shown in Example 4-20, then the code works. The 32-bit representation of the expression (a + b) is cast into the 16-bit representation of the **short** variable c.

Example 4-20 *Casting and Conversion*

```
short a, b, c;
a = 1;
b = 2;
c = (short)(a + b);
```

No casts occur between integer types and the **boolean** type. Some languages, most notably C and C++, allow numeric values to be interpreted as logical values. This is not permitted in the Java programming language. When a **boolean** type is required, only **boolean** values (**true** and **false**) can be used.

Character and String Data

To represent textual data, Java provides two options. Text data can be represented as a single character stored in a primitive data type **char** or as a string of characters in an object of the classes String or StringBuffer. This section contains the following topics:

- Character data type
- Introduction to String and StringBuffer classes

Character Data Type

The *char data type* stores a single 16-bit Unicode character. It must have its literal (that is, the character) enclosed in single quotes ('), as in 'A' to represent the letter *A*.

Use the backslash (escape character) to represent the literal for nonprinting and special-meaning characters, as shown in Table 4-15.

Table 4-15 Character Data Type

NOTE

Note that you also can use Unicode to represent these nonprinting and special-meaning characters. For more information on Unicode, go to www.unicode.org.

Syntax	Description	Unicode
\b	Backspace	\u0008
\t	Tab	\u0009
\n	Linefeed	\u000a
\r	Carriage return	\u000d
\"	Double quote	\u0022
\'	Single quote	\u0027
\\	Backslash	\u005c

Some of the declarations and the assignment of **char** data are shown in Example 4-21.

Example 4-21 *Character Data Type*

```
Char letterGrade = 'C'; // declares a primitive letterGrade
                           and assigns a value C
char choice1, choice2;  // declares two primitives
choice1 = 'Y';          // assigns primitive choice1  Y
choice2 = 'n';          // assigns primitive choice2  n
```

Introduction to `String` and `StringBuffer` Class

Java provides two core classes for the storing and manipulation of textual data: the `String` and `StringBuffer` classes. This section covers these two classes briefly. Chapter 6, "System, String, StringBuffer, Math, and Wrapper Classes," explores all the methods and attributes of these classes. The classes are introduced at this stage because some of the data needs to be stored as text. Additionally, the System class member out and its method println are used to print the data. As mentioned in previous chapters, the println method accepts a String as its argument. Thus, even the simplest of tasks to print data requires some understanding of the String class.

String

A simple definition of a *String* is the collection of one or more Unicode characters stored in an object. All **char** data types store a single Unicode character, which are enclosed in single quotes.

String objects are immutable. After a String object is created, its value cannot change. For example, consider the code shown in Example 4-22.

Example 4-22 *Immutable* String

```
String aphrase = "Teacher";
aphrase = "Teacher" + " Loves teaching ";
```

In this example, the reference variable aphrase is assigned the string of characters "Teacher". Note that String literals are always enclosed in double quotes ("). In the second statement, the String object's data is changed to add the phrase "Loves teaching". Actually, the JVM makes a copy of the data in the object and creates a new object that will contain the result of the operation of adding the two String objects. The reference to this new object is assigned to the reference variable aphrase. The + operator in Java is considered an "overloaded" operator. The concept of overloading is explored in Chapter 5, "Basics of Defining and Using Classes." A simple definition of *overloading* in Java is that the operator or method can perform more than the same action with different types of data. In this example, the + operator, which was used in adding numeric data, can also be used to combine String objects. This often is referred to as *concatenation*. The + operator is the only overloaded operator in the Java language.

Some guidelines for using String objects are shown in Example 4-23.

Example 4-23 String *Objects*

```
1 //Create Strings for fixed string data
2 String s = "text";
3 String s = new String("text");
4
```

continues

Example 4-23 String *Objects (Continued)*

```
 5 //Strings can be concatenated using the + operator
 6 String s = "Now";
 7 String s2 = "Then";
 8 String phrase = s + " and " + s2;
 9
10 //The System.out.println() method accepts a String as its argument
11 System.out.println(s + " and " + s2);
```

StringBuffer Class

Because `String` objects are immutable and cannot be changed, concatenation operations on `String` objects are memory-intensive. The Java core class *StringBuffer* provides for the storage of string data that will change. Use of the `StringBuffer` class generally is recommended to store string data that will change.

In a `Teacher` object, for example, the name of the course probably would not change, but the name of the teacher might. In this case, use the `StringBuffer` object to store the `Teacher` name and the `String` object to store the course name.

Control Structures

No matter what procedure or progression of logical actions the computer is to perform, all programming logic can be broken down into one of three control structures: sequence, selection or decision, and repetition. This section consists of the following topics:

- Decision making and repetition
- Logic
- Multiple-condition **if**
- Nested **if**
- **switch** statements
- Loop
- **do**-**while** statement
- **while** statement
- **for** statement
- Use of **break**, **continue**, and label

Decision Making and Repetition

A *control structure* is a standard progression of logical steps to control the execution sequence of statements. The purpose of these structures is to define the logic flow of the procedure. All these structures can nest inside each other. A sequence structure can nest inside a selection, a selection and sequence can nest inside a repetition, and so on.

An important distinction between object-oriented languages and procedural languages is that control structures are used only in the methods of a class. In procedural languages, the entire program implements control structures. Procedural programming languages impose a textual order to the execution of instructions. The program will begin executing at the first statement and continue sequentially until a control structure is encountered that causes the program to change the flow of execution. In object-oriented programming, the textual order of instructions is imposed with a method. In a class definition, the textual order of method definitions (that is, the order in which methods are defined) are a matter of coding convention and do not impose a specific sequence or order by which the methods will be executed. In a class definition, methods can be organized in any order. Some programmers prefer to organize it alphabetically, and some prefer to organize by actions, using classifications such as "setters" and "getters." An object's methods are called in no particular order. However, the instructions inside a method are procedural. A Java programmer employs control structures inside a method.

Chapter 3 introduced the Student and Teacher classes. This section adds a new attribute (pointsEarned) and a new method (getPoints()) to the Student class, as shown in Example 4-24.

Example 4-24 *Decision Making and Repetition*

```
1  /** Student Class establishes the student id, name and grade
2   *  @author Cisco Teacher
3   *  @version 2002
4   */
5  public class Student
6  {
7       private final String studentName;
8       private String grade;
9       private int pointsEarned;
10      private int studentID;
11      public static final int courseNumber = 12345;
12
```

NOTE

The full version of the abbreviated code shown in this example can be viewed using the book's accompanying CD-ROM.

continues

Example 4-24 *Decision Making and Repetition (Continued)*

```
13      // null constructor
14      public Student( )
15      {
16         studentName = "";
17      }
18
19      // constructor with 2 arguments
20      /**
```

These additions will be used to demonstrate decision-making and repetition control structures, using the main method of the Teacher class. The current Teacher class is shown in Example 4-25.

Example 4-25 *Decision Making and Repetition*

```
 1 /** Teacher Class creates students
 2  *   @author Cisco Teacher
 3  *   @version 2002
 4  */
 5 public class Teacher
 6 {
 7    // Main method
 8            public static void main(String[] args)
 9            {
10                  Student s1, s2, s3, s4;
11                  s1 = new Student();
12                  s2 = new Student();
13                  s3 = new Student("Mary Jane", "A");
14                  s4 = new Student("Mary Martin", "B", 12345);
15            }
16 }// End of Teacher class
```

Logic

The most basic control structure is *sequence*. In Example 4-26, the actions are performed in sequence until all actions have completed successfully.

Example 4-26 *Sequence Logic*

```
 1 /** Teacher Class creates students
 2  *  @author Cisco Teacher
 3  *  @version 2002
 4  */
 5 // sample code version 1
 6 public class Teacher
 7 {
 8    public static void main (String[ ] args)
 9    {
10       int totalPoints = 200;
11       Student s1=  new Student("Mary Martin", "B", 12345);
12       int score = s1.getPoints() * 100 / totalPoints;
13       System.out.println("Student name is " + s1.getName() +
14       " and grade percentage is " + s1.getPoints() + "%");
15    }
16 }
```

The *selection control structure* is used to tell a program which action to perform based on a certain condition. Two types of selection control are used in Java: **if**-then-**else** structures and **case** control or **switch** structures.

The *repetition control structure* is used to instruct the computer to repeatedly perform a set of actions. This structure also is called looping or iteration (which means "to repeat"). Three repetition structures are available in Java: **for** <loop>, **while** <loop>, and **do** <loop>.

if Statement

Conditional statements allow for the selective execution of portions of the program according to the value of some expressions. The Java programming language supports the *if statement* for two-way alternatives, as shown in Figure 4-2.

In an **if** statement, actions are performed based on a certain condition. The condition is a **boolean** expression or a **boolean** value. Therefore, the condition must evaluate to a **true** or **false**.

Figure 4-2 `if` Statement

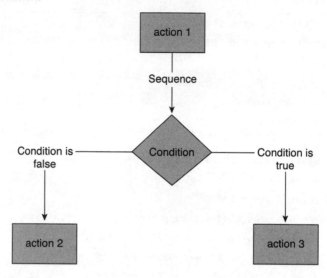

The basic syntax for an **if-else** statement is shown in Example 4-27.

Example 4-27 `if` *Statement Syntax*

```
1  /*
2  The basic syntax for an if/else statement is as follows:
3
4    if (boolean expression)
5    {
6      statement or block;
7    }
8    else
9    {
10     statements;
11   }
12 */
13 //an example
14 int a = 1;
15 int b = 2;
16
17 if(a < b)
18 {
```

Example 4-27 *if Statement Syntax (Continued)*

```
19   System.out.println("a is less than b");
20 }
21 else
22 {
23   System.out.println("a is not less than b");
24 }
```

When using a nested **if**, the short-circuit operator can also be used instead of an **if** statement, as shown in Example 4-28.

Example 4-28 *if Statement*

```
// sample code using if statements
String s = "Student Name";
if(s != null) {
    if(s.length() <= 20) {
        System.out.println(s);
    }
}
// sample code using the short-circuit operators
String s = "Student Name";
if(s != null) && (s.length() <= 20) {
    System.out.println(s);
}
```

In some instances, the conditional operator can be used instead of an **if** statement, as shown in Example 4-29.

Example 4-29 *if Statement*

```
// Examples using the Conditional Operator
 2 // sample code version 1
 3 public class Teacher
 4 {
 5     public static void main (String[ ] args)
 6     {
 7         int totalPoints = 200;
```

continues

Example 4-29 `if` *Statement (Continued)*

```
8              Student s1=  new Student("Mary Martin", "B", 12345);
9              int score = s1.getPoints() * 100 / totalPoints;
10             if(score >= 70 )
11             { s1.setGrade("P"); }
12             else
13             { s1.setGrade("F"); }
14        }
15 }
16
17 // sample code version 2
18 public class Teacher
19 {
20     public static void main (String[ ] args)
21     {
22         int totalPoints = 200;
23         Student s1=  new Student("Mary Martin", "B", 12345);
24         int score = s1.getPoints() * 100 / totalPoints;
25         String lgrade = (score >=70) ? "P" : "F";
26         s1.setGrade(lgrade);
27     }
28 }
29
30 // sample code version 3
31 public class Teacher
32 {
33     public static void main (String[ ] args)
34     {
35         int totalPoints = 200;
36         Student s1=  new Student("Mary Martin", "B", 12345);
37         int score = s1.getPoints() * 100 / totalPoints;
38         s1.setGrade( (score >=70) ? "P" : "F");
39     }
40 }
41
```

All three of the Teacher class examples contained the following assignment:

```
int score = s1.getPoints() * 100 / totalPoints;
```

Although the division and multiplication operators have the same group precedence and are left-to-right–associative, this statement might be more easily understood using parentheses:

```
int score = (s1.getPoints() * 100) / totalPoints;
```

This reinforces that the student's points, multiplied by 100, are being divided by the totalPoints to generate a percentage.

Multiple-Condition `if`

The **if** statement also can be used to chain a series of conditions, as shown in Figure 4-3.

Figure 4-3 `if-else` Structure

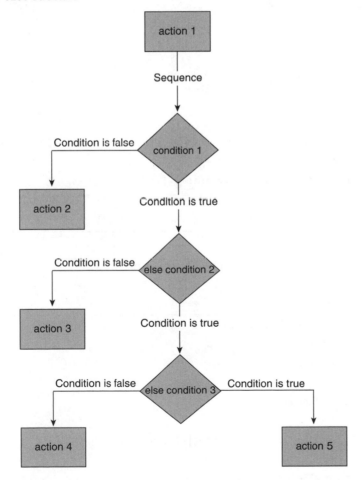

The basic syntax for a multiple-condition **if** structure is shown in Example 4-30.

Example 4-30 **if-else** *Structure*

```
1 /*
2 The syntax for multiple conditions is as follows:
3
4   if (Boolean expression)
5     {statement or block;}
6   else if (Boolean expression)
7     {statement or block;}
8   else
9     {statement or block;}
10
11 */
12
13 int a = 3;
14 int b = 2;
15 int c = 1;
16
17 if(a < b)
18 {System.out.println("a is less than b");}
19 else if(a < c)
20 {System.out.println("a is less than c");}
21 else
22 {System.out.println("a is not less than b or c");}
```

Sample code using **if** structures is shown in Example 4-31.

Example 4-31 **if-else** *Code*

```
1 /** Teacher Class creates students
2  *  @author Cisco Teacher
3  *  @version 2002
4  */
5 public class Teacher
6 {
7    public static void main (String[ ] args)
8    {
9        int totalPoints = 200;
```

Example 4-31 `if-else` *Code (Continued)*

```
10       Student s1=  new Student("Mary Martin", "B", 12345);

11       int score = s1.getPoints() * 100 / totalPoints;

12       if (score >= 90)

13          { s1.setGrade("A"); }

14        else if (score >= 80 )

15           { s1.setGrade("B"); }

16        else if (score >= 70)

17           { s1.setGrade("C"); }

18        else

19           { s1.setGrade("P"); }   //everyone passes this course

20     }

21 }//end Teacher class

22
```

Nested `if`

The nesting of `if` can be noted as a flowchart, as shown in Figure 4-4.

Figure 4-4 Nested `if`

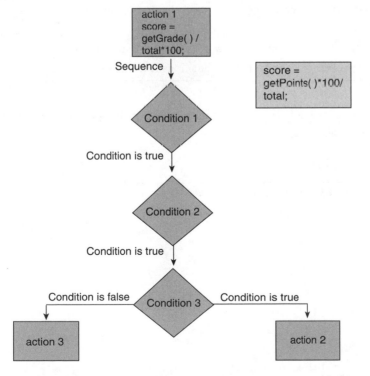

The flowchart from Figure 4-4 is implemented with the nested **if** structure in Example 4-32.

Example 4-32 *Nested* **if**

```
1  /*
2   if (Boolean condition)
3    if (Boolean condition)
4       if (Boolean condition)
5         { statements }
6         else { statements }
7 */
8
9 int a = 1;
10 int b = 2;
11 int c = 3;
12 ind d = 4;
13 if(a < b)
14   if(a < c)
15     if(a < d)
16       {System.out.println("a is less than b, c, and d");}
17     else
18       {System.out.println("a is less than b and c");
19         System.out.println("a is not less than d");}
```

This conditional testing is the same as using the & or && operators. The same code could be written as shown in Example 4-33.

Example 4-33 *Nested* **if**

```
if(condition1) && (condition2 ) && (condition 3 )
{
    statement;
}
else
{
    statement;
}
```

Example 4-33 *Nested* `if` *(Continued)*

```
Sample Code:
if((cookies > 144) && (cakes > 36) && (breadLoaves > 144))
{
    System.out.println("The baker has finished his daily
    baking requirements.");
}
else
{
    System.out.println("The baker is still baking.");
}
```

The use of braces to enclose a block of statements is strongly recommended, although it is not required if a single statement is executed. In Example 4-34, Statement 1 is executed if the condition is **true**. Statement 2 is executed all the time.

Example 4-34 *Nested* `if`

```
if(condition)
    Statement1 ;
    Statement2 ;
Sample Code:
if(tirePressure < 32)
    System.out.println("Add air to the car's tire.");
    System.out.println("Drive Safely."); //this line will print
                                          //regardless of the
                                          //tirePressure value
```

The lack of braces makes the sequence of the code unclear, and a programmer might have difficulty tracing the logic of the program to correct errors or problems. The correct use of braces is shown in Example 4-35.

Example 4-35 *Nested* `if`

```
if(condition)
{
    Statement1;
}
```

continues

Example 4-35 *Nested* **if** *(Continued)*

```
Statement2;


Sample Code:
if(tirePressure < 32)
{
    System.out.println("Add air to the car's tire.");
}
//much clearer code
System.out.println("Drive Safely.");
```

switch Statements

switch statements are also known as branching statements, or *case-control statements*. This is a special kind of selection-control structure that allows for more than two choices when the condition is evaluated.

The basic **switch** control syntax is shown in Example 4-36.

Example 4-36 **switch** *Syntax*

```
switch (expr1){
   case constant1:
      statements;
      break;
   case constant2:
      statements;
      break;
   default:
      statements;
      break;
}
```

Several keywords and symbols must be used in the **switch** control structure.

switch

switch begins the selection. The open brace follows the expression.

case

For each **case**, the condition is equal to the constant. The colon (:) at the end of this statement is required.

break

A **break** ends the sequence of actions and exits from the **switch** control structure.

default

A **default** is the set of actions that will be executed if no match was found between the expression and each constant.

In the **switch** (expr1) statement, expr1 must be assignment-compatible with an **int**, **byte**, **short**, or **char** type. Floating-point, **long** expressions, or class references (including String objects) are not permitted. The optional **default** label specifies the code segment to be executed when the value of the variable or expression cannot match any of the **case** values. If there is no **break** statement, as in the last statement in the code segment for a certain **case**, the execution continues into the code segment for the next **case** without checking the **case** expression's value.

The sample code shown in Example 4-37 configures a Car object based on the **int** variable carModel. If the carModel variable is equal to the integer constant DELUXE (its value is 1), air conditioning is added to the car, as are a radio, wheels, and an engine. However, if the carModel variable is equal to the integer constant STANDARD (its value is 2), only a radio, wheels, and an engine are added.

Example 4-37 switch *Statements*

```
final static int DELUXE = 1;
final static int STANDARD = 2;


switch (carModel ){

  case DELUXE:
     addAirConditioning();
     addRadio();
     addWheels();
     addEngine();
     break;
```

continues

Example 4-37 `switch` *Statements (Continued)*

```
    case STANDARD:
       addRadio();
       addWheels();
       addEngine();
       break;

    default:
       addWheels();
       addEngine();
}
```

In this example, some methods are repeated, making them redundant. Reduce the redundant code by organizing the sequence of the **case** statements to use key methods in an incremental manner and eliminating the **break** statement. The syntax for this would be as shown in Example 4-38.

Example 4-38 `switch` *Syntax*

```
switch (expr1){

    case constant1:

            statement1;
            statement2;

    case constant2:

            statement3;
            statement4;

    case constant3:

            statement5;


}
```

The sample code in Example 4-39 eliminates the redundancy allowing the flow of control to descend through multiple **case** blocks. For example, if the carModel variable is equal to the integer constant THE_WORKS, the gold package and seven-way adjustable seats are added to this car, along with floor mats, air conditioning, a radio, a defroster, wheels, and an engine. However, if the carModel variable is equal to only the integer constant STANDARD, only a radio, a defroster, wheels, and an engine are added. Nine out of ten **switch** statements required breaks in each **case** block. Forgetting the **break** statement causes the most logical programming errors in using **switch** statements.

Example 4-39 switch *Statements*

```
switch ( carModel ) {

    case THE_WORKS:
        addGoldPackage();
        add7WayAdjustableSeats();

    case DELUXE:
        addFloorMats();
        addAirConditioning();

    case STANDARD:
        addRadio();
        addDefroster();

    default:
        addWheels();
        addEngine();

}
```

Example 4-40 provides an additional example illustrating why it might be useful to have **case** statements fall through. This code derives the number of days in a month.

Example 4-40 *Calculating the Days in a Month*

```
1 public class Test
2 {
3     public static void main(String[] args)
```

continues

Example 4-40 *Calculating the Days in a Month (Continued)*

TIP

The switch syntax evaluates either a **char**, an **int**, a **byte** or a **short** data type. Example 4-40 evaluates the variable month, which explicitly was declared and defined before the **switch** statement. The evaluation also can be against a returned value from a method or an expression, as long as the data type of the returned value (or expression) matches the data type of the **case** condition.

```
4      {
5          // initialize month and year
6          int month = 8;
7          int year = 2000;
8
9          // holds max days for the month in question
10         int numDays = 0;
11
12         switch (month)
13         {
14             case 1:
15             case 3:
16             case 5:
17             case 7:
18             case 8:
19             case 10:
20             case 12:
21             // months with 31 days
22                 numDays = 31;
23                 break;
24             case 4:
25             case 6:
26             case 9:
27             case 11:
28             // months with 30 days
29             numDays = 30;
30             break;
31             case 2:
32             // check for leap year
33             if ( ((year % 4 == 0) && !(year % 100 == 0))
34                 || (year % 400 == 0) )
35                 numDays = 29;
36             else
37                 numDays = 28;
38             break;
39         }
```

Example 4-40 *Calculating the Days in a Month (Continued)*

```
40          System.out.println("The number of days is " + numDays + ".");
41     }
42 }
```

The output is: `The number of days is 31.`

Loop

Loop structures allow for the repeated execution of blocks of statements. The Java programming language supports three types of loop constructs: *for*, *while*, and *do loops*. Before executing the loop body (a pretest loop), **for** and **while** loops test the loop condition. To check a condition after the loop executes, **do** loops (a post-test loop) are utilized. This implies that the **for** and **while** loops might not execute the loop body even once, whereas **do** loops execute the loop body at least once.

Use the **for** loop when the loop is to be executed a predetermined number of times. Use the **while** and **do** loops when this is not predetermined.

All loop structures have four elements or actions that occur, as listed here:

1. Initialization
2. Testing of a condition or expression
3. Execution of statements
4. Alteration of the condition or expression to exit the loop

Each loop structure implements these elements a little differently. Ignoring these elements is the major cause of logic problems. A programmer who uses these structures diligently must ensure that all four of these elements have been addressed.

do while Statement

The syntax for the **do while** loop structure is shown in Example 4-41.

Example 4-41 **do while** *Loop*

```
1 /*
2 This is the syntax for a do while loop
3
4   do {
5     statement or block;
```

continues

Example 4-41 `do while` *Loop (Continued)*

```
 6    } while (Boolean test);

 7

 8 */

 9

10 //an example

11 int i = 0;

12 do{

13    System.out.println("Are you finished yet?");

14    i++;

15    }while(i < 10);

16    System.out.println("Done");
```

The syntax describes two out of the three elements. The programmer inserts the other two elements. The initialization statement in a **do** loop is defined before the loop structure. This loop does a test before executing the statements. This loop executes at least once.

Note the statement i++; in the example. The **do** loop in this example is controlled by testing the value of the variable i. This variable was initialized on Line 11. If the i++; is omitted, this loop will execute endlessly. The control to stop a loop comes from changing the condition to **false**. In a **do** loop, the programmer must ensure that the condition will result in **false** at some point. The change in the value of i using the increment operator eventually will cause the value of i to equal 10. When this value equals 10, the loop will stop repeating the statement "Are you finished yet?" and will display the statement "Done".

When using **do** loops, ensure that the loop control variable is initialized appropriately, updated in the body of the loop, and properly tested.

while Statement

The syntax for the **while** loop is shown in Example 4-42.

Example 4-42 `while` *Loop*

```
1 /*

2 This is the syntax for a while loop

3

4   while (Boolean test)
```

Example 4-42 `while` *Loop (Continued)*

```
 5   {
 6     statement or block;
 7   }
 8
 9 */
10
11 //an example
12 int i = 0;
13 while(I < 10);
14 {
15   System.out.println("Are you finished yet?");
16   I++;//updates the control variable
17 }
18 System.out.println("Done");
```

Ensure that the loop control variable is initialized appropriately before the loop body begins execution, and ensure that the loop condition is **true** at the beginning if the loop must be entered at least once. The control variable must be updated appropriately to prevent an infinite loop.

for Statement

The syntax for the **for** loop structure is shown in Example 4-43.

Example 4-43 `for` *Loop*

```
 1 /*
 2 This is the syntax of a for loop
 3
 4   for (init_expr; Boolean test; alter_expr)
 5   {
 6     statement or block;
 7   }
 8
 9 */
10
11 //an example using one incremented variable
```

continues

Example 4-43 **for** *Loop (Continued)*

```
12 for(int i = 0; i < 10; i ++)
13 {
14   System.out.println("Are you finished yet?");
15 }
16 System.out.println("Done");
17
18 //an example using two incremented variables
19 for(int i = 0, j = 20; i < j; i++, j--)
20 {
21     System.out.println("Are you finished yet?");
22 }
23 System.out.println("Done");
```

In this example, **int** i is declared and defined within the **for** block.

The variable i is accessible only within the scope of this particular **for** block. The Java programming language allows the comma separator in the **for**() loop syntax. The last example shown is legal; it initializes both i and j to 0. After executing the loop body, it increments i and decrements j.

Use of break, continue, and Label

Use the following statements to further control loop statements:

- break [label];
- continue [label];
- [label:] statement;, where the statement should be a loop

Use the **break** statement to exit prematurely from **switch** statements, loop statements, and labeled blocks. Use the **continue** statement to skip over and jump to the end of the loop body, and then return control to the loop control statement.

The label statement identifies any valid statement to which control must be transferred. With regard to a labeled **break** statement, the label can identify any statement. With regard to a labeled **continue** statement, the label must identify a loop construct.

Use the **break** statement as it is used in Example 4-44. In this case, when the **if** condition is **true**, the **break** statement is executed and the flow of execution would go to the next statement after the loop structure, statement3. The code in statement 2 is not executed.

Example 4-44 *Use of* **break**, **continue**, *and* Label

```
do{
    statement1;
    if(boolean expression){
        break;
    }
    statement2;
}while(boolean expression);


statement3;
```

The use of the **continue** statement is shown in Example 4-45. In this case, when the **if** condition is **true**, flow of control goes directly to the **while** condition.

Example 4-45 *Use of* **break**, **continue**, *and* Label

```
do{
    statement1;
    if(boolean expression){
        continue;
    }
    statement2;
}while(boolean expression);
```

Example 4-46 shows the **break** statement with a label named outer. When the **if** condition is **true** (in the innermost **do** structure), the **break** statement is executed and control leaves the labeled block (the outermost **do** structure).

Example 4-46 *Use of* **break**, **continue**, *and* Label

```
outer:
do{
    statement;
    do{
        statement;
        if (boolean expression){
            break outer;
        }
```

continues

Example 4-46 *Use of* **break**, **continue**, *and* Label *(Continued)*

```
        statement;
    }while(boolean expression);
    statement;
}while(boolean expression);


statement;
```

Example 4-47 shows the **continue** statement with a label named test. When the **if** condition is true (in the innermost **do** structure), flow of control goes directly to the last **while** condition (of the outermost structure).

Example 4-47 *Use of* **break**, **continue**, *and* Label

```
test:
do{
    statement;
    do{
        statement;
        if (boolean expression){
            continue test;
        }
        statement;
    }while(boolean expression);
    statement;
}while(boolean expression);
```

Use Figure 4-5 to practice tracing the flow of the different loop control structures. How many times will each loop execute? In some cases, it could be an infinite number of times.

For Figure 4-5, you can check your answers by accessing the full, interactive graphic for this figure on the book's accompanying CD-ROM. The title of the activity is "Use of **break**, **continue**, and Label" in e-Lab Activities.

Figure 4-5 Use of **break**, **continue**, and *Label*

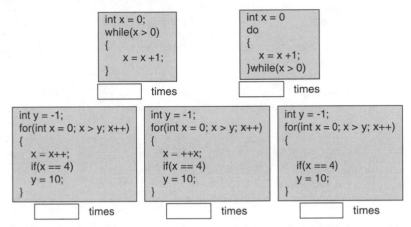

Exploring the `java.lang.System` **Class Member** `in` **and** `out`

Java provides the `System` class to access properties of the underlying operating system devices, including data from the keyboard and output to the display. This section primarily addresses the `java.lang.System` class.

The `java.lang.System` Class

Many features in Java can be used for obtaining input from users and printing output. Complex activities, such as accepting input on GUI screens or printing output to printers, require the use of the Java classes in the Swing and AWT (Abstract Window Toolkit) API.

Programmers must view the results of the class methods or input data and test object behaviors, so they need classes that can accept or read from simple input devices on the computer and display information to devices such as the console or screen.

In Java, data flowing in and out of a program is called a stream. Java provides the *System class* to access properties of the underlying operating system devices to stream data in and out of the program. The `System` class contains references to three useful objects: the static objects *in*, *out*, and *err*, as shown in Table 4-16. Static means that the value is based on the class—that is, no object is needed to use this member. Objects of the type `System` do not need to be created to access the member objects in, out, or err. These objects can send and receive data from default input and output devices. In general, the default input device is the keyboard, and the default output device is the screen.

Table 4-16 The java.lang.System **Class**

Class	Function	Methods Used	Default Device
System.in	Accepts data from the keyboard buffer	read()	Keyboard buffer
System.out	Sends output to the display or redirects to a designated file	print() println() flush()	Monitor
System.err	Sends output to the monitor, used for prompts and error messages	print() flush()	Monitor

The out object (an object of the class PrintStream) prints using either the print method or the println method. The code shown in Example 4-48 might be used in the Teacher class to generate a single line of output.

Example 4-48 *The* java.lang.System *Class*

```
System.out.print("Your Grade is "); // prints and does not
                                    // start a newline.


System.out.println("A"); // prints next to the previous
                         // text, and then starts a newline.
```

The in object (an object of the class InputStream) accepts a single character from the keyboard. The character is stored as an **int**. It is usually far more useful to provide a program with values at runtime, which is when the program is executing. A program that accepts values at runtime is interactive because it exchanges communication, or interacts, with the user. The programs seen thus far do not interact with the user. To support this interaction, there must be a way to get the input from the keyboard. The System.in object has methods to do that. Sample code of the in object is shown in Example 4-49.

Example 4-49 *The* java.lang.System *Class*

```
1 /** GetUserInput retrieves user input
2    *  @author Cisco Teacher
3    *  @version 2002
```

Example 4-49 *The* `java.lang.System` *Class (Continued)*

```
4    */
5    public class GetUserInput
6    {
7       public static void main (String[ ] args) throws Exception
8       {
9          char userInput;
10         System.out.print("Please enter a character: ");
11         userInput = (   char)System.in.read();
12         System.out.println("You entered " + userInput);
13      }
14   }
```

For Example 4-49, you can view the explanatory text by accessing the full, interactive graphic for this example on the book's accompanying CD-ROM. The title of the activity is "The java.lang.System Class" in e-Lab Activities.

Dissecting Sample Code

This section explores some sample code to help you better understand the use of operators and control structures.

Sample Code Using Operators and Control Structures

Review the code for the class `SuperRide`, shown in Example 4-50. Note the following explanations of the logic selection structures:

In Line 15, the outer **if** selection structure tests whether a rider is eligible to ride on the `SuperRide`.

In Line 20, the inner **if** selection structure tests whether the eligible rider is heavy enough to sit in the front seat.

Example 4-50 **if** *Structure*

```
1  /**
2   * SuperRide Class
3   * @author Cisco Teacher
4   * @version 2002
```

continues

Example 4-50 if *Structure (Continued)*

NOTE

The full version of the abbreviated code shown in this example can be viewed using the book's accompanying CD-ROM.

```
 5   */
 6   public class SuperRide
 7   {
 8     // Main method
 9     //Secures weight and height data for a potential rider and
10     //determines whether rider is eligible to ride on the SuperRide, and if
11     //so, if the rider can sit in the front row.
12     public static void main(String[] args)
13     {
14         int weight = Console.readInt("\nEnter your weight in pounds:");
15         int height = Console.readInt("Enter your height in inches:");
16         //checks for weight greater than 100 or height greater than 60 inches
17         if(weight > 100 || height > 60)
18         {
19             System.out.print("\nCongratulations, you can go on SuperRide");
20             if(weight > 150)
```

For Example 4-50, you can view the explanatory text by accessing the full, interactive graphic for this example on the book's accompanying CD-ROM. The title of the activity is "**if** Structure" in e-Lab Activities.

Review the code in Examples 4-51, 4-52, and 4-53 for three different loop structures (**for**, **while**, and **do while**), which produce the same results. The output for these loops is shown in Example 4-54.

Example 4-51 *Loop Structure—***for** *Loop*

NOTE

The full version of the abbreviated code shown in this example can be viewed using the book's accompanying CD-ROM.

```
1  /** ForLoopSquare Class
2   *   @author Cisco Teacher
3   */
4  public class ForLoopSquare
5  {
6          // Main method
7          // Request range of integers from user and then presents the square
8          // for each integer
9          public static void main(String[] args)
```

Example 4-51 *Loop Structure—***for** *Loop (Continued)*

```
10              {
11                      int start = Console.readInt
12                      ("\nEnter starting integer for loop:");
13                      int stop = Console.readInt
14                      ("Enter stopping integer for loop:");
15                      int increment = Console.readInt
16                      ("Enter increment integer for loop:");
17                      for(int i = start; i <= stop; i += increment)
18                      {
19                              System.out.println
20                              ("   The square of " + i + " is " + i * i);
```

Example 4-52 *Loop Structure—***while** *Loop*

```
 1 /** WhileSquare Class
 2  *   @author Cisco Teacher
 3  */
 4 public class WhileSquare
 5 {
 6       // Main method
 7       // Request range of integers from user and then presents the square
 8       // for each integer
 9       public static void main(String[] args)
10       {
11               int start = Console.readInt
12               ("\nEnter starting integer for loop:");
13               int stop = Console.readInt
14               ("Enter stopping integer for loop:");
15               int increment = Console.readInt
16               ("Enter increment integer for loop:");
17               int i = start;
18               while( i <= stop)
19               {
20                       System.out.println
```

NOTE

The full version of the abbreviated code shown in this example can be viewed using the book's accompanying CD-ROM.

Example 4-53 *Loop Structure—***do while** *Loop*

```
1  /** DoWhileSquare Class
2   *   @author Cisco Teacher
3   */
4  public class DoWhileSquare
5  {
6          // Main method
7          // Request range of integers from user and then presents the square
8          // for each integer
9          public static void main(String[] args)
10         {
11                 int start = Console.readInt
12                 ("\nEnter starting integer for loop:");
13                 int stop = Console.readInt
14                 ("Enter stopping integer for loop:");
15                 int increment = Console.readInt
16                 ("Enter increment integer for loop:");
17                 int i = start;
18                 do
19                 {
20                         System.out.println
```

Example 4-54 *Loop Structure—Output*

```
Enter starting integer for loop: -1
Enter stopping integer for loop: 12
Enter increment integer for loop: 3
    The square of -1 is 1
    The square of 2 is 4
    The square of 5 is 25
    The square of 8 is 64
    The square of 11 is 121
```

Review the code for the class GetUserName, shown in Example 4-55. Using loop and
logic, users can obtain input from the keyboard, test the value entered, and perform
some action based on the data entered. Note this statement on Line 17:

```
name += letter;
```

This line uses a `String` to modify the text for the user's name. In Chapter 6, we cover the classes `String` and `StringBuffer` in more detail. At this point, be aware that programmers should use the `StringBuffer` class to create and modify text data and, when the data is in its final form, store it in `String` objects. Example 4-56 incorporates the use of the more efficient `StringBuffer` class (in building the user's name) in the class `GetUserName1`.

Example 4-55 *Console Input and Selection Based on Input Using String Objects*

```
1 /** GetUserName Class
2 *   @author Cisco Teacher
3 */
4 public class GetUserName
5 {
6     public static void main (String args[]) throws Exception
7     {
8         String name = "";
9
10        System.out.print("Please enter your name, one character at a time
11        (enter the character '*' to end): ");
12        char letter = (char) System.in.read();
13        System.in.read(); //clears line feed out of the buffer
14
15        do
16        {
17            name += letter;  //using String object to build the user's name
18            System.out.print
19            ( "Please enter the next character in your name: ");
20            letter = (char) System.in.read();
21            System.in.read(); //clears line feed out of the buffer
22        }while(letter != '*');
23
24 System.out.println("\nThe name you entered is: " + name);
25     } // end of main
26 } // end of GetUserName class
27
```

The output for this code is shown in Figure 4-6.

Figure 4-6 Console Input and Selection Based on Input Using `String` Objects—Output

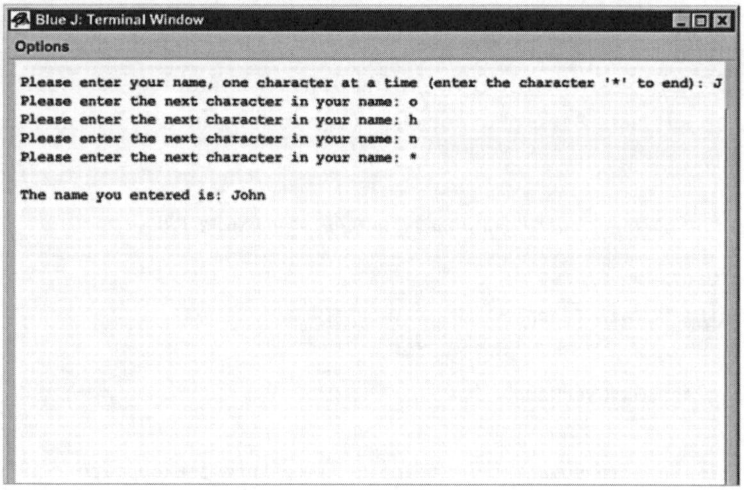

Review the code for the class `GetUserName1`, shown in Example 4-56. When obtaining input from the keyboard, each character needs to be stored in a `StringBuffer` object until all the characters have been entered. This code shows the use of the `StringBuffer` class. Note this statement on Line 13:

```
name.append(letter);
```

It uses a `StringBuffer` object to modify the text for the user's name. When the text data is in its final form, the `toString()` method, shown on Line 22, can be used to convert the `StringBuffer` object to a `String` object.

Example 4-56 *Console Input Using* `StringBuffer`

```
 1 public class GetUserName1
 2 {
 3     public static void main (String args[]) throws Exception
 4     {
 5         StringBuffer name = new StringBuffer();
 6
 7         System.out.print("Please enter your name, one character at a time
 8         (enter the character '*' to end): ");
 9         char letter = (char) System.in.read();
10         System.in.read(); //clears line feed out of the buffer
11         do
```

Example 4-56 *Console Input Using* StringBuffer *(Continued)*

```
12          {
13              name.append(letter);
14              System.out.print
15              ( "Please enter the next character in your name: ");
16              letter = (char) System.in.read();
17              System.in.read(); //clears line feed out of the buffer
18          }while(letter != '*');
19
20          //name.toString() converts the StringBuffer object back to a String
21          //object
22         System.out.println("\nThe name you entered is: " + name.toString());
23     } // end of main
24 } // end of GetUserName1 class
25
```

The output for this code is shown in Figure 4-7.

Figure 4-7 Console Input Using StringBuffer—Output

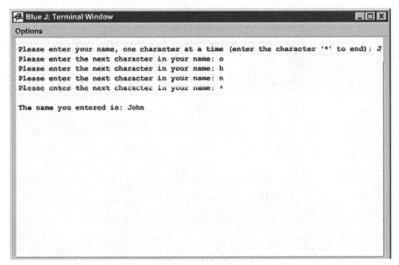

Summary

This chapter introduced the concepts of Java language operators and control structures. Students learned that there are arithmetic, unary, **boolean**, comparison, logical,

and assignment operators. Precedence gives some operators priority over others so that the evaluation of a statement is predictable and consistent. Operators also have associative properties. Some statements are evaluated from left to right, and others are evaluated from right to left.

The other major topic of this chapter dealt with the three control structures: sequence, selection, and repetition. Selection constructs are the `if` and `switch` statements. The constructs for repetition are the `do`, `while`, and `for` loops.

Java provides the `System` class to access properties of the underlying operating system devices to stream data in and out of the program. The `System` class contains references to three useful static objects: `in`, `out`, and `err`. These objects can send data and receive data from default input and output devices.

Syntax Summary

++ and --	Increase or decrease a value by 1.
Prefix++	Changes the value before use.
Postfix++	Changes the value after use.
=	Assigns the value on the right of the = to the variable on the left of the =.
*=	Multiplies the value on the left of the *= by the value on the right and assigns the product to the variable on the left of the *=.
/=	Divides the value on the left of the /= by the value on the right and assigns the quotient to the variable on the left of the /=.
%=	calculates the modulus (left value % right value) and assigns this value to the variable on the left of the %=.
==	Equality of two values.
!=	Inequality of two values.
Escape characters	Represent a literal for nonprinting and special meaning characters:
	\b: Backspace
	\t: Tab
	\n: Linefeed
	\r: Carriage return

\": Double quotes

\': Single quotes

\\: Backslash

if statement:

```
if(boolean)
{
(statement or block;)
}
else
{
(statements;)
}
```

if-else statement:

```
if(boolean)
{
(statement or block;)
}
else if(boolean)
{
(statement or block;)
}
else
{
      (statement or block;)
}
```

Nested **if**:

```
    if (boolean)
    {
        if (boolean)
        {
            if (boolean)
            {
                (statements;)
            }
            else
            {
                (statements;)
            }
        }
    }
```

switch statement:

```
    switch(expression1) // begins selection
    {
            case constant1: //(If the condition is true, the
                            // program goes to the break
                            // statement and ends the sequence
                            // of actions.
```

```
                        (statements;)
                         break;

            case constant2:
                        (statements;)
                         break;

            default: // If no match is found in one of the
                     // constants, the default statements
                     // will execute.
                     (statements;)
        }
```

do while loop:

```
    do
    {
       (statements or block;)
    }while(boolean test);
```

while loop:

```
while (boolean test)
{
(statements or block;)
}
```

for loop:

```
    for (init_expression; boolean test; alter_expression)
    {
            (statements or block;)
    }
```

System.out.print(....);   Prints and does not start a new line

System.out.println(...); Prints next to the previous text and then starts a new line

throws Exception   Is used in the main method to allow it to compile when
                          the enclosed code might throw an exception

System.in.read   returns the keyboard's strokes as an **int** and
                          converts to a **char**

Key Terms

associative property   Determines whether the operation of the operator is performed left to right or right to left. Arithmetic expressions are performed left to right. Assignment operators are performed right to left.

boolean *data type*   A primitive data type that stores a single-bit representation of the values **true** or **false**.

char *data type*   A primitive data type that stores a single 16-bit Unicode character.

concatenation   Process of using the overloaded + operator, which is also used in adding numeric data, to combine **String** objects.

control structure   A standard progression of logical steps to control the execution sequence of statements.

> *sequence*   Actions are performed in sequence or in order until successfully completed.
>
> *selection*   A program is told which action to perform based upon a certain condition. Two types of selection control are used in Java:
>
> — ***if***-then-**else** structures
> — *case-control* or ***switch*** structures
>
> *repetition*   Instructs the computer to repeatedly perform a set of actions. This structure is also called looping or iteration (which means "to repeat"). Three repetition structures are available in Java:
>
> — ***for*** loop
> — ***while*** loop
> — ***do*** loop

operator precedence grouping   A set of rules or priorities that Java imposes on the use of operators.

operators:

> *arithmetic operators*   Operators needed to execute a computation, such as a plus sign. The arithmetic operators include +, -, *, /, and %.
>
> *Assignment operators*   These operators include =, +=, -=, *=, /=, %=, &=, |=, ^=, <<=, >>=, and >>>=.
>
> *bitwise shift operators*   Perform bit shifts of the binary representation of the left operand. The bitwise shift operators include <<, >>, and >>>.

bitwise logical operators—Provide multiple comparisons of binary representations and return a binary representation:

- — *& (AND)*—For a given bit comparison, 1 and 1 produces 1, and all others produce 0.
- — *| (OR)*—For a given bit comparison, 0 and 0 produces 0, and all others produce 1.
- — *^ (XOR)*—For a given bit comparison, 1 and 0 produces 1, as does 0 and 1. All others produce 0.

boolean *logical operators*—Provide multiple **boolean** comparisons, and return a **boolean** result:

- — *& (AND)*—All expressions must be true for a true result.
- — *| (OR)*—If one expression is true, the result is true.
- — *^ (XOR)*—The result is true when one expression is true and the other expression is false. The result is false when both expressions are true or both expressions are false.
- — *&& (short-circuit AND)*—If the first expression is false, the result is false without regard for the second expression.
- — *|| (short-circuit OR)*—If the first expression is true, the result is true without regard for the second expression.

casting and conversion of data types   Operation with primitive data types that assigns a value of one data type to a variable of another data type. If the two types are compatible, Java does the conversion automatically.

comparison operators   Operators that test the relative values of two operands and return a **boolean** result:

- — *ordinal*   Tests the relative values of two numeric values: < (less than), > (greater than), >= (greater than or equal to), or <= (less than or equal to)
- — *equality*   Uses the symbols == (equal to) and != (not equal to) for comparing two values.
- — *object-type*   Uses the keyword **instanceof** to determine whether the runtime type of an object is of a particular class or subclass.

conditional operator (?:)—Used to assign one of two different values to a variable based upon a condition.

object operators:

- — The *new* operator is used to create a new object (instance) of a class.
- — The *dot operator* is used to access methods or member data of an object.

unary operators   Requires only one operand. The unary operators include +, -, ++ (prefix), ++ (postfix), --(prefix), --(postfix), ~, !, and (cast operator).

overloading   When an operator or method can perform more than the same action with different types of data. The + operator, which is used in adding numeric data, also can be used to combine String objects. This often is referred to as concatenation.

String   A collection of one or more Unicode characters stored in an object. String objects are immutable. After a String object is created, its value cannot change.

StringBuffer   Class that provides for the storage of string data that will change.

System class objects   Objects used to access properties of the underlying operating system devices to stream data in and out of the program.

> *in*   Accepts data from the keyboard buffer.

> *out*   Sends output to the display or redirects to a designated file.

> *err*   Sends output to the monitor. Used for prompts and error messages.

Check Your Understanding

1. Which operator is used to obtain the remainder of integer division?

   A. /

   B. ^

   C. &

   D. %

2. Which Java statement correctly increments Value by 4?

   A. Value = 4;

   B. Value += 4;

   C. Value =+ 4;

   D. Value + 4;

3. Which of the following Java operators is not a comparison operator?

   A. >

   B. >=

   C. =

   D. !=

4. What is the result of this expression?

```
16 >= 16.0
```

A. 0

B. `true`

C. `false`

D. 5

5. What is the result of the following expression?

```
true && true ^ true
```

A. `true`

B. `false`

6. Which of the following expressions results in a **true** value?

A. `(7 < 5) && (true)`

B. `false || (5 == 5)`

C. `(7 < 5) && (5 == 5)`

D. `false || (7 < 5)`

7. In the following statement, if x evaluates to **false**, what will the value of a be?

```
a = x ? b : c;
```

A. x

B. a

C. b

D. c

8. What is the other name for bitwise operators?

A. Shift operators

B. Logic operators

C. Assignment operators

D. Byte operators

9. Which of the following is not one of the bitwise operators?

A. `<<`

B. `<<<`

C. `>>`

D. `>>>`

10. Which assignment statement is the proper way to cast a **double** value, double-Value, to an **int** value?

A. `int myValue = (int)doubleValue;`

B. `int myValue = new int(doubleValue);`

C. `int myValue = doubleValue;`

D. `int myValue = doubleValue.toInt();`

11. Which class can be used to store and manipulate textual data?

A. `String`

B. `StringBuffer`

C. `char`

D. Both the `String` and `StringBuffer` classes

12. How many `String` objects are created in memory with the following Java statements?

```
String xyz = new String ("XYZ");
String abc = new String ("ABC");
String def = abc;
```

A. 3

B. 2

C. 5

D. 6

13. Which of the following is not one of the Java repetition structures?

A. `do`

B. `for`

C. `while`

D. `case`

14. What are the four keywords associated with the **switch** statement?

A. `switch, case, break, continue`

B. `switch, break, continue, default`

C. `switch, case, default, break`

D. `switch, case, break, while`

15. The **switch** statement evaluates which of the following types of data?

    A. **int** only

    B. **char** or **int** only

    C. **char**, **int**, or **byte** only

    D. **char**, **int**, byte, or **short** only

16. Which of the following is a post-test loop structure?

    A. **if**

    B. **do**

    C. **for**

    D. **while**

17. Which of the following is a correct example of a **for** loop?

    A. `for(int x = 0; x < 5; x++)`

    B. `for(int x: x < 5: x++)`

    C. `for(int x = 0, x < 5, x++)`

    D. `for (int x = 0; x < 5; x++)`

18. Which statement can be used to exit from a loop structure?

    A. `continue;`

    B. `exit;`

    C. `break;`

    D. `terminate;`

19. Which object in the **System** class can be used to display text on the screen?

    A. `out`

    B. `println()`

    C. `in`

    D. `printer`

20. When the **System.in** object accepts a character from the keyboard, it is stored as a(n):

    A. **int**

    B. **char**

    C. **byte**

    D. `String`

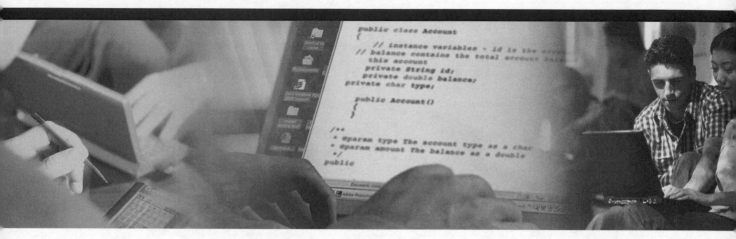

Upon completion of this chapter, you will be able to

- Identify the four steps in creating objects
- Understand attributes (class and instance)
- Define encapsulation
- Understand constructors
- Identify method types and syntax
- Use the variable **this**
- Understand method data and encapsulation
- Define overloading
- Understand the Java type lifespan
- Apply the Java language concepts that you have learned in this chapter to the JBANK case study

Basics of Defining and Using Classes

This chapter explains the elements that define classes and methods, exploring in detail the syntax and best practices for managing the attributes of a class and the methods of a class. Several classes are described in this chapter to illustrate the definition process and the use of objects and object methods. Students will also learn that a programmer manages the attributes of a class using variables. Variables, or identifiers, identify storage locations in memory where data can be stored and allow access to object data.

This chapter also discusses the concepts of scope, life, and encapsulation of data and objects. The scope of access to data stored in a variable is affected by where the variable is created. The life of a variable is how long it remains in memory, and this is closely tied to the scope of a variable. Knowing the scope and lifetime of an object can influence the program design and help determine where and when an object is created. Accessibility of data determines the encapsulation of an object. The keywords **public** and **private** can be used to set the accessibility of an object's data or methods.

Objects that are no longer necessary can be destroyed. Objects are removed from storage by the garbage collector, which is part of the JVM. A programmer can request garbage collection on an object and can define tasks to be completed before the object is removed from memory.

Review

This section reviews concepts related to classes and objects that were presented in earlier chapters.

A Review of Class and Object Definitions

As demonstrated in earlier chapters, it is possible to use a class without needing to know how it is implemented. All that must be known is the syntax of the methods. The first predefined class that students used in this book was in the statement System.out.println. In the System.out.println statement, students accessed the System class and an object out of the PrintStream class. Note that the out object is an attribute of the System class. These are part of the Java language API. Students have used the String class to create and store textual data in String objects. Students have also used their own Teller class to create and use Customer and Account objects. This chapter further explores the syntax and rules for implementing object-oriented principles with Java classes.

Concepts related to classes and objects of a class include these:

- A class is a template, or blueprint, for an object.
- A class defines the object behavior and its attributes.
- An object knows something and knows how to do something.
- A class defines the knowledge that is common to certain types of objects.
- A class is also referred to as a Java type.
- Each object stores information about what it currently knows or looks like. This is usually called the object's state. The state of an object is the object data.
- When an object from a class is created, it is said that an instance of the class has been created.
- The data of an object is stored in instance variables or fields.
- Each object of a class has a variable or identifier that stores the address of the object in memory. This variable is known as the object reference or the object identity. Two objects can have the same data with different references. That is, they can have the same state but different identities or different object references.
- The behavior of an object is defined by the message it accepts. Behaviors of an object are also known as methods, and the message that it accepts is the method argument.
- All interaction between two objects occurs through the use of the object reference to send messages.
- Programs should never directly access the data of an object; this data should be hidden. This is known as encapsulation.
- An object can be related to another type of object through association or inheritance. These are also referred to as "has a" and "is a" relationships.

As a review, in Figure 5-1 match the key terms at the bottom of the figure with their appropriate definition or explanation.

Figure 5-1 Review—Class and Object Definitions

Software Characteristics	
Request for an object to perform a task, a method call	
A common set of attributes	
Envelope or hide data of an object	
Name, return type, and arguments	
Derived attributes and methods	
Its data is stored in instance variables	

Class	Object message	Encapsulation
Object	Inheritance	Method signature

NOTE

For Figure 5-1, you can check your answers by accessing the full, interactive graphic for this figure on the book's accompanying CD-ROM. The title of the activity is "Drag and Drop Table" in e-Lab Activities.

Four Steps to Creating Objects

Proper design of classes is critical to effective implementation of their objects and ongoing management of changes and errors. This section covers the following topics:

- Designing classes
- Defining a class
- Creating an object
- Using an object

Designing Classes

The four steps necessary in creating objects are as follows:

Step 1   Design the attributes and behaviors of the object.

Step 2   Define the object. Create a *class definition*, or a blueprint, that addresses the attributes and behaviors identified in Step 1.

Step 3   Create an object.

Step 4   Use the object.

Those new to object-oriented languages often start by creating very few classes and having a class perform too many complex tasks. The key to skilled object definition is to handle this trade-off between doing too much and keeping the number of classes manageable. Remember, the more encompassing a class definition is, the harder it is to manage changes and errors. Having many robust classes is preferable to having fewer classes that break each time a change is introduced.

Applications and Objects

NOTE

For Exercise 5-1, you can check your answers by accessing the full, interactive graphic for this exercise on the book's accompanying CD-ROM. The title of the activity is "Discovering Objects" in the e-Lab Activities.

An application is a program that solves a business problem. How do programmers begin to discover the objects needed to create an application? In discovering the classes needed to solve a problem, one place to start is to use the activity in Exercise 5-1. Several nouns have been underlined in the activity's description. Identify the possible objects defined by this narrative. Not all the nouns underlined make sense when used as a potential object.

Exercise 5-1   Discovering Objects
A <u>construction company</u> would like to handle a <u>customer's order</u> for a new <u>home</u>. The customer can select one of four <u>models</u> of a home: Model A for 10,000, Model B for 120,000, Model C for 180,000, or Model D for 250,000. Each model can have one, two, three, or four <u>bedrooms</u>.

Having discovered the necessary objects, the next step for the programmer is to design the blueprint for each object. This means designing the class. Nouns and adjectives can point the programmer to the possible data or attributes of the object. Verbs can lead the programmer to selecting methods or behaviors. In Figure 5-2, use the highlighted text in the description to identify the attributes (nouns) and behaviors (verbs) for a Subscriber.

Figure 5-2 Identifying Nouns and Verbs or Attributes and Behaviors

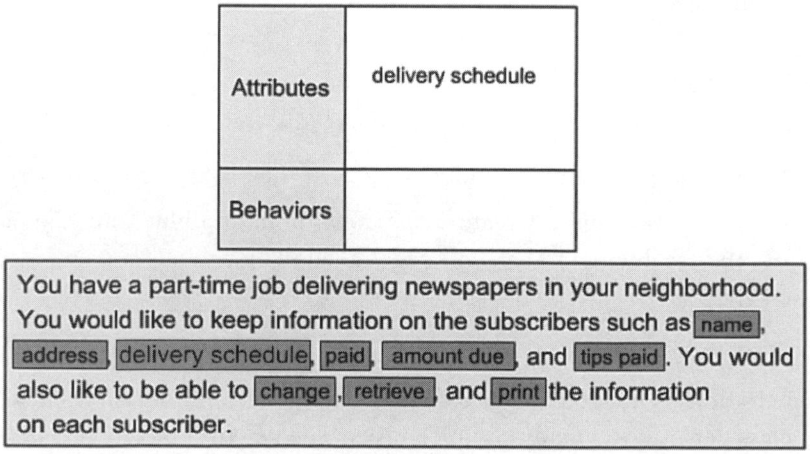

NOTE

For Figure 5-2, you can check your answers by accessing the full, interactive graphic for this figure on the book's accompanying CD-ROM. The title of the activity is "Identifying Nouns and Verbs or Attributes and Behaviors" in e-Lab Activities.

Attributes	delivery schedule
Behaviors	

You have a part-time job delivering newspapers in your neighborhood. You would like to keep information on the subscribers such as name, address, delivery schedule, paid, amount due, and tips paid. You would also like to be able to change, retrieve, and print the information on each subscriber.

Define a Class

Java is a tightly cast language. This means that the Java language has very specific rules regarding the ways in which data is stored, how much storage is allocated for each data value, and where data is stored. The Java compiler enforces many of these rules. Students will discover that applying the following guidelines will result in fewer code errors:

- Objects are created based on a class definition. A Java source file can have only one **public** class definition. The name of the **public** class and the name of the source file must be the same. The syntax for class definition follows. The class definition begins with this statement:

  ```
  <modifiers> class classname {
  ```

  A java source file with the name Subsriber.java must also have the following matching class statement:

  ```
  public class Subscriber {
  ```

- A Java source file can contain more than one class definition, as long as the previous guideline is followed. The file `PayCalculator.java` contains two classes. Only one class is **public**. The name of the file is the same as the name of the **public** class, `PayCalculator`. The compiler will create a class file for `Pay.class` and for `PayCalculator.class`. The `PayCalculator.class` file contains the main method. This will be the class that is executed first, as shown in Example 5-1.

Example 5-1 *Syntax for Class Definition*

```
1  /**
2   * Class Pay, File name PayCalculator.java
3   * @author Cisco Teacher
4   * @version 2002
5   * This class calculates the pay
6   */
7 class Pay
8 {
9      /**
10      * @param hrs The number of hours worked as a double
11      * @param pr The pay rate per hour as a double
12      * @param wr The withholding rate as a double
13      * @return The computed amount of pay as a double
14      */
```

continues

Example 5-1 *Syntax for Class Definition (Continued)*

```
15     public double computeNetPay(double hrs, double pr, double wr)
16     {
17         return (hrs * pr) - (hrs * pr * wr);
18     }
19
20 }   // end of class Pay
21
22 /**
23  * Class PayCalculator, File name PayCalculator.java
24  * @author Cisco Teacher
25  * @version 2002
26  * This class calculates uses the Pay class
27  * to calculate different NetPay amounts
28  */
29 public class PayCalculator
30 {
31     public static void main (String [] args)
32     {
33         double aNetpay;
34         /*
35         The default constructor Pay()
36         inserted by the compiler is used by the new operator
37         */
38         Pay p = new Pay ();
39
40         /*
41         calculate the pay for 20 hours at 13.00 an hour
42         and with a witholding tax rate of 20 % (.20)
43         */
44         aNetpay = p.computeNetPay(20.00, 13.00, .20);
45
46         /*
47         Print the result of calculating the net pay for 20 hours
48         at 15.00 an hour and with a witholding tax rate of 20 % (.20)
49         */
```

Example 5-1 *Syntax for Class Definition (Continued)*

```
50          System.out.println ( " The NetPay for 20 hours at $15.00" +
51              " per hour is " + p.computeNetPay(20.00, 15.00, .20));
52      }
53 } // end of PayCalculator class
```

A class definition includes several constructs, or structures, as shown in Example 5-2:

Example 5-2 *Code with No Constructor, Using the Default Constructor*

```
 1 /**
 2  * Class Pay, File name PayCalculator.java
 3  * @author Cisco Teacher
 4  * @version 2002
 5  * This class calculates the pay
 6  */
 7 class Pay
 8 {
 9     /**
10      * @param hrs The number of hours worked as a double
11      * @param pr The pay rate per hour as a double
12      * @param wr The withholding rate as a double
13      * @return The computed amount of pay as a double
14      */
15     public double computeNetPay(double hrs, double pr, double wr)
16     {
17         return (hrs * pr) - (hrs * pr * wr);
18     }
19
20 }    // end of class Pay
21
22 /**
23  * Class PayCalculator, File name PayCalculator.java
24  * @author Cisco Teacher
25  * @version 2002
26  * This class calculates uses the Pay class
```

continues

Example 5-2 *Code with No Constructor, Using the Default Constructor (Continued)*

```
27  * to calculate different NetPay amounts
28  */
29 public class PayCalculator
30 {
31    public static void main (String [] args)
32    {
33        double aNetpay;
34        /*
35        The default constructor Pay()
36        inserted by the compiler is used by the new operator
37        */
38        Pay p = new Pay ();
39
40        /*
41        calculate the pay for 20 hours at 13.00 an hour
42        and with a witholding tax rate of 20 % (.20)
43        */
44        aNetpay = p.computeNetPay(20.00, 13.00, .20);
45
46        /*
47        Print the result of calculating the net pay for 20 hours
48        at 15.00 an hour and with a witholding tax rate of 20 % (.20)
49        */
50        System.out.println ( " The NetPay for 20 hours at $15.00" +
51            " per hour is " + p.computeNetPay(20.00, 15.00, .20));
52    }
53 } // end of PayCalculator class
```

- **Declaration of the attributes**—The variables that identify the data that is stored in the object typically are declared either at the start of the class definition (before constructors or methods) or at the end of the class definition. Object data can be primitives or references to other objects.

■ **Definition of the constructors**—Class definitions can include one or more constructor method(s). The purpose of the *constructor* method is to define the specifics of object creation. A constructor method has some unique features, such as those that follow:

— Constructor methods must have the same name as the class.

— Programmers can choose to define none, one, or many constructors for a class, as illustrated in Examples 5-3 and 5-4.

Example 5-3 *Null Constructor*

```
1  /**
2   * Class Household1, File HouseHold1.java
3   * @author Cisco Teacher
4   * @version 2002
5   */
6
7  // Demonstrate use of constructor with no arguments
8
9  public class Household1
10 {
11     private int occupants;
12     private double annualIncome;
13
14     public Household1()
15     {
16         occupants = 1;
17         annualIncome = 0.0;
18     }
19
20     /**
21      * @return The number of occupants as an int
22      */
23     public int getOccupants()
24     {
25         return occupants;
26     }
27
```

continues

Example 5-3 *Null Constructor (Continued)*

```
28      /**
29       * @param occ The number of occupants as an int
30       */
31      public void setOccupants(int occ)
32      {
33          occupants = occ;
34      }
35
36      /**
37       * @return The household's annual income as a double
38       */
39      public double getAnnualIncome()
40      {
41          return annualIncome;
42      }
43
44      /**
45       * @param inc The household's annual income as a double
46       */
47      public void setAnnualIncome(double inc)
48      {
49          annualIncome = inc;
50      }
51
52      public static void main (String [] args)
53      {
54          Household1 ahome = new Household1 ( );
55          ahome.setAnnualIncome ( 30000.00);
56          System.out.println( " A Household has " +
57              ahome.getOccupants() +
58              " occupants and an Annual Income of " +
59              ahome.getAnnualIncome() ) ;
60      }
61 } //end of Household1 class
```

Example 5-4 *Class with Multiple Constructors*

```java
1 /**
2  * class VideoItem.java, File VideoItem.java
3  * @author Cisco teacher
4  * @version 2002
5  */
6 public class VideoItem
7 {
8     int id;
9     double price;
10    String title;
11    String location = "Stock check table";
12
13    /**
14     * @param aId The video's id number as an int
15     * @param aPrice The video's price as a double
16     * @param aTitle The video's title as a String
17     * @param aLocation The location of the video as a String
18     */
19    public VideoItem(int aId, double aPrice, String aTitle, String aLoc)
20    {
21        id = aId;
22        price = aPrice;
23        title = aTitle;
24        location = aLocation;
25    }
26
27    /**
28     * @param aId The video's id number as an int
29     * @param aPrice The video's price as a double
30     * @param aTitle The video's title as a String
31     */
32    public VideoItem(int aId, double aPrice, String aTitle)
33    {
34        id = aId;
35        price = aPrice;
```

continues

Example 5-4 *Class with Multiple Constructors (Continued)*

```
36          title = aTitle;
37      }
38
39      /**
40       * @param aId The video's id number as an int
41       * @param aPrice The video's price as a double
42       */
43      public VideoItem(int aId, double aPrice)
44      {
45          id = aId;
46          price = aPrice;
47      }
48      public VideoItem(){}
49  }  // end of VideoItem class
```

— Constructors do not have a return value.

— Constructors are executed only once at object creation.

■ **Definition of standard methods (accessor and mutator)**—When a class definition declares the data of the object to be hidden, it restricts the access to the data using the keyword **private**. The only way to access this hidden data is through methods. The programmer can then define methods to access or change only certain data. Methods to access data in an object are referred to as accessors. Methods to change the data in an object are referred to as mutators. Other terms used to describe accessor and mutator methods are getters and setters, as shown in Examples 5-5 and 5-6.

Example 5-5 *Code Standard Methods—*VideoItem *Class*

```
1 /**
2  * class VideoItem.java, File VideoItem.java
3  * @author Cisco teacher
4  * @version 2002
5  */
6
7 public class VideoItem
8 {
9      int id;
```

Example 5-5 *Code Standard Methods—*VideoItem *Class (Continued)*

```
10     double price;
11     String title;
12     String location = "Stock check table";
13
14     // constructor
15     /**
16      * @param aId The video's id number as an int
17      * @param aPrice The video's price as a double
18      * @param aTitle The video's title as a String
19      *@param aLocation The location of the video as a String
20      */
21     public VideoItem(int aId, double aPrice, String aTitle, String aLoc)
22     {
23         id = aId;
24         price = aPrice;
25         title = aTitle;
26         location = aLocation;
27     }
28
29     /**
30      * @return The video's id number as an int
31      */
32     public int getVideoId()
33     {
34         return id;
35     }
36
37     /**
38      * @param amount The video's price as a double
39      */
40     public void setVideoPrice(double amount)
41     {
42         price = amount;
43     }
44
```

continues

Example 5-5 *Code Standard Methods—*VideoItem *Class (Continued)*

```
45    /**
46     * @param amount The video's title as a String
47     */
48    public void setVideoTitle(String aTitle)
49    {
50        title = aTitle;
51    }
52
53    /**
54     * @return All of the video's information as a String
55     */
56    public String displayVideoInformation  ( )
57    {
58        return (" The title for video number + id"
      + " is " + title +
      ". The Price of the Video is $" + price);
59    }
60
61    /**
62     * @return The video's title and location as a String
63     */
64    public String displayVideoTitleandLocation ()
65    {
66        return (title + ":  " + location);
67    }
68
69 } //end of VideoItem class
```

Example 5-6 *Code Standard Methods—* Household *Class*

```
1 /**
2  * Household.java
3  * @author Cisco Teacher
4  * @version 2002
5  */
6
7 // Demonstrating standard accessor and mutator methods
```

Example 5-6 *Code Standard Methods—* Household *Class*

```
 8 public class Household
 9 {
10     int occupants;
11     double annualIncome;
12
13     /**
14      * @param occ The occupants as an int
15      * @param inc The annual income as a double
16      */
17     public Household(int occ, double inc)
18     {
19         occupants = occ;
20         annualIncome = inc;
21     }
22
23     /**
24      * @return The number of occupants as an int
25      */
26     public int getOccupants()
27     {
28         return occupants;
29     }
30
31     /**
32      * @param occ The number of occupants as an int
33      */
34     public void setOccupants(int occ)
35     {
36         occupants = occ;
37     }
38
39     /**
40      * @return The household's annual income as a double
41      */
42     public double getAnnualIncome()
```

continues

Example 5-6 *Code Standard Methods—* Household *Class*

```
43   {
44        return annualIncome;
45   }
46
47   /**
48    * @param inc The household's annual income as a double
49    */
50   public void setAnnualIncome(double inc)
51   {
52        annualIncome = inc;
53   }
54
55 } //end of Household class
```

- **Definition of custom methods (implementing business rules or modeling the business tasks)**—Methods that implement the business rules for which the application is being developed are part of the class definition. An example might be a method calcGPA for a Student object or a method calcInterest for a CreditCardAccount object, as shown in Example 5-7.

Example 5-7 *Code Custom Methods—*CreditCardAccount *Class*

```
1 /**
2  * CreditCardAccount.java
3  * @author Cisco Teacher
4  * @version 2002
5  */
6
7 public class CreditCardAccount
8 {
9     private static int nextAccountNumber = 0;
10    private int accountNumber;
11    private double balance;
12    public double creditLimit;
13    private static double interestRate = .24;
14
```

Example 5-7 *Code Custom Methods—*CreditCardAccount *Class (Continued)*

```
15      /**
16       * @param limit The credit card limit as a double
17       */
18      public CreditCardAccount(double limit)
19      {
20          accountNumber = ++nextAccountNumber;
21          creditLimit = limit;
22      }
23
24
25      public void display()
26      {
27          System.out.println("The Credit Card account number is "
28              + accountNumber
29              + ", the credit limit is " + creditLimit);
30      }
31
32      public void calcInterest()
33      {
34          double financeCharge = (balance * interestRate);
35          balance = balance + financeCharge;
36          System.out.println("The current Finance charge is "
37              + financeCharge
38              + ", the new balance is " + balance);
39      }
40
41      public static void reportStatus()
42      {
43          System.out.println("The current interest rate is "
44              + interestRate
45              + ", the last account number was " + nextAccountNumber);
46      }
47
48  } //end of CreditCardAccount class
```

Create an Object

Objects are created when the **new** operator is used. There are almost no restrictions governing when an object can be created. Objects can be created in methods of other classes, as a part of the attribute definition of another class, and within the definition of the class of the object (typically the main method). The creation of an object is also referred to as instantiation. An *instance* of the class thus is created.

The creation of an object using two statements is shown in Example 5-8. The first statement declares a variable to hold the reference to the object, and the second uses the **new** operator to create the object. The reference is declared as part of the class definition, and the object is created in a method of the class. The class creating the object is Teacher, and the object being created is a Student object.

Example 5-8 *Using Two Statements to Create an Object*

```
1 /**
2  * class Teacher.java
3  * @author Cisco Teacher
4  * @version 2002
5  */
6 public class Teacher
7 {
8     // delare variable to hold object reference
9     Student s1 ;
10
11    /**
12     * @param name The student's name as a String
13     * @param grade The student's grade as a String
14     */
15    public void createStudent(String name, String grade)
16    {
17
18        //new operator creates the object,
19        //and = operator assigns the object reference
20        //to variable s1
21
22        s1 = new Student(name, grade);
23    }
24 } // end of Teacher class
```

Another variation of this is the declaration of the variable to hold the reference to the object and the creation of the object in the method of a class, as shown in Example 5-9.

Example 5-9 *Using Two Statements to Create an Object*

```
1 /**
2  * class Teacher.java
3  * @author Cisco Teacher
4  * @version 2002
5  */
6 public class Teacher
7 {
8     /**
9      * @param name The student's name as a String
10     * @param grade The student's grade as a String
11     */
12    public void createStudent (String name, String grade)
13    {
14        Student s1 ;
15        s1 = new Student(name, grade);
16    }
17 } // end of Teacher class
```

The decision to create an object as a class attribute or in a method is influenced by how long the object data needs to be available to the class creating the object. Lifespan and scope of data are explored further in a later section of this chapter, "Java Type Lifespan."

The declaration of a variable to hold a reference to an object can be combined with the creation of an object into one statement, as shown in Example 5-10. In this example, the Student object exists as soon as the Teacher object is instantiated.

Example 5-10 *Using One Statement*

```
1 /**
2  * class Teacher.java
3  * @author Cisco Teacher
4  * @version 2002
5  */
6 public class Teacher
```

continues

Example 5-10 *Using One Statement (Continued)*

```
 7 {
 8     // creates a Student object using the null constructor
 9     Student s1 = new Student( );
10     /**
11      * @param grade The student's grade as a String
12      */
13     public void changeStudentGrade(String grade)
14     {
15         s1.setGrade(grade);
16     }
17 } // end of Teacher class
18
```

The next example shows the use of a single statement in a method. The Student object comes into existence only when this method is called; it cannot be referred to after the method is completed, as shown in Example 5-11.

Example 5-11 *Using One Statement to Create an Object*

```
 1 /**
 2  * class Teacher.java
 3  * @author Cisco Teacher
 4  * @version 2002
 5  */
 6 public class Teacher
 7 {
 8     /**
 9      * @param name The student's name as a String
10      * @param grade The student's grade as a String
11      */
12     public void createStudent(String name, String grade)
13     {
14         // creates a Student object using the constructor
15         Student s1 = new Student(name,"");
16         s1.setGrade(grade);
17     }
18 } // end of Teacher class
```

Creating Objects in the main Method of the Same Class

Objects of a class also can be created in the main method of the same class. When a class such as the Teacher class has a main method, the class is considered an entry point for the application. If the Teacher class were used to create many Teacher objects with their own unique data, the Teacher objects would need to be created as part of the main method. This is so that when the program starts, the Teacher objects can be created. Sample code illustrating this concept is shown in Example 5-12. In this example, the Teacher class has data and a main method. Teacher objects are created in the main method of the Teacher class. The **new** operator uses the constructor in the Teacher class to create the objects. Figure 5-3 shows the output for the Teacher class.

Example 5-12 Teacher *Class Creating Objects in the* main *Method*

```
 1 /**
 2  * class Teacher.java
 3  * @author Cisco Teacher
 4  * @version 2002
 5  */
 6 public class Teacher
 7 {
 8     String teacherName;
 9     String classroom;
10
11     // constructor
12     /*
13         @param aName The teacher's name as a String
14         @param aClassroom The teacher's classroom as a String
15     */
16     public Teacher(String aName, String aClassroom)
17     {
18         teacherName = aName;
19         classroom = aClassroom;
20     }
21
22     public static void main(String [] args)
23     {
24         Teacher one = new Teacher( "Peter Gray", "Room 208");
25         Teacher two = new Teacher ( "Penelope Masters" , "Mathematics" );
```

continues

Example 5-12 Teacher *Class Creating Objects in the* main *Method (Continued)*

```
26          System.out.println("Teacher " + one.teacherName +
27              " is in classroom " + one.classroom);
28          System.out.println( "Teacher " + two.teacherName +
29              " is in classroom " + two.classroom);
30      }
31 } // end of Teacher class
```

Figure 5-3 Teacher Class Creating Objects in the main

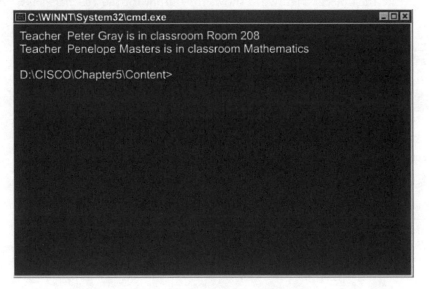

Using the Object

Objects are created to interact with one another to accomplish a task. This interaction occurs when one object uses the **public** methods of the other object to retrieve or change the information it needs. To gain access to these methods, the dot operator is used. It is important to understand that object instance data is accessed through the objects reference variable, and class data is accessed through the use of the class name. Class data is qualified with the use of the keyword **static**. Syntax of the dot operator in accessing instance information is shown in Example 5-13.

Example 5-13 *Syntax for Accessing Object Instance Information*

```
 1 /*
 2 For instance data or methods
 3    Object-reference.member
 4    Object-reference .method( )
 5 */
 6 Student s1 = new Student();
 7 // access variable (member or instance data)
 8 //through the reference variable(s)
 9 s1.studentName;
10 // access a method through the reference variable(s)
11 s1.setGrade();
```

Syntax of the dot operator in accessing class information is shown in Example 5-14.

Example 5-14 *Syntax Sample*

```
 1 /*
 2      For class (static) data or methods
 3          Class-name.member
 4          Class-name.method( )
 5 */
 6
 7 // accessing the variable out of the System class.
 8 // This is a static variable.
 9 System.out
10
11 // accessing the method gc of the System class.
12 // This is a static method.
13 System.gc()
```

Only nonprivate data or methods are accessible to other objects. Other objects can be objects of the same class or a different class.

The sample code shown for the CiscoStudent and Teacher classes in Example 5-15 demonstrates the use of nonprivate object data and methods.

Example 5-15 *Using Object Data (**public** Data)*

```
1 /**
2 * Class CiscoStudent
3 * @author Cisco Teacher
4 * @version 2002
5 **/
6 class CiscoStudent
7 {
8     int studentID;
9     private String name;
10    public String classroom;
11    String teachername;
12
13    /*
14        @param aId The student's id number as an int
15    */
16    public CiscoStudent (int aId)
17    {
18        studentID = aId;
19    }
20
21    /*
22        @param aId The student's id number as an int
23        @param aName The student's name as a String
24    */
25    public CiscoStudent (int aId, String aName)
26    {
27        studentID = aId;
28        name = aName;
29    }
30
31    /*
32        @param aName The student's name as a String
33    */
34    public void setName(String aName)
35    {
36        name = aName;
```

Example 5-15 *Using Object Data (**public** Data) (Continued)*

```
37      }
38
39      /*
40          @return The student's name as a String
41      */
42      public String getName()
43      {
44          return name;
45      }
46  } // end of CiscoStudent class
47
48  /**
49   * Teacher class with main method
50   * @author Cisco Teacher
51   * @version 2002
52   */
53  public class Teacher
54  {
55      String name;
56      String classroom;
57
58      /**
59       * @param aName The teacher's name as a String
60       * @param aClassroom The teacher's classroom as a String
61       */
62      Teacher ( String aName, String aClassroom)
63      {
64          name = aName;
65          classroom = aClassroom;
66      }
67
68      /**
69       * @return The teacher's name as a String
70       */
71      public String getName()
```

continues

Example 5-15 *Using Object Data (**public** Data) (Continued)*

```
72      {
73          return name;
74      }
75
76      public static void main (String [] args)
77      {
78          // Teacher class creates teacher objects
79          Teacher one = new Teacher(" Peter Gray ", "Room 208");
80          Teacher two = new Teacher (" Penelope Masters " , " Mathematics " );
81
82          // Teacher class creates student objects
83          CiscoStudent s1 = new CiscoStudent (97887 );
84          CiscoStudent s2 = new CiscoStudent (46573 );
85
86          s1.classroom = "Room 208 ";
87          s2.classroom = "Mathematics ";
88          s1.teachername = one.getName();
89          s2.teachername = two.getName();
90          s1.setName( " Mark Novell" );
91          s2.setName( " Maria Lee " );
92
93          System.out.println(s1.getName( ) + " is in classroom "
94          + s1.classroom + " meeting with " + s1.teachername );
95      }
96 } // end of Teacher class
```

In Example 5-15, the Teacher class creates and uses the CiscoStudent objects. The classroom variable of the CiscoStudent object is **public** and accessible to the Teacher class directly. The Teacher class changes the values of these variables.

The second class within Example 5-15 requires no arguments for the getName method. The method is called for each Teacher object. This method returns a String object that stores the name of the teacher and then is assigned to the String object teachername, an attribute of the CiscoStudent object. In this example, the teachername variable in the CiscoStudent class references a name, not the Teacher object.

In Table 5-1, the `s1.getName()` method is used to obtain **private** data from the Cisco-Student object. The method `println` is using data returned from the `CiscoStudent` method `getName()`.

Table 5-1 Using Object Methods

Syntax	Description
`s1.teachername = one.getName ( );` `s2.teachername = two.getName ( );`	The `Teacher` class method `getName` requires no arguments. The method is called for each `Teacher` object. This method returns a `String` object that stores the name of the teacher. This name then is assigned to the `String` object `teachername` referenced by the `CiscoStudent` objects. In this example, the `teachername` variable in the `Cisco-Student` class references a name, not the `Teacher` object.
`s1.setName( " Mark Novell" );` `s2.setName( " Maria Lee " );`	The `CiscoStudent` class method `set-Name` requires a `String`. The text for the `String` object is provided inside the quotes—for example, `" Mark Novell"` and `" Maria Lee "`.

`System.out.println(s1.getName( ) +`
 `"is in classroom " + s1.classroom +`
 `" meeting with " + s1.teachername );`
	The `s1.getName()` method is used to obtain **private** data from the `Cisco-Student` object. The method `println` is using data returned from the `Cisco-Student` method `getName()`.

Attributes (Class and Instance)

An *attribute* is a piece of data stored in an object. This data can relate to the entire class (class data) or to the individual object of the class (instance data). This section contains the following topics:

- Overview
- Variables
- Instance variables
- Class data and static variables
- Immutability

Overview

Attributes are declared using variables to identify storage of data. Data can be a reference to any of the eight primitive data types (**boolean, char, byte, short, int, long, float**, or **double**). Data also can be a reference or an identifier for another object. The syntax for declaring an object is shown here:

```
type identifier;
identifier = value;
or
type identifier = value;
//type is any Java type.
int x ; //refers to the datatype int referenced by the variable x
```

Example 5-16 shows types of attributes in the LabelText class. The attribute MAX_TEXT is of the primitive type, while the attribute label references a String object.

Example 5-16 *Class Definition: Attributes of the Type Primitive and Reference*

```
1 /**
2   * A Java class for text labels of arbitrary length limit
3   * @author Cisco Teacher
4   * @version 2002
5   */
6 public class LabelText
7 {
8     private static final int MAX_TEXT = 20;
9     private String label;
10
11    /**
12     * @param inputText The text to be assigned to the label as a String
13     */
14    public LabelText(String inputText)
15    {
16        System.out.println( "Creating a LabelText object");
17        if ( inputText.length() <= MAX_TEXT )
18        {
19            label = inputText;
20        }
21        else
22        {
23            System.err.println("Input label text is too long!");
24
```

Example 5-16 *Class Definition: Attributes of the Type Primitive and Reference*

```
25                //NOTE: next line extracts 20 chars at index 0 to 19
26                label = inputText.substring( 0, MAX_TEXT );
27          }
28      }
29 } // end of LabelText class
```

Definitions of Attributes

Definitions of attributes can be placed at the beginning of classes or at the end. Although neither placement affects the compiling or executing of the code, it is best for novice programmers to define attributes at the beginning of a class definition so that they can be referenced easily in coding the rest of the class. The `PublicData` and `PrivateData` classes shown in Example 5-17 demonstrate placement of code for the definition of attributes.

Example 5-17 *Placement of Code for the Definition of Attributes*

```
 1 /**
 2  * Java Program PublicData.java
 3  * @author Cisco Teacher
 4  * @version 2002
 5  */
 6
 7 import java.util.Date;
 8
 9 class PublicData
10 {
11     public int a;
12     private double dollar;
13     private String name;
14     Date d;
15
16     // constructor
17
18     // other methods
19
20 } //end of PublicData class
```

continues

Example 5-17 *Placement of Code for the Definition of Attributes (Continued)*

```
21
22 /**
23  * Java Program: PrivateData.java
24  * @author Cisco Teacher
25  * @version 2002
26  */
27
28 class PrivateData
29 {
30     public int a;
31     Date d;
32
33     // constructor
34
35     // other methods
36
37     private double dollar;
38     private String name;
39
40 } //end of PrivateData class
```

The graphic in Figure 5-4 illustrates the relationship among design, define, and use for the CreditCardAccount class.

The standards for identifiers include the following:

- The first character must be any nonnumber of the Unicode character set.
- Lowercase must be used for the starting letter or word, and upper case must be used for the start of each separate word in the name. No spaces or other symbols, such as _ or -, are used to separate words.
- Use all uppercase for identifiers that are used to reference constants.
- Define all attributes of a class at the start of the class definition. This improves readability of the code.

Figure 5-4 UML, Source Code, and Object Picture

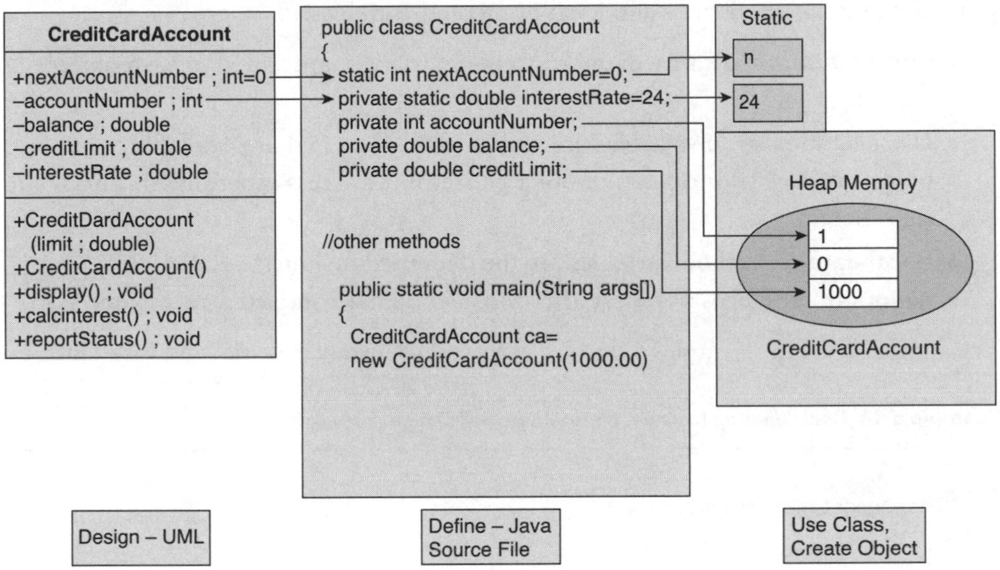

Variables

Students might recall that data stored in memory is accessed through an identifier or a label. This is also known as a variable. As discussed in earlier chapters, the five aspects of a variable are data type, identifier, scope, address, and value. Which one of the facets would properly complete the statements in Figure 5-5?

Figure 5-5 Facets of a Variable

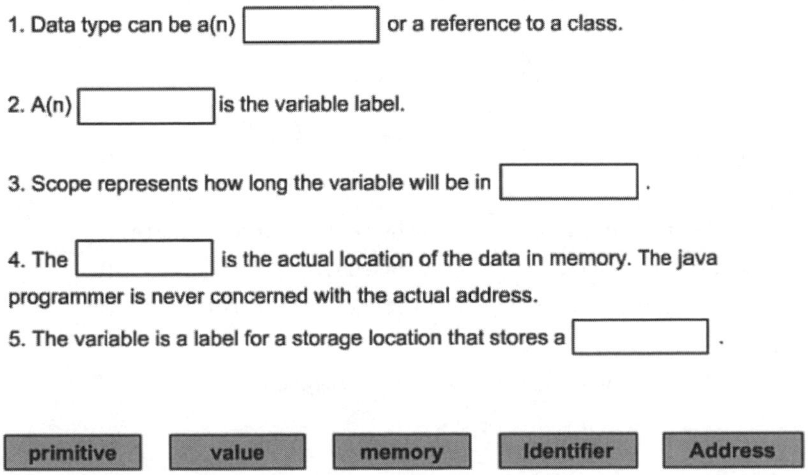

1. Data type can be a(n) [   ] or a reference to a class.

2. A(n) [   ] is the variable label.

3. Scope represents how long the variable will be in [   ].

4. The [   ] is the actual location of the data in memory. The java programmer is never concerned with the actual address.

5. The variable is a label for a storage location that stores a [   ].

primitive   value   memory   Identifier   Address

NOTE

For Figure 5-5, you can check your answers by accessing the full, interactive graphic for this figure on the book's accompanying CD-ROM. The title of the activity is "Facets of a Variable" in e-Lab Activities.

Class definition can include three categories of variables: instance or object variables, static data or class variables, and local or method variables:

- *Object data*, or instance data or instance variables, are stored in each object of a class.

- *Class data* or static variables are stored in the class and are available to all objects of a class or objects of other classes if the access is permitted. This is shared data.

- Local data or method variables are the data used in a method. This data is temporary and does not exist after the method has completed execution.

The sample code in Examples 5-18 and 5-19 shows instance, static, and local data.

NOTE

For Example 5-18, you can view the explanatory text by accessing the full, interactive graphic for this example on the book's accompanying CD-ROM. The title of the activity is "Code Showing Instance, Static, and Local Data" in e-Lab Activities.

Example 5-18 *Code Showing Instance, Static, and Local Data*

```
1  /**
2   * CreditCardAccount.java
3   * @author Cisco Teacher
4   * @version 2002
5   */
6
7  public class CreditCardAccount
8  {
9      private static int nextAccountNumber = 0;
10     private int accountNumber;
11     private double balance;
12     public double creditLimit;
13     private static double interestRate = .24;
14
15     //Constructors and some other methods...
16
17     public void calcInterest()
18     {
19         double financeCharge = (   balance *    interestRate);
20         balance =    balance +    financeCharge;
21         System.out.println("The current Finance charge is "
22             +    financeCharge
23             + ", the new balance is " +    balance);
24     }
```

Example 5-18 *Code Showing Instance, Static, and Local Data (Continued)*

```
25
26     //Some other methods...
27
28 } //end of CreditCardAccount class
```

Example 5-19 *Code Showing Instance, Static, and Local Data*

```
 1 /**
 2  * Java Program: CreditCardUser.java
 3  * @author Cisco Teacher
 4  * @version 2002
 5  */
 6 public class CreditCardUser
 7 {
 8     public static void main (String args [ ])
 9     {
10         CreditCardAccount c1 = new CreditCardAccount(10000.00);
11         CreditCardAccount c2 = new CreditCardAccount(2000.00);
12
13         c1. display();
14         c2.display ();
15
16         c1.calcInterest ();
17         c2.calcInterest ( );
18
19         c1. reportStatus();
20         c2. reportStatus();
21     }
22 } // end of CreditCardUser class
```

Storage of Data

Three areas of storage are of interest to the Java programmer: the storage of local or method data, the storage of object data, and the storage of class data.

- All objects are created in RAM. The area of storage that is used is referred to as heap storage.

- All method data also are created in RAM. That area is called the stack storage.

- All class data also are created in RAM. The area of storage that is used is referred to as static storage.

The graphic in Figure 5-6 illustrates the impact on stack and heap storage areas when using the `CreditCardUser` and `CreditCardAccount` classes, shown in Examples 5-18 and 5-19.

Figure 5-6 Memory Access—Stack and Heap

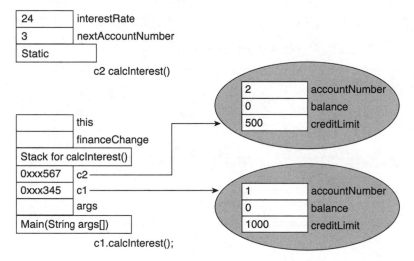

Instance Variables

Instance variables identify the data stored in each object of the class. They are also referred to as instance fields, instance data, and data members. Students will find the term *field* more commonly used to refer to instance variables.

A class is a blueprint for an object. When one or more objects of a class are created in memory, each object has a copy of the instance variables and stores its own value for the variable. For example, if two `Student` objects are created, each Student object stores data for a single student. It is possible for two students to have the same name or the same grade. Even in this situation, each object represents only one student, and each student has a copy of the same value.

The object is an instance of the class. Each variable in the object is owned by that specific instance. The values stored in the instance variables differentiate the object from others of the same class, giving each object its individuality. Even if the values were the same in two objects, their identifiers would be different. When a value in an object changes, it does not affect the value in other objects of the same class.

The data stored in an object can be either a primitive (**boolean**, **char**, **byte**, **short**, **long**, **int**, **float**, or **double**) or a reference to another object.

When one object stores the reference to another object, it is described as having a reference. This relationship between the two objects is also referred to as a "has a" relationship. This means that an association between the two objects exists through the reference data. The LabelText class stores an **int** and a reference to a String object.

To reference an instance variable within the class definition, use the variable name, as shown in Example 5-20.

Example 5-20 *Accessing Instance Data*

```
 1 /**
 2  * Java Program: CreditCardAccount.java
 3  * @author Cisco Teacher
 4  * @version 2002
 5  */
 6
 7 public class CreditCardAccount
 8 {
 9     private static int nextAccountNumber = 0;
10     private int accountNumber;
11     private double balance;
12     public double creditLimit;
13     //for this example the creditLimit variable is public
14     private static double interestRate = .24;
15
16     /**
17      * @param limit The credit card limit as a double
18      */
19     public CreditCardAccount(double limit)
20     {
21         accountNumber = ++nextAccountNumber;
22         creditLimit = limit;
23     }
24
25     public void display()
```

continues

NOTE

For Example 5-20, you can view the explanatory text by accessing the full, interactive graphic for this example on the book's accompanying CD-ROM. The title of the activity is "Accessing Instance Data" in e-Lab Activities.

Example 5-20 *Accessing Instance Data (Continued)*

```
26    {
27        System.out.println("The Credit Card account number is "
28        + accountNumber
29        + ", the credit limit is " + creditLimit);
30    }
31
32    public void calcInterest()
33    {
34        double financeCharge = (   balance * interestRate);
35        balance = balance + financeCharge;
36        System.out.println("The current Finance charge is "
37        +    financeCharge
38        + ", the new balance is " + balance);
39    }
40
41    public static void reportStatus()
42    {
43        System.out.println("The current interest rate is "
44        + interestRate
45        + ", the last account number was " + nextAccountNumber);
46    }
47
48 } //end of CreditCardAccount class
```

NOTE

For Example 5-21, you can view the explanatory text by accessing the full, interactive graphic for this example on the book's accompanying CD-ROM. The title of the activity is "Accessing Instance Data" in e-Lab Activities.

To reference the variable of an object by another object, use the dot notation, as shown in Example 5-21.

Example 5-21 *Accessing Instance Data*

```
1 /**
2  * Java Program: CreditCardCardUser.java
3  * @author Cisco Teacher
4  * @version 2002
5  */
6 public class CreditCardUser
7 {
8    public static void main (String args [ ])
```

Example 5-21 *Accessing Instance Data (Continued)*

```
 9    {
10        CreditCardAccount c1 = new CreditCardAccount(10000.00);
11        CreditCardAccount c2 = new CreditCardAccount(2000.00);
12
13        c1. display();
14        c2.display ();
15        c1.creditLimit = 2000.00;
16        // c2.balance = 2500.00;  illegal statement,
17        // balance is a private attribute
18        c1.calcInterest();
19        c2.calcInterest();
20
21        c1. reportStatus();
22        c2. reportStatus();
23    }
24 } // end of CreditCardUser class
```

The sample code shown in Examples 5-20 and 5-21 for the CreditCardUser and CreditCardAccount classes illustrates the access of variables within a class and the access of variables from outside the class by another object.

Class Data and Static Variables

Variables that are associated with a class and that are shared by all objects of the class are known as class or static variables. A given class has only one copy of each of its class variables. The class variables exist even if no objects of the class have been created. If the value of the class variable is changed, the new value is available to all objects. This is quite different from instance variables, in which changing a value for one object does not affect the values in other objects. The keyword **static** is used as a qualifier to define a class variable.

The sample code shown in Examples 5-22 and 23 for the CreditCardUser and CreditCardAccount classes illustrates the use of the keyword **static** and the impact of shared data on object data.

Example 5-22 *Impact of Static and Object Data—*`CreditCardUser` *Class*

```
1 /**
2  * CreditCardCardUser.java
3  * @author Cisco Teacher
4  * @version 2002
5  **/
6 public class CreditCardUser
7 {
8      public static void main (String args [ ])
9      {
10         CreditCardAccount c1 = new CreditCardAccount(10000.00);
11         System.out.println (" The Next account number is "
12             + CreditCardAccount.nextAccountNumber + 1);
13         CreditCardAccount c2 = new CreditCardAccount( 2000.00);
14         System.out.println (" The Next account number is "
15             + CreditCardAccount.nextAccountNumber + 1);
16         System.out.println (" The Next account number is "
17             + ++ CreditCardAccount.nextAccountNumber);
18     }
19
20 } // end of class CreditCardUser
```

Example 5-23 *Impact of Static and Object Data—*`CreditCardAccount` *Class*

```
1 /**
2  * CreditCardAccount.java
3  * @author Cisco Teacher
4  * @version 2002
5  */
6
7 public class CreditCardAccount
8 {
9      static int nextAccountNumber = 0;
10     private int accountNumber;
11     private double balance;
12     //for this example the creditLimit variable is public
13     public double creditLimit;
14     private static double interestRate = .24;
```

Example 5-23 *Impact of Static and Object Data—*CreditCardAccount *Class (Continued)*

```
15
16      /*
17          @param limit The credit card limit as a double
18      */
19      public CreditCardAccount(double limit)
20      {
21          accountNumber = ++nextAccountNumber;
22          creditLimit = limit;
23      }
24
25      public void display()
26      {
27          System.out.println("The Credit Card account number is "
28              + accountNumber
29              + ", the credit limit is " + creditLimit);
30      }
31
32      public void calcInterest()
33      {
34          double financeCharge = (balance * interestRate);
35          balance = balance + financeCharge;
36          System.out.println("The current Finance charge is "
37              + financeCharge
38              + ", the new balance is " + balance);
39      }
40
41      public static void reportStatus()
42      {
43          System.out.println("The current interest rate is "
44              + interestRate
45              + ", the last account number was " + nextAccountNumber);
46      }
47
48  } //end of CreditCardAccount class
```

Immutability

Consider a situation in which the data for an object or class must not change. This feature represents the mutability (changeability) of object (and class) data or methods. In the Java language, *final* is used to qualify a class attribute or method as *immutable* (unchangeable). Data that is fixed, or **final**, is also referred to as constant data or as constants. The coding convention in Java is to name such data with identifiers in uppercase. The use of the term **final** instructs the JVM to assign an unchangeable value to the variable.

The attributes of an object that have been declared as **final** cannot be changed after an instance (object) of the class has been constructed. For instance attributes, each object of the class has its own copy of the attribute. The value of the constant for each object can be different. To be capable of doing this, the value would be initialized in the constructor method of the class.

The sample code for the ObjectNoChange class demonstrates the use of **final** for constants (instance). In Example 5-24, the variables objectNumber and objectSecondNumber are instance variables and have been declared as **final**. These are constants. When the objects referenced by ob1 and ob2 are created, the values for variables objectNumber and objectSecondNumber are fixed and cannot be changed. Although objectSecondNumber is **public**, an attempt to change its value results in a compiler error. Figure 5-7 shows the output for the ObjectNoChange class.

Example 5-24 **final** *Instance Variable—Code View*

```
1 /**
2  * ObjectNoChange.java
3  * @author Cisco Teacher
4  * @version 2002
5  **/
6 public class ObjectNoChange
7 {
8     private final int objectNumber ;
9     private String objectName;
10    public final int objectSecondNumber ;
11
12    /**
13     *  @param i Object number as an int
14     *  @param j Object section number as an int
15     *  @param s Object name as a String
```

Example 5-24 `final` *Instance Variable—Code View (Continued)*

```
16      */
17      ObjectNoChange(int i,int j, String s)
18      {
19          objectNumber = i;
20          objectSecondNumber  = j;
21          objectName = s;
22      }
23
24      /*
25          @return The object's name as a String
26      */
27      public String getName()
28      {
29          return objectName;
30      }
31
32      /*
33          @return The object's number as an int
34      */
35      public int getNumber ()
36      {
37          return objectNumber;
38      }
39
40      public static void main (String args [])
41      {
42          ObjectNoChange ob1 = new ObjectNoChange (15,30, "Scooter");
43          ObjectNoChange ob2 = new ObjectNoChange (25,10, "Tester");
44          ob1.objectSecondNumber ++;
45      }
46  }// end of ObjectNoChange class
```

Figure 5-7 `final` Instance Variable—Output View

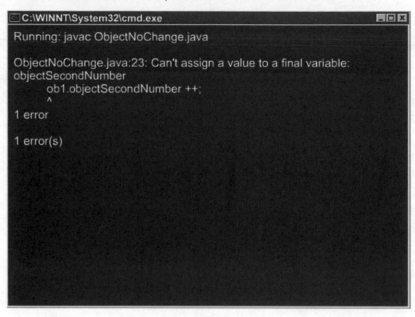

Each object, referenced by ob1 and ob2, stores its own copy of the constants. When the constant is to be shared among all objects of the class, the attribute is qualified as both **final** and **static**.

The sample code for the `CreditCardUser` and `CreditCardAccount` classes demonstrates the use of **final static** constants. In Example 5-25, the constant MAX_TEST is static. All `LabelText` objects will use this constant; the value of the constant cannot be changed. Objects of another class will access this constant using the syntax `LabelText.MAX_TEXT`.

Example 5-25 *Use of* **final** *and* **static** *for Constants*

```
1 /**
2  * A Java class for text labels of arbitrary length limit
3  * @author Cisco Teacher
4  * @version 2002
5  */
6 public class LabelText
7 {
8     private static final int MAX_TEXT = 20;
9     private String label;
10
```

Example 5-25 *Use of* `final` *and* `static` *for Constants (Continued)*

```
11     /**
12      * @param inputText The text to be assigned to the label as a String
13      */
14     public LabelText(String inputText)
15     {
16         System.out.println( "Creating a LabelText object");
17         if ( inputText.length() <= MAX_TEXT )
18         {
19             label = inputText;
20         }
21         else
22         {
23             System.err.println("Input label text is too long!");
24
25             //NOTE: next line extracts 20 chars at index 0 to 19
26             label = inputText.substring( 0, MAX_TEXT );
27         }
28     }
29 } // end of LabelText class
```

Encapsulation

Encapsulation in Java is defined as the localization of knowledge within a module. Because objects encapsulate data and implementation, the user of an object can view the object as a black box that provides services. This section covers the following topics:

- The concept of encapsulation
- Access modifiers

The Concept of Encapsulation

The simple definition of the concept of encapsulation is the act of enclosing or making into a capsule. In Java, this term has a special meaning of hiding information. One of the most important expectations users have of objects is for them to provide consistent, reliable, and predictable behavior. If object data can be changed directly by another object, it might become unreliable. The idea is to keep data members encapsulated to prevent the public and other objects from modifying them. Encapsulation is implemented through access modifier keywords.

Access Modifiers

Four *access modifiers* have been defined to access class or object information. The words **public**, **private**, and **protected** are keywords used to define three types of access. Additionally, default access is implied when none of these keywords is used. Table 5-2 reflects the influence of access modifiers.

Table 5-2 Access Modifiers

Keyword	Who Has Access
public	All classes and objects of the class
protected	Subclasses and objects of the class
private	Methods of the object
default or no access modifier	Object of the class, classes in the same directory or package

The arrows in Figure 5-8 show access to and denial of the data.

Figure 5-8 Influence of Access Modifiers

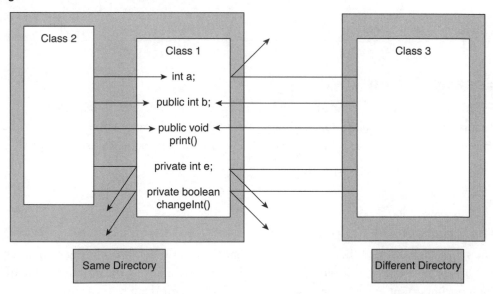

In general, data or attributes of a class should be **private**, and methods should be accessible to the outside. Class-based data also can be accessible to the outside, especially if the data does not change—that is, if a constant is declared with the keyword **final**. A class member should be explicitly specified as **public** or **private** rather than omitting access modifiers.

The variables in a **public** class should be **private**, and the methods that will be called from the outside should be **public**. Even when access to the values of the variables from outside the class is necessary, a simple **public** accessor or "getter" method can return the value of the data. A few exceptions must be considered:

- Methods intended to be used internally only by other methods in the same class can be declared **private**.
- Methods or members that are class based, static, generally are used from the outside and might be declared **public**.

Access modifiers apply in the same manner whether the variable is an instance variable or a static variable, as shown in Example 5-26. Consider the business rule that the `CreditCardAccount` class needs access to an interest rate. However, the `CreditCard-Account` objects should not be capable of changing the interest rates directly. In this situation, the `interestRate` should be stored as a static variable. It should be hidden from other objects by declaring its access **private**. The variable `interestRate` can be accessed directly only by other methods within the `CreditCardAccount`. These methods access the variable using its name, `interestRate`.

Example 5-26 CreditCardAccount.*java*

```
 1 /**
 2  * CreditCardAccount.java
 3  * @author Cisco Teacher
 4  * @version 2002
 5  */
 6 public class CreditCardAccount
 7 {
 8      // non-private static variable
 9      static int nextAccountNumber = 0;
10      private int accountNumber;
11      private double balance;
12      public double creditLimit;
13      // private static variable
```

continues

Example 5-26 CreditCardAccount.*java (Continued)*

```
14      private static double interestRate = .24;
15
16      /**
17       * @param limit The account limit as a double
18       */
19      public CreditCardAccount(double limit)
20      {
21          accountNumber = ++nextAccountNumber;
22          creditLimit = limit;
23      }
24
25      public void display()
26      {
27          System.out.println("The Credit Card account number is "
28                  + accountNumber
29                  + ", the credit limit is " + creditLimit);
30      }
31
32      public void calcInterest()
33      {
34          double financeCharge = (balance * interestRate);
35          balance = balance + financeCharge;
36          System.out.println("The current Finance charge is "
37                  + financeCharge
38                  + ", the new balance is " + balance);
39      }
40      public static void reportStatus()
41      {
42          System.out.println("The current interest rate is "
43                  + interestRate
44                  + ", the last account number was " + nextAccountNumber);
45      }
46
47 } //end of CreditCardAccount class
```

The CreditCardAccount class stores account numbers for each instance of the class (each credit card issued). These numbers could be a sequential set of numbers. Every instance of the class will obtain one of these sequential numbers. To ensure that the assigned numbers do not duplicate (no two cards result in the same number), the variable nextAccountNumber is maintained as a static attribute of the class. All objects of the CreditCardAccount class will share this attribute.

To make the nextAccountNumber accessible by other classes, the access is declared as nonprivate. In this example, it is provided the default access. Other classes within the same package or directory can access this attribute.

Another class using the class-name.member syntax can access the nextAccountNumber variable. Therefore, all objects (those in the class and those in the same package or directory) will be capable of accessing and changing this variable.

The **private static** modifier for the variable interestRate is more restrictive, allowing accessibility to the variable interestRate only from inside the CreditCardAccount class.

The influence of access modifiers applies in the same manner for both instance variables and static variables.

Constructors

In the Java programming language, constructors are instance methods (with the same name as their class) that construct an object. Constructors are invoked using the keyword **new**. This section covers the following topics:

- The constructor process
- Default constructors
- Defined constructors

The Constructor Process

Object construction starts when the **new** operator is used. Calling the **new** operator, as in the following statement:

```
Student s1 =  new Student ( 23559, " Mary Martin", "A");
```

results in allocation of space for the new object in this sequence:

Step 1   Space for the new object is allocated. Instance variables are initialized to their default values.

Step 2 Explicit initialization is performed. Variables initialized in the attribute declaration have the default values replaced with this initial value.

Step 3 A constructor is executed. Variable values can be reset or set in the constructor. Constants should be set here.

Step 4 A variable assignment is made to reference the object. That is, a reference value for the object is stored in the variable.

An important concept in Java is understanding variable default values. To begin, a default value for an attribute is a value that is stored in memory and that is based on some predefined rules. This value can be changed. When an object is created in Java, it is created in heap memory. Each variable default value is determined by the type of data that the variable references. Table 5-3 shows the default values for primitive and reference data types. Although instance variables are initialized to their default values in Step 1 of the object construction sequence described previously, it is a good programming practice to explicitly initialize variables (Step 2) instead of relying on their default values.

Table 5-3 Default Values

Data Type	Default Value
byte	0
short	0
int	0
long	0
float	0.0
double	0.0
boolean	false
char	\u0000
reference	null

Revisit the creation of an object by examining the sample code for the VideoItem class in Example 5-27.

Example 5-27 *Class* VideoItem

```
1  /**
2   * VideoItem.java
3   * @author Cisco Teacher
4   * @version 2002
5   */
6  public class VideoItem
7  {
8      int id;
9      double price;
10     String title;
11     // explicit initialization
12     String location = "Stock check table";
13
14     // constructor
15     /**
16      * @param aId The video's id number as an int
17      * @param iPrice The video's price as a double
18      * @param aTitle The video's title as a String
19      * @param aLocation The video's location as a String
20      */
21     public VideoItem(int aId, double aPrice,
22                 String aTitle, String aLocation)
23     {
24         id = aId;
25         price = aPrice;
26         title = aTitle;
27         location = aLocation;
28     }
29
30     // additional methods
31
32  } // end of VideoItem class
33
```

It is very important to note that variables declared in a method are not assigned any default values. The programmer is responsible for ensuring that all variables in a method have assigned values before use. Variables in a method are created in stack memory. Note in Figure 5-9 that the variable s1 (declared in the main method) is not assigned a default value. Not until Step 4 is a variable assignment made to s1.

Figure 5-9 Initial Values

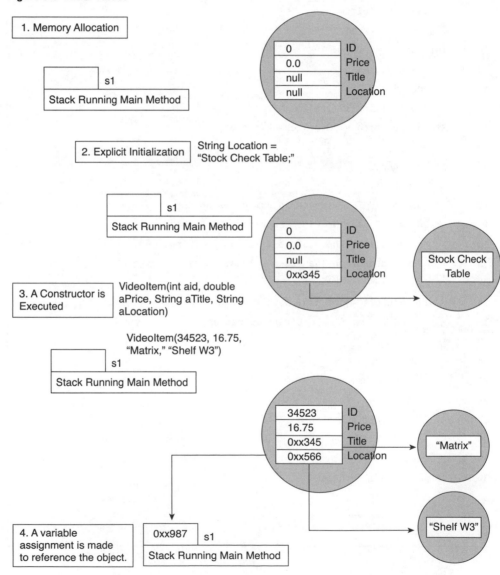

Default Constructor

Students have seen sample code in which no constructor is defined. If a constructor is not defined, how is an object created? The Java compiler inserts a constructor (*default constructor*) in the class definition. This constructor has the same name as the class and requires no arguments. This constructor does not have any specialized instructions. This type of a constructor also is referred to as the null constructor; it does nothing. Example 5-28 shows the TimeClock class, which has no constructor.

Example 5-28 *No Constructor Defined*

```
1 /**
2  * TimeClock.java
3  * @author Cisco Teacher
4  * @version 2002
5  */
6 public class TimeClock
7 {
8     private int hours;
9     private int minutes;
10    private int seconds;
11
12    public void setTime(int hour, int minute, int second)
13    {
14        hours = hours;
15        minutes - minute;
16        seconds = second;
17    }
18
19    public static void main(String args[])
20    {
21        /*
22        the Java compiler will insert a null constructor
23        when no constructor has been explicitly defined.
24        */
25        TimeClock myTime = new TimeClock();
26        myTime.setTime(7, 30, 5);
27    }
28 }//end TimeClock class
```

An object created using the null constructor has all the member data initialized to their default values or to the initialization values that explicitly are assigned in the declaration section of the class or an initializer block.

Defined Constructor

When a class definition includes an explicit constructor (*defined constructor*), the compiler uses the constructor. The compiler does not insert a null constructor in the class definition. The rules and the insertion of multiple constructor definitions in a class are discussed later in this chapter in the section "Overloading Constructors." Example 5-29 shows the `TimeClock` class, which now has an explicitly defined constructor.

Example 5-29 *Explicitly Defined Constructor*

```
 1 /**
 2  * TimeClock.java
 3  * @author Cisco Teacher
 4  * @version 2002
 5  */
 6 public class TimeClock
 7 {
 8    private int hours;
 9    private int minutes;
10    private int seconds;
11
12    public TimeClock(int hour)
13    {
14       hours = hour;
15       minutes = 0;
16       seconds = 0;
17    }
18
19    public void setTime(int hour, int minute, int second)
20    {
21       hours = hours;
22       minutes = minute;
23       seconds = second;
24    }
25
```

Example 5-29 *Explicitly Defined Constructor (Continued)*

```
26    public static void main(String args[])
27    {
28        /*
29        the Java compiler will not insert a null constructor
30        when no constructor has been explicitly defined.
31        use of 'TimeClock myTime = new TimeClock();' would
32        cause an error.
33        */
34        TimeClock myTime = new TimeClock(5);
35        myTime.setTime(7, 30, 5);
36    }
37 }//end TimeClock class
```

Method Types and Syntax

A method is a set of instructions executed by an object. Methods also are referred to as behaviors that describe what objects can do. This section covers the following topics:

- Method syntax
- Method body
- Method name
- Return value
- Method arguments
- Concept of pass-by value
- main method
- Instance methods
- Class methods

Method Syntax

Method syntax can be understood in terms of three sections or parts, as shown in Figure 5-10:

1. The method identifier elements, which include modifiers, qualifiers, return-type, and name.

2. The method arguments, which include data types received by the method defined inside the parentheses ( ).

3. The method body defined inside opening and closing braces { }.

NOTE

For Figure 5-10, you can view the explanatory text by accessing the full, interactive graphic for this figure on the book's accompanying CD-ROM. The title of the activity is "Syntax of Methods" in e-Lab Activities.

Figure 5-10 Syntax of Methods

①   ②   ③

```
<modifiers> <qualifiers> return-type method-name (<<qualifier>
java-type variable>, <<qualifier> java-type variable>,...)
{
   "// body of the method-procedural statements
   <return java-type; >
}
```

When objects send messages to other objects, they are said to be calling the method of an object. The caller object identifies the object, the reference, and the name of the method, and provides the data required for the method. When several objects of a class are created, each object has its own copy of the instance variables. However, only one copy of the methods of the class is loaded in memory and shared by all the objects.

NOTE

For Figure 5-11, you can view the text associated with the highlighted words by accessing the full, interactive graphic for this figure on the book's accompanying CD-ROM. The title of the activity is "Sample Methods in the Core API Classes" in e-Lab Activities.

One technique for having a strong understanding of method signatures and recognizing the elements of a method is to read the API docs for the core Java classes. Some samples of the Java core class definitions are shown in Figure 5-11.

Figure 5-11 Sample Methods in the Core API Classes

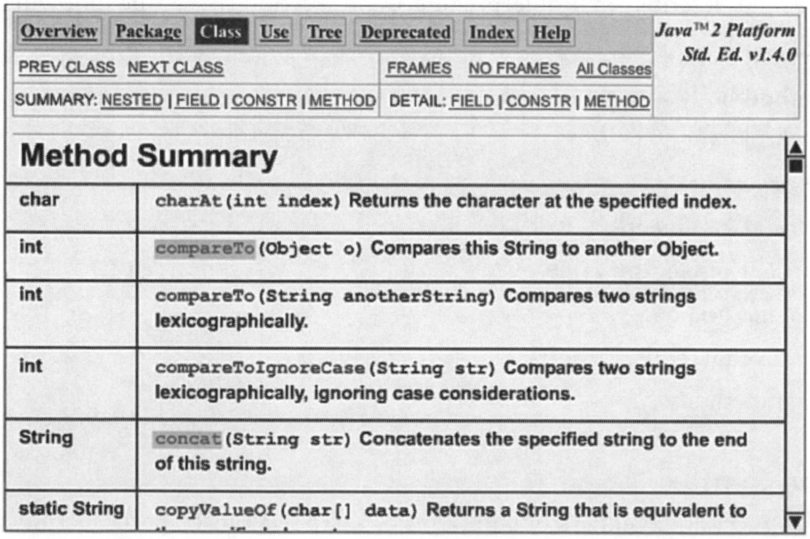

Overview	Package	**Class**	Use	Tree	Deprecated	Index	Help	*Java™ 2 Platform Std. Ed. v1.4.0*

PREV CLASS   NEXT CLASS   FRAMES   NO FRAMES   All Classes

SUMMARY: NESTED | FIELD | CONSTR | METHOD   DETAIL: FIELD | CONSTR | METHOD

Method Summary

char	`charAt(int index)` Returns the character at the specified index.
int	`compareTo(Object o)` Compares this String to another Object.
int	`compareTo(String anotherString)` Compares two strings lexicographically.
int	`compareToIgnoreCase(String str)` Compares two strings lexicographically, ignoring case considerations.
String	`concat(String str)` Concatenates the specified string to the end of this string.
static String	`copyValueOf(char[] data)` Returns a String that is equivalent to

To send a message to an object or to use the method of a class, the caller class needs to be aware of the method signature. The syntax of a method describes the method signature. It is important to remember that almost all uses of a class and objects of a class are through its methods. A strong understanding of the syntax of a method is essential to programming with Java.

The method syntax includes several required elements. These include the return type and the method name. The method syntax also includes several optional elements. These are described inside the < > symbols, as shown in Figure 5-10:

- The modifiers can be omitted. Modifiers define the accessibility of the method. Leaving out this definition declares the method to have default access. Classes within the same directory can therefore access the methods of this class of objects.
- The qualifiers can be omitted. Qualifiers (also known as *qualifier modifiers*) define special limitations or capabilities of the method. The keywords used here include the following:
  - **static**—An object of this class does not need to exist, and the method can be called by referencing `class-name.method()`.
  - **final**—The method definition cannot be changed. This qualifier is used primarily while implementing inheritance or subclasses.
  - **native**—The method calls procedures or programs in another language. This is an advanced Java language feature that is not covered in this course.
  - **synchronized**—This keyword is used in the context of multithreading (see Chapter 15, "Threads").
- The arguments of a method are the message or data that a caller needs to provide.

Method Body

The methods in a class define the procedures and tasks that an object or class can perform. The body of the method, or method body, contains the procedures. The body of the method is enclosed between the opening and closing braces ({ }). Methods include many Java language constructs, such as object creation; use of Java operators; use of sequence, selection, or logic constructs; and use of repetition with **do**, **for**, and **while** loops. Although all or some of these can be included in a method, from the outside the user of the class needs to know only three elements of the method's syntax: the method identifier or name, the return value, and the method arguments. Example 5-30 shows the method body for three methods in the `Student` class: `printData`, `setGrade`, and `main`.

Example 5-30 *Accessing Instance Data*

```
1  /**
2   * Student Class establishes the student id, name and grade
3   * @author Cisco Teacher
```

continues

Example 5-30 *Accessing Instance Data (Continued)*

```
4  * @version 2002
5  */
6 public class Student
7 {
8      private final String studentName;
9      private String grade;
10     private int studentID;
11     public static final int courseNumber = 12345;
12
13     // null constructor
14     public Student( )
15     {
16         studentName = "";
17     }
18
19     // constructor with 2 arguments
20     /**
21      * @param name The student's name as a String
22      * @param grd The student's grade as a String
23      */
24     public Student(String name, String grd)
25     {
26         studentName = name;
27         grade = grd;
28         studentID = 99999;
29     }
30
31     // constructor with 3 arguments
32     /**
33      * @param name The student's name as a String
34      * @param grd The student's grade as a String
35      * @param id The student's id as an int
36      */
37     public Student(String name, String grd, int id)
38     {
39         studentName = name;
```

Example 5-30 *Accessing Instance Data (Continued)*

```
40          grade = grd;
41          studentID = id;
42      }
43
44      // Print student name and grade
45      public void printData()
46      {
47          System.out.println("Student name is: " + studentName +
48              " Grade is: " + grade);
49      }
50
51      // set student's grade
52      /**
53       * @param newGrade The student's new grade as a String
54       */
55      public void setGrade(String newGrade)
56      {
57          grade = newGrade;
58      }
59
60      // Main method
61      public static void main(String[] args)
62      {
63          Student s1, s2;
64          s1 = new Student("Mary Jane", "A");
65          s2 = new Student("Mary Martin", "B", 12345);
66          s1.setGrade("B");
67          s2.printData();
68      }
69
70 }// End of Student class
```

Method Name

A method name can be any unique identifier. This is a required element of the method signature.

The rules for Java identifiers require that the first character be any letter or connecting punctuation of the Unicode character set. Coding convention among Java programmers varies. Some organizations establish standards that programmers working on a team must follow. For example, the Java core classes have a set of standards for identifiers. Standards help communicate the capabilities of the method by its name. This course frequently follows these Java-coding standards. The course encourages students to become familiar with these standards. Students will see these implemented in the Java Development Kit, which means all the Java packages, core classes, and most IDEs.

The coding standard used in this course for naming methods is as follows:

- Use of lower case for the starting letter and upper case for the start of each separate word in the name. No spaces or other symbols such as, _ or -, are used to separate words.
- Use of the word getXXX, where XXX is the identifier for the data returned and get signifies that the method is a getter or accessor method.
- Use of the word setXXX, where XXX is the identifier for the data of an object that will be changed by the method.
- The name explains what the method does.
  Examples:
  getStudentName, not getName or Name
  calcGradePointAverage, or calcGPA, or calculateGradePointAverage, or calculateGPA, not GPA or gradePointAverage

Return Value

The return value is a required element of the method signature. The return type declares what type of data (reference data type or primitive data type) will be returned by the method to the caller of this method. If the method has no data to return, as in the case of many setter or mutator methods, the keyword **void** must be used. If the method returns a specific data type, this must be defined using the keyword **return** in the body of the method.

The keyword **return** is used in two different formats:

- return value;
- return;

In the first format, the return type identifies the data that is to be returned, such as x, a reference to a primitive or another object, or **this**, a reference to the current object whose method is called.

The compiler automatically provides the second format (at the end of the method block) when the return type of the method is **void**. On special occasions programmers will use the second format. This is demonstrated in a later example that uses this format to end the method abruptly and exit from the method before all the instructions have been completed. This can occur if some condition was not met for the code to continue execution.

Specific Java types are primitives and Java classes. A common mistake made in method signatures is to describe the return type as the reference variable to an object or primitive. If a method returns a reference to an object, the method signature declares only the class of the object, not the object reference. If a method returns a primitive, the method signature declares the primitive data type, not the variable name.

A method can return only one value. A return statement can return a value referenced by a variable or the result of an expression. In all instances, the data type of the values must be assignment compatible to the data type declared as the return type in the method signature.

The sample code shown in Example 5-31 for the `LabelText` class demonstrates the return type **void**. When the `print()` method of the `LabelText` class is called in the `main` method, the object `String` variable `label` is printed. Because the return type for this method is **void**, the `print()` method does not return any value when used. Note that there is no return statement in the `print()` method.

Example 5-31 *Return Type*—**void**

```
1 /**
2  * A Java class for text labels of arbitrary length limit
3  * @author Cisco Teacher
4  * @version 2002
5  */
6 public class LabelText
7 {
8     public static final int MAX_TEXT = 20;
9     private String label;
10
11    /**
12       * @param inputText The text to be assigned to the label
13     */
14    public LabelText( String inputText )
```

continues

Example 5-31 *Return Type—**void** (Continued)*

```
15      {
16          System.out.println("Creating a LabelText object" );
17          if ( inputText.length() <= MAX_TEXT )
18          {
19              label = inputText;
20          }
21          else
22          {
23              System.err.println( "Input label text is too long!");
24              //NOTE: next line extracts 20 chars at index 0 to 19
25              label = inputText.substring( 0, MAX_TEXT );
26          }
27      }
28
29      public void print()
30      {
31          System.out.println( label );
32      }
33
34      public static void main( String[] args )
35      {
36          LabelText a = new LabelText( "Capital Losses" );
37          LabelText b = new LabelText( "Really Big Capital Gains" );
38          a.print();
39          b.print();
40      }
41 } // end of LabelText class
```

A method can return a reference to a primitive or any Java class.

The sample code shown in Example 5-32 for the MyStock class demonstrates the return type primitive.

Example 5-32 *Return Type—Returning a Primitive*

```
1 /**
2  * Java Program: MyStock.java
3  * @author Cisco Student
```

Example 5-32 *Return Type—Returning a Primitive (Continued)*

```
 4  * @version 2002
 5  */
 6 public class MyStock
 7 {
 8      private int stockNumber;
 9      private float price;
10
11      /**
12       * @return The item's stock number as an int
13       */
14      public  int getStockNumber()
15      {
16          return stockNumber;
17      {
18
19      /**
20       * @return The item's price as a float
21       */
22      public float getPrice()
23      {
24          return price;
25      {
26
27 } // end of MyStock class
28
```

The sample code shown in Example 5-33 for the modified `MyStock` class demonstrates the return type Java class. In this code, the keyword **this** is used as a placeholder for the current objects whose methods are called. At compile time, no objects are created. The keyword **this** serves as a placeholder variable for the compiler, which will be assigned as an object reference at runtime. Section "The Variable **this**," presented later in this chapter, explores the use of **this** in further detail.

Example 5-33 *Return Type—Returning a Java Class*

```
1 /**
2  * Java Program: MyStock.java
```

continues

Example 5-33 *Return Type—Returning a Java Class (Continued)*

```
3  * @author Cisco Student
4  * @version 2002
5  */
6 public class MyStock
7 {
8      private int stockNumber;
9      private float price;
10
11     /**
12      * @return The item's stock number as a MyStock type
13      */
14     public MyStock setStockNumber(int stockNumber)
15     {
16         this.stockNumber = stockNumber;
17             return this;
18     }
19
20     /**
21      * @return The item's price as a MyStock type
22      */
23     public MyStock setPrice(float price)
24     {
25         this.price = price;
26         return this;
27     }
28
29     /**
30      * @return The item's number as an integer
31      */
32     public int getStockNumber()
33     {
34         return this.stockNumber;
35     }
36
37     /**
38      * @return The item's price as a float
```

Example 5-33 *Return Type—Returning a Java Class (Continued)*

```
39        */
40      public float getPrice()
41      {
42              return this.price;
43      }
44
45 } // end of MyStock class
```

In addition to declaring the return value, the body of the method must include the return statement in the code. The sample code shown in Example 5-34 demonstrates the correct and incorrect placement of the return statement.

Example 5-34 *Placement of a Return Statement*

```
1 /**
2 * Java Program: SumIntegers.java
3 * @author Cisco Teacher
4 * @version 2002
5 */
6 public class SumIntegers
7 {
8     /**
9      * @param x Any number as an int
10     * @param y Any number as an int
11     */
12      public static int getSum(int x, int y)
13      {
14          int sum = 0;
15          for(int i = x; i <= y; i++)
16          {
17              sum += i;
18              //return sum;   incorrect placement of the return
                    statement
19          }
20          //correct placement of the return statement
21          return sum;
22      }
```

continues

NOTE

For Example 5-34, you can view the explanatory text by accessing the full, interactive graphic for this example on the book's accompanying CD-ROM. The title of the activity is "Placement of a Return Statement" in e-Lab Activities.

Example 5-34 *Placement of a Return Statement (Continued)*

```
23
24
25        // Main method
26        public static void main(String[] args)
27        {
28            System.out.println("\nPlease enter the integer range "
29                + "for which you want to calculate the sum.");
30            int start = Console.readInt("Enter starting integer for count:");
31            int stop = Console.readInt("Enter stopping integer for count:");
32            System.out.println("Sum of numbers from " + start + " to "
33                + stop + " is " + getSum(start,stop));
34        }// end of main
35 }// end of SumIntegers class
```

Method Arguments

The method arguments can be omitted by declaring the method to have no arguments using the syntax (). The empty parentheses following the method name indicates that there are no arguments for the method. A frequent use of this type of argument declaration is with getXXX methods.

The method can have one or more arguments defined in the method signature. When defining one or more arguments, the syntax for each argument includes the use of qualifiers, Java data type, and the name of the argument method variable that will store the data. A comma separates each argument. Methods can include arguments in which the data type is the same. If a method requires more than one argument, the syntax for each argument (the use of qualifiers, the Java data type, and the name of the method variable) is required for each argument, even if the Java data type for the arguments is the same. Finally, the naming of the argument method variable must be different for each argument. The following sample code demonstrates correct and incorrect argument syntax.

```
public int myMethod(String s1, String s2, int x, int y);  //correct syntax
public int myMethod(String s1, s2, int x, y);  //incorrect syntax
public  int myMethod(s1, s2, x, y);  //incorrect syntax
```

The arguments in the method definition also are referred to as formal parameters, and the data values provided when calling the method are known as actual values. The actual values sent by the caller are stored in the method variables defined by the formal parameters. The following sample code demonstrates the use of method arguments.

The method setAccountData:

```
public void setAccountInfo(String s1, String s2, int x, int y);
```

can be called as follows:

```
//passing literals as arguments to a method
setAccountInfo("John", "Doe", 1117, 150);
//passing variables as arguments to a method
setAccountInfo(fname, lname, accountID, initialDeposit);
//passing expressions as arguments to a method
setAccountInfo(customer.getFirstName(), customer.getLastName(),
getNextAccoutNumber(), customerDeposit + 50);
```

Concept of Pass-by-Value

A method call can include literal data or the reference to an object or primitive. When the method call uses a variable, the JVM makes a copy of the value stored in memory and assigns it to the method variable. This is known as passing the value, or pass-by-value. The original variable is not changed. Java acts upon data received using the pass-by-value and not pass-by-reference rule. In pass-by-reference, the method can change the data in the original location.

The sample code shown in Example 5-35 for the MyDate class and Example 5-36 for the PassTest class demonstrates the concept of pass-by-value.

Example 5-35 *Pass-by-Value in* MyDate *Class—*MyDate.java

```
 1 /**
 2  * Java Program: MyDate.java
 3  * @author Cisco Teacher
 4  * @version 2002
 5  */
 6 public class MyDate
 7 {
 8     private int day;
 9     private int month;
10     private int year;
11
12     /**
13      * @param day The day as an int
14      * @param month The month as an int
15      * @param year The year as an int
16      */
```

continues

Example 5-35 *Pass-by-Value in* MyDate *Class—*MyDate.java *(Continued)*

```java
17      public MyDate(int day, int month, int year)
18      {
19          this.day = day;
20          this.month = month;
21          this.year = year;
22      }
23
24      // set day method
25      /**
26       * @param day The day as an int
27       */
28      public void setDay(int day)
29      {
30          this.day = day;
31      }
32
33      // set month method
34      /**
35       * @param month The month as an int
36       */
37      public void setMonth(int month)
38      {
39          this.month = month;
40      }
41
42      // set year method
43      /**
44       * @param year The year as an int
45       */
46      public void setYear(int year)
47      {
48          this.year = year;
49      }
50
51      // display method for MyDate
52      public void displayDate()
```

Example 5-35 *Pass-by-Value in* MyDate *Class—*MyDate.java *(Continued)*

```
53    {
54          System.out.println("The date is: " + month
55              + "/" + day + "/" + year);
56    }
57
58 } // end of MyDate class
```

Example 5-36 *Pass-by-Value in* MyDate *Class—*PastTest.java

```
 1 /**
 2  * Java Program: PassText.java
 3  * @author Cisco Teacher
 4  * @version 2002
 5  */
 6 public class PassTest
 7 {
 8     // Methods to change the current values
 9     /**
10      * @param value A value as an int
11      */
12     public static void changeInt(int value)
13     {
14         value = 55;
15     }
16
17     /**
18      * @param ref A date as a MyDate type
19      */
20     public static void changeObjectRef(MyDate ref)
21     {
22         ref = new MyDate(1, 1, 2000);
23     }
24
25     /**
26      * @param ref A day reference as MyDate type
27      */
```

continues

Example 5-36 *Pass-by-Value in* MyDate *Class—*PastTest.java *(Continued)*

```
28      public static void changeObjectAttr(MyDate ref)
29      {
30          ref.setDay(4);
31      }
32
33      public static void main(String args[])
34      {
35          MyDate date;
36          int val;
37
38          // Assign the int
39          val = 11;
40
41          // Try to change it
42          changeInt(val);
43
44          // What is the current value?
45          // val will retain its value of 11
46          System.out.println("Int value is: " + val);
47
48          // Assign the date
49          date = new MyDate(22, 7, 1964);
50
51          // Try to change it
52          /* At the start of the changeObjectRef method execution,
53             ref has the same value as the object reference date.
54             However, the very first instruction in the changeObjectRef
55             method assigns a new object reference value to ref.
56             The value held by the date object
57             reference has not been changed.
58          */
59          changeObjectRef(date);
60
61          // What is the current value?
62          /* Since the date object reference did not get modified
63             by the previous line of code, what is displayed by
```

Example 5-36 *Pass-by-Value in* MyDate *Class*—PastTest.java *(Continued)*

```
64              this method is the unchanged object data referenced
65              by the object reference date.
66      */
67      date.displayDate();
68
69      // Now change the day attribute through the object reference
70      changeObjectAttr(date);
71
72      // What is the current value?
73      /* Since the changeObjectAttr method accesses the non-private
74         method setDay of the MyDate class, this method can
75         change object data.
76      */
77      date.displayDate();
78    }
79 }// end of PassTest class
```

When the data sent is a Java primitive (**char, boolean, int, short, double**, and so on), only the copy of the value is acted on. When the data sent is a reference to an object—that is, the address of an object—the method does have access to the nonprivate data of that object through the reference. Therefore, it can change the values of the object data. However, the original reference, or the address of the object, cannot be changed. The value passed to the method is a copy of the reference or address of the object.

Suppose that a student provided an electronic copy of a term paper to her teacher. The teacher can change the copy, but the student still has the original. This is an analogy of a pass-by-value action. However, if a friend was provided with the location of the term paper on the student's computer and the friend was given access to this computer, any changes the friend made to the term paper in the computer would occur because the student provided the reference. The student also has a copy and access to the same term paper, so the student could change the contents of the term paper. Depending on who got there last, the contents of the term paper would reflect these changes. Although both the student and the friend are able to reference the term paper, the information that the student gave the friend is not the term paper, but a copy of the location. That is a reference to the term paper.

Often this is confused as a pass-by-reference action. Actually, a method is given a copy of the address to the object. So, even with reference variables, the action is still considered a pass-by-value.

`main` Method

By now, students have used the `main` method many times in this course. Some of the options for placement of the `main` method now are explained further. The `main` method signature is defined by Java language rules. All other methods are considered user-defined methods. The `main` method signature is specific because the JVM is programmed to look for this signature. Any class defining a `main` method, such as the `Student` class shown in Example 5-37, is considered an entry point in an application that can consist of many classes.

Example 5-37 `main` *Method*

```
1 /**
2  * Student Class establishes the student id, name and grade
3  * @author Cisco Teacher
4  * @version 2002
5  */
6 public class Student
7 {
8      private final String studentName;
9      private String grade;
10     private int studentID;
11     public static final int courseNumber = 12345;
12
13     // null constructor
14     public Student( )
15     {
16         studentName = "";
17     }
18
19     // constructor with 2 arguments
20     /**
21      * @param name The student's name as a String
22      * @param grd The student's grade as a String
23      */
24     public Student(String name, String grd)
```

Example 5-37 main *Method (Continued)*

```
25    {
26        studentName = name;
27        grade = grd;
28        studentID = 99999;
29    }
30
31    // constructor with 3 arguments
32    /**
33     * @param name The student's name as a String
34     * @param grd The student's grade as a String
35     * @param id The student's id as an int
36     */
37    public Student(String name, String grd, int id)
38    {
39        studentName = name;
40        grade = grd;
41        studentID = id;
42    }
43
44    // Print student name and grade
45    public void printData()
46    {
47        System.out.println("Student name is: "
48            + studentName + " Grade is: " + grade);
49    }
50
51    // set student's grade
52    /**
53     * @param newGrade The student's new grade as a String
54     */
55    public void setGrade(String newGrade)
56    {
57        grade = newGrade;
58    }
59
```

continues

Example 5-37 main *Method (Continued)*

```
60      // Main method
61      public static void main(String[] args)
62      {
63          Student s1, s2;
64          s1 = new Student("Mary Jane", "A");
65          s2 = new Student("Mary Martin", "B", 12345);
66          s1.setGrade("B");
67          s2.printData();
68      }
69 }// End of Student class
```

The main method signature includes the access modifier **public**, the qualifier **static**, the return type of **void**, and a single argument that describes a data type of String array and a variable to store this data. An array is a reference to more than one object of the same Java data type. For this discussion, String[] declares the data type to be one or more String objects. Each is a separate object that is accessible through array indexes. Sometimes the String array is defined using the format String args[]. The array symbol is attached to the variable name, not the Java type. This does not change the meaning of the argument; it still defines the argument to be a reference to an array of String objects.

The coding convention is to use the label args for the variable in the method argument. (String [] s), (String s[]), (String dataFromConsole[]), or (String [] dataFrom-Console) will still work, however. In each of these examples, the variable label is different, but the data type has not changed. Use of the args label is recommended for most cases.

To test a class, a programmer often includes the main method in every class. This makes it very easy to test the class, but it also introduces confusion in organizing classes and identifying an entry point for an application. To tightly control which class should be loaded in memory first, avoid including a main method in more than one class. If the main method has been inserted for the purposes of testing a class, be sure to comment out this method when the classes are working. The sample code for the Student class demonstrates the use of the main method for testing the class.

Instance Methods

Methods that can be accessed only through an object of a class are known as *instance methods*. If the qualifier **static** is not declared in the method signature, the method is considered an instance method. The familiar Student class illustrates the definition and use of instance methods. Instance methods can access any data members of the class just by using the appropriate name. Each object of a class shares the methods of the class and retains its own copy of the data. Instance methods can access other methods of the same class, including static methods. Instance methods can also access nonprivate methods and variables of other classes. Almost all of the methods used in the classes so far have been instance methods, such as those methods highlighted in the Student class shown in Example 5-38.

Example 5-38 *Instance Methods*

```
1 /**
2  * Student Class establishes the student id, name and grade
3  * @author Cisco Teacher
4  * @version 2002
5  */
6 public class Student
7 {
8      private final String studentName;
9      private String grade;
10     private int studentID;
11     public static final int courseNumber = 12345;
12
13     // null constructor
14     public Student( )
15     {
16         studentName = "";
17     }
18
19     // constructor with 2 arguments
20     /**
21      * @param name The student's name as a String
22      * @param grd The student's grade as a String
23      */
24     public Student(String name, String grd)
25     {
26         studentName = name;
27         grade = grd;
```

continues

Example 5-38 *Instance Methods (Continued)*

```
28              studentID = 99999;
29      }
30
31      // constructor with 3 arguments
32      /**
33       * @param name The student's name as a String
34       * @param grd The student's grade as a String
35       * @param id The student's id as an int
36       */
37      public Student(String name, String grd, int id)
38      {
39              studentName = name;
40              grade = grd;
41              studentID = id;
42      }
43
44      // Print student name and grade
45      public void printData()
46      {
47              System.out.println("Student name is: "
48                      + studentName + " Grade is: " + grade);
49      }
50
51      // set student's grade
52      /**
53       * @param newGrade The student's new grade as a String
54       */
55      public void setGrade(String newGrade)
56      {
57              grade = newGrade;
58      }
59
60      // Main method
61      public static void main(String[] args)
62      {
63              Student s1, s2;
```

Example 5-38 *Instance Methods (Continued)*

```
64          s1 = new Student("Mary Jane", "A");
65          s2 = new Student("Mary Martin", "B", 12345);
66          s1.setGrade("B");
67          s2.printData();
68      }
69 }// End of Student class
```

Class Methods

Class methods (also known as *static methods*) require that no objects of the class be created to use these methods. Instance variables and nonstatic methods cannot be directly accessed by static methods of the same class. This is a very important concept and can cause some confusion when using the main method. Recall that the main method is a static method. This method cannot access instance data, but it can access static variables. This is because the main method can be executed when no objects of the class have been created and, therefore, no instance variables exist. Static methods can access instance methods or instance data only after an instance of the class is created—that is, after an object has been created. The sample code for the Commission class, shown in Example 5-39, illustrates the definition and use of class methods.

Example 5-39 *Class Methods*

```
 1 /**
 2  *  Java Program: Commission.java
 3  * @author Cisco Teacher
 4  * @version 2002
 5  */
 6 // example of class or static methods.
 7
 8 class Commission
 9 {
10     /**
11      * @param s A number as a double
12      * @param t A number as a double
13      */
14     public static double computeCommission(double s, double r)
15     {
```

continues

Example 5-39 *Class Methods (Continued)*

```
16          return (( (double) r / 100.0) * s);
17    }
18
19 } //end of Commission class
20
21 /**
22  * Java Program: AnotherClass.java
23  * @author Cisco Teacher
24  * @version 2002
25  */
26 public class AnotherClass
27 {
28     public static void main(String[] args)
29     {
30         double comm = Commission.computeCommission(2000.00,.30);
31         System.out.println("The Commisssion is " + comm);
32     }
33 }  // end of AnotherClass class
```

The Variable this

In the Java programming language, the keyword **this** can be used to represent an instance of the class in which it appears. This section covers the use of the keyword **this** in constructors and methods

Using this in Constructors and Methods

When several objects of a class are created, each object has its own copy of the instance variables. However, only one copy of the methods of the class is loaded in memory and shared by all the objects. How does a method keep track of which object is using the method currently? Every instance method has a variable with the name **this**, which refers to the current object for which the method is applied. Each time an instance method is called, the **this** variable is set to the reference for the particular class object.

The variable **this** is prefixed by the compiler for every instance variable in the class. Some programmers manually insert the **this** reference for every use of the instance variable. Students do not need to do this. However, students do need to use the **this** reference in many situations. If the instance variable name and one of the method arguments variable names are the same, for example, the **this** variable clarifies which variable the method should work on. A common use of the **this** reference is in constructors. If students find it confusing, they can create different names for the argument variables.

The sample code shown in Example 5-40 for the MyStock class demonstrates the use of **this** to clarify a method variable from the object variable. Another use of **this** is to return a reference to the object itself. For example, if a method needs to return a reference to the object that owns the method, then return the **this** variable. The reference **this** also is used when implementing GUI classes and nested and inner classes. These topics are covered later in Chapter 10, "Creating GUI Applications Using AWT."

Example 5-40 MyStock.java

```
1 /**
2  * Java Program: MyStock.java
3  * @author Cisco Teacher
4  * @version 2002
5  */
6 public class MyStock
7 {
8     private int stockNumber;
9     private float price;
10
11    /**
12     * @param stockNumber The stock number as an int
13     * @param price The stock price as a float
14     */
15    public MyStock(int stockNumber, float price)
16    {
17        this.stockNumber = stockNumber;
18        this.price = price;
19    }
20
21    // additional methods
22
23 } // end of MyStock class
```

NOTE

For Example 5-41, you can view the explanatory text by accessing the full, interactive graphic for this example on the book's accompanying CD-ROM. The title of the activity is "MyStock.java" in e-Lab Activities.

The expanded sample code in Example 5-41 for the MyStock class demonstrates the use of return this; as a return value of a method.

Example 5-41 MyStock.java

```java
1 /**
2  * Java Program: MyStock.java
3  * @author Cisco Teacher
4  * @version 2002
5  */
6 public class MyStock
7 {
8      private int stockNumber;
9      private float price;
10
11     /**
12      * @param stockNumber The stock number as an int
13      * @param price The stock price as a float
14      */
15     public MyStock(int stockNumber, float price)
16     {
17         this.stockNumber = stockNumber;
18         this.price = price;
19     }
20
21     /**
22      * @param stockNumber The stock number as an int
23      */
24     public MyStock setStockNumber(int stockNumber)
25     {
26         this.stockNumber = stockNumber;
27         return this;
28     }
29
30     /**
31      * @param price The stock price as a float
32      */
33     public MyStock setPrice(float price)
```

Example 5-41 MyStock.java *(Continued)*

```
34      {
35          this.price = price;
36          return this;
37      }
38
39      /**
40       * @return The stock number as an int
41       */
42      public int getStockNumber()
43      {
44          return this.stockNumber;
45      }
46
47      /**
48       * @return The stock price as a float
49       */
50      public float getPrice()
51      {
52          return this.price;
53      }
54 } // end of MyStock class
```

Method Data and Encapsulation

The data available to the programmer when writing code for a method can come from a number of sources. In addition, the programmer can restrict access to the method using access modifiers. This section covers the following topics:

- Data sources
- Encapsulation using methods

Data Sources

Four different potential sources of data are available when writing code for a method:

- Arguments passed to the methods—referred to by using the method arguments variable names or formal parameter names
- Data members—both instance variables and class variables, which are referred to by their names

- Local variables—declared in the body of the method
- Values—returned by other methods that are called from within the method

The sample code for the TelNumber class illustrates the use of the different data sources in a method (see Example 5-42).

Example 5-42 *Data Sources in a Method*

```
1 /**
2  * Java Program: TelNumber.java
3  * @author Cisco Teacher
4  * @version 2002
5  */
6 public class TelNumber
7 {
8     /**
9      * @param s The telephone number as a string
10     */
11    public static void printTelNumber(String s)
12    {
13        // check for digits only
14        for ( int i = 0; i < s.length(); i++ )
15        {
16            if ( ! Character.isDigit( s.charAt( i ) )
17            {
18                System.out.println( "Not valid: " + s );
19                /*
20                this will return control to the calling
21                environment. The remaining code in this
22                method will not be executed, since the
23                String s has been determined to be invalid.
24                */
25                return;
26            }
27        }
28         // format string into (ddd) ddd-dddd
29        StringBuffer sb = new StringBuffer(s);
30        while (sb.length() < 10)
```

Example 5-42 *Data Sources in a Method (Continued)*

```
31          {
32               sb.insert(0, '0');
33          }
34          sb.insert( 6, '-' );
35          sb.insert( 3, ") " );
36          sb.insert( 0, '(' );
37          System.out.println( sb );
38      }
39 } // end of TelNumber class
```

Implementing Encapsulation Using Methods

Encapsulation occurs in methods naturally. The user of a method knows the signature of the method, but not how it works. In addition to this, the access to the method can be restricted through the use of access modifiers (**private**, **protected**, or no access modifier [default]). Encapsulation in general applies to hiding object information. For the majority of the time, instance variables should be declared as **private** and methods should be declared as **public**. Hidden instance data of an object still might need to be accessed or changed. This can be done through getters (accessor methods) and setters (mutator methods).

Getters and setters can be created for **private** attributes of the object. The setting and retrieving of data also can be combined where it makes sense. When students combine, they might lose some flexibility. In general, you should provide setters only for attributes that need to change. For example, when a Student object is created, the student name does not change. This should be declared **final**, and its value should be set in the constructor method. Because studentName is **final** and **private**, a set method for studentName is not required. A get method still might be required. The sample code shown in Example 5-43 for the Student class demonstrates encapsulation and the use of set and get methods.

Example 5-43 *Implementing Encapsulation and Using the set and get Methods*

```
1 /**
2  * Student Class establishes the student id, name and grade
3  * @author Cisco Teacher
4  * @version 2002
5  */
```

continues

Example 5-43 *Implementing Encapsulation and Using the set and get Methods (Continued)*

```
 6 public class Student
 7 {
 8      private final String studentName;
 9      private String grade;
10      private int studentID;
11      public static final int courseNumber = 12345;
12
13      // null constructor
14      public Student( )
15      {
16          studentName = "";
17      }
18
19      // constructor with 2 arguments
20      /**
21       * @param name The student's name as a String
22       * @param grd The student's grade as a String
23       */
24      public Student(String name, String grd)
25      {
26          studentName = name;
27          grade = grd;
28          studentID = 99999;
29      }
30
31      // constructor with 3 arguments
32      /**
33       * @param name The student's name as a String
34       * @param grd The student's grade as a String
35       * @param id The student's id as an int
36       */
37      public Student(String name, String grd, int id)
38      {
39          studentName = name;
40          grade = grd;
41          studentID = id;
```

Example 5-43 *Implementing Encapsulation and Using the set and get Methods (Continued)*

```
42      }
43
44      // Print student name and grade
45      public void printData()
46      {
47          System.out.println("Student name is: "
48              + studentName + " Grade is: " + grade);
49      }
50
51      // get student's name
52      /**
53       * @return The student's name as a String
54       */
55      public String getStudentName()
56      {
57          return studentName;
58      }
59
60      // set student's grade
61      /**
62       * @param newGrade The student's new grade as a String
63       */
64      public void setGrade(String newGrade)
65      {
66          grade = newGrade;
67      }
68
69      // get student's grade
70      /**
71       * @return The studen's grade as a String
72       */
73      public String getGrade()
74      {
75          return grade;
76      }
```

continues

Example 5-43 *Implementing Encapsulation and Using the set and get Methods (Continued)*

```
77
78      // set student's id
79      /*
80          @param id The student's id as an int
81      */
82      public void setStudentID(int id)
83      {
84          studentID = id;
85      }
86
87      // get student's id
88      /**
89       * @return The student's id as an int
90       */
91      public int getStudentID()
92      {
93          return studentID;
94      }
95
96      // Main method
97      public static void main(String[] args)
98      {
99          Student s1, s2;
100         s1 = new Student("Mary Jane", "A");
101         s2 = new Student("Mary Martin", "B", 12345);
102         s1.setGrade("B");
103         s2.printData();
104     }
105 }// End of Student class
```

Overloading

Overloading is defined as using one identifier to refer to multiple items in the same scope. In the Java programming language, you can overload methods and constructors. This section covers the following topics:

- Overloading methods
- Overloading constructors

Overloading Methods

Two or more methods can be defined in the same class and can be given the same name. This is called *method overloading*. Both methods and constructors can be overloaded. Methods typically are overloaded because the user wants to have different versions of a method accept different input but have the same name because they have similar functions.

The rules for overloading methods or constructors are as follows:

- Names must be the same.
- The number of arguments must be different, or if the number of arguments is the same, at least one argument (by position) must have a different data type.
- Changing only the return type for a method with the same name, same number of arguments, and same data type of arguments (by position) is not a valid overloaded method.

As previously stated, overloading is done to obtain different input. The differences, therefore, need to be in the input received. Although overloading can be used to vary the order of the arguments, this is not advisable. Maintaining code for all possible orders of a long list of arguments can be cumbersome and difficult. The sample code shown in Example 5-44 for the Commission class demonstrates the use of overloaded methods.

Example 5-44 *Overloaded Methods*

```
1 /**
2  * Java Program: Commission.java
3  * @author Cisco Teacher
4  * @version 2002
5  */
6 public class Commission
7 {
8     public static void main(String[] args)
9     {
10         double sales = 50000.0;
11         double commission = 0.0;
12         int rate = 5;
13         /* since rate is an int variable, the second method
14          would be called */
15         commission = computeCommission(sales, rate);
```

continues

Example 5-44 *Overloaded Methods (Continued)*

```
16
17          System.out.println("Commission on sales of "
18              + sales
19              + " with a rate of " + rate + "%"
20              + " is "
21              + commission);
22      }
23
24      /**
25       * @param s A number as a double
26       * @param r A number as a double
27       */
28      public static double computeCommission(double s, double r)
29      {
30          return (( (double) r / 100.0) * s);
31      }
32
33      /**
34       * @param s A number as a double
35       * @param r A number as an int
36       */
37      public static double computeCommission(double s, int r)
38      {
39          return (( (double) r / 100.0) * s);
40      }
41
42 } // end of  Commission class
```

How does the JVM know which method or constructor to use? The compiler uses a process called name mangling to generate distinct internal names for the methods. The name-mangling process involves adding characters to the name to represent the enclosed argument types.

Overloaded methods of the StringBuffer class, from the API docs, are shown in Figure 5-12.

Figure 5-12 Overloaded Methods API Docs

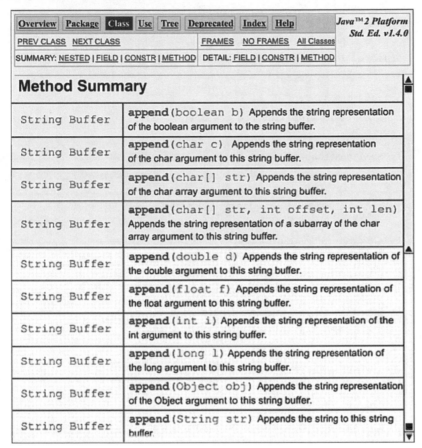

Overloading Constructors

The sample code shown in Example 5-45 for the Student class demonstrates the use of overloaded constructors.

Example 5-45 *Overloaded Constructors*

```
1 /**
2  * Student Class establishes the student id, name and grade
3  * @author Cisco Teacher
4  * @version 2002
5  */
```

continues

Example 5-45 *Overloaded Constructors (Continued)*

```
 6 public class Student
 7 {
 8     private final String studentName;
 9     private String grade;
10     private int studentID;
11     public static final int courseNumber = 12345;
12
13     // null constructor
14     public Student( )
15     {
16         studentName = "";
17     }
18
19     // constructor with 2 arguments
20     /**
21      * @param name The student's name as a String
22      * @param grd The student's grade as a String
23      */
24     public Student(String name, String grd)
25     {
26         studentName = name;
27         grade = grd;
28         studentID = 99999;
29     }
30
31     // constructor with 3 arguments
32     /**
33      * @param name The student's name as a String
34      * @param grd The student's grade as a String
35      * @param id The student's id as an int
36      */
37     public Student(String name, String grd, int id)
38     {
39         studentName = name;
40         grade = grd;
41         studentID = id;
42     }
```

Example 5-45 *Overloaded Constructors (Continued)*

```
43
44     // Print student name and grade
45     public void printData()
46     {
47         System.out.println("Student name is: "
48             + studentName + " Grade is: " + grade);
49     }
50
51     // set student's grade
52     /**
53      * @param newGrade The student's new grade as a String
54      */
55     public void setGrade(String newGrade)
56     {
57         grade = newGrade;
58     }
59
60     // Main method
61     public static void main(String[] args)
62     {
63         Student s1, s2;
64         s1 = new Student("Mary Jane", "A");
65         s2 = new Student("Mary Martin", "B", 12345);
66         s1.setGrade("B");
67         s2.printData();
68     }
69 }// End of Student class
```

The sample code shown in Example 5-46 for the Employee class demonstrates the use of overloaded constructors that call each other using the **this** variable.

Example 5-46 *Overloaded Constructors Using the* **this** *Variable*

```
1 /**
2  * Java Program: Employee.java
3  * @author Cisco Teacher
```

continues

Example 5-46 *Overloaded Constructors Using the* **this** *Variable (Continued)*

```
 4  * @version 2002
 5  */
 6
 7 import java.util.Date;
 8
 9 public class Employee
10 {
11      private static final double BASE_SALARY = 15000.00;
12      private String name;
13      private double salary;
14      private Date birthDate;
15
16      /**
17       * @param name The employee name as a String
18       * @param salary The employee salary as a double
19       * @param DoB The employee date of birth as a Date
20       */
21      public Employee(String name, double salary, Date DoB)
22      {
23          this.name = name;
24          this.salary = salary;
25          this.birthDate = DoB;
26      }
27
28      /**
29       * @param name The employee name as a String
30       * @param salary The employee salary as a double
31       */
32      public Employee(String name, double salary)
33      {
34          this(name, salary, null);
35      }
36
37      /**
38       * @param name The employee name as a String
39       * @param DoB The employee date of birth as a Date
```

Example 5-46 *Overloaded Constructors Using the* **this** *Variable (Continued)*

```
40      */
41      public Employee(String name, Date DoB)
42      {
43          this(name, BASE_SALARY, DoB);
44      }
45
46      /**
47       * @param name The employee name as a String
48       */
49      public Employee(String name)
50      {
51          this(name, BASE_SALARY);
52      }
53
54      // more Employee code...
55
56 } // end of Employee class
```

Java Type Lifespan

Earlier in this chapter, we discussed the scope, or lifespan, of a variable. This section expands on this topic by addressing the following topics:

- Data initialization
- Scope of variables
- Lifetime of an object
- Mutability of an object
- Destruction of an object
- Finalizers

Initializing Data

Object instance data is initialized upon creation of the object. The **new** operator creates an object. During each stage of object creation, values are assigned to the variables. Static variables of a class are initialized before any object is created. The construction process ensures that no member or class data for an object is without known value. If the programmer does not specify an initial value, default values are applied. The primitive data types **byte**, **short**, **int**, and **long** are set to **0**; **double** and **float** are set to **0.0**; **boolean** is set to **false**; **char** is set to \u0000; and reference is set to **null**.

Some things cannot be initialized with a single statement. If a large number of variables are to be initialized with some calculated value or be based on testing some condition, a code block must be created. This code block has no name, it is not a method, and it is executed before an object is created. This is also known as an *initialization block*.

Two types of initialization blocks exist: static and nonstatic. A *static initialization block* is used to initialize static variables of a class. This block is executed only once when the class is loaded at runtime. The static block is defined using the keyword **static**. This block can initialize only static variables of the class. The sample code shown in Example 5-47 for the ConstantThings2 class demonstrates the use of a static initialization block.

Example 5-47 *Using a Static Initialization Block*

```
1 /**
2 * Java Program: ConstantThings2
3 * @author Cisco Teacher
4 * @version 2002
5 */
6 public class ConstantThings2
7 {
8     private static final int ARRAY_SIZE;
9
10     public static void main(String[] args)
11     {
12         String[] stringThings;
13         stringThings = new String[ARRAY_SIZE];
14         stringThings[0] = "Howdy pardner";
15         System.out.println( stringThings[0] );
16     }
17
18     static
19     {
20             ARRAY_SIZE = 57;
21     }
22
23 }// end of ConstantThings2
```

Nonstatic Initialization Block

A *nonstatic initialization block* is executed for each object that is created and, thus, can initialize instance variables in a class. Nonstatic initialization blocks can initialize both static and instance variables. Object data always is initialized when an object is created. The sample code shown in Example 5-48 for the Account class demonstrates the usage of a nonstatic initialization block.

Example 5-48 *Using a Nonstatic Initialization Block*

```
1  /**
2   * Java Program: Account.java
3   * @author Cisco Teacher
4   * @version 2002
5   */
6  import java.util.*;
7  import java.text.*;
8
9  public class Account
10 {
11     private String name;
12     private int accountID;
13     private double balance;
14     private int numSequenceOnFirstCheck = 1001;
15     private Date dateOpened;
16     private Date nextBillingDate;
17
18     /*
19     Non-static initialization block to automatically
20     calculate the date opened and next billing date
21     for each new instance of the class Account.
22     Relieves the user of the class from passing this
23     data as an argument to the Account constructor.
24     */
25     {
26         Calendar c = Calendar.getInstance();
27         dateOpened = c.getTime();
28         c.add(Calendar.DATE, 30);
29         nextBillingDate = c.getTime();
30     }
```

continues

Example 5-48 *Using a Nonstatic Initialization Block (Continued)*

```
31
32     // Constructor
33     /**
34      * @param name The name on the account as a String
35      * @param id The account id as an int
36      * @param initialDeposit The initial deposit as a double
37      */
38     public Account(String name, int id, double initialDeposit)
39     {
40        this.name = name;
41        accountID = id;
42        balance = initialDeposit;
43     }
44
45     //Additional methods for Account class
46
47 }// end of Account class
```

Method data must be initialized in the code of a method. Data for a method can come from four different sources: as arguments, as local to the method, as returned by another method, or as data from an object. Arguments in a method reference variables that also are known as parameters. Parameter variables are initialized when the method is called. The programmer does not need to explicitly initialize a method's argument variable. The programmer of the code of the method must initialize local variables that are used in the method. Local variables cannot be used before they are initialized. The compiler enforces this and displays an error. The sample code for the doComputation method, shown in Example 5-49 (correct) and Example 5-50 (incorrect), demonstrates the importance of method data initialization.

Example 5-49 *Method Data Initialization—Correct*

```
1 /**
2  * Java Program: Computation.java
3  * @author Cisco Teacher
4  * @version 2002
5  */
```

Example 5-49 *Method Data Initialization—Correct (Continued)*

```
 6 public class Computation
 7 {
 8     public void doComputation()
 9     {
10         int x = (int)(Math.random() * 100);
11          // Code to verify compilation
12         int y = (int)(Math.random() * 100);
13         int z;
14         if (x > 50)
15         {
16             y = 9;
17         }
18         /*
19         This statement will not cause an
20         error when y has been initialized.
21         */
22         z = y + x;
23     }
24 }//end Computation class
```

Example 5-50 *Method Data Initialization—Incorrect*

```
 1 /**
 2  * Java Program: Computation.java
 3  * @author Cisco Teacher
 4  * @version 2002
 5  */
 6 public class Computation
 7 {
 8     public void doComputation()
 9     {
10         int x = (int)(Math.random() * 100);
11         int y;
12         int z;
13         if (x > 50)
```

continues

Example 5-50 *Method Data Initialization—Incorrect (Continued)*

```
14         {
15             y = 9;
16         }
17         /*
18         Use of the local variable y before
19         initialization will create compilation error
20         */
21         z = y + x;
22     }
23 }//end Computation class
```

Scope of Variables

Variables that define member data are available as long as the object that holds the data is being referenced or is being used. Class variables are available as long as the class is loaded in memory, as shown in Example 5-51 for the StudentMath101 class and Example 5-52 for the Teacher class. However, method variables have a temporary existence. Variables of a method are known as automatic, temporary, and local.

Example 5-51 *Class Variables and Instance Variable Scope—StudentMath101 Class*

```
1/**
2  * Java Program: StudentMath101.java
3  * @author Cisco Teacher
4  * @version 2002
5  */
6 public class StudentMath101
7 {
8      private String name;
9      private int studentID;
10     private int studentPoints;
11     private static String course = "Math 101";
12     private static int coursePoints = 600;
13
14     /**
15      * @param name The student's name as a String
16      * @param id The student' id as an int
17      */
```

Example 5-51 *Class Variables and Instance Variable Scope—*StudentMath101 *Class (Continued)*

```
18    public StudentMath101(String name, int id)
19    {
20        this.name = name;
21        studentID = id;
22    }
23
24    /**
25     * @param score The student's score as an int
26     */
27    public void addPoints(int score)
28    {
29        coursePoints += score;
30    }
31
32    //Additional methods
33
34 }// end of Studuentmath101 class
```

Example 5-52 *Class Variables and Instance Variable Scope—*Teacher *Class*

```
1 /**
2  * Java Program: Teacher.java
3  * @author Cisco Teacher
4  * @version 2002
5  */
6 public class Teacher
7 {
8     public static void main(String[] args)
9     {
10        StudentMath101 s1; //class loaded in memory
11        s1 = new StudentMath101("John", 12345);
12        s1.addPoints(85);
13        s1 = null;
14    }
15 }// end of Teacher class ... class no longer loaded in memory
```

Variables defined inside a method automatically are created in stack memory. A declaration of the variable in the method or in the argument of the method automatically creates a storage space for the variable on the stack. If the variable is an argument, its value is initialized when the method is called. If the variable is defined within the method, its initial value is unknown until it is explicitly defined within the code.

Method variables are local, are available only to the method, and can be accessed only within the method. An argument's method variable can be accessed through the entire duration of a method. Other local variables can be accessed only in the code block in which they were defined.

Method variables that are local to a block of code exist only for the block of code. When the block of code has finished executing, the variables inside the block are said to be out of scope. In general, the *scope* of an object variable or method variable is for the duration of the code block within which it is defined. Use the sample code shown in Example 5-53 for the ScopeExample class and Example 5-54 for the TestScoping class to track the scope of each method variable.

Example 5-53 *Scope of Method Variables—*ScopeExample *Class*

```
1  /**
2   * Java Program ScopeExample.java
3   * @author Cisco Teacher
4   * @version 2002
5   */
6  public class ScopeExample
7  {
8      private int i=1;
9
10     public void firstMethod()
11     {
12         int i=4, j=5;
13         this.i = i + j;
14         secondMethod(7);
15     }
16
17     public void secondMethod(int i)
```

Example 5-53 *Scope of Method Variables—ScopeExample Class (Continued)*

```
18      {
19          int j=8;
20          this.i = i + j;
21      }
22 } // end of ScopeExample class
```

Example 5-54 *Scope of Method Variables—TestScoping Class*

```
 1 /**
 2  * Java Program: TestScoping.java
 3  * @author Cisco Teacher
 4  * @version 2002
 5  */
 6 public class TestScoping
 7 {
 8      public static void main(String[] args)
 9      {
10          ScopeExample scope = new ScopeExample();
11          scope.firstMethod();
12      }
13 } // end of TestScoping class
```

Lifetime of an Object

An instance variable that references an object as part of a class definition ties the *lifetime* of that referenced object to the lifetime of an object of the enclosing class. If the variable that references an object is part of a method, the object reference dies when the block of code within the method has finished executing. As long as there is a reference to an object, the object lives and its data is accessible through the reference. The sample code shown in Examples 5-55, 5-56, and 5-57 demonstrates the lifetime of an object.

NOTE

For Example 5-55, you can view the explanatory text by accessing the full, interactive graphic for this example on the book's accompanying CD-ROM. The title of the activity is "Lifetime of an Object - Teacher Class" in e-Lab Activities.

Example 5-55 *Lifetime of an Object—Teacher Class*

```
 1 /**
 2  * Sample code for Teacher class with 3 students
 3  * @author Cisco Teacher
```

continues

Example 5-55 *Lifetime of an Object*—Teacher Class (Continued)

```
 4  * @version 2002
 5  */
 6 public class Teacher
 7 {
 8     private String teacherName;
 9     private String courseName;
10     private int courseID;
11     private static String school = "Cisco";
12
13     private Student s1 = new Student("Mary Smith", 12321);
14     private Student s2 = new Student("John Jones", 12454);
15     private Student s3 = new Student("Susan Johnson", 12554);
16
17     /**
18      * @param name The student's name as a String
19      * @param id The course id as an int
20      */
21     public Teacher(String name, String course, int id)
22     {
23         teacherName = name;
24         courseName = course;
25         courseID = id;
26     }
27
28     //Assign grades to students
29     public void assignGrades()
30     {
31         s1.setGrade('A');
32         s2.setGrade('C');
33         s3.setGrade('B');
34     }
35
36     //Display student grades
37     public void displayGrades()
38     {
39         System.out.println(s1.getName()
```

Example 5-55 *Lifetime of an Object*—Teacher *Class (Continued)*

```
40              +  " has a grade of " + s1.getGrade());
41          System.out.println(s2.getName()
42              +  " has a grade of " + s2.getGrade());
43          System.out.println(s3.getName()
44              +  " has a grade of " + s3.getGrade());
45      }
46
47      // Additional methods
48
49      public static void main(String[] args)
50      {
51          Teacher t = new Teacher("Mark Jenkins", "Math", 101);
52          t.assignGrades();
53          t.displayGrades();
54      }
55
56 } // end of Teacher class
```

Example 5-56 *Lifetime of an Object*—Teacher *Class*

```
 1 /**
 2  * Sample code for Teacher class with 3 students
 3  * @author Cisco Teacher
 4  * @version 2002
 5  */
 6 public class Teacher
 7 {
 8     private String teacherName;
 9     private String courseName;
10     private int courseID;
11     private static String school = "Cisco";
12
13     private Student s1, s2, s3;
14
15     /**
16      * @param name The student's name as a String
```

continues

NOTE

For Example 5-56, you can view the explanatory text by accessing the full, interactive figure for this example on the book's accompanying CD-ROM. The title of the activity is "Lifetime of an Object - Teacher Class" and in e-Lab Activities.

Example 5-56 *Lifetime of an Object*—Teacher *Class*

```
17      * @param id The course id as an int
18      */
19     public Teacher(String name, String course, int id)
20     {
21         teacherName = name;
22         courseName = course;
23         courseID = id;
24     }
25
26     //Assign grades to students
27     public void assignGrades()
28     {
29         s1 = new Student("Mary Smith", 12321);
30         s2 = new Student("John Jones", 12454);
31         s3 = new Student("Susan Johnson", 12554);
32         s1.setGrade('A');
33         s2.setGrade('C');
34         s3.setGrade('B');
35     }
36
37     //Display student grades
38     public void displayGrades()
39     {
40         System.out.println(s1.getName() +  " has a grade of " +
41             s1.getGrade());
42         System.out.println(s2.getName() +  " has a grade of " +
43             s2.getGrade());
44         System.out.println(s3.getName() +  " has a grade of " +
45             s3.getGrade());
46     }
47
48     // Additional methods
49
50     public static void main(String[] args)
51     {
52         Teacher t = new Teacher("Mark Jenkins", "Math", 101);
```

Example 5-56 *Lifetime of an Object*—Teacher Class

```
53          t.assignGrades();
54          t.displayGrades();
55      }
56
57 } // end of Teacher class
```

Example 5-57 *Lifetime of an Object*—Teacher Class

```
 1 /**
 2  * Sample code for Teacher class with 3 students
 3  * @author Cisco Teacher
 4  * @version 2002
 5  */
 6      public class Teacher
 7 {
 8      private String teacherName;
 9      private String courseName;
10      private int courseID;
11      private static String school = "Cisco";
12
13      private Student s1, s2, s3;
14
15      /**
16       * @param name The student's name as a String
17       * @param id The course id as an int
18       */
19      public Teacher(String name, String course, int id)
20      {
21          teacherName = name;
22          courseName = course;
23          courseID = id;
24      }
25
26      //Assign grades to students
27      public void assignGrades()
```

continues

NOTE

For Example 5-57, you can view the explanatory text by accessing the full, interactive graphic for this example on the book's accompanying CD-ROM. The title of the activity is "Lifetime of an Object - Teacher Class" in e-Lab Activities.

Example 5-57 *Lifetime of an Object*—Teacher Class (Continued)

```
28      {
29          Student s1 = new Student("Mary Smith", 12321);
30          Student s2 = new Student("John Jones", 12454);
31          Student s3 = new Student("Susan Johnson", 12554);
32          s1.setGrade('A');
33          s2.setGrade('C');
34          s3.setGrade('B');
35      }
36
37      //Display student grades
38      public void displayGrades()
39      {
40          System.out.println
41              (s1.getName() +  " has a grade of " + s1.getGrade());
42          System.out.println
43              (s2.getName() +  " has a grade of " + s2.getGrade());
44          System.out.println
45              (s3.getName() +  " has a grade of " + s3.getGrade());
46      }
47
48      // Additional methods
49
50      public static void main(String[] args)
51      {
52          Teacher t = new Teacher("Mark Jenkins", "Math", 101);
53          t.assignGrades();
54          t.displayGrades();
55      }
56 } // end of Teacher class
```

Mutability of an Object

Objects can be defined as immutable, and classes can be defined as immutable. When a class is defined as immutable using the keyword **final**, the class cannot be inherited (or derived) as a subclass or child class. By declaring the class **final**, the programmer has restricted the use of the class in an inheritance context. The objects of a class can also be defined as immutable by declaring all the attributes (data, fields) of the class as

final. After an object is created from a class where all the attributes have been declared as **final**, the object is immutable. If an object is declared to be immutable, the data of the instantiated objects is unchangeable. The String class provides an example of the use of immutability in both the context of inheritance and instantiation. The String class is declared **final**. Programmers cannot extend or derive from the String class. The attributes of the String class (the characters that form the string) are also declared as immutable with the use of the keyword **final** in the class definition. This means that after any object of the type String is created, it cannot change its values. String objects are considered immutable, as highlighted in the API docs shown in Figure 5-13.

Figure 5-13 String Docs API—the String Class Is Declared **final**

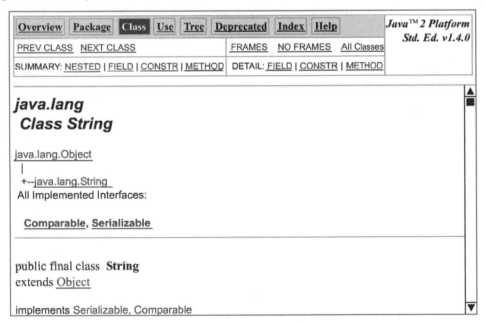

Students can also define instance variables of an object to be immutable. In this case, only the variable qualified with the keyword **final** is unchangeable. When the object is created, the value that is assigned during the creation process is **final** and cannot be changed. A common use of **final** is with the keyword **static**. A variable that is **final** can be initialized through the use of code initialization blocks.

Destruction of an Object

The value of a reference variable can be reset to **null**. The variable no longer refers to an object; the object that it originally referenced will be destroyed if no more references to it exist. Although the object has been discarded, the reference variable continues to exist for the block of code that it is executing. This variable can be used to reference a different object. The lifetime of an object is determined by whether any variable anywhere in the program still references it. The sample code shown in Example 5-58 for the ToManyStrings class demonstrates the creation of a String object, the use of **null**, and the reassignment of a reference variable.

Example 5-58 String *Object*

```
1  /**
2   * Java Program TooManyStrings.java
3   * @author Cisco Teacher
4   * @version 2002
5   */
6  public class TooManyStrings
7  {
8      public static void main(String[] args)
9      {
10         String a, b, c;
11         a = " Hello ";
12         b = " Good bye";
13         c = "Have a nice day";
14
15         System.out.println(a + c);
16         System.out.println(b + c);
17
18         a = null;
19         b = null;
20         c = null;
21         a = "Why a String?";
22     }
23 }//end TooManyStrings class
```

The act of removing objects from memory is called garbage collection. Garbage collection is automatic in Java. A garbage-collector program sweeps through the list of objects periodically and reclaims resources held by unreferenced objects. Every object is associated with a count of references to that object. When this count reaches 0, the object is eligible for garbage collection. When does this count reach 0? When the object is out of scope, or when any remaining references to the object are set to **null**. This does not necessarily mean that the object disappears immediately from memory. Users cannot rely on the memory occupied by the object becoming available immediately.

When does the garbage collection actually occur? The JVM decides on the need to run the garbage-collection program. This is generally when memory is running low. If the program makes modest demands of memory, the garbage collection might never run.

Students cannot depend on garbage collection or the use of the method gc() from the System class to destroy objects and release memory for the program. Nor should they write code that is dependent on the timing of garbage collection. A call to the gc() method suggests to the JVM that it run garbage collection soon, but the JVM is free to disregard this advice. Because the JVM decides on the need to run the garbage-collection program, even if you do not call the gc() method, the garbage-collection method cannot be prevented from running. The sample code shown in Example 5-59 for the FinalizerClass class demonstrates how the System class's gc() method is used.

Example 5-59 System *Class* gc() *Method*

```
 1 /**
 2  * A Java class to demonstrate how the garbage collection
 3  *   method is defined and used.
 4  * @author Cisco Teacher
 5  * @version 2002
 6  */
 7 public class FinalizerClass
 8 {
 9     private int a, b;
10
11     /* Class default constructor method */
12     public FinalizerClass()
13     {
14         a = 1;
15         b = 2;
16         System.out.println( "Constructing an object!" );
17     }
```

continues

Example 5-59 System *Class* gc() *Method (Continued)*

```
18
19     // Test method for the class
20     public static void main(String[] args)
21     {
22         FinalizerClass x = new FinalizerClass();
23         FinalizerClass y = new FinalizerClass();
24         x = null;
25         y = null;
26         System.gc();
27     }
28 } // end of FinalizerClass class
```

When the value of a reference variable is set to **null**, the JVM is notified that the user is finished with an object. Any object reference can be tested to see if its value equals **null**. The following code checks to ensure that the object reference is not **null** before checking the String's length.

```
//sample code using the short-circuit operators
```

```
String s = " Student name";
if ((s != null) && (s.length() > 20)) {
System.out.println(s);
```

Finalizers

Finalizers are methods that perform whatever actions should be completed before objects are discarded by the JVM garbage-collection program. Because the finalize method is called by the JVM just before running the garbage-collection program, programmers cannot predict when the finalize method will be called. Although the static runFinalization method of the System class (System.runFinalization()) can be used to run the finalize methods of objects that have been discarded but whose finalize methods have not yet been run, this is performed on a "best effort" basis by the JVM.

Because the JVM frees memory when objects are destroyed, finalizers often are not needed. Generally, finalizers are used for clean-up tasks other than reallocating memory and should be used sparingly.

The main reason is that programmers have no control over the schedule of the garbage-collection schedule. If a Java object is used to establish a network connection and the instructions to close the connection are in the finalize() method of the object, the connection might never get closed if the garbage collector was not needed by the program. This would cause open connections to a bank account or bank data in a banking application. Although this almost never happens in actual business practice, it is an example of what could occur when a programmer depends on the `finalize()` method.

Close or Dispose Method

An alternative to the `finalize()` method (and the "best efforts" of the `runFinalization()` method) is to define a close or dispose method. When called by the programmer, it performs necessary cleanup. Classes that are used to create GUI objects use such methods to ensure that images and resources used by GUI objects are released and cleared from the screen.

Every class inherits from the superclass `Object`. The concept of inheritance is explored in more detail in Chapter 8, "Classes and Inheritance." Inheritance is a simple concept with complex implementation possibilities. A class can derive many of its methods and attributes from another class. This enables a programmer to organize classes in such a manner that when a class is defined, tested, and working, another class can be created just like it with additional methods or attributes. The second class is considered to derive or inherit its properties from the first class. All classes in the Java language inherit from the superclass `Object`. The `Object` class includes several methods that are automatically part of any defined class. The `finalize()` method is one such method. The code of the `finalize()` method can be replaced with the programmer's own; however, the exact signature of the method is required. The API docs provide documentation on the `Object` class.

The sample code shown in Example 5-60 for the `FinalizerClass` class demonstrates how the `Object` class' `finalize()` method is defined and used.

Example 5-60 *The* `finalize` *Method of the* `Object` *Class*

```
1 /**
2  * A Java class to demonstrate how a
3  *   finalizer method is defined and used
4  * @author Cisco Teacher
5  * @version 2002
6  */
7 public class FinalizerClass
8 {
9     private int a, b;
```

continues

Example 5-60 *The* `finalize` *Method of the* `Object` *Class (Continued)*

```
10
11      /* Class default constructor method */
12      public FinalizerClass()
13      {
14          a = 1;
15          b = 2;
16          System.out.println( "Constructing an object!" );
17      }
18
19      /*
20       * @exception Throwable Any exception at all
21       */
22      protected void finalize() throws Throwable
23      {
24          System.out.println( "Doing object cleanup!" );
25      }
26
27      // Test method for the class
28      public static void main( String[] args )
29      {
30          FinalizerClass x = new FinalizerClass();
31          FinalizerClass y = new FinalizerClass();
32          x = null;
33          y = null;
34          System.gc();
35          System.runFinalization();
36      }
37 } // end of FinalizerClass class
```

Case Study: JBANK Application

The JBANK application introduced in Chapter 1, "What Is Java?", provides students with an opportunity to apply the Java language concepts learned throughout this course. In the JBANK labs for Chapter 5, "Basics of Defining and Using Classes," students will finish all the JBANK Phase1 classes per the UML specified. Students will implement overloaded constructors and instantiate objects using overloaded constructors. Students will apply **static final** fields to the Bank class so that any other classes can use it.

The JBANK Application

The JBANK application uses the Bank class to store static data that will be required by all other classes. This class needs to be loaded and have its data ready as soon as the JBANK is ready for business. In a bank, a bank manager would be responsible for maintaining all this information.

The data in the Bank class will be **static** and **final**. This represents information that should not be changed. For example, the change in the name of a bank happens with great consideration. Although many mergers and acquisitions (banks merging to become a large bank) occur, these activities and changes are implemented with special attention to detail. In the same manner, the data to be stored by the Bank class should be done with some thought, and changes to data should be made infrequently.

The attributes and behaviors of the Customer and Account classes will continue to be expanded. For example, a customer ID number is not expected to change after it has been set. Information such as date of birth also is not expected to change. This can be ensured by using **final** as a qualifier.

Phase I is completed in this chapter. The definition and design of the Bank and Customer class will be completed as well. However, the next phase implements inheritance models with the Account class that will provide a Customer access to many different types of bank products (account services) available to the customer.

Figures 5-14 and 5-15 display what the JBANK application might look like at the end of the course.

Figure 5-14 JBANK Application

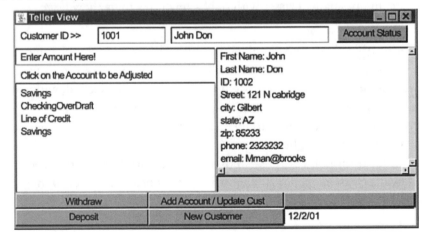

Figure 5-15 JBANK Application

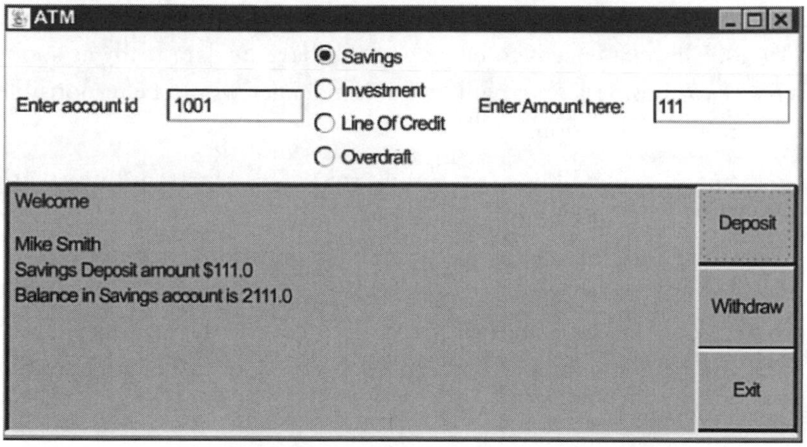

Summary

This chapter introduced the basics of defining and using classes. When defining a class, four steps are involved: declaration of attributes, definition of constructors, definition of standard methods, and definition of custom methods. After the class has been defined, students should remember to always initialize data, keep data **private** so as not to violate the principle of encapsulation, and use names that reflect the tasks of that class. Each class and object has an access modifier (**public**, **private**, **protected**) or default and a qualifier modifier (**static** and **final**). Finally, the chapter demonstrated that it is better to have many smaller classes with only a few tasks than a few large classes with multiple tasks.

The definitions of methods and variables also were discussed in this chapter. Among the items that students learned are that methods must declare a return value and can have none, one, or many arguments. Methods also can be overloaded, with more than one version defined to allow for multiple types of input. Variables can be instance, class, or local. Instance and class variables are initialized with default values, and local variables must be initialized. Instance variables are created on the heap portion of memory, and local variables are created on the stack. Furthermore, the special **this** variable is available to all methods. The variable **this** has a reference to the object currently using the method.

Finally, garbage collection was discussed. Students learned that the programmer does not control garbage collection. However, garbage collection can be scheduled by calling the gc() method. Cleanup of resources used by an object can be defined with the finalize() method of a class.

Syntax Summary

Class definition:

begins with the statement:

```
<modifiers> class classname {
```

A Java source file with the name Subsriber.java must also have the following matching class statement:

```
public class Subscriber {
```

Accessing instance data or methods:

```
/*
For instance data or methods
Object-reference.member
Object-reference.method( )
*/

Student s1 = new Student();

// access variable (member or instance data)
//through the reference variable(s)
s1.studentName;

// access a method through the reference variable(s)
s1.setGrade();
```

Accessing class (static) data or methods:

```
/*
For class (static) data or methods
Class-name.member
Class-name.method( )
*/

// accessing the variable out of the System class.
// This is a static variable.
System.out

// accessing the method gc of the System class.
// This is a static method.
System.gc()
```

Syntax for declaring an object:

```
type identifier;
identifier = value;
```

or

```
type identifier = value;
//type is any Java type.
int x ; //refers to the datatype int referenced by the variable x
```

Coding conventions for identifiers include the following:

- The first character must be any nonnumber of the Unicode character set.

- Lowercase must be used for the starting letter or word, and uppercase must be used for the start of each separate word in the name. No spaces or other symbols, such as _ or -, are used to separate words.
- Use all uppercase for identifiers that are used to reference constants.
- Define all attributes of a class at the start of the class definition. This improves readability of the code.

Object creation:

```
Student s1 -= new Student(23559, "Mary Martin", "A");
```

Syntax of methods:

```
<modifiers> <qualifiers> return-type method-name(<<qualifier> java-type
    variable>, <<qualifier>  java-type variable>, ………)
{
    //body of the method-procedural statements
    <return java-type;>
}
```

Where:

- <modifiers>—The keywords are: **public**, **private**, and **protected**
- <qualifiers>—The keywords are: **static**, **final**, **native**, and **synchronized**
- return-type—This is a required element of the method syntax, and can be any Java primitive, class, or the keyword **void**. If the method has no data to return, as in the case of many setter or mutator methods, then the keyword **void** must be used.

The coding standard used in this course for naming methods follows:

- Use of lowercase for the starting letter and uppercase for the start of each separate word in the name. No spaces or other symbols such as, _ or -, are used to separate words.
- Use of the word getXXX, where XXX is the identifier for the data returned and get signifies that the method is a getter or accessor method.
- Use of the word setXXX, where XXX is the identifier for the data of an object that will be changed by the method.
- The name explains what the method does.

  Examples:

  getStudentName, not getName or Name

  calcGradePointAverage, or calcGPA, or calculateGradePointAverage, or calculateGPA, not GPA or gradePointAverage

Use of method arguments:

The method `setAccountData`:

```
public void setAccountInfo(String s1, String s2, int x, int y);
```

can be called as follows:

```
//passing literals as arguments to a method
setAccountInfo("John", "Doe", 1117, 150);

//passing variables as arguments to a method
setAccountInfo(fname, lname, accountID, initialDeposit);

//passing expressions as arguments to a method
setAccountInfo(customer.getFirstName(), customer.getLastName(),
getNextAccoutNumber(), customerDeposit + 50);
```

Nonstatic initialization block:

```
{
Calendar c = Calendar.getInstance();
dateOpened = c.getTime();
c.add(Calendar.DATE, 30);
nextBillingDate = c.getTime();
}
```

Static initialization block:

```
static
{
ARRAY_SIZE = 57;
}
```

Key Terms

access modifiers   Identify different levels of encapsulation. They define the level of access to the class, data, or method.

> *private*   Only methods of the object have access. Access to private data by a method of another class may be available by using one of the class's non-private accessor (getter) methods.

> *public*   All classes and objects of the class have access.

> *default*   Objects of the class and classes in the same directory or package have access.

> *protected*   Subclasses and objects of the class have access.

attributes   The data that describes an object.

class data   Also known as static variables. Stored in the class and are available to all objects of a class or objects of other classes if access is permitted.

class definition   Defines the object's behavior and its attributes.

constructors   Are methods to construct an object; they define the specifics of object creation.

> *default*   If a constructor is not defined for a class, the Java compiler inserts a constructor in the class definition. This constructor will have the same name as the class, requires no arguments, and will not have any specialized instructions. This type of a constructor is also referred to as the null constructor. All member data are initialized to their default values or to the initialization values that explicitly are assigned in the declaration section of the class or an initializer block.

> *defined*   When a class definition includes an explicit constructor, the compiler will use the constructor. The compiler will not insert a null constructor in the class definition. Member data can be defined in the constructor method.

destruction of an object   An object is considered available for garbage collection when the object is out of scope, or all reference variables to the object are reset to **null**. The reference variable(s) still exists within the block of code.

encapsulation   Packaging an object's attributes into a cohesive unit that can be used as a complete entity. In Java this has a special meaning of hiding information, such that an object's attributes cannot be changed directly by another object.

finalizers   Methods that perform actions to be completed before objects are discarded by the JVM's garbage collector.

immutability   In the Java language, **final** is used to qualify a class attribute or method as immutable (unchangeable). Data that is fixed or **final** also is referred to as constant data or as constants.

initialization block   Two types of initialization blocks exist:

> *static initialization block*   is used to initialize static variables. This block is executed only once at runtime. The other type of initialization is the nonstatic block that is executed for each object created and that initializes instance variables in a class. Nonstatic blocks can initialize both static and nonstatic instance variables.

> *nonstatic initialization block*   is executed for each object created and initializes both static and instance variables.

instance   *An object of a particular class. An instance of a class is created using the new operator followed by the class name.*

method syntax   Can be understood in terms of three sections or parts:

- The method identifier elements, which include modifiers, qualifiers, return-type, and name.
- The method arguments, which include data types received by the method defined inside the parentheses ( ).
- The method body defined inside opening and closing braces { }.

When no arguments are used in a method, the syntax is ( ). When defining arguments, the qualifiers for each argument are defined within the ( ).

methods:

> *instance*   Can be accessed only through an object of a class

> *main*   The entry point in an application

> *overloading*   Two or more methods defined in the same class and given the same name.

> *static*   Require that no objects of the class be created to use these methods. Instance variables and nonstatic methods cannot be directly accessed by static methods of the same class (an instance of the class must be created within the static method to access instance variables and nonstatic methods).

mutability of an object   Objects can be defined as immutable, and classes can be defined as immutable. When a class is defined as immutable using the keyword **final**, the class cannot be inherited (or derived) as a subclass or child class. The objects of a class can also be defined as immutable by declaring all of the attributes (data, fields) of the class as **final**.

new   Keyword used to define and reserve memory for the creation of a new object.

object data (or instance variables)   Stored in each object of a class.

qualifier modifiers for methods   Define special limitations or capabilities of the method. The keywords used include the following:

> *final*   The method definition cannot be changed. This qualifier is used primarily while implementing inheritance or subclasses.
>
> *static*   An object of this class does not need to exist, and the method can be called by referencing `class-name.method()`.

scope and lifetime   Class variables are available for as long as the class is in memory. The scope of an object variable or method variable is for the duration of the code block. When the block has finish executing, the variables inside the block are said to be out of scope. When an instance variable references an object as part of a class definition, the lifetime of the referenced object is tied to the lifetime of the object of the enclosing class.

this variable   Java programming language keyword that can be used to represent an instance of the class in which it appears. The keyword **this** can be used to access class variables and methods.

Check Your Understanding

1. Which of the following is a true statement about object-oriented programming?

   A. An object should be responsible for as many functions as possible.

   B. An object is created from a class.

   C. A class is created from an object.

   D. An application with few, complex objects is easier to maintain than an application with many simple objects.

2. How many **public** classes can a Java source file contain?

   A. A Java source file can contain multiple **public** classes, as long there is one **private** class.

   B. All of the classes in a Java source file must be **public**.

   C. A Java source file with multiple classes can contain only one **public** class.

   D. A Java source file is not required to contain a **public** class.

3. Which of the following rules must be followed when creating a constructor method?

   A. The constructor method must have a return type of `void`.

   B. The constructor method must be declared `private`.

   C. The constructor method must be declared in a class.

   D. The constructor method must have the same name as the class.

4. If a class is the entry point of an application, what must it contain?

   A. At least one constructor method

   B. An accessor and mutator method

   C. The `main` method

   D. A custom method with the same name as the class

5. Which statement correctly instantiates an object from the class `Student`?

   A. Student 1Student = new Student();

   B. Student aStudent = Student();

   C. Student aStudent = new Student;

   D. Student aStudent = new Student();

6. When declaring attributes of a class

   A. They must be declared inside a `main` method.

   B. They must be declared inside a constructor method.

   C. They must be declared outside of any method.

   D. They must be declared inside a mutator method.

7. Which type of data is stored in an object?

   A. Static data

   B. Class data

   C. Local data

   D. Instance data

8. Which type of data is shared among objects?

   A. Static data

   B. Instance data

   C. Local data

   D. Method data

9. Which Java keyword is used to denote a constant or immutable variable?

   A. `const`

   B. `static`

   C. `final`

   D. `class`

10. What is the correct way to declare a constant that can be shared by all objects of a class?

    A. `public static CONSTANT = 5;`

    B. `public static int CONSTANT = 5;`

    C. `public final int CONSTANT = 5;`

    D. `public static final int CONSTANT = 5;`

11. Which type of access is implied when no access modifier has been explicitly defined?

    A. `public`

    B. `private`

    C. default

    D. `protected`

12. What happens when a class that has no constructor defined is compiled by the JVM?

    A. The JVM inserts a constructor method.

    B. A compile error is generated.

    C. A runtime error is generated.

    D. The class compiles, but no objects can be instantiated.

13. Which of the following methods correctly returns the **double** value of myDouble?

    A. ```
       public myDouble method1()
          {return myDouble;}
       ```

    B. ```
       public Double method1()
       {return myDouble;}
       ```

    C. ```
       public double method1()
       {return myDouble;}
       ```

    D. ```
       public method1()
       {return myDouble;}
       ```

14. What is the correct syntax for declaring a method that has two arguments of type `int`?

    A. `public void method2(int x; int y)`

    B. `public void method2(int x, int x)`

    C. `public void method2(x,y)`

    D. `public void method2(int x, int y)`

15. Which of the following statements about instance methods is false?

    A. An instance method is accessed through an object reference.

    B. Instance methods must be declared with the `static` qualifier.

    C. Instance methods can access other methods of the same class.

    D. Examples of instance methods are getters and setters.

16. Which of the following statements about class methods is false?

    A. An object must be instantiated to access a class method.

    B. Class methods are declared with the keyword `static`.

    C. Class methods can access the static data of a class.

    D. Class methods can access instance data only after an object has been created.

17. For methods to be overloaded, the class must contain:

    A. Multiple methods with different names, but the same argument lists

    B. Multiple methods with the same names and the same argument lists

    C. Multiple methods with different names and different argument lists

    D. Multiple methods with the same names but different argument lists

18. What is a limitation of the static initialization block?

    A. A static initialization block can be used only to instantiate objects.

    B. A static initialization block can be used only to initialize instance data.

    C. A static initialization block can be used only to initialize class data.

    D. A static initialization block is inefficient because it is executed each time an object is instantiated.

19. Which of these statements will cause the compiler to generate an error if the class `MyClass` is inherited?

    A. `public class MyClass`

    B. `public final MyClass`

    C. `public static class MyClass`

    D. `public final class MyClass`

20. What is the purpose of the `System.gc()` method?

    A. When called, this method removes all objects from memory.

    B. The method prevents the garbage collector from running.

    C. The method informs the JVM that an object is ready for destruction.

    D. The method immediately destroys inactive objects from memory.

Upon completion of this chapter, you will be able to

- Use the System class
- Use the String class
- Use the StringBuffer class
- Understand input selection and repetition using the System, String, and StringBuffer classes
- Use wrapper classes
- Use the Math class
- Use the math package
- Work with dates and random numbers
- Apply the Java language concepts that you have learned in this chapter to the JBANK case study

Chapter 6

System, String, StringBuffer, Math, and Wrapper Classes

In this chapter, students learn to use the API documentation and create classes that use objects of the System, String, StringBuffer, Math, and wrapper classes. Students will use the methods and attributes of each of these classes. The Date, DateFormat, and Calendar classes are also featured. The purpose of this chapter is to familiarize students with the Java API documentation and to demonstrate its value. Students will find that the Java API documentation is a valuable tool that they will use in this course and for most Java programming projects.

System Class

One of the core classes of the Java platform is the *System class*. The System class can be used to read input from the keyboard and display output. This section covers the following topics:

- Use of the System class for input and output
- Input using System.in
- Output using System.out

Use of the System Class for Input and Output

The System class is a Java core class that is part of the Java language package. Students will learn about packages and the directory management of classes in Chapter 9, "Understanding Packages." For this chapter, students should know that most of the classes explored here are automatically available and loaded when they are cited within the code. However, some are stored in packaged directories. Java programmers will need to organize their own files and import the files that others have created. The use of the **import** statement is introduced in the code.

Documentation for the System class describes its attributes (fields), constructor, and methods, as shown in Figures 6-1 and 6-2. The System class is used for many operations that require data about the underlying operating system settings or that require a change to an operating system setting. The System class also has a method to request garbage collection using the static method gc().

Figure 6-1 System API

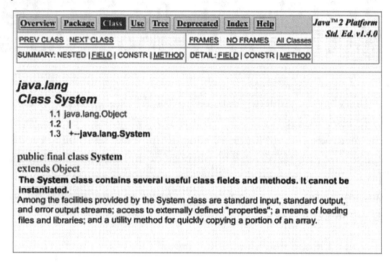

Figure 6-2 System API Field and Method Summary

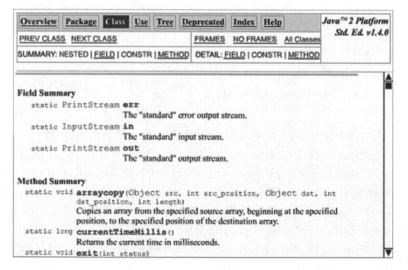

As illustrated in Figure 6-3, input of data to a program can come from many sources, including files, databases, other computers on the network, and end users interacting with GUIs or using keyboards.

Figure 6-3 Sources of Input

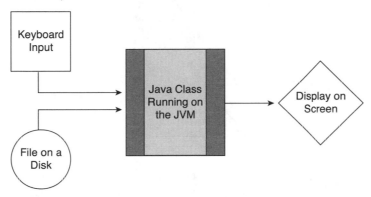

Keyboard input is also referred to as stdin (standard input) in a console-based (non-GUI) program. When using GUIs, the Java programmer does not spend time writing code to read input from the keyboard or display output to the console. This is handled by many useful classes that form the GUI set of packages and are called the Java Foundation Classes.

A program outputs two types of information to a monitor. First, an application displays information that a programmer has coded for display on the console. A program also displays information or messages about its status, errors, and the completion of the program. The target locations for this information are known as standard output and standard err, or stdout and stderr. Until programmers are ready to work with those, they need a mechanism to read data from the keyboard and display data to the screen. This is done using a console window, also known as the DOS window, terminal window, or command prompt. Here, the class that is being used sends data to an object that has methods to display the data in any console window that has been opened. The out object from the `System` class has been used to do this.

In Java, data enters the program as a stream of bytes, which can be thought of as a flow of pieces of information through a pipe. When the bytes arrive at the other end of the pipe, they are put together to form a meaningful piece of data. Several classes in the Java API process the streams of data in and out of the program. For now, the chapter focuses on three stream objects that all Java programs can use. These objects are the *in, out, and err fields of the System class*. These fields are static and are designed to connect to the underlying stdin, stdout, and stderr devices, as illustrated in Figure 6-4.

Figure 6-4 Uses of System Class

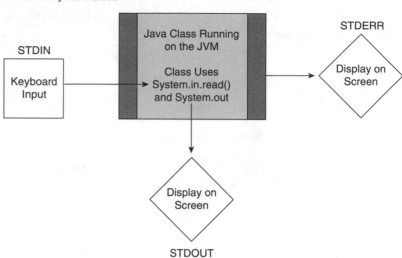

Input Using `System.in`

Reading input from the keyboard is difficult in plain Java because it uses the language core classes. The Java platform includes the Java language, core classes, and additional libraries. It provides additional GUI solutions for reading input from users.

Consider a common task such as reading a floating-point number that a user enters from the keyboard. This requires many complex instructions. For example, consider the number −14.26. This requires reading one character at a time, holding it in memory, and joining each new character to the next until all data has been input. The string of characters must then be converted to the **float** −14.26 before being processed.

The OneCharInput class, shown in Example 6-1, tests whether the value of the user's input from the keyboard is an A, B, C, or Q. If it is a Q, the program ends. The One-CharInput class reads and processes one character at a time. The System.in object can be used to read one character at a time. The in object has several methods for reading data. The data returned from the read() method has an **int** data type. The **int** needs to be converted to (that is, cast as) a **char**. Even if the user typed in a number, the **int** value is the Unicode for the symbol for the number; it is not the value of the number. For example, if the number typed were a 7, the **int** would not be a 7, but the Unicode of the character 7, which is 55. Refer to the appendix for a table of Unicode character values and ASCII character values. Note that the ASCII character set is a subset of the broader Unicode character set. The output from the code is shown in Figure 6-5.

Example 6-1 System.in.read() *Method*—OneCharInput *Code*

```
1  /**
2   * Java Program: OneCharInput.java
3   * @author Cisco Teacher
4   * @version 2002
5   */
6  public class OneCharInput
7  {
8      /**
9       * @exception Exception Any exception at all
10      */
11     public static void main (String args[]) throws Exception
12     {
13         char selection = 'x';
14
15         while (selection != 'Q')
16         {
17             System.out.print("Enter Selection (A, B, C, Q): ");
18             selection = (char)System.in.read();
19             System.in.read();
20             System.in.read();
21
22             switch(selection)
23             {
24             case 'Q':
25                 break;
26             case 'A': case 'B': case 'C':
27                 System.out.println("Good Job!");
28                 break;
29             default:
30                 System.out.println("Invalid selection");
31             }
32         }
33     }
34
35 } // end of OneCharInput class
```

For Example 6-1, you can view the explanatory text by accessing the full, interactive graphic for this example on the book's accompanying CD-ROM. The title of the activity is "`System.in.read()` Method—`OneCharInput` Code" in e-Lab Activities.

Figure 6-5 `System.in.read()` Method—`OneCharInput` Output

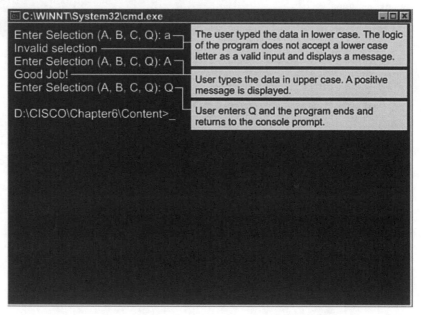

When working with the `System.in.read()` method, cast the value read to a **char**. The `MoreThanOneCharInput` class, shown in Example 6-2, together with its output shown in Figure 6-6, reflects this change.

Example 6-2 `System.in.read()` *Method*—`MoreThanOneCharInput` *Code*

```
1 /**
2  * Java Program: MoreThanOneCharInput.java
3  * @author Cisco Teacher
4  * @version 2002
5  */
6 public class MoreThanOneCharInput
7 {
8     /**
9       * @exception Exception Any exception at all
```

Example 6-2 `System.in.read()` *Method*—`MoreThanOneCharInput` *Code (Continued)*

```
10      */
11      public static void main (String[] args) throws Exception
12      {
13          int selection = 0;
14          String userinput = " ";
15
16          System.out.print
17          ("Enter a three digit number.(Press enter when you are done): ");
18
19          while (selection != 10 && selection != 13)
20          //check for carriage return or new line
21          {
22              selection = System.in.read();
23              userinput += (char) selection;
24          }
25
26          if(selection == 13)
27          {
28              System.in.read();
29              //if selection == carriage return, flush out new line
30          }
31
32          System.out.println (userinput);
33      }
34 } // end of MoreThanOneCharInput class
```

For Example 6-2, you can view the explanatory text by accessing the full, interactive graphic for this example on the book's accompanying CD-ROM. The title of the activity is "`System.in.read()` Method—`MoreThanOneCharInput` Code" in e-Lab Activities.

Figure 6-6 System.in.read() Method MoreThanOneCharInput Output

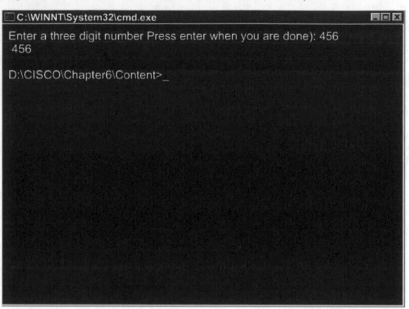

Working with input in Java without the benefit of the classes that support GUI can be difficult. To store more than one set of keyboard characters as one value in a variable, include repetition of the simple `System.in.read()` instruction until the user has typed in all of the information and pressed the Enter key, as shown in Examples 6-3 and 6-4.

Example 6-3 Employee *Class*

```
1 /**
2 * Java Program: Employee.java
3 * @author Cisco Teacher
4 * @version 2002
5 */
6 public class Employee
7 {
8     static private int COMPANY_ID = 12345;
9     private int empNum;
10     private double empSalary;
11
12     /**
13      * @exception Exception Any exception at all
```

Example 6-3 Employee *Class (Continued)*

```
14      */
15      Employee( ) throws Exception
16      {
17          System.out.print("Enter 3-digit employee number: ");
18
19          // temp chars to accept bytes from input stream
20          char a1, a2, a3;
21          // temp numbers used in converting the chars
22          int n1, n2, n3;
23          // a dummy variable to throw away the Enter key
24          int ta;
25
26          a1 = (char)System.in.read();    // read first digit
27          a2 = (char)System.in.read();    // read second digit
28          a3 = (char)System.in.read();    // read third digit
29          ta = System.in.read();          // get rid of newline char
30          ta = System.in.read();          // get rid of newline char
31
32          n1 = Character.digit(a1, 10);   // convert to a number
33          n2 = Character.digit(a2, 10);   // convert to a number
34          n3 = Character.digit(a3, 10);   // convert to a number
35
36          // put the number back together
37          empNum = (n1*100) + (n2*10) + n3;
38
39          System.out.println("empNum is " + empNum);
40      }
41
42  } // end of Employee class
```

For Example 6-3, you can view the explanatory text by accessing the full, interactive graphic for this example on the book's accompanying CD-ROM. The title of the activity is "Employee Class" in e-Lab Activities.

Example 6-4 Password3 *Class*

```
1 /**
2  * Java Program: Password3
3  * @author Cisco Teacher
4  * @version 2002
5  */
6 public class Password3
7 {
8     /**
9      * @exception Exception Any exception at all
10     */
11    public static void main(String[] args) throws Exception
12    {
13        char p1, p2, p3, p4;
14        boolean passTest = true;
15
16        System.out.println("Enter a four-character password, press Enter:");
17
18        p1 = (char)System.in.read();
19        p2 = (char)System.in.read();
20        p3 = (char)System.in.read();
21        p4 = (char)System.in.read();
22
23        System.out.println("Your password is: " + p1 + p2 + p3 + p4);
24
25        if (p1 != 'B')
26            passTest = false;
27        if (p2 != 'O')
28            passTest = false;
29        if (p3 != 'L')
30            passTest = false;
31        if (p4 != 'T')
32            passTest = false;
33
34        if (passTest == true)
35            System.out.println("Valid password");
```

Example 6-4 `Password3` *Class (Continued)*

```
36        else
37            System.out.println("Invalid password");
38    }
39 } //end of Password3 class
```

Output Using `System.out`

Students have used the `System.out` object in almost all of their classes. This section covers some additional features of this object.

The out object is an object of the class `PrintStream`. This class has overloaded methods *print* and *println* that are particularly useful for console output. The differences between these are that `println` adds a line separator to produce a complete line of output. The `print` method does not add the line separator, so one line of output can be built up with several calls to the `print` method, as shown in Example 6-5 and Figure 6-7.

Example 6-5 `print` *and* `println` *Code*

```
 1 /**
 2  * Java Program: Teacher.java
 3  * @author Cisco teacher
 4  * @ version 2002
 5  * Class implements the toString method inherited
 6  * from the Object class. When a Teacher object is
 7  * provided as the argument to the print or println
 8  * method a call is made to the toString method
 9  * to obtain the String to be printed.
10  */
11 public class Teacher
12 {
13     String name;
14     String classroom;
15
16     /**
17      * @param aName The teachers name as a String
18      * @param aClassroom The teachers classroom as a String
19      */
20     Teacher (String aName, String aClassroom)
```

continues

Example 6-5 print *and* println *Code (Continued)*

```
21     {
22          name = aName;
23          classroom = aClassroom;
24     }
25
26     /**
27      * @return The teacher and classroom info as a String
28      */
29     public String toString()
30     {
31          return   ("Teacher " + name + " is in classroom " + classroom );
32     }
33
34     public static void main (String [] args)
35     {
36          Teacher one = new Teacher( " Peter Gray ", "Room 208");
37          Teacher two = new Teacher ( " Penelope Masters " , " Mathematics " );
38          System.out.println( one );
39          System.out.println( two );
40     }
41 }     // end of Teacher class
```

For Example 6-5, you can view the explanatory text by accessing the full, interactive graphic for this example on the book's accompanying CD-ROM. The title of the activity is "print and println Code" in e-Lab Activities.

The print and println methods are overloaded to create different versions specifically for the primitive types, the **char**[](**char**[] is an array of **char** data) and the String class. All other reference types implement the *toString() method* inherited from the Object class in their class definition. To render an object as a String, implement the toString method in the class.

The Teacher class implements the toString method and prints data from an object.

Figure 6-7 print and println Output

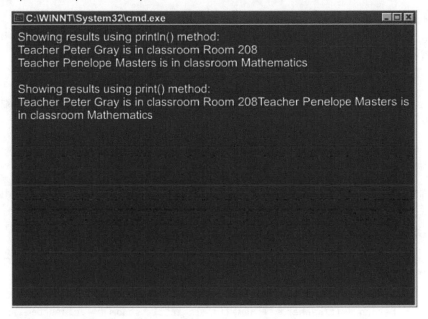

String Class

In Java, the *String class* has been designed to handle a sequence of characters, also known as a string. This section covers the following topics:

- Creating String objects
- String methods
- Casting and conversion

Creating String Objects

Strings are a sequence of characters, such as the "hello" string. Java does not have a built-in data type (primitive) for strings. Instead, the String class serves to create and store a sequence of characters as a String object. Each of the quoted strings shown in Example 6-6 is an instance of the String class.

String objects can be created using either of the two syntax rules shown in Example 6-6. String objects can also be created without a reference, as in the return statement of the toString methods of the Teacher class. String objects are also created with the println method.

Example 6-6 String *Syntax*

```
//Quoted strings

String e = " " ;  // an empty string

String greet = "HI There";


//String syntax

String s = "text ";


//Or


String s = new String (" text" );


//String syntax in a return statement


public String toString()
    {
        return   ("Teacher " + name + " is in classroom " + classroom );
    }


//String syntax in the println method

System.out.println ("Hello Student" );
```

The String class is defined as **final**. This means that any objects created of this class are considered immutable or unchangeable. The individual characters of the String class cannot be changed. Just as the number 9 is always the number 9, the String "Yes" will always contain the characters Y, e, and s.

When creating a variable that references a String object, a different String object can be assigned to the reference variable, as shown in Example 6-7. In the first example, the String "Polly" is referenced by the variable named name. In the second statement, the String "David" is referenced by the same variable, name. The String "Polly" no longer has a reference to it. In the next example, the variable name again references a String object "Polly". On the following line, the operation causes the (literal) creation of the String " Pocket". The concatenation on this line creates a third String, "Polly Pocket". This simple operation has resulted in the creation of several String objects. This seems inefficient, and it is. However, because String objects are immutable, they can be shared. When a String is created using a literal assignment, the String is stored in a memory space that all objects can share. This often is referred to as the String pool.

Example 6-7 *Additional Examples of* String *Syntax*

```
String  name = "Polly";
name = "David";



int x = 10;
x += 20;

String name = "Polly";
name = name + " Pocket";



String name = "Polly";
name = name + " Pocket";
String name2, name3;


name2 = "Polly";


name3 = " Pocket";



String name = new String("Movie");
name = " Video";
String name2 = "Movie";
```

Contrast the use of a reference to a String object with a reference to a primitive type. In Example 6-7, the **int** x is assigned a 10. The += operator adds a 20 to the 10, and x stores the value 30. Only one copy of x has been used here.

Because "Polly" and " Pocket" are shared String objects, they can be reused and referenced by the variables name2 and name3. This is not guaranteed, but, in general, as long as there is memory and the garbage-collection activity has not occurred, the assignment of a String to a String object reference results in a search of the String pool for a match and reuse of the String in the pool.

Consider what happens when the **new** operator is used to create a String. Here, the name variable references a String object that will be created in heap memory, not in the String pool. When name is reassigned a reference to the String "Video", "Video" is stored in the shared area, the String pool. When name2 is assigned a reference to the String "Movie", it is referencing a String object from the String pool, not the String object created on the heap and originally assigned to name.

In general, you should write your programs to avoid creating many String objects. Use String to store data that will be shared by many objects and that does not change. The alternative to using String objects is to use StringBuffer objects.

String Methods

TIP

The substring()
method requires as
arguments a begin-
ning and ending
index. In other lan-
guages, you provide
a beginning index
and a length in char-
acters. The site http://
www.javaranch.com/
maha/Resources/
gotchas_1_.html
expands on the reasons
that support doing it
this way.

String objects can be operated on using the + operator. Testing equality of String objects using the == operator tests only the equality of the references. In Example 6-8, the first result is false because both reference different objects. The second line prints true because both reference the same object in the shared area called the String pool. The third line prints false because "Polly" is a different object from "polly".

Example 6-8 String *Methods*

```
String a, b, c, d;
a = "Polly";
b = new String("Polly");
c = "Polly";
d = "polly";


System.out.println( a==b? "true": "false";);
System.out.println( a==c? "true": "false";);
System.out.println( a==d? "true": "false";);
```

The use of == to compare object data is considered a shallow comparison; it tells whether the reference values are the same. To perform a deeper comparison of the data in these String objects, use the compareTo() method of the String class.

You should know and use several methods in the String class. The table shown in Table 6-1 describes the signature of the method and offers some suggestions for use. Remember that String objects are immutable. Any method in this table that describes a change to the String actually results in a copy of the String being created with the change. This can result in many String objects being created to make the change desired. For this reason, it is suggested that the StringBuffer class be used for string data that needs to be changed frequently.

Table 6-1 Discussing the Different Methods

Method	Code

int length()	```java
	String city = "Phoenix";
	int length = city.length();
	
	// length = 7
	``

char charAt(**int** index)	```java
	String name = "Smith";
	char c = name.charAt(2);
	
	 // c = 'i'
	``

boolean equals(Object anObject)	```java
	String s1 = new String("Jones");
	String s2 = new String ("James");
	String s3 = s1;
	String s4 = s3;
	if (s1.equals(s2))
	    System.out.println("s1 equal to s2");
	else
	    System.out.println("s1 not equal to s2");
	if (s4.equals(s1))
	    System.out.println("s4 equal to s1");
	else
	    System.out.println("s4 not equal to s1");
	// s1 not equal to s2
	// s4 equal to s1
	``

boolean equalsIgnoreCase(String anotherString)	```java
	String s1 = "Hello";
	String s2 = "hello";
	if (s1.equalsIgnoreCase(s2))
	System.out.println ("s1 is equal to s2");
	else
	  System.out.println("s1 is not equal to s2");
	
	// s1 equal to s2
	``

int compareTo(String anotherString)	```java
	String s1 = "and";
	String s2 = "ant";
	int n = s1.compareTo(s2);
	if (n == 0)
	    System.out.println("s1 is equal to s2");
	else if (n < 0)
	    System.out.println("s1 precedes s2");
	else
	    System.out.println("s2 precedes s1");
	
	// s1 precedes s2
	// The Unicode value of 'd' in s1
	// precedes Unicode value of 't' in s2.
	``

continues

Table 6-1 Discussing the Different Methods (Continued)

Method	Code
| **int** compareTo(Object o) | ```java
String s1 = new String("one");
String s2 = s1;
int n = s1.compareTo(s2);
if(n == 0)
  System.out.println("s1 equal to s2");
else if (n < 0)
  System.out.println("s1 precedes s2");
else
  System.out.println("s2 precedes s1");

// s1 equal to s2
``` |
| **int** compareToIgnoreCase (String str) | ```java
String s1 = "ANT";
String s2 = "ant";
int n = s1.compareToIgnoreCase(s2);
if (n == 0)
    System.out.println("s1 equal to s2");
else if (n < 0)
    System.out.println("s1 precedes s2");
else
    System.out.println("s2 precedes s1");

// s1 equal to s2
``` |
| **boolean** startsWith(String prefix) | ```java
String s1 = "sea shells";
if (s1.startsWith("sea"))
    System.out.println("String starts with sea ");

// String starts with sea
``` |
| **boolean** startsWith(String prefix, **int** offset) | ```java
String s1 = "sea shells";
if (s1.startsWith("she", 4))
 System.out.println("s1 starts with prefix
(she) at index 4");

// s1 starts with prefix (she) at index 4
``` |
| **int** indexOf(**int** ch) | ```java
String s = "Oklahoma";
int index = s.indexOf('k');

 // index = 1
``` |
| **int** indexOf(String str) | ```java
String s = "Mississippi";
int index = s1.indexOf("is");

// index = 1
``` |

Table 6-1 Discussing the Different Methods (Continued)

Method	Code
| String substring(**int** beginIndex) | ```
String s1 = "Black and Blue";
String value = s1.substring(10);

// value = "Blue"
``` |
| String substring(**int** beginIndex, **int** endIndex) | ```
String s1 = "Black and Blue";
String value = s1.substring(5,9);

// value = " and"
``` |
| String concat(String str) | ```
String firstName = "Jones";
String lastName = "Smith";
String name = firstName.concat(lastName);

// name = "JonesSmith"
``` |
| **static** String valueOf(Object obj) | ```
Integer id = new Integer(234);

String idStr = String.valueOf(id);

// idStr = "234";
``` |

Casting and Conversion

String objects can be operated on using the methods in the String class and using the + operator. The + operator is considered an overloaded operator in the Java language. As an operand for the operator, it accepts numeric values and String values.

All data types can be converted to a String. The String class does the conversion of primitives as an implicit cast to a String. A primitive cannot be assigned to a String directly; it can be concatenated with a String (*concatenation*), and the result can be stored in a String object. When a String is concatenated (using the overloaded + operator) with a value that is not a String, the latter is converted to a String. Every object can be converted to a String if it implements the toString() method.

The code shown in Example 6-9 for the AllStrings class, together with its output shown in Figure 6-8, illustrates the incorrect assignment of primitives to a String.

Example 6-9 *Incorrectly Assigning Primitives—Code*

```
1 /**
2  * Java Program: AllStrings.java
3  * @author Cisco Teacher
4  * @version 2002
5  */
6 class AllStrings
7 {
8     public static void main (String[] args)
9     {
10        char c = 'a';
11        boolean b = true;
12        int i = 10;
13        double d = 50.23;
14        float f = 34.5f;
15        short s = 35;
16        /*
17        The following statements cause
18        compile errors
19        */
20        String s1 = c;
21        String s2 = b;
22        String s3 = i;
23        String s4 = d;
24        String s5 = f;
25        String s6 = s;
26    }
27
28 } // end of AllStrings class
```

Figure 6-8 Incorrectly Assigning Primitives—Output

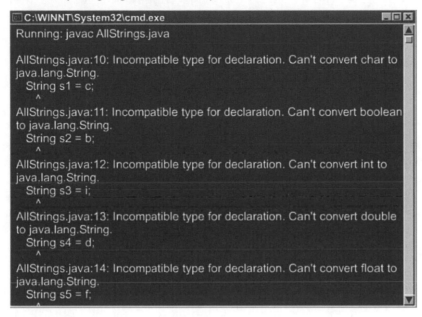

The correct assignment of primitives and objects to a `String` requires linking the primitive or objects with a `String`. The corrected `AllStrings` class shown in Example 6-10, together with its output shown in Figure 6-9, illustrates this.

Example 6-10 *Correctly Assigning Primitives—Code*

```
1 /**
2  * Java Program: AllStrings.java
3  * @author Cisco Teacher
4  * @version 2002
5  */
6 class AllStrings
7 {
8     public static void main (String[] args)
9     {
```

continues

Example 6-10 *Correctly Assigning Primitives—Code (Continued)*

```
10          char c = 'a';
11          boolean b = true;
12          int i = 10;
13          double d = 50.23;
14          float f = 34.5f;
15          short s = 35;
16          Teacher t = new Teacher ("Cisco teacher", "Cisco lab");
17          String s1 = c + "";
18          String s2 = "" + b + "";
19          String s3 = "" + i + "";
20          String s4 = "" + d + "";
21          String s5 = "" + f + "";
22          String s6 = "" + s + "";
23          String st1 = t.toString();
24          String st2 = " " + t;
25
26          System.out.println ("All Strings from primitives \n"
27              + s1 + "\n"
28              + s2 + "\n"
29              + s3 + "\n"
30              + s4 + "\n"
31              + s5 + "\n"
32              + s6 );
33
34          System.out.println ("All Strings from Objects\n"
35              + st1 + "\n"
36              + st2 + "\n" );
37      }
38
39 } // end of AllsStrings class
```

Figure 6-9 Correctly Assigning Primitives—Output

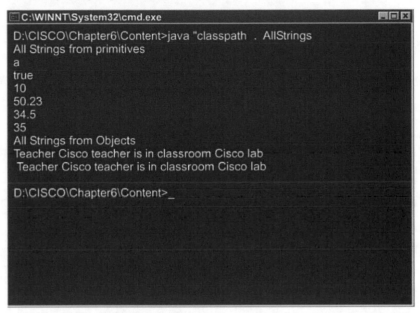

The use of the + operator with String objects has some side effects. These examples illustrate the way in which the operator behaves. Again, the AllStrings class has been modified to demonstrate these side effects. Consider the way in which the + operator will behave. If it has numbers as both its operands, a numeric calculation occurs. If one of the operands is a String, the result is a concatenation operation, as shown in Example 6-11 and Figure 6-10.

Example 6-11 String *and the + Operator—Code*

```
1 /**
2  * Java Program: AllStrings.java
3  * @author Cisco Teacher
4  * @version 2002
5  */
6 class AllStrings
```

continues

Example 6-11 String *and the + Operator—Code (Continued)*

```
 7 {
 8     public static void main (String args[])
 9     {
10         char c = 'a';
11         boolean b = true;
12         int i = 10;
13         double d = 50.23;
14         float f = 34.5f;
15         short s = 35;
16         System.out.println (10 + d + " printing 10 + d");
17         System.out.println (" printing 10 + d  "+ 10 + d );
18     }
19 } // end of AllStrings class
```

Figure 6-10 String and the + Operator—Output

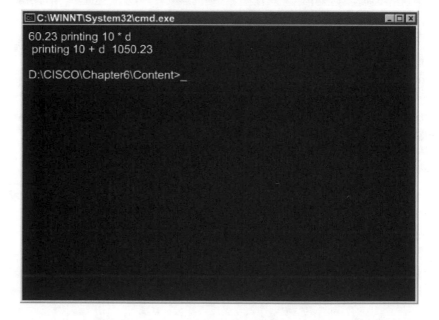

StringBuffer **Class**

The *StringBuffer class* also has been designed to create and store strings. This section explores the methods of the StringBuffer class and reviews when to use the String and StringBuffer classes.

Methods

String and StringBuffer are independent classes with many different methods. Use the StringBuffer class as the working space for manipulating the characters, and use the String class as the place where the final result is placed.

Every StringBuffer object has a maximum capacity or size. However, if additional characters are added to a StringBuffer so that it exceeds its capacity, Java provides a larger capacity.

You should know and use several methods in the StringBuffer class. Table 6-2 describes the signature of the method and offers some suggestions for use.

Table 6-2 Methods of the StringBuffer Class

Method	Code
StringBuffer append(**char** c)	```StringBuffer s1 = new StringBuffer("How are you"); s1.append('?');``` `// s1 = "How are you?"`
StringBuffer delete(int start, **int** end)	```StringBuffer number = new StringBuffer("67.7890"); number.delete(2,7);``` `// number = "67"`
StringBuffer deleteCharAt(**int** index)	```StringBuffer number = new StringBuffer("67.7890"); number.deleteCharAt(5);``` `// number = 67.780`
StringBuffer replace(**int** start, **int** end, String str)	```StringBuffer number = new StringBuffer("67.7890"); number.replace(2,6, "8.31");``` `// number = "678.310"`

Table 6-2 Methods of the `StringBuffer` Class (Continued)

Method	Code
String substring (**int** start)	```StringBuffer subject = new` `StringBuffer("Science");` `String s1 = subject.substring` `(3).toString();``` `// s1 = "ence"`

String substring
(**int** start, **int** end)
	`StringBuffer subject = new`
	`StringBuffer("Science");`
	`String s1 = subject.substring`
	`(2,4).toString();`
	
	`// s1 = "ie"`

StringBuffer insert
(**int** offset, String
str)
	`StringBuffer s1 = new`
	`StringBuffer("Fast Furious");`
	`s1.insert(4, "and");`
	
	`// s1 = "Fast and Furious"`

StringBuffer
reverse()
	`StringBuffer s1 = new`
	`StringBuffer("stop");`
	`s1.reverse();`
	
	`// s1 = "pots"`

String toString()	`StringBuffer s1 = new`
	`StringBuffer("Java Programming");`
	`String s = s1.toString();`
	
	`// s = "Java Programming"`

Overriding the equals() Method in the StringBuffer Class

The `equals()` method of the `StringBuffer` class does not override the `equals()` method of the Java `Object` class. As a result, `StringBuffer.equals()` checks only the identity of the referred object. Look at the following examples using the `String` and the `StringBuffer` classes:

```
String stringTest = "Good Day!";
String stringA = new String(stringTest);
String stringB = new String(stringTest);
```

In this example, `stringA.equals(stringB)` results in **true**.

However, using the `StringBuffer` equals() method yields different results:

```
StringBuffer sbuffer1 = new StringBuffer(stringTest);
StringBuffer sbuffer2 = new StringBuffer(stringTest);
```

TIP

The site http://
www.javaworld.com/
javaworld/jw-03-2000/
jw-0324-javaperf.html
expands on the rea-
sons why the String-
Buffer class is more
efficient than the
String class.

Now, `sbuffer1.equals(sbuffer2)` results in **false** because the `Object equals()` method does only a shallow comparison.

To do a comparison with `StringBuffer` objects, you could convert them to `String` objects and then use the `String.equals()` method:

```
String compareA = sbuffer1.toString();   // convert StringBuffer contents to a String
String compareB = sbuffer2.toString();

if(compareA.equals(compareB))  // use the String class equals method
                               // which returns a boolean value
    System.out.println("equal");
else
    System.out.println("Not equal");
```

Another more shorthand way to do this would be to combine methods:

```
if(sbuffer1.toString().equals(sbuffer2.toString() )
    System.out.println("equal");
else
    System.out.println("Not equal");
```

In the previous example, the **if** statement evaluates as follows:

> sbuffer1.toString() returns a String class object from the StringBuffer object sbuffer1.

> To the resulting `String` object returned from `sbuffer1.toString()`, use the `String`'s `equals()` method to do the comparison against the `String` object returned from `sbuffer2.toString()`.

This format is more efficient if you do not need to keep a reference and access the `String` objects at a later time in the program.

Input Selection and Repetition Using the Console Class

The task of obtaining input from the keyboard without any GUI classes is quite difficult and tedious. Because the goal of the Java language is to encourage extensive reuse, a `Console` class will be created and used for collecting input from the console.

The Console Class

The methods of the `Console` class are static, which makes this class very useful and easy to use. The methods of the `Console` class are shown in Table 6-3.

Table 6-3 Methods of the Console Class

Syntax	Description
static void printlnPrompt(String prompt)	Prints a prompt on the console.
static String readLine()	Reads a string of data from the console until it reaches a line break.
static String readLine(String prompt)	Reads a string of data from the console until it reaches a line break.
static int readInt(String prompt)	Reads an integer from the console.
static double readDouble(String prompt)	Reads a floating-point number from the console.

The Console class can be used to display any prompt to the user and collect input from the user. The code for the Console class is shown in Example 6-12.

Example 6-12 Console *Class - Code*

```
 1 /**
 2 * Java Program: Console.java
 3 * @author Cisco Teacher
 4 * @version 2002
 5 */
 6 public class Console
 7 {
 8     /**
 9     * print a prompt on the console but don't print a newline
10     * @param prompt the prompt string to display
11     */
12     public static void printPrompt(String prompt)
13     {
14         System.out.print(prompt + " ");
15         System.out.flush();
16     }
17
18     /**
19     * read a string from the console.
20     * The string is terminated by a newline
```

Example 6-12 Console *Class - Code (Continued)*

```
21       * @return the input string (without the newline)
22       */
23      public static String readLine()
24      {
25          int ch;
26          String r = "";
27          boolean done = false;
28          while (!done)
29          {
30              try
31              {
32                  ch = System.in.read();
33                  if (ch < 0 || (char)ch == '\n')
34                      done = true;
35                  else if ((char)ch != '\r')
36                      r = r + (char) ch;
37              }
38              catch(java.io.IOException e)
39              {
40                  done = true;
41              }
42          }
43          return r;
44      }
45
46      /**
47       * read a string from the console.
48       * The string is terminated by a newline
49       * @param prompt the prompt string to display
50       * @return the input string (without the newline)
51       */
52      public static String readLine(String prompt)
53      {
54          printPrompt(prompt);
55          return readLine();
56      }
```

continues

Example 6-12 Console *Class - Code (Continued)*

```
57
58    /**
59     * read an integer from the console.
60     * The input is terminated by a newline.
61     * @param prompt the prompt string to display
62     * @return the input value as an int
63     * @exception NumberFormatException if bad input
64     */
65    public static int readInt(String prompt)
66    {
67        while(true)
68        {
69            printPrompt(prompt);
70            try
71            {
72                return Integer.valueOf(readLine().trim()).intValue();
73            }
74            catch(NumberFormatException e)
75            {
76                System.out.println("Not an integer. Please try again!");
77            }
78
79        }
80    }
81
82    /**
83     * read a floating point number from the console.
84     * The input is terminated by a newline
85     * @param prompt the prompt string to display
86     * @return the input value as a double
87     * @exception NumberFormatException if bad input
88     */
89    public static double readDouble(String prompt)
90    {
91        while(true)
```

Example 6-12 Console *Class - Code (Continued)*

```
 92          {
 93              printPrompt(prompt);
 94              try
 95              {
 96                  return Double.parseDouble(readLine().trim());
 97              }
 98              catch(NumberFormatException e)
 99              {
100                  System.out.println("Not a floating point number. "+
101                      "Please try again!");
102              }
103          }
104      }
105 }//end Console class
```

The code shown in Example 6-13 for the Investment class also demonstrates the use of the Console class.

Example 6-13 Investment *Class using* Console *Class Methods*

```
 1 /**
 2  * Java Program: Investment.java
 3  * @author Cisco Teacher
 4  * @version 2002
 5  */
 6 public class Investment
 7 {
 8     public static void main(String[] args)
 9     {
10         double goal;
11         double interest;
12         double payment;
13         int years = 0;
14         double balance = 0;
15
```

continues

Example 6-13 Investment *Class using* Console *Class Methods (Continued)*

```
16          goal = Console.readDouble("How much money do you want to earn?");
17          payment = Console.readDouble("How much money will you invest ?");
18          interest = Console.readDouble("Interest rate in % :") / 100;
19
20          while (balance < goal)
21          {
22              balance = (balance + payment) * (1 + interest);
23              years++;
24          }
25
26          System.out.print("You will reach your goal for earnings in: ");
27          System.out.println(years + " years.");
28      }
29 } // end of Investment class
```

Wrapper Classes

TIP

The site http://
www.glenmccl.com/
tip_040.htm provides
additional information
on the use of wrapper
classes.

The Java programming language does not look at primitive data types as objects. Numeric, Boolean, and character data are treated in the primitive form for the sake of efficiency. The Java programming language provides *wrapper-classes* to manipulate primitive data elements as objects. Such data elements are "wrapped" in an object that is created around them. This section consists of the following topics:

- Introduction to wrapper classes
- Wrapper classes and their associated methods

Introduction to Wrapper Classes

Each Java primitive data type has a corresponding wrapper class in the java.lang package. Each wrapper class object encapsulates a single primitive value, as shown in Table 6-4.

Table 6-4 Wrapper Classes

Primitive Data Type	Wrapper Class
char	Character
boolean	Boolean
byte	Byte

Table 6-4 Wrapper Classes (Continued)

Primitive Data Type	Wrapper Class
short	Short
int	Integer
long	Long
float	Float
double	Double

Construct a wrapper class object by passing the value to be wrapped into the appropriate constructor, as shown in Example 6-14.

Example 6-14 *Wrapper Constructors*

```
Integer  in = new Integer( 25 );

Boolean condition = new Boolean( true);

Character ch  = new Character ('Y');

Float fl = new Float( 34.56f);  //remember that the default for floating point
is a double not a float.

Double db = new Double ( 56.7 );
```

These wrapper classes implement immutable objects. This means that after the primitive value is initialized in the wrapper object, there is no way to change that value. Wrapper classes are useful when converting primitive data types because of the many wrapper class methods available. In other cases, the primitive must be used. For example, wrapper classes cannot be used with arithmetic operators or conditions. The code examples shown in Example 6-15 would each cause a compile error. To be used in the instances shown, the primitive values first must be extracted using methods from the wrapper classes.

Example 6-15 *Syntax Errors with Wrapper Classes*

```
Integer x = new Integer(5);
Integer y = new Integer(10);
x = x + y;
```
```
Boolean b = new Boolean("true");
if(b)
System.out.println("Java is fun");
```
```
Double d = new Double(4.9);
Double e = new Double(10.5);
double f = e / d;
```

Wrapper Classes and Their Associated Methods

The methods for some of the more commonly used wrapper classes are illustrated in this section.

Integer

The methods for the `Integer` class are described in Table 6-5.

Table 6-5 Integer Class Methods

Method	Code
static String toString(**int** i)	String number = Integer.toString(23); // number = "23"

static int
 parseInt(String s)
 throws
 NumberFormatException
	String num = "789";
	 try
	 {
	   int n = Integer.parseInt(num);
	 }
	 catch (NumberFormatExceptione)
	 {
	   System.out.println("parse error");
	 }
	
	 // n = 789

Table 6-5 Integer Class Methods (Continued)

Method	Code
| **static** Integer valueOf(String s, **int** radix) **throws** NumberFormatException | ```java
String num = "343";
try
{
  Integer n =
    Integer.valueOf(num, 10);
}
catch (NumberFormatExceptione)
{
  System.out.println ("parse error");
}

// value of Integer n = 123
``` |
| **double** doubleValue() | ```java
Integer i = new Integer(25);
double d = i.doubleValue();

// d = 444
``` |
| **boolean** equals (Object obj) | ```java
Integer integer1 = new Integer(2);
Integer integer2 = new Integer(3);
Integer integer3 = integer1;
Integer integer4 = integer3;
if (integer1.equals(integer2))
{
  System.out.println( "integer1 equals
to integer2");
}
else
{
  System.out.println("integer1 not
equal to integer2");
}

if (integer4.equals(integer1))
{
  System.out.println( "integer4 equals
to integer1");
}
else
{
  System.out.println("integer4 not
equal to integer1");
}

// integer1 not equals to integer2
// integer4 equals to integer1
``` |
```

Double

The methods for the Double class are described in Table 6-6.

Table 6-6 Double Class Methods

Method	Code
| **static** String<br>toString(**double** d) | ```java
double d = 768.90;
String s = Double.toString(d);
``` |
| **static** Double<br>valueOf(String s)<br>**throws**<br>NumberFormatException | ```java
String num = "543.467";
try
{
  Double n =
    Double.valueOf(num);
}
catch (NumberFormatExceptione)
{
  System.out.println("parse error");
}

//Double n = 543.467;
``` |
| **static double**<br>parseDouble(String s)<br>**throws**<br>NumberFormatException | ```java
String num = "789.456";
try
{
  double d =
    Double.parseDouble(num);
}
catch (NumberFormatExceptione)
{
  System.out.println("parse error");
}

// d = 789.456
``` |
| String toString() | ```java
Double d = new Double (189.944);
String s = d.toString();

//s = "189.944"
``` |
| **int** intValue() | ```java
Double d = new Double(67.890);
int n = d.intValue();
``` |
| **double**<br>doubleValue() | ```java
Double d = new Double(67.897);
double e = d.doubleValue();
``` |

Table 6-6 Double Class Methods (Continued)

Method	Code
| **boolean** equals(Object obj) | ```java
Double d1 = new Double(12.678);
Double d2 = new Double(53.345);
Double d3 = d1;
Double d4 = d3;
if (d1.equals(d2))
{
  System.out.println( "d1 equals to d2");
}
else
{
  System.out.println("d1 not equal to d2");
}
if (d4.equals(d1))
{
  System.out.println( "d4 equals to d1");
}
else
{
  System.out.println("d4 not equal to d1");
}

// d1 not equals to d2
// d4 equals to d1
``` |
| **int** compareTo(Double anotherDouble) | ```java
Double d1 = new Double(901.373);
Double d2 = new Double(562.839);
int n = d1.compareTo(d2);
if (n == 0)
System.out.println("d1 equals to d2");
else if (n < 0)
System.out.println("d1 precedes d2");
else
System.out.println("d2 precedes d1");
``` |
| **int** compareTo(Object o) | ```java
Double d1 = new Double(34.890);
Double d2 = d1;
int n = d1.compareTo(d2);
if (n == 0)
System.out.println("d1 equals to d2");
else if (n < 0)
System.out.println("d1 precedes d2");
else
System.out.println("d2 precedes d1");
``` |
```

Character

The methods for the Character class are described in Table 6-7.

Table 6-7 Character Class Methods

Method	Code

char charValue()	```Character ch = new Character('c');```
	```char c = ch.charValue();```
	
	```// c = 'c'```

boolean equals(Object obj)	```Character c1 = new Character('A');```
	```Character c2 = new Character('C');```
	```if(c1.equals(c2))```
	``` System.out.println("c1 equals to c2");```
	```else```
	``` System.out.println("c1 not equal to C2");```
	
	```// c1 not equals to c2```

String toString()	```Character c1 = new Character('A');```
	```String s = c1.toString();```
	
	```// s = "A"```

static boolean isLowerCase(**char** ch)	```char c = 'a';```
	```if (Character.isLowerCase(c))```
	``` System.out.println("lower case");```
	```else```
	``` System.out.println("upper case");```
	
	```// lower case```

static boolean isUpperCase(**char** ch)	```char c = 'A';```
	```if (Character.isUpperCase(c))```
	``` System.out.println("upper case");```
	```else```
	``` System.out.println("lower case");```
	
	```// upper case```

static boolean isDigit(**char** ch)	```char c = 'a';```
	```if (Character.isDigit(c))```
	``` System.out.println("is a digit");```
	```else```
	``` System.out.println("not a digit);```
	
	``` // not a digit```

static char toLowerCase(**char** ch)	```char c =``` ```Character.toLowerCase('A');```

Table 6-7 Character Class Methods (Continued)

Method	Code
static char toUpperCase(**char** ch)	```char c = Character.toLowerCase('A');```
static int getNumericValue(**char** ch)	```char c = 'a';int n = Character.getNumericValue(c);```
int compareTo(Character anotherCharacter)	```Character c1 = new Character('a');Character c2 = new Character('A');int n = c1.compareTo(c2);if (n == 0) System.out.println("c1 equals to c2");else if (n < 0) System.out.println("c1 precedes c2");else System.out.println("c2 precedes c1");// c1 precedes c2```
int compareTo(Object o)	```Character c1 = new Character('c');Character c2 = c1;int n = c1.compareTo(c2);if (n == 0) System.out.println("c1 equals to c2");else if (n < 0) System.out.println("c1 precedes c2");else System.out.println("c2 precedes c1");// c1 equals to c2```

Boolean

The methods for the Boolean class are described in Table 6-8.

Table 6-8 Boolean Class Methods

Method	Code
boolean booleanValue()	```Boolean bObject = new Boolean ("true");boolean b = bObject.booleanValue ( );```
static Boolean valueOf(String s)	```Boolean.valueOf("True") returns true.Boolean.valueOf("yes") returns false.Boolean.valueOf("False") returns false.Boolean.valueof("true") returns true.```

continues

Table 6-8 Boolean Class Methods (Continued)

Method	Code

String toString()	```boolean a = 30 * 12.35 > 70 ? true : false;```
	```boolean A = new Boolean (a);```
	```String result = A.toString( );```

boolean equals(Object obj)	```boolean a = 30 * 12.35 > 70 ? true : false;```
	```boolean b = 46 * 11.37 > 90 ? true : false;```
	```Boolean A = new Boolean (a);```
	```Boolean B = new Boolean (b);```
	```Boolean C = new Boolean (A.equals(B));```

Converting Comma-Separated String Floating-Point Values

Often, you need to work with floating-point values that come in with comma punctuation—for example, the user entered data through a GUI. The Double wrapper class methods parseDouble(String val) and Double(String val).doubleValue() cannot handle comma punctuation (as in 1,234.50) and will throw a NumberFormatException.

An alternative is to use the DecimalFormat class (part of the java.text package), calling its parse(String val) method, as shown in Example 6-16.

Example 6-16 parse(String val) *Method of the* DecimalFormat *Class*

```
Class String val = "1,234.50";

DecimalFormat df = new DecimalFormat();

Number n = df.parse(val);


if(n instanceof Double) Double dval = (Double) n;


A short cut is the following code:

double dval = new DecimalFormat().parse(val.trim()).doubleValue();
```

You must use the trim() method to eliminate any leading or trailing blanks; the DecimalFormat class's parse() method does not like blanks. To be safe, always include the trim() option.

Math Class

The *Math class* is a very useful class for many mathematical operations. This section covers the operations performed by the static methods of the Math class.

Static Methods

The Math class, shown in Figure 6-11, has many methods, all of which are static. Creating an instance of this class is not necessary to use its *static methods*.

Figure 6-11 Math Class API

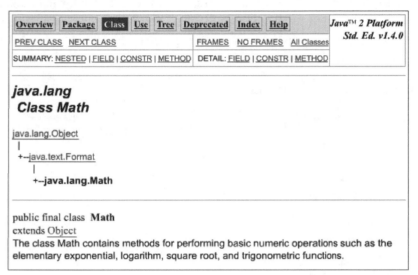

Use the Math class for the operations shown in Table 6-9 and other operations.

Table 6-9 Math Class Operations

Operation	Method to Use
Power of (exponentiation)	pow()
Returns the greater of two values	max()
Returns the smaller of two values	min()
Generate a random number	random()
Round numbers	round()
Find the square root	sqrt()

Some of these methods take parameters, while some do not require any parameters. Explore the Java API documentation to find out how these methods are used.

math Package

The precision of the basic integer and floating-point types is not sufficient for some applications. When the operations on the number need to maintain a high level of precision, a large fractional portion of a number or a very large number, the programmer can use the *BigDecimal and BigInteger classes*. These classes are for manipulating numbers with an arbitrarily long sequence of digits. The documentation for these classes can be found in the section on the java.*math package* in the Java API documentation, shown in Figure 6-12.

Figure 6-12 java.math Package API Docs

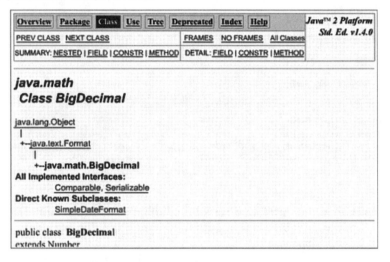

Storing Numeric Data in Objects

The BigDecimal and BigInteger classes are useful for applications such as security keys (numbers or codes for security of a program, a building, or an account), very large monetary values, and scientific calculations with large numbers. There is a price to pay for this precision, though: Computations using the BigDecimal and BigInteger classes are slower than when using primitives.

BigDecimal

The BigDecimal class implements arbitrary precision floating-point arithmetic. BigDecimal can perform calculations that might result in numbers larger than a 64-bit storage number such as a **double**. BigDecimal holds signed decimal numbers that are accurate to an arbitrary level of precision and are useful for currency operations. This class gives programmers control over rounding and scaling behavior, and provides methods for performing basic operations.

To create a `BigDecimal`, use the constructor and provide a `String` of numbers. The familiar mathematical operators cannot be used. The methods in the class must be used, as shown in Example 6-17.

Example 6-17 `BigDecimal` *Constructor and Methods*

```
//Sample constructor use :
BigDecimal   d = new BigDecimal("123.45678912344567887890");
//To store an ordinary number in a BigDecimal use the method:
BigDecimal d = BigDecimal.valueOf(1234059);
//The difference is that the constructor accepts a String as a parameter and
the valueOf accepts a long as a parameter.
```

The `BigDecimal` class has some remarkable capabilities. Notice that Java programmers typically get used to using the **double** numeric type to perform almost any kind of mathematical computations. Using the **double** Java type for large-scale numeric computations can lead to much trouble and confusion, unless you understand the limitations of this Java primitive numeric type. The precision scale for values of the type **double** is fixed at 15 digits. After that, it is a best approximation in scientific notation.

As an example, suppose that you had to calculate the product of the following two floating-point numbers:

9876543256789098765678.45673009876

8876543897654328967.9876098432645

You could tackle it as shown in Example 6-18:

Example 6-18 `BigDecimal`—*Calculating Very Large Numbers to a High Degree of Precision*

```
public class BigNumberCalc
{
    public static void main(String[] args)
    {
    // For illustration purposes, the double value here is hard-coded.
    // It may have come in as input from a user through a GUI component
    // as well.  This would make the value and scale unpredictable.
    // wrap values in a Double wrapper class using the wrapper class built-in
    // string conversion method - GUI input comes in as text.
```

continues

Example 6-18 `BigDecimal`—*Calculating Very Large Numbers to a High Degree of Precision (Continued)*

```
        Double val1 = new Double.valueOf("9876543256789098765678.45673009876");
        Double val2 = new Double.valueOf("8876543897654328967.9876098432645");
        // create a new wrapper class to hold result.
        Double result = val1.doubleValue() * val2.doubleValue();
        System.out.println("Answer is " + result.toString());
        }
}
//The output will be:
//Answer is 8.766956977597029E40


//Disappointing answer, right?



//Lets do this with BigDecimal:
public class BigNumberCalc2
{
    public static void main(String[] args)
    {
    BigDecimal val1 = new BigDecimal("9876543256789098765678.45673009876");
    BigDecimal val2 = new BigDecimal("8876543897654328967.9876098432645");
    // use built-in multiplication method
    BigDecimal result = val1.multiply(val2);
    System.out.println("Answer is " + result.toString());
    }
}
//The output will be:
//Answer is 87669569775970286821113136221976620139131.35050199800154320580202
```

The precision and scale of `BigDecimal` are both 32-bit signed integer values. That translates to 2,147,483,647 digits.

The `BigInteger` class is very much like the `BigDecimal` class and provides the same arbitrary precision characteristics.

The `BigDecimal` class has numerous capabilities for rounding, based on your scale of precision. Refer to the `BigDecimal` class in the Java API for more specifics. Example 6-19 is a simple example that uses one number (`0.255`) with and without a rounding factor and scale applied.

Example 6-19 BigDecimal—*How to Round a* BigDecimal *Number*

```
//----------------------------------------------------------------------


//  create a BigDecimal instance using default parameters.
BigDecimal a = new BigDecimal("0.255");


// create another BigDecimal instance setting a precision scale of 2
// (two places behind the decimal point).
// ROUND_HALF_UP is a rounding mode to round towards "nearest neighbor"
// unless both neighbors are equidistant, in which case round up. This is the
// rounding mode that most of us were taught in grade school.
// Note: this second object uses the number from the first object
BigDecimal b = a.setScale(2, BigDecimal.ROUND_HALF_UP);


System.out.println("Unrounded: " + a);
System.out.println("Rounded: " + b);


//Output is:
//Unrounded: 0.255
//Rounded: 0.26
//----------------------------------------------------------------------
```

The BigDecimal class has four constructor signatures, as shown in Example 6-20.

Example 6-20 BigDecimal *Class—Using the Correct Constructor*

```
//Translates a BigInteger into a BigDecimal.
BigDecimal(BigInteger val)
//Translates a BigInteger unscaled value and an int scale into a BigDecimal.
BigDecimal(BigInteger unscaledVal, int scale)
//Translates a double into a BigDecimal.
BigDecimal(double val)
//Translates the String representation of a BigDecmal into a BigDecimal.
BigDecimal(String val)
```

Of special interest are the last two—BigDecimal(**double** val) and
BigDecimal(String val). In BigDecimal(**double** val), the results of the

constructor can be somewhat unpredictable. You might assume that **new** BigDecimal(.1) is exactly equal to .1, but it is actually equal to .1000000000000000055511151231257827021181583404541015625. This is so because .1 cannot be represented exactly as a **double** (or, for that matter, as a binary fraction of any finite length). Thus, the long **double** value that is being passed *in* to the constructor is not exactly equal to .1, appearances notwithstanding.

The (String) constructor, on the other hand, is perfectly predictable: new BigDecimal(".1") is *exactly* equal to .1, as one would expect. Therefore, it is generally recommended that the BigDecimal(String val) constructor be used instead of to BigDecimal(**double** val).

BigInteger

The BigInteger class implements arbitrary precision integer arithmetic. The phrase "arbitrary precision" means that the precision is not predictable. Keep in perspective that the Java language is a strongly typed language; the precision of storage for each data type is known. BigInteger can perform calculations that might result in numbers larger than a 64-bit storage number.

To create a BigInteger, use the constructor and provide a String of numbers. Familiar mathematical operators cannot be used. The methods in the class must be used, as shown in Example 6-21.

Example 6-21 BigInteger *Constructor and Methods*

```
//Sample constructor use:
BigInteger b = new BigInteger("12345678912345678912345678912345678912");
//To store an ordinary number in a BigInteger use the method:
BigInteger d = BigInteger.valueOf(1234059);
//The difference is that the constructor accepts a String as a parameter and the
valueOf //accepts a long as a parameter.
```

To perform mathematical operations on BigInteger objects, use the methods of the object, as shown in Example 6-22.

Example 6-22 BigInteger *Mathematical Operations*

```
//A Simple addition of c = a + b would be implemented using this code.
BigInteger c = a.add(b) ;
//A calculation of d = c * (b + 2) would be implemented using this code.
BigInteger d = c.multiply(b.add(BigInteger.valueOf(2)));
```

The code shown for the `BigIntegerTest` class in Example 6-23 demonstrates the use of the `BigInteger` class. The `Console` class is used to accept input from the user. If a programmer provided 60 numbers out of a selection of 400 numbers, this program would say that the odds are 1 in a very large number (more than 30 digits long).

Example 6-23 *Sample Program Using* `BigInteger`

```
1 /**
2  * Java Program: BigIntegerTest
3  * @author Cisco Teacher
4  * @version 2002
5  */
6
7 import java.math.*;
8
9 public class BigIntegerTest
10 {
11     /**
12      * @param high A high int
13      * @param number A second int
14      */
15     public static BigInteger lotteryOdds(int high, int number)
16     {
17         BigInteger r = new BigInteger("1");
18         int i;
19         for (i = 1; i <= number; i++)
20             {
21             r = r.multiply(BigInteger.valueOf(high));
22             r = r.divide(BigInteger.valueOf(i));
23                 high--;
24         }
25         return r;
26     }
27
28     public static void main(String[] args)
29     {
30         int numbers = Console.readInt
31             ("How many numbers do you need to draw?");
```

continues

Example 6-23 *Sample Program Using* BigInteger (Continued)

```
32          int topNumber = Console.readInt
33              ("What is the highest number you can draw?");
34          BigInteger oddsAre = lotteryOdds(topNumber, numbers);
35
36          System.out.println
37              ("Your odds are 1 in " + oddsAre + ". Good luck!");
38      }
39
40  }   // end of BigIntegerTest class
```

For Example 6-23, you can view the explanatory text by accessing the full, interactive graphic for this example on the book's accompanying CD-ROM. The title of the activity is "Sample Program Using BigInteger" in the e-Lab Activities.

Working with Dates and Random Numbers

Dates can be used in many applications to document identities for individuals, such as date of birth, date hired, the date a course was started, and the date a course was completed. Dates can also be used to identify significant events, such as the date of a wedding, the date of a friend's party, or the due date of a homework paper. Businesses use dates to identify significant events, such as the date a customer placed an order, opened an account, received a shipment of goods or services, paid a balance on an invoice, and so on.

Random numbers are used in many different applications, from generating unique IDs for students or customers to shuffling a deck of cards.

This section consists of the following topics:

- Creating dates
- Setting dates
- Formatting dates
- Generating random numbers

Creating Dates

Three classes in the Java API documentation are concerned with dates: the *Date, Calendar, and DateFormat classes*. The Date class creates a Date object. The Calendar class sets or changes the date for a Date object. The DateFormat class displays the date in different formats. The `Date` and `Calendar` classes are located in the `java.util` package. The `DateFormat` class is part of the `java.text` package. When using these classes, specify the location of these using the following statements before the class header:

```
import java.util.*;
import java.text.*;
```

The Java API documentation for the `Date`, `Calendar`, and `DateFormat` classes is shown in Figures 6-13, 6-14, and 6-15. Review the constructors and methods for each class, and create a `Date` instance using the `Calendar` class.

NOTE

The `GregorianCalendar` is a direct concrete subclass of `Calendar`. It implements many useful features and should be the choice of programmers.

Figure 6-13 Date Class

Figure 6-14 Calendar Class

Figure 6-15 DateFormat Class

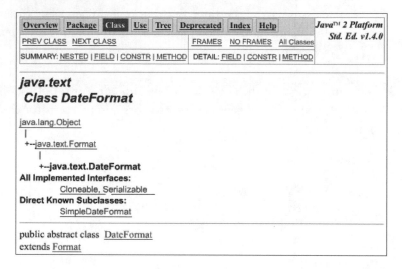

The Date class can be used to create objects that hold date values. The date stored is a specific instance in time to the nearest millisecond. The no-args constructor Date() creates an object based on the current time from the computer clock to the nearest millisecond, as shown in Example 6-24.

Example 6-24 parse() *Method of the* DateFormat *Class*

```
 1 /**
 2  * Java Program: DateDemo.java
 3  * @author Cisco Teacher
 4  * @version 2002
 5  */
 6
 7 import java.util.*;
 8 import java.text.*;
 9
10 public class DateDemo
11 {
12      public static void main (String args [ ])  throws ParseException
13      {
14          Date today = new Date();
15
16          Date someDate;
```

Example 6-24 `parse()` *Method of the* `DateFormat` *Class (Continued)*

```
17          DateFormat df =  DateFormat.getDateInstance
18             (DateFormat.FULL, Locale.US);
19          someDate = df.parse("Monday, May 30, 2002");
20      }
21 }
```

For Example 6-24, you can view the explanatory text by accessing the full, interactive graphic for this example on the book's accompanying CD-ROM. The title of the activity is "parse() Method of the `DateFormat` Class" in the e-Lab Activities.

A `Date` object also can be obtained from a `String` using the `DateFormat` class. The parse() method of the `DateFormat` class, shown in Example 6-24, can be used to interpret a date represented in a `String` as a `Date` object. If an error occurs, this method **throws** an exception. Because the parse method is called from within the main() method, you must declare that your main method can also **throw** that exception. Recall that this phrase was included in the use of the `System.in.read()` method for reading input from the console. Exceptions are explained further in Chapter 12, "Exceptions."

Example 6-25 *Using the* `Calendar` *Class*

```
Calendar newCal = new Calendar();
// this will generate a "java.util.Calendar is abstract: cannot be instantiated."
// compiler error message.
```

> **NOTE**
>
> The `Calendar` class is an abstract class. Therefore, you cannot create a direct instance of `Calendar`, as shown in Example 6-25.

Setting Dates

Note that almost all of the `Date` methods that would help to change dates have been marked deprecated in the API documentation. This means that these are old and are not as dependable as methods in other classes that accomplish the same task. To set the date of a `Date` object to a new date, use the methods in the `Calendar` class, which uses the Gregorian calendar. To change the date of a `Date` object, create a `Calendar` object and use its getTime() method to get the most current date values for the `Date` object, as shown in Example 6-26.

Example 6-26 *Using the* Calendar *and* GregorianCalendar *Classes*

```
//Create a calendar with any one of these statements.
Calendar rightNow = Calendar.getInstance();
//The getInstance method of the Calendar class returns an object of the class
//Calendar.

//A calendar can also be created using this statement.
GregorianCalendar calendar = new  GregorianCalendar ();
//This will be set to the current instance in time.
//Retrieve this as a Date object by using the getTime method of the
GregorianCalendar //object.

GregorianCalendar calendar = new GregorianCalendar();
Date someDate = new Date();
//the value of someDate can be changed with this statement.
someDate = calendar.getTime();
```

Formatting Dates

The DateFormat object can hold specific data regarding formatting styles for a date. To format a Date object, start with the same steps that were used to convert a String to a Date object using the parse() method. Example 6-27 shows the format() method of the DateFormat class converting the Date object someDate to the String object formatDate, which can then be printed.

Example 6-27 *Using* DateFormat *Class to Format a* Date *Object*

```
GregorianCalendar calendar = new  GregorianCalendar ();

Date someDate;
DateFormat df =  DateFormat.getDateInstance(DateFormat.FULL, Locale.US);

someDate =  calendar.getTime ( );
String formatDate = df.format( someDate) ;
System.out.println ( "The date is " + formatDate);
```

Example 6-28 shows how to get today's date.

Example 6-28 *Calendar How-To: Finding Today's Date*

```
//-----------------------------------------------------
GregorianCalendar calendar = new GregorianCalendar();
int day = calendar.get(Calendar.DATE);
int month = calendar.get(Calendar.MONTH);
int year = calendar.get(Calendar.YEAR);
System.out.print("Month: " + month + " Day: "+ day + " Year: " + year);


//Output is the following if today's date is 05/20/2002:
Month: 4 Day: 20 Year: 2002
//-----------------------------------------------------
```

Example 6-29 shows a slightly different approach, adjusting the MONTH value.

Example 6-29 *Calendar How-To: Finding a Date*

```
//-----------------------------------------------------
GregorianCalendar calendar = new GregorianCalendar();
System.out.println("The current date is "
    + calendar.get(Calendar.YEAR) + " "
    + (calendar.get(Calendar.MONTH) + 1) + " "
    + calendar.get(Calendar.DATE));


//Output is the following if today's date is 05/20/2002:


The current date is 2002 05 20
//-----------------------------------------------------
```

Formatting a Date to a Specific Format Pattern Using SimpleDateFormat

SimpleDateFormat is a concrete class for formatting and parsing dates in a locale-sensitive manner. It allows for formatting a date to text and parsing text to a date. SimpleDateFormat enables you to start by choosing any user-defined patterns for date-time formatting.

The short code snippet shown in Example 6-30 expects a date in the yyyy-mm-dd format and reformats it to the mm/dd/yyyy format. In this example, the input date could have come in from a GUI date field entered by a user. This example uses the SimpleDateFormat class.

TIP

The site http://www.javaworld.com/javaworld/jw-12-2000/jw-1229-dates-p2.html provides additional information on the methods in the GregorianCalendar class that can be used to manipulate dates.

Example 6-30 *Calendar How-To: Formatting a Date*

```java
import java.text.SimpleDateFormat;
import java.util.Date;

public class DateFormatTest
{
    public static void main( String[] args ) throws Exception
    {
    // note the MM in the "yyyy-MM-dd" and "MM/dd/yyyy" format patterns.
    // Capital MM stands for Month, while lower case "m" identifies minutes.

    // set format patterns for the input and output.
    SimpleDateFormat sdfInput = new SimpleDateFormat( "yyyy-MM-dd" );
    SimpleDateFormat sdfOutput =  new SimpleDateFormat ( "MM/dd/yyyy" );

    // input date - from GUI input text box.  Refer to section on AWT (Abstract
    // Window Toolkit
    String textDate = dateTextField.getText(); // value is "2001-01-04";

    Date aDate = sdfInput.parse( textDate );    // instantiate Date object passing
                                                // date in the constructor
    // use the format method in the output SimpleDateFormat
    // object to re-format the date
    System.out.println("The date is: " +  sdfOutput.format( aDate ) );
    }
}


//The output looks like this:
//The date is: 01/04/2001.

//If you prefer, you can replace the last two lines of code with
//System.out.println( sdfOutput.format(  sdfInput.parse(textDate) ) );
```

The SimpleDateFormat editing patterns are extremely robust and flexible; refer to the Java API for all specifics. Of special note is the MM vs. MMM vs. MMMM format character strings. Refer to the previous format patterns, yyyy-MM-dd and MM/dd/yyyy. If you use MM, the formatter produces and expects a numeric month, such as 04 for April. If you use MMM, the formatter produces and expects the standardized three-character text representation of the month, such as Apr for April. Finally, if you use a character pattern of greater than three M's, the formatter produces and expects a full-month String designation, such as April for April, and September for September.

You can test this by just changing the format pattern in Example 6-30:

```
SimpleDateFormat sdfOutput = new SimpleDateFormat ( "MM/dd/yyyy" );
```

All you need to do is change the MM to MMM or MMMM to get the different output formats.

Random Numbers

Random numbers in the Java language can be generated either using the random() method of the Math class or using objects of the Random class. Random number generators (methods or classes) take a "seed" number and "grow" a sequence of numbers. The random number can be of the type **int, long, float**, or **double**. The same seed number generates the same set of random numbers. The sequence of numbers generated is distributed uniformly over the range of the type of numbers. Floating-point values are distributed between 0.0 and 1.0.

Initializing the random number algorithm with the same number produces the same sequence.

The Java language provides two classes for generating random numbers. The Math class provides the static method random(). The Math.random() method returns a **double** value with a positive sign that is greater than or equal to 0.0 and less than 1.0. Returned values are chosen pseudorandomly with (approximately) uniform distribution from that range.

The java.util package includes the Random class, with different algorithms for generating random numbers. The Random class has two constructors. One constructor uses the time from the clock in the computer as the seed value, and the other accepts an argument of the type **long** as a seed to generate the random numbers.

If the no-args constructor is used, the sequence of numbers is different each time. However, if a Random object is generated within the same program, it is possible for the sequence to be the same. The difference in the time of the computer might be in milliseconds and might not be enough to generate a different sequence of numbers. When the constructor is used with the **long** argument, two Random objects with the same "seed" number generate the same sequence.

After a `Random` object has been created, the methods of the object can be used to generate the next number. Table 6-10 describes the methods of the `Random` class.

Table 6-10 Some Random Class Methods

Method	Description
`int nextInt()`	Returns the next pseudorandom, uniformly distributed **int** value from this random number generator's sequence. All 2^{32} possible **int** values are produced with (approximately) equal probability.
`int nextInt(int n)`	Returns a pseudorandom, uniformly distributed **int** value between **0** (inclusive) and the specified value (exclusive), drawn from this random number generator's sequence. All n possible **int** values are produced with (approximately) equal probability.
`long nextLong()`	Returns the next pseudorandom, uniformly distributed **long** value from this random number generator's sequence. All 2^{64} possible **long** values are produced with (approximately) equal probability.
`boolean nextBoolean()`	Returns the next pseudorandom, uniformly distributed **boolean** value from this random number generator's sequence. The values **true** and **false** are produced with (approximately) equal probability.
`float nextFloat()`	Returns the next pseudorandom, uniformly distributed **float** value between **0.0** and **1.0** from this random number generator's sequence. All 2^{24} possible **float** values of the form m x 2^{-24}, where m is a positive integer less than 2^{24}, are produced with (approximately) equal probability.
`double nextDouble()`	Returns the next pseudorandom, uniformly distributed **double** value between **0.0** and **1.0** from this random number generator's sequence. All 2^{53} possible **float** values of the form m x 2^{-53}, where m is a positive integer less than 2^{53}, are produced with (approximately) equal probability.
`void setSeed(long seed)`	Sets the seed of this random number generator using a single **long** seed.

The sample code for the `LuckySix` class, shown in Example 6-31, simulates the throwing of dice in the **for** loop. For each throw, a random number between 1 and 6 is needed for each die. Do this by adding 1 to the random number modulus 6. Because the random number generated with the `nextInt()` method will be any integer number, positive or negative, the `abs()` method from the `Math` class is used to ensure that there is a positive number for the throw of the die. The output for `LuckySix.java` is shown in Figure 6-16.

Example 6-31 `LuckySix.java`—*Code*

```
1 /**
2  * Java Program: LuckySix.java
3  * @author Cisco Teacher
4  * @version 2002
5  */
6 import java.util.*;
7 import java.io.*;
8
9 public class LuckySix
10 {
11     public static void main(String args[])
12     {
13         System.out.println( "You have six throws of a pair of dice.  \n" +
14         "If you get a pair you can try again. \n" +
15         "Try to get a lucky six when the dice are both at six. \n" +
16         "Good Luck! \n\n");
17         Random dicenumbers = new Random();
18         String[] athrow - {"One", "Two", "Three", "Four", "Five", "Six"};
19         int die1=0, die2=0;
20         int throwNumber = 0;
21         boolean winner = false;
22         while (throwNumber < 6  && winner == false)
23         {
24             die1= 1 + (Math.abs(dicenumbers.nextInt())) % 6;
25             die2= 1 + (Math.abs(dicenumbers.nextInt())) % 6;
26             System.out.println("Throw " + athrow[throwNumber] +
                   " resulted in " + die1 + "," + die2);
27
28             if (die1 == 6 && die2 == 6)
29             {
30                 winner = true;
```

continues

Example 6-31 LuckySix.java—*Code (Continued)*

```
31                    continue;
32                }
33
34            if (die1 == die2)
35            {
36                System.out.println("You win another turn!");
37                throwNumber = 0;
38                continue;
39            }
40
41            throwNumber++;    // increment throw count
42        }
43
44        //Print out results
45        if(winner == true)
46        {
47            System.out.println("You win a Lucky six! ");
48        }
49        else
50        {
51            System.out.println("Sorry you lost...");
52        }
53    }
54 }
55
56
```

Figure 6-16 `LuckySix.java`—Output

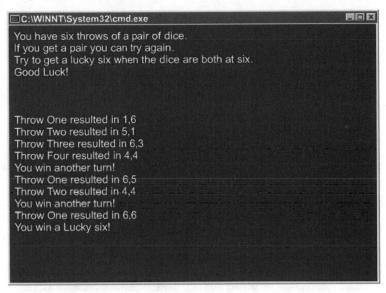

Case Study: JBANK Application

The JBANK application introduced in Chapter 1, "What Is Java?", provides students with an opportunity to apply the Java language concepts learned throughout this course. In the JBANK labs for Chapter 6, students

- Read `Customer` data from standard input using `System.in`
- Output `Customer` data to standard output using `System.out`
- Use `String` and `StringBuffer` classes to store, retrieve, and manipulate data
- Use the `Console` class provided in the Resource folder to read `Customer` data
- Include a menu system in the `Teller` class
- Use the `Date` class to set the hours of operation for the bank and the customers' DOB (date of birth) field
- Use `BigDecimal` and `BigInteger` for manipulating numbers with arbitrarily long sequences of digits to calculate the interest on the account balance
- Use the wrapper classes to convert string data to primitive data types

The JBANK Application

The JBANK application uses string, date, and currency values in many objects, as shown in Figures 6-17 and 6-18.

Figure 6-17 JBANK Application

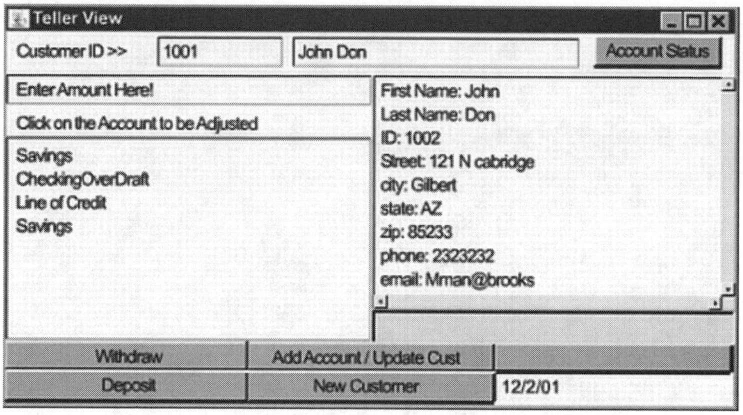

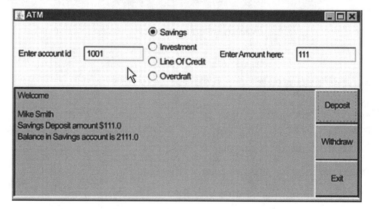

Figure 6-18 JBANK Application

This chapter prepares students to use many of the useful Java classes in their application. The `Date` class is implemented to maintain real date values in the objects. Later, while working with GUIs or user input programs, students will use the code presented in this chapter to convert string data into different forms:

- `Date`-Uses the parse method of the `DateFormat` class
- **int**-Uses the `Integer.parseInt` methods
- **double**-Uses the `Double.parseDouble` method

In addition to these, many currency calculations require precise storage of decimal values. The `BigDecimal` objects will help to store bank financial data to arbitrary precision.

Summary

This chapter focused on the Java library of classes. It introduced the System, String, StringBuffer, Math, and wrapper classes. The System class allows programmers to accept input from users. The String class holds immutable character (text) data. The StringBuffer class holds mutable character (text) data. The Math class has static methods for calculating different types of numbers. Wrapper classes manipulate primitive data types. Every primitive data type has a corresponding wrapper class. The wrapper classes for the numeric primitives are also useful for converting string data into primitives. Finally, the chapter discussed classes for creating, manipulating, and storing dates.

Syntax Summary

System class - input and output:

```java
//The read method reads the first character typed on the keyboard. This is read as an
//int. The (char) cast explicitly requests the conversion of the int to the Unicode
//char, which is stored in the char variable selection.
char selection = (char) System.in.read( );
```

```java
//The print method does not add the line separator, so one line of output can be
//built up with several calls to the print method.
System.out.print("message");
```

```java
//The println method adds a line separator to produce a complete line of output.
System.out.print("message");
```

String class:

```java
//Empty String
String a = "";
//String in a return statement:
    public String toString( )
    {
        return   "statements";
    }
//String class with + operator:
int score = 95;
System.out.println("The student's test score is: " + score);
```

String class methods:

```java
int length()
char charAt(int index)
boolean equals(Object anObject)
boolean equalsIgnoreCase(String anotherString)
int compareTo(String anotherString)
int compareTo(Object o)
int compareToIgnoreCase(String str)
boolean startsWith(String prefix)
boolean startsWith(String prefix, int offset)
int indexOf(int ch)
```

```
int indexOf(String str)
String substring(int beginIndex)
String substring(int beginIndex, int endIndex)
String concat(String str)
static String valueOf(Object obj)
```

StringBuffer class methods:

```
StringBuffer append(char c)
StringBuffer delete(int start, int end)
StringBuffer deleteCharAt(int index)
StringBuffer replace(int start, int end, String str)
String substring(int start)
String substring(int start, int end)
StringBuffer insert(int offset, String str)
StringBuffer reverse()
String toString()
```

Console class methods:

```
static void printlnPrompt(String prompt)
static String readLine()
static String readLine(String prompt)
static int readInt(String prompt)
static double readDouble(String prompt)
```

Integer class methods:

```
static String toString(int i)
static int parseInt(String s) throws NumberFormatException
static Integer valueOf(String s, int radix) throws NumberFormatException
double doubleValue()
boolean equals(Object obj)
```

Double class methods:

```
static String toString(double d)
static Double valueOf(String s) throws NumberFormatException
static double parseDouble(String s) throws NumberFormatException
String toString()
int intValue()
double doubleValue()
boolean equals(Object obj)
int compareTo(Double anotherDouble)
int compareTo(Object o)
```

Character class methods:

```
char charValue()
boolean equals(Object obj)
String toString()
static boolean isLowerCase(char ch)
static boolean isUpperCase(char ch)
static boolean isDigit(char ch)
static char toLowerCase(char ch)
static char toUpperCase(char ch)
static int getNumericValue(char ch)
int compareTo(Character anotherCharacter)
int compareTo(Object o)
```

Boolean class methods:

```
boolean booleanValue()
static Boolean valueOf(String s)
String toString()
boolean equals(Object obj)
```

Math class methods:

```
static double pow(double a, double b)
static double max(double a, double b) (also overloaded for float, int and long)
static double min(double a, double b) (also overloaded for float, int and long)
static double random()
static long round(double a)
static int round(float a)
static double sqrt(double a)
```

BigDecimal and BigInteger classes:

```
//the program must first import the java.math package

//BigDecimal constructor
BigDecimal d1 = new BigDecimal("123.45678912344567887890");

//To store an ordinary number in BigDecimal
BigDecimal d2 = BigDecimal.valueOf(1234059);

//BigInteger constructor
BigInteger a = new BigInteger("12345678912345678912345678");

//To store an ordinary number in BigInteger:
BigInteger b = BigInteger.valueOf(1234059);

//Mathematical operations (addition): c = a + b
BigInteger  c = a.add(b);

//Mathematical operations (multiplication): d = c * (b + 2)
BigInteger d = c.multiply(b.add(BigInteger.valueOf(2)));
```

Date, Calendar, GregorianCalendar and DateFormat classes:

```
//Date class no-args constructor

//Allocates a Date object and initializes it so that it represents the time
//at which it was allocated, measured to the nearest millisecond (based on
//the current time on the computer clock).
Date someDate = newDate();

//Create a Calendar object using the getInstance() method of the Calendar class.
//The Calendar object returned is based on the current time in the default time zone
//with the default locale.
Calendar calendar1 = Calendar.getInstance()

//Create a GregorianCalendar object using the no-args constructor
//Constructs a GregorianCalendar object using the current time in the default
//time zone with the default locale.
GregorianCalendar calendar2 = new GregorianCalendar();

//The date held by the Date object referenced by the variable someDate can
//be changed with the getTime() method of the Calendar class.
someDate = calendar1.getTime();
```

```
//Format a Date object
//The parse() method of the DateFormat class can be used to convert a String
//object to a Date object; in this example, the String "Monday, May 30, 2002"
//is converted to a Date object and then assigned to the Date object reference
someDate.
DateFormat df = DateFormat.getDateInstance(DateFormat.FULL, Locale.US);
someDate = df.parse("Monday, May 30, 2002");

//The format() method of the DateFormat class can be used to convert a Date
//object to a String object; in this example, the Date object someDate is /
/converted to a String object and then assigned to the String object
reference formatDate.
String formatDate = df.format(someDate);
System.out.println ("The date is " + formatDate);
```

Key Terms

BigDecimal `class`   Class that implements arbitrary precision floating-point arithmetic.

BigInteger `class`   Class that implements arbitrary precision integer arithmetic.

`Calendar` class   Class that sets or changes the date for a `Date` object. Part of the `java.util` package.

casting and conversion   Process that assigns a value of one data type to a variable of another data type. If the two types are compatible, Java converts it automatically.

concatenation   Process of putting together two values (where at least one of the values is a `String`) into a new `String`. When a `String` is concatenated (using the overloaded + operator) with a value that is not a `String`, the latter value is converted to a `String`.

`Date` class   Class that creates a `Date` object. Part of the `java.util` package.

`DateFormat` class   Class that displays the date in different formats. Part of the `java.text` package. The `parse()` method of the `DateFormat` class can be used to convert a date represented in a `String` object into a `Date` object. This method requires the declaration of a **throws** `ParseException`. The `format()` method of the `DateFormat` class can be used to convert a `Date` object into a `String` object.

`in` field of the `System` class   A reference to an `InputStream` object, typically used to stream in data from keyboard input or another input source specified by the host environment or user. The `read()` method of the `InputStream` object referenced by the `in` variable can be used to read one character at a time. The data returned from the `read()` method has an **int** data type; it must be converted to a **char**. The (**char**) cast explicitly requests the conversion of the **int** to the Unicode **char**. The `read()` method can be used to flush out keystrokes, such as carriage return or new line.

`err` field of the `System` class   A reference to a `PrintStream` object used to display error messages.

`Math` class   Class that contains static methods to perform mathematical operations.

`math` package   Package that contains the `BigDecimal` and `BigInteger` classes that are useful for maintaining a high level of precision and manipulating a long sequence of numbers, such as scientific calculations or security codes.

static methods   Methods that require that no objects of the class be created to use these methods.

String class   Class used to create and store a sequence of immutable character (text) data. The String class is defined as **final**, so any objects created of this class are considered immutable or unchangeable. The individual characters of the String class cannot be changed.

StringBuffer class   Class that holds mutable character (text) data.

System class   A Java core class, used for many operations that require data about the underlying operation system settings. The System class has three **public static final** fields, in, out, and err. These fields are designed to connect to the underlying system's stdin, stdout, and stderr devices. The System class also has a method to request garbage collection using the static method gc().

out field of the System class   A reference to a PrintStream object used to stream out data for printing output. Two commonly used methods of the PrintSteam object referenced by the out variable include:

> println()   Adds a line separator to produce a complete line of output

> print()   Does not add the line separator, so one line of output can be built up with several calls to the print method

toString method   Method inherited from the Object class that renders an object as a String. Unless the method is overridden, it will return a String consisting of the name of the class of which the object is an instance, the at-sign character '@', and the unsigned hexadecimal representation of the hash code of the object.

wrapper classes   Classes that manipulate primitive data elements as objects. After the primitive value is initialized in the wrapper object, it cannot be changed. Wrapper classes are useful because of the many wrapper class methods available; however, wrapper classes cannot be used with arithmetic operators or conditions.

Check Your Understanding

1. Which of these is not one of the standard fields of the System class for input/output operations?

    A. in

    B. error

    C. out

    D. err

2. Which method prints text and a carriage return to the console?

   A. `System.print();`

   B. `System.in.println();`

   C. `System.out.print();`

   D. `System.out.println();`

3. Which class should be used to create a string of characters that will be altered frequently?

   A. `char`

   B. `String`

   C. `StringBuffer`

   D. `toString`

4. Which class should be used to create a string of characters that will not be altered?

   A. `char`

   B. `String`

   C. `StringBuffer`

   D. `toString`

5. Which Java statement incorrectly assigns a `String` value to the identifier `myString`?

   A. `String myString - 'Hello Student';`

   B. `String myString = Teacher.toString();`

   C. `String myString = new String("Hello Student");`

   D. `String myString = "Hello" + "Student";`

6. Using the `==` operator to compare object data is known as:

   A. Deep comparison

   B. Shallow comparison

   C. Assignment comparison

   D. Static comparison

7. What is the resulting value of name after these two lines of code have been executed?

```
String name =  new String ("Michael");
name = name.substring(2,5);
```

   A. ich

   B. ichae

   C. chael

   D. cha

8. Which set of classes is used to treat primitive values as objects?

   A. Standard classes

   B. Wrapper classes

   C. Object classes

   D. Numeric classes

9. Which statement correctly instantiates a Double object?

   A. double x = 15.5;

   B. Double x = 15.5;

   C. Double x = new Double (15.5);

   D. double x = new double (15.5);

10. Which method of the Character class identifies whether the value is a lowercase character?

   A. toLowerCase()

   B. isLowerCase()

   C. LowerCase()

   D. notUpperCase()

11. What type of value does the compareTo() method in the Double class return?

   A. double

   B. void

   C. Double

   D. int

12. Which of the following is a false statement about the Math class?

    A. The Math class contains methods useful for arithmetic operations.

    B. A programmer must instantiate an object from the Math class before using its methods.

    C. All methods in the Math class are static methods.

    D. random() is a method in the Math class that generates a random number

13. What is the value of answer after the following statement is executed?

    ```
    double answer = Math.pow(2,3);
    ```

    A. 2.0

    B. 4.0

    C. 6.0

    D. 8.0

14. What type of argument does the constructor for BigInteger accept?

    A. `int`

    B. `Integer`

    C. `String`

    D. `Long`

15. Which of these **import** statements will allow you to use the BigDecimal class?

    A. `import java.math.*;`

    B. `import java.util.*;`

    C. `import java.BigDecimal.*;`

    D. No **import** statement is needed.

16. Which **import** statement will allow you to use the Date and Calendar classes?

    A. `import java.util.*;`

    B. `import java.Date.*;`

    C. `import java.text.*;`

    D. `import java.io.*;`

17. Which Java statement does not cause a compiler error?

    A. `DateFormat myDateFormat = new DateFormat();`

    B. `Date myDate = new Date();`

    C. `Calendar myCalendar = new Calendar();`

    D. All of these statements cause a compiler error.

18. Which class in the `java.util` package can be used to generate random numbers?

    A. `RandomNumber`

    B. `Number`

    C. `Random`

    D. `Math`

19. What does the no-args constructor for a `Random` object use as the seed for its random number?

    A. It randomly selects a seed between 0 and 1.

    B. It uses the computer clock value as the seed.

    C. It always uses 1 as the seed.

    D. It always uses 0 as the seed.

20. What type of value does `Math.random()` return?

    A. `int`

    B. `double`

    C. `float`

    D. `long`

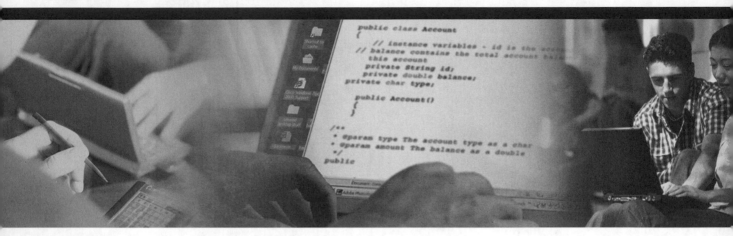

Upon completion of this chapter, you will be able to

- Understand arrays
- Declare and initialize arrays
- Use arrays
- Use multidimensional arrays
- Apply the Java language concepts that you learned in this chapter to the JBANK case study

Chapter 7

Arrays

Introduction

This chapter focuses on arrays, which are logical, organized mechanisms for storing data of objects of the same data type. The Java language also supports multidimensional arrays, also known as an array of arrays.

Arrays provide enormous flexibility in programming. The data in arrays can be accessed, processed, and sorted quickly and efficiently by using loops. The use of loops and arrays reduces the number of instructions that a programmer must code and the number of instructions that the compiler must compile.

Students will learn how to create, initialize, and use arrays in this chapter.

Arrays

The array object is a built-in object, defined by the developers of the Java language. The array object creates and stores data of the same data type in a sequential set of storage locations. This data (primitive or object) is accessed through the index of the element in the array. This section consists of the following topics:

- Introduction to arrays
- Variables in arrays
- Index
- Arrays of primitives
- Arrays of objects

Introduction to Arrays

Java has several methods to hold references to objects and variables that reference primitive data type values. One method is to create separate references for each and process each reference with separate instructions. Other methods use predefined classes in the API library known as collection classes or containers. These are examined in Chapter 14, "Collections." The method discussed in this chapter uses arrays. An array object creates and stores data in a sequential set of storage locations.

Why do programmers use arrays? Consider the case of a teacher's grade book. Several objects are needed to hold information about each student in a class. Programmers need to create a separate variable with a unique name for each. To print student data or to change student data, separate instructions must be written for each student object. Every time a new student is enrolled in the class, the code must be changed. Now consider that there are more than 20 students in a class and that code must be written to manipulate all of these student objects. This code involves many more lines of code repeating the same set of instructions for each object.

The code for the Teacher class shown in Example 7-1 demonstrates that even with three students, there is a significant increase in the number of lines of code that must be retyped. This is just the process for creating the Student object, setting data, and printing data. Consider the process for doing more than this, such as calculating scores and grade-point averages or storing data for many Student objects in memory or to a file. The number of lines of code to manipulate one Student object could run into many lines. The number of lines increases dramatically as this is repeated for each object. This introduces the potential for errors of omission, with the programmer forgetting to set the data of one or more of the Student objects.

NOTE

The full version of the abbreviated code shown in this example can be viewed using the book's accompanying CD-ROM.

Example 7-1 *Array Variables, Reference, Sequence*

```
1 /**
2  * Teacher Class creates students
3  * @author Cisco Teacher
4  * @version 2002
5  */
6 public class Teacher
7 {
8      // Main method
```

Example 7-1 *Array Variables, Reference, Sequence (Continued)*

```
9      public static void main(String[] args)
10     {
11         Student s1, s2, s3;
12         s1 = new Student("Mary Jane", "U");
13         s2 = new Student("Mary Martin", "U");
14         s3 = new Student("John Smith", "U");
15         s1.setGrade("C");
16         s2.setGrade("A");
17         s3.setGrade("B");
18         s1.printData();
19         s2.printData();
20         s3.printData();
```

Programmers need to create programs that are efficient and that run fast. They also need to code programs quickly and efficiently. Programmers constantly face the demand to create solutions quickly. With Java, they can do this by using prebuilt data types such as the array data type to build an array object to hold a large number of objects and a small number of lines of code to manipulate these objects.

Thus, the array is the most efficient way to store and randomly access a sequence of objects (object references). In Figure 7-1, the references to Student objects are stored in an array. A programmer would need to access the object references through the array. These arrays can be used in loops to perform the same actions on each object.

Variables in Arrays

Variables are used to reference data. A variable references a single primitive data value or a single reference to an object. An array is an object that references many primitive values or objects as a collection. The array itself is referenced through a single variable. An array gives programmers the capability to handle sets of values of the same data type with one name.

Figure 7-1 Array Variables, Reference, Sequence

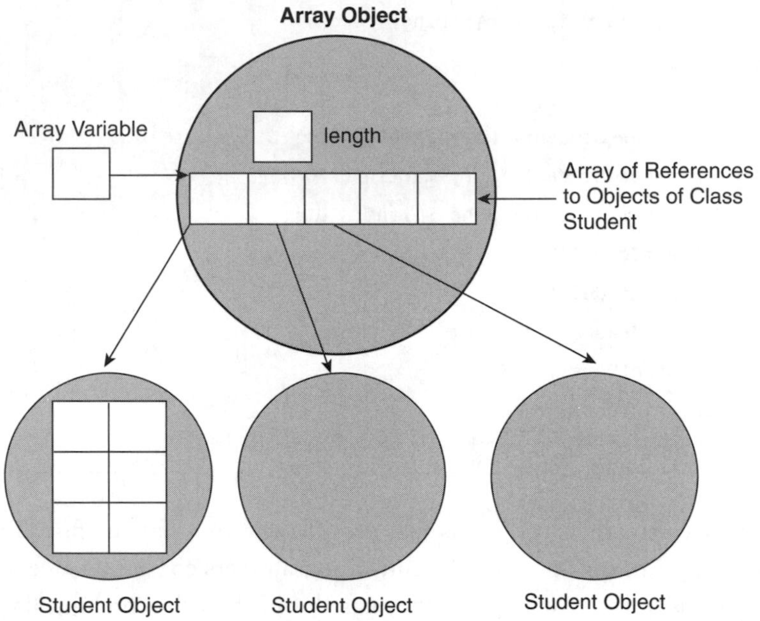

Array Object

Array Variable

length

Array of References
to Objects of Class
Student

Student Object   Student Object   Student Object

Figure 7-2 Array Length and Elements

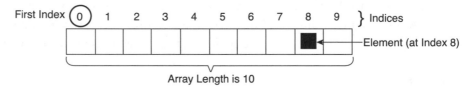

Every primitive or object can be accessed through a variable. In all of the programs
shown so far in this course, each variable has had a unique name. An array object
holds the references to these values of the same data type. Some Java programmers
think of this as a set of objects that share a group name; the manager of the group is
the array object.

Regardless of what type of array the programmer is working with, the array variable is
a reference to an object that is created on the heap. Access to the data is through this
array object. The array object has a unique variable identifier. Access to the primitives
and objects is through the array variable. The array object can reference one or more
objects and primitives of the same data type as a sequence of items. For example, an

array of integers is a sequence of primitives of the data type **int** stored next to each other. All of the primitive data types and references to objects can be stored in an array. A simple illustration of an array is shown in Figure 7-3.

Figure 7-3 Accessing Primitives with Arrays

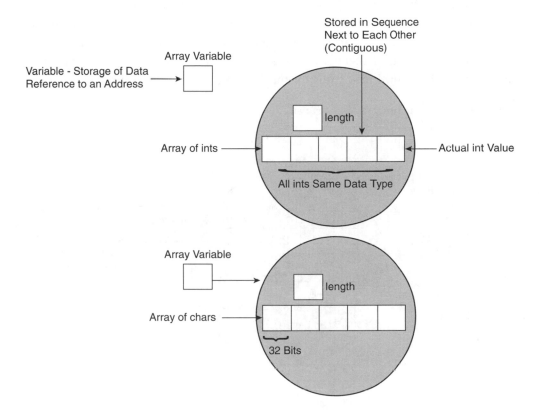

An array of characters is a sequence of **char** primitives. Some classes specialize in storing a sequence of **char** primitives. The String and StringBuffer classes, for example, store text as a sequence of **char** primitives.

Index

The array object is a built-in object. This means that the developers of the language have defined attributes for it. Because Java is a strongly typed language, keeping the items referenced by an array object of the same data type makes it fast and efficient. No special calculations are needed to figure out the next location for storage. To keep this an efficient operation, the array object must know exactly how many objects or primitives to reference. The fixed number of objects or primitives therefore determines the size of an array or the number of storage locations that the array will reference (*array length*). This information is stored in a **final int** variable of the array object labeled length. This variable is read only (**final**). After the array object is created, its length is fixed and cannot be changed (*fixed size*).

Although array objects create references to other objects or storage for primitives contiguously, they can access these in any order. They use an *index* to know which object or primitive to access. In an array, each primitive or reference to an object is known as an element. Each array element is assigned an **int** value in the sequence in which it was created. This is the index value for the element, as shown in Figure 7-4.

Figure 7-4 Creating an Array Reference to an Array of ints

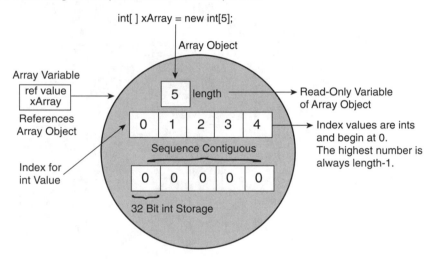

Array Elements

NOTE

Array indexes cannot be of type **long**. Because only non-negative integers can be used as indexes, this effectively limits the number of elements in an array to 2,147,483,648, or 2^{31}, with a range of indices from 0 to $2^{31} - 1$.

When creating an array of primitives or objects, the data (primitive or object) is accessed through the index of the element in the array. The first element in the array is always assigned the number 0, the next element is assigned the number 1, and so on (*zero-based indexing*). The length of the array determines the total number of elements created. The last element in the array has an index equal to the length of the index minus one (length of index – 1). So, if the array contains 15 elements, then the last element has an index of 14 (15 – 1). It is important to note that the index begins at 0, not 1, as shown in Figure 7-5.

Figure 7-5 Creating an Array Reference to an Array of Objects

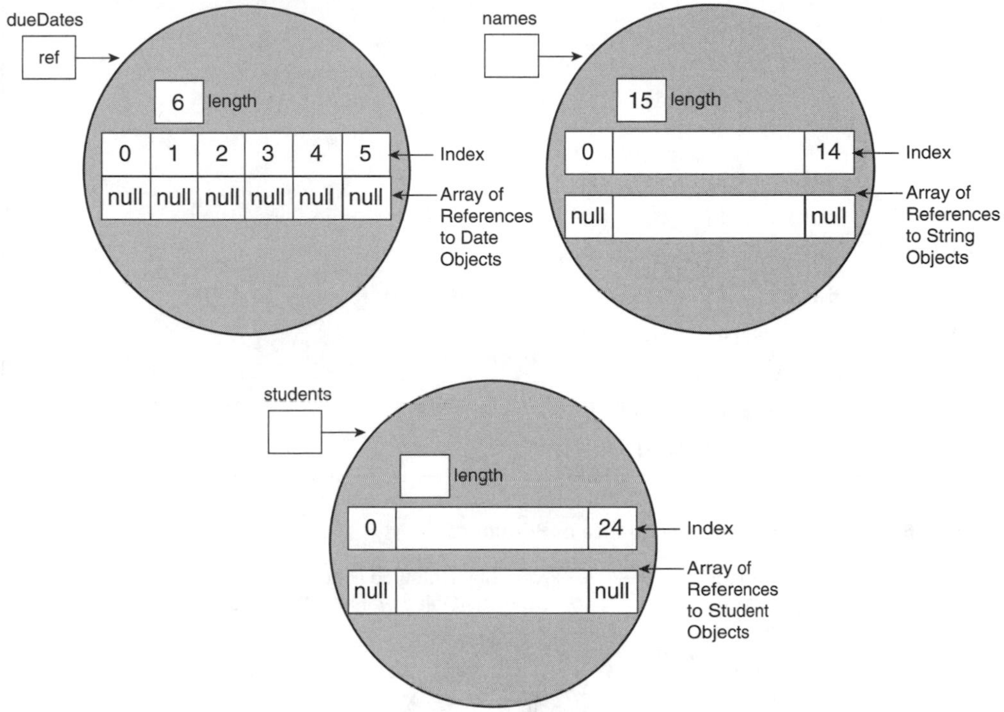

Arrays of Primitives

Arrays can represent a set of variables that store primitive data (*array of primitives*). In the code and graphic shown for the `PrimitiveArrays` class in Example 7-2 and Figure 7-6, an array of **int** primitives and an array of **char** primitives are being created. Arrays of **long**, **float**, **double**, **boolean**, **byte**, or **short** primitive data types also could be created.

Example 7-2 *Creating an Array of Primitives*

```
1 /**
2  * PrimitiveArrays Class creates students
3  * @author Cisco Teacher
4  * @version 2002
5  */
6 public class PrimitiveArrays
7 {
8     public static void main(String[] args)
```

continues

NOTE

The full version of the abbreviated code shown in this example can be viewed using the book's accompanying CD-ROM.

Example 7-2 *Creating an Array of Primitives (Continued)*

```
9      {
10         int[] intArray = new int[5];
11         char[] charArray = new char[6];
12
13         intArray[0] = 6;
14         intArray[1] = 3;
15         intArray[2] = 2;
16         intArray[3] = 4;
17         intArray[4] = 9;
18         charArray[0] = 'a';
19         charArray[1] = 'l';
20         charArray[2] = 'k';
```

Figure 7-6 Array Referencing a Sequence of Primitives

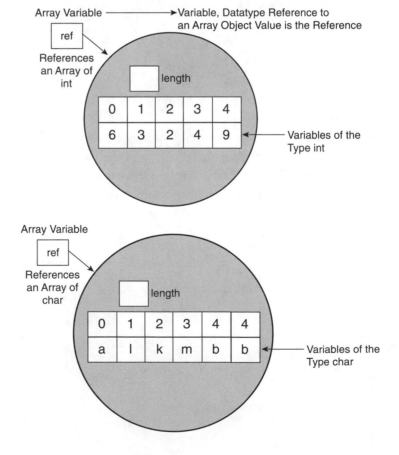

Arrays of Objects

An *array of objects* is a little more complex. In this case, the array variable references an array of data type references. The data in the array object is a sequence of references to the actual objects. Both the array object and the objects that it references are created on the heap part of memory.

Figure 7-7 shows two examples. One is an array of Student objects. The other is an array of Date objects, which are references to objects of the class Date. The Date class is described in the Java language API documents as part of the java.util package of classes. As discussed in earlier chapters, a package is the Java language term to describe and identify access to an organization of classes.

Figure 7-7 Array of Object References

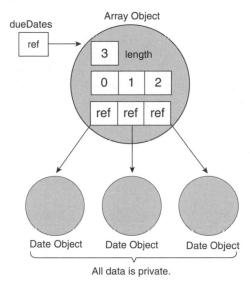

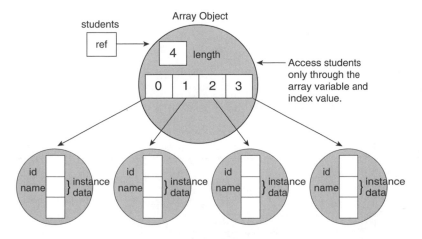

The next sections of the chapter address the creation and use of array objects.

Declaring and Initializing Arrays

Before an array object can be used, it must be declared and initialized. This section consists of the following topics:

- Declaring arrays
- Using subscripts to access elements of an array

Declaring Arrays

Creating an array includes two steps:

Step 1   Declare the variable.

Step 2   Initialize the array object.

The first step is to declare the variable that will reference the array object. Two forms exist for the declaration of the variable, as shown in Example 7-3. Note that the set of braces can be placed after the data type or after the identifier. Either form is acceptable.

Example 7-3 *Declaring Arrays*

```
Declaration of an array, the first concept is the creation of a variable.


int[ ]  quantity;
double[ ] amount;
char[ ]  choices;
Date[ ] duedates;
String[ ] names;


Another form of declaration is,


int quantity[ ];
double amount[ ];
char choices[ ];
Date duedates[ ];
String names[ ];
```

TIP

For array declaration, the brackets can be in one of two places: `int[]` variable and `int` variable`[]`. The first says that the variable is of type `int[]`. The latter says that the variable is an array and that the array is of type `int`.

The form `int[]` var1, var2; declares two variables that are `int` arrays, whereas int var1[], var2; declares one variable of type `int` array and another variable just of type `int`.

The first form is to identify the data type as an array by adding square brackets ([ ]) after the data type. In the examples shown, the primitives are identified by the keywords **int**, **double**, and **char**. For nonprimitives, the class that they belong in (String and Date, in this case) identifies the array objects. When reading this format, the type of objects that the array object references is clear. The variables referencing the array objects are quantity, amount, choices, duedates, and names. These statements create the variable, not the array object.

The second form adds the square brackets ([ ]) after the name of the variable. This is also an acceptable syntax for declaring arrays. The first form makes clear the data type referenced by the array object. The second form is similar to the way in which the array will be referenced for use. Programmers can choose to use either. You might find that the first form helps to keep focus on the data type of the array object.

The second step is the *initialization of the array object*, as shown in Example 7-4.

Example 7-4 **new** *Operator Syntax in Arrays*

```
int[ ]  quantity;
quantity = new int[3];


double[ ] amount;
amount = new double[2];



char[ ]  choices;
choices = new char[3];
```

The **new** operator is used to create an array object. In creating arrays, the number of elements, or the length of the array, must be defined. In the examples shown, the elements of the array are defined within the square brackets ([ ]). The **new** operator creates storage for each item. For example, amount = new double[2]; creates storage for two primitives of the type **double**. Each primitive stores a default value. The default values are 0 for integer, 0.0 for floating point, \u0000 for **char**, and **false** for **boolean**. Thus, the amount array stores the two default values 0.0, as shown in Figure 7-8.

Figure 7-8 Default Values Assigned to the Primitive Arrays

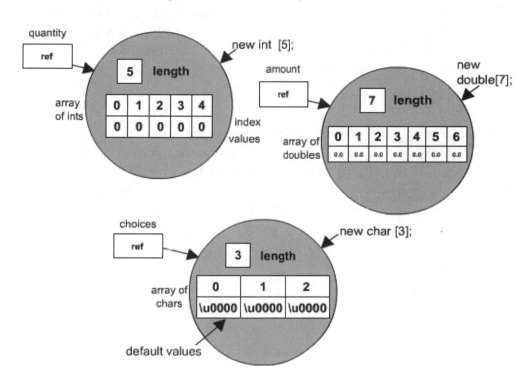

NOTE

Declaring an array type variable as **final** means that the array variable will always reference the same array. It does not mean that the elements of the array cannot be changed.

Figure 7-9 shows the arrays after a value has been assigned to each element of the array.

When creating an array of references to objects, the procedure includes a few more steps. The array object is created first, and then each object that the array references is created.

Answer the questions in Example 7-5 as they relate to the code that illustrates the creation of the array object and its object data. You can check your answers using an interactive graphic on the book's accompanying CD-ROM. The title of the activity is "**new** Operator Syntax in Arrays, Single Statement" in the e-Lab Activities.

Figure 7-9 Primitive Arrays After Values Assigned to Each Element

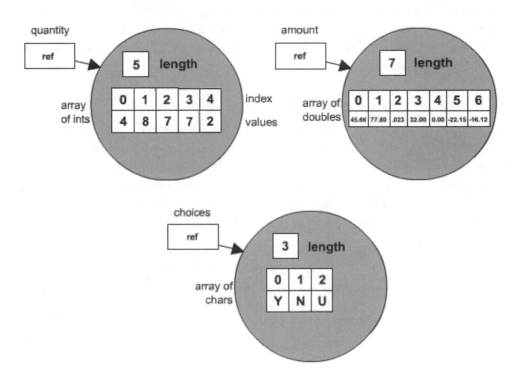

Example 7-5 **new** *Operator Syntax in Arrays, Single Statement*

```
int[] quantity = new int[3];
double[] amount = new double[2];
char[] choices = new char[3];
```

What is the name of the variable referencing the quantity values?

How many separate values of quantity will be referenced by the array?

The new operator in line 3 above creates what type of an object?

Which type of value is stored in the object created in line 3?

What are the default values of the items stored in line 3?

The Java statements for creating an array object that references other objects are the same as those for creating an array of primitives. The array variable and the number of elements must be defined. The default value for the reference data type is **null**. Hence, each of the elements of the array contains the value **null**. It is important to understand that, at this point, no objects that the array references have been created yet.

Using Subscripts to Access Elements of an Array

NOTE

If you try to create an array in which the length is negative, the run-time exception *NegativeArray-SizeException* will be thrown. Zero-length arrays are valid, however.

Each element of an array is assigned an index value (*subscript*) that is of the type **int**. Access to this value is through the use of an **int** value or an expression that results in an **int** value. Example 7-6 shows how an array element is accessed using a value. The index value is shown inside the array symbol (square brackets following the identifier) in the statement. The name of the array variable and the index value together provide a reference to an individual element of the array. The index value can be an expression that results in an **int**.

It is important to note the difference between the "nth element of the array" and "array element n." Because array subscripts (the number representing the index value) begin at 0, the "nth element of the array" has a subscript of n–1, while the "array element n" has a subscript of n and is actually the n+1 element of the array. Thus, in an array of ten elements, the seventh element of an array has a subscript of 6, and the eighth array element has a subscript of 7. This confusion is a source of "off-by-one" errors.

Example 7-6 new *Operator*

```
Creating the array object

int [ ]  quantity = new int[3];
double[ ] amount = new double[2];
String[ ] names = new String[15];


Referencing the array element using a value


System.out.println("Student  " + names[1] +  " has ordered " + quantity[1] + "
   books  for the price of " + amount[1]);
```

The example in Example 7-7 demonstrates the use of an expression to access an array element. The main method creates an array object of **int** and an array object of **double**. Each element in the array object of **int** is assigned the default 0, and each element in the array object of **double** is assigned the default 0.0. An **int** variable indexElement is created as a local variable in the **for** loop code block. This loop executes several times and prints the value for array elements referenced by the value of indexElement. How many array objects are created?

Example 7-7 *Accessing by Using Expression*

```
 1 public static void main(String[ ] args)
 2 {
 3       int[ ] quantity = new int[8]
 4       double[ ] amount = new double[8]
 5
 6       for (int IndexElement = 1;indexElement<4; ++indexElement)
 7       {
 8           System.out.printin("The quantity is " + quantity[indexElement] +
 9           "books for the price of " + amount[indexElement];
10       }
11 }
```

You can check your answer using an interactive graphic on the book's accompanying CD-ROM. The title of the activity is "Accessing by Using Expression" in e-Lab Activities.

Initializing Arrays

The previous section discussed the initialization of the array object with the default value for the data type being stored. This section discusses initializing array objects with values for an array of primitives, and reference variables for an array of objects. This section consists of the following topics related to initializing arrays:

- Array of primitives
- Array of objects
- Initializer blocks

Array of Primitives

When creating an array object to reference primitives, the primitive values are stored in the array object and are initialized to the default values for the primitive. The values of an array of primitives can be initialized as part of the creation of the array object. In the example shown in Example 7-8, the actual values of the primitives are provided in the code block ({ }). The length of the array is fixed to the number of items separated by commas described inside the code block ({ }). The quantity array has a length of 5. In this example, how many array objects are created?

TIP

Before an array can be used, it must be created using the **new** operator. A compiler error is generated if the type of an expression in an array initializer is not assignment-compatible with the data type of the array.

You can check your answer using an interactive graphic on the book's accompanying CD-ROM. The title of the activity is "Arrays with Initialization Values" in e-Lab Activities.

Example 7-8 *Arrays with Initialization Values*

```
 1 public static void main(String arg [ ])
 2 {
 3     int[ ]  quantity = {4, 5, 6, 78,100};
 4     double[ ] amount = {45.66, 77.89, .023, 32.00, 0.00, -22.15, -16.12 };
 5     char[ ]  choices = { 'Y', 'N', 'U', 'Z' };
 6
 7     for (int indexElement = 1; indexElement < 4; ++indexElement)
 8     {
 9        System.out.println("The quantity is "  + quantity[indexElement] +
10        " and the price is " + amount[indexElement]);
11     }
12 }
```

The values can also be changed from default to some other value after the array object has been created. The code in Example 7-9 uses three **for** loops to store data. The first **for** loop stores data in each element of the array object of **char**, obtaining input from the user using the prebuilt class `Console`. The `Console` class was discussed in Chapter 6, "System, String, StringBuffer, Math, and Wrapper Classes." The second **for** loop uses the value of the index element in an expression to calculate and store data in each element of the array object of **int**. This technique often is used to store identification values in an array. The third **for** loop uses the result of the expression (element of quantity multiplied by the value 2.50). This technique often is used to create parallel values. A quantity value corresponds to an amount value. Both are stored in the same element of parallel arrays. That is, the amount in element 0 represents a meaningful value for the quantity in element 0. An example of this use is product, quantity, and price in an object that stores a list of prices and quantities.

NOTE

The full version of the abbreviated code shown in this example can be viewed using the book's accompanying CD-ROM.

Example 7-9 *Arrays with Initialization Values*

```
 1 /**
 2 * Java Program ArrayExample.java
 3 * @author Cisco Teacher
 4 * @version 2002
 5 */
```

Example 7-9 *Arrays with Initialization Values (Continued)*

```
 6 public class ArrayExample
 7 {
 8     public static void main(String[] args)
 9     {
10         int[] quantity = new int[4];
11         double[] amount = new double[4];
12         char[] choices = new char[5];
13
14         for (int  i = 0; i < choices.length; ++i)
15         {
16             choices[i] = Console.readChar
17                 ("Please enter a character: ");
18         }
19         for (int  i = 0; i < quantity.length; ++i)
20         {
```

The **for** loop creates a variable i of the type **int**. The first value in this variable is 0. The value is increased when ++i is executed. The loop is controlled by comparing the value of the variable i against the value of the length variable for the array (quantity.length, choices.length, or amount.length).

When processing arrays, always use the length variable of an array to ensure that the code does not try to access an element beyond the size of the array. If the code references an element of an array for which there is no index, an error occurs and the program ends. This type of error, named *IndexOutOfBoundsException*, is unknown until runtime. Chapter 12, "Exceptions," discusses how to manage such errors.

Any of the loops can be used to store values in an array. The process of storing values in an array is also referred to as populating the array. In the sample code shown in Example 7-10, the **do** and **while** loops also are used to populate each of the array elements. Note that the value of x is incremented using the postfix increment operator ++. The value of x is used as an index value and is incremented in preparation for the next repetition of the loop.

Example 7-10 *Arrays with Initialization Values*

```
 1 /**
 2  * Java Program: ArrayExample2.java
 3  * @author Cisco Teacher
```

continues

NOTE

The full version of the abbreviated code shown in this example can be viewed using the book's accompanying CD-ROM.

Example 7-10 *Arrays with Initialization Values (Continued)*

```
 4  * @version 2002
 5  */
 6 public class ArrayExample2
 7 {
 8     public static void main(String[] args)
 9     {
10         int[] quantity = new int[4];
11         double[] amount = new double[4];
12         char[] choices = new char[5];
13
14         for (int i = 0; i < choices.length; ++i)
15         {
16             choices[i] = Console.readChar
17             ("Please enter a character: ");
18         }
19         int x = 0;
20         do
```

Array of Objects

In populating an array to reference objects, a few more steps are needed. First, the array object and its length are determined. At this stage, each element of the array is a reference variable with the value **null**. Each object referenced by the array must be created, and its reference must be stored as the value of an array element.

The sample code shown in Example 7-11 for the Teacher class demonstrates this process. The Teacher class creates the variable studentsInTheClass to store the reference to the array object. The length of the array is 3. This array object will hold references for three Student objects.

Example 7-11 *Array of Objects*

NOTE

The full version of the abbreviated code shown in this example can be viewed using the book's accompanying CD-ROM.

```
1 /**
2  * Java Program: Teacher.java
3  * @author Cisco Teacher
4  * @version 2002
5  */
6 public class Teacher
7 {
8     public static void main(String[] args)
```

Example 7-11 *Array of Objects (Continued)*

```
9      {
10         /*
11         create the variable studentsInTheClass
12         to store the reference to the array object
13         */
14         Student[] studentsInTheClass = new Student [3];
15
16         /*
17         Student object is created, and a reference
18         to this object is stored in the first
19         element of the array
20         */
```

A Student object then is created, and a reference to this object is stored in the first element of the array. This is repeated for the second and third Student objects. The reference to these objects is stored in the second and third elements of the array. To retrieve data on a specific student, the methods of the Student class are accessed using the element of the studentsInTheClass array that holds the reference to the specific Student object, as shown in Example 7-12.

Example 7-12 *Object Initialization in a Loop*

```
1 /**
2  * Java Program: ObjectArrayExample
3  * @author Cisco Teacher
4  * @version 2002
5  */
6 public class ObjectArrayExample
7 {
8    public static void main (String[] args)
9    {
10       int numOfStudents;
11       /*
12       use the readInt() method of the Console class
13       to get a number that will be used to set
14       the length of the array. the argument to the
```

continues

NOTE

The full version of the abbreviated code shown in this example can be viewed using the book's accompanying CD-ROM.

Example 7-12 *Object Initialization in a Loop (Continued)*

```
15        readInt() method is a String that will be used
16        as a prompt to the user
17        */
18        numOfStudents = Console.readInt
19           ("Enter number of Students to be created");
```

For Example 7-12, you can view the explanatory text by accessing the full, interactive graphic for this example on the book's accompanying CD-ROM. The title of the activity is "Object Initialization in a Loop" in e-Lab Activities.

Initializer Blocks

Member and class data can be initialized as part of the class declaration through the use of the constructer method. If the programmer does not specify an initial value, default values are applied.

Some things cannot be initialized with a single statement. If a large number of variables are to be initialized with some calculated value or are to be based on testing some condition, a code block would need to be created. This code block has no name, is not a method, and is executed before an object is created or as part of the object-creation process. This is also known as an initialization block.

Two types of initialization blocks exist: static and nonstatic. A *static initialization block* is useful for initializing an array of objects or primitives. It can initialize only static variables; therefore, the variable referencing the array object must be declared **static** to use a static initialization block. This block is executed only once when the class is loaded at runtime. The static block is defined using the keyword **static**. Static blocks are especially useful for initializing an array of static data. Static data of a class is created and available before any object of the class is created. If a class contains static array data and a loop construct is to be used to initialize the data, this construct is enclosed in a static block. This construct is executed and the data that it creates is available before any object of the class is created.

In Example 7-13, the students in the JavaStudent class complete five tests. The points for each test are based on a maximum number of points for the test. The JavaStudent objects store points for each test separately. The JavaStudent objects also store the test scores in percentages. To calculate the percentage, an array of maximum scores must be available for each JavaStudent object. The maximum scores for each test are the same for all students and, thus, need to be shared by each JavaStudent object.

Example 7-13 *Static Initialization Block*

```
 1  /**
 2   * Java Program: JavaStudent.java
 3   * @author Cisco Teacher
 4   * @version 2002
 5   */
 6
 7  import java.util.*;
 8  import java.text.*;
 9
10  public class JavaStudent
11  {
12      // data to be shared by all JavaStudent objects
13      static int numOfTests;
14      static Date[ ] testDate;
15      static String[ ] testName;
16      static int[ ] maxPoints;
17
18      // data for each student object
19      private final int id;
20      private String name;
```

NOTE

The full version of the abbreviated code shown in this example can be viewed using the book's accompanying CD-ROM.

For Example 7-13, you can view the explanatory text by accessing the full, interactive graphic for this example on the book's accompanying CD-ROM. The title of the activity is "Static Initialization Block" in e-Lab Activities.

The JavaStudent class can be defined as in the example. Three static arrays are declared in this definition. The testDate array stores data on the date of each test. The testName array references String objects that store data that represents a title for each test, and the maxPoints array stores the maximum points to be earned for each test.

A *nonstatic initialization block* can be used to initialize nonstatic data and update static data. In the case of the JavaStudent class, the elements of the array testScore and the array percentage do not need to be initialized. Primitive data stored on the heap automatically is initialized to default values. However, the String array testComments might or might not be initialized. The sample code shown in Example 7-14 illustrates the usage of a nonstatic block to initialize the array testComments. In this code sample, the static variable numOfTests is used to set the array length of the instance (nonstatic) arrays. Static variables are created before any object is created, so numOftests is available for use in this code block.

Example 7-14 *Nonstatic Initialization Block*

NOTE

The full version of
the abbreviated code
shown in this example
can be viewed using
the book's accompa-
nying CD-ROM.

```
1 /**
2  * Java Program: JavaStudent.java
3  * @author Cisco Teacher
4  * @version 2002
5  */
6
7 import java.util.*;
8 import java.text.*;
9
10 public class JavaStudent
11 {
12     // data to be shared by all JavaStudent objects
13     static int numOfTests;
14     static Date[ ] testDate;
15     static String[ ] testName;
16     static int[ ] maxPoints;
17
18     // data for each student object
19     private final int id;
20     private String name;
```

For Example 7-14, you can view the explanatory text by accessing the full, interactive
graphic for this example on the book's accompanying CD-ROM. The title of the activity is "Nonstatic Initialization Block" in e-Lab Activities.

The next section demonstrates the use of the JavaStudent class and the impact of the
initialization blocks on the JavaStudent objects.

Using Arrays

When the array object has been created and initialized, the programmer can utilize
the storage capabilities of the array object in their program. This section consists of the
following topics:

- Accessing array elements
- Passing an array to a method
- Using parallel arrays

- Searching and sorting an array
- Reusing an array

Accessing Array Elements

To access an array element, the syntax requires using the array variable and a value that represents the index of the element. The value can be stored in a variable of type **int**, **byte**, or **short**, or it can be the result of an expression. The expression must result in an integer. Recall that with implicit casting, an expression that uses a **short** or a **byte** also results in an integer.

In the sample code shown in Example 7-15, an element of an array is accessed directly.

Example 7-15 *Accessing Array Elements*

```
1      /*
2      The general syntax for accessing an array element is:
3
4      array-identifier[int-index-value]
5
6      */
7
8      Student astudent  = new JavaStudent(123444, " Mary Post");
9
10     System.out.println(" Percentage score for student  " +
11                     aStudent.getName() + " on test " +
12                     JavaStudent.testName[1] + " is " +
13                     aStudent.percentage[1]);
```

The sample code for the JavaStudent class shown in Example 7-16 demonstrates accessing elements of an array directly and changing object data using class data.

Example 7-16 *Array of References to Objects*

```
1 /**
2 * Java Program: JavaStudent.java
3 * @author Cisco Teacher
4 * @version 2002
5 */
6
```

continues

NOTE

The full version of the abbreviated code shown in this example can be viewed using the book's accompanying CD-ROM.

Example 7-16 *Array of References to Objects (Continued)*

```
 7 import java.util.*;
 8 import java.text.*;
 9
10 public class JavaStudent
11 {
12
13     /*
14     code for JavaStudent class definition
15     */
16
17
18     /*
19     main method - demonstrates accessing elements of
20     an array directly and changing object data using
```

For Example 7-16, you can view the explanatory text by accessing the full, interactive graphic for this example on the book's accompanying CD-ROM. The title of the activity is "Array of References to Objects" in e-Lab Activities.

One array also can be used to initialize another array. In this instance, both array variables reference the same array object. The sample code shown in Example 7-17 demonstrates this initialization. Note that elements of the array are accessed through the use of the index variable i, which is an **int**.

Example 7-17 *System Class API - arraycopy() Method*

NOTE

The full version of the abbreviated code shown in this example can be viewed using the book's accompanying CD-ROM.

```
 1 /**
 2  * Java Program: Teacher.java
 3  * @author Cisco Teacher
 4  * @version 2002
 5  */
 6 public class Teacher
 7 {
 8     public static void main (String args [ ])
 9     {
10             JavaStudent[]  groupOne, specialGroup;
11             groupOne = new JavaStudent[ 3];
```

Example 7-17 *System Class API - arraycopy() Method (Continued)*

```
12
13              for ( int i = 0; i < groupOne.length; i ++)
14              {
15                  int aID = Console.readInt
16                      ("Enter student id");
17                  String aName = Console.readLine
18                      ("Enter student name: ");
19
20                  groupOne[0] = new Student(aID, aName);
```

Arrays are fixed in length. To create groups of references that can change in size, explore the classes in the Collections library. These are discussed in Chapter 14, "Collections."

More Information
If you try to access before the beginning or after the end of an array, an `ArrayIndexOutOfBounds-Exception` will be thrown. As a subclass of `IndexOutOfBoundsException`, `ArrayIndexOutOfBounds-Exception` is a run-time exception.

The `System` class provides a method for copying arrays. This method, the `arraycopy()` method, allows elements of an array to be copied to a new array, as shown in Table 7-1.

Table 7-1 System Class API - `arraycopy()` Method

Method Summary	
static void	arraycopy (`Object` src, int src_position, `Object` dst, int dst_position, int length) Copies an array from the specified source array, beginning at the specified position, to the specified position of the destination array.
static void	currentTimeMillis ( ) Returns the current time in milliseconds.
static void	exit(int status) Terminates the currently running Java Virtual Machine.
static void	gc( ) Runs the garbage collector.

The syntax for the `arraycopy()` method is shown in Example 7-18.

Example 7-18 *Syntax for* `arraycopy()` *Method*

```
1    public static void arraycopy(Object src,
2                             int src_position,
3                             Object dst,
4                             int dst_position,
5                             int length)
```

For Example 7-18, you can view the explanatory text by accessing the full, interactive graphic for this example on the book's accompanying CD-ROM. The title of the activity is "Syntax for `arraycopy()` Method" in e-Lab Activities.

This is a static method and can be accessed by referencing the class name, as in `System.arraycopy();`. The sample code shown in Example 7-19 illustrates the use of the `arraycopy()` method.

Example 7-19 *Using the* `arraycopy()` *Method*

NOTE

The full version of the abbreviated code shown in this example can be viewed using the book's accompanying CD-ROM.

```
1 /**
2  * Java Program: CopyDemo
3  * @author Cisco Teacher
4  * @version 2002
5  */
6
7 public class CopyDemo
8 {
9     public static void main(String[] args)
10    {
11        char gradeArray[] =  {'a','b','c','d','y','z'};
12        char vowelArray[] =  {'e','i','o','u'};
13
14        // new larger array of grades and vowel;
15        char lettersArray[] = new char [10];
16
17        /*
18        copy all of the gradeArray to the lettersArray
19        array, starting with the 0th index
20        */
```

> **More Information**
>
> One use for the `System.arraycopy` method is to add or remove elements in the middle of an array. To add a new element at position `i` into the variable data, first move all elements from `i` onward one position up. Then insert the new value:
>
> ```
> System.arraycopy(data, i, data, i + 1, data.length - i -1);
> data[i] = x;
> ```
>
> Note that the value in the last element in the array is lost.
>
> To remove the element at a position i, copy the elements above the position downward:
>
> ```
> System.arraycopy(data, i + 1, data, i, data.length - i- 1);
> ```
>
> Note that the value in the last element in the array is also in the next-to-last element in the array.

Passing an Array to a Method

An array element can be passed to a method requesting a single value. A method that converts a percentage to a corresponding letter grade is one example. In Example 7-20, the `letterGradePerc` method is in the `Teacher2` class. This method converts the percentage to a letter grade. Two methods are defined in this example of the `Teacher2` class: One is `letterGradeInt`, and the other is `letterGradePerc`. Both methods accept a single value and return a **char**. These two methods can be accessed using the syntax shown. A copy of the value in an array element is passed to the methods.

Example 7-20 *Passing an Array to a Method*

```
System.out.println("Student " + aStudent.getName() + " has earned a grade of " +
   letterGradeInt(aStudent.testScore[3]) + " on the test " + JavaStudent.testName[3]);


System.out.println("Student " + aStudent.getName() + " has earned a grade of " +
   letterGradePerc(aStudent.percentage[3]) + " on the test " + JavaStudent.testName[3]);
```

For Example 7-20, you can view the rollover text associated with aStudent.testScore[3] and aStudent.percentage[3] by accessing the full, interactive graphic for this example on the book's accompanying CD-ROM. The title of the activity is "Passing an Array to a Method" in e-Lab Activities.

The `Teacher2` class can also include one method to calculate the average percentage of a student across all tests or the average percentage of a test for all students in the class, as shown in Example 7-21. To do the first calculation, the method is passed a reference to one student object. To calculate the average percentage for all students on a specific test, the method is passed a value for the test number and a reference to the `JavaStudent` array object that holds the references for all the students.

Example 7-21 *Passing an Array to a Method*

NOTE

The full version of the abbreviated code shown in this example can be viewed using the book's accompanying CD-ROM.

```
1  /**
2   * Java Program: Teacher.java
3   * @author Cisco Teacher
4   * @version 2002
5   */
6  public class Teacher2
7  {
8      /**
9       * @param aStudent A student as a JavaStudent type
10      */
11     private static double averageStudentPerc (JavaStudent aStudent)
12     {
13         double sum = 0;
14         for (int i =0; i < aStudent.percentage.length; i++)
15         {
16             sum += aStudent.getPercent(i);
17         }
18         return sum/aStudent.percentage.length;
19     }
```

For Example 7-21, you can view the explanatory text by accessing the full, interactive graphic for this example on the book's accompanying CD-ROM. The title of the activity is "Passing an Array to a Method" in e-Lab Activities.

Several design principles are presented here. The first is that the instance data for the JavaStudent object is **private**. To access a specific field, a get or set method needs to be used. The array references, therefore, are used to send messages to the object methods. The Teacher2 class is the entry point for this application that uses Teacher2 and JavaStudent data. This Teacher2 class defines the methods as static. This enables the Teacher2 class to be useful without having any Teacher2 objects created. Additionally, the main method is a static method. Static methods access other static methods in the same class directly but need an instance of the class to access other nonstatic methods. For example, the methods averageStudentPerc() and averageClassPercentage() are declared static in the Teacher2 class and can be accessed directly in the main method of the Teacher2 class.

More Information
If you want to construct an array and pass it on to a method that expects an array parameter, you can initialize an anonymous array as follows: `new int[] {3, 6, 8, 1}`

Using Parallel Arrays

In the JavaStudent class, each of the arrays can be thought of as a *parallel array*. That is, the value in one element of the array has corresponding meaning for the value of the same element in another array.

For example:

- testDate[0], testName[0], and maxPoints[0] all hold different information about the first test.
- testScore[0] and percentage[0] contain the scores and percentages of a specific student for the first test.

This parallel relationship between the arrays can be used to process and handle these arrays in the same loop construct, the same **if** statement, or any other method or statement. The sample code shown in Example 7-22 demonstrates this concept.

Example 7-22 *Processing Parallel Arrays*

```
 1 /**
 2  * Java Program: Teacher
 3  * @author Cisco Teacher
 4  * @version 2002
 5  */
 6 public class Teacher
 7 {
 8     /**
 9      * @param aStudent A student as a JavaStudent type
10      */
11     private static double averageStudentPerc (JavaStudent aStudent)
12     {
13         double sum = 0;
14         for (int i =0; i < aStudent.percentage.length; i++)
```

continues

NOTE

The full version of the abbreviated code shown in this example can be viewed using the book's accompanying CD-ROM.

Example 7-22 *Processing Parallel Arrays (Continued)*

```
15          {
16                  sum += aStudent.getPercent(i);
17          }
18          return sum/aStudent.percentage.length;
19      }
```

Searching and Sorting an Array

NOTE

An important computer application is the sorting of data into some particular order, such as ascending or descending order. A bank sorts all checks by account number so that it can prepare individual bank statements at the end of each month. Telephone companies sort their lists of accounts by last name and, within the last name, by first name, to make it easy to find phone numbers. Virtually every organization must sort some data and, in many cases, massive amounts of data. Sorting data is an intriguing problem that has attracted some of the most intense research efforts in the fields of computer science.

Sorting is the process of arranging a series of objects in some logical order. When objects are placed in an order beginning with the lowest value and ending at the highest value, they are being sorted in ascending order. Sorting character data can be influenced by the case of the character. When objects are placed in an order beginning with the highest value and ending with the lowest value, they are being sorted in descending order.

Use Example 7-23 to identify ascending and descending order of numbers and characters.

Example 7-23 *Searching and Sorting an Array*

```
Which of the following lists is in descending order?
19,14,8,3,1
4,6,8,99
2,7,1,9
3,4,4,3,5
z,y,x,Z
z,Y,x,W


Which of the following lists is in ascending order?
d,f,m,y
Z,T,S,F
a,A,b,B
z,y,x,Z
W,x,Y,Z
```

In the examples used so far in this chapter, the array elements have been manipulated in the sequence in which they were created. For example, the `Student` object was printed starting with the first student. To print the students in alphabetical order or by the value of their scores or percentages, the array must be sorted in some order (ascending or descending).

Bubble Sort and Sinking Sort

The code in Examples 7-24 and 7-25 illustrates a commonly used programming technique called a *bubble sort*. This particular technique relies on being able to compare pairs of values, assuming that the values can be organized into some order. In this technique, two values are compared. If the values are out of order, they are swapped. The three variables x, y, and z hold integer values and are printed in an ascending and then a descending order. A temporary variable is used to swap the values in x, y, and z, if necessary.

Example 7-24 *Bubble Sorting Three Numbers in Ascending Order*

```
int x =5, y =4, z =6, temp;
for(int a = 0; a <2; a++)
{
      if  ( x > y )
      {
            temp = x;
            x = y;
            y = temp;
      }
      if (y > z )
      {
            temp = y;
            y = z;
            z = temp;
      }
}
System.out.println ( " values in ascending order are " + x + y + z);
```

Example 7-25 *Bubble Sorting Three Numbers in Descending Order*

```
int x =5, y =4, z =6, temp;
for(int a = 0; a <2; a++)
{
      if  ( x < y )
      {
            temp = x;
            x = y;
```

continues

Example 7-25 *Bubble Sorting Three Numbers in Descending Order (Continued)*

```
            y = temp;
        }
    if (y < z )
      {
            temp = y;

            y = z;

            z = temp;

      }

}
System.out.println ( " values in ascending order are " + x + y + z);
```

Sorting two or three values is fairly simple. Sorting a large number of values without the use of arrays can be a difficult task. The simple swap technique can be used to process an array several times until the values are in the necessary order. The technique to do this is called a bubble sort. In this technique, the array is processed until the largest or the smallest number is assigned to the first element. The lowest or highest value bubbles to the start of the array. Each processing of the array includes comparing pairs of values and swapping the values, if needed.

The sample code in Example 7-26 demonstrates a bubble sort using a simple array of integers. The array references 10 numbers. The array is processed by comparing two numbers to each other. It starts with the first two elements in the array, then the second and third elements, and so on. The values are swapped as needed. The array is processed until there are no more swaps to be done. This example sorts the array in ascending order, from low to high.

NOTE

The full version of the abbreviated code shown in this example can be viewed using the book's accompanying CD-ROM.

Example 7-26 *Bubble Sorting in Ascending Order*

```
1 //Main method

2 public static void main(String[] args)

3 {

4   int[]  tenNumbers = {75, 35, 92, 12, 44, 32, 4, 99, 67, 10};

5 int temp;

6

7 // processing the array  as many times as

8 // the number of elements in the array

9 for ( int i = 0; i <= tenNumbers.length -1; i++)

10 {
```

Example 7-26 *Bubble Sorting in Ascending Order (Continued)*

```
11 // processing each element in the array and
12 // comparing it to the next element (pairs)
13 for ( int j = 0; j < tenNumbers.length -1; j++)
14 {
15 if(tenNumbers[j + 1] < tenNumbers[j])
16  {
17  temp = tenNumbers[j];
18 tenNumbers[j]  = tenNumbers[j + 1];
19  tenNumbers[j +1 ] = temp;
20 }
```

Bubble sorting got its name because the smaller values gradually "bubble" to the top of the array (toward the first element) like air bubbles rising in water, while the larger values sink to the bottom (end) of the array.

The chief virtue of the bubble sort, also known as the sinking sort, is that it is easy to program. However, the bubble sort runs slowly. This becomes apparent when sorting large arrays. Some simple modifications can be made to the bubble sort to improve its performance. Let's consider an array with 10 elements (length = 10, with the last index value 9):

1. You expect to make nine passes through the array. After the first pass, the largest number is guaranteed to be in the highest–numbered element of the array; after the second pass, the two highest numbers are in place, and so on. Instead of making every paired comparison on each pass, modify the sort to reduce the number of comparisons by one in each pass. So, in the first pass, nine comparisons are made; in the second pass, eight are made, and so on.

2. The data already might be in the proper order, or near proper order, so why make nine passes through the array if fewer will suffice? Modify the sort check at the end of each pass to check whether any swaps have been made. Use a **boolean** variable to flag any swaps. If no swaps have been made, the data already must be in proper order, so the method or program should terminate. If swaps have been made, at least one more pass is needed.

Several other sort algorithms to explore are described in the following subsections; they include the bucket sort, the selection sort, and the quick sort.

Bucket Sort

A bucket sort begins with a single subscripted array of positive integers to be sorted and a double subscript array of integers with rows subscripted from 0 to 9 and columns subscripted from 0 to $n-1$, where n is the number of values in the array to be sorted. Each row of the double-subscripted array is referred to as a bucket. The following steps describe a bucket sort of an integer array:

Step 1 Place each value of the single subscripted array into a row of the bucket array based on the value's one digit. For example, 97 is placed in Row 7, 3 is in Row 3, and 100 is in Row 0. This is called the distribution pass.

Step 2 Loop through the bucket array row by row, and copy the values back to the original array. This is called the gathering pass. The new order of the preceding values in a single subscripted array is 100, 3, 97.

Step 3 Repeat this process for each subsequent digit position (tens, hundreds, thousands, and so on).

On the second pass, 100 is placed in Row 0, 3 is in Row 0 (3 has no tens digits), and 97 is in Row 9. After the gathering pass, the values in the single subscripted array are 100, 3, and 97. On the third pass, 100 is in row 1, 3 is in Row 0, and 97 is in Row 0 (after 3). After the last gathering pass, the original array is in sorted order.

Note that the double-scripted array of buckets is ten times the size of the integer array being sorted. This sorting technique provides better performance than a bubble sort but requires more memory. The bubble sort requires space for only one additional element: the swap variable. This is an example of the space-time trade-off.

Selection Sort

A selection sort searches an array looking for the smallest element in the array and then swaps that element with the first element of the array. The process is repeated for the subarray beginning with the second element. Each pass of the array places one element in its proper location. For an array of n elements, $n-1$ passes must be made, and for each subarray, $n-1$ comparisons must be made to find the smallest value. When the subarray being processed contains one element, the array is sorted. Example 7-27 shows sample code for a selection sort using an array of integer values.

Example 7-27 *Selection Sort Using an Array of Integer Values*

```
public class SelectionSorter{
      private static void swap(int[] a, int i, int j)
      {
            if ( i == j) return;
```

Example 7-27 *Selection Sort Using an Array of Integer Values (Continued)*

```
                int temp = a[j];
                a[j] = a[i];
                a[i] = temp;
        )
        public static void sort(int[] a)
        {
                for (int i = a.length-1; i > 0; i--)
                { int j=0;
                        for ( int k=1; k <= i; k++)
                        if (a[k] > a[j]) j = k;
                        swap (a, I, j);
                }
        ]
        public static void main (String[] args)
        {
sort (new int[] {3, 6, 8, 1});
}
}// end of class
```

Quick Sort

A recursive sorting technique often used is the quick sort. The basic algorithm for a single subscripted array of values is as follows:

- Partitioning steps: For the first element of the unsorted array, determine its final location in a sorted array. Now one element is in its proper location, with two unsorted arrays left.
- Recursive step: Perform the first step on each unsorted subarray.

Each time the first step is performed on a subarray, another element is placed in its final location of the sorted array and two unsorted subarrays are created. When a subarray consists of one element, it must be sorted; therefore, that element is in its final location. Example 7-28 shows sample code for a quick sort.

Example 7-28 *Quick Sort*

```
public class QuickSort{

        private static void swap(int[] a, int i, int j)
```

continues

Example 7-28 *Quick Sort (Continued)*

```
        {
                if ( i == j) return;
                int temp = a[j];
                a[j] = a[i];
                a[i] = temp;
        )
        public static void sort(int[] a)
        {
                if (a.length >1)
                sort (a, 0, a.length);
        }
        public static void sort(int[] a, int k, int n)
        {
                if (n < 2) return;
                int pivot = a[k];
                int i =k;
                int j = k + n;
                while ( i < j )
                {
                        while ( i+1 < k+n && a[++i] < pivot) ;
                        while (a[--j] >pivot);
                        if (i < j)
                                swap(a,i,j);
                }
                swap (a,k,j);
                sort(a,k,j-k);
                sort (a,j+1,k+n-j-a);
        }

        public static void main (String[] args)
        {
            sort (new int[] {3, 6, 8, 1});
        }
}// end of class
```

Sorting objects is not much different than sorting primitives. Objects generally are sorted based on the value of some data in the object. For example, if the teacher wanted to sort the students in the class by ID, the `JavaStudent` array would be processed comparing the ID for each of the students. The only difference here is that the `temp` variable is of the type `JavaStudent`, and the comparison for swapping uses the `method` `getId()` to compare the ID for each student.

Example 7-29 `sort()` *Method of the* `Arrays` *Class*

```java
import java.util.*;
import java.awt.*;

class Sort1 {
    // Sorts an array of random double values.
    public static void main(String[] args) {
        double[] dblarr = new double[10];
        for (int i=0; i<dblarr.length; i++) {
            dblarr[i] = Math.random();
        }
        // Sort the array.
        Arrays.sort(dblarr);
        //Print the array
        for (int i=0; i<dblarr.length; i++){
            System.out.println(dblarr[i]);
        }
    }
}
```

TIP

Sorting arrays of primitive types is easy. Seven methods in the class `Arrays` are used for sorting arrays of each of the seven primitive types: **byte**, **char**, **double**, **float**, **int**, **long**, and **short**. Example 7-29 sorts an array of **double** values, using the `sort()` method of the `Arrays` class.

Shuffling

A simple algorithm to shuffle a set of letters in an array is shown in Example 7-30. Shuffling algorithms use random number generators to determine the specific element in the array to retrieve.

Shuffling algorithms can be used in programs that simulate card games; in word games in which a shuffled set of characters are presented, such as word scramble; or in scramble grams, as shown in Example 7-30.

NOTE

Of course, to really make this interesting, the array of letters would contain duplicates or multiples of some characters. If you want to try these, you could use the number of tiles assigned for each letter in the popular board game Scrabble. This shuffling also could be used to assign a set of letters to a group of players engaged in an electronic version of Scrabble.

Example 7-30 *Shuffling Algorithms*

```
1 public  class ScrambleGram{
2 // this array can hold the letters of the alphabet.
3     char[] letters ={'a','b','c','d','e','f','g','h','i','j','k','l','m',
      'n','o','p','q',
4     'r','s','t','u','v','w','x','y','z'};
5    /*  the shuffle method accepts an int that will be used to set the size of the
6        shuffled array.
7        The method returns an array of char's of the size specified in the
           argument.
8    */
9
10    public char[] shuffle(int  size)
11    {
12        char[] shuffledLetters = new char[size];
13        int index;
14        // populate the shuffledLetters array with letters
15        for (int x=0; x < size; x++)
16        {
17            index =  (int) (Math.random() * 26);
18            shuffledLetters[x] =  letters[index];
19        }
20        // Shuffle the array
21        // for each letter, pick another random letter from the array and
           swap them.
22        for (int first = 0; first < shuffledLetters.length; first ++)
23        {
24            int second = (int) (Math.random() * size);
25            char temp = shuffledLetters[first];
26            shuffledLetters[first] = shuffledLetters[second];
27            shuffledLetters[second] = temp;
28        }
29        return shuffledLetters;
30    }
31
32    public static void main(String[] args)
33    {
34        ScrambleGram sg = new ScrambleGram();
```

Example 7-30 *Shuffling Algorithms (Continued)*

```
35          System.out.println("What word(s) do these letters represent");
36          System.out.println(sg.shuffle(5));
37      }
38 }
```

Reusing an Array

The array variable is separate from the array itself. It is similar to the way an ordinary variable can access different values at different times. You can use array variables to access different arrays at different points in the program. For example, a teacher could have several courses for which data is being stored. The code for the `main` method of the `Teacher` class reuses the array variable that is a reference to an array object of `JavaStudent` object references, as shown in Example 7-31.

Example 7-31 *Reuse of an Array*

```
1 /**
2  * Java Program: TeacherExample
3  * @author Cisco Teacher
4  * @version 2002
5  */
6 public class TeacherExample
7 {
8     public static void main (String args [ ])
9     {
10        int number = Console.readInt("number of students?");
11        JavaStudent [] studentsInaCourse =
12            new JavaStudent[number];
13        for (int i = 0; i < studentsInaCourse.length; i++)
14        {
15            int id = Console.readInt
16                ("Enter student number: ");
17            String name = Console.readLine
18                ("Enter student name: ");
19            studentsInaCourse [i] = new JavaStudent(id, name);
20        }
```

NOTE

The full version of the abbreviated code shown in this example can be viewed using the book's accompanying CD-ROM.

In Example 7-31, it is assumed that the `Teacher` class saves the `JavaStudent` arrays in a file. It is not implied that a teacher has to create this student information repeatedly. Chapter 13, "Files, Streams, Input, and Output," demonstrates how to save object data in memory in a file. This allows the data to persist beyond the program.

Multidimensional Arrays

NOTE

Because each element in the outermost array of a multidimensional array is an object reference, nothing requires your arrays to be rectangular (or cubic, for three-dimensional arrays). Each inner array can have its own size.

The Java language supports multidimensional arrays. This section consists of the following topics:

- Initializing multidimensional array objects
- Traversing a multidimensional array

Initializing Multidimensional Array Objects

Multidimensional arrays have a number of useful applications for storing data. For example, a teacher has a number of students attending class, each receiving different test scores for the test given in the class. The `Teacher` object can store the scores of a test in a two-dimensional array. A student array can hold references for the addresses of test arrays, and each test array stores the test scores for the specific student, as illustrated in Tables 7-2 and 7-3.

Table 7-2 Creation and Initialization of Multidimensional Arrays

Names	Test1	Test2	Test3	Test4	Test5	Test6
Mary Post	66	78	78	89	88	90
Peter Lei	76	80	80	82	90	90
Polly Pocket	90	92	87	83	99	94

Table 7-3 Creation and Initialization of Multidimensional Arrays

[] []	0	1	2	3	4	5
0	66	78	78	89	88	90
1	76	80	80	82	90	90
2	90	92	87	83	99	94

A multidimensional array is also known as an array of arrays. The syntax for a two-dimensional array contains two sets of brackets, as shown in Example 7-32.

Example 7-32 *Creation and Initialization of Multidimensional Arrays*

```
int [ ] [ ] scores = {{66, 78, 78, 89, 88, 90},
                      {76, 80, 80, 82, 90, 90},
                      {90, 92, 87, 83, 99, 94} };
```

The first set of brackets holds the index reference to the elements of the first dimension of the array, and the second set of brackets holds the index reference to the elements of the second dimension.

Table 7-2 presents data for three students. Each item could be stored as a separate element in one array. This would make it hard to identify which particular test and which student the test was associated with. A two-dimensional array would allow the test number to be referenced as one dimension and the student to be referenced as another dimension.

Each score then could be uniquely identified as associated with the student and the test based on the index value of the dimensions. For example, in Table 7-3, a reference of [2][3] would identify the fourth test score for the third student (`Polly Pockets`, `Test4`, score of `83`).

Creating and initializing multidimensional arrays require that each dimension (the outer dimension) be created before initializing values for the next (next inner) dimension. The sample code shown in Example 7-33 illustrates this initialization process. Some `JavaStudent` objects then can be created and related to the multidimensional scores array.

Example 7-33 *Multidimensional Arrays*

```
1 /**
2  * Java Program: Array3D_Example
3  * @author Cisco Teacher
4  * @version 2002
5  */
6 public class Array3D_Example
7 {
8     public static void main (String args [ ])
```

continues

Example 7-33 *Multidimensional Arrays (Continued)*

```
 9      {
10          int array3D[][][] = new int[5][4][3];
11          for (int x = 0; x < array3D.length; x ++)
12              for(int y = 0; y < array3D[x].length; y++)
13                  for (int z = 0; z < array3D[x][y].length; z++)
14                  {
15                      array3D[x][y][z] = 0;
16                  }
17      } // end main
18 } // end class
```

Multidimensional arrays can have different length arrays in each dimension. As shown in Example 7-34, the first dimension of the array can have a length of 3, and each of the next dimensional arrays can have different lengths. When processing arrays of irregular lengths, use the length variable of the array to process the array. The sample code in Example 7-34 illustrates another form of initializing arrays of irregular length.

Example 7-34 *Multidimensional Arrays with Different Lengths*

```
int [ ] [ ] numbers =  { {2,3,4,5},
                         { 2,3},
                         {3,4,5,6,7,8,9} };
```

Traversing a Multidimensional Array

To reference a single element of a multidimensional array, reference the index value for each dimension. For example, to obtain the information for Mary Post's score on a specific test, the score might be referenced as score[0][3], as shown in the sample code in Example 7-35.

Example 7-35 *Referencing a Single Element of a Multidimensional Array*

```
1 /*
2 This is an example of the syntax to access one
3 element of a multidimensional array
4 */
5
6 public static void main(String args[])
7 {
```

Example 7-35 *Referencing a Single Element of a Multidimensional Array (Continued)*

```
8     //lots of other statements
9
10    //accessing the multidimensional array
11    System.out.println("The score on " +
12        JavaStudent.testName[3] + "  is  " + score[0][3]);
13
14 }
```

To access more than one element of a multidimensional array, nested **for** loops can be used. Each loop processes elements of one dimension. In the sample code shown in Example 7-36, the first loop processes one element of the first dimension, which then is referenced to one JavaStudent in the JavaStudent dimension. The nested loop processes all the scores for that one JavaStudent object. When the nested loop is complete, the outer loop processes the next element of the JavaStudent dimension.

Example 7-36 *Accessing More Than One Element of a Multidimensional Array*

```
1 /*
2 This is an example of the syntax to access one
3 element of a multidimensional array
4 */
5
6 public static void main(String args[])
7 {
8     //lots of other statements
9
10
11    for (int a = 0; a <3; ++a)
12    {
13        System.out.println( students[a].getName() +
14            "Scores for the tests are: ");
15        for (int b = 0; b < scores[a].length; b++)
16        {
17            System.out.println(JavaStudent.testName[b] +
18                "  is  " + score[a][b] );
19        }
20    }
21 }//end main method
```

Example 7-37 shows sample code for a class and a test program for playing Tic-Tac-Toe.

Example 7-37 *Sample Code for Playing Tic-Tac-Toe*

```
1  /**
2   * A 3 by 3 tic-tac-toe board.
3   *
4   */
5  public class TicTacToe
6  {
7      private static final int ROWS = 3;
8      private static final int COLUMNS = 3;
9      private final char[][] board = new char[ROWS][COLUMNS];
10     /** Constructs an empty board */
11     public TicTacToe()
12     {
13         board = new char[ROWS][COLUMNS];
14
15         //fill with spaces
16         for(int i = 0; i < ROWS; i++)
17             for(int j = 0; j < COLUMNS; j++)
18                 board[i][j] = ' ';
19     }
20     /**
21      * Sets a field in the board. The field must be unoccupied.
22      * @param i the row index
23      * @param j the column index
24      * @param player the player ('x' or 'o')
25      */
26     public void set(int i, int j, char player)
27     {
28         if(board[i][j] != ' ')
29             // Exception handling will be covered in a later chapter
30             throw new IllegalArgumentException("Position occupied");
31         board[i][j] = player;
32
33     }
34
```

Example 7-37 *Sample Code for Playing Tic-Tac-Toe (Continued)*

```
35      /**
36       * Creates a string representation of the board such as
37       * | x   o |
38       * |   x   |
39       * |     o|.
40       * @return the string representation
41       */
42      public String toString()
43      {
44          String r = "";
45          for(int i = 0; i < ROWS; i++)
46          {
47              r = r + " ";
48              for (int j = 0; j < COLUMNS; j++)
49              {
50
51                  if( j < 2)
52                      r = r + board[i][j] + " | ";
53                  else
54                      r = r + board[i][j];
55              }
56              if(i < 2)
57                  r = r + "\n" + "------------\n";
58          }
59          return r;
60      }
61 }
62
63 /**
64  * Write a description of class TicTacToeTest here.
65  *
66  * @author (your name)
67  * @version (a version number or a date)
68  */
69 public class TicTacToeTest
```

continues

Example 7-37 *Sample Code for Playing Tic-Tac-Toe (Continued)*

```
70 {
71
72     public static void main(String[] args)
73     {
74         char player = 'x';
75         TicTacToe game = new TicTacToe();
76         while(true)
77         {
78           System.out.println(game);    //calls game.toString()
79           int row = Console.readInt("Enter a row for " + player);
80            int column = Console.readInt("Enter a column for " + player);
81           try
82           {
83               game.set(row, column, player);
84               if (player == 'x')
85                  player = 'o';
86               else
87                  player = 'x';
88           }
89           // Exception handling will be covered in a later chapter
90           catch(IllegalArgumentException iae)
91           {
92               System.out.println(iae.getMessage());
93           }
94         }
95     }
96 }
```

Case Study: JBANK Application

The JBANK application introduced in Chapter 1 ("What Is Java?") provides students with an opportunity to apply the Java language concepts learned throughout this course. In the JBANK lab for Chapter 7, students will create an array to hold information for 20 customers. To locate a customer, the program must read each customer ID in the array until the customer is located. The use of loop structures is essential for efficient processing of arrays. A **for** loop is used to process the elements of the Customer array. Nested loops are used to process each account for the customer retrieved.

This section addresses primarily using an array within the JBANK.

Using an Array Within the JBANK

The banking application affords several useful implementations of arrays. A bank has many customers, so an array of Customer objects is created for the bank. Each Customer can have more than one Account (but not more than four). Again, an array object can be used to hold the references to the Account objects. Figures 7-10 and 7-11 display what the JBANK application might look like at the end of the course.

Figure 7-10 JBANK Application

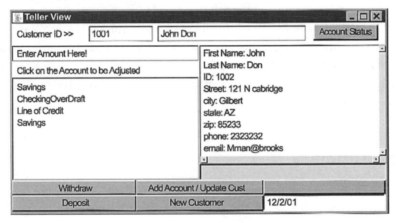

Figure 7-11 JBANK Application

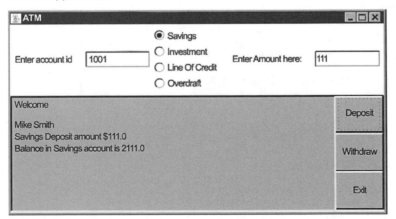

Summary

This chapter explained the concept of arrays. Arrays are special Java built-in objects that provide a way to manage several items of the same data type. Arrays can be one-dimensional (holding only one type of data) or multidimensional (holding several types of information for each object).

It is important that students understand how each element is numbered and how to access, process, and sort elements of the array. The first element of the array is indexed at the value 0, and the last element is indexed at the value that is one less than the length of the array. Array elements often are accessed or processed using loop constructs. Loops that process arrays must ensure that the code block does not try to access an index value larger than the length of the array or less than 0. If an array is accessed beyond its last element or with a negative index, the JVM ends the program and produces an error message, IndexOutOfBoundsException. Finally, arrays can be sorted using a number of sorting algorithms, including the bubble sort, the bucket sort, the selection sort, and the quick sort.

Syntax Summary

Array of primitives:

```
int [ ] intArray = new int[5];

intArray[0] = 5;
intArray[1] = 2;
intArray[2] = 3;
intArray[3] = 4;
intArray[4] = 8;
```

Array of objects:

```
Student[] studentsInTheClass = new Student [20];
//or
String[] studentName = new String[20];

studentName[0] = "Mary Post";
studentName[1] = "Peter Lei";
studentName[2] = "Polley Pocket";
//etc…
```

Array variable declaration:

```
int[ ] quantity;    or  int quantity[ ];
double[ ] amount;   or  double amount[ ];
char[ ] choices;    or  char choices[ ];
Date[ ] duedates;   or  Date duedates [ ];
String[ ] names;    or  String names [ ];
```

Initialization of the array object:

```
quantity = new int[2];
amount = new double[4];
choices = new char[5];
duedates = new Date[2];
names = new String[3];
```

Array with initialization values:

```
int[ ] quantity = {4, 5, 6, 7, 100};
```

Static initialization block:

```
static
{
//initialize static data
}
```

Nonstatic initialization block:

```
{
//initialize nonstatic data and update static data.
}
```

Passing an array to a method:

```
private static double avgPercent(javaStudent[ ] students, int num)
```

Parallel array:

```
int[ ] quantity = { 79, 80, 90, 100, 110, 220};
double[ ] price = { 0.89, 1.23, 5.79, 3.19, 1.26, 8.00};
```

Ascending Order Bubble Sort:

```
int x =5, y =4, z =6, temp;
for(int a = 0; a <2; a++)
{
    if  ( x > y )
    {
        temp = x;
        x = y;
        y = temp;
    }
    if (y > z )
    {
        temp = y;
        y = z;
        z = temp;
    }
}
System.out.println ( " values in ascending order are " + x + y + z);
```

Multidimensional array:

```
int [ ] [ ] scores = {{66, 78, 78, 89, 88, 90},
                      {40, 50, 60, 70, 80, 90},
                      {50, 55, 60, 65, 70, 75}};
```

Key Terms

array length   The fixed number of storage locations (for either primitive values or object references) that the array object will reference. This information is stored in a `final int` variable of the array object labeled `length`.

array of objects   The data in the array object is a sequence of object references, all of which are of the same data type. The array object is referenced through a single variable.

array of primitives   The data in the array object is a sequence of primitive values, all of which are of the same data type. The array object is referenced through a single variable.

bubble sort   Method of comparing two values. If the values are out of order, they are swapped to place them in order.

fixed size   After the array object is created, its length is fixed, or `final`.

index   The value inside the square brackets, used to access a specific array element. The index value is an `int`.

IndexOutOfBoundsException   Error that occurs when the code references an element of an array for which there is no index. The program then ends.

initialization of the array object   Process done with the `new` operator. The number in the square brackets creates storage for the amount of a particular data type.

multidimensional array   An array of arrays. The first set of brackets holds the index reference to the elements of the first dimension of the array. The second set of brackets holds the index reference to the elements of the second dimension.

NegativeArraySizeException   Exception thrown when you try to create an array with a negative size. The JVM ends the program and issues an error message.

nonstatic initialization block   Used to initialize nonstatic data and update static data.

parallel array   The value in one element of the array has corresponding meaning for the value of the same element in another array.

sorting   The process of arranging a series of objects in some logical order.

static initialization block   Used to initialize static data.

subscript   An integer contained within square brackets that indicates one of an array's elements.

zero-based indexing   All arrays start with an index of `0` for the first element.

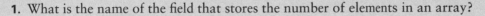

Check Your Understanding

1. What is the name of the field that stores the number of elements in an array?

   A. `size`

   B. `LENGTH`

   C. `getSize`

   D. `length`

2. What is the value for the index of the first element in an array?

   A. `1`

   B. `0`

   C. The value is variable depending on the size of the array.

   D. It is equal to the `length` minus 1.

3. Which is a true statement about the size of an array?

   A. The size of an array can be any positive number.

   B. The size of an array is fixed and cannot be changed.

   C. This size of an array cannot be `0`.

   D. The size of an array can be changed with the `setSize()` method.

4. Which of the following Java statements correctly declares an array of 10 **int** values?

   A. `int[10] myArray = new int[10];`

   B. `int myArray[10] = new int[];`

   C. `int myArray = new myArray[10];`

   D. `int[] myArray = new int[10];`

5. What is the default value stored for each element of an array of **double** objects?

   A. `0`

   B. `0.0`

   C. `null`

   D. `\u0000`

6. What is the default value stored for each element of an array of `String` objects?

   A. `""` – empty String

   B. `\u0000`

   C. `null`

   D. `0`

7. What is the correct syntax to access the third element in an array called `intArray`?

   A. `intArray(3)`

   B. `intArray[3]`

   C. `intArray[4]`

   D. `intArray[2]`

8. How many objects are created with this Java statement?

   `String[] stringArray = new String[9];`

   A. 1: One array object is created.

   B. 10: Nine `String` objects and one array object are created.

   C. 11: Ten `String` objects and one array object are created.

   D. 9: Nine `String` objects are created.

9. Which exception is thrown when a programmer uses the index 12 to access an element in an array of only 10 elements?

   A. `NoSuchIndexException`

   B. `ArrayIndexOutOfBoundsException`

   C. `Exception`

   D. `NegativeArraySizeException`

10. What is a difference between an array of objects and an array of primitives?

    A. The objects are stored in the array, whereas only references to the primitives are stored in the array.

    B. The primitives are stored in the array, whereas only references to the objects are stored in the array.

    C. The size of an array of primitives is fixed, whereas the size of an array of objects is flexible.

    D. The size of an array of objects is fixed, whereas the size of an array of primitives is flexible.

11. Which areas of memory are used for an array of integers?

   A. The array object is created on the stack, and each of the **int** values is created on the heap.

   B. The array object is created on the heap, and each of the **int** values is created on the stack.

   C. The array object is created on the heap, and each of the **int** values is created on the heap.

   D. The array object is created on the stack, and each of the **int** values is created on the stack.

12. Which of these statements is a true statement about static initialization blocks?

   A. A static initialization block is executed once for each object that is created from the class.

   B. A static initialization block can be used only to initialize object data.

   C. A static initialization block can be used only to initialize class data.

   D. A static initialization block is not executed until at least one object has been instantiated.

13. Which class contains the `arraycopy()` method?

   A. `Array`

   B. `Util`

   C. `Object`

   D. `System`

14. What is the correct way to define the header for a method that will accept an array of ten integers as a parameter?

   A. `public static void myMethod(int array){}`

   B. `public static void myMethod(int[] array){}`

   C. `public static void myMethod(array[]){}`

   D. `public static void myMethod(int[10] array){}`

15. What is the correct way to call `myMethod()` from question 14?

   A. `myMethod(myArray[]);`

   B. `myMethod(myArray[10]);`

   C. `myMethod(myArray);`

   D. `myMethod(int[] myArray);`

16. When the values of one array correspond to the values of another array, the arrays are.

    A. Specified arrays

    B. Related arrays

    C. Multidimensional arrays

    D. Parallel arrays

17. Which of the sorting techniques uses a recursive approach?

    A. Bubble sort

    B. Quick sort

    C. Selection sort

    D. Bucket sort

18. Which of the following array declarations could be used to hold 12 elements?

    A. `int[] myArray = new int[12];`

    B. `int[][] myArray = new int[6][2];`

    C. `int[][] myArray = new int[3][4];`

    D. All of the above

19. What is the correct way of accessing the third column in the second row in the following multidimensional array?

    ```
    int row = 5;
    int column = 4;
    int[][] myArray = new int[row][column];
    ```

    A. `myArray[3][2]`

    B. `myArray[2][3]`

    C. `myArray[2][1]`

    D. `myArray[1][2]`

20. How many loop structures are needed to individually access each element in a three-dimensional array?

    A. One

    B. Two

    C. Three

    D. Four

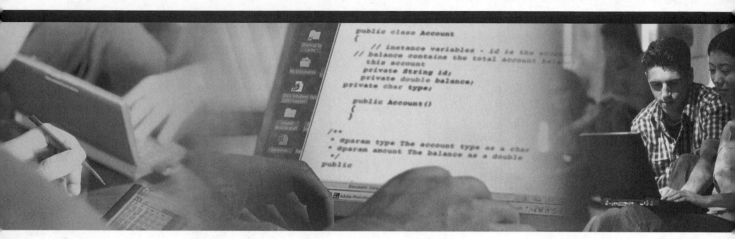

Upon completion of this chapter, you will be able to

- Understand inheritance and object-oriented programming
- Describe Java language support for inheritance
- Explain access modifiers and inheritance
- Understand the concept of overriding
- Use the keywords **this** and **super**
- Understand inheritance and constructors
- Describe the concept of extending classes
- Implement interfaces
- Understand polymorphism, dynamic binding, and virtual method invocation
- Apply the Java language concepts that you have learned in this chapter to the JBANK case study

Chapter 8

Classes and Inheritance

This chapter discusses inheritance, a key concept that helps increase flexibility when designing classes. With *inheritance*, general classes can be created from which other classes can derive behaviors and attributes. The class at the top of a hierarchy of classes is known as the *superclass*. Classes that derive from this class are known as *subclasses* or *child classes*. All classes in Java derive from the superclass Object. A subclass inherits all nonprivate attributes and methods of the superclass. However, attributes and methods with default access can only be accessed if the subclass is in the same package as the superclass. Data and methods can be referenced as if they were declared as normal members of the class. A subclass does not inherit superclass constructors, and it can override the methods of the superclass.

This chapter also discusses interfaces and polymorphism. An *interface* can contain only constants and abstract methods. A class can implement more than one interface, and unrelated classes can implement the same interface. If several classes implement a common interface, the methods declared as members of the interface can be executed polymorphically. Polymorphism provides a programmer with enormous flexibility: A method can be defined to accept a general class type or interface as an argument. Any class that **extends** from the general class or that **implements** the interface then can be passed as an argument to the method.

Inheritance and Object-Oriented Programming

The technique of deriving new class definitions from an existing class definition is known as *inheritance*. The reasons for using inheritance include these:

- Reuse of predefined, well-tested classes
- Standardization of behaviors across a group of classes
- Capability to use members of a family of classes interchangeably in methods

This section consists of the following topics:

- Inheritance
- Abstraction
- The problem of multiple inheritance

Inheritance

When using inheritance to derive a new class definition from an existing class, the methods of the existing classes can be reused or changed. New fields (data members) and methods can be added to adapt them to new situations.

Inheritance defines "is a" relationships among classes and objects. Every object represents this "is a" relationship to its class. All objects inherit from the class that defines them. For example, in the code shown in Figure 8-1, the object referenced by f1 "is a" Fish. It inherits from the class Fish. The following code snippet creates an instance of a Fish object and assigns the object reference to the variable f1:

```
Fish f1 = new Fish("Flipper");
```

Figure 8-1 Fish Class and Object Reference

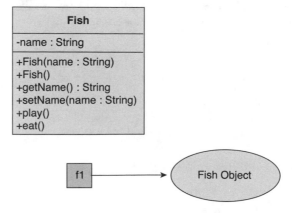

In Figure 8-2, the object referenced by c1 "is a" Cat, and it inherits its data and behavior from the class Cat. The following code snippet creates an instance of a Cat object and assigns the object reference to the variable c1:

```
Cat c1 = new Cat("Sylvester");
```

Figure 8-2 Cat Class and Object Reference

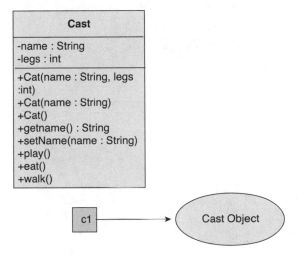

The Fish and Cat classes define both common and different behaviors and data. The commonality of behaviors across some classes is the basis for inheritance. The programmer defining these classes also could define a class named Animal that describes the data and behaviors common to the Fish and Cat classes. The inheritance model applied to these classes would be one in which the Animal class is the parent class. The parent class would define common behaviors for the Fish and Cat classes. The Fish and Cat classes each would inherit common behaviors from the parent class. The Fish and Cat classes also would define their own adaptation of these behaviors, which include new data and new behaviors. There exists an "is a" relationship between Animal, Fish, and Cat. A Fish is an Animal, and a Cat is an Animal. This "is a" relationship is the cornerstone concept of inheritance in object-oriented technology. Java allows "is a" relationships to exist between classes. The Java API defines all classes as inheriting from the Object class, which is at the root of all class hierarchies. When defining class hierarchy, it is not necessary to define explicit inheritance from the Object class; the Animal class automatically **extends** Object. Thus, because the Fish class **extends** from Animal, the Fish class has all the methods and attributes of the Object class.

NOTE

Although we state that there exists an "is a" relationship among Animal, Fish, and Cat, we can think of this relationship as *"is a, plus additional functionality."* Cat and Fish are examples of subclasses of the Animal class that provide additional functionality, such as the name attribute, the getName() method, and the Cat class's play() method.

With inheritance, the "is a" relationship extends to the root of the hierarchy. The object referenced by f1 "is a" Fish and "is a" Animal. The object referenced by c1 "is a" Cat and "is a" Animal, and the Animal "is an" Object. (See Figure 8-3.)

Figure 8-3 Inheritance—Animal, Fish, and Cat Objects

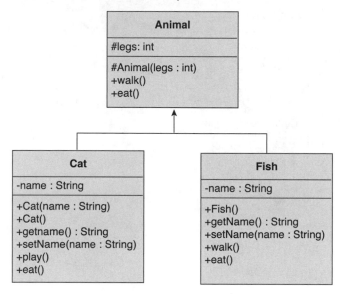

Abstraction

The very same Animal class also can be used to derive a Spider class. Although this new class does not have a name attribute like the Fish or the Cat classes, the fact that all of these classes share some similar behaviors allows the programmer to derive their definitions from a general class of Animal, as shown in Figure 8-4. In this example, the Animal class serves a limited use. The Animal class could not provide the functionality needed for a Fish object or the functionality needed for a Cat object. The class is an abstract representation of the classes that inherit from it. Placing common behaviors in an abstract class is another component of inheritance. The Fish, Cat, and Spider classes represent concrete classes from which a useful object can be created.

Programmers arrive at abstract and concrete designs of classes in one of two ways:

- Generalization, or discovery of general behaviors among classes
- Specialization, or identification of a specific adaptation of general behaviors or adoption of new behaviors in an inherited class

Figure 8-4 Inheritance—Animal, Fish, Cat, and Spider Objects

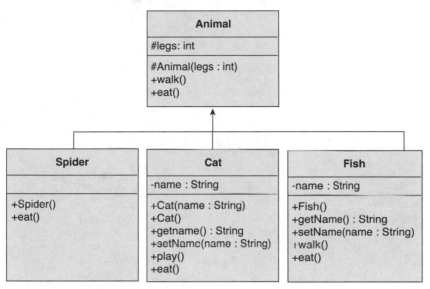

Generalization Through Superclasses

When designing classes, common fields and behaviors lead to generalizations about the classes. These generalizations can be implemented through the design of parent classes that also are known as superclasses. Superclasses then can be designed to describe required and optional fields and behaviors. A superclass can be an abstract representation of common behaviors and data (*abstraction*). When a superclass is an abstract representation, the superclass cannot actually be used as an object. Objects demonstrate behaviors of an abstract superclass through concrete implementations of these behaviors in subclasses. The Animal class can define common behaviors for Fish, Cat, and Spider objects. Creating an object of the Animal class has almost no practical use; instead, a programmer uses a specific instance of one of the derived classes. In object-oriented programming, the term *concrete* means a class from which an object can be created and used.

The term *abstract* is applied to classes from which no objects are expected to be created. In a program that manages data for an aquarium, the Fish class is derived as a concrete implementation of the Animal class. The term *concrete implementation* refers to classes from which objects *are* expected to be created. In a veterinarian application, the Cat object is a concrete implementation of the Animal class. In this manner, an abstract representation such as the Animal class can be used in two unrelated applications. The Animal class shown in Figure 8-5 is an abstract class and is not designed for the creation of objects; objects are instantiated only through its subclasses—Spider, Cat, and Fish. The concepts of abstract and concrete are defined in the following section.

Figure 8-5 Inheritance—Abstract and Concrete Implementation of Classes

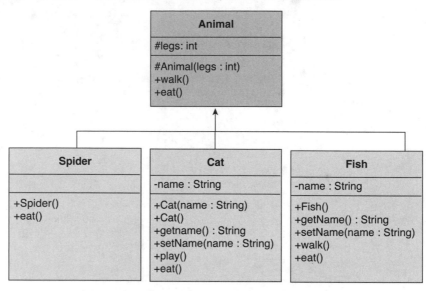

Generalizations of classes into a superclass can be either concrete or abstract. For example, an application can design classes to include an `Employee` class and two derived classes called `Manager` and `Programmer` (see Figure 8-6). In this application, managers are represented using objects of the `Manager` class, and programmers are represented using objects of the `Programmer` class. All other employees are represented using objects of the `Employee` class. Here, all the classes in the inheritance hierarchy are *concrete* classes. That is, each class can be used to create objects of the class. In this model, the object referenced by e1 is an `Employee`, the object referenced by m1 is a `Manager` and an `Employee`, and the object referenced by p1 is a `Programmer` and an `Employee`.

Specialization Through Subclasses

Although fish, cats, and spiders are indeed animals, their anatomy and behaviors are different. Fish swim and have fins instead of legs. Spiders have eight legs, and cats only have four. These differences among fish, cats, and spiders represent specializations of the general and abstract class `Animal`. `Fish`, `Cat`, and `Spider` classes are subclasses of the parent superclass `Animal`. In the same sense, `Manager` and `Programmer` are subclasses of the parent class `Employee`.

NOTE

A subclass must override methods that are declared **abstract** in the superclass, or the subclass itself must be abstract.

Figure 8-6 Inheritance—Concrete Implementation of All Classes

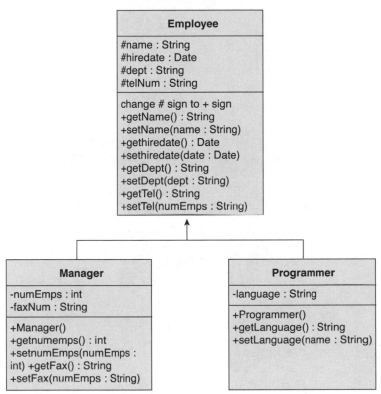

The Problem of Multiple Inheritance

In some object-oriented languages, such as C++, a class can derive from multiple parent classes or superclasses (*multiple inheritance*). In Java, a class may not have multiple superclasses. As illustrated in Figure 8-7, if a `Programmer` object is both a member of the `Person` and `Employee` classes, and if both the `Person` and `Employee` classes have a field name and a method `getName()`, the JVM does not know which `getName()` method to use for a `Programmer` object. To avoid such confusion, and because Java is a strongly typed language, a class can derive from only one parent class. A form of multiple inheritance is provided through the use of interfaces, which are described later in this chapter.

Figure 8-7 Person, Employee, and Programmer—No Multiple Inheritance

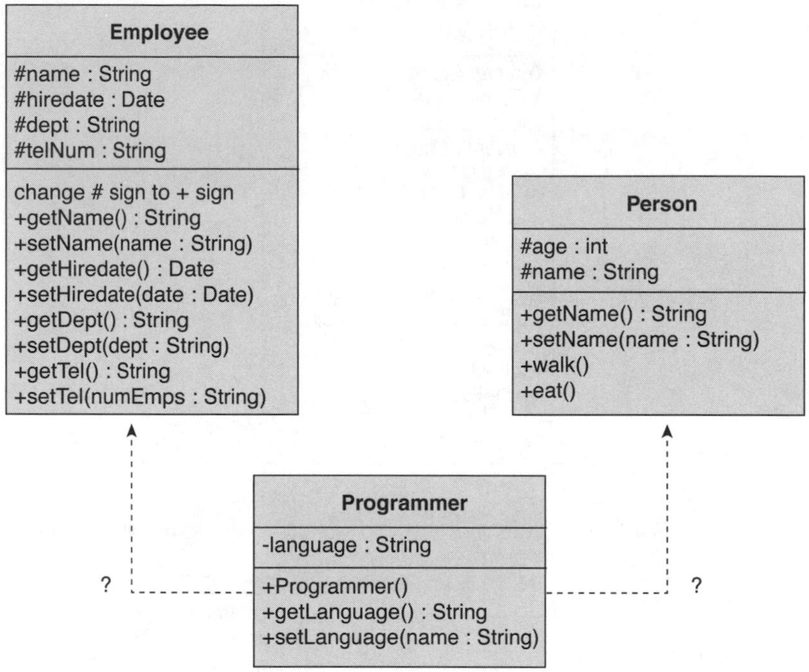

Inheritance hierarchies show the relationship between classes. A hierarchy can show that the Programmer class is a subclass of the Employee class, which is a subclass of the Person class. In the same regard, this shows that the Person class is a superclass to the Employee class, the Programmer class, and all other classes that are subclasses of the Employee class or even the Programmer class.

Figures 8-8, 8-9, and 8-10 illustrate the four-level hierarchy path for the TextField class, a class that is used in a graphical user interface (GUI). GUIs include items such as windows and dialog boxes to facilitate user input. They are a vital aspect of virtually all applications.

Figure 8-8 Inherited Hierarchy of the API Class `TextField`

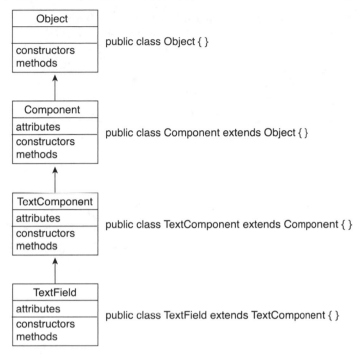

Figure 8-9 Inherited Hierarchy of the API Class `TextField`—API Docs

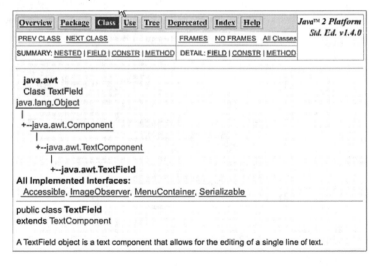

Figure 8-10 TextField—Inherited Methods from API Docs

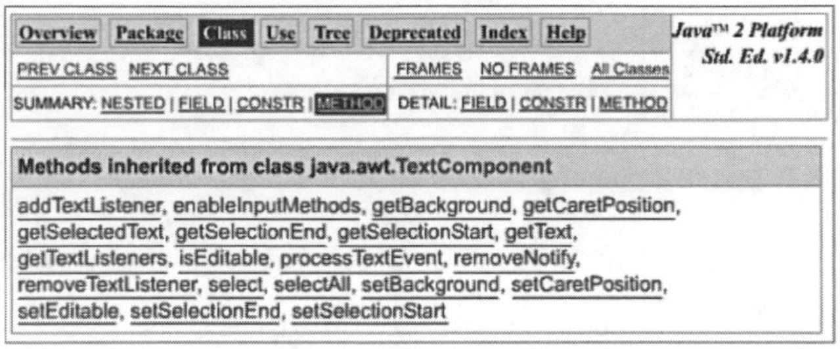

Java Language Support for Inheritance

The Java language provides specific keywords to support inheritance, as well as a robust set of API classes that can be used as superclasses. This section consists of the following topics:

- Java language and keywords in inheritance
- Object class

Java Language Keywords in Inheritance

The most important keyword provided by the Java language for inheritance is *extends*. When a class **extends** from another class, it is considered a subclass; likewise, extending from another class also is known as subclassing. The idea behind the keyword **extends** is that the class definition includes all of the nonprivate attributes and behaviors of the parent class and other attributes and behaviors that are unique to the class.

Another keyword used with inheritance is *super*, which enables the programmer to access methods and data of the parent class. Because Java does not permit multiple inheritances, there is only one parent class. The keyword **super** can be used to access the data and methods of this parent class. The **private** methods and data of the parent class, while part of the subclass object, are not accessible by the subclass; this includes either overriding or overloading of methods. The keyword **super** functions in the same manner as the keyword **this**; it provides a reference to the derived attributes of the object.

In Exercise 8-1, identify the Java keywords, at the top of the example, that are associated with each inheritance statement.

Exercise 8-1 Java Keywords for Inheritance

Java keywords for inheritance:

implements, extends, super, protected, abstract

1. The keyword _____ is used to signify that one class is a subclass of a parent class.

2. _____ is a keyword used within a subclass to refer to data and methods from the parent class.

3. A class that is declared _____ cannot actually be used to instantiate an object.

4. More than one interface can be implemented by a class. The keyword _____ is used with interfaces.

5. Similar to **private**, the access modifier _____ restricts access to data members and methods, but unlike **private**, subclasses are allowed access to these data members and methods.

You can check your answers using an interactive graphic on the book's accompanying CD-ROM. The title of the activity is "Java Keywords for Inheritance" in e-Lab Activities.

Object Class

The Java language provides comprehensive support for inheritance through the API of classes. Almost any Java program that creates and uses GUIs uses inheritance models that are implemented in the classes that form the Abstract Window Toolkit (AWT) of classes.

Each class that has been created **extends** from the Object class, which is the superclass of all classes.

The list that follows shows all of the methods of the Object class.

- clone()
- equals(Object obj)
- finalize()
- getClass()

- hashCode()
- notify()
- notifyAll()
- toString()
- wait()
- wait(long timeout)
- wait(long timeout, int nanos)

Every object's attributes and behaviors are defined by its class, its superclass, the superclass's superclass, and so on. Because the Object class is the superclass of all classes in Java, the attributes and behaviors defined in Object are present in all Java objects. As a result, Object class behaviors and attributes are inherited by all new objects. The fact that the created classes are subclasses of the Object class makes them useable in many of the predefined API classes. Any method of any class that receives an Object as its argument also can use a reference to any object because all objects inherit Object class behaviors and attributes.

Each class that is created includes all the methods of the Object class. Although every class **extends** the Object class, this information never has to be declared in the class definition. It is assumed that the class Programmer **extends** the class Object and, therefore, does not have to be declared.

Some methods of the Object class, the equals() and toString() methods, require special consideration. These methods perform very generic actions when executed. For example, the *equals()* method compares its reference value with that of another object. This is a comparison of the addresses of two objects, not the data. The *toString()* method converts the reference value of an object to a String. Both of these methods might not be very useful when comparing or printing object data, however. A later section in this chapter, "Overriding of Object Class Methods," explores the ways of changing these methods.

Figure 8-11 identifies all of the *derived methods* (inherited methods) of the Programmer class from its parent class, Employee. Note that all the derived methods from the Object class also are identified.

Figure 8-11 Derived Methods from the `Employee` Class and the `Object` Class

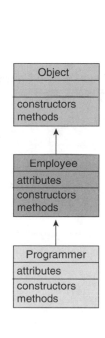

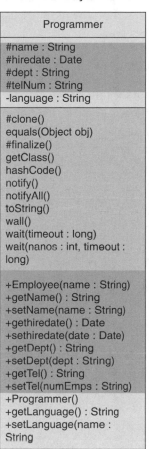

Access Modifiers and Inheritance

Access modifiers of the superclasses methods and attributes play an important role in inheritance. This section covers the role of access modifiers in inheritance.

Role of Access Modifiers in Inheritance

So what do subclasses inherit? Access modifiers control which superclass attributes and methods are inherited by the subclass. A subclass cannot inherit methods or data that are **private**. All other nonprivate data and methods can be inherited, excluding default access when the superclass is in a different package than the subclass. Table 8-1 describes access modifiers and their impact on inheritance. The table shows the access to class members based on the modifier used. The instance referred to in the table is an instance of another class.

Table 8-1 Access Modifiers and Inheritance

Access Modifier	Instance in the same package	Instance in a different package	Subclass in the same package	Subclass in a different package
`public`	Yes	Yes	Yes	Yes
`private`	No	No	No	No
`protected`	Yes	No	Yes	Yes
default	Yes	No	Yes	No

Figure 8-12 shows the impact of inheritance when a subclass is in the same package as the parent class and when the subclass is in a different package than the parent class.

Figure 8-12 Influence of Access Modifiers in an Inheritance Model

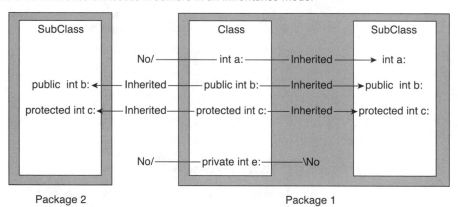

It is important to understand that all methods and data from a parent class exist in the subclass object. However, the `private` attributes and methods are inaccessible to the subclass object. In the code example shown in Example 8-1, a `private` attribute in the Parent class is not directly accessible to the subclass. The nonprivate method of the Parent class is directly accessible, however. The nonprivate method accesses the `private` attribute. This code illustrates that inaccessibility does not mean that the `private` methods and data do not exist.

Example 8-1 Parent *and* Child *Classes*

```
Parent:
 1 /**
 2  * Java Program: Parent.java
 3  * @author Cisco Teacher
 4  * @version 2002
 5  */
 6 public class Parent
 7 {
 8     private  int x;
 9     public int y;
10
11     /**
12     * @param aNum A random number as an int
13     */
14     Parent(int aNum)
15     {
16         x = aNum * (int) Math.random();
17     }
18
19     /**
20     * @return The new number as an int
21     */
22     public int getX()
23     {
24         return x;
25     }
26 }
27


Child:
 1 /**
 2  * Java Program: Child.java
 3  * @author Cisco Teacher
 4  * @version 2002
```

NOTE

If a subclass declares an attribute or method with the same name as the superclass's attribute or method, the subclass "hides" the attribute or overrides the method of the superclass. The keyword **super** can be used to access the superclass's hidden attributes and overridden methods.

continues

Example 8-1 Parent *and* Child *Classes (Continued)*

```
 5  */
 6 public class Child extends Parent
 7 {
 8     int parentX;
 9
10     /**
11     * @param theNum A random number as an int
12     */
13     Child (int theNum)
14     {
15         super(theNum);
16     }
17
18     /*
19     the private variable X of the parent is inherited,
20     although not directly accessible.  The getX method
21     of the parent class is public and inherited. It is
22     used to access the parent class value.
23     */
24     public void setX()
25     {
26         parentX = super.getX();
27         System.out.println( "Parent value X is "
28             + parentX + " Y is " + super.y);
29     }
30 } // end class
31
```

Overriding

An important functionality of inheritance is the capability to redefine or customize the definition of a parent class method. This section consists of the following topics:

- Method overriding
- Overriding of Object class methods
- Overloading versus overriding

Method Overriding

Although inheritance provides extensive support to reuse of existing classes, many of the methods and behaviors of a superclass might need customizing. For example, the Object class methods of equals() and toString() have a limited use if they only compare or print the addresses of objects. A toString() method that prints the actual data of an object in a formatted manner or an equals() method that compares the values of two objects would be more practical. The capability of a programmer to redefine or customize the definition of a parent class method is known as *overriding*. This is another component of inheritance. Any method that is inherited can be overridden, except for nonprivate methods that have been declared **final** in the parent class. Recall that access modifiers influence inheritance. Only methods that are inherited can be overridden.

The following list outlines and describes the rules for overriding parent class methods:

- A parent method can be overridden only once in the subclass.
- Overridden methods must have argument lists of identical type and order; otherwise, they are treated as overloaded methods. The method name, type, and order of arguments must be identical to those of the parent class.
- The return type of the overridden method must be identical to that of the method that it overrides.
- The accessibility must not be more restricted than the original method. For example, if the parent method is declared **public**, the overridden method cannot be anything less than **public**. Therefore, it also must be **public**. However, if the parent class method is **protected** or default, the overridden method can be declared **public**.
- Exceptions are specialized classes that determine errors or problems that arise when a method is executing. An overriding method cannot **throw** checked exceptions that are not of the same class or subclasses of the original method.

Returning to the Animal class, although all of the subclasses eat, they do so in different manners. Therefore, the eat method has been overridden in each of the subclasses. Both the Spider and the Cat objects use the walk method defined in the Animal class, which describes how many legs are used to walk. However, because Fish objects do not walk, the walk method is overridden in the Fish class. Figure 8-13 illustrates the parent (Animal) class methods that have been overridden in each of the subclasses. A method with the same signature in both the superclass and subclass, but defined with a different set of statements in the subclass, is an overridden (superclass or parent class) method.

Figure 8-13 Overridden Parent (Animal) Class Methods

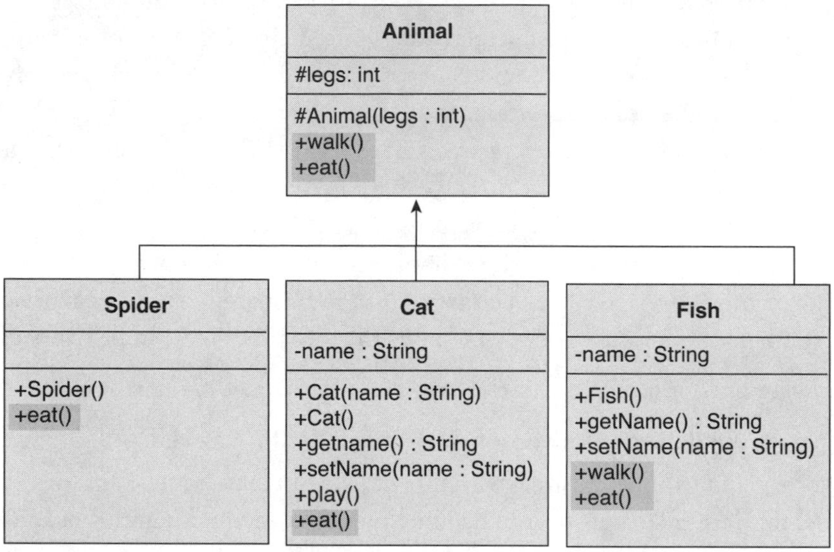

Overriding of `Object` Class Methods

In general, class design should include overriding of the `equals()`, `hashCode()`, and `toString()` methods. Note, the `hashCode()` method returns a hash code value for the object. Example 8-2 and Figure 8-14 apply this to the `Student` class used in previous examples.

Example 8-2 *Inherited "as-is" Object Methods—Code*

```
 1 /** * Student Class establishes the student id, name and grade
 2  * @author Cisco Teacher
 3  * @version 2002
 4  */
 5 public class Student
 6 {
 7     private final String studentName;
 8     private String grade;
 9     private int studentID;
10     public static final int courseNumber = 12345;
11
12     // null constructor
13     public Student( )
```

Example 8-2 *Inherited "as-is" Object Methods—Code (Continued)*

```
14    {
15        studentName = "";
16    }
17
18    // constructor with 2 arguments
19    /**
20     * @param name The student's name as a String
```

For Example 8-2, you can view the explanatory text by accessing the full, interactive graphic for this example on the book's accompanying CD-ROM. The title of the activity is "Inherited 'as-is' Object Methods" in e-Lab Activities.

Figure 8-14 Inherited "as-is" Object Methods—Output

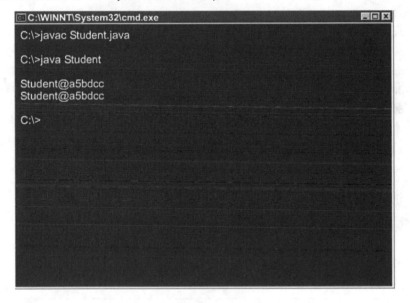

NOTE

Your classes might want to override the following Object methods. The equals/hashCode methods are listed together because they must be overridden together:

- clone
- equals/hashCode
- finalize
- toString

Your class cannot override these Object methods (they are **final**):

- getClass
- notify
- notifyAll
- wait

The Student class has methods to access **private** data. The Student class inherits the equals() method and the toString() method from the Object class. Note that using these methods with Student objects produces information that is not useable. For example, both Student objects contain the same data. However, each Student object has a different address and causes the method to return **false**. The System.out.println() method uses the toString() method of an object to print information about the object. Because the toString() method in the Object class returns the memory address of the object only as a String, this is what is printed.

To address these limitations, you can override the `toString()`, `equals()`, and `hash-Code()` methods in the `Student` class. The `System.out` class uses the `toString()` method of an object to print information about the object. The `Student` version of the `toString()` method shown in Example 8-3 and Figure 8-15 returns a `String` that represents the student's name, identification, and other information. When the `System.out.println()` method is provided a reference to the `Student` object, it uses the overridden `toString()` method to print student information that is useful.

Example 8-3 `toString()` *Method Overridden—Code*

```
1 /**
2 * Student Class establishes the student id, name and grade
3 * @author Cisco Teacher
4 * @version 2002
5 */
6 public class Student
7 {
8     private final String studentName;
9     private String grade;
10     private int studentID;
11     public static final int courseNumber = 12345;
12
13     // null constructor
14     public Student( )
15     {
16         studentName = "";
17     }
18
19     // constructor with 2 arguments
20     /**
```

For Example 8-3, you can view the explanatory text by accessing the full, interactive graphic for this figure on the book's accompanying CD-ROM. The title of the activity is "`toString()` Method Overridden" in e-Lab Activities.

Figure 8-15 `toString()` Method Overridden—Output

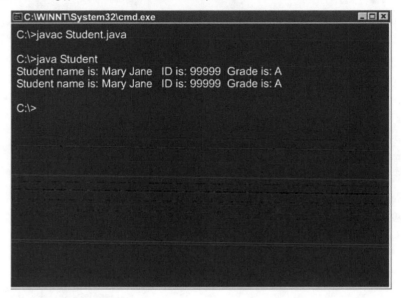

Because two `Student` objects will need to be compared to ensure that none of the student information is duplicated, the `equals()` method is overridden. It is possible for two `Student` objects to have the same data, but because they are not the same object, they will have different memory addresses. The address of an object is calculated using a hashing algorithm, which is a unique identifier given to each object on the heap. The hashing algorithm is in the code of the method. To ensure that this unique identifier is the same, the `hashCode()` method of the object needs to be overridden. In this example, the `hashCode()` method uses the student identification to determine a hashvalue. The method returns an integer as the hashvalue of the object. The `equals()` method is overridden to compare the data in the fields of the two objects. If all fields are equal, the method returns a **true**. A test of the hashvalue of the objects is also included.

In Example 8-4 and Figure 8-16, the `equals()` method is overridden, but the `hashCode()` method is not. Although the objects contain the same data, each has been assigned a different hashvalue and thus are considered different objects.

Example 8-4 *Overridden* `equals()` *Method—Code*

```
1 /**
2  * Student Class establishes the student id, name and grade
3  * @author Cisco Teacher
```

continues

Example 8-4 *Overridden* `equals()` *Method—Code (Continued)*

```
 4   * @version 2002
 5   */
 6  public class Student
 7  {
 8     private final String studentName;
 9     private String grade;
10     private int studentID;
11     public static final int courseNumber = 12345;
12
13     // null constructor
14     public Student( )
15     {
16        studentName = "";
17     }
18
19     // constructor with 2 arguments
20     /**
```

For Example 8-4, you can view the explanatory text by accessing the full, interactive graphic for this example on the book's accompanying CD-ROM. The title of the activity is "Overridden `equals()` Method" in e-Lab Activities.

Figure 8-16 Overridden `equals()` Method—Output

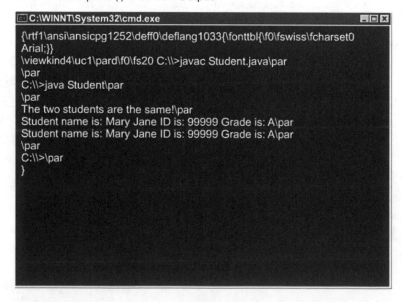

In Example 8-5 and Figure 8-17, the hashCode() and equals() methods are both over-ridden. This yields a more accurate result of comparing the two objects.

Example 8-5 *Overridden* hashCode() *Method—Code*

```
 1 /**
 2  * Student Class establishes the student id, name and grade
 3  * @author Cisco Teacher
 4  * @version 2002
 5  */
 6 public class Student
 7 {
 8    private final String studentName;
 9    private String grade;
10    private int studentID;
11    public static final int courseNumber = 12345;
12
13    // null constructor
14    public Student( )
15    {
16       studentName = "";
17    }
18
19    // constructor with 2 arguments
20    /**
```

For Example 8-5, you can view the explanatory text by accessing the full, interactive graphic for this example on the book's accompanying CD-ROM. The title of the activity is "Overridden hashCode() Method" in e-Lab Activities.

Overloading versus Overriding

Table 8-2 presents a comparison of overloading and overriding techniques. Both can be used in classes that form an inheritance hierarchy.

Figure 8-17 Overridden hashCode( ) Method—Output

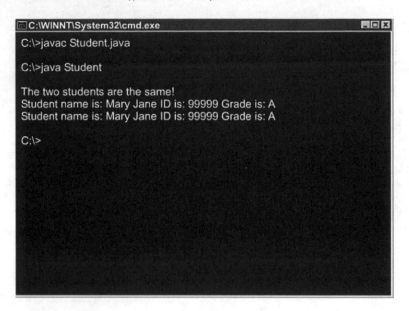

Table 8-2 Comparison of Overloading and Overriding

Overloading	Overriding
Method must be in same class.	Method must be in subclass.
Method must have same name *but* must have different parameters (either number of parameters or data types).	Method must have the same name *and* the same parameters (both number of parameters and data types).
Return type *may be* different. (Different return type alone is not enough to overload the method; parameters must be different, too.)	Return type *must be* the same.
Different method signature is used.	Same method signature is used.
Method's access modifier *can* be more private than the parent method's.	Method's access modifier *cannot* be more private than the parent method's.

Table 8-2 Comparison of Overloading and Overriding (Continued)

Overloading	Overriding
Exceptions *may be* different. (Different exceptions alone are not enough to overload the method; parameters must be different, too.)	Method must **throw** exceptions that are the *same* type as the parent method's or child exceptions of the parent method's exceptions.
Methods *can* **throw** more exceptions than the parent method that they override. (Different number of exceptions alone are not enough to overload the method; parameters must be different, too.)	Methods *cannot* **throw** more exceptions than the parent method they override.

Use of this and super

The Java language keywords **this** and **super** enable the programmer to access superclass and subclass attributes and methods. This section addresses the use of **this** and **super** in inheritance.

Accessing Parent and Subclass Methods and Data

A subclass object should be viewed as containing the parent class's object methods and data within it. Example 8-6 illustrates the subclass SportsCoupe and the parent class BaseModelAuto. In actuality, there are two objects. To reference the methods and data of each object, use the variables **this** and **super** in the methods. All of the methods of the subclass include the **this** variable and the **super** variable. The **this** variable contains a reference to the subclass object. The **super** variable contains a reference to the parent object.

In Example 8-6, **this** and **super** are used in two places. Here, the parent-class method is overridden in the subclass. The main method calls the parent-class method using the **super** variable and then the **this** variable to call the overridden version of the subclass.

NOTE

The use of **super** is not required for inherited attributes and methods that have not been overridden by the subclass.

Example 8-6 *Identifying* **this** *and* **super**

```
SportsCoupe:
 1 /**
 2  * Java Program: SportsCoupe.java
 3  * @author Cisco Teacher
 4  * @version 2002
```

continues

Example 8-6 *Identifying* **this** *and* **super** *(Continued)*

```
 5  */
 6 public class SportsCoupe extends BaseModelAuto
 7 {
 8         protected String accessories = "Moon roof\n";
 9
10         //constructor
11
12         /**
13          * @return The car's accessories as a String
14          */
15         public String getAccessories() //overridden method
16         {
17             return super.getAccessories() + accessories;
18         }
19
20         /**
21          * @param options The car's options as a String
22          * @return The car's accessories as a String
23          */
24         public String getAccessories(String options) //overloaded method
25         {
26             return this.getAccessories() + options;
27         }
28         //additional methods
29
30         public static void main(String[] args)
31         {
32             SportsCoupe myCar = new SportsCoupe();
33             System.out.println("\nList of options includes:\n"
34             + myCar.getAccessories());
35             System.out.println("\nList of options includes:\n"
36             + myCar.getAccessories("Chromeplated Wheels"));
37         }
38 } // end of SportsCoupe class
39
```

Example 8-6 *Identifying* **this** *and* **super** *(Continued)*

```
BaseModelAuto:
 1  /**
 2   * Java Program: BaseModelAuto.java
 3   * @author Cisco Teacher
 4   * @version 2002
 5   */
 6  public class BaseModelAuto
 7  {
 8      protected String accessories;
 9      accessories = "Power Steering\nPower Windows\n";
10
11      //constructor
12
13      /**
14       * @return The accessories as a String
15       */
16      public String getAccessories()
17      {
18          return accessories;
19      }
20
21      //additional methods
22  } // end of BaseModelAuto class
23
```

More Information

Sometimes, you don't want to completely override a method. Instead, you want to add more functionality to it. You can do this by calling the overridden method using the **super** keyword. For example, the getAccessories method in the subclass SportsCoupe adds functionality to the getAccessories method in the superclass BaseModelAuto with the code shown here:

```
public String getAccessories()
{
    return (super.getAccessories() + " " + accessories);
}
```

Inheritance and Constructors

Constructors are not inherited in the same way as methods and attributes are inherited by the subclass. Constructors must be defined for each subclass. This section consists of the following topic:

- Handling constructors in inheritance
- Performing initialization with inheritance

Handling Constructors in Inheritance

Inheritance makes nonprivate code and data defined in the parent class accessible to the subclass. The only exception is constructors, which are not inherited in the normal way, even if they are nonprivate. Instead, constructors must be defined for each subclass. Example 8-7 demonstrates the use of the **new** operator to construct an object and the matching constructor that is used. In this example, the code for MyClass includes overloaded constructors. Overloading means that different versions of the same method exist in the same class.

Example 8-7 *Constructors in a Sample Class, MyClass*

```
1 /** * Java Program: MyClass.java
2  * @author Cisco Teacher
3  * @version 2002
4  */
5
6 public class MyClass
7 {
8     private int studentID;
9     private int creditHoursEarned;
10    private double tuitionBalance;
11    private String studentName;
12    private String studentAddress;
13
14    //Overloaded Constructors, demonstrating "name mangling"
15    public MyClass()
16    {
17    }
18
19    /**
20     * @param id The student's id as an int
```

When the inheritance model is applied to a class definition, if the parent class includes a constructor that is not a null constructor (and does not include a no-args constructor), the subclass also must explicitly include code for constructors and cannot depend on a null constructor creation through the compiler. Each constructor in the subclass must include a call to the parent constructor. The word *extends* means that an object of the parent class is constructed and then extended to include the data and methods of the subclass.

When a programmer does not include a constructor in a class definition, the compiler inserts a null constructor. A null constructor is a constructor that does not take any arguments. In the case of subclasses, the matter is more complicated. If the programmer does not include a constructor, the compiler tries to insert a null constructor. In this null constructor, a call will be made to the null constructor of the parent. If the parent class does not have a null constructor, the class will fail to compile.

The following list identifies the different conditions for using constructors from subclasses and superclasses:

- Constructors are not inherited in the same way as normal methods. An object can be created only with the **new** operator and an argument list that matches one of the constructors defined in the class.

- The compiler provides a default constructor that takes no arguments when no constructors have been explicitly defined in the class. This is also known as the null constructor.

- If a class contains even one constructor, the compiler will not insert a null constructor. In the case of inheritance, it is imperative that the null constructor be defined explicitly in the parent class, if any of the subclasses are permitted null constructors.

- Constructors can be overloaded with different argument lists. One constructor can call another constructor using the syntax **this**(arguments…).

- A constructor delays running the body of its code until the parent parts of the class have been initialized. This commonly happens because of an implicit call to **super**() added by the compiler. If the parent class does not include a null constructor, the call to **super**() will fail.

- A call to a constructor of the superclass can be included in the method body of a constructor in the subclass. The call must match one of the argument lists of the parent class and must be the first statement in the subclass constructor.

- When overloading constructors, the call to another constructor with the statement **this**() must be the first statement. In these cases, initialization of the parent class is performed in the overloaded constructor.

The call to a parent constructor is through the use of the keyword **super**. The format of the statement matches at least one argument list of a constructor of the parent class. The name for the parent class is not used in this call. Because Java does not permit multiple inheritance, there can be only one parent to any subclass. The variable **super** has a reference to the parent class object and its definition.

The sample code shown in Examples 8-8 and 8-9 demonstrates the correct and incorrect use of the keyword **super** and constructors in the construction of a subclass.

Example 8-8 *Incorrect Use of* **super** *and Constructors*

```
 1 class Parent
 2 {
 3      String name;
 4
 5      // constructor
 6      Parent (String s)
 7      {
 8          name = s;
 9      }
10
11 // some methods
12 }
13
14 class Child extends Parent
15 {
16     // NO CONSTRUCTORS
17     // OTHER METHODS
18 }
```

For Example 8-8, you can view the explanatory text by accessing the full, interactive graphic for this example on the book's accompanying CD-ROM. The title of the activity is "Incorrect Usage of **super** and Constructors" in e-Lab Activities.

Example 8-9 *Correct Use of* **super** *and Constructors*

```
 1 class Parent
 2 {
 3     String name;
 4
```

Example 8-9 *Correct Use of* **super** *and Constructors (Continued)*

```
 5     // constructor
 6     Parent (String s)
 7     {
 8         name = s;
 9     }
10
11 // some methods
12 }
13
14 class Child extends Parent
15 {
16    // null constructor
17    Child()
18    {
19        super("name unknown");
20    }
```

For Example 8-9, you can view the explanatory text by accessing the full, interactive graphic for this example on the book's accompanying CD-ROM. The title of the activity is "Correct Usage of **super** and Constructors" in e-Lab Activities.

The Child class in Example 8-8 will not compile. The compiler will try to insert a null constructor and an implicit call to **super**(). Note that the Parent class does not have a null constructor; this is because the Parent class has an explicitly defined constructor.

The Child class in Example 8-9 will compile. The null constructor of the Child class has been overridden to call the Parent constructor, using **super** and passing the argument required by the Parent constructor.

Constructors in subclasses can be overloaded. Example 8-10 illustrates the use of overloaded constructors that call the **super** constructor.

Example 8-10 *Overloaded Subclass Constructor, Using* **this** *and* **super**

```
1 /**
2 * Java Program Person.java
3 * @author Cisco Teacher
4 * @version 2002
```

continues

Example 8-10 *Overloaded Subclass Constructor, Using* **this** *and* **super**

```
 5 */
 6 public class Person
 7 {
 8    String name;
 9
10    // null constructor
11    Person (){}
12
13    // some methods
14 }
15
16 /**
17 * Java Program: Person.java
18 * @author Cisco Teacher
19 * @version 2002
20 */
```

For Example 8-10, you can view the explanatory text by accessing the full, interactive graphic for this example on the book's accompanying CD-ROM. The title of the activity is "Overloaded Subclass Constructor, Using **this** and **super**" in e-Lab Activities.

Extending Classes

As presented earlier in this chapter, in some cases, a superclass is not expected to be used to create objects. Instead, it is used to set boundaries for definitions of other subclasses. Also, the use of the keyword **final** in the superclass's class definition, its methods, and its attributes has special implications in inheritance.

This section consists of the following topics:

- Abstract classes
- Use of **final** in Inheritance

Abstract Classes

As the programmer moves up the inheritance hierarchy, classes become more general and probably more abstract. At some point, the ancestor class becomes so general that it is thought of as a guideline for other classes rather than as a definition for an object that can be used. When the class in a hierarchy serves as a framework or guideline for other classes, the class is defined as **abstract**. In this case, the class is not expected to be used to create objects that store data and do work. The class is used to set boundaries for definitions of other subclasses. It is viewed as a common framework for a set of related subclasses.

Consider an electronic-messaging system, such as fax, e-mail, voice mail, and postal mail. The common feature of all the messaging classes is having a message. An inheritance hierarchy is shown in Figure 8-18. A Message object must have information on how a message will be transported. Thus, the Message class serves as an abstract framework for all the other subclasses.

Figure 8-18 Messaging System Diagram

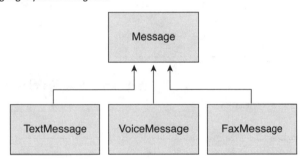

The ultimate goal of OOP design is to factor out the common operations and data to a higher level in the inheritance hierarchy. As the common operations are factored out, it might become apparent that the details of how the operations are implemented cannot be specified in the higher-level class. For example, in the message system, the display() method can be implemented in all the subclasses. How is this implemented for the Message class? Clearly, the method display() is an abstract concept. It is a framework to define inclusion of such a method in the subclass definitions. An abstract method is declared using the syntax shown in Example 8-11. An abstract method does not have any body of code. A class that has an abstract method must be declared **abstract**.

Example 8-11 *Abstract Syntax*

```
1 /*
2 An abstract method is declared using the following syntax:
3
4   abstract method-name (arguments);
```

continues

Example 8-11 *Abstract Syntax (Continued)*

```
5
6 An abstract method does not have any body of code.
7 A class that has an abstract method must be declared abstract.
8
9   abstract class ClassName {}
10
11    */
12
13    public abstract class AbstractDemo{
14
15        public abstract double calculateInterest(double balance);
16
17 }//end AbstractDemo
```

The sample code shown in Example 8-12 presents the Message class definition, including the abstract display method.

Example 8-12 *The* Message *Class Definition*

```
1 /**
2  * Java Program: Message.java
3  * @author Cisco Teacher
4  * @version 2002
5  */
6 abstract class Message
7 {
8     String sender;
9     String receiver;
10    String subject;
11
12    /**
13     * @param from The from tag of a message as a String
14     * @param to The to tag of a message as a String
15     * @param topic The topic of a message as a String
16     */
```

Example 8-12 *The* Message *Class Definition (Continued)*

```
17    public Message(String from, String to, String topic)
18    {
19        sender = from;
20        receiver = to;
```

The list that follows sets out the guidelines for the creation of abstract classes. In the case of the messaging system, the abstract class Message can store sender, receiver, and subject information as data values. These are concrete data. Programmers of many GUI classes use the abstract class design to move as many common methods and data into the superclass as possible.

- Any high-level class that includes an abstract method must be declared as **abstract**. The subclasses that extend from it must implement some code in this method.

- Abstract classes can have abstract methods and concrete methods and data. A class can be declared **abstract** even if it does not have a single abstract method.

- Abstract classes force any nonabstract subclasses to provide an implementation for the abstract methods. The abstract method serves as a placeholder.

- Although it is common to think of abstract classes as having only abstract methods, this is not true. In general, you should move as many common methods and data as possible into an abstract superclass.

Use of `final` in Inheritance

The keyword *final* was introduced in the definition of data values as constants. The keyword **final** always indicates that the object, method, or data cannot be changed. In inheritance models, when **final** is applied to the methods of a class, it prevents the method from being overridden by any subclass.

When applied to a class definition, **final** prevents a class from being used as a superclass; this class cannot be extended. Several classes in the Java language have been declared **final**. One of the most commonly used is the String class, shown in Figure 8-19. A programmer does not expect to have this class extended to some other unpredictable extension of the String class. If the classes must be used in a controlled manner, you must declare it to be **final**.

Figure 8-19 API Docs—`String` Class

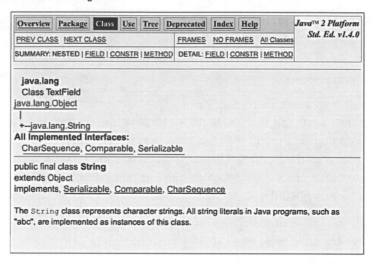

The wrapper classes examined in Chapter 6, "`System`, `String`, `StringBuffer`, `Math`, and Wrapper Classes," which wrap object methods around Java primitives, also are declared **final** and cannot be extended. (See Figure 8-20.)

Figure 8-20 API Docs—`Integer` Wrapper Class

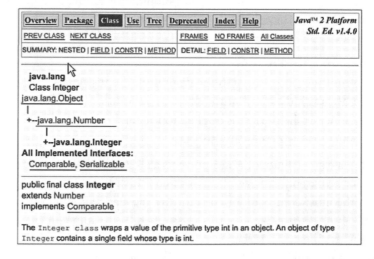

Interfaces

As stated earlier, in the Java language, a class can extend from only a single superclass. This constraint is addressed with the use of interface classes. This section consists of the following topics:

- The what and why of interfaces
- How to implement interfaces

What and Why of Interfaces

Since Java does not allow for multiple inheritance, a `Programmer` class cannot extend from both a `Person` class and an `Employee` class, even though a programmer is both a person and an employee. However, the Java language provides interface classes for implementing inheritance from two unrelated sources.

Interfaces are Java types much like classes are Java types defining attributes and methods. An interface is a Java type that defines only **public abstract** methods, and **static** constants. The purpose of an interface is to serve as a design document for external features of a class. All the methods in an interface must be **public**. The Java programmer can define all the methods that must exist in many of the classes in a `Personnel` application. Interfaces provide a mechanism for a subclass to define behaviors from sources other than the direct and indirect superclasses.

Consider the example of classes that describe things that fly. Flying includes actions such as taking off, landing, and flying. A class can be created that defines all of these actions in abstract. Things that fly can include a bird, an airplane, and a helicopter. However, each object takes off, lands, and flies differently. The bird flaps its wings, the airplane uses the thrust from an engine, and the helicopter utilizes a rotor blade. Each flying thing implements a different procedure for what seems to be common and similar actions. An interface, such as the `Flyer` interface, can define these common methods. Each of the classes then can implement this interface. Figure 8-21 shows the inheritance relationship between the `Flyer` interface and the classes.

In addition to implementing a `Flyer` interface, each of these objects is part of its own superclass/subclass hierarchy. Figure 8-22 illustrates how the classes relate to their inheritance hierarchies and to the interface implementations. In this example, one can agree that although an `Airplane` is not an `Animal` and a `Bird` is not a `Vehicle`, a `Bird` and an `Airplane` are both `Flyer` objects.

TIP

Interfaces are useful for capturing similarities among unrelated classes without artificially forcing a class relationship, declaring methods that one or more classes are expected to implement, and revealing an object's programming interface without revealing its class.

NOTE

A class must implement all the methods that are declared in the interface, or the class itself must be defined as abstract.

Figure 8-21 Things That Can Fly and Classes That Can Implement a `Flyer`

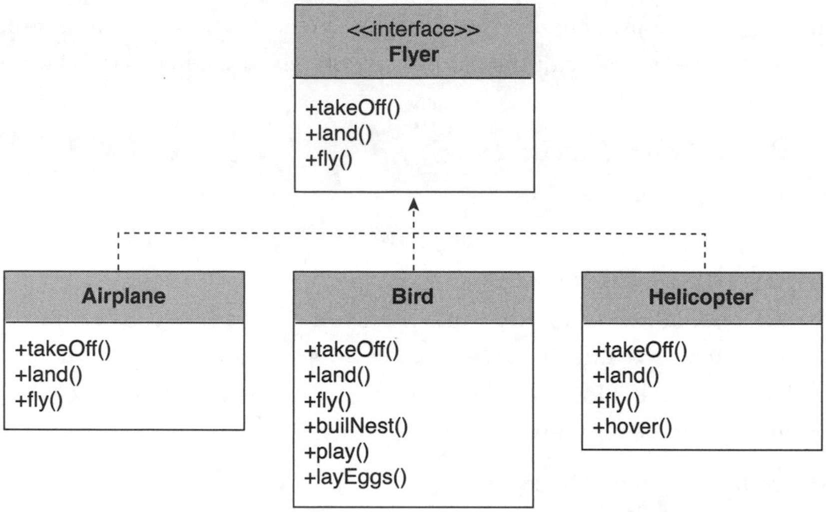

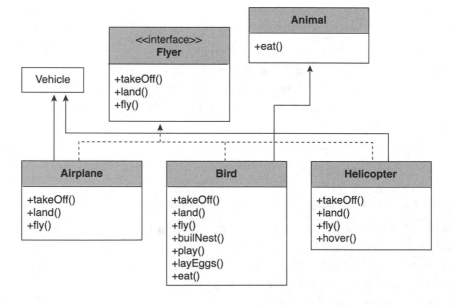

Figure 8-22 Interfaces and Inheritance

In the Animal inheritance hierarchy, some of the subclasses—specifically, the `Fish` and `Cat` classes—can be considered pets. These classes have common behaviors that relate to being a pet. Thus, a `Pet` interface class could be added to the class design to address these common methods. Figure 8-23 illustrates the inheritance relationship between this new `Pet` interface class and the other classes in the `Animal` inheritance hierarchy.

Figure 8-23 Interfaces and Inheritance—Adding a New Pet Interface Class

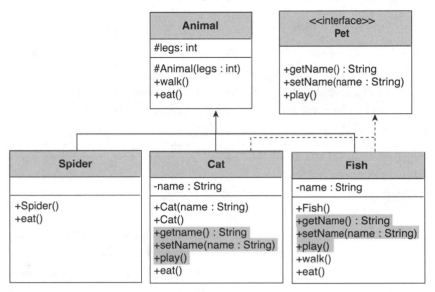

Implementing Interfaces

The syntax for implementing an interface includes the use of the keyword ***implements*** in the class definition statement. However, implementing interfaces is more than the declaration in the class definition statement. This declaration is viewed as a contract between the class that **implements** the interface and the interface itself. The compiler enforces this contract by ensuring that all methods declared in the interface also are implemented in the class. In some cases, this might include a null implementation, which is an implementation of a method definition without any procedural code. For example, because fish do not play, a null method implementation is used to satisfy this contract between the `Fish` class and the `Pet` interface class, as shown in Figure 8-24.

Figure 8-24 Syntax for Method and Use of the Null Method Definition

```
              Fish
  -name : String
  +Fish(name : String)
  +Fish()
  +getName() : String
  +setName(name : String)
  +play()
  +walk()
  +eat()
```

NOTE

Methods declared in an interface are always **public**. Even when the **public** access modifier is not used, the default access value for a method declaration in an interface is **public**. When implementing an interface method in a class, it is a common error to use the default access modifier similar to the interface declaration. This results in a compiler error because the default access modifier for a class method is package access, which the compiler identifies as a weaker access level than the required **public** access.

For Figure 8-24, you can view the text associated with the highlighted play() method by accessing the full, interactive graphic for this figure on the book's accompanying CD-ROM. The title of the activity is "Syntax for Method and Use of the Null Definition" in e-Lab Activities.

The list that follows summarizes the implementation of an interface:

- A **public** interface is a contract between the client code (that is, the code in the interface class) and the class that **implements** the interface.
- A Java interface is a formal declaration of a contract in which all methods contain no implementation. That is, all methods are abstract.
- Many unrelated classes can implement the same interface.
- A class can implement many interfaces.
- A class that **implements** an interface "is a" instance of the interface class. The "is a" relationship that exists between superclasses and subclasses also applies to classes that implement interfaces.
- All methods of an interface are declared **public** and are automatically abstract. The keyword **abstract** is not required to define the methods as such.
- An interface cannot include methods with qualifiers such as **native**, **static**, **synchronized**, or **final**. These keywords imply implementation code, and methods cannot be implemented in an interface.
- An interface also can declare constants: **public**, **static**, and **final**. If you omit the qualifiers, the Java compiler provides them for you.
- Interfaces can extend other interfaces.

Polymorphism, Dynamic Binding, and Virtual Method Invocation

Polymorphism literally means "many forms." Polymorphism is a mechanism in the Java language that adds enormous flexibility to programs. This section consists of the following topics:

- Polymorphism
- Virtual method invocation or dynamic method binding

Polymorphism

In general terms, polymorphism allows the same code to have different effects at runtime, depending on the context. Polymorphism takes advantage of inheritance and interface implementations. Polymorphism is best understood in the context of code.

In Example 8-13, polymorphism is employed in object creation. At runtime, the JVM will assign e1 an `Employee` object and will assign t1 and e2 `Teacher` objects.

Example 8-13 *Polymorphism in Object Creation*

```
// class definition
//


Employee e1 = new Employee();
Teacher t1 = new Teacher();
Employee e2 = new Teacher();
```

In this example, assume that the `Employee` class and the `Teacher` class both have a method named `getDetails()`. The code for each is different. The `Employee getDetails()` method returns a `String` containing the employee's identification and name. The `Teacher getDetails()` method returns an identification, name, classroom, and grade. If `e1.getDetails()` and `t1.getDetails()` are called, different behaviors are exhibited and different results are returned. It is not obvious what happens with e2. The object referenced by e2 is an example of polymorphism. Here, the variable e2 is of the type `Employee`. The actual object created and the resulting object reference assigned to e2 is a `Teacher` object. At runtime, `e2.getDetails()` will result in the invocation of the `Teacher` object's `getDetails()` method.

In Example 8-14, the `School` class has a method `display(Employee e)`. This method accepts objects of the type `Employee`. The call to this method in Line 37 passes the reference to an `Employee` object, and Line 38 passes a reference to a `Teacher` object. This works in this statement because a `Teacher` is an `Employee`. Line 39 passes the variable e2, which is of the type `Employee` but holds a reference to a `Teacher` object.

Example 8-14 *Polymorphism in Method Calls*

```
1 /**
2  * This class uses Employee and Teacher objects
3  * @author Cisco Teacher
4  * @version 2002
5  */
6 public class School
7 {
8     /**
```

continues

Example 8-14 *Polymorphism in Method Calls (Continued)*

```
 9     * @param e The Employee object
10     */
11     public String display(Employee e)
12     {
13         System.out.println(" The employee information is: ");
14         System.out.println(e.getDetails());
15     }
16
17     /**
18     * @param t The Teacher object
19     */
20     public String setClassroom(Teacher t)
```

The class named School has the method setClassroom(Teacher t). This method accepts references to objects of the type Teacher. Line 41 will work because t1 references a Teacher object. Line 47 will not work. Although a Teacher is an Employee, not all employees are Teachers. As a result, the Employee object is not always a Teacher object. Inheritance works in only one direction: from superclass to subclass. A method that receives an object of a type can be called with objects that are subclasses of that type, but not more general objects or superclasses of the type. Line 54 works because it holds a reference to a Teacher object, even though the variable e2 is of type Employee.

Virtual Method Invocation or Dynamic Method Binding

The technique of resolving the behaviors of an object at runtime is known as *dynamic method binding* or *virtual method-invocation*. This is a key feature of polymorphism. In the code for the School class, Line 29 creates a variable that is a reference of the type Employee. However, at runtime, the call to e2.getDetails() on Line 35 invokes the method of the Teacher class. This is because, on Line 29, the object that was created is a Teacher object.

Dynamic binding resolves which method to call at runtime when more than one class in an inheritance hierarchy has implemented the method. The JVM looks at the type of object for which the call is made, not the type of object reference in the calling statement. So, in Line 29, e2 is a reference of the type Employee in the calling statement, but the object actually being called is a Teacher object. Therefore, the Teacher version of the getDetails() method is used.

Dynamic binding also resolves the handling of the arguments being passed to a method. Again, the JVM looks at the type of object being passed by value as an argument, not the reference type of the variable being passed as an argument to the method. In Line 54, the method argument e2 is a reference variable of the type Employee. However, the object actually being referenced is a Teacher object, and the method setClassroom(), which requires a Teacher argument, is invoked successfully.

Case Study: JBANK Application

The JBANK application introduced in Chapter 1, "What Is Java?", provides students with an opportunity to apply the Java language concepts learned throughout this course. In the JBANK lab for Chapter 8, "Classes and Inheritance," students implement several subclasses, each inheriting from the Account class, yet implemented differently. When the banking application needs to process account information, regardless of the type of account, methods can be defined that allow for polymorphic arguments. This feature (polymorphism) is implemented in this lab. Several future labs (in Chapter 10, "Creating GUIs Using AWT") also implement polymorphic behavior.

The JBANK Application

The banking application provides many opportunities for implementing an inheritance model, with the more common behaviors abstracted into a superclass.

Students begin by redesigning the Account class to become the superclass for all types of accounts that are held by Customers. All accounts have an account number, a balance, a withdrawal method, and a deposit method. However, the different types of checking and savings accounts provide different services for withdrawing money and for calculating interest on the balance of the account.

The Account class serves as an abstract class. From this class, two other classes are derived: a concrete Savings account class and an abstract Checking account class. The bank provides two types of savings accounts for the customer to choose from: a regular savings account (Savings class) and a premium savings account (Investment class). Because a customer could have a Savings account or an Investment account, the Investment account is a subclass of Savings, and both are designed as concrete classes.

The bank rules are that a customer can have only one of two types of checking accounts: a checking account with overdraft protection or an account with a line of credit. The Checking class is thus designed as an abstract class, from which subclasses are created for the overdraft protection and line of credit accounts (LineofCredit class and OverDraftProtection class).

In each of the subclasses of the `Account` class, either the `deposit` or the `withdrawal` method is overridden to implement the specific business rules for each type of account.

Figures 8-25 and 8-26 display what the JBANK application might look like at the end of the course.

Figure 8-25 JBANK Application

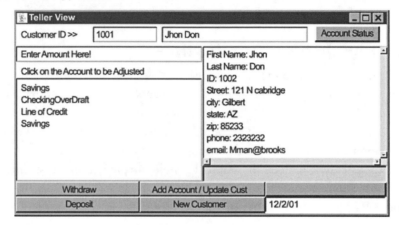

Figure 8-26 JBANK Application

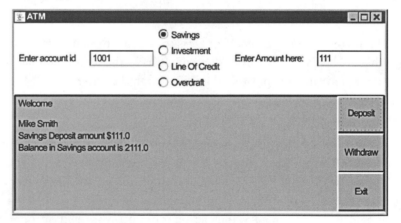

Summary

This chapter introduced inheritance, the creation of general classes from which other classes derive attributes and behaviors. The class at the top of a hierarchy of classes is known as the superclass. Classes that derive from this class are known as subclasses or child classes.

Access modifiers control which superclass attributes and methods are inherited by the subclass. A subclass cannot inherit methods or data that are **private**. All other nonprivate data and methods can be inherited, excluding default access when the superclass is in a different package than the subclass. Additionally, a subclass does not inherit the superclass constructors. A subclass can override the methods of the superclass.

Inheritance defines "is a" relationships among classes and objects. Every object represents this "is a" relationship to its class. All objects inherit from the class that defines them.

When designing classes, common fields and behaviors lead to generalizations about the classes. Generalizations of classes into a superclass can be either concrete or abstract, where the term *abstract* is applied to classes from which no objects are expected to be created. Abstract classes contain abstract methods that must be implemented in subclasses.

The Java language provides specific keywords to support inheritance, as well as a robust set of API classes that can be used as superclasses. Keywords introduced in this chapter include **extends**, **implements**, **abstract**, **protected**, and **super**.

The class Object is the superclass from which all objects inherit data and methods. In general, class design should include overriding of the equals(), hashCode(), and toString() methods.

In inheritance models, when **final** is applied to the methods of a class, it prevents the method from being overridden by any subclass. When applied to a class definition, **final** prevents a class from being used as a superclass. The String class is one of the most commonly used classes that have been declared **final**.

Although Java does not allow for multiple inheritance, the Java language provides interface classes for implementing inheritance from two unrelated sources. Interface classes contain only constants and abstract methods.

This chapter also introduced polymorphism, which allows the same code to have different effects at runtime, depending on the context. The technique of resolving the behaviors of an object at runtime is known as dynamic method binding or virtual method invocation.

Syntax Summary

Parent and child classes:

```
public class Parent
{
    private int x;
    public int y;
```

```
        /**
        * @param aNum A random number as an int
        */
        Parent(int aNum)
        {
            x = aNum * (int) Math.random();
        }

        /**
        * @return The new number as an int
        */
        public int getX()
        {
            return x;
        }
}

public class Child extends Parent
{
    int parentx;
    Child(int theNum)
    {
        super(theNum);
    }
}
```

toString() method overridden:

```
// overridden toString method
public String toString()
{
    return ("Student name is: " + studentName + " ID is: "
      + studentID + " Grade is: " + grade);
}
```

equals() method overridden:

```
// overridden equals method
public boolean equals(Student s)
{
    boolean test = false;
    if(s.studentName == studentName
       && s.studentID == studentID
       && s.grade == grade)
    {
        test = true;
    }
    return test;
}
```

Using **this** and **super** in inheritance:

```
public class SportsCoupe extends BaseModelAuto
{
    protected String accessories = "Moon roof\n";
```

```
//constructor

/**
 * @return The car's accessories as a String
 */
public String getAccessories() //overridden method
{
    return super.getAccessories() + accessories;
}

/**
 * @param options The car's options as a String
 * @return The car's accessories as a String
 */
public String getAccessories(String options) //overloaded method
{
    return this.getAccessories() + options;
}

//additional methods

public static void main(String[] args)
{
    SportsCoupe myCar = new SportsCoupe();
    System.out.println("\nList of options includes:
        \n" + myCar.getAccessories("Chromeplated Wheels"));
}
} // end of SportsCoupe class
```

Abstract syntax:

An abstract method is declared using the following syntax:

```
abstract  method-name (arguments);
```

An abstract method does not have any body of code.

A class that has an abstract method must be declared abstract using the following syntax:

```
abstract class ClassName { }
```

Example:

```
public abstract class AbstractDemo
{
    public abstract double calculateInterest(double balance);
}//end AbstractDemo
```

Polymorphism:

```
Employee e1 = new Employee();
Teacher t1 = new Teacher();
Employee e2 = new Teacher();
```

To resolve which method to call at run time when more than one class in an inheritance hierarchy has implemented the method: the JVM looks at the type of object for which the call is made, not the type of object reference in the calling statement.

To resolve the handling of the arguments being passed to a method: the JVM looks at the type of object being passed by value as an argument, not the reference type of the variable being passed as an argument to the method.

Key Terms

abstract   A keyword used in a class definition to specify that a class is not to be instantiated, but rather inherited by other classes. An abstract class can have abstract methods that are not implemented in the abstract class, but in subclasses.

abstraction   When designing classes, common fields, and behaviors lead to generalizations about the classes. These generalizations can be implemented through the design of parent classes that also are known as superclasses. Superclasses then can be designed to describe required and optional fields and behaviors. A superclass can be an abstract representation of common behaviors and data.

derived methods   Methods inherited from the parent class.

dynamic binding or virtual method invocation   A technique of resolving the behaviors of an object at runtime. Also resolves the handling of the arguments being passed to a method.

extends   A keyword used to signify that one class is a subclass of a parent class.

final   A keyword used to define an entity once. In inheritance models, when `final` is applied to the methods of a class, it prevents the method from being overridden by any subclass. When applied to a class definition, `final` prevents a class from being used as a superclass.

implements   The keyword optionally included in the class declaration to specify any interfaces that are implemented by the current class.

inheritance   The process of deriving new class definitions from an existing class definition. Defines "is a" relationships among classes and objects.

inheritance hierarchies   Shows the relationship between classes (superclasses and subclasses).

interfaces   The Java language provides interface classes for implementing inheritance from two unrelated sources. Interface classes contain only constants and abstract methods.

multiple inheritance   The ability to inherit from more than one class. In the Java language, a capability provided through the use of interfaces.

null method definition   An implementation of a method definition without any procedural code.

Object class   The superclass from which all objects inherit data and methods. In general, class design should include overriding of the `equals()`, `hashCode()`, and `toString()` methods:

> *equals() method*   Compares its reference value with that of another object. This is a comparison of addresses, not data.

> *hashCode() method*   Returns a hash code value in the form of an **int** for the object.

> *toString() method*   Converts the reference value of an object to a `String`.

overriding   The capability of a programmer to redefine or customize the definition of a parent-class method.

polymorphism   A mechanism in Java that allows the same code to have different effects at runtime, depending on the context.

subclass or *child class*   A class that is derived from a parent class and that shares common attributes and behaviors with the parent class.

protected   A keyword used in a method or variable declaration. It signifies that the method or variable can be accessed only by elements residing in its class, subclasses, or classes in the same package.

super   A keyword used within a subclass to refer to data and methods from the parent class.

superclass   A class from which a particular class is derived, perhaps with one or more classes in between. A superclass can be either a concrete or an abstract class.

this   A keyword used to represent an instance of the class in which it appears. The **this** variable can be used to access class variables and methods.

Check Your Understanding

1. The process of creating new classes from existing classes is called

    A. Polymorphism

    B. Inheritance

    C. Abstraction

    D. Derivation

2. What kind of relationship does the inheritance model implement?

   A. "is a" relationship

   B. "has a" relationship

   C. "abstract" relationship

   D. "direct" relationship

3. What type of class is not instantiated directly?

   A. Inherited class

   B. Concrete class

   C. Abstract class

   D. Polymorphic class

4. Which methods from the superclass must a subclass override if the subclass is not abstract?

   A. Constructor methods

   B. Custom methods

   C. Static methods

   D. Abstract methods

5. Which keyword is used in the class header to signify that one class inherits from another class?

   A. `super`

   B. `extends`

   C. `inherits`

   D. `is`

6. Which keyword is used to access data and methods from the parent class?

   A. `this`

   B. `parent`

   C. `extends`

   D. `super`

7. Which class is at the top of the Java inheritance hierarchy?

    A. `Class`

    B. `Object`

    C. `Component`

    D. `Collection`

8. Which data and methods are inherited from the parent class?

    A. All `private` data and methods only

    B. All `public` data and methods only

    C. All nonprivate data and methods only

    D. All data and methods are inherited

9. When a method is given new functionality in a subclass, the method is said to be

    A. Inherited

    B. Overloaded

    C. Overridden

    D. Abstract

10. What is true about two methods that are overloaded?

    A. They must have the same signature.

    B. They must have different signatures.

    C. They must be declared `abstract`.

    D. They must be declared `public`.

11. What is true about two methods that are overridden?

    A. They must have the same signature.

    B. They must have different signatures.

    C. They must be declared `abstract`.

    D. They must be declared `public`.

12. If a parent class and subclass each have a method `getName()`, how is the parent method accessed from the subclass?

    A. `this.getName();`

    B. `getName();`

    C. `super.getName();`

    D. `getName.super();`

13. Which is the correct syntax for declaring an abstract method?

   A. `public final double getDouble(){}`

   B. `public abstract double getDouble(){}`

   C. `public double getDouble();`

   D. `public abstract double getDouble();`

14. How can a programmer ensure that a method is not overridden in a subclass?

   A. Use **abstract** in the method header.

   B. Use **public** in the method header.

   C. Use **final** in the method header.

   D. Use **protected** in the method header.

15. Which of the following is a false statement about interfaces?

   A. Interfaces are Java types defining attributes and methods.

   B. Interfaces are used to inherit functionality from multiple unrelated sources.

   C. Interfaces are implemented using the keyword **implements.**

   D. All methods in an interface must be **private**.

16. When a class **implements** an interface

   A. Only the constructor of the interface must be implemented in the class.

   B. Only the **private** methods of the interface must be implemented in the class.

   C. All of the methods of the interface must be implemented in the class.

   D. The class must be an abstract class to implement an interface.

17. When no access modifier is specified for a method in an interface, what is the implied level of access?

   A. `private`

   B. default

   C. `protected`

   D. `public`

18. Does an interface have to contain methods?

    A. Yes, an interface must have a constructor.

    B. Yes, an interface must have an abstract method.

    C. No, an interface must have at least one data member.

    D. No, an interface class body can be entirely blank.

19. Is the following Java statement syntactically correct?

    ExampleClass e1 = new DemoClass();

    A. Yes, if `ExampleClass` is a subclass of `DemoClass`.

    B. Yes, if `DemoClass` is a subclass of `ExampleClass`.

    C. Yes, if `DemoClass` **implements** `ExampleClass` as an interface.

    D. No, the class name must be the same on each side of the assignment operator.

20. Resolving method behavior at runtime is known as

    A. Dynamic resolution

    B. Polymorphic resolution

    C. Dynamic binding

    D. Polymorphic binding

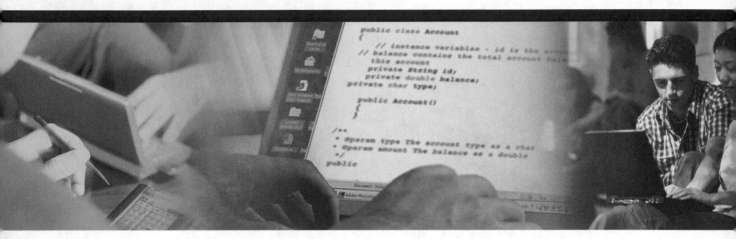

Upon completion of this chapter, you will be able to

- Understand Java packages
- Understand packaging and names in programs
- Access packages
- Use AWT
- Apply the Java language concepts that you have learned to the JBANK case study

Chapter 9

Understanding Packages

This chapter focuses on organizing classes into packages. *Packages* are entities that help manage classes as a collection. The Java language uses packages to hold collections of classes that share a common function.

Classes in packages can inherit from other classes in the same package or other classes in other packages. The modifier **protected** influences the inheritance of classes from other packages.

Packages can be stored as one archive file using the jar utility. By default, the jar utility compresses the packages, but this is optional. This jar file is easily accessed by the Java platform.

For the classes in files to be loaded properly, the classes must include a **package** statement in their definition and an **import** statement for classes not in their package. The operating system variable CLASSPATH must be set properly to access the JDK programs and classes that form the Java platform API.

GUIs provide a context for exploring the Java platform packages, class hierarchies, design principles of Model View Controller, and event-driven programming.

Java Packages

Java classes can be stored in collections called packages. To access classes stored in packages, they must be imported into the program using a **package** statement. The compiler and interpreter then search the specified packages when another class is referenced.

This section consists of the following topics:

- What a collection of classes is
- How class loading works
- How to locate explicit package declarations

A Collection of Classes

A package is a collection of classes. It groups classes together.

Java packaging manages classes in a group. For the classes in files to be loaded properly, the classes must include a **package** statement in their definition and an **import** statement for classes not in their package.

Two main reasons exist for creating Java packages. The primary reason is that the Java interpreter locates and loads the classes for the program using namespaces. Namespaces are identifiers of a class and its methods. For example, assume that two classes, Bank and CreditCard, are being used. If both include a class method named getMoney(), the Java interpreter associates the method with the separate namespaces. In this case, each unique getMoney() method is associated with the name of the class in which it is defined.

It is important that students have control over the namespaces in Java. Perhaps they are downloading Java programs from the Internet that use classes that have the same name as classes on their machine. Or they could be planning to create libraries or programs that are friendly or that are used by other classes. In any case, the students must prevent using identical names.

For instance, imagine that a class named Printer is created, but another class with the name Printer already exists in the Java language API. How can the conflicts that the Printer class has with the API Printer class be prevented? Is it possible for two or more unrelated classes to have the same class and method names? It is if the class files are stored in different directories. Most operating systems do not permit two files to have the same name in the same directory. The Printer class can be in a separate directory from the API classes. To use both classes, however, each class must be identified with some unique name. To enable both classes to be loaded in different namespaces and to avoid conflicts in method calls, the Java language provides the package construct.

A second reason to consider organizing classes into packages is to manage the program as a collection of classes. Recall the concept of a working Java program. In the JBANK banking application, the working program (launched by the student) is the Teller program. This program uses a number of classes, such as Customer, Bank, Account, String, and Date. A school application uses a number of classes, such as Teacher and Student.

These working programs can be viewed as a collection of classes. This ensures that classes that are used by one another are identified as being colocated (near each other). The directory structures for operating systems provide this capability. Organizing related classes in directories and subdirectories, as shown in Figure 9-1, is, therefore, the first step. However, this does not ensure that the interpreter knows where to look for the classes.

Figure 9-1 Class, Package, and Directory Structure

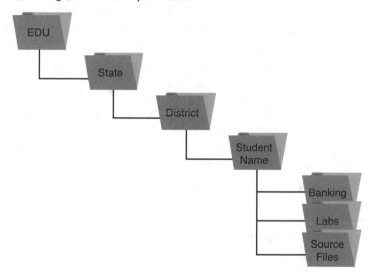

The keyword **package** in the Java language allows these collections of classes to be identified as belonging with each other. The keyword **import** ensures that the interpreter knows where the classes that are referenced are located. A **package** statement using the keyword **package** defines an *explicit package declaration*; it is used to declare the unique namespaces for the classes.

Packaging classes provides a way of enforcing scope above the class level. Unless classes from a package are imported using the **import** statement, the class does not have access to them.

Class Loading and How it Works

The classes created so far in the labs have been placed in a specific *directory*. The lab instructions specified a directory to work in. This directory is known as the *default directory*. The source files created are stored in this directory, and the class files created are stored in the same directory. Students work in the default package.

When a source code file is created, it is commonly called a *compilation unit*. The file-name for each source code file or compilation unit must end with .java. Inside this compilation unit, there can only be one **public** access class definition. There can be one or more nonpublic class definitions. When you compile the source file, the result is a class file (a file ending in .class) for each class defined in the source file. The Java compiler and interpreter are responsible for finding, loading, and interpreting these files.

To understand the concept of class locations, you must understand some important related concepts of PATH and CLASSPATH. All operating systems use variables to store names of directories to search when a user is trying to load or launch programs. For the Java run-time environment, the two variables that affect access to class files and JDK programs are the PATH variable and the CLASSPATH variable.

The term *path* is used to identify the specific list of directories that a program will search for the location of a file. For example, on the Windows operating system, the Java compiler and the Java interpreter are the program files javac.exe and java.exe. These two files generally are stored in a directory structure identified by c:\jdk#.#.#\bin\javac.exe and c:\jdk#.#.#\bin\java.exe. Figure 9-2 shows a view of the directory hierarchy for the files java.exe and javac.exe.

Figure 9-2 Location of bin Directory

On certain platforms, the *PATH variable* is an operating system variable that contains the paths to the directories where many executable files are located. The operating system on a machine uses these paths to locate executable files that need to run. For example, to ensure that the operating system can locate the javac.exe and java.exe files, the name of the directory where these files can be found, c:\jdk#.#.#\bin, needs to be added to the PATH variable. Figure 9-3 shows the use of a command console window for locating information on the PATH variable. Information about this variable can also be obtained in the properties window of computers running Windows.

Figure 9-3 DOS Window and PATH Command

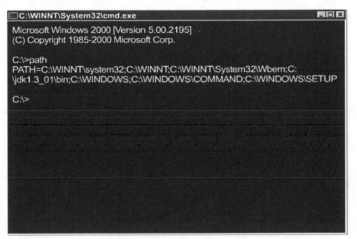

The Java compiler and the interpreter use the variable CLASSPATH to locate classes and packages. The *CLASSPATH variable* can contain paths to many directories that contain packages. The JDK directory structure contains several subdirectories that automatically are used to search for classes. These directories are known as the standard directories. These directories do not need to be defined in the CLASSPATH variable. It is possible, although not recommended, to store class files in one of these directories. Class files should be managed in a directory structure created by the programmer. Figure 9-4 identifies the standard directories and the location of *standard classes*, the core API classes.

Because separate directories will almost always be created to store the created class files, paths to these directories must be included in the CLASSPATH variable. The line CLASSPATH=d\javacourse\lab assigns CLASSPATH at the operating system level.

How does the interpreter find, load, and interpret classes needed by a program? The flowchart in Figure 9-5 shows this process.

Figure 9-4 Location of Standard Directories

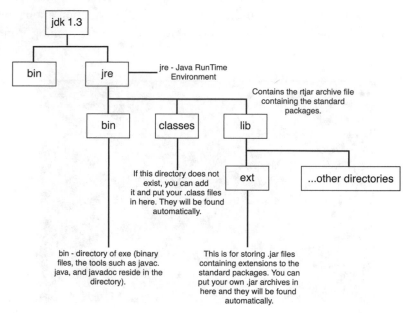

When *class loading* occurs, two locations searched are the default location and the explicitly identified package locations. The interpreter performs the following procedure:

1. Looks for files in the standard directories.

2. Looks for all the files in the *current working directory*. In most operating systems, the (.) symbol references the current working directory.

3. Uses the directory paths defined in the CLASSPATH variable to look for files. A programmer must explicitly specify directory paths in the CLASSPATH variable if they are to be searched.

4. Looks for files in the packages declared in the **package** statement of the class. Searches for these packages are only in the directories identified in the CLASS-PATH variable.

Locating Standard Classes

The classes that form the java.lang package are automatically accessed and do not need specific identification of the location of the java.lang package. The System, String, and StringBuffer classes are all part of the java.lang package.

Figure 9-5 Class with Reference to Other Classes

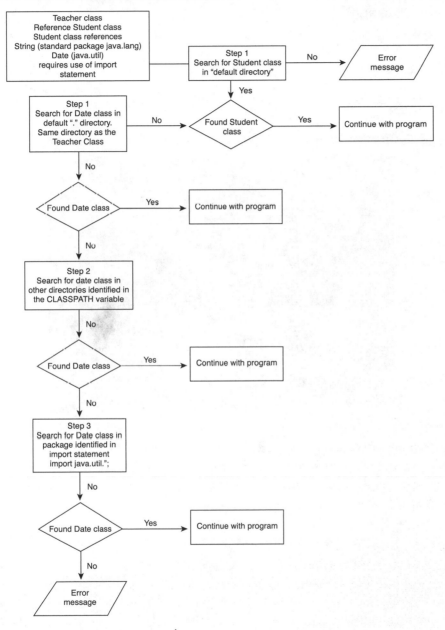

Locating User-Defined Classes in the Current Directory (Default Package)

Assume that the source file Teacher.java, shown in Figure 9-6, does not contain any references to packages. This class uses the Student class. The Teacher class is in the default package. The current directory where the class is located is considered the default package. The Teacher.Java file is the compilation unit. The Teacher class accesses the Student class. The compiler searches first for all the files in the default package.

Figure 9-6 Compilation Unit Teacher.java

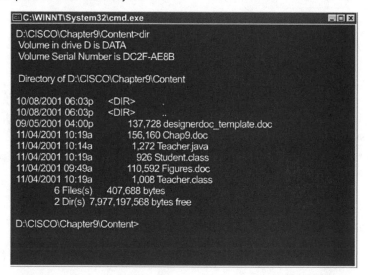

If the Student class file is not located in the same directory as the Teacher class file, an error message is generated. Figure 9-7 shows that the Student class file is missing from the current directory. When this Teacher class is compiled, the error message in Figure 9-8 will be generated.

Locating Explicit Package Declarations

If the classes needed for a program are located in a specific directory and have been identified as part of a package, the location of these classes can be identified using two forms. The first and simplest is the use of the **import** statement. The Student class in Example 9-1 defines two **import** statements. The second way to locate these classes is to identify the package name in each use of the classes in the program. The Student class references the Date class. The code in Example 9-2 shows the access to the Date class. The Date class is located in the package java.util. These packages of classes are generally located in the jdk#.#/jre/lib directories.

Figure 9-7 Student File Not in Default Package

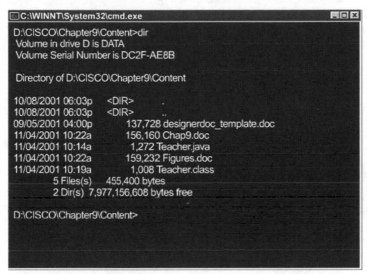

Figure 9-8 Error Message, Unable to Locate the `Student.class` File

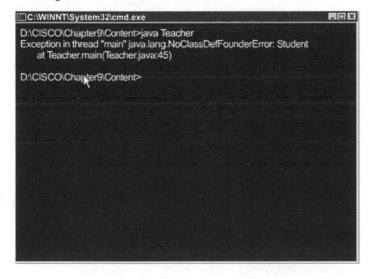

Example 9-1 *Using the* **import** *Statement to Access Classes in a Package*

```
1 /**
2  * Student Class establishes the student id, name and grade
3  * @author Cisco Teacher
4  * @version 2002
5  */
6 import java.util.*;
7 import java.text.*;
8
9 public class Student
10 {
11     // data to be shared by all Student objects
12     static int numOfTests;
13     static Date[ ] testDate;
14     static String[ ] testName;
15     static int [ ] maxPoints;
16
17     //more statements....
18 }//end Student class
```

Example 9-2 *Using Explicit Reference to Access Classes in a Package*

```
1 /**
2  * Student Class establishes the student id, name and grade
3  * @author Cisco Teacher
4  * @version 2002
5  */
6
7 public class Student
8 {
9     // data to be shared by all Student objects
10     static int numOfTests;
11     static java.util.Date[ ] testDate;
12     static String[ ] testName;
13     static int [ ] maxPoints;
14
15     //more statements....
16 }//end Student class
```

For Example 9-2, you can view the highlighted code by accessing the full, interactive graphic for this example on the book's accompanying CD-ROM. The title of the activity is "Using Explicit Reference to Access Classes in a Package" in the e-Lab Activities.

Consider an example in which the Student and the Console classes are located in the same directory. However, the classpath defined for this machine does not include a reference to the default directory—that is, the current directory—indicated by the period (.). Note that the classpath directories on the top half of the screen do not include the default directory. Therefore, the call to the compiler results in the error message shown in Figure 9-9.

NOTE

The CLASSPATH variable can be overridden by using the -classpath option when using the compiler and using the -cp option or the –classpath option when using the interpreter.

Figure 9-9 Compile Fails, Cannot Access the Console File

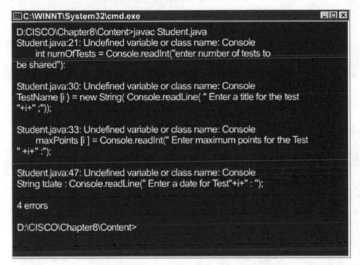

```
C:\WINNT\System32\cmd.exe

D:CISCO\Chapter8\Content>javac Student.java
Student.java:21: Undefined variable or class name: Console
        int numOfTests = Console.readInt("enter number of tests to
be shared"):

Student.java:30: Undefined variable or class name: Console
TestName [i } = new String( Console.readLine( " Enter a title for the test
"+i+" ;"));

Student.java:33: Undefined variable or class name: Console
        maxPoints [i ] = Console.readInt(" Enter maximum points for the Test
" +i+" :");

Student.java:47: Undefined variable or class name: Console
String tdate : Console.readLine(" Enter a date for Test"+i+" : ");

4 errors

D:\CISCO\Chapter8\Content>
```

The call to the compiler using the -classpath option provides a class path reference to the default directory. Note the use of the period (.) after -classpath in Figure 9-10; this overrides the CLASSPATH variable for this particular compilation of the class.

The -cp option also can be used to declare a specific CLASSPATH for the interpreter to use. In the example shown in Figure 9-11, the Console class is in the same directory as the Student and Teacher classes (indicated by the period after -cp). To use the Teacher program, the CLASSPATH needs to be set to the current directory.

Figure 9-10 Compile with the `-classpath` Option

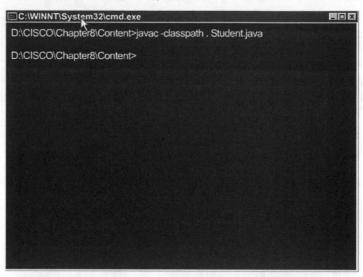

Figure 9-11 Running the Class with the `-cp` Option

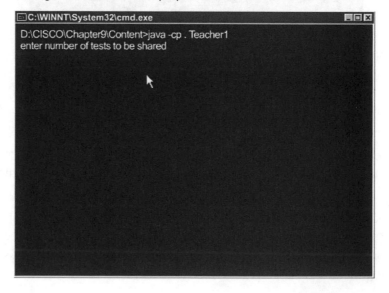

Packages and Names in Programs

Packaging classes is an efficient way to manage class files. In addition, a programmer can enforce stricter access to a class by using packages. The Java keyword **package** is used to create class packages.

This section consists of the following topics:

- Three effects of packages on object-oriented design
- How to package classes

Three Effects of Packages on Object-Oriented Design

Packages have three effects on object-oriented design:

1. Enable definition of stricter access control. The use of the keyword **protected** for inner class or method access ensures that only other subclasses in the inheritance hierarchy have access to the class, method, or attribute. When no access modifiers are used, the class, method, or attribute is considered to have default access. Classes in the same package, therefore, can access this class.

2. Make it easier to reuse common names. For example, a class named `Printer` might exist in the API classes, in the `Bank` package, and in the `Teacher` package. The common name `Printer` is reused to define specific printing features available in each collection, or package, of classes.

3. Collect classes so that they can be shared more easily between applications. For example, the `Date` class is packaged with other utility classes. The `Date` class serves a utility function for many programs in handling data of type date. This class can be shared and used by many other classes. This class is used in the `Student` class and in the `Customer` and `Bank` classes. The bank application is unrelated to the teacher application, yet both can share and use the classes in the utility package.

How are unique names selected for the packages? This is relatively simple if all the classes that will ever be worked with are created by one person. This is quite rare. Most frequently, programs will be accessed over the Internet, and these programs might use class and package names that conflict with the ones already selected. If a programmer were asked to deliver an application (programs) to another machine, there could also be conflict in directory or package names. To avoid this, it might be best to use a *unique domain* name.

Figure 9-12 shows one way to create packages in directories' structures. In this example, the package identifier is `edu.state.district.studentname.banking`. The collection of classes being packaged is actually in the Banking directory. To keep this package uniquely different from any other `Banking` package, the parent directory names are included as part of the package name.

Figure 9-12 Naming Packages in Unique Domain Name Directories

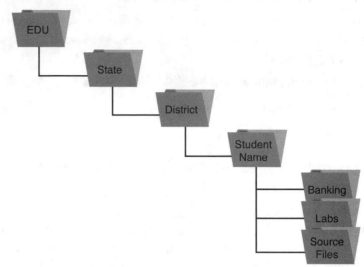

Packaging Classes

The following steps outline the process of packaging classes:

Step 1   To package classes and identify each class as a member of the package, include the statement **package** <packagename> as the very first statement of the source file. As shown in Example 9-3, this statement causes the compiler to insert the package reference in the class bytecode. The code in Example 9-4 will cause an error because the **package** statement is not the first statement in the class.

Example 9-3 *Source File with* **package** *Statement (Correct)*

```
 1 /*   Student Class establishes the student id, name and grade
 2  *   @author Cisco Teacher
 3  */
 4         package edu.state.district.studentname.banking;
 5         import java.util.*;
 6
 7         public class Customer
 8         {
 9 //attributes
10
```

Example 9-3 *Source File with* **package** *Statement (Correct) (Continued)*

```
11 // constructors
12
13 // methodsetc
```

For Example 9-3, you can view the explanatory text by accessing the full, interactive graphic for this example on the book's accompanying CD-ROM. The title of the activity is "Source File with Package Statement (Correct)" in the e-Lab Activities.

Example 9-4 *Source File with* **package** *Statement (Incorrect)*

```
1 /*  Student Class establishes the student id, name and grade
2  *  @author Cisco Teacher
3  */
4       import java.util.*;
5       package edu.state.district.studentname.banking;
6
7       public class Customer
8       {
9 //attributes
10
11 // constructors
12
13 // methodsetc
```

For Example 9-4, you can view the explanatory text by accessing the full, interactive graphic for this example on the book's accompanying CD-ROM. The title of the activity is "Source File with Package Statement (Incorrect)" in the e-Lab Activities.

Step 2   Create the directories in which the classes will be saved. The example in Figure 9-13 identifies the directory for the Banking package.

Figure 9-13 Identify the Directory for the Banking Package

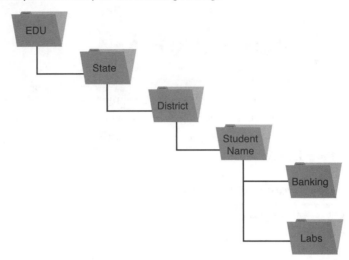

Step 3   Place the source code in a separate directory.

Step 4   By using the -d option with the javac command, you can create class files and place them in the package directory. The path to the package directory is defined by the argument after the -d option, which stands for "destination." This should not include the directories reference in the **package** statement of code.

Step 5   Set the CLASSPATH variable to point to the root of the package identifier.

One suggested organization of classes is shown in Figure 9-14.

Figure 9-14 Location of Source Files Example

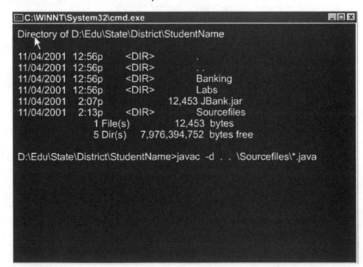

All the files in a package also can be combined into a single file using the *jar* utility. This is a utility program that packs all the class files in the directory and the directories into one file. This file is known as an archive file. Jar is an acronym for Java Archive. "Jar-ing" the files can tremendously improve the management and delivery of the classes. The jar utility was developed for applets. Applets that contain several code and graphics files are compressed for quicker download. The Java compiler and interpreter can access classes archived in a jar file directly. The syntax for the **jar** command is as follows:

```
jar [options] [manifest] destination input-files
```

Table 9-1 identifies options for the **jar** command.

Table 9-1 Options for the **jar** Command

Options for jar Command	
c	Creates a new or empty jar file.
t	Types a list of contents of an existing jar file.
x	Extracts files from an existing jar file.
f	Gives the jar filename named in the jar file command.
m	Includes manifest information.
0	Does not compress the files. (If you leave this out, files are compressed.)
M	Does not create a manifest file.
v	Sets verbose status.

The following steps outline the process of creating a jar file using the options of the jar utility.

Step 1   Set the current working directory. The files in the Banking directory will form the `Banking` package.

Step 2   Use the **jar** command, as shown in Figure 9-15.

Figure 9-15 Creating a jar File of the Banking Directory

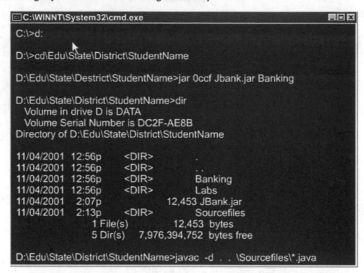

The **jar** command in Figure 9-16 is used to list the contents of the jar file.

Figure 9-16 Listing Contents of a jar File

The following is a guide for creating jar files:

Step 1 First, create all the class files in the particular package structure that has been chosen (follow the steps described previously).

Step 2 Use the `jar` utility to jar all the files in the package. Be sure to work in the directory above the package directory.

Step 3 Verify the contents of the jar file.

Step 4 Adjust the CLASSPATH to point to the directory in which the jar file is placed.

Step 5 Use `import` statements that point to the classes in the jar file.

NOTE

Do You Know: Use the **jar** command to view the contents of the `rt.jar` file, located in the `jdk#.#.#/jre/lib` directory. You should be able to identify the class files of the Java 2 Platform Packages.

Accessing Packages

To access the classes stored in packages, you must include an **import** statement within the class definition that references the classes. Generally, **import** statements are written after any **package** statements but before the class header. The wildcard (*) symbol can be used to access all classes within a package.

Accessing Packages

Two important steps are involved in accessing packages. The first is to ensure that the CLASSPATH variable is assigned the proper directory path to the location of the package. The second is to include the **import** statement in the class definition. As shown in Example 9-5 and Example 9-6, the **import** statement must be after any **package** statement in the class.

Example 9-5 *Source File with* **package** *Statement (Correct)*

```
1 /*  Student Class establishes the student id, name and grade
2  *   @author Cisco Teacher
3  */
4        package edu.state.district.studentname.banking;
5        import java.util.*;
6
7        public class Customer
8        {
9 //attributes
10
11 // constructors
12
13 // methodsetc
```

For Example 9-5, you can view the explanatory text by accessing the full, interactive graphic for this example on the book's accompanying CD-ROM. The title of the activity is "Source File with **package** Statement (Correct)" in the e-Lab Activities.

import statements must provide the names of the packages. They do not identify directories or locations of files.

Example 9-6 *Source File with **package** Statement (Incorrect)*

```
 1 /*  Student Class establishes the student id, name and grade
 2  *  @author Cisco Teacher
 3  */
 4      import java.util.*;
 5      package edu.state.district.studentname.banking;
 6
 7      public class Customer
 8      {
 9 //attributes
10
11 // constructors
12
13 // methodsetc
```

For Example 9-6, you can view the explanatory text by accessing the full, interactive graphic for this example on the book's accompanying CD-ROM. The title of the activity is "Source File with **package** Statement (Incorrect)" in the e-Lab Activities.

When an **import** statement is included in the class definition, the compiler and the interpreter search the directories and jar files on the CLASSPATH for the classes that belong to the imported packages as one of the search steps.

Case Study: Banking Application, Building Packages

Now that you have explored many features of packages, the concept can be applied to the JBANK application. The API specification documents all of the classes included in the Java language. This is a valuable resource for understanding how classes and packages are related.

This section consists of the following topics:

- Exploring the API packages
- Creating a banking package

Exploring the API Packages

On most computers, the API documentation is located in the directory `c:\jdk#.#.#\docs\api`. When the index.html page in this directory is loaded in a web browser, the student can navigate links to all of the classes and packages in the Java language.

Location of the Classes

Many *API packages* are used throughout this class and in most of the programs that are created. Understanding the package structures and the classes in the packages will help students quickly locate the classes they need.

Classes are packaged based on their commonality of use. Inheritance does not affect the capability of package classes with different inheritances in the same package.

In Table 9-2 and Table 9-3, selecting a specific package narrows the listing of the classes to those in the package.

Table 9-2 API Docs—Java 2 Platform Packages

Java.applet	Provides the classes necessary to create an applet and the classes an applet uses to communicate with its applet context.
Java.awt	Contain all of the classes for creating user interfaces and for painting graphics and images.
Java.awt.color	Provides classes for color spaces.
Java.awt.datatransfer	Provides interfaces and classes for transferring data between and within applications.
Java.awt.dnd	Drag and Drop is a direct manipulation gesture found in many Graphical User Interface systems that provides a mechanism to transfer information between two entities logically associated with presentation elements in the GUI.
Java.awt.event	Provides interfaces and classes for dealing with different types of events fired by AWT components.
Java.awt.font	Provides classes and interface relating to fonts.
Java.awt.geom	Provides the Java 2D classes for defining and performing operations on objects related to two-dimensional geometry.

Table 9-3 Package java.awt—Interface Summary

ActiveEvent	An interface for events that know how to dispatch themselves.
Adjustable	The interface for objects that have an adjustable numeric value contained within a bounded range of values.
Composite	The Composite interface, along with CompositeContext, defines the methods to compose a draw primitive with the underlying graphics area.
Composite Context	The CompositeContext interface defines the encapsulated and optimized environment for a compositing operation.
Item Selectable	The interface for objects that contain a set of items for which zero or more can be selected.
LayoutManager	Defines the interface for classes that know how to lay out Containers.
LayoutManager2	Defines an interface for classes that know how to lay out Containers based on a layout constraints object.
MenuContainer	The super class of all menu-related containers.
Paint	This Paint interface defines how color patterns can be generated for Graphics2D operations.
PaintContext	The PaintContext interface defines the encapsulated and optimized environment to generate color patterns in device space for fill or stroke operations on a Graphics2D.
PrintGraphics	An abstract class, which provides a print graphics context for a page.
Shape	The Shape interface provides definitions for objects that represent some form of geometric shape.
Stroke	The Stroke interface allows a Graphics2D object to obtain a Shape that is the decorated outline, or stylistic representation of the outline, of the specified Shape.

The class definition in Figure 9-17 shows both the package location and its superclasses. Note that in this example, the inheritance is from a class in the same package. The Button class is a subclass of the Component class. The Button class and the Component class are in the same package, java.awt.

Figure 9-17 API Docs

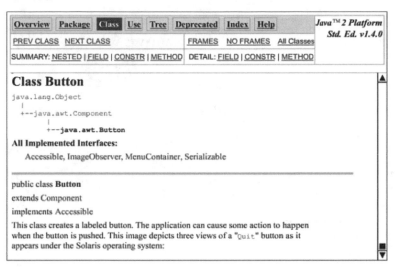

The AWTEXception class's definition shows that it inherits from a class in a different package. The documentation for this class is shown in Figure 9-18. The AWTException class is a subclass of the Exception class, located in the java.lang package. The Applet class is in the java.applet package, as shown by the documentation in Figure 9-19; it inherits from, or is subclassed from, the Panel class in the java.awt package. In each of these packages, the classes have been grouped for commonality of use and can be subclassed from packages in other classes.

Figure 9-18 API Docs

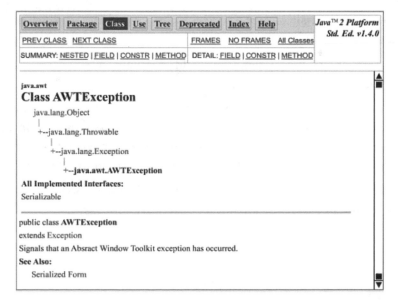

Figure 9-19 API Docs

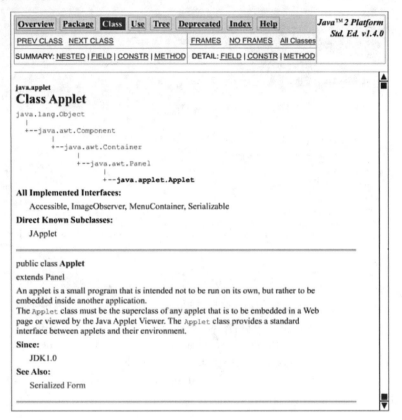

The keyword **protected** allows access by subclasses of the class in which **protected** members are defined.

The access modifiers can have a significantly different impact when classes are collected into packages.

As shown in Figure 9-20, classes that belong to the same package inherit all default, **protected**, and **public** attributes of the parent class. Subclasses that are in a different package inherit only the **public** and **protected** attributes of the parent class. Attributes of the parent class that are declared **private** are not inherited by any subclass.

Access to attributes of a class also is influenced by packages. Classes can access **public** and default attributes of other classes in the same package.

Figure 9-20 Creating a jar File of the Banking Directory

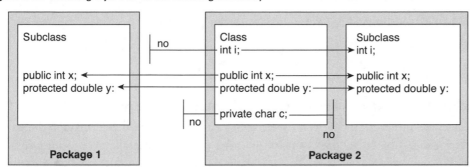

Creating a Banking Package

Many classes have been created for the banking application JBANK. The first several classes were stored in the Phase I directory. Storage for the next set of classes took place in Phase II. In this portion of the case study, students will create a directory structure that helps to organize the classes into a Banking package.

The goal of this section of the case study is to first help students organize their classes by phase into separate subdirectories under the Banking directory. Students will then use **package** statements and **import** statements to access the classes in these packages. More classes will be added to the banking application, such as GUIs, I/O, and utility classes, that are in the API set of packages. The **import** statement becomes very important to make the classes compile and run properly.

The subdirectories for the classes will be created first. Then the source files will be modified to add the package statements. After these changes have been made, the classes will be recompiled using the -d option so that they are compiled in the proper directory. A jar file for the Phase I classes in the banking application also will be created.

Using AWT

A very useful package included in the Java platform is the java.awt package, or AWT package. Graphical programs can be constructed using the Abstract Window Toolkit (AWT). The AWT package is a collection of classes such as buttons and text fields that can be combined to create an interactive program.

This section consists of the following topics:

- Understanding the Model View Controller program
- Applying inheritance concepts
- Understanding AWT hierarchy

Understanding the Model View Controller Program

Much of the interaction between the program and the user has been through the use of the `System.in` object. A `Console` class has been provided to make user input interaction easier for students to program into their classes. In most real-world applications, such interactions are impractical. Program users expect more graphical representations of data and input interactions. Users expect to find a specific box on a screen to input data, a button to activate actions, scrollbars to view large amounts of information, and progress charts or bars that inform them of the progress of an activity. Users also expect to see pictures and images, hear sound, and even view video clips.

Creating classes that will draw images, produce digitized sounds, and show movement of text and graphics can be very daunting. The Java platform provides a set of APIs commonly known as the Java Foundation Classes that provide many predefined programs that draw graphics and manage user interaction. The Swing classes also can be used to create graphical components. Much like a Lego block set, these classes can be used to build customized user interfaces (screens). These are commonly known as graphical user interfaces (GUIs).

To program a GUI, students must understand the following:

- Event-driven programming
- The Model View Controller pattern
- GUI terminology

Event-Driven Programming

All input and output should pass through the program's GUI. The GUI, therefore, consists of what the user will see on the screen and the code to process user actions. These actions can include moving a mouse over an object, selecting an item from a menu, entering text in a box, pressing a graphic that resembles a button, or closing or resizing a window. These represent a few of the possible user interactions that the code must be prepared to handle.

GUI programs are event driven. The user initiates an action by pressing a key on the keyboard or clicking a mouse. The GUI program always must be responsive to user input and must take directions from the user.

In designing a GUI, keep in mind these principles:

- The user initiates all actions.
- The user must be able to initiate an action and receive a reasonable response.
- You should display graphical objects that suggest actions that the user can perform.
- You should provide responses whenever a user initiates an action.

To implement these principles, students need to master event-driven programming. They must design classes and write code that listens for events (actions) initiated by the user and that then responds to these actions.

In Java, events can be associated with GUI components and non-GUI components. One such example is an application that includes a class that observes network connections and notifies the client class when the network connection is closed, or a class that observes writing data to a file and notifies the client class when the file is closed. Figure 9-21 demonstrates a simple program that responds to interaction with a button.

Figure 9-21 Interacting with a GUI: Event-Driven Programming

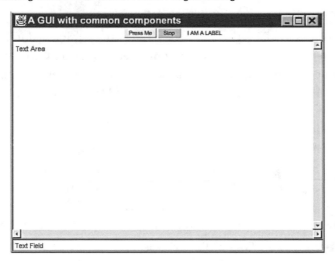

For Figure 9-21, you can view the full, interactive graphic for this figure on the book's accompanying CD-ROM. The title of the activity is "Interacting with a GUI: Event-Driven Programming" in the e-Lab Activities.

Model View Controller Pattern

To be consistent with object-oriented design, you must separate the program's GUI from the program's processing. The program should use one class to present the graphics, another class to process the data (that is, the user input), and one class to handle the events that occur with user interaction.

For example, a program that allows a customer to withdraw money from an account would have a GUI class to present the window (screen for the user) to input customer ID, account information, and the amount to be withdrawn. A button on this screen could be used to initiate the withdrawal process. Another class, the Customer class, might contain the account information and a method to access account data. The Customer and the Account classes form the model, or the business classes. The GUI that displays the screen is the view, and the class that handles interaction with the button is the controller. The controller provides the connection between the model and the view.

The design of classes separating the class that presents the data from the class that holds the data and the class that controls the transfer of data between the user and the model is known as the *Model View Controller pattern.*

The advantage of this model is that the same model can be presented in different views. For example, the Customer objects can be connected to a Teller GUI or an ATM GUI. A single Customer class holds the data for the customer, but there are different view and controller classes for handling the Teller and ATM implementations.

GUI Terminology

Components form a major part of a GUI. In Java, components are predefined standard elements such as buttons, text fields, frames, windows, menus, menu items, text areas, and dialog boxes. Figure 9-22 shows a GUI that utilizes many of these components. The display space on the screen is also a component. Like all GUI-based applications, the Java display space is a frame window. Frame windows have a title, a border, and buttons for closing, minimizing, and maximizing the window. As shown in Figure 9-23, a frame window can be constructed using the Frame and Window classes.

Figure 9-22 Identifiers for Buttons, Text Areas, and Labels

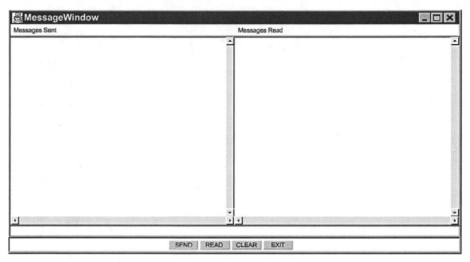

Figure 9-23 A Java Program Displaying a Window

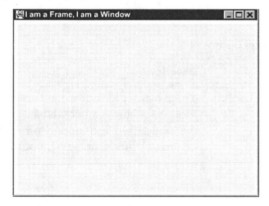

Some of the components are used to hold other components. For example, a dialog box can hold a label and a button. A window can hold a dialog box and other buttons and components. Components that can hold other components are called containers. For example, the frame component in Figure 9-24 is a container; it holds other panel components.

Figure 9-24 Containers and Components

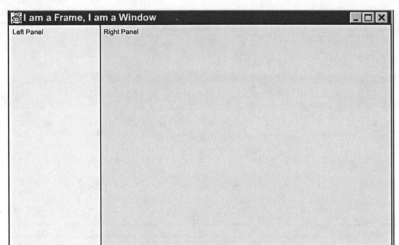

In response to popular demand to support GUIs, the Java platform provides the Java Foundation Classes. The five APIs that form the Java Foundation Classes are described in Table 9-4.

Table 9-4 Java Foundations Classes API

API	Description
Abstract Windowing Toolkit	The Abstract Windowing Toolkit was the original toolkit for developing GUIs. This toolkit provides the foundation and support for colors, fonts, graphics, images, events, listeners, layout managers, and other utility programs.
Swing	This is an extensive set of classes for building GUIs. These components build on top of the AWT component classes that feature a pluggable look and feel. The study and use of Swing components requires more time than is afforded in this course.
Java2D	The Java2D API provides a variety of painting styles and features for defining complex shapes and controlling the rendering process.

Table 9-4 Java Foundations Classes API (Continued)

API	Description
Accessibility	The Accessibility API provides an interface that allows assistive technologies such as screen readers, screen magnifiers, and speech recognition to be integrated easily into applications.
Drag and Drop	The Drag and Drop API provides the capability to move data between programs created with the Java language.

This course focuses on the *AWT classes*. The Abstract Window Toolkit (AWT) API and the Swing API form the foundation of classes used to create GUIs. If students master the AWT classes, the transition to using Swing classes is quite simple.

Applying Inheritance Concepts

This section explores the AWT package and the set of classes that are part of this package. This package, shown in Table 9-5, contains many of the classes used to create GUIs. The Button class is part of the java.awt package. The documentation for this class is shown in Figure 9-25. Inheritance is an important concept in AWT. Examine the inheritance hierarchy of the Frame class shown in Figure 9-26.

The purpose of this exploration is to familiarize students with the location of these classes. When the students are ready to create GUIs, they will know where to look for these classes.

Table 9-5 Package java.awt — Interface Summary

ActiveEvent	An interface for events that know how to dispatch themselves.
Adjustable	The interface for objects that have an adjustable numeric value contained within a bounded range of values.
Composite	The Composite interface, along with CompositeContext, defines the methods to compose a draw primitive with the underlying graphics area.
Composite Context	The CompositeContext interface defines the encapsulated and optimized environment for a compositing operation.
Item Selectable	The interface for objects that contain a set of items for which zero or more can be selected.

continues

Table 9-5 Package `java.awt` — Interface Summary (Continued)

LayoutManager	Defines the interface for classes that know how to lay out Containers.
LayoutManager2	Defines an interface for classes that know how to lay out Containers based on a layout constraints object.
MenuContainer	The super class of all menu-related containers.
Paint	This Paint interface defines how color patterns can be generated for Graphics2D operations.
PaintContext	The PaintContext interface defines the encapsulated and optimized environment to generate color patterns in device space for fill or stroke operations on a Graphics2D.
PrintGraphics	An abstract class, which provides a print graphics context for a page.
Shape	The Shape interface provides definitions for objects that represent some form of geometric shape.
Stroke	The Stroke interface allows a Graphics2D object to obtain a Shape that is the decorated outline, or stylistic representation of the outline, of the specified Shape.

Figure 9-25 Some Common GUI Components: `Button`

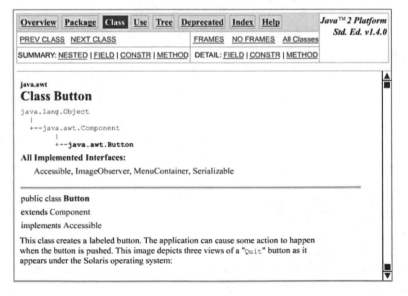

Figure 9-26 Some Common GUI Components: `Frame`

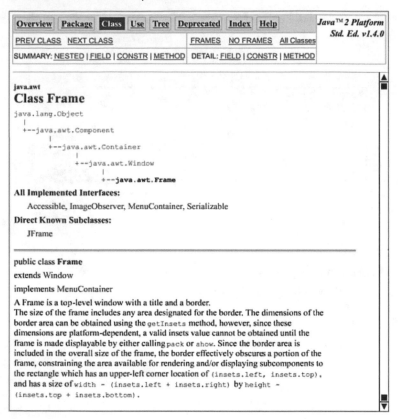

Computer users now demand that application programs provide GUIs. When a program has GUIs, a large portion of the code services the GUI. It builds the GUI and repaints graphics when the windows are moved or when new information needs to be displayed. Programming for the GUI sometimes can become the largest part of the code for the application. Consider the GUI for the JBANK application shown in Figure 9-27.

The Swing set of classes provides more sophisticated GUI capabilities than those of AWT. Swing classes build on the features of the AWT classes. Understanding the AWT classes prepares students for the use of Swing classes. Sun Microsystems' Java website, java.sun.com, has a tutorial on the use of Swing. Students might want to go through this tutorial to explore the possibilities of using the Swing set of classes.

Figure 9-27 Common GUI Components in the JBANK GUI

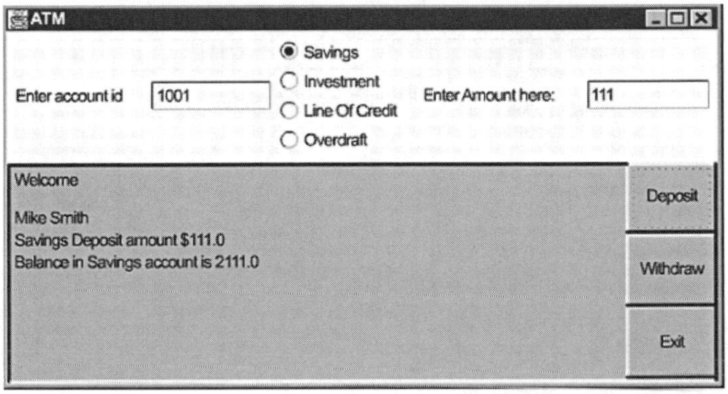

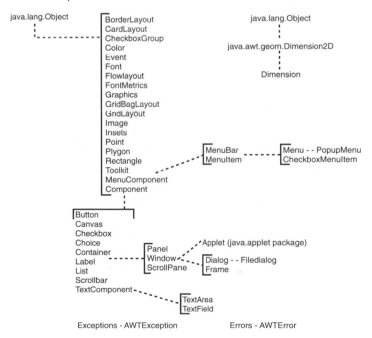

AWT Hierarchy

The AWT classes can be viewed under several categories. Figure 9-28 illustrates the AWT hierarchy and presents a map of the classes.

Figure 9-28 AWT Hierarchy

Numerous classes in the AWT hierarchy can be used to create graphical user interfaces. Each class has unique features that can be applied to interactive applications. The following list identifies many of the classes included in the `java.awt` package.

- Classes that draw graphics or manipulate images:

```
Graphics
Image
Insets
Point
Polygon
Rectangle
```

- Classes that can be used to position visual elements:

```
BorderLayout
CardLayout
CheckboxGroup
FlowLayout
GridBagLayout
GridLayout
```

- Classes that can be used to change properties of visual elements:

```
Toolkit
Color
Font
FontMetrics
CheckboxGroup
```

- Classes that create graphical components:

```
MenuComponent
Component
MenuBar
MenuItem
Menu
PopupMenu
CheckboxMenuItem
Button
Canvas
Checkbox
Choice
Label
List
Scrollbar
TextComponent
TextArea
TextField
```

- Classes that can hold other components or containers:

```
Container
Panel
Window
ScrollPane
Dialog
Frame
Applet (java.applet package)
FileDialog
```

Case Study: JBANK Application

The JBANK application introduced in Chapter 1 ("What Is Java?") provides students with an opportunity to apply the Java language concepts learned throughout this course. Using the concepts of packages, AWT, and the API, students can improve the functionality of the JBANK application. Including a graphical user interface makes the JBANK application more versatile and easier to use. In the JBANK labs for Chapter 9, "Understanding Packages," students will review the API and familiarize themselves with the graphics components needed to create an ATM GUI and a Teller GUI. Using only paper and pen or pencil, students will select all of the necessary components and lay them out in a design that will become the ATM GUI and the Teller GUI.

JBANK GUI

In this lab, you begin by designing the GUI windows for the Teller and ATM activities. These GUIs will be launched using classes that implement the Model View Controller design pattern. Completing the Model View Controller pattern are a class to present the GUI and a class to handle user interaction with the GUI components and connect them to the model of the business using the `Teller`, `Account`, and `Customer` classes. Figure 9-29 and Figure 9-27, shown previously, display what the JBANK application's `TellerGUI` and `ATMGUI` might look like.

The purpose of this lab is to ensure that the GUI components are placed in locations that follow good design principles for creating user interfaces. This lab is focused on design. Time that is spent designing and researching the capabilities of the GUI components shortens the time needed in creating classes that use these features.

Figure 9-29 JBANK Application

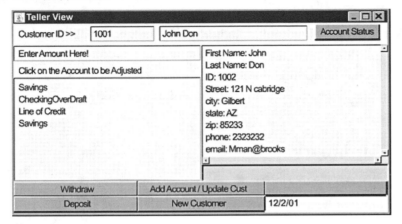

Summary

This chapter covers the features in the Java language that help to organize classes.

A package is an entity that is used to collect classes or group classes. Selecting which classes should belong in a package depends upon their commonality of use, not necessarily their inheritance relationship.

Classes that are in packages can be archived and compressed into one single file using the jar utility.

The **package** statement must be the first statement in a class definition, excluding comments. The source file that contains the class definition is known as the compilation unit. A compilation unit can have only one class declared as **public**.

The compiler loads classes by searching directories identified in the CLASSPATH variable. The CLASSPATH variable can be overridden to search the current directory. Finally, the compiler searches the directories identified by the **package** statement. Classes that belong to the Java language are loaded automatically and are not affected by the CLASSPATH settings.

The CLASSPATH can be redefined at compile time by using the -classpath option, or at run-time by using the -cp option. When using jar files, the CLASSPATH must point to the exact location of the jar file and must include the jar file in the CLASSPATH.

The **import** statement is used to identify the package names for classes that are not in the default directory and are not part of the standard packages. The **import** statement must be inserted after the **package** statement and before any class-definition statements.

GUIs provide user interfaces that display data and obtain user input using graphics. The AWT classes provide flexible and extensive support for programming GUIs. In designing GUI programs and classes, use the Model View Controller pattern.

This design approach separates the classes that present the data (GUI) from the classes that hold the data (model) and the classes that control the transfer of data between the user and the model (controller); it is known as the Model View Controller pattern.

Syntax Summary

Explicit reference to access classes:

```
public class ClassName
{
  static int numOfTests;
  static java.util.Date[ ] testDate;
  static String[ ] testName;
  static int[ ] maxPoints;
}
//end of class
```

Using **import** statements:

```
import java.util.*;
import java.text.*;

public class ClassName
{
  static int numOfTests;
  static Date[ ] testDate;
  static String[ ] testName;
  static int[ ] maxPoints;
}
//end of class
```

The **package** statement:

```
package edu.state.district.studentName.banking;
import java.util.*;
```

Key Terms

API packages   Packages that contain all the classes included with the Java language.

AWT classes   Classes found in the `java.awt` package that enable a programmer to construct graphical user interfaces.

class loading   Process in which the Java interpreter loads a Java class and any class referenced by the class by searching directories specified on the CLASSPATH for the `.class` files.

CLASSPATH variable   An environmental variable that tells the Java Virtual Machine where to find the class libraries, including user-defined class libraries.

compilation unit   A source file for a java class named with the `.java` extension.

current working directory   The location, specified by a period (`.`), where the compiler will search for `.class` files to be loaded.

default directory   Location where a source file without an explicit package declaration is saved.

directory   A unit of the file-management structure that specifies a location to store files.

explicit package declaration   The process of specifying a package to which the class will belong, using a **package** statement as the first statement in the definition.

GUI   Graphical user interface. Refers to the techniques involved in using graphics, along with a keyboard and a mouse, to provide an easy-to-use interface to some program.

import *statement*   A statement used at the beginning of a source file that can specify classes or entire packages to be referred to later without including their package names in the reference.

jar   Utility included with the Java Development Kit deployment, used to pack several classes into one archive.

Model View Controller pattern   An object-oriented concept in which the code to display a graphical user interface, the code to respond to user interaction, and the code to define the nature of the program are created separately.

packages   A collection of classes.

PATH variable   An operating system variable that specifies the directories that contain many executable files, including the Java compiler and interpreter.

standard classes   The core classes that belong to the Java language, located automatically and unaffected by the CLASSPATH variable.

unique domain   Using packages to create a unique namespace for classes prevents name collisions when these classes are shared.

Check Your Understanding

1. A unique _____ identifies a specific class and its method.

   A. Package

   B. Namespace

   C. Path

   D. Definition

2. What is the purpose of packaging Java classes?

   A. It allows classes to be managed as a collection.

   B. It declares unique namespaces for the classes.

   C. It ensures that the interpreter can locate the classes.

   D. All of the above are true.

3. What is another name for the file containing the Java source file?

   A. CLASSPATH

   B. Compilation unit

   C. Inheritance hierarchy

   D. Bytecode file

4. Which variable is used to store the paths to the directories where executable files are stored?

   A. CLASSPATH variable

   B. PATH variable

   C. SYSTEM variable

   D. CLASS variable

5. Which variable is used to store the paths of the directories where packages are stored?

   A. CLASSPATH variable

   B. PATH variable

   C. SYSTEM variable

   D. CLASS variable

6. The CLASSPATH variable can be redefined at compile time by using which option?

   A. The `-cp` option.

   B. The `-classpath` option.

   C. CLASSPATH is static and cannot be redefined.

   D. The CLASSPATH can be redefined only at run time.

7. Where does the interpreter search first for classes needed by a program?

   A. The default package

   B. The directories identified in the CLASSPATH variable

   C. The standard directories

   D. The directory identified in the `package` statement

8. Which is not an effect of packaging on object-oriented design?

   A. Packaging allows fewer classes to be designed.

   B. Packaging enables stricter access control.

   C. Packaging allows reuse of common class names.

   D. Packaging allows classes to be managed as collections.

9. Which access modifier is used to limit access only to those classes in the same package?

   A. `private`

   B. default

   C. `public`

   D. `protected`

10. Where must the **package** statement be placed within a source file?

    A. After any **import** statements

    B. As the first line in the source file

    C. As the last line in the source file

    D. Within the Javadoc comments for the class

11. Which utility compresses classes into a single file?

    A. `java`

    B. `javadoc`

    C. `javac`

    D. `jar`

12. Which Java keyword is used to access packages?

    A. `extends`

    B. `include`

    C. `import`

    D. `package`

13. Which package are the Button and Component classes in?

    A. `java.gui`

    B. `java.awt`

    C. `java.io`

    D. `java.util`

14. If a subclass and superclass belong to the same package, which data and methods are not inherited by the subclass?

    A. **public** data and methods

    B. **private** data and methods

    C. default data and methods

    D. **protected** data and methods

15. With what concept is event-driven programming associated?

    A. Packaging

    B. GUI

    C. Procedural programming

    D. Abstract methods

16. Which function is not one of the three functions separated in the Model View Controller pattern?

    A. GUI design

    B. Data processing

    C. Event handling

    D. Package definition

17. In Java, buttons, menus, windows, and text fields are all

    A. EVT components

    B. IUD components

    C. GUI components

    D. JAR components

18. Which component can hold other components?

    A. `ScrollPane`

    B. `TextArea`

    C. `Scrollbar`

    D. `Checkbox`

19. What does the acronym AWT stand for?

    A. Advanced Window Toolkit

    B. Abstract Written Tools

    C. Abstract Window Toolbox

    D. Abstract Window Toolkit

20. Which class can be used to change the properties of visual components?

    A. `Component`

    B. `GridLayout`

    C. `Font`

    D. `PopupMenu`

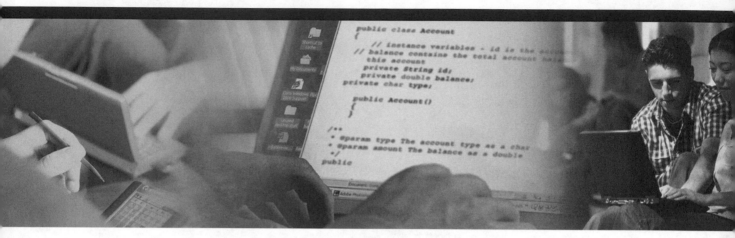

Upon completion of this chapter, you will be able to

- Use the Abstract Window Toolkit
- Create a GUI
- Understand GUI functionality
- Apply the Java language concepts that you have learned in this chapter to the JBANK case study

Chapter 10

Creating GUIs Using AWT

Overview

This chapter continues exploring the *Abstract Window Toolkit (AWT)* and the creation of *graphical user interfaces (GUIs)*. Most interactions between a user and an application are through GUIs. These interfaces provide a means for the program to display data and to obtain input from the user. The Java platform provides an extensive library of classes for a programmer to use in building GUIs.

A GUI is a display of information on the screen in a frame referred to as a window. A GUI can be as simple as a message box that displays some message to the user, or as complex as a window that displays text. GUIs can also be textboxes for users to input data, or buttons for users to select specific actions or to display moving images, pictures, and sound. A useful GUI has several basic features: *graphics* (text, pictures, images, buttons, and so on), the components that a user will interact with, and action results that occur when the user interacts with the GUI.

Managing user interaction with a GUI is possible through an event delegation model. In such a model, the component that is presented to the user does not actually perform the actions; instead, it instructs another object to perform the action. This enables the component to monitor further actions of the user while another class is completing the action currently requested.

The Model-View-Controller design pattern is used extensively in applications that implement GUIs. This design pattern emphasizes the separation of display information, actions, and responses to user interactions into separate classes. The view is implemented in classes that display information. The model is implemented in classes that hold and manipulate business data. The control is implemented in classes that monitor user interaction and respond with the correct model actions. The model represents the class that holds the business data, such as a `Customer` class. GUIs that display graphics represent the view. Classes that implement the listener interfaces represent the controller.

Working with GUIs results in the creation of many class files. One way to manage these is to create tightly associated classes through the use of inner class and anonymous class designs. This chapter explores the use of these designs in creating GUI applications.

Reviewing AWT

Computer users now demand that application programs provide GUIs, making them easier to use. When a program has a GUI, a large portion of the code services (builds) the GUI. It also repaints graphics when the windows are moved (or new information needs to be displayed). Programming for the GUI sometimes becomes the largest part of the code of the application.

NOTE

GUIs can be used in applications, which are standalone Java programs, and also in applets, which are Java programs that run inside a web browser.

The `java.applet` package contains the `Applet` class, which provides a standard interface between applets and their environment. An applet is a small program that is intended not to be run on its own, but to be embedded inside another application. Applets typically run within web pages in web browsers that can read HTML tags. We explore the creation and use of applets in Chapter 11, "Creating Applets and Graphics."

The Java platform provides extensive support for programming GUIs through the classes that form the Abstract Window Toolkit (AWT). This toolkit consists of classess in the `java.awt` package. Take a moment to locate the `java.awt` package in the Java API documents. The chapter content and labs require that you spend a significant amount of time researching the classes in this package. This section addresses the AWT classes.

The AWT Classes

To create GUIs, you use the classes in the `java.awt` and `java.awt.event` packages. When creating applications that include GUIs, include the **import** statements shown in Example 10-1 in the source file. Recall from Chapter 9, "Understanding Packages," that **import** statements must follow **package** statements and precede all other code. These two lines most commonly are found at the start of GUI source code.

Example 10-1 *Commonly Used Statements That Define GUI Applications*

```
import java.awt.*;
import java.awt.event.*;
```

For the purposes of creating GUIs, the extensive set of classes that make up the AWT can be categorized as classes that manage and create graphics and classes that create components. *Components* are objects that display a graphic image and can monitor user interactions with the image.

Another categorization of the AWT classes is shown in Table 10-1.

Table 10-1 Types of Graphic Classes

Classes That Draw Graphics or Manipulate Images	Classes That Can Be Used to Position Visual Elements	Classes That Can Be Used to Change Properties of Visual Elements
Graphics	BorderLayout	Toolkit
Image	CardLayout	Color
Insets	FlowLayout	Font
Point	GridBagLayout	FontMetrics
Polygon	GridLayout	
Rectangle		

Reading from left to right, the first box shows the classes used to create graphic objects. These are not GUI components. These classes include the following:

- Graphics class—The Graphics class is the abstract base class for all graphics contexts. It is used to draw on onscreen and off-screen components.
- Image class—The abstract class Image is the superclass of all classes that represent graphical images. The image must be obtained in a platform-specific manner.

The second box refers to the classes that are used to manage the layout of the graphic elements. These classes include the following:

- BorderLayout class—A BorderLayout lays out a container, arranging and resizing its components to fit in five regions: North, South, East, West, and Center. When adding a component to a container with a BorderLayout, you can use one of these five names to control which part of the container the component gets added to. If you do not specify a region, the component is added to the Center.
- FlowLayout class—A FlowLayout arranges components in a left-to-right flow, much like lines of text in a paragraph. FlowLayout is typically used to arrange Buttons in a Panel left to right until no more Buttons fit on the same line. Each line is centered.

Finally, the third box refers to the classes that set the properties of graphics and GUI components. These classes include the following:

- Color class—This class encapsulates colors using the RGB format. In this format, the red, blue, and green components of a color are each represented by an integer in the range 0–255. The value 0 indicates no contribution from this primary color. The value 255 indicates the maximum intensity of this color component.

■ Font class—This class represents fonts, which are used to render text in a visible way.

Figure 10-1 shows the most commonly used GUI components. These components were created using the classes in the `java.awt` package. An example of a commonly used GUI component is a window. A frame is a window that has a title, a button to maximize or minimize, and a button to close the window. Another example is a `button`, which is usually a rounded polygon–shaped figure that a user clicks with a mouse to initiate some action. The textbox is a GUI component that accepts input from the user as text. Textboxes can be a single-line box (also known as a `TextField`) or a multiline box, with or without scroll bars, known as a `TextArea`. Other components (not shown in this figure) include menus in a menu bar and choice boxes (in which a list of choices can be presented).

Figure 10-1 Most Commonly Used GUI Components

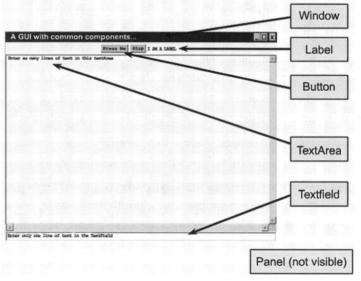

GUIs can be used to display custom forms. In Figure 10-2, a word-processing program uses the form shown to display information about the document.

GUIs also form the displays seen in browsers and World Wide Web documents, as shown in Figure 10-3. Each of these examples shows the use of components to give the user a way of interacting with the information. Nothing happens until the user interacts with the GUI.

Figure 10-2 Sample Form

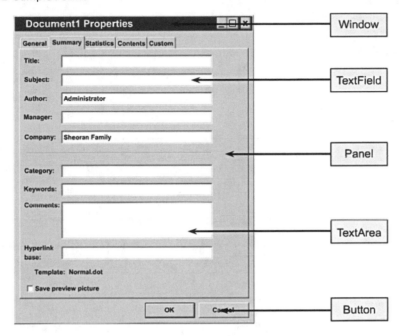

Figure 10-3 Web Page with Form, Button, and TextArea

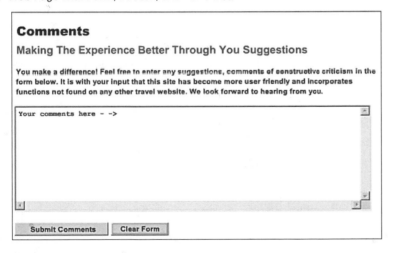

You already have encountered many of these components. Screens now can be created and components can be placed in design layouts to meet the programmer's needs. A programmer can program functionality for these components by creating classes that handle events generated by user interactions with these components.

Table 10-2 shows some classes that create GUI components. The root of all of these classes is the *Component class*; all of the other classes inherit from this class. Recall from Chapter 8, "Classes and Inheritance," that subclasses inherit nonprivate methods and data from the parent class. When using these classes, always read the list of inherited methods and data. Most components inherit from the `Component` class. `MenuComponent` is the superclass for `MenuBar` and `MenuItem`.

Table 10-2 The AWT Class Hierarchy

Object					
→→→→	Component				
	→→→→	Button			
	→→→→	Canvas			
	→→→→	Checkbox			
	→→→→	Choice			
	→→→→	Container			
		→→→→	Panel		
			→→→→	Applet (java.applet package)	
		→→→→	ScrollPane		
		→→→→	Window		
			→→→→	Dialog	
				→→→→	FileDialog
			→→→→	Frame	
	→→→→	Label			
	→→→→	List			
	→→→→	Scrollbar			
	→→→→	TextComponent			
		→→→→	TextArea		
		→→→→	TextField		

Table 10-2 The AWT Class Hierarchy (Continued)

→→→→ MenuComponent				
	→→→→	MenuBar		
	→→→→	MenuItem		
		→→→→	CheckboxMenuItem	
		→→→→	Menu	
			→→→→	PopupMenu

GUI component classes include both the code to draw the graphic image that is visible on the screen and **public** methods to provide user interaction functionality. The most common methods that you will encounter in the GUI component classes include the following:

- add()
- remove()
- setText()
- getText()
- setLabel()
- getLabel()

Most components need a surface on which to be displayed. Among the Component subclasses is a Container class. All classes that derive from the Container class serve as *containers* for other components or other containers. These containers display the components added to the container.

Among the containers that can hold other components are the Panel, Applet, Dialog, and Frame classes. Each of these containers implements enhancements over the class it derives from. Except for the Panel class, which is a free-floating container, all other classes display the components directly. The Panel class must be added to another container to be displayed.

Steps to Create a GUI

A step-by-step process should be followed when creating GUIs. This section details each of these steps and provides sample code for each step. This section addresses the following topics:

- Designing the class

- Creating the components
- Selecting the containers
- Using layout managers
- Sizing components and containers
- Displaying the GUIs

Designing the Class

When creating GUIs, follow these steps:

Step 1   Design the GUI on paper. Get feedback on functionality and clarity from the users of the application.

Step 2   Create the references for the GUI components.

Step 3   Select a container for all the components.

Step 4   Select a layout manager for each of the containers.

Step 5   Create the component objects and add the components to the container. Do this in a subassembly order. That is, begin with the container that holds components, and then containers that hold containers. (This works like packing a series of small to large boxes one inside the other.)

Step 6   Register the event listener with the component.

Step 7   Set the size for the container.

Step 8   Make the container visible.

Designing GUIs requires a great deal of interaction with the users of the application. A good GUI results in effective user interaction. The goal is not to clutter up the screen with every component that you want to display, but to break up the screen into separate areas. Draw a rough sketch of the GUI. Many commercial integrated development environments (IDEs) provide a visual component editor that let a programmer place and move components. That is, these programs are GUIs for creating other GUIs.

One technique to use is to layer the GUI into panels. Then each panel can be designed to have different functionality. Panels are containers that can hold other panels and other components. Panels are an effective way of sectioning the screen area (also known as display real estate). Take a look at a simple GUI application to send and receive messages that is similar to a chat window. This is not a fully working application because it does not have the network connectivity to send messages to other computer users. The purpose of introducing this example is to provide a simple application to illustrate the concepts in this chapter.

Based on user input, a rough sketch of the `MessageGUI` window is shown in Figure 10-4. There is an area for displaying messages that have been sent and an area for displaying messages received. This is a chat window. The expectation is that one or two sentences can be transmitted back and forth. The users have asked for a window in which a message can be typed in one area and an immediate response can be displayed in another area. The window includes buttons to allow the user to command the sending, reading, and clearing of messages, as well as exiting from the program.

Figure 10-4 Rough Sketch of `MessageGUI` Window

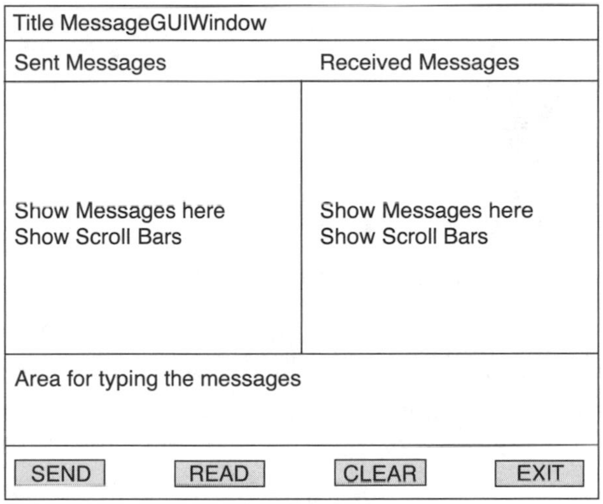

Identify the components used in the diagram for Figure 10-5. Note the many layers that are required to create this GUI.

For Figure 10-5, you can view the answers associated with the numbered buttons by accessing the full, interactive graphic for this figure on the book's accompanying CD-ROM. The title of the activity is "Identify GUI Components" in the e-Lab Activities.

Creating the Components

Defining the GUI class begins with creating references for all of the component objects. The component's references can be created, and then each component object can be constructed, or the reference and the object can be created at the same time. This is a matter of coding style.

Figure 10-5 Identify GUI Components

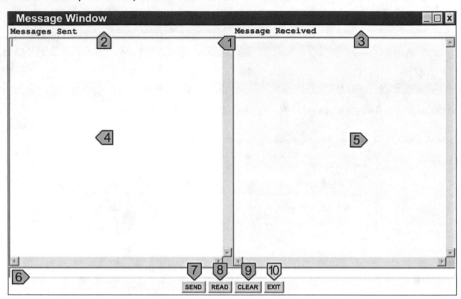

The example shown in Example 10-2 uses the sketch designed in the previous section and creates the references for all of the components. The components used for this GUI are `Button`, `Label`, `TextArea`, `TextField`, `Panel`, and `Frame`. Locate the documents for each of these classes in the API documents before reading any further.

Example 10-2 `MessageGUI` *Class Code Showing the Components Used*

```
 1 /**  The MessageGUI class presents a user interface for
 2  * sending and receiving messages
 3  *
 4  * @author Cisco Teacher
 5  * @version 2002
 6  */
 7
 8 //Required import statements
 9
10 import java.awt.*;
11 import java.awt.event.*;
12
13 public class MessageGUI implements ActionListener,WindowListener
```

Example 10-2 `MessageGUI` *Class Code Showing the Components Used (Continued)*

```
14 {

15

16        TextArea sent, received;

17        Label sentLabel, RecdLabel;

18        TextField message;

19        Button send, read, clear, exit;

20

21        //...more statements

22

23 }
```

Button

The `Button` class provides two constructors and several methods. Figure 10-6 shows the `Button` class API. The `Button` class has several methods that are useful for programming event handling, including `setLabel(String s)`, to change the text that displays as the label on a button, and `setActionCommand(String s)`, to set a specific `String` that represents an action on the button. In addition to these are the methods to add a listener to the component or remove a listener from the component. The `Button` class extends the `Component` class. Be sure to review the methods that it inherits from the `Component` class.

Figure 10-6 Button Class API

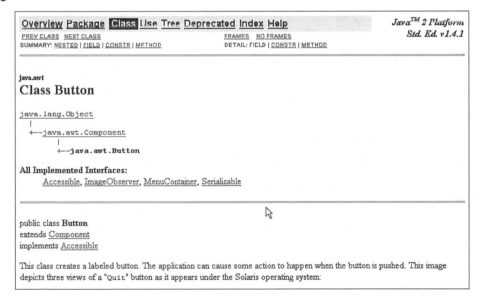

A button on the screen has three elements, as follows:

- The image of the button (the graphic)
- The code that monitors the interaction of the user with the button (whether the user pressed the button or just moved the mouse over the button, and so on)
- The code that performs some action based on the user's interaction with the button

The behavior of the button can be controlled by using various methods provided in the `Button` class. The following is a list of some of the methods and what they do:

- `addActionListener(ActionListener l)`—Adds the specified action listener to receive action events from this button
- `addNotify()`—Creates the peer of the button
- `getAccessibleContext()`—Gets the `AccessibleContext` associated with this button
- `getActionCommand()`—Returns the command name of the action event fired by this button
- `getActionListeners()`—Returns an array of all the action listeners registered on this button
- `getLabel()`—Gets the label of this button
- `getListeners(Class listenerType)`—Returns an array of all objects currently registered as *Foo*`Listeners` upon this button
- `paramString()`—Returns a string representing the state of this button
- `processActionEvent(ActionEvent e)`—Processes action events that occur on this button by dispatching them to any registered `ActionListener` objects
- `processEvent(AWTEvent e)`—Processes events on this button
- `removeActionListener(ActionListener l)`—Removes the specified action listener so that it no longer receives action events from this button
- `setActionCommand(String command)`—Sets the command name for the action event fired by this button
- `setLabel(String label)`—Sets the button's label to be the specified string

TIP

A `Label` object is a component for placing text in a container. A label displays a single line of read-only text. The text can be changed by the application, but a user cannot edit it directly.

Label

The `Label` class is used to display text as labels on the screen. Labels can be changed using the `setText()` method. Figure 10-7 shows the `Label` class API.

Figure 10-7 Label Class API

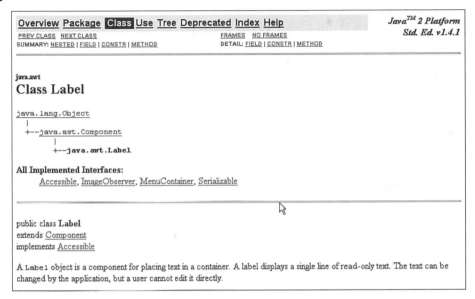

The behavior of the label can be controlled by using various methods provided in the Label class. The following lists some of the methods and what they do:

- addNotify()—Creates the peer for this label
- getAccessibleContext()—Gets the AccessibleContext associated with this label
- getAlignment()—Gets the current alignment of this label
- getText()—Gets the text of this label
- paramString()—Returns a String representing the state of this label
- setAlignment(int)—Sets the alignment for this label to the specified alignment
- setText(String text)—Sets the text for this label to the specified text

TextComponent, TextArea, and TextField

The *TextComponent* class is subclassed into TextField and TextArea. The *TextArea* is an area in which the user can enter several lines of text. TextAreas can be set to have a length of rows and width of characters. Figure 10-8 shows the TextArea class API.

Figure 10-8 TextArea API

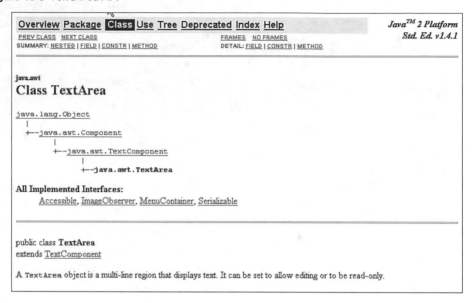

Both a vertical and a horizontal scrollbar can be displayed to the right and bottom, respectively, of the TextArea. A *TextField* is a single line of text. Figure 10-9 shows the TextField class API. The size of the field can be set. When a user presses Enter, the input to the TextField is considered complete.

Figure 10-9 TextField API Documentation

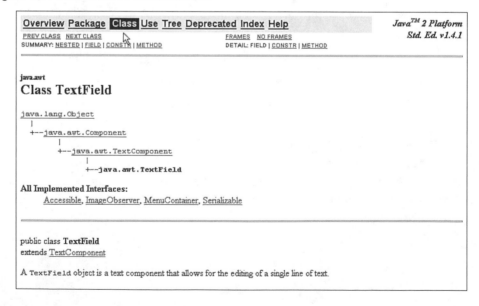

Several other components can be chosen. Each of the components includes constructors and methods to add listeners to the components. Only the most commonly used components have been selected for this application.

At least two possible approaches exist for the creation of GUI components. Some programmers like to define the references to GUI components first, define a constructor that calls a build() method, and thus build the GUI in this method. Others prefer to build the GUI in the constructor for the class. Either method is acceptable.

Two examples of code for the MessageGUI class are presented in Examples 10-3 and 10-4. The first builds the GUI in the constructor. The second calls the build() method in the constructor. Note the placement of the code. Creating an instance of the MessageGUI class automatically launches the GUI, regardless of which coding pattern is used.

Example 10-3 *Build the GUI in a Constructor*

```
 1 /**
 2  * The SimpleGUI class presents a simple user interface
 3  * @author Cisco Teacher
 4  * @version 2002
 5  */
 6
 7 // Required import statements
 8
 9 import java.awt.*;
10 import java.awt.event.*;
11
12 public class SimpleGUI extends WindowAdapter
13 {
14              // Step 2 Creating references for components
15              TextArea  t = new TextArea("Enter as multiple lines " +
16                                    "of text here");
17              Label la = new Label("I AM A LABEL");
18              TextField tf = new TextField("Enter one line of text here");
19              Button b1, b2;
20              Panel p1,p2;
```

NOTE

The full version of the abbreviated code shown in this example can be viewed using the book's accompanying CD-ROM.

For Example 10-3, you can view the explanatory text by accessing the full, interactive graphic for this example on the book's accompanying CD-ROM. The title of the activity is "Build the GUI in a Constructor" in the e-Lab Activities.

Example 10-4 *Build the GUI in a Method*

NOTE

The full version of the abbreviated code shown in this example can be viewed using the book's accompanying CD-ROM.

```
 1 /**
 2  * The SimpleGUI2 class presents a simple user interface
 3  * @author Cisco Teacher
 4  * @version 2002
 5  */
 6
 7 // Required import statements
 8
 9 import java.awt.*;
10 import java.awt.event.*;
11
12 public class SimpleGUI2 extends WindowAdapter
13 {
14        // Step 2 Creating references for components
15        TextArea  t;
16        Label la;
17        TextField tf;
18        Button b1, b2;
19        Panel p1,p2;
20        Frame f;
```

Selecting Containers

The containers used in the MessageGUI application are shown in Figure 10-10. This section discusses the properties of these objects and the appropriate selection of these to hold and display other components.

Two main types of containers exist: Window and Panel, each of which is described in the following sections.

Figure 10-10 Containers Used in the MessageGUI Application

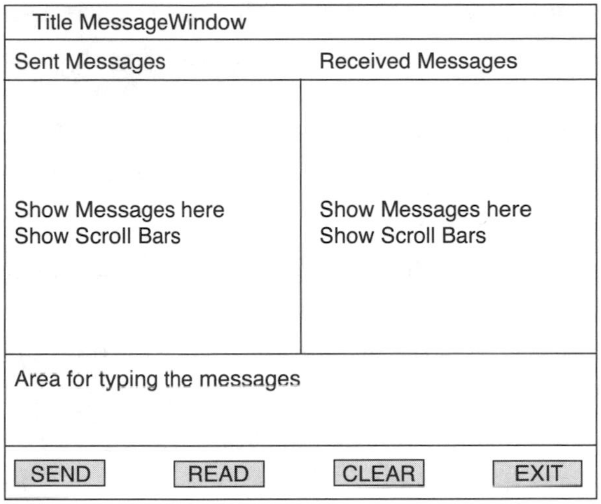

```
┌──────────────────────────────────────────────┐
│ Title MessageWindow                            │
├────────────────────────┬───────────────────────┤
│ Sent Messages          │ Received Messages      │
├────────────────────────┼───────────────────────┤
│                        │                        │
│                        │                        │
│                        │                        │
│ Show Messages here     │ Show Messages here     │
│ Show Scroll Bars       │ Show Scroll Bars       │
│                        │                        │
│                        │                        │
├────────────────────────┴───────────────────────┤
│ Area for typing the messages                    │
│                                                 │
├─────────────────────────────────────────────────┤
│ [ SEND ]    [ READ ]    [ CLEAR ]    [ EXIT ]   │
└─────────────────────────────────────────────────┘
```

Window

A Window is a freestanding native window on the display that is independent of other containers. Two important types of Window exist: *Frame* and *Dialog*. Dialog does not have a menu bar. Although it can be moved, it cannot be resized. Frame is a Window with a title and resizing corners. Frame is a subclass of Window. Frame inherits from Container, so the programmer can add components to a Frame using the *add method*. The constructor Frame(String s) in the Frame class creates a new, invisible Frame object with the title specified by the String object referenced by the variables. Add all the components to the Frame while it is still invisible. You can view examples of Window, Frame, and Dialog by accessing the full, interactive graphic on the book's accompanying CD-ROM. The title of the activity is "Windows, Frames, and Dialog Boxes," and it is found under the e-Lab Activities.

More Information

A Frame is a top-level window with a title and a border. The default layout for a frame is Border-Layout. Frames are capable of generating the following types of window events: WindowOpened, WindowClosing, WindowClosed, WindowIconified, WindowDeiconified, WindowActivated, and WindowDeactivated.

The following is a list of methods for the Frame class, with a brief mention of what each method does:

- addNotify()—Makes this frame displayable by connecting it to a native screen resource.

- `finalize()`— We have to remove the (hard) reference to `weakThis` in the `Vector`; otherwise, the `WeakReference` instance will never be garbage-collected.
- `getAccessibleContext()`—Gets the `AccessibleContext` associated with this frame.
- `getCursorType()`—Deprecated.
- `getExtendedState()`—Gets the state of this frame.
- `getFrames()`—Returns an array containing all frames created by the application.
- `getIconImage()`—Gets the image to be displayed in the minimized icon for this frame.
- `getMaximizedBounds()`—Gets maximized bounds for this frame.
- `getMenuBar()`—Gets the menu bar for this frame.
- `getState()`—Gets the state of this frame (obsolete).
- `getTitle()`—Gets the title of the frame.
- `isResizable()`—Indicates whether this frame is resizable by the user.
- `isUndecorated()`—Indicates whether this frame is undecorated.
- `paramString()`—Returns a `String` object representing the state of this frame.
- `remove(MenuComponent m)`—Removes the specified menu bar from this frame.
- `removeNotify()`—Makes this frame undisplayable by removing its connection to its native screen resource.
- `setCursor(int cursorType)`—Deprecated.
- `setExtendedState(`**int** `state)`—Sets the state of this frame.
- `setIconImage(Image image)`—Sets the image to be displayed in the minimized icon for this frame.
- `setMaximizedBounds(Rectangle bounds)`—Sets maximized bounds for this frame.
- `setMenuBar(MenuBar mb)`—Sets the menu bar for this frame to the specified menu bar.
- `setResizable(`**boolean** `resizable)`—Sets whether this frame is resizable by the user.
- `setState(`**int** `state)`—Sets the state of this frame (obsolete).
- `setTitle(String title)`—Sets the title for this frame to the specified `String` object referenced by the variable `title`.
- `setUndecorated(`**boolean** `undecorated)`—Disables or enables decorations for this frame.

More Information

A `Dialog` is a top-level window with a title and a border that typically is used to take some form of input from the user. The default layout for a `Dialog` is `BorderLayout`. A `Dialog` must have either a `Frame` or another `Dialog` defined as its owner when it is constructed. When the owner window of a visible `Dialog` is hidden or minimized, the `Dialog` automatically is hidden from the user. When the owner window is subsequently reopened, the `Dialog` is made visible to the user again. Dialogs are capable of generating the following `Window` events: `WindowOpened`, `WindowClosing`, `WindowClosed`, `WindowActivated`, and `WindowDeactivated`.

A *Panel* is a free-floating container and must be displayed on another container such as a `Window`, `Frame`, or `Dialog` (or inside a web browser's window in an applet). `Panel` identifies a rectangular area into which other components are placed. The `Panel`s shown in Figure 10-11 are displayed on a `Frame`, and the `Frame` is displayed on a `Window`. The colors for the `Panel`s were set using the `setBackground()` method of the component classes.

TIP

`Panel` is the simplest container class. A `Panel` provides space in which an application can attach any other component, including other `Panel`s. The default layout manager for a `Panel` is the `FlowLayout` layout manager.

Figure 10-11 `Panel`

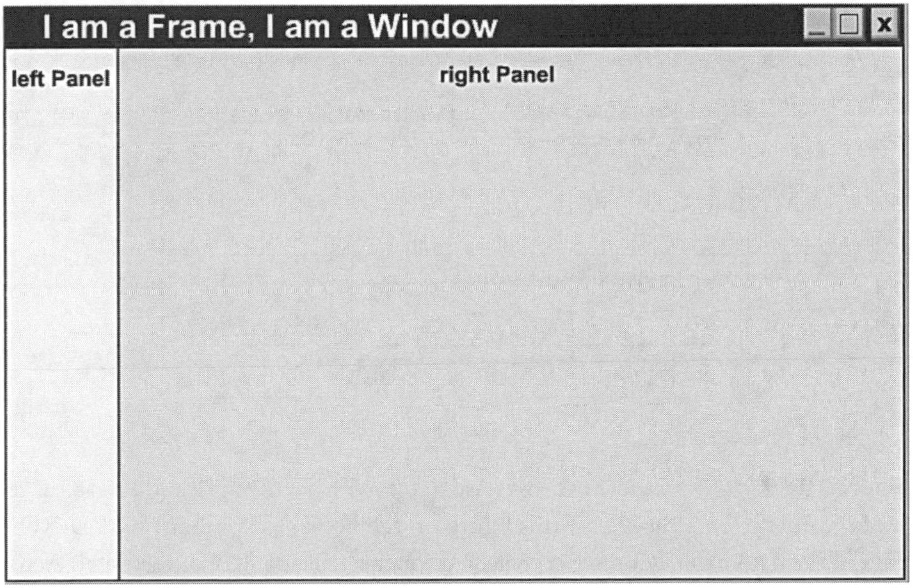

The fact that a container can hold not only components, but also other containers, is fundamental to building complex layouts. The `Panel` container is used to layer a GUI display. In the chat window shown in Figure 10-12, the following layers were employed to display each of the components and manage each without unduly changing the location or size of others:

- A `Frame` forms the base for displaying all the components.
- Two large `Panels` are placed on the `Frame`: `messageBase` and `messageAction`.
- The `Panel` `messageBase` is used to contain two additional `Panels`: `labelArea` and `messageDisplay`.
- The `labelArea` `Panel` will display two `Label` objects.
- The `messageDisplay` `Panel` will display two `TextArea` objects.
- The `Panel` `messageAction` is used to contain the `buttonArea` `Panel` and display a `TextField`.
- The `buttonArea` `Panel` will display the four `Button` objects.

Figure 10-12 Containers Selected for the `MessageGUI` Application

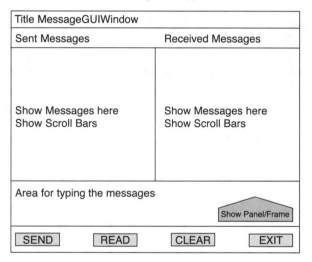

For Figure 10-12, you can view the text associated with each `Panel` and `Frame` by accessing the full, interactive graphic for this figure on the book's accompanying CD-ROM. The title of the activity is "Containers Selected for the `MessageGUI`" in the e-Lab Activities.

Note that what seems like a simple GUI required several layers of panels to display the desired components.

In designing the GUI, the programmer must consider the context in which the GUI will be displayed. Will the GUI be displayed in a web page or as part of a standalone application? Java provides the `Applet` class to display GUIs in web pages. However, the context might be a standalone program that is not part of a web page. In this case, the `Frame` class can build a window on the screen to display components. What if the programmer is expected to create a GUI that can be displayed in either? In this case, the programmer can select the Panel class as a container for all the GUI components. An object of this class then can be displayed either in a Frame or an Applet. This provides the most flexibility and reuse of code.

Using Layout Managers

Each container object adds other components or containers when the add() method of the container is called and a component object reference is passed to it. Each container has a default LayoutManager object that sets the position for displaying each component. LayoutManager objects figure out location and size based on predefined instructions. A *layout manager* usually governs the layout of components in a container. Each container (such as a panel or frame) has a default layout manager associated with it that can be changed by calling the *setLayout method*. The layout manager is responsible for deciding the layout policy and size of each of its containers' child components. The default layout manager for Panel is FlowLayout, and for Frame it is BorderLayout.

The programmer can select a layout manager in the following ways:

- Use the default.
- Select an alternate layout manager from the predefined layout manager classes using the setLayout() method—for example, setLayout(**new** BorderLayout()) or setLayout(**new** GridLayout(2,3)).
- Create a custom layout manager extending from LayoutManager. Set the layout to this custom layout manager.
- Place each component using setLocation(). This requires that the default layout manager is not used by using setLayout(**null**).

The layout managers manage components according to the rules shown in the list that follows. The following are the available container layout managers:

- FlowLayout—Left to right, top to bottom. Maintains dimensions of components.
- BorderLayout—Container area managed in five regions: North, South, East, West, and Center.
- GridLayout—Uses a grid of rows and columns. Fills each grid with one component, from left to right and top to bottom.
- CardLayout—Uses each Panel like a deck of cards. A tab panel is an example of this layout.
- GridBagLayout—Uses a grid of rows and columns. You can place components across several grid areas.

Selecting the proper layout manager can make placing the components and controlling the resizing and movement of the components a lot easier.

The BorderLayout manager breaks up the area into five regions, as shown in Figure 10-13. The layout manager controls the sizes of the regions. Each component is placed in the entire region. The North and South regions maintain the component's height and expand its width to occupy the entire region. The East and West regions maintain the width but increase or decrease the height to occupy the whole region. When objects are placed in only one region, the Center region takes up the rest of the space.

Figure 10-13 The Five Regions of the BorderLayout Manager

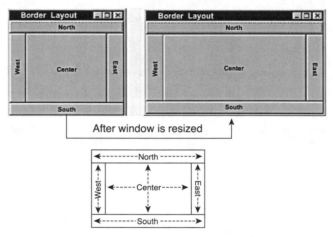

When selecting the BorderLayout manager, be sure to use the Center region for at least one of the components. BorderLayout manager proprieties are described in the following list:

- This is the default layout for the Frame class.
- Each region holds only one component.
- Components are added to a specific region using the syntax add(component,REGION). The regions are specified using the constants NORTH, SOUTH, EAST, WEST, and CENTER.
- The syntax to add a region is add(component, BorderLayout.NORTH) or add(component,"North");. Using capitals and case is critical. Either of these formats can be used.
- North, South, and Center regions adjust horizontally. East, West, and Center regions adjust vertically.

The setLayout(new BorderLayout()); method creates a new instance of the Border-Layout object for the specific container. The add(Component, Region); statement adds a specific component in the region specified.

The sample code in Example 10-5 implements a simple BorderLayout.

Example 10-5 *Implementing a Simple* BorderLayout

```
1 import java.awt.*;
2 public class ButtonDir extends Panel {
3   public ButtonDir () {
4     setLayout(new BorderLayout());
5     add("North",  new Button("North"));
6     add("South",  new Button("South"));
7     add("East",   new Button("East"));
8     add("West",   new Button("West"));
9     add("Center", new Button("Center"));
10  }
11  public static void main(String[] args)
12  {
13    Frame f = new Frame();
14    ButtonDir  bd = new ButtonDir();
15    f.add(bd);
16    f.setSize(200,400);
17    f.setVisible(true);
18  }
19 }
20
```

The FlowLayout manager places the components from left to right. In Figure 10-14, resizing the window does not change the size of the components. The default alignment is centered. The constructor for the FlowLayout manager accepts settings for the behavior of the layout manger.

NOTE

Resizing the window might not always change the size of the components.

Figure 10-14 FlowLayout Manager

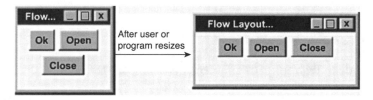

The FlowLayout manager has the following properties:

■ It is the default layout for the Panel class.

■ Components are added from left to right and top to bottom.

- The default alignment is centered to the area. This can be changed.
- The component's preferred sizes are used.

The constructor arguments for the FlowLayout manager are described in Example 10-6.

Example 10-6 FlowLayout *Constructors*

```
1 //setLayout(new FlowLayout(int align,int hgap,int vgap));
2
3 //The value of align must be FlowLayout.LEFT, FlowLayout.RIGHT, or
4 //FlowLayout.CENTER
5
6 //The following statement constructs a FlowLayout with right alignment,
7 //a 20 unit horizontal gap and 40 unit vertical gap
8
9 setLayout(new FlowLayout(FlowLayout.RIGHT, 20, 40))
10
11 //setLayout(new FlowLayout(int align))
12
13 //The default gap is a five unit horizontal gap and five unit vertical gap
14
15 //The following statement constructs a FlowLayout with left alignment, a 5
16 //unit horizontal gap and a 5 unit vertical gap
17
18 setLayout(new FlowLayout(FlowLayout.LEFT))
19
20 //The default alignment is FlowLayout.CENTER
21 //The folowing statement constructs a FlowLayout with a centered alignment,
22 //a 5 unit horizontal gap and a 5 unit vertical gap
23
24 setLayout(new FlowLayout());
```

The sample code in Example 10-7 implements a simple FlowLayout.

Example 10-7 *Implementing a Simple* FlowLayout

```
1 import java.awt.*;
2 public class ButtonOnFrame extends Frame {
3   Button button1, button2, button3;
```

Example 10-7 *Implementing a Simple* FlowLayout (Continued)

```
4    public ButtonOnFrame(){
5      setLayout(new FlowLayout());
6      button1 = new Button("Ok");
7      button2 = new Button("Open");
8      button3 = new Button("Close");
9      add(button1);
10     add(button2);
11     add(button3);
12   }
13   public static void main(String[] args)
14   {
15     ButtonOnFrame bof = new ButtonOnFrame();
16     bof.pack();
17     bof.setVisible(true);
18   }
19 }
20
```

In addition to the FlowLayout and the BorderLayout managers, the GridLayout manager provides more control over the location of components, as illustrated in Figure 10-15.

Figure 10-15 GridLayout Manager

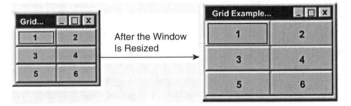

The properties of a GridLayout manger could look similar to the following:

- Components are added left to right and top to bottom.
- All regions are sized equally.
- The constructor specifies the rows and columns.

The sample code in Example 10-8 implements a simple `GridLayout`.

Example 10-8 *Implementing a Simple* `GridLayout`

```
1 import java.awt.*;
2 public class ButtonGrid extends Frame {
3   public ButtonGrid() {
4     setLayout(new GridLayout(3,2));
5     add(new Button("1"));
6     add(new Button("2"));
7     add(new Button("3"));
8     add(new Button("4"));
9     add(new Button("5"));
10    add(new Button("6"));
11  }
12  public static void main(String[] args)
13  {
14    ButtonGrid bg = new ButtonGrid();
15    bg.setSize(300,600);
16    bg.setVisible(true);
17  }
18 }
19
```

Selecting specific panels and layouts for each of the panels can further refine the chat window class. Selecting the proper combination of panels, frames, and layout managers provides greater control over the components on the screen, as shown in the list that follows:

- A `Frame` forms the base to display all the components.
- Two large `Panels` are placed on the `Frame`: messageBase and messageAction.
- The `Panel` messageBase is used to contain two additional panels: labelArea and messageDisplay.
- The labelArea will display two `Label` objects, and the messageDisplay `Panel` will display two `TextArea` objects.
- The `Panel` messageAction is used to contain the buttonArea `Panel` and display a `TextField`.
- The buttonArea `Panel` will display the four buttons.

The following shows containers and their layout managers:

```
Frame messageWindow  -- BorderLayout (default)


Panel  messageBase  -- BorderLayout (not the default)

Panel  messageAction -- BorderLayout

Panel  messageDisplay -- GridLayout (not the default)

Panel  buttonArea -- FlowLayout (default )

Panel  labelArea -- GridLayout (not the default)
```

You can select a layout manager by using the `setLayout()` method of the container. Example 10-9 shows the use of this method in the `MessageGUI` class.

Example 10-9 *Code for Selecting a Layout Manager*

```
 1 /** The MessageGUI class presents a user interface for
 2  * sending and receiving messaages
 3  *
 4  * @author Cisco Teacher
 5  * @version 2002
 6  */
 7
 8 //Required import statements
 9
10 import java.awt.*;
11 import java.awt.event.*;
12
13 public class MessageGUI implements ActionListener,WindowListener
14 {
15
16        Panel messageBase;
17        Panel messageAction;
18        Panel labelArea;
19        Panel messageDisplay;
20        Panel buttonArea;
```

NOTE

For Example 10-9, you can view the explanatory text by accessing the full, interactive graphic for this example on the book's accompanying CD-ROM. The title of the activity is "Code for Selecting a Layout Manager" in the e-Lab Activities.

NOTE

The full version of the abbreviated code shown in this example can be viewed using the book's accompanying CD-ROM.

After the layout managers have been selected, components can be added to the containers. The sequence in which they are added is critical. Take time to review the code and the sequence in which the components are added.

Table 10-3 presents a comparison of the layout managers.

Table 10-3 Comparing Layout Managers

FlowLayout	BorderLayout	GridLayout	CardLayout
Components are added from left to right and top to bottom.		Components are added from left to right cells and top to bottom cells.	
Center is the default alignment.		Center is the default alignment.	
The preferred size of components added to it is honored.	North and South: Preferred height is honored, but not preferred width. East and West: Preferred width is honored, but not preferred height. Center: Preferred width and height are ignored.	All components are equal in size, ignoring preferred width and height.	
Many components can be held.	Each region can have only one component.	Each region (cell) can have only one component.	This is made up of multiple panels, which can own layout manager and components.
Components can move from one row to the next if the panel is resized vertically or horizontally.	Components stay put within their region as the panel is resized.	Components stay put within their region as the panel is resized.	

More Information
The CardLayout manager is very useful for managing panels that will be stacked on top of each other. This layout manager displays a different panel as requested. As with a deck of cards, the CardLayout manager can display one card at a time. The card here is represented by a Panel with all of its components. The design of a GUI using the CardLayout manager requires the creation of a base Panel to which the layout manager is assigned. Then, each of the display Panels references is added to the layout manager. The methods show() and add() are used to create a CardLayout-managed display.

Sizing Components and Containers

A layout manager determines the position and size of a component in a container. A container keeps a reference to a particular instance of a layout manager. When the container needs to position a component, it invokes the layout manager to do so. The same delegation occurs when deciding on the size of a component. The layout manager takes full control of all of the components within the container. It is responsible for computing and defining the preferred size of the object in the context of the actual screen size. For example, the preferred size of a button is the size of the label text plus the border space and the shadowed decorations that mark the boundary of the button. The preferred size depends on the platform.

Because the layout manager is generally responsible for the size and position of components on its container, the size and position should not be changed. If this is tried (using methods such as setLocation, setSize, or setBounds), the layout manager can override the decision. For these methods to size and position the components, the layout manager must be set to null using the syntax setLayout(null).

In addition to using the *setSize() method*, the pack() method can be used to place all the components within a small Panel or Frame. A call to the pack() method of a container does not change the placement of the components if a layout manager is installed. However, the size of the components might be impacted by the use of the pack() method.

Displaying the GUI

It is best to display the GUI after all of the components have been built and added to the `Panels`, `Frames`, and `Windows`. The *setVisible method*, shown in the step examples that follow, is used to display components:

```
Making the Container Visible
// Step 7 Sizing the container    messageWindow.setSize(200,300);

// Step 8 Making the container visible
   messageWindow.setVisible(true);
```

This method accepts the **boolean** value **true** to make the components visible and **false** to hide them. The `setVisible` method can be used on a specific component or on the base container that contains all other components. The `MessageGUI` class consists of a base `Frame`, `messageWindow`. The `setVisible` method of the `messageWindow` is called, and all of the components contained in this base `Frame` (`messageWindow`) are displayed on the screen.

GUI Functionality

In the last section, you learned how to create a GUI. This section looks into how the GUI handles actions initiated by a user, known as events. This section consists of the following topics:

- The event-delegation model
- Event objects
- Listener classes
- Adapter classes
- Inner classes
- Anonymous classes

NOTE

Examples of event objects include `ActionEvent`, `Window-Event`, `Component-Event`, `ItemEvent`, `TextEvent`, `KeyEvent`, and `MouseEvent`.

Event-Delegation Model

An event is an action initiated by a user. Some common events are pressing (or clicking) a button and changing text. Figure 10-16 illustrates the concept of an event. When the user performs an action at the user interface level (clicks a mouse or presses a key), this causes an event to be issued. Events are objects that describe what has happened. A variety of event classes exist to describe different categories of user action.

Figure 10-16 Source of an Event, the Event, and the Handler

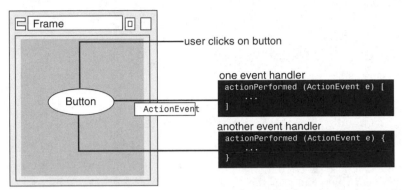

In Java, event objects derive from the `java.awt.AWTEvent` class. The first experience that most programmers have with event-driven programming is in the context of GUIs and managing user interactions. However, many other types of events can be created to handle non–GUI-related business tasks. Classes that handle events can be found in the `java.awt.event` package, as well as in other packages.

The Java language uses an *event-delegation model* to handle events. Figure 10-16 illustrates the objects that are used in this model:

- Source of an event (*event source*)—This is an object that can generate an event object.
- Event (*event object*)—This is an event object that encapsulates information about the event.
- Handler (*event handler*)—This is the object that can handle the event, which is performing some task.

The implementation of the event-delegation model includes:

- Events are not handled accidentally. The objects that want to listen to particular events on a particular GUI component register themselves with that component.
- When an event occurs, only the objects that were registered receive a message that the event occurred.
- The delegation model is good for the distribution of work among classes.

For example, to implement the delegation model for the button in Figure 10-16:

- Define and create the component that the user will interact with—in this case a `Button`:

  ```
  Button b = new Button("ok");
  ```

- Define a class that implements the listener interface (*event listener*). Some components might generate more than one event object. In this case, if the programmer needs to handle all of these event objects, a class must implement all the appropriate listener interfaces.

- Register an instance of the class that implements the interface with the component object that generates the event object. This is accomplished by having the component object call an *addXXXXListener(Object o); method*. The XXXX is replaced with the name of the listener interface.

The button is the source and generates the `ActionEvent` object when the user initiates an action. The handler is the class that implements the specific interface that is appropriate for the event.

TIP

The MVC pattern uses three main components: model, view, and controller.

The model represents the logical structure of data in the application and does not contain any information about the user interface.

The view represents elements in the user interface.

The controller represents classes that connect the model and the view, and is used to communicate between model classes and view classes.

The code that the programmer will write to implement the event-driven model consists of the previous three steps. The event-delegation model can be implemented all in one class. In other words, the class that contains the GUI components also implements the listener interfaces. In general, when implementing a proper Model-View-Controller (MVC) pattern, the GUI should be defined in one class, the business logic should be defined in a separate class, and the listener methods should be defined in another class.

In some cases, if the handler for the event is specific to a GUI and its components, the programmer can use two special types of class definitions, the inner class and the anonymous class, to handle the events. A later section describes these classes and their use.

Event Objects

User interaction with a component is the source of an event for GUI programs. Each of the component classes can generate specific event objects. The type of event object generated depends on the component. For example, the `Button` object generates an `ActionEvent` object, and the `TextComponent` object generates a `TextEvent` object.

Table 10-4 shows the component and the event objects that they generate.

Table 10-4 Component and Event Objects

Event/Method	Generated By
ACTION_EVENT/action	ButtonListMenuItem TextField
	Checkbox CheckboxMenuItem Choice
WINDOW_DESTROY WINDOW_EXPOSE WINDOW_ICONIFY WINDOW_DEICONIFY	Dialog Frame
WINDOW_MOVED	Dialog Frame
SCROLL_LINE_UPSCROLL_LINE_DOWNSCROLL_PAGE_ UPSCROLL_PAGE_DOWNSCROLL_ABSOLUTESCROLL_BEGIN SCROLL_END	Scrollbar
LIST_SELECT LIST_DESELECT	Checkbox CheckboxMenuItem Choice List
MOUSE_DRAG/mouseDrag MOUSE_MOVE/mouseMove	Canvas Dialog Frame Panel Window
MOUSE_DOWN/mouseDownMOUSE_UP/mouseUpMOUSE_ ENTER/mouseEnter MOUSE_EXIT/mouseExit	Canvas Dialog Frame Panel Window

In the ChatWindow class, the only components of interest to the programmer are the interaction of the users with the button and the closing of windows. In general, the Window component (which, in this class, is a Frame) is not programmed to close automatically.

The minimize feature and maximize feature are built-in features for the window. So, to close the window, the programmer must use an event handler to handle window events.

Although the ChatWindow includes a TextField and a TextArea, the programmer pays attention only to the buttons that are pressed. This reduces the amount of work that the object must do to listen to user events. In this example, the user's entry into the TextArea is of less interest than when the user notifies the object to send the text.

The Frame object is a Window and generates a WindowEvent object. The Button objects generate ActionEvent objects.

Listener Classes

A handler class is any class that implements a listener interface that is appropriate for the type of event object generated by the component. Components generate event objects when a Listener object is registered with the component.

The method of the component that accomplishes this is the addXXXListener method. The XXX represents the name of the specific listener.

The listener interface specifies the methods by which the event object can be handled. The class must implement the code for these methods. Table 10-5 shows the listener interfaces that can be implemented and their methods.

NOTE

Interfaces are contracts between two classes. The interface is the client contract, and the user of the interface is the class that implements the interface. When declaring that a class implements an interface, that class must implement all of the abstract methods declared in the interface. Event handling in Java is arrived at by creating interfaces. These interfaces define the methods that must be implemented by the classes that want to handle events. The JVM looks for these implementations to communicate between components and handler classes.

Table 10-5 Event Objects and Listener Interfaces

Category	Interface Names	Methods
Action	ActionListener	actionPerformed(ActionEvent)
Item	ItemListener	itemStateChanged(ItemEvent)
Mouse	MouseListener	mousePressed(MouseEvent) mouseReleased(MouseEvent) mouseEntered(MouseEvent) mouseExited(MouseEvent) mouseClicked(MouseEvent)
Mouse motion	MouseMotionListener	mouseDragged(MouseEvent) mouseMoved(MouseEvent)
Key	KeyListener	keyPressed(KeyEvent) keyReleased(KeyEvent) keyTyped(KeyEvent)

Table 10-5 Event Objects and Listener Interfaces (Continued)

Category	Interface Names	Methods
Focus	FocusListener	focusGained(FocusEvent) focusLost(FocusEvent)
Adjustment	AdjustmentListener	AdjustmentValueChanged(AdjustmentEvent)
Component	ComponentListener	componentMoved(ComponentEvent) componentHidden(ComponentEvent) componentResized(ComponentEvent) componentShown(ComponentEvent)
Window	WindowListener	windowClosing(WindowEvent) windowOpened(WindowEvent) windowIconified(WindowEvent) windowDeiconified(WindowEvent) windowClosed(WindowEvent) windowActivated(WindowEvent) windowDeactivated(WindowEvent)
Container	ContainerListener	componentAdded(ContainerEvent) componentRemoved(ContainerEvent)
Text	TextListener	textValueChanged(TextEvent)

For example, to handle window events such as window closing, implement the WindowListener interface. This interface has seven methods. Although only one of these methods is of interest, the class must implement all of them.

The listener interfaces are part of the java.awt.event package. An **import** statement, import java.awt.event.*;, must be inserted at the start of the source file.

The listener interfaces for event handling can be implemented either in the class that constructs the GUI or in a separate class. The MVC design pattern suggests that these be kept separate; code is shown that uses both. In Example 10-10, the MessageGUI class implements the listener interfaces needed to handle the component-generated events. This class defines the GUI components, constructs the GUI, places the GUI on a Frame for display, and implements the listener interfaces. One class does it all. Here, the **this** variable identifies the class itself as being the handler. First, let us look at the two interfaces, WindowListener and ActionListener. The WindowListener is being used to close the window. This interface has many methods, but the programmer needs only to use the windowClosing method. Notice that all of the methods of the interface have been implemented. Only the windowClosing method has executable code inside the code

NOTE

For Example 10-10, you can view the highlighted code by accessing the full, interactive graphic for this example on the book's accompanying CD-ROM. The title of the activity is "Listener Interfaces in the MessageGUI Class" in e-Lab Activities.

NOTE

The full version of the abbreviated code shown in this example can be viewed using the book's accompanying CD-ROM.

NOTE

The ActionListener interface is the listener interface for receiving action events. The class that is interested in processing an action event implements this interface, and the object created with that class is registered with a component, using the component's addActionListener method. When the action event occurs, that object's action-Performed method is invoked.

block; the rest of the methods are implemented with empty code blocks ({}). The ActionListener interface has only one method. This method is implemented with code that changes the display (for example, the contents of the TextAreas, the TextField, or both).

Example 10-10 *Listener Interfaces in the* MessageGUI *Class*

```
1  /**
2   * Java Program: MessageGUI.java
3   * @author Cisco Teacher
4   * @version 2002
5   */
6
7  import java.awt.*;
8  import java.awt.event.*;
9
10 public class MessageGUI implements ActionListener, WindowListener
11 {
12
13     // step1 assignements
14     Button send = new Button();
15     Button read = new Button();
16     Button clear = new Button();
17     Button exit = new Button();
18     Frame messageWindow = new Frame();
19     TextArea sent = new TextArea();
20     TextField message = new TextField();
```

The second example follows the suggested MVC pattern of keeping the handling of the interaction separate. Here, a class known as the Handler implements the interfaces. The MessageGUI class registers an object of the Handler class with each component that a user interacts with and that is of interest to the programmer.

The MVC pattern introduces some complexity into this application. The MessageGUI class can use an external handler for its window-closing activity. To use an external handler for the actionPerformed method, a reference to the object that displays the button must be available. In the code shown in Example 10-11, the ActionListener is handled within the MessageGUI class, and the WindowListener is handled with another class called the Handler.

Example 10-11 MessageGUI *and* Handler *Classes*

NOTE

The full version of the abbreviated code shown in this example can be viewed using the book's accompanying CD-ROM.

```
1  /**
2   * Java Program: MessageGUI.java
3   * @author Cisco Teacher
4   * @version 2002
5   */
6
7  import java.awt.*;
8  import java.awt.event.*;
9
10 public class MessageGUI implements ActionListener
11 {
12
13     // step1 assignements
14     Button send = new Button();
15     Button read = new Button();
16     Button clear = new Button();
17     Button exit = new Button();
18     Frame messageWindow = new Frame();
19     TextArea sent = new TextArea();
20     TextField message = new TextField();


1  /**
2   * Java Program: Handler.java
3   * @author Cisco Teacher
4   * @version 2002
5   */
6
7  import java.awt.event.*;
8
9  public class Handler implements WindowListener
10 {
11     /**
12      * @param e An event as a WindowEvent data type
13      */
14     public void windowClosing(WindowEvent e)
```

continues

Example 10-11 `MessageGUI` *and* `Handler` *Classes (Continued)*

```
15    {
16          System.exit(0);
17    }
18
19    // Interface methods not used
20    public void windowOpened(WindowEvent e) {}
```

For Example 10-11, you can view the full, interactive graphic for this example on the book's accompanying CD-ROM. The title of the activity is "`MessageGUI` and `Handler` Classes" in e-Lab Activities.

A handler class contains the code logic for responding to user interaction. This also is known as the business logic. This class represents part of the model classes that form the MVC pattern. In these examples, the business logic is implemented in the methods `actionPerformed()` and `windowClosing()`. The `windowClosing(0)` method calls the `System.exit(0)` method. This static method of the `System` class closes the window and releases resources used by the program. The `actionPerformed()` method assesses the source of the action. In other words, it identifies the button pressed and performs tasks. When the Send, Clear, or Read button is pressed, the `TextArea` and `TextField` component are changed to display new information. Note the use of `StringBuffer`, `setText()`, and `getText()` to accomplish this.

Multiple listeners can be registered with a component. For example, if the programmer was interested in text change in a `TextComponent` and any specific key pressed by the user, the programmer could register a `TextListener` object with a `TextArea` component and a `KeyListener` with the same component.

Adapter Classes

The `MessageGUI` application **implements** the `WindowListener` interface to close the window. The `WindowListener` interface includes several methods that are not needed for this application. The Java platform provides *adapter classes*. These are abstract classes that implement the methods for a specific listener interface. In providing these classes, the Java platform reduces the number of methods that a programmer needs to implement. The class that extends the adapter class can override the methods that are useful. The programmer can create a handler class that extends from one of these adapter classes. The adapter classes have the name of the `ListenerInterface` and the word `Adapter`. Table 10-6 shows the adapter classes.

NOTE

The methods of the `WindowAdapter` class are the same as those defined in the `WindowListener` interface. The only difference between the adapter and the listener is that the methods listed in the `Listener` class are implemented (albeit as empty methods) in the `Adapter` class. This makes it unnecessary for the programmer to implement each of the methods in the `Listener` class. The programmer can extend from the `Adapter` class and override only the desired method(s).

Table 10-6 Adapter Classes

Listener	Adapter
WindowListener	WindowAdapter
MouseListener	MouseAdapter
KeyListener	KeyAdapter

The MessageGUI application now is modified to use the adapter classes. Here the adapter class can be used easily. The one drawback to using an adapter class is that the class can extend only from this, not any other class. For example, a class cannot be extended from both a `Panel` and a `WindowAdapter`. Example 10-12 shows the use of the adapter class in the `MessageGUI` application (where the class handles all the events).

Example 10-12 *Adapter Class Use in the* `MessageGUI` *Application*

```
1  /**
2   * Java Program: MessageGUI.java
3   * @author Cisco Teacher
4   * @version 2002
5   */
6
7  import java.awt.*;
8  import java.awt.event.*;
9
10 public class MessageGUI extends WindowAdapter
11 {
12
13     // step1 assignements
14     Button send = new Button();
15     Button read = new Button();
16     Button clear = new Button();
17     Button exit = new Button();
18     Frame messageWindow = new Frame();
19     TextArea sent = new TextArea();
20     TextField message = new TextField();
```

NOTE

The `ActionListener` is not implemented as an adapter class because it has only one method.

NOTE

The full version of the abbreviated code shown in this example can be viewed using the book's accompanying CD-ROM.

NOTE

For Example 10-12, you can view the explanatory text by accessing the full, interactive graphic for this example on the book's accompanying CD-ROM. The title of the activity is "Adapter Class Usages in the `MessageGUI` Application" in e-Lab Activities.

Example 10-13 shows the `Handler` class, which is used by the `MessageGUI` class.

Example 10-13 Handler *Class Uses Adapter*

```
 1 public class MessageGUI  implements ActionListener{

 2

 3 // the rest of the code is the same, except for the listener.

 4 // the listener interface ActionListener is implemented in this class.

 5 // Step 6 Registering the event-listener with the component

 6       /*  We are only interested in the user interactions with

 7           the buttons.

 8       *   The buttons will be registered with a class that implements

 9           the ActionListener interface

10      *   This interface is implemented within this class

11      * the 'this' reference identifies the current class as

12         implementing the listener interface

13      *

14      *   we are also interested in closing the window.

15         So we will register the frame with this class also

16      */

17      // This class implements the ActionListener, therefore the

18         class is registered with the button objects using the

19         keyword this

20      send.addActionListener(this);
```

For Example 10-13, you can view the explanatory text by accessing the full, interactive graphic for this example on the book's accompanying CD-ROM. The title of the activity is "`Handler` Class Uses Adapter" in e-Lab Activities.

In the next chapter, students learn about applets, which are GUIs that display in browser applications. Here, the GUI class is `Applet`, which **extends** from `Panel`, and therefore cannot extend from a `WindowAdapter`. With applets, event handling is accomplished best through the use of separate handler classes.

Inner Classes

The creation of a GUI resulted in many classes to handle the GUI, its events, and its display context. The Java language provides programmers with the facility to define a class within another class. These classes are called *inner or enclosed classes*. Some simple ideas surround inner classes. Example 10-14 and Figure 10-17 show the creation of inner classes in two ways. Inner classes can be defined inside or outside a method. When defined inside a method, the inner classes have access to the fields of the outer class but not the variables of the method. A source file (`.java` file) that defines an outer class and an inner class result in two class files. In this example, a file named `Outer.class` and a file named `Outer$Inner.class` are generated.

Example 10-14 *Syntax for Defining Inner Classes*

```
 1 /**
 2  * This class shows the effects of declaring
 3  * Inner classes defined within another class.
 4  *
 5  * @author Cisco Teacher
 6  * @version 2002
 7  */
 8 public class Outer
 9 {
10
11     // data  for outer class
12     //class defined within the definition
13     class Inner
14     {
15        // data
16        // method
17     }  // end of inner class definition
18
19
20     // class defined with a method
```

NOTE

The full version of the abbreviated code shown in this example can be viewed using the book's accompanying CD-ROM.

For Example 10-14, you can view the explanatory text by accessing the full, interactive graphic for this example on the book's accompanying CD-ROM. The title of the activity is "Syntax for Defining Inner Classes" in e-Lab Activities.

Figure 10-17 Syntax for Defining Inner Classes

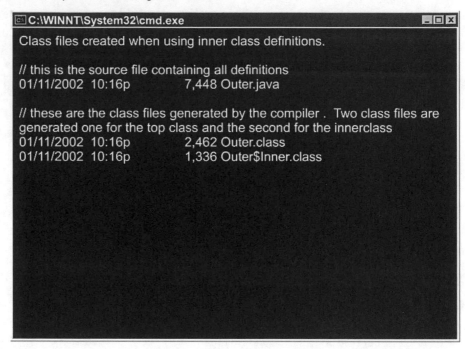

In Example 10-15, the inner class definitions are applied to the MessageGUI application. The ButtonHandler class implements the ActionListener, and the WindowHandler extends the WindowAdapter. A listing of the class files generated is shown in Figure 10-18.

Example 10-15 *Syntax for Defining Inner Classes*

NOTE

The full version of the abbreviated code shown in this example can be viewed using the book's accompanying CD-ROM.

```
1
2  /**
3   * The MessageGUI class presents a user interface for
4   * sending and receiving messages
5   *
6   * @author (Cisco Teacher )
7   * @version (Version 2002.1)
8   */
9
10 // Required import statements
11
12 import java.awt.*;
13 import java.awt.event.*;
14
```

Example 10-15 *Syntax for Defining Inner Classes (Continued)*

```
15 public class MessageGuiOuter
16 {
17    // Step 2 Creating references for components
18    TextArea  sent, recieved;
19    Label sentLabel, recdLabel;
20    TextField message;
```

Figure 10-18 Syntax for Defining Inner Classes

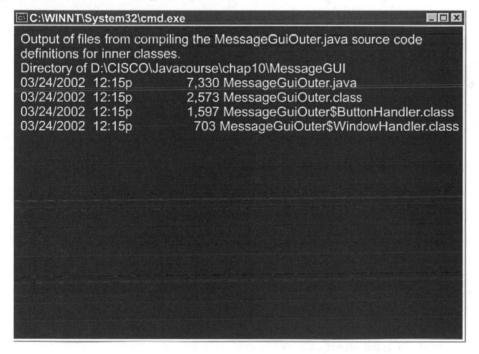

The enclosed classes fall into one of the following categories:

- Nested top-level classes, also known as outer class
- Member inner classes
- Local inner classes, defined as part of a method

Member inner classes are defined inside another class. Local inner classes are defined inside a method of a class. Member inner classes must be instantiated as part of an instance of their enclosing class. That is, a member inner class object cannot be instantiated unless an object of the outer class has been instantiated. The programmer can qualify the **new** keyword with an object reference to specify the enclosing object. Example 10-16 illustrates the use of outer and inner classes.

Example 10-16 *Syntax for Defining Classes*

NOTE

The full version of the abbreviated code shown in this example can be viewed using the book's accompanying CD-ROM.

```
 1
 2  /**
 3   * This class shows the use of instances of the inner class
 4   * The sample code maintains information on a customer.
 5   *  The top level class is InnerOuter.  This holds the
 6      name of the customer
 7   * The inner class is Inner and this holds the address.
 8   * The main method of the InnerOuter class instantiates the
 9      InnerOuter object
10   * this method also instatiates an object of the Inner class.
11      This code is
12   * to demonstrate the creation of an inner object in the context
13      of an outer object.
14   * @author CiscoTeacher
15   * @version 2002
16   */
17  public class InnerOuter
18  {
19      String name;
20      Inner addressObject;  // contains a reference to the Inner object
```

Local inner classes are defined within a method, and their definitions are private to that method. After an object of a local inner class has been created, its lifetime continues even after the scope of the method in which the class is declared ends.

The compelling reason for inner classes is that each inner class can inherit independently from an implementation. Thus, the inner class is not limited to whether the outer class already inherits from an implementation. The inner class completes the solution to the multiple-inheritance problem. A closure is a callable object that retains information from the scope in which it was created. The inner class holds a reference to the outer class (the scope in which it was created) and has permission to manipulate all the members, even **private** ones of the outer class.

> **More Information**
>
> Why did Sun go through so much trouble to add this fundamental language feature? Typically, the inner class inherits from a class or **implements** an interface, and the code in the inner class manipulates the object within which it was created. The inner class provides a "window" to the outer class. You might wonder, if you needed to implement a specific interface, why not have the outer class do it? Well, if that was your intention, you could do so. However, if the outer class inherits from a specific implementation and another class that manipulates the data of the outer class needs to inherit from a different implementation, how would you get these two classes to work together? For example, an outer class might represent the visual elements of a GUI. An inner class might perform the event handling for the GUI. However, the inner class needs to access the components of the outer class to display, change, redraw, and so on. The outer class might extend from a Frame, and the inner class might extend from a Window-Adapter. This allows the two classes to be "tightly coupled" to work together to provide both the display and user response functionality to the class.

Your class has these additional features with the use of an inner class:

- The inner class can have multiple instances, each with its own state information that is independent of the information in the outer class object.

- A single outer class can have several inner classes, each of which implements the same interface or inherits from the same class in a different way.

- The point of creation of the inner class object is not tied to the creation of the outer class object.

- There is no potentially confusing "is-a" relationship with the inner class; it is a separate entity.

Anonymous Classes

A programmer can include an entire class definition within the scope of an expression. This approach defines what is called an *anonymous inner class* and creates the instance all at once. Anonymous inner classes generally are used with AWT event handling and are used to extend from one of the adapter classes. In the code example shown in Example 10-17, the addXXXListener method is provided with a call to a constructor for an adapter class, and a method of the adapter class is overridden.

NOTE

Adapter classes are abstract classes and must be implemented before use.

NOTE

The full version of the abbreviated code shown in this example can be viewed using the book's accompanying CD-ROM.

Example 10-17 *Simple Use of an Anonymous Class*

```
1 /**
2  * Java Program: HelloWorld.java
3  * @author Cisco Teacher
4  * @version 2002
```

continues

Example 10-17 *Simple Use of an Anonymous Class (Continued)*

```
 5  */
 6
 7 import java.awt.*;
 8 import java.awt.event.*;
 9
10 public class HelloWorld extends Frame
11 {
12     /**
13      * @param titleText window's title bar text
14      */
15     public HelloWorld(String titleText)
16     {
17         super(titleText);
18
19         /*
20         creates an anonymous class
```

For Example 10-17, you can view the explanatory text by accessing the full, interactive graphic for this example on the book's accompanying CD-ROM. The title of the activity is "Simple Use of an Anonymous Class" in e-Lab Activities.

Anonymous inner classes are local inner classes that do not have a name. Anonymous inner classes do not have constructors, but their fields can be initialized with instance initializer blocks.

In the MessageGUI application, the class is modified and the WindowAdapter class is created as an expression within the call to the addWindowListener method. In the code example shown in Example 10-18, the MessageGUI class implements the Action-Listener interface and uses the anonymous class definition to handle window closing.

Example 10-18 *The Anonymous Class in the* MessageGUI *Application*

NOTE

The full version of the abbreviated code shown in this example can be viewed using the book's accompanying CD-ROM.

```
1 /**
2 * Java Program: MessageGUI.java
3 * @author Cisco Teacher
4 * @version 2002
5 */
6
7 import java.awt.*;
```

Example 10-18 *The Anonymous Class in the* `MessageGUI` *Application (Continued)*

```
 8 import java.awt.event.*;
 9
10 public class MessageGUI extends WindowAdapter
11 {
12
13     // step1 assignements
14     Button send = new Button();
15     Button read = new Button();
16     Button clear = new Button();
17     Button exit = new Button();
18     Frame messageWindow = new Frame();
19     TextArea sent = new TextArea();
20     TextField message = new TextField();
```

The syntax for this code is a little tricky. The first thing to note is that () encloses the entire definition. These () belong to the syntax of the method called addWindowListener(). The class definition is enclosed as an expression inside the parentheses. The next set of symbols and code to note is the use of { } embedded inside the call to a constructor. The code includes a call to the **new** operator, and the call to the WindowAdapter() constructor includes a class definition inside the code braces ({ }).

More Information

This strange syntax means, "Create an object of an anonymous class that is inherited (**extends**) from WindowAdapter." The reference returned by the **new** expression automatically is upcast to a WindowAdapter reference. This anonymous class is a shortcut for this syntax:

```
class MyWindowAdapter extends WindowAdapter{
  public void windowClosing(WindowEvent w)
    { System.exit(0); }
}
```

Anonymous classes do not have a name. In this example, the WindowAdapter class, which is abstract, is being implemented in an anonymous concrete class with the windowClosing method overridden in the code. In this context, the compiler inserts an anonymous class that extends from the WindowAdapter class. The last thing to note is the overriding of the windowClosing method inside the class definition. The final set of braces and); end the statement that began with messageWindow.addWindowListener().

Study: Banking Application

The JBANK application introduced in Chapter 1, "What Is Java?", provides students with an opportunity to apply the Java language concepts learned throughout this course. In the JBANK lab for Chapter 10, students will finalize the Model-View-Controller Pattern for the ATMGUI class and complete the ATMGUI application. As part of this lab, code will be added to allow customers to withdraw and deposit money into their accounts. Several opportunities will be given to include many Java language constructs of logic and loop.

Banking Application

In previous chapters, all interactions between a teller and a customer, or a customer and his or her accounts, have been through the Console class. In addition, all input has used the System.in object. These are fine for programmers to test their applications. When end users have to use the applications, extensive GUIs must be provided. The banking application includes the creation of two GUIs: a TellerGUI and an ATMGUI. Figures 10-19 and 10-20 display what the JBANK application's TellerGUI and ATMGUI might look like. The tellers of the bank will use the TellerGUI, which gives the teller the ability to retrieve information about customer accounts, add new customers, change customer and account data, and conduct withdrawal and deposit transactions. The ATMGUI provides a user interface for customers. This interface provides less functionality than the TellerGUI. Customers can query balances, withdraw money, and deposit money into their accounts.

Figure 10-19 The JBANK Application

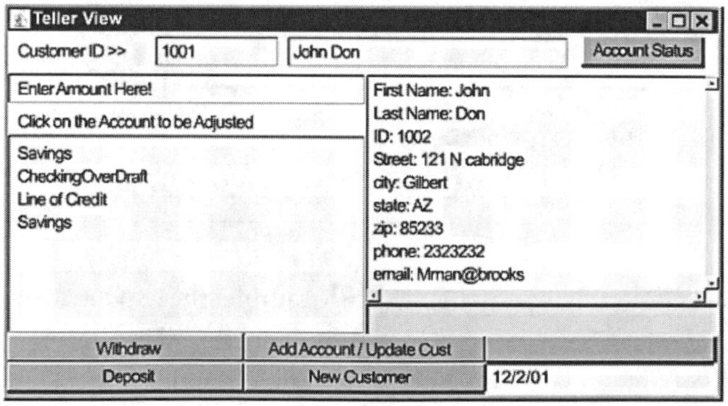

Figure 10-20 The JBANK Application

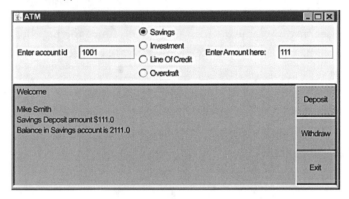

Throughout this chapter, the code for the TellerGUI class has been provided. Now complete the code for the ATMGUI adding the business logic to these classes. This requires modifying the handler and controller classes to include code for conducting customer account transactions.

The Model-View-Controller design pattern is employed in these labs. The need for a connection between the view class and the handler class is implemented through the use of an interface controller. This interface serves as a marker interface; it is a way of labeling classes as being of the same kind. This interface does not have any methods declared. Implement this interface in the lab to help connect the model, view, and controller classes. Read the instructions regarding this implementation carefully.

Summary

The Java language provides extensive support for creating graphical user interfaces (GUIs) through the java.awt package. In this chapter, students learned that GUIs are built using component objects and container objects. A programmer can add components to containers by creating objects of the component class and calling the add method of the container, passing the component as an argument. Components are added to a container using a layout manager. Although a programmer can set the specific location and size of a component, the recommended approach is to use one of the predefined layout managers to arrange the components in a way that adjusts for screen resolutions and window resizing. Each container has a default layout manager.

Students also learned that GUIs are programmed to respond when the user moves the mouse, clicks the mouse, or types on the keyboard. These kinds of user input are called events. The Java language uses the event-delegation model for programming event handling. To handle an event, define a class to implement the appropriate listener interface. Call a method for the component to register the listener with the component. Use adapter classes that implement the interfaces to reduce the number of methods that must be implemented to only those events that are of interest.

Key Terms

Abstract Window Toolkit (AWT)   The Java platform provides extensive support for programming GUIs through the classes found in the `java.awt` package.

adapter classes   Abstract classes that implement the methods for a specific listener interface.

add() method   Method that adds other components or containers to each container object.

addXXXListener() method—Method that implements the listener of a particular event. The XXX represents the name of a specific listener.

anonymous inner classes   Using an entire class definition within the scope of an expression.

button   A rounded polygon-shaped figure that a user clicks to initiate an action.

Component   The abstract class that is at the root of all the classes that create GUI components objects.

components   Objects that display a graphic image and can monitor user interactions with the image.

container   Component that holds other components so that a group of components can be treated as a single entity.

event-delegation model   Model that Java uses to handle events. It is composed of event source, event objects, and event handlers.

> *event source*   Object that generates an event object.
>
> *event object*   Object describes what action has happened; derived from the `java.awt.AWTEvent` class.
>
> *event handler*   Object that handles the event, performing some task.

event listener   Object that is interested in a particular event.

Frame   A subclass of the `Window` class. `Frames` are created so that other objects can be placed in them for display.

graphics   Text, pictures, images, buttons, and so on.

graphical user interface (GUI)   Provides a means for the program to display data and to obtain input from the user.

inner or enclosed classes   Defining a class within another class, either inside or outside a method.

Label   Noncontainer object of the `Component` class that holds text that can be displayed.

layout manager   Sets the position for displaying each component.

>   *BorderLayout*   Breaks up the area into five regions: North, South, East, West, and Center. The layout manager controls the size of each region.

>   *FlowLayout*   Places components from left to right, top to bottom.

>   *GridLayout*   Uses a grid of rows and columns. It fills each grid with one component from left to right and top to bottom.

Panel   A free-floating container that must be displayed on another container such as a `Window`, `Frame`, or `Dialog` (or inside a web browser's window in an applet).

setLayout() method   Method used to change the default layout manager for each container.

>   *setSize()method*   Method to set the physical size of a component.

>   *setVisible() method*   Method used to display components.

TextArea   Multiline textbox with scrollbars, which accepts input from the user.

TextComponent   Parent class for `TextArea` and `TextField`.

TextField   Single-line textbox that accepts input from the user.

Window   A freestanding native window on the display that is independent of other containers. Two important types of `Window` exist: `Frame` and `Dialog`.

Check Your Understanding

1. Which of the following classes is not in the `java.awt` package?

   A. `GridLayout`

   B. `Graphics`

   C. `Frame`

   D. `ActionEvent`

2. Which abstract class is used to draw on components in GUI applications?

   A. `Image`

   B. `Graphics`

   C. `AWT`

   D. `Color`

3. `Panel`, `ScrollPane`, and `Window` are all subclasses of

   A. `Component`

   B. `Container`

   C. `MenuContainer`

   D. `LayoutManager`

4. An effective way to design a GUI is to divide the display area into meaningful regions; each region is a _____.

   A. `Panel`

   B. `Frame`

   C. `Window`

   D. `Graphic`

5. Which statement could be used to change the text on an existing `Button` object, b1, to "Finish?"

   A. `Button b1 = new Button("Finish");`

   B. `setText("Finish");`

   C. `Button.setText("Finish");`

   D. `b1.setLabel("Finish");`

6. Which statement could be used to change the text on an existing `Label` object, L1, to "Finish"?

   A. `Label L1 = new Label("Finish");`

   B. `L1.setText("Finish");`

   C. `Label.setText("Finish");`

   D. `L1.setLabel("Finish");`

7. What is the default layout manager for a `Frame` object?

   A. `FlowLayout`

   B. `DefaultLayout`

   C. `BorderLayout`

   D. `GridBagLayout`

8. What is one difference between a `Dialog` object and a `Frame` object?

   A. A `Dialog` has a default `FlowLayout`, while a `Frame` has a default `GridBagLayout`.

   B. A `Dialog` has a `Frame` or other `Dialog` defined as its owner, but a `Frame` does not.

   C. A `Dialog` does not have a title bar, but a `Frame` does.

   D. A `Dialog` does not have a border, but a `Frame` does.

9. If a programmer must design a GUI that can be used as an applet or a standalone application, which type of container should be used to hold the components?

   A. `Frame`

   B. `Applet`

   C. `Panel`

   D. `Window`

10. Which Java statement will add a `Panel` object, `myPanel`, to the upper region of a `Frame`, `myFrame`, with a `BorderLayout`?

    A. `myFrame.add(this.myPanel);`

    B. `myFrame.add(myPanel, NORTH);`

    C. `myFrame.add(myPanel, BorderLayout.North);`

    D. `myFrame.add(myPanel, BorderLayout.NORTH);`

11. Which of the following is not one of the layout managers used in GUI development?

    A. `BorderLayout`

    B. `CardBagLayout`

    C. `FlowLayout`

    D. `GridLayout`

12. Which of the following is false about the `FlowLayout`?

    A. It is the default layout for the `Frame` class.

    B. It adds components from left to right.

    C. It centers components by default

    D. All of the above.

13. Which statement can be used so that a `Frame` object, `myFrame`, allows absolute positioning of components?

    A. `myFrame.setLayout(new AbsoluteLayout());`

    B. `myFrame.setLayout("");`

    C. `myFrame.setLayout(new BorderLayout());`

    D. `myFrame.setLayout(null);`

14. Which of the following is a false statement about the MVC pattern?

    A. The model exists independently from any GUI displays.

    B. The view contains all of the graphical components of an application.

    C. The controller is used to communicate between the model and the view.

    D. The model is used to communicate between the view and the controller.

15. Which of the following is false about the listener interfaces?

    A. An appropriate listener interface must be implemented to handle events.

    B. The listener interfaces are part of the `java.awt.listener` package.

    C. The listener interfaces are part of the `java.awt.event` package.

    D. All of the methods from the listener interface must be defined by the class in which the interface is implemented.

16. Which listener interface must be implemented to handle the event generated by a button click?

    A. `ActionListener`

    B. `ClickListener`

    C. `ItemListener`

    D. All of the above

17. Which method in the `ActionListener` interface is invoked when an `ActionEvent` is generated?

    A. `mouseClicked()`

    B. `action()`

    C. `actionPerformed()`

    D. `actionEvent()`

18. Which of the following is true about `WindowAdapter` and `WindowListener`?

    A. `WindowAdapter` is an abstract class and `WindowListener` is an interface.

    B. `WindowAdapter` has null implementations of the `WindowListener` methods.

    C. `WindowAdapter` is utilized by extending the class and implementing only those methods that are necessary.

    D. All of the above.

19. Which of the following is a false statement about inner classes?

    A. Inner classes can be defined inside a method.

    B. An inner class defined inside a method has access to variables of the outer class, but not method variables.

    C. An inner class defined inside a method has access to variables of the method, but not variables of the outer class.

    D. Inner classes can be defined outside a method.

20. What is the distinguishing characteristic of anonymous inner classes?

    A. They can be used to handle events.

    B. They extend adapter classes.

    C. They override methods of the class from which they inherit.

    D. They do not have a name.

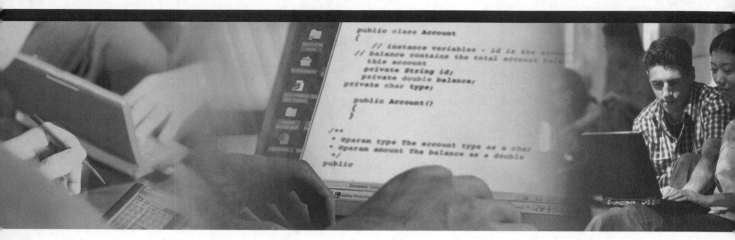

Upon completion of this chapter, you will be able to

- Understand applets
- Create an applet
- Understand the `Applet` class hierarchies
- Use and understand `Applet` class methods
- Understand and apply GUI components in applets
- Understand applets and event-driven programming
- Understand graphic objects
- Apply the Java language concepts that you have learned in this chapter to the JBANK case study

Applets and Graphics

This chapter focuses on applets and graphics. *Applets* are Java programs that display and run in a web browser. A browser is a program used to display HTML documents from the World Wide Web. The applet is embedded in an HTML document and then can be accessed.

Applets provide programmers with a way to display Java programs in any browser window. Applets include graphical user interface (GUI) components, graphics, and event-handling objects and code.

Creating applets requires using classes in the java.applet package and other classes in the java.awt package. The Java 2 SDK provides the appletviewer utility to test applets.

The second topic of this chapter is graphics. The Java platform provides many classes for creating graphics. The Graphics class has methods for drawing lines, rectangles, and ovals as basic shapes. From these basic shapes, a programmer can create many complex graphics. GUI components are drawn on the screen using Graphics objects, as well as the paint, repaint, and update methods. The Applet class also uses these methods to display the applet's graphics in the browser window.

Applets

The early popularity of the Java language is attributed to its use of Java applets. An applet is a small program (application) that is run within a web browser such as Netscape Navigator or Microsoft Internet Explorer.

This section consists of the following topics:

- Defining applets
- Launching applets
- Applying security to applets
- Embedding a Java applet

Defining Applets

NOTE

Traditionally, the word *applet* has come to mean any small application. A Java applet is any program that is launched from a web document— that is, from an HTML file. Java applications, on the other hand, are programs that run from the command line, independent of a web browser. A Java applet has no limit in size or in complexity. However, on the Internet, where communication speed is limited and download times are long (narrow bandwidth), applets often are designed to be small by necessity.

The popularity of Java applets was largely the result of the widespread use of the World Wide Web. This vast network has made information accessible through documents that use a special markup language of the Internet known as the *Hypertext Markup Language (HTML)*. These documents can be static (providing static information) or dynamic, with content presentations that include graphics and symbols that a user can interact with. One such user-interactive technology that can be embedded in an HTML document is the Java applet.

The Java programming language enables developers to create powerful software tools. These tools can run either standalone—that is, inside the user's Java Virtual Machine— or inside other programs. A Java program that runs standalone is called a Java application. An applet is a Java program that requires another program, a web browser, to run it. Web browsers are applications (programs) that are used to display information (web pages) from other computers. These other computers are connected to the network of computers on the Internet, known as the World Wide Web. It is possible to embed a Java applet within one of these web pages so that when the user views the web page, the embedded Java applet starts automatically. In this manner, Java programs can be a resource that is made available to Internet users. Applets are the Java technologies that make this happen.

Applets represent container objects. These containers can display the graphics and other GUI components in a frame.

Launching Applets

In all of the classes thus far, the main method is the starting point of the program. The Java interpreter begins the application by locating the main method in the class and then executing the code in this method. Running an applet is more complex than running an application; simply typing in a command cannot run an applet.

The basic steps followed in the creation and use of applets are outlined here:

Step 1   Design the GUI that you want to display.

Step 2   Create a class that extends from the `Applet` class.

Step 3   Compile the applet.

Step 4   Create an HTML file. Insert the statements that call the `Applet` class.

Step 5   Open a browser or use the `appletviewer` program and call the HTML file.

Review the code shown in Example 11-1.

Example 11-1 `TodayIS.java` *Program*

```
 1 /**
 2  * TodayIS.java
 3  * @author Cisco Teacher
 4  * @version 2002
 5  */
 6
 7 import java.applet.*;
 8 import java.awt.*;
 9 import java.awt.event.*;
10 import java.util.*;
11
12 public class TodayIS extends Applet implements ActionListener
13 {
14     Label banner = new Label("");
15     Font theFont = new Font("TimesRoman",Font.BOLD, 12);
16     Button button1 = new Button("Press ME");
17
18     public void init()
19     {
20          banner.setFont(theFont);
```

NOTE

The full version of the abbreviated code shown in this example can be viewed using the book's accompanying CD-ROM.

This Java class is an applet. This simple applet, `TodayIS`, provides a button and displays a message. Launching an applet follows the steps shown in Figure 11-1.

Figure 11-1 How the Applet Loads

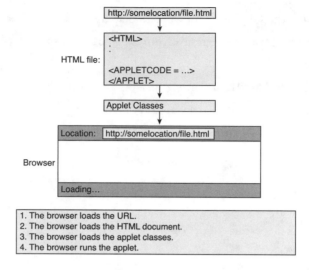

The four basic steps shown in Figure 11-1 are as follows:

1. The browser loads the URL.

2. The browser loads the HTML document.

3. The browser loads the applet classes.

4. The browser runs the applet.

Figures 11-2 and 11-3 show two different ways of launching Lights.java, the applet shown in Example 11-2.

Figure 11-2 Launching an Applet

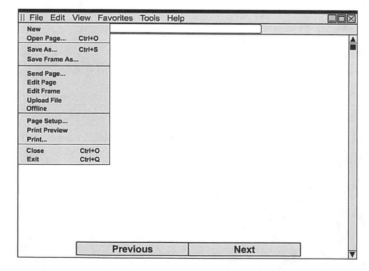

Figure 11-3 Launching an Applet

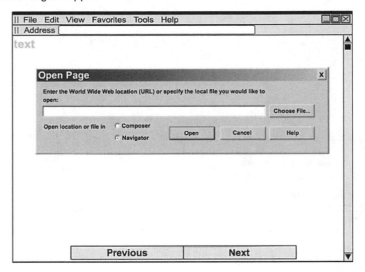

For Figures 11-2 and 11-3, you can view the full, interactive graphic for these two figures on the book's accompanying CD-ROM. The title of the activity is "Launching an Applet," and it is found under the e-Lab activities.

Example 11-2 *Code for Creating the Java Applet*

```
1  import java.applet.*;
2  import java.awt.*;
3  import java.net.*;
4     public class Lights extends Applet {
5
6          final int ON = 1;
7          final int OFF = -1;
8          final int WIDTH = 200;
9          protected int light [][];
10         protected int counterOn = 0;
11         protected int counterOFf = 0;
12         int end = 0;
13
14         public void init() {
15             end = 0;
16             light = new int[5][5];
```

continues

Example 11-2 *Code for Creating the Java Applet (Continued)*

```
17                    for (int i = 0; i < 5; I++) {
18                        for (int j = 0; j < 5; j++) {
19                            light[I][j] = OFF;
20                        }
21                    }
22            countLight();
23      }
24
25      public void start() {
26            setBackground(Color.white);
27      }
28
29      public void paint(Graphics g) {
30            g.setColor(Color.blue);
31            g.fill3Drect(210, 165, 60, 20 true);
32            g.setColor(Color.red);
33            g.drawString("RESTART", 214, 180);
34            drawBoard(g);
35            for (int i = 0; i < 5; I++) {
36                for (int j = 0; j < 5; j++) {
37                    if (light[I][j] != 0){
38                        drawLight(I, j, g);
39                    }
40                }
41            }
42            drawCountLight(g);
43      }
44
45      Public void drawBoard(Graphics g) {
46            g.setColor(Color.black);
47            g.drawLine(0,0, 0,WIDTH);
48            g. drawLine(WIDTH,0, WIDTH,WIDTH);
49            g.drawLine(0,0, WIDTH,0);\
50            g.drawLine(0,WIDTH, WIDTH,WIDTH);
51            for (int i = 1; i < 5; I++) {
52                g.drawLine(WIDTH*i/5,0, WIDTH*i/5,WIDTH);
```

Example 11-2 *Code for Creating the Java Applet (Continued)*

```
53                      g.drawLine(0,WIDTH*i/5, WIDTH,WIDTH*i/5);
54              }
55      }
56
57      public void drawLight(int column, int row, Graphics g) {
58              if (light[column][row] == ON) {
59                      g.setColor(Color.yellow);
60              } else if (light[column][row] == OFF) {
61                      g.setColor(Color.gray);
62              }
63              g.fillRect(column * WIDTH / 5 + 2, row * WIDTH / 5 + 2,
64                              WIDTH / 5 - 3, WIDTH / 5 - 3);
65      }
66
67      void countLight() {
68              counterOn = 0;
69              counterOff = 0;
70              for (int i = 0; i <5; I++) {
71                      for (int j = 0; j < 5; j++) {
72                              if(light[I][j] == ON) counterON++;
73                              if(light[I][j] == Off) counterOff++;
74                      }
75              }
76              if (counterON == 25) {
77                      endGame(getGraphics());
78              }
79      }
80
81      public void endGame(Graphics g) {
82              update(getGraphics());
83                      for (int i = 0; i < 5; I++) {
84                              for (int j = 0; j < 5; j++) {
85                                      light[I][j] = OFF;
86                                      update(getGraphics());
87                              }
88                      }
```

continues

Example 11-2 *Code for Creating the Java Applet (Continued)*

```
89                for (int i = 0; i < 5; I++) {
90                    for (int j = 0; j < 5; j++) {
91                        light[I][j] = ON;
92                        update(getGraphics());
93                    }
94                }
95                g.setColor(Color.yellow);
96                g.fillRect(65, 98, 10);
97                g.setColor(Color.black);
98                g.drawString("Congratulations!!", 65, 105);
99                end = 1;
100        }
101
102    void drawCountLight(Graphics g) {
103            g.setColor(Color.white);
104            g.fill3DRect(WIDTH+15, 50, 30,20, false);
105            g.fill3DRect(WIDTH+15, 110, 30,20, false);
106            g.setColor(Color.gray);
107            g.fill3DRect(WIDTH+5, 85, 20,20, true);
108            g.setColor(Color.yellow);
109            g.fill3DRect(WIDTH+5, 20, 20,20, true);
110            g.setColor(Color.black);
111            g.drawString("LightOn", WIDTH+30, 35);
112            g.drawString("LightOff", WIDTH+30, 100);
113            g.drawString(Integer.toString(counterOn), WIDTH+20, 65);
114            g.drawString(Integer.toString(counterOff), WIDTH+20, 125);
115    }
116
117    public boolean mouseUp(Event event, int x, int y) {
118            if (end == 1) {
119                init();
120                update(getGraphics());
121            } else {
122                if (x > 210 && x < 270 && y > 165 && y < 185) {
123                    init();
124                    update(getGraphics());
```

Example 11-2 *Code for Creating the Java Applet (Continued)*

```
125                        }
126                        int column = (int)(x / (WIDTH / 5));
127                        int row = (int) (y / (WIDTH / 5));
128                        light[column][row] = -light[column][row];
129                        try {
130                                light[column+1][row] = -light[column+1][row];
131                        } catch(Exception e) {
132                        }
133                        try {
134                                light[column-1][row] = -light[column-1][row];
135                        } catch(Exception e) {
136                        }
137                        try {
138                                light[column][row+1] = -light[column][row+1];
139                        } catch(Exception e) {
140                        }
141                        try {
142                                light[column][row-1] = -light[column][row-1];
143                        } catch(Exception e) {
144                        }
145                        countLight();
146                        if (end == 0) {
147                                update(getGraphics());
148                        }
149                }
150             return true;
151        }
152 }
153
154 <HTML>
155 <APPLET CODE = "Lights.class" WIDTH = 300 HEIGHT =  200 >
156 </APPLET>
156 </HTML>
```

To launch an applet, begin by loading a browser and pointing the browser to a *URL* (a specific address for an HTML document). The URL could be either a reference to a directory on the programmer's machine or an Internet address for another machine.

NOTE

The differences between an applet and an application stem from the context in which they run. A Java application runs in the simplest of environments—its only input from the outside world is a list of command-line parameters. On the other hand, a Java applet receives a lot of information from the web browser. It needs to know when it is initialized, when and where to draw itself in the browser window, and when it is activated and deactivated. User movement from one page of the browser to another must be communicated to the applet.

A browser loads the URL and locates the HTML document. It loads the HTML document and interprets it. Then it locates the applet classes referenced by the HTML document, loads them, and runs them.

The Java applet differs from all the Java standalone programs that have been created so far. An applet cannot be run directly; it requires an HTML file and a browser to display the HTML file. The sample code presented in this figure represents two files: the .java file and the HTML file. The format of the HTML file is described in the next sections.

Table 11-1 shows a comparison between a Java application and a Java applet.

Table 11-1 Java Application Versus Java Applet

Differences	Java Application	Java Applet
Use of graphics	Optional.	Inherently graphical.
Memory requirements	Minimal Java application requirements (JVM).	Java applet requirements plus web browser requirements.
Distribution	Loaded from the file system or by a custom class-loading process.	Linked via HTML and transported via HTTP.
Environmental input	Command-line parameters (input through GUIs are after the application is launched).	Browser client location and size parameters embedded in the Host document. (The HTML file can define user input parameters that then are passed to the applet.)
Startup method	`main`: startup method.	`init`: initialization method. `start`: startup method. `stop`: pause/deactivate method. `destroy`: terminate method. `paint`: drawing method.

Table 11-1 Java Application Versus Java Applet (Continued)

Differences	Java Application	Java Applet
Typical use	Network server, multimedia kiosks, developer tools, appliance and consumer electronics control and navigation, such as PDAs and text-based wireless phones.	Public-access order-entry systems for the web—e-commerce, e-learning, online multimedia presentations, web page animation.
Version control	Features of newer Java versions might not be supported by the current operating system. Software such as newer versions of Windows might not provide automatic support for the JVM, and users might have limited capabilities.	In an intranet (network within a corporation), there tends to be more control over software versions, and you can know what versions are available and develop accordingly.

The Java platform also provides the `appletviewer` program to test-run the applets. Figures 11-4 and 11-5 show that an applet can be launched from the command line with the appletview program.

Figure 11-4 Code for Creating the Java Applet Lights—Code

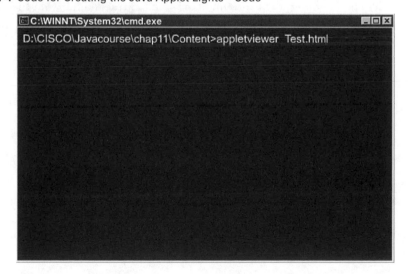

NOTE

For Figures 11-4 and 11-5, you can view the full, interactive graphics on the book's accompanying CD-ROM. The title of the activity is "Code for Creating the Java Applet Lights" in the e-Lab Activities.

Figure 11-5 Code for Creating the Java Applet Lights—Output

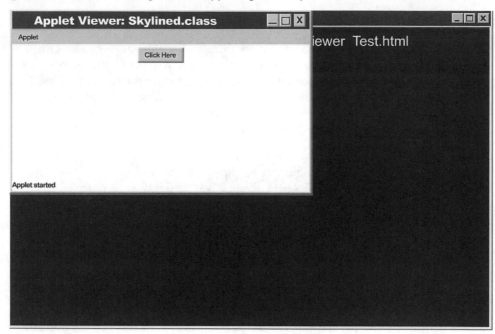

One of the features of an applet is that data, or parameters from the browser, can be sent to the applet. This concept is used extensively in Java Server Pages (JSP) and servlet technologies. In an applet, the following command extracts data from the browser, through the parameters defined in the HTML document:

```
String s = getParameter("p").
```

The getParameter method of the applet class accepts a String. This String represents the name (as in the variable name) of the parameter that will be passed by the browser. This variable is declared in the HTML document as follows:

```
<applet code="AnyApplet.class" width=100 height=200>
<param name="p" value="some text">
</applet>
```

You also can send messages from the applet to the browser for display in the browser's message area. The showStatus() method of the applet is used to display a message in the browser's status area, as in this example:

```
showStatus("This applet is safe, and will not access files from your computer");
```

Applets and Security

When a user downloads an applet in a browser, the applet runs in the memory of the user's computer. Browsers launch a copy of the JVM to run these applets. As such, the code of the applet is inherently dangerous because the applet is loaded over a network and is resident in the client's memory. Several security concerns exist. What if the class that was downloaded wrote to the storage drives using a filename that was the same as the name of the documents? What if someone writes a malicious class that reads personal files and sends them over the Internet? What if the applet is coded to erase important files on the computer? What if the applet class name is the same as the name of some other class that is running?

The threat of malicious damage to computers and networks has resulted in most browsers implementing security measures against code that is downloaded from another machine. The depth to which security is controlled is implemented at the browser level. Most browsers (including Netscape Navigator) prevent several actions by default. The following list shows the security actions prevented (by default) for applets accessed over the Internet (*applet security*):

- File I/O
- Calls to any native methods
- Attempts to open a socket to any system except the host that provided the applet

An applet loaded from the local file system has more privileges. A remotely loaded applet that attempts to perform any of these actions causes exceptions to be thrown, and the applet will fail to load.

Embedding a Java Applet

The HTML language has many features and commands for presenting content. Comprehensive coverage of the HTML language requires a separate study. The use of special tags to create HTML files when documenting classes has already been illustrated. The javadoc utility converts the comment tags to HTML tags, which then can be displayed by a browser. In a similar manner, a document is created and HTML tags are inserted to set the size of the applet to be displayed and the specific applet class to run, among a few other parameters.

HTML commands are used to format text for display as a web page, to import graphics and images, and to link a page to other web pages. HTML commands are also known as tags, which are special keywords enclosed in < > symbols. A tag includes a keyword that starts the markup command and a tag to end the markup command. To run a Java applet, a programmer must learn only two tags: HTML and APPLET.

An HTML document always begins with the tag that identifies the HTML block of content. This is the <HTML> tag. The document ends with the </HTML> closing tag.

To embed applets in an HTML document, the two sets of tags used are *<HTML> </HTML>* and *<APPLET> </APPLET>*. Place the attributes CODE, WIDTH, and HEIGHT inside the applet tag, as shown in Figure 11-6. CODE is the attribute that points to the name of the Java class file. WIDTH is the width of the applet on the screen. HEIGHT is the height of the applet on the screen.

Figure 11-6 HTML Tags and Syntax

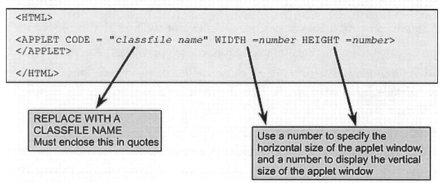

```
<tag> -- //HTML keyword enclosed in < > angle brackets
</tag> -- //Same HTML key word enclosed in </ > symbols. The / indicates end of
action for that command.

<HTML> //some information  </HTML> //Begin and end tags
<Applet>  </Applet> //begin and applet information.

//HTML language, unlike java, is not case-sensitive and the whitespaces between the
tags are generally ignored.

<APPLET CODE= "class name" WIDTH = 300  HEIGHT = 400 > //Defines the
applet command
</APPLET> //ending tag for the applet command
```

```
<HTML>

<APPLET CODE = "classfile name" WIDTH =number HEIGHT =number>
</APPLET>

</HTML>
```

REPLACE WITH A
CLASSFILE NAME
Must enclose this in quotes

Use a number to specify the
horizontal size of the applet window,
and a number to display the vertical
size of the applet window

TIP

Generally, an applet should be less than 800 pixels wide and 600 pixels tall. Most computers support these dimensions.

The height and width of the applet are measured in pixels. Pixels (picture elements) are the number of lighted dots required to display the image. Most common monitors display 640 pixels horizontally and 480 pixels vertically. A statement such as WIDTH = 300 and HEIGHT = 200 would be approximately half the size of the screen. Although many monitors can display higher resolution (pixels per inch), it is recommended to keep the applet size within the 640 × 480 pixels resolution. Keep in mind that browsers display titles, menus, messages, and so on. The applet should be viewed easily alongside these other objects, and the titles, menus, and other items should be accessible to the user.

Before running the HTML document, make sure that the class file is compiled.

More Information

Placing additional characters such as commas (,) between the attributes in the <APPLET> tag can cause the appletviewer or the browser to produce a MissingResourceException when loading the applet.

Forgetting the ending </APPLET> tag prevents the applet from loading into the appletviewer or browser properly.

The MissingResourceException can be addressed by checking the <APPLET> tag in the HTML file carefully for syntax errors.

Running the appletviewer with a filename that does not end with .html or .htm is an error that will prevent your applet from loading.

Historical Overview

In 1998, Sun Microsystems separated the browser and the virtual machine. The virtual machine was then and currently is packaged as the Java Runtime Environment, which is to be installed in a standard place on each computer that supports Java. Browser developers are encouraged to use the JRE, not their own Java implementation, to execute applets. This way, users can update Java implementations and browsers separately. If your browser operates this way, you will be able to execute the applets without problems. Netscape and Opera work this way.

However, Microsoft's Internet Explorer does not support the most recent version of the JVM. To solve this problem, Sun Microsystems provides the Java plug-in, a tool that uses the Microsoft ActiveX component architecture to add Java support to Internet Explorer. To display your applet inside Internet Explorer, download the Java plug-in from java.sun.com/products/plugin/index.html. Additionally, the HTML required to activate the browser is not the simple applet tag described in this chapter. Sun has developed the Java plug-in HTML converter to translate HTML pages that contain applet tags to HTML pages with the appropriate tags to launch the Java plug-in. You should download the converter from java.sun.com/products/plugin/1.3/converter.html.

NOTE

The first versions of browser programs that supported Java contained a built-in Java Virtual Machine. That turned out to be not such a great idea because, as new versions of Java appeared rapidly, the browser developers were unable to keep up, or the browser developers made changes to the Java implementations, causing incompatibilities.

Creating an Applet

Up to this point, what an applet is, how to launch it, and how to embed an applet in an HTML document has been discussed. This section describes how to create an applet.

Creating an Applet

To create an applet, start by creating a class using the form displayed in Example 11-3.

Example 11-3 *Applet Class Coding Form*

```
import java.applet.*;
public class HelloWorld extends Applet{
```

The applet's class must be **public,** and its name must match the name of the file it is in. In this case, the file is named HelloWorld.java. The class must be derived from the class Applet that is in the java.applet package.

Writing an applet class requires several things, such as these:

- Adding more **import** statements (in addition to others such as java.awt.*; and java.awt.event.*)
- Adding components
- Implementing the methods to handle what happens to the applet when resized or minimized
- Including the use of the Font and Color classes to set the properties of text and graphics
- Including the use of the Graphics class to draw images on the display
- Implementing event handling through the event-delegation model, which involves using WindowListener and ActionListener objects to handle events

In Example 11-3, the Applet class is imported from the java.applet package with the use of an **import** statement. The class-definition statement uses the keyword **extends** to show that this class is an applet.

Applet **Class Hierarchies**

This section describes the class hierarchies of the Applet class.

Class Hierarchies

The Applet class is part of the Component subclasses, and it inherits from the *Panel* class. Recall that Panel is a free-floating container and cannot be displayed by itself. Panel usually is displayed in a Frame or a Window. Because an Applet is a Panel, it must be displayed in a Container that can render its graphical components. The browser window or frame serves as this container. The Applet is a Panel (subclassed from the Panel class) that inherits the default layout manager FlowLayout from the Panel class. All components are added from left to right. The FlowLayout manager maintains the size of the component; it is not changed when the user resizes the Panel or Frame.

The applet inherits methods from the Component, Container, and Panel classes. Example 11-4 and Figure 11-7 illustrate the inheritance of the Applet class.

Example 11-4 Applet *and AWT Class Hierarchies*

```
java.lang.Object
        java.awt.Component
                java.awt.Container
                        java.awt.Panel     →     java.applet.Applet


                        java.awt.Window    →     java.awt.Frame
```

Figure 11-7 AWT Hierarchies

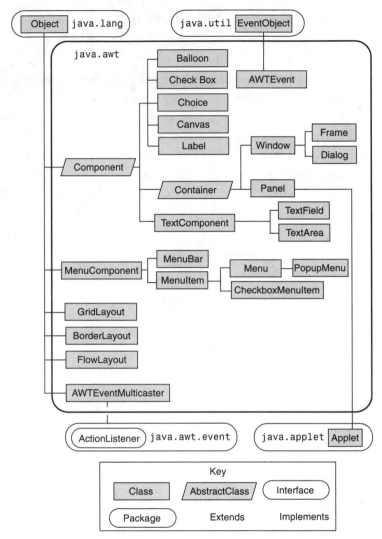

Applet Methods

The Applet class has inherited methods as well as its own defined methods. This section consists of the following topics:

- Applet inherited methods
- Applet life cycle methods

Applet Inherited Methods

The Applet class inherits methods from the Component, *Container*, and Panel classes. Figure 11-8 displays the inherited methods. In addition to these, the Applet class has its own methods for initializing an applet and closing or destroying the applet object. Applets have add methods to add components, set methods to set values and properties of components, get methods to retrieve values of components, and addXXXListener and removeXXXListener methods to implement event handling. Like all Component objects, the applet includes methods to paint, repaint, and update the graphics of the applet.

Figure 11-8 Methods Inherited from Container and Component

continues

Figure 11-8 Methods Inherited from `Container` and `Component` (Continued)

Methods inherited from class java.awt.Component

action, add, addComponentListener, addFocusListener, addHierarchyBoundsListener,
addHierarchyListener, addInputMethodListener, addKeyListener, addMouseListener,
addMouseMotionListener, addMouseWheelListener, bounds, checkImage, checkImage,
coalesceEvents, contains, contains, createImage, createImage, createVolatileImage,
createVolatileImage, disable, disableEvents, dispatchEvent, enable, enable,
enableEvents, enableInputMethods, firePropertyChange, firePropertyChange,
firePropertyChange, getBackground, getBounds, getBounds, getColorModel,
getComponentListeners, getComponentOrientation, getCursor, getDropTarget,
getFocusCycleRootAncestor, getFocusListeners, getFocusTraversalKeysEnabled,
getFont, getFontMetrics, getForeground, getGraphics, getGraphicsConfiguration,
getHeight, getHierarchyBoundsListeners, getHierarchyListeners, getIgnoreRepaint,
getInputContext, getInputMethodListeners, getInputMethodRequests, getKeyListeners,
action, add, addComponentListener, addFocusListener, addHierarchyBoundsListener,
addHierarchyListener, addInputMethodListener, addKeyListener, addMouseListener,
addMouseMotionListener, addMouseWheelListener, bounds, checkImage, checkImage,
coalesceEvents, contains, contains, createImage, createImage, createVolatileImage,

createVolatileImage, disable, disableEvents, dispatchEvent, enable, enable,
enableEvents, enableInputMethods, firePropertyChange, firePropertyChange,
firePropertyChange, getBackground, getBounds, getBounds, getColorModel,
getComponentListeners, getComponentOrientation, getCursor, getDropTarget,
getFocusCycleRootAncestor, getFocusListeners, getFocusTraversalKeysEnabled,
getFont, getFontMetrics, getForeground, getGraphics, getGraphicsConfiguration,
getHeight, getHierarchyBoundsListeners, getHierarchyListeners, getIgnoreRepaint,
getInputContext, getInputMethodListeners, getInputMethodRequests, getKeyListeners,
getLocale, getLocation, getLocation, getLocationOnScreen, getMouseListeners,
getMouseMotionListeners, getMouseWheelListeners, getName, getParent, getPeer,
getPropertyChangeListeners, getPropertyChangeListeners, getSize, getSize, getToolkit,
getTreeLock, getWidth, getX, getY, gotFocus, handleEvent, hasFocus, hide,
imageUpdate, inside, isBackgroundSet, isCursorSet, isDisplayable, isDoubleBuffered,
isEnabled, isFocusable, isFocusOwner, isFocusTraversable, isFontSet, isForegroundSet,
isLightweight, isOpaque, isShowing, isValid, isVisible, keyDown, keyUp, list, list, list,
location, lostFocus, mouseDown, mouseDrag, mouseEnter, mouseExit, mouseMove,
mouseUp, move, nextFocus, paintAll, postEvent, prepareImage, prepareImage, printAll,
processComponentEvent, processFocusEvent, processHierarchyBoundsEvent,
processHierarchyEvent, processInputMethodEvent, processKeyEvent,
processMouseEvent, processMouseMotionEvent, processMouseWheelEvent, remove,
removeComponentListener, removeFocusListener, removeHierarchyBoundsListener,
removeHierarchyListener, removeInputMethodListener, removeKeyListener,
removeMouseListener, removeMouseMotionListener, removeMouseWheelListener,
removePropertyChangeListener, removePropertyChangeListener, repaint, repaint,
repaint, repaint, requestFocus, requestFocus, requestFocusInWindow,
requestFocusInWindow, reshape, resize, resize, setBackground, setBounds, setBounds,
setComponentOrientation, setCursor, setDropTarget, setEnabled, setFocusable,
setFocusTraversalKeysEnabled, setForeground, setIgnoreRepaint, setLocale,
setLocation, setLocation, setName, setSize, setSize, setVisible, show, show, size,
toString, transferFocus, transferFocusUpCycle

An applet is a `Container`, so it can contain numerous `Panels` with different layout managers. Other components, such as `Labels`, `Buttons`, `TextFields`, and `Scrollbars`, can be added to these `Panels` or to the applet directly. In addition to methods for adding components, the `set` methods can be used to set the properties of the components, such as color, font, and size. The listener objects can be registered with the components that will generate event objects using the `addXXXListener` methods. (XXX stands for the name of the listener for the event generated by the component.) The steps to create the GUI features of an applet are no different than the steps used to create standalone applications that present GUIs. Review the sections in Chapter 10, "Creating GUIs Using AWT," that describe steps for creating GUIs.

Applet Life Cycle Methods

The painting and repainting of an applet are also known as the *life cycle methods*. When an applet is launched, the graphics that form the applet must be painted on the screen for the first time. When the applet window is resized or minimized, the graphics must be redrawn. When the user moves from the current document to a different HTML document and then returns to the HTML with the applet, the applet must be painted.

The life cycle methods of the applet are listed as follows:

- *init()*
- *start()*
- *stop()*
- *destroy()*

The `Applet` class provides a general outline to be used by any browser when it runs an applet. In an application, the `main()` method calls other methods. With an applet, the browser calls many methods automatically. Every applet includes the four methods shown previously. If code is not written for one of these methods, the compiler creates them automatically. The methods that the compiler creates do not do anything special; they are created with empty braces (`{ }`).

The first method the browser calls is the `init()` method. This is the method in which code must be written to present the components. Other key methods are called depending on the actions being performed. A simple flow of the life cycle methods is shown in Figure 11-9. When the window is closed, the `destroy()` method is called. In this method, the program should initiate actions to release resources and to close input/output streams and any network connections. The `stop()` and `destroy()` methods do not have to be written. Any tasks that must be performed when the applet is no longer visible can be defined in the applet's `stop()` and `destroy()` methods.

Figure 11-9 Key Applet Life Cycle Methods

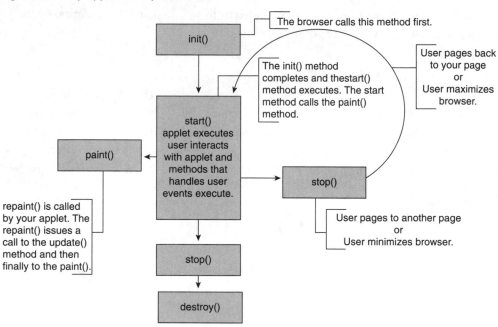

More Information

The only statements that should be placed in an applet's `init` method are those that are related directly to the one-time initialization of an applet's instance variables. The applet's results should be displayed from other methods of the `Applet` class. Results that involve drawing should be displayed from the applet's `paint` method.

The statements to be placed in the `paint` method should be only those that are related directly to drawing (calls to methods of the `Graphics` object) and the logic of drawing. Dialog boxes should not be displayed from an applet's `paint` method. The `paint` method should do as little computation as possible.

Every applet must subclass `Applet`, as shown for the `AnyApplet` class in Example 11-5.

Example 11-5 AnyApplet *Class*

```
import java.applet.*;
import java.awt.*;
public class AnyApplet extends Applet{
  public void init()
    {// called once by the browser when it starts the applet.}
```

Example 11-5 AnyApplet *Class (Continued)*

```
  public void start()
    {// called whenever the page containing the applet is made visible.}
  public void stop()
    {//called whenever the page containing this applet is not visible}
  public void destroyed()
    {//called whenever the browser destroys this applet.}
  public void paint(Graphics g)
    {//called whenever the applet needs to repaint itself.}
  // other handler methods can be defined here, or utility methods, and or inner
classes.
} // end of applet class definition


This is the applet's accompanying HTML file
<html>
<applet code = "AnyApplet.class" width=200 height = 100>
</applet>
</html>
```

GUI Components in Applets

The Applet class extends from Panel, which extends from Container. So, an Applet is a Container. Any Abstract Window Toolkit (AWT) component can be added to the applet. Code also can be included to set the font and color of some of the components. In addition to AWT components, graphic objects can be included using the Graphics class to draw simple shapes or combine simple shapes to create complex images. Some simple uses of Graphics objects are described later in this chapter. This section consists of the following topics:

- GUI components
- Color
- Font
- Other Applet methods

GUI Components

The following code in Example 11-6 demonstrates the use of Label, TextField, and Button objects in an applet. This program presents the user with TextFields to enter a username and password. The username and password are checked against a list. The applet returns a message if the entry is correct. The actual verification of usernames and passwords in a business application can be far more complex than this example. Often, this includes retrieving data from a database to verify that the information the user has provided is correct. Here, it can be assumed that only a single password, rosetime, is acceptable to the program.

Example 11-6 *PasswordTest.java*

NOTE

The full version of the abbreviated code shown in this example can be viewed using the book's accompanying CD-ROM.

```
 1 import java.applet.*;

 2 import java.awt.*;

 3 import java.awt.event.*;

 4

 5 public class PasswordTest extends Applet implements ActionListener

 6 {

 7     Label banner1 = new Label("Enter username: ");

 8     TextField un = new TextField("",10);

 9     Label banner2 = new Label("Enter password: ");

10     TextField pw = new TextField("",10);

11     Button button1 = new Button("ENTER");

12

13     public void init()

14     {

15         add(banner1);

16         add(un);

17         add(banner2);

18         add(pw);

19         add(button1);
```

Samples of output from the program are shown in Figure 11-10. The class definition includes references to **import** classes from three sources: java.applet.* to use the Applet class, java.awt.* to use the Component class and its subclasses, and java.awt.event.* to use listener interfaces and event objects. This applet implements the ActionListener interface. The applet includes the labels banner1, banner2, and result. The first two labels are used to display a prompt to the user and label the TextField. The third label is added to the applet in the actionPerformed method of the applet.

Figure 11-10 Output from `PasswordTest.class` and `PasswordTest.html`

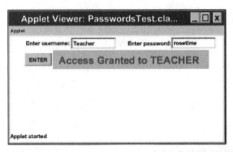

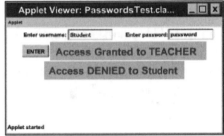

These concepts are demonstrated by the following code:

- Components are added in the `init()` method. The `init()` method is followed by the `start()` method, which calls the `paint()` method to draw the graphics for each component.

- The `PasswordTest` object (referenced by the keyword **this**) implements the `ActionListener` interface: `button1.addActionListener(this)`. The listener object handles any `ActionEvent` objects that are generated by `button1`. This statement can be described as registering an `ActionListener` object with a component (`button1`) that generates events. When a user presses the button on the applet screen, an `ActionEvent` object will be generated.

- The focus (that is, the cursor is positioned in the `TextField`) is requested for the object referenced by un: `un.requestFocus();`.

- The `actionPerformed` method is implemented because this is the only method declared in the `ActionListener` interface. In the `actionPerformed` method, the code verifies the data provided by the user, changes the text for the `Label` object referenced by `result`, and adds this label component to the applet.

- Because components of the applet have changed, the *invalidate()* method is called to mark the applet as invalid or out-of-date, and then a call to the *validate()* method is made to redraw the window and implement the addition of the new label referenced by `result`.

Color

The `color` of a component is a property of the graphics of that component. The Java language provides the *Color* class in the AWT package. The `Color` class includes several constants that define the combination of red, green, and blue as integer values. Each integer value represents a specific color. To set the color of a graphic object, the programmer either can provide her own `Color` object or can use one of the **static final** predefined objects of the `Color` class shown in Example 11-7. Unlike the standard naming convention of using uppercase for constants, these are all named in lowercase.

A `Color` object also can be created using one of the constructors. For example, `Color(int r, int g, int b)` creates an opaque object with different intensities of red (r), green (g), and blue (b). The values for each integer are between 0 and 255. Some computers cannot display all of the colors. There are 16 million possible colors; each computer displays the closest color it can.

NOTE

The full version of the abbreviated code shown in this example can be viewed using the book's accompanying CD-ROM.

Example 11-7 TestColors

```
1 /**
2  * @author Cisco Tacher
3  * @version 2002
4  */
5
6 import java.applet.*;
7 import java.awt.*;
8 import java.awt.event.*;
9
10 public class TestColors extends Applet
11 {
12     TextField t1 = new TextField(20);
13     Button b1 = new Button("Button");
14     Label l1 = new Label("message");
15     Font f1 = new Font("TimesRoman",Font.ITALIC,20);
16     Font f2 = new Font("TimesRoman",Font.ITALIC+ Font.BOLD,20);
17     Font f3 = new Font("TimesRoman", Font.BOLD, 36);
18
19     public void init()
20     {
```

Text associated with Example 11-7 can be viewed by accessing the full, interactive graphic for this example on the book's accompanying CD-ROM. The title of the activity is `TestColors`, and it is found under the e-Lab activities.

Coloring text and objects requires some attention to the type of component being colored. `Labels`, `Buttons`, and `TextFields` can be set to different colors using the `setBackground()` and `setForeground()` methods. The foreground changes the color of the text in a `TextField` object, the label of a `Button` object, or the text of a `Label` object.

Table 11-2 Predefined Colors in the `Color` Class and Their RGB Values

Color	RGB Value
Color.black	0.0f, 0.0f, 0.0f
Color.blue	0.0f, 0.0f, 1.0f
Color.cyan	0.0f, 1.0f, 1.0f
Color.gray	0.5f, 0.5f, 0.5f
Color.darkGray	0.25f, 0.25f, 0.25f
Color.lightGray	0.75f, 0.75f, 0.75f
Color.green	0.0f, 1.0f, 0.0f
Color.magenta	1.0f, 0.0f, 1.0f
Color.orange	1.0f, 0.8f, 0.0f
Color.pink	1.0f, 0.7f, 0.7f
Color.red	1.0f, 0.0f, 0.0f
Color.white	1.0f, 1.0f, 1.0f
Color.yellow	1.0f, 1.0f, 0.0f

NOTE

When you first start drawing shapes, all shapes are drawn with a black pen. To change the color, an object of the type `Color` is used. Java uses the RGB model—that is, you specify a color by the amounts of the primary colors—red, green, and blue—that make up the color. The amounts are given as **float** values, and they range from `0.0f` (primary color not present) to `1.0f` (maximum amount of primary color present). Some of the predefined colors and their RGB values are shown in Table 11-2.

Font

Fonts represent the technology for displaying symbols of the written language in different shapes, sizes, and styles. Two terms frequently are used to describe the features of fonts: character and glyph. A *character* is a symbol that represents items such as letters and numbers in a particular writing system. For example, lowercase g is a character. When a particular character has been rendered, a shape now represents this character. This shape is called a glyph.

A font is a collection of shapes for representing characters (glyphs). A font can have faces such as heavy, medium, oblique, gothic, and regular. All of these faces have similar typographic design. Thus, a font includes the shape (glyph), the face, and the size. The typographical design (glyph shapes) is known as the font family. For example, Courier and Helvetica are examples of the font family names.

Face Name, Style, and Point Size

A font is described by its face name, style, and point size. The face name is one of the five logical face names—Serif, SanSerif, Monospaced, Dialog, or DialogInput—or the name of the typeface that is available on your computer, such as those shown in Table 11-3.

Table 11-3 provides a comparison of the font family names used in Java across different OS platforms.

Table 11-3 Comparison Chart of Java Font Family Names

JavaFont	MS Windows Font	Windows Font X	Macintosh Font
Monospaced	Courier New	Adobe-courier	Courier
Dialog	MS Sans Serif	b&h-lucida	Geneva
DialogInput	MS San Serif	b&h-lucidatype-writer	Geneva
SansSerif/Helvetica	Arial	Adobe-Helvetica	Helvetica
Symbol	WingDings	itc-zapfdingbats	Symbol
Serif/TimesRoman	Times New Roman	Adobe-times	Times Roman

The font styles are plain, bold, and italic. Italic can be combined with plain and bold.

The size of a string depends on the font face, the point size. The ascent of the font is the height of the largest letter above the baseline. The descent of the font is the depth below the baseline of the letter with the lowest descender. These describe the vertical extent of the string. The horizontal extent depends on the individual letters in a string. In a proportionally spaced font, different letters have different widths.

Fonts are set for the text of any component or graphics objects using Font objects. A Font object contains data regarding the font face (that is, the style of the font), the style (such as bold, italic, or plain), and the size. Three different names can be obtained from a Font object: the logical font, the font face name, or the font name, for short (which is the name of a particular font face, such as Helvetica Bold). The family name is the name of the font family that determines the typographic design across several faces, such as Helvetica. It is important to note that the font face name is the one that should be used to specify fonts. This name signifies actual fonts in the host system.

Font Class

The Font class represents an instance of a font face from a collection of font faces. These font faces are present in the system resources of the host system. For example, Arial Bold and Courier Bold Italic are font faces. Several Font objects can be associated with a font face, each differing in size, style, transform, and font features. The getAllFonts method of the GraphicsEnvironment class returns all of the font faces available in the system.

Integer Values and Fonts

Integer values represent the style of the fonts. The Font class stores data in static members to represent the font style. These integers are Font.ITALIC, Font.BOLD, and Font.PLAIN. These integers are added to obtain combination styles such as italics and bold using Font.BOLD + Font.ITALIC. The Toolkit class can also be used to obtain information about the fonts on the computer; however, the better option is to utilize the GraphicsEnvironment class.

Font objects then can be used as arguments to the setFont() methods of components.

The font can also be set by obtaining the names of the fonts from the system (*system fonts*) and then using these to create a Font object.

You can obtain a list of fonts available from your system by using the following code:

```
GraphicsEnvironment grenv = GraphicsEnvironment.getLocalGraphicsEnvironment();
String[] fontNames = grenv.getAvailableFontFamilyNames();
for (int i=0; i <fontNames.length; i++)
{
    System.out.println(fontNames[i]);
}
```

You can evaluate the elements of the String array to determine the specific Font object to create. The String list can also be used to "load" a list of choices in a Choice component. You can present the user with these, and the specific choice made could be used to create a Font object and set the text of some field or a label to this font.

Other Applet Methods

In addition to the key methods, the graphics of the applet are painted and repainted, as shown in Table 11-4.

Table 11-4 Painting, Repainting, and Updating the Graphics

Action	Browser
The browser starts your applet class file.	init()
The init() method completes.	start()
The start() method is invoked.	paint()
Exposure by another window occurs.	paint()
Exposure by another window occurs.	paint()
Your applet code explicitly asks it to repaint(). (For example, the user clicks the Clear button on your GUI.)	repaint() → update() → paint()
A user pages to another page.	stop()
A user pages back to your page.	start() → paint()
A user minimizes the browser.	stop()
A user maximizes the browser.	start() → paint()

When adding components to an applet, you must implement additional methods. The init() method lays out all the components of the applet. The init() method is called only once when the applet loads. If the applet code adds or removes components, two methods must be called to have the applet redraw the components. These are the invalidate() and validate() methods.

The invalidate() and validate() Methods

When moving out of the window or resizing the window, the applet knows that the window needs to be redrawn. It redraws based on the original information about the components. When a component is added, the applet does not know that its information is outdated. The programmer must call the invalidate() method for the applet, as shown in Example 11-8. This marks it as out-of-date. The validate() method then redraws any invalid windows, allowing the changes to take effect.

Example 11-8 *Use of the* validate() *and* invalidate() *Methods*

```
 1 // TodayIS.java
 2 import java.applet.*;
 3 import java.awt.*;
 4 import java.awt.event.*;
 5 import java.util.*;
 6
 7 public class TodayIS extends Applet implements ActionListener
 8 {
 9         Label banner = new Label("");
10         Font theFont = new Font("TimesRoman",Font.BOLD, 12);
11         Button button1 = new Button("Press ME");
12
13 public void init()
14 {
15         banner.setFont(theFont);
16         add(banner);
17         add(button1);
18         button1.addActionListener(this);
19 }
```

NOTE

For Example 11-8, you can view the highlighted code by accessing the full, interactive graphic for this example on the book's accompanying CD-ROM. The title of the activity is "Use of the validate() and invalidate() Methods" in the e-Lab Activities.

NOTE

The full version of the abbreviated code shown in this example can be viewed using the book's accompanying CD-ROM.

setLocation() Method

The FlowLayout manager manages the placement of the components on an applet. Because an applet is a Panel, this is the default layout manager for all Panels and their subclasses. The FlowLayout manager places the components from left to right and top to bottom when each row is filled.

Control can be exercised over the placement of the components using the setLocation() method, inherited from the java.awt.Component class. The applet window consists of horizontal and vertical pixels on the screen. Each component has several location and size values. The upper-left corner of the applet display area has the value of 0,0. These two numbers represent the horizontal position, known as the x-axis, and the vertical position, known as the y-axis. Just as the display's top-left corner is set to 0,0 for both the x-axis and the y-axis, each component is placed within this display; its location can be described as some value from the 0,0 position of the display, as illustrated in Figures 11-11 and 11-12.

Figure 11-11 Show the Applet Axis

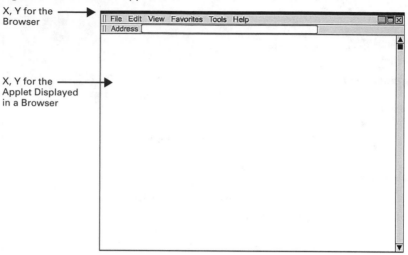

Figure 11-12 Show the Applet Axis

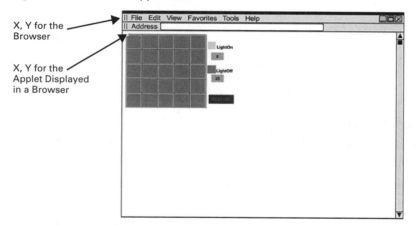

The **public void** setLocation(**int** x, **int** y) method provides a way to control the position of the components in the applet display area. The method arguments include an integer to define the x value and another integer to define the y value, as shown in Example 11-9 and Figure 11-13.

Example 11-9 SetLocation() *Place Components—Code*

```
import java.applet.*;
import java.awt.*;
import java.awt.event.*;
```

Example 11-9 `SetLocation()` *Place Components—Code (Continued)*

```
public class ComponentLocation extends Applet implements ActionListener
{
      Label banner = new Label("Press this button for Lucky number ");
      Button button1 = new Button("Lucky");

      public void init()
      {
<html>
<head>
</head>
<body>
<APPLET>
   CODE="ComponentLocation.class"
   WIDTH=450
   HEIGHT=200>
</APPLET>
</body>
</html>
         add(button1);
         button1.addActionListener(this);
      }
      public void actionPerformed(ActionEvent e)
      {
         button1.setLocation(20 , 40);
}
```

NOTE

The full version of the abbreviated code shown in this example can be viewed using the book's accompanying CD-ROM.

Figure 11-13 `SetLocation()` Place Components—Output

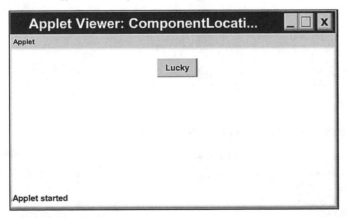

setEnabled() Method

Components also can be made available or unavailable, and visible or hidden. The setEnabled() method makes the component available if a **boolean true** is supplied to the method, and unavailable if the **boolean false** is supplied to the method. When a component is unavailable, it is still visible, but the user cannot interact with it.

setVisible() Method

NOTE

For Example 11-10, you can view the highlighted code by accessing the full, interactive graphic for this example on the book's accompanying CD-ROM. The title of the activity is "setVisible() Method" in the e-Lab Activities.

The setVisible() method was introduced in the previous chapter to make all the components of a Frame visible. This method can also be used on components of an applet to make them visible or hidden, as shown in Example 11-10.

Example 11-10 setVisible() *Method*

```
 1  import java.applet.*;
 2  import java.awt.*;
 3  import java.awt.event.*;
 4
 5  public class HideAndSeek extends Applet implements ActionListener
 6  {
 7     Label banner = new Label ("Press this button to play hide and seek");
 8     Button start = new Button("Activate Button");
 9     Button stop = new Button("Stop");
10     Button hide = new Button("hide");
11
12     public void init()
13     {
14        add(banner);
15        add(start);
16        add(stop);
17        add(hide);
18        hide.addActionListener(this);
19        start.addActionListener(this);
20        stop.addActionListener(this);
```

NOTE

The full version of the abbreviated code shown in this example can be viewed using the book's accompanying CD-ROM.

Applets and Event-Driven Programming

Applets can be designed to respond to user-initiated actions. The user actions can be actions on components such as pressing a button, entering text in a text field, or moving a mouse over a label. The response to the user action is delegated to some object that has a method that is executed. This section addresses primarily applets and event-driven programming.

Event-Driven Programming

Figure 11-14 displays the event-delegation model implemented by the Java 2 platform.

Figure 11-14 Event-Delegation Model

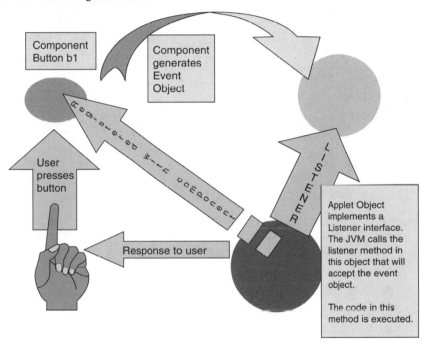

The *event-delegation model* consists of the following items:

- A component that generates an event object
- A listener object that implements a listener interface and that also implements the methods that accept the event object and execute some code representing a response to the user action
- A listener object being registered with the component

The code shown in Example 11-11 provides event handling with the applet object implementing the listener interfaces. In this figure, the applet is the listener and responds to the actions of the user on specific components. The first example shown in Figure 11-15 accepts a value that represents miles; when the button is pressed, the applet uses this value to calculate a conversion to kilometers. The value entered is text. A `Double` object is created using this value. (`Double` is the wrapper class for the primitive **double**.) This `Double` object's parse method is called to retrieve the value of the actual **double** primitive and to calculate the kilometers.

Example 11-11 *Sample Code Implementing the Event-Delegation Model*

NOTE

The full version of the abbreviated code shown in this example can be viewed using the book's accompanying CD-ROM.

```
1  /**
2   *   Java Program: ConvertMiles.java
3   * @author Cisco Teacher
4   * @version 2002
5   */
6
7  import java.applet.*;
8  import java.awt.*;
9  import java.awt.event.*;
10
11 public class ConvertMiles extends Applet implements ActionListener
12 {
13
14     Label banner = new Label("Enter miles: ");
15     TextField number = new TextField("",9);
16     TextField answer = new TextField("",10);
17     Button button1 = new Button("Calculate Kilometers");
18
19     public void init()
20         {
```

In Example 11-12 and Figure 11-16, the applet listens for `ActionEvent` objects from several components. Here, the `actionPerformed` method handles actions from all of the components. The code in this method uses the `getSource()` method of the `Action-Event` object to determine which object generated the event and the action to be performed.

Figure 11-15 Output of the `ConvertMiles` Class

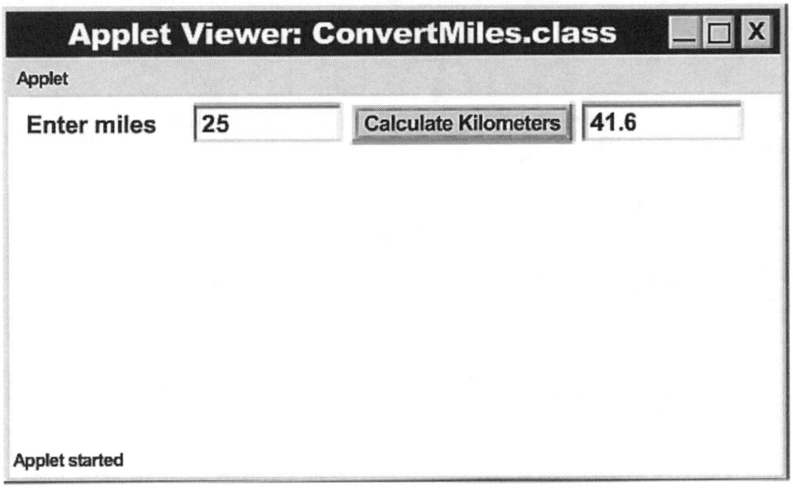

Example 11-12 `HideAndSeek` *Class*

```
1 import java.applet.*;
2 import java.awt.*;
3 import java.awt.event.*;
4
5 public class HideAndSeek extends Applet implements ActionListener
6 {
7       Label banner = new Label ("Press this button to play hide and seek");
8        Button start = new Button("Activate Button");
9        Button stop = new Button("Stop");
10       Button hide = new Button("hide");
11
12       public void init()
13       {
14          add(banner);
15          add(start);
16          add(stop);
17          add(hide);
18          hide.addActionListener(this);
19          start.addActionListener(this);
20          stop.addActionListener(this);
```

NOTE

The full version of the abbreviated code shown in this example can be viewed using the book's accompanying CD-ROM.

NOTE

For Figure 11-16, you can view the full, interactive graphic for this figure on the book's accompanying CD-ROM. The title of the activity is "Output of HideAndSeek" in the e-Lab Activities.

Figure 11-16 Output of HideAndSeek

More Information

Always test an applet in the appletviewer and ensure that it is executing correctly before load-ing the applet into a browser. Browsers often save a copy of the applet in memory until the cur-rent browsing session terminates—that is, until all browser windows are closed. So, if you change an applet and do not see the changes in the browser, the browser might be executing a previously loaded applet. Close all your browser windows to remove the old version of the applet from memory, and then open a new browser to see your changes.

Try to test your applet in every browser used by people who view your applet.

Graphic Objects

TIP

You draw graphical shapes in an applet by placing the drawing code inside the paint method. The paint method is called whenever the applet needs to be refreshed.

The Java platform provides the *Graphics* class and the Canvas class to support draw-ing onto components. This section consists of the following topics:

- Creating graphic objects
- Painting and repainting graphics

Creating Graphic Objects

Each component has a Graphics object, and any component can be drawn in. A Graphics object is an instance of the Graphics class. A Panel, Frame, or applet can be drawn in. The AWT also provides a Canvas class specifically for the purpose of draw-ing. Typically, a subclass of Canvas is created and the paint() method is overwritten.

A constructor cannot be called to create a `Graphics` object. To create a `Graphics` object, there must be a context in which this `Graphics` object can be drawn. This is usually a `Component` such as a `Panel`. These classes provide the `getGraphics()` method that provides a graphics context. This context then can be used to draw on. Imagine the context as a surface on which images will be drawn. Without this surface, the images cannot be visible. In an applet, the `getGraphics()` method provides the applet surface as the context. In a `Frame`, the `Frame` itself provides the context.

The `Graphics` class provides many methods to draw shapes. Figure 11-17 shows the methods and a sample of the shape drawn.

Figure 11-17 Drawing Methods

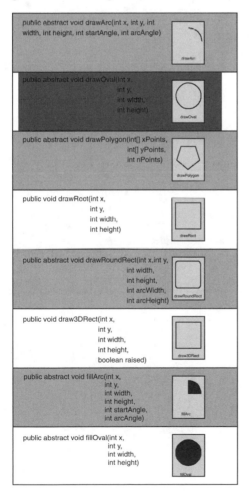

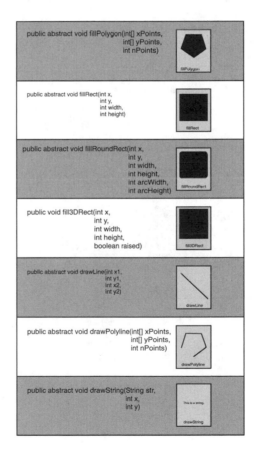

In addition to the methods for drawing shapes, the `clearRect()` method can be used to draw what appears to be a clear, or empty, rectangle. The `clearRect()` method draws a rectangle using the current background color. This is what creates the appearance of an empty rectangle.

Two sample programs are provided here—the `Monogram` program and the `Skylined` program, as described and exemplified in the sections that follow.

Monogram Program

The `Monogram` program, shown in Example 11-13 and Figure 11-18, is a simple applet that draws filled-in ovals and rectangles.

Example 11-13 `Monogram.java`—*Code*

NOTE

The full version of the abbreviated code shown in this example can be viewed using the book's accompanying CD-ROM.

```
 1 /**
 2  * Java Program: Monogram.java
 3  * @author Cisco Student
 4  * @version 2002
 5  */
 6
 7 import java.applet.*;
 8 import java.awt.*;
 9 import java.awt.event.*;
10
11 public class Monogram extends Applet
12 {
13 /**
14   * @param gr A graphic as a Graphics type
15  */
16 public void paint(Graphics gr)
17 {
18     gr.setColor(Color.red);
19     gr.fillRect(10,10,20,80);
20     gr.fillOval(30,50,40,40);
```

Figure 11-18 Monogram.java—Output

Skylined Program

The Skylined program, shown in Example 11-14 and Figure 11-19, sets an integer to count the number of times the button is clicked. For each even number, the colors of the shapes arc changed and the background for the graphic is changed. In this applet, the paint() method is called when the applet starts and again when the action-Performed method is executed. In this method, the paint(gr) method is called so that the shapes can be painted with different colors.

Example 11-14 *Shapes and Colors—Code*

```
 1 /**
 2  * Java Program: Skylined
 3  * @author Cisco Teacher
 4  * @version 2002
 5  */
 6 import java.applet.*;
 7 import java.awt.*;
 8 import java.awt.event.*;
 9
10 public class Skylined extends Applet implements ActionListener
```

continues

NOTE

The full version of the abbreviated code shown in this example can be viewed using the book's accompanying CD-ROM.

Example 11-14 *Shapes and Colors—Code (Continued)*

```
11 {
12      int x=0;
13      Button aButton = new Button("Click here");
14
15      public void init()
16      {
17              setBackground(Color.white);
18              add(aButton);
19              aButton.addActionListener(this);
20      }
```

Figure 11-19 Shapes and Colors—Output

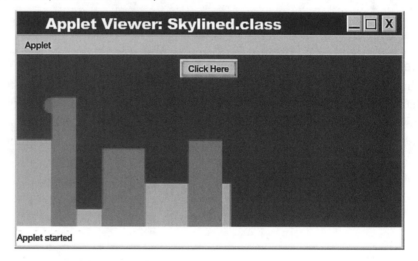

Painting and Repainting Graphics

In addition to the basic life cycle methods, an applet has other important methods related to its display. These methods are declared and documented for the AWT `Compo-nent` class. Exposure handling occurs automatically and results in a call to the `paint()` method. A facility of the `Graphics` class, called a clip rectangle, optimizes the `paint()` method. The painting and repainting of images is performed by the `paint()`, `update()`, and `repaint()` methods.

Displaying the graphics on the screen is also known as exposure. Figure 11-20 illustrates what occurs. The `start()` method calls the `paint()` method. This is the first exposure of the graphics. The next time the graphics are redrawn is if the window loses focus (that is, if the user has moved to another window, minimized, and so on). For these conditions, the start() method is called, which then calls the paint() method. The second exposure happens if the programmer wants to make changes to the display. The area that is changed is considered a damaged area—that is, it is now different from when the area was first painted. The program must be capable of updating the display at any time. When the display is updated, the old image first might need to be removed.

Figure 11-20 How the paint(), repaint(), and update() Methods Are Related

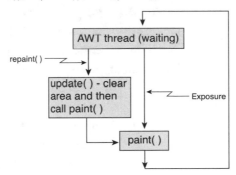

The methods that draw the images or handle image painting are described as follows:

- paint()—Updates are not made over the entire area of the graphics (unless necessary). Instead, these updates are restricted to the region that has been damaged or changed. Override the paint() method to control what is painted on the applet. In the Skylined example, the paint() method is used to change the colors of the rectangles, the oval, and the background for the graphics. The signature for this method is paint(Graphics g).

- repaint()—A call to the repaint() method notifies the system that the programmer wants to change the display. These methods do not repaint the entire graphics; they repaint only the part that has been changed. Programs that include frequent repainting can reduce the flickering of images with the paint() method by calling the repaint() method.

- update()—The repaint() method causes a call to this component's update() method as soon as possible. The update() method usually clears the current display and calls paint(). The update() method can be modified, for example, to reduce flicker by calling paint() without clearing the display.

Case Study: Banking Application

The JBANK application introduced in Chapter 1, "What Is Java?," provides students with an opportunity to apply the Java language concepts learned throughout this course. In the JBANK lab for Chapter 11, "Applets and Graphics," students will create an ATM applet. As part of this lab, the student will discover the flexibility in design introduced by creating the ATM as a `Panel`. The ATM `Panel` will now be displayed in an applet. In the previous chapter, this was displayed on a `Frame`. This lab completes the creation of GUIs to support the banking application.

Applying Concepts to the Banking Application

Two GUIs will be created in the banking application. One GUI is to represent the user interface for a bank employee who will manage the teller activity. Another GUI is the creation of an ATM user interface. The primary users of this interface will be customers. Figures 11-21 and 11-22 display what the JBANK application's `TellerGUI` and `ATMGUI` might look like. In Chapter 10, these interfaces were created using the AWT classes. In this lab, the `ATMGUI` will be modified to run as an applet. An HTML file will be created to launch the applet. Today, most banks provide customers with online banking access. The customers use their Internet connections to conduct banking transactions. This lab provides the experience to create a simple applet.

Figure 11-21 The JBANK Application

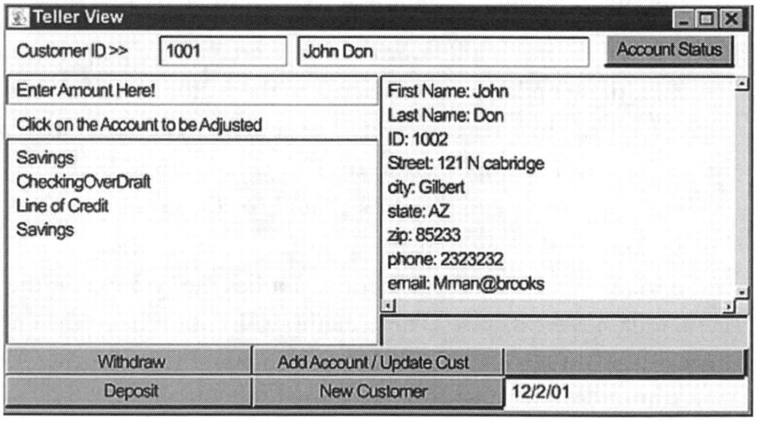

Figure 11-22 The JBANK Application

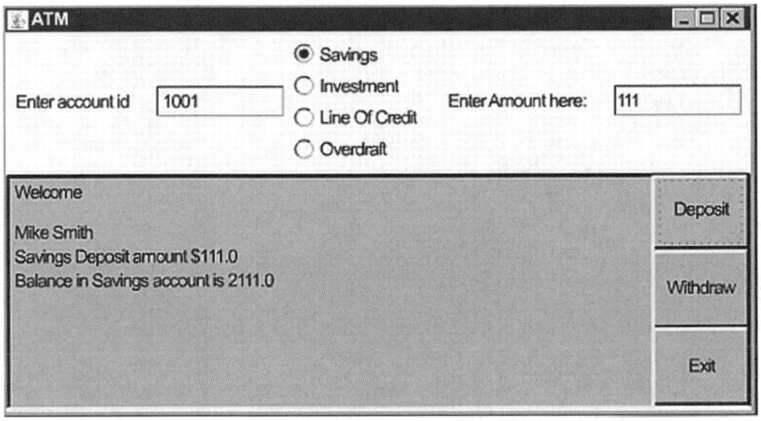

Summary

This chapter focused on Java applets and graphics. An applet is a Java program that runs in another application, such as a web browser. Applets are useful for making programs available to Internet users. They are secure, and they do not permit access to files or data from the client's computer. Furthermore, the applet is destroyed when the user closes the applet. Students also learned that applets have many methods that are executed automatically. A programmer can override these methods to execute specific instructions. Programmers can test and run applets using a utility called `appletviewer` in the Java SDK toolkit.

Graphics are created using the `Graphics` class of the `java.awt` package. The `Graphics` class provides many methods to draw shapes. Custom shapes also can be created. In addition, the `Color` and `Font` classes can be used to enhance applets and graphics in the application.

Syntax Summary

Applet:

```
//import statements
import java.applet.*;
import java.awt.*;
import java.awt.event.*;
import java.util.*;
```

```
public class ClassName extends Applet implements ActionListener
{
    Label banner = new Label(" ");
    Font theFont = new Font("TimesRoman",Font.BOLD, 12);
    Button button1 = new Button("Press Me");
    //first applet method init()
    public void init( )
    {
      banner.setFont(theFont);
      add(banner);
      add(button1);
      button1.addActionListener(this);
      button1.setBackground(Color.red);
     }

    public void actionPerformed(ActionEvent e)
     {
         Date today = new Date( );
         banner.setText("Today is " + today);
         invalidate( );
         validate( );
     }
}
//end of class

<HTML> // start of HTML
<APPLET CODE = "ClassName.class" WIDTH = 300 HEIGHT =  400>
</APPLET>
</HTML>//end of HTML
```

Key Terms

applet   A Java program that typically executes and displays in a web browser but can execute in a variety of other applications or devices that support the applet programming model.

applet security   The following list shows the security actions prevented (by default) for applets accessed over the Internet:

> File I/O
>
> Calls to any native methods
>
> Attempts to open a socket to any system except the host that provided the applet

A remotely loaded applet that attempts to perform any of these actions causes exceptions to be thrown, and the applet will fail to load.

<APPLET> </APPLET>   To embed applets in an HTML document, the two sets of tags used are `<HTML> </HTML>` and `<APPLET> </APPLET>`. Place the attributes `CODE`, `WIDTH`, and `HEIGHT` inside the applet tag. `CODE` is the attribute that points to the name of the Java class file. `WIDTH` is the width of the applet on the screen. `HEIGHT` is the height of the applet on the screen.

appletviewer   The Java 2 SDK provides the `appletviewer` utility to test applets.

character   A symbol that represents items such as letters and numbers in a particular writing system. For example, lowercase g is a character.

Color   Class within the AWT package. An integer value represents the various colors within the class. The constant colors are red, green, and blue. The integer range is 0 through 255.

Container   A subclass of the `Component` class. A `Container` object can hold other components; a group of components can be treated as a single entity.

event-delegation model   Model that Java uses to handle events. It is composed of event source, event objects, and event handlers.

font   The technology for displaying symbols of the spoken language in different shapes, sizes, and styles.

glyph   When a particular character has been rendered, a shape now represents this character (glyph).

Graphics   The abstract base class for all graphics contexts that allow an application to draw onto components. The method `getGraphics()` of the `Component` class creates a graphics context for a component.

<HTML> </HTML> To embed applets in an HTML document, the two sets of tags used are <HTML> </HTML> and <APPLET> </APPLET>. The <HTML> tag is always the beginning of an HTML program. The </HTML> tag is the closing tag of an HTML document.

Hypertext Markup Language (HTML) A special markup language for hypertext documents on the Internet.

invalidate() Method that marks an applet as outdated when changes have occurred on the applet.

life cycle methods The painting and repainting of an applet. The life cycle methods are init(), start(), stop(), and destroy(). These methods do not have to be written in a program; Java automatically creates them:

> *init()* The first method used to create an applet. The code for presenting the components is included in this method.

> *start()* Method that starts the applet program.

> *stop()* Method that stops the program when completed.

> *paint()* Method called by the start() method. This method is running when Java displays the applet. It is generated automatically by Java or can be overridden by the programmer.

Panel A subclass of the Container class, it is a free-floating Container that cannot be displayed by itself. It usually is displayed in a Window or Frame.

repaint() Method used when it is necessary to update a window. This method calls another method named update(), which calls paint().

system fonts A collection of shapes for representing characters in a host software.

update() Method called by repaint(). The update() method clears the current display and calls paint() to produce another image.

URL (uniform resource locator) A standard for writing a text reference to an arbitrary piece of data on the World Wide Web. A specific address for HTML documents.

validate() Method that redraws any invalid window when changes to the applet are made.

Check Your Understanding

1. Which of the following is a true statement about Java applets?

   A. A Java applet typically is run from the command line using the `java` command.

   B. A Java applet can be executed only in a web browser.

   C. A Java applet is viewed on the Internet with an HTML document that references the class.

   D. Java applets can be graphical or nongraphical, depending on the user's needs.

2. Which is not one of the attributes needed in the applet tags of an HTML document to embed an applet?

   A. `CODE`

   B. `WIDTH`

   C. `HEIGHT`

   D. `CLASS`

3. What is the correct way to write the applet tags for an applet, `myApplet`, in an HTML document?

   A. `<APPLET>CLASS="myApplet.class" HEIGHT=200 WIDTH=200</APPLET>`

   B. `<APPLET>CODE="myApplet.class" HEIGHT=200 WIDTH=200</APPLET>`

   C. `<APPLET>CODE="myApplet.java" HEIGHT=200 WIDTH=200</APPLET>`

   D. `<APPLET>CODE="myApplet.class" HEIGHT=200 WIDTH=200<APPLET>`

4. The dimensions `HEIGHT` and `WIDTH` for an applet are measured in:

   A. Inches

   B. Centimeters

   C. Picas

   D. Pixels

5. What is the difference between the security privileges for locally loaded and remotely loaded applets?

   A. A locally loaded applet has more security privileges than a remotely loaded applet.

   B. A remotely loaded applet has more security privileges than a locally loaded applet.

   C. A locally loaded applet has the same security privileges as a remotely loaded applet.

   D. A remotely loaded applet can perform file I/O, but a locally loaded applet cannot.

6. When using the `appletviewer` from the command line, which file is executed?

   A. The `.java` file containing the source code for the applet

   B. The `.class` file containing the bytecode for the applet

   C. The `.applet` file containing the applet code

   D. The `.html` file containing a reference to the class file for the applet

7. From which class must a programmer extend to design an applet?

   A. `Object`

   B. `Applet`

   C. `Panel`

   D. `Frame`

8. From which class does `Applet` extend?

   A. `Object`

   B. `Applet`

   C. `Panel`

   D. `Frame`

9. Which **import** statement must be included in an applet to access the components of the Abstract Windowing Toolkit?

   A. `import java.applet.*;`

   B. `import java.awt.event.*;`

   C. `import java.util.*;`

   D. `import java.awt.*;`

10. Which class is used to draw images on the applet?

   A. `Applet`

   B. `Graphics`

   C. `Color`

   D. `Drawing`

11. Which method is called first when an applet is launched?

    A. `main()`

    B. `run()`

    C. `init()`

    D. `actionPerformed()`

12. Which method in an applet is called when the browser window is closed?

    A. `main()`

    B. `kill()`

    C. `init()`

    D. `destroy()`

13. In which method should components be added to the applet?

    A. `main()`

    B. `start()`

    C. `init()`

    D. `paint()`

14. Which of the following references is used to access the constant for the color white?

    A. `Color("WHITE")`

    B. `Color.white`

    C. `Color.WHITE`

    D. `Color(white)`

15. What color is represented by the following?

    `Color(255,0,0)`

    A. `Blue`

    B. `Red`

    C. `Green`

    D. `Black`

16. What is the name for a shape that is drawn to represent a number or letter?

   A. Character

   B. Char

   C. Glyph

   D. Font

17. What is the default layout manager for an applet?

   A. `BoxLayout`

   B. `FlowLayout`

   C. `BorderLayout`

   D. `AppletLayout`

18. In event-driven programming, which method is called from the `actionPerformed()` method to identify the component that generated an event object?

   A. `getComponent()`

   B. `setSource()`

   C. `event()`

   D. `getSource()`

19. Can a constructor be called for a `Graphics` object?

   A. No, it is an abstract class.

   B. Yes, in the form of `Graphics(Applet a)`.

   C. Yes, in the form of `Graphics(Panel p)`.

   D. Yes, in the form of `Graphics(Applet a, Panel p)`.

20. Which class is used to insert audio media in an applet?

   A. `Audio`

   B. `AudioMedia`

   C. `MediaClip`

   D. `AudioClip`

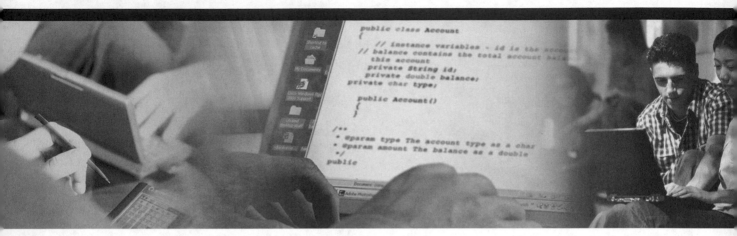

Upon completion of this chapter, you will be able to

- Understand the idea behind exceptions
- Identify the types of exceptions
- Understand how exception handling works
- Work with exception objects
- Describe when and how to deal with exceptions
- Understand how to structure a method and the execution sequence
- Understand and describe overriding and exceptions
- Apply the Java language concepts that you have learned in this chapter to the JBANK case study

Chapter 12

Exceptions

Errors are a common occurrence during compilation and runtime. Traditional methods for identifying and handling possible errors involved using many variables to flag errors. Sometimes the code could run into thousands of lines and had to be rewritten for each program. The Java platform provides the `Throwable` class for handling errors. In Java, errors are known as exceptions. Exceptions identify errors that arise in programs. They represent an exception to the normal flow of processing of a program.

This chapter covers the set of classes that inherit from the `Throwable` class and their uses. The keywords **try**, **catch**, **finally**, **throw**, and **throws** are used to manage exceptions.

Idea Behind Exceptions

A fundamental premise of good programming is that badly formed code should not run. In Java, badly formed code *will* not be run. The ideal time to catch an error is at compile time, before the program is run. Not all errors can be detected at compile time, however. As user interfaces are included in programs through GUIs, and data is accessed from files and over networks, the possibilities of errors at runtime increase.

This section consists of the following topics:

- The limitations of traditional methods of exception handling
- Error handling in the Java platform

The Limitations of Traditional Methods of Exception Handling

In a perfect world, users would never enter data in the wrong form, files would always exist, network URLs would always be correct, and code would never have bugs. Most of the code written thus far presents such an idealistic picture. When errors have been encountered at runtime, the program has been run again or the logic of the code has been changed to accommodate the error.

NOTE

Implementations of exception handling go back to the operating systems in the 1960s and even to BASIC's on error goto. With C++, exception handling was based on ADA; Java's is based primarily on C++, although it often is seen as being similar to Object Pascal.

When an error occurs at runtime, some formality is required in informing the user of the error and sending a message indicating the nature of the event that caused the error. If a user loses all the work done during a program because of program error, that user might not use the program again. At the very least, the following steps must be taken:

Step 1   Notify the user of the error.

Step 2   Save all the work.

Step 3   Allow users to exit from the program.

Traditional procedural languages include lengthy lines of code to identify possible run-time error conditions. Traditional approaches for detecting errors consist of using variables that are set to on, off, true, or false. This technique commonly is referred to as flagging because it uses flag variables (on, off, true, and false). The code to catch and handle errors can become quite complicated, and the number of variables that must be flagged can be large. Additionally, similar error conditions must be handled repeatedly in each program. Although cutting and pasting of code provides reusability, it does not ensure that the code logic is correct for the new use.

With object-oriented languages such as Java, classes can be designed to specifically handle error conditions. In most cases, these classes hold a message and information as data about the particular code that was executing when the error occurred. In addition, by handling the error, the program is not abruptly terminated. However, program termination will occur without error handling.

Objects of these exception classes then can be created when an error occurs, and methods in these objects can be used to inform the user of the error. Reusing classes and objects for the notification of errors greatly enhances the speed of code development and enforces a level of formality in communicating error situations.

Error Handling in the Java Platform

The Java platform provides a formal and disciplined approach to proactive error handling. An exception is a representation of an error condition or any situation that is not the expected result of a method. The key idea is that errors occur during method execution. In these situations, the programmer must include code to trap potential errors and code to attend to these errors. This coding technique can be thought of as the test-handle or **try/catch** technique. In the **try/catch** technique, code statements are tried and, if they cause errors, the programmer catches the error and includes code to handle the error.

In Java, any unexpected situation is known as an exception. Exceptions can be errors at runtime. They can also represent an unexpected user response or the unexpected results of an expression. They are called exceptions because they signal some unusual event in the program, as shown in Example 12-1 and Figure 12-1.

Example 12-1 *Java Runtime Exception—Code*

```
1  /**
2   * Java Program: SimpleExceptions.java
3   * @author Cisco Teacher
4   * @version 2002
5   */
6  public class SimpleExceptions
7  {
8       /**
9        * @exception Exception Any exception at all
10       */
11      //this syntax will be explained a little later
12      public static void main(String[] args) throws Exception
13      {
14              int x = Console.readInt("Enter a number");
15              int y = Console.readInt("Enter a number");
16              System.out.println("Before division X is " + x +
17                  " and  y is " + y);
18              x /= y;
19              System.out.println("After division X is " + x +
20                  " and  y is " + y);
21      }
22  } // end of class
```

Figure 12-1 Java Runtime Exception—Output

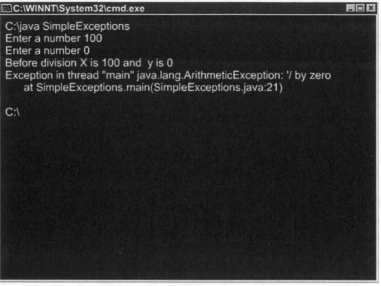

```
C:\WINNT\System32\cmd.exe                                    _ □ X

C:\java SimpleExceptions
Enter a number 100
Enter a number 0
Before division X is 100 and  y is 0
Exception in thread "main" java.lang.ArithmeticException: '/ by zero
     at SimpleExceptions.main(SimpleExceptions.java:21)

C:\
```

More Information

The word *exception* is meant to represent an exception to something; this is not in the sense of "exception to the rule," but in the sense of "I take exception to that." The second example also implies that the exception can cause something to halt.

An exceptional condition is a problem that prevents the continuation of a method or scope that you are in. In general, exceptions in code represent the point where a problem occurs, and you do not know what to do with it (because you do not have enough information in the current context). However, you do know that you just can't continue execution of the rest of the code until this exception is addressed. You stop and locate somebody somewhere to figure out what to do.

The central theme of exception handling is as follows:

1 You stop what you were doing because you do not have enough information in the current context to complete the execution of the code. (Execution of the current code terminates.)

2 You look for someone else (in a higher context—in the calling method block or in another code block that has been designated as a handler code for the exception) to handle the exception. That is, you locate a handler for the exception situation.

Handling unexpected situations or exceptions is delegated to a section of the code that is separate from the main processing of the code. As shown in Example 12-2 and Figure 12-2, this separates the code that deals with the errors from the code where things are processing normally.

Example 12-2 *try/catch Block*

```
1 /**
2  * Java Program: SimpleExceptions.java
3  * @author Cisco Teacher
4  * @version 2002
5  */
6 public class SimpleExceptions
7 {
8      /**
9       * @exception Exception Any exception at all
10      */
11     public static void main (String[] args) throws Exception
12     {
13         int x= 1, y = 9;
14         try
15         {
16             x = Console.readInt("Enter a number");
17             y = Console.readInt("Enter a number");
18             System.out.println("Before division X is " + x +
19                 " and y is " + y);
20             x /= y;
```

NOTE

The full version of the abbreviated code shown in this example can be viewed using the book's accompanying CD-ROM.

Figure 12-2 `try/catch` Block

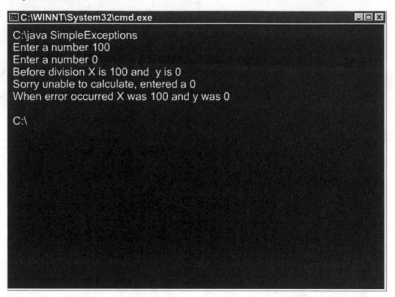

The Java language provides a set of classes that a programmer can use to handle exceptions. Objects of these classes are created when an exception occurs. The programmer only needs to test the existence of an exception object and code statements to attend to the exception. Many of the classes used so far include methods that create exceptions. For example, in the `DateConversion` class shown in Example 12-3, the `System.in.read()` method creates an `IOException` object if the method cannot read input from the keyboard.

Example 12-3 *Creation of Exception Objects*

NOTE

The full version of the abbreviated code shown in this example can be viewed using the book's accompanying CD-ROM.

```
 1 /**
 2  * Java Program: DateConversion.java
 3  * @author Cisco Teacher
 4  * @version 2002
 5  */
 6 import java.util.*;
 7 // ParseException class is in the java.text package
 8 import java.text.*;
 9 // IO Exception class is in the java.io package
10 import java.io.*;
11
```

Example 12-3 *Creation of Exception Objects (Continued)*

```
12 public class DateConversion
13 {
14      /**
15       * @exception IOException Object can not be created
16       * @exception ParseException Date can not be parsed
17       */
18      public static void main (String[] args) throws IOException,
19      ParseException
20      {
```

The `DateFormat` method `parse()` creates and throws a `ParseException` object when it receives a `String` that does not represent a date.

Types of Exceptions

Not all errors—and how they are handled—are the same in Java programming. This section covers the types of errors.

Types of Errors

Four major types of errors exist in Java programming, as included in the following list:

- Some Java errors occur with the JVM and are often the result of program errors.
- Code or data errors include these:
    - Improperly casting data or objects.
    - Accessing array indexes beyond the last element of the array.
    - Dividing integral primitives (**byte**, **short**, **int**, **long**) by 0.
    - Code defensively to avoid such errors. Be prepared and ensure that all the data needed for the task is correct and available. Include **if** conditions to test code defensively. Also, test code many times with different data.
- Standard errors are errors that are known and expected to occur during method processing. These errors can be errors in accessing files, in obtaining network connections, in receiving data from a database, and in sending instructions to a database, as well as actions that occur during the processing of an applet (application in a browser window).

- User-defined errors specifically are designed by the programmer to implement exceptions to normal business rules or activities. An example might be a student test score that is more than the maximum for the test, or a customer withdrawal against an account with no balance.

More Information

Use exceptions to do the following:

1 Fix the problem and call the method that caused the exception again.

2 Patch things up and continue without retrying the method.

3 Calculate some alternative result instead of what the method was supposed to do.

4 Do whatever you can in the current context (code block) and rethrow the same exception to a higher context (a `catch` block or the calling method).

5 Do whatever you can in the current context and throw a different exception to the higher context.

6 Terminate the program.

7 Simplify.

8 Make your library and programs safer, a long-term investment in the robustness of your program.

When used to their best advantage, exceptions can improve a program's readability, reliability, and maintainability.

NOTE

In Java, you are required to inform the client programmer who calls your method of the exception that might be thrown by your method. Even if the source code was available to the client programmer (which it often is not), the programmer would still have to dig through the code to locate the error-handling code and the **throw** clause. The Java compiler enforces such "civilized" code and enforces the syntax for declaring exception throwing through the exception specification. The exception specification is part of the method declaration and appears after the argument list. By enforcing exception specifications from top to bottom, Java ensures exception correctness at compile time.

How Exception Handling Works

Up to this point, the need for error handling and the different types of Java programming errors have been discussed. This section looks at how Java exception handling works, including throwing and handling exception objects.

Throwing and Handling Exception Objects

The act of detecting an abnormal condition and generating an exception is called throwing an exception. In Java, throwing an exception results in the creation of an object that encapsulates data about the unexpected condition. The act of throwing an exception causes the normal processing of the code to halt and search for a handler. The handler is a section of code that identifies the type of exception object to handle and the associated instructions on what to do.

The compiler enforces exception handling. If the class uses any method that has been defined to throw exception objects, the compiler must be notified of the intentions regarding this object. This requirement of the language commonly is known as the "handle and declare" rule (also known as the "catch and declare" rule). As shown in Example 12-4, there are many ways to handle an exception and declare the intention of passing the exception to another method.

Example 12-4 *Throwing and Handling Exception Objects*

```
1 /**
2 * Java Program: SimpleExceptions.java
3 * @author Cisco Teacher
4 * @version 2002
5 */
6 public class SimpleExceptions
7 {
8     /**
9      * @exception Exception Any exception at all
10     */
11     public static void main (String[] args) throws Exception
12     {
13         int x= 1, y = 9;
14         try
15         {
16             x = Console.readInt("Enter a number");
17             y = Console.readInt("Enter a number");
18             System.out.println("Before division X is " + x +
19                 " and y is " + y);
20             x /= y;
```

NOTE

The full version of the abbreviated code shown in this example can be viewed using the book's accompanying CD-ROM.

The objects that encapsulate exception conditions derive from the inheritance hierarchy described in the following section.

The information about the error is represented both inside the exception object and implicitly in the type of exception object chosen. Inside an exception object, a message can be stored as a String, and additional attributes can be added to hold specific data regarding the exception situation. However, often the only information stored is the type of exception object, and nothing meaningful is stored within the exception object. Typically, you throw a different type of exception for each different type of error.

Exception Objects

This section looks at the inheritance hierarchy for exception objects and consists of the following topics:

- The `Throwable` class
- `Exception` and its subclasses
- `RuntimeException` class
- Fatal errors

Class `Throwable`

The inheritance hierarchy for the *Throwable class* and its subclasses is shown in Figure 12-3.

Figure 12-3 Throwable—Class Hierarchy

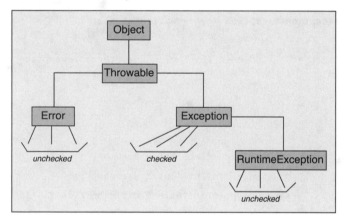

Only objects that are instances of the `Throwable` class (or one of its subclasses) are thrown by the Java Virtual Machine or can be thrown by the Java **throw** statement. Only this class or one of its subclasses can be the object type referenced by the handler code, also known as the **catch** clause. The Java language does not allow primitives or any other class of objects to be thrown.

All member data for this class is **private**. This class contains a snapshot of the execution stack of its thread at the time it was created. In other words, an object of this class contains information about the particular method that was executing when the error occurred. It also can contain a message String that gives more information about the error.

An execution stack represents all the methods invoked that led to the particular error. The Java programming language keeps track of methods that are active at any one time, so the last method called is always the last method on the list. This tracking area in memory is known as the *call stack*. For example, in Example 12-5, the main method here calls the setName method, which calls the Console2.readline() method, which, in turn, calls the System.in.read() method. The call stack shows the last method called as the read() method. If an exception occurs when the read() method tries to read data from the keyboard, the JVM unwinds the call stack until a handler for the method is found, as shown in Example 12-5 and Figure 12-4.

Example 12-5 *Unwinding the Call Stack—Code*

```
 1  import java.io.*;

 2

 3  class Student2

 4  {

 5      private String name;

 6      public void setName() throws IOException

 7      {

 8              name = Console2.readLIne("");

 9      }//  end of setname

10      public String getName ()

11      {

12              return name;

13          }// end of getName

14  } // end of Student2 class
```

> 2. Call stack unwound to this method and searches for handler in this method. Does not find any handler and returns to main at Student2.setName(CallStack1.java:7)

continues

Example 12-5 *Unwinding the Call Stack—Code (Continued)*

```
15
16
17  class Console2
18  {
19      public static String readLine(String prompt) throws IOException
20      {
21      int ch;
22      String x = "";
23      boolean done = false;
24      if (prompt.compareTo("") == 0)
25         throw new IOException();
26      System.out.println(prompt);
27      while (!done)
28      {
29          ch = System.in.read();
30          if (ch < 0 || (char)ch == '\h')
31             done = true;
32          else if ((char)ch != '\r')
33             r = r + (char) ch;
34      }
35      return r;
36   }//end of readLine
37  } // end of Console2 class
38
39
40 public class CallStack1
41 {
42      public static void main (String args [ ]) throws IOException
43              {
44          Student2 aStudent = new Student2() ;
```

> 1. Exception thrown here first, and handler searched in this code block. Does not find any handler and unwinds the call stack to the setName method
>
> Console2.readLine(CallStack1.java, Compiled Code

Example 12-5 *Unwinding the Call Stack—Code (Continued)*

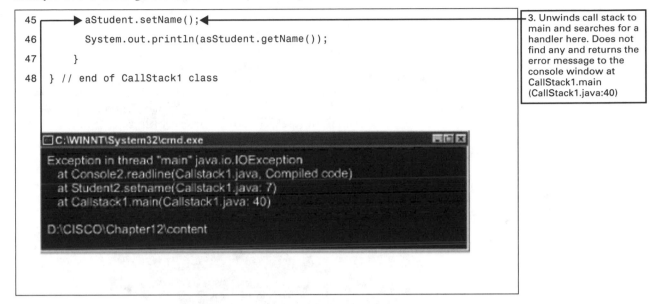

```
45        aStudent.setName();
46           System.out.println(asStudent.getName());
47        }
48  } // end of CallStack1 class
```

3. Unwinds call stack to main and searches for a handler here. Does not find any and returns the error message to the console window at CallStack1.main (CallStack1.java:40)

```
C:\WINNT\System32\cmd.exe                              _ □ ×

Exception in thread "main" java.io.IOException
  at Console2.readline(Callstack1.java, Compiled code)
  at Student2.setname(Callstack1.java: 7)
  at Callstack1.main(Callstack1.java: 40)

D:\CISCO\Chapter12\content
```

Figure 12-4 Unwinding the Call Stack—Graphic

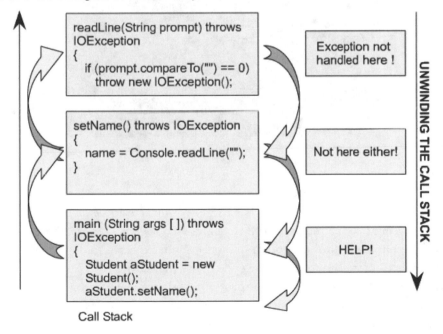

```
readLine(String prompt) throws
IOException
{
    if (prompt.compareTo("") == 0)
        throw new IOException();
```

Exception not handled here !

```
setName() throws IOException
{
    name = Console.readLine("");
}
```

Not here either!

```
main (String args [ ]) throws
IOException
{
    Student aStudent = new
    Student();
    aStudent.setName();
```

HELP!

UNWINDING THE CALL STACK

Call Stack

The Throwable class has some very useful methods that are described in Table 12-1.

Table 12-1 Throwable Class Method

Method	Description
String getMessage()	Returns a message stored in the exception object.
void printStackTrace()	An overloaded method that prints a representation of the call stack. This method can print to the standard output device or any other printer devices.

Figure 12-5 illustrates the getMessage() and printStackTrace methods.

Figure 12-5 Using Throwable Class Methods

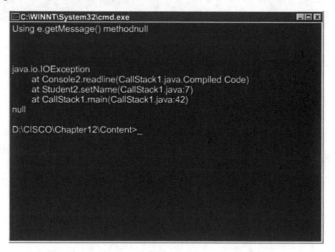

Types of Throwable Objects

Two general types of Throwable objects exist: *Error* objects and *Exception* objects. Error objects are used to represent run-time and system errors. Error and its subclasses represent conditions that programmers are not expected to do anything about. Programmers do not need to write any code that handles the error. Instead, they should let the JVM handle the error or pass it to the run-time environment. The JVM handles Error objects automatically. Exceptions have many subclasses. The Exception subclasses include the *RuntimeException* class and its subclasses, as well as others.

The compiler enforces exception handling by checking the code to ensure that any known Exceptions (but not Errors) have been handled or declared in the code. Except for the RuntimeException class and its subclasses, the compiler checks all other Exception subclasses. These Exception subclasses are known as *checked exceptions*. The code will not compile if there is a call to any method that throws a checked exception and the exception has not been declared or handled.

The IOException is a common checked exception that you will encounter during this course. The inheritance hierarchy shown in Table 12-2 describes the IOException class found in the java.io package.

Table 12-2 IOException Class Hierarchy in the java.io Package

IOException Class Hierarchy
class java.io.IOException
class java.io.CharConversionException
class java.io.EOFException
class java.io.FileNotFoundException
class java.io.InterruptedIOException
class java.io.ObjectStreamException
class java.io.InvalidClassException
class java.io.InvalidObjectException
class java.io.NotActiveException
class java.io.NotSerializableException
class java.io.OptionalDataException
class java.io.StreamCorruptedException
class java.io.WriteAbortedException
class java.io.SyncFailedException
class java.io.UnsupportedEncodingException
class java.io.UTFDataFormatException

Exception and Its Subclasses

The Exception subclass consists of the RuntimeException class and all other subclasses. Extending from the Exception class also can create custom exception classes. The compiler checks all Exception subclasses except for RuntimeException. Figure 12-6 shows the Throwable hierarchy. The RuntimeException is a common unchecked exception that you will encounter during this course. The inheritance hierarchy shown in Table 12-3 describes the RuntimeException class (and its subclasses) found in the java.lang package.

Figure 12-6 Throwable-Class Hierarchy Checked Exception

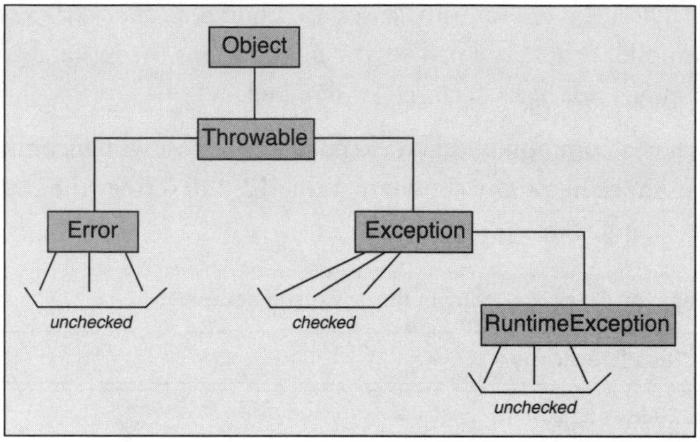

Table 12-3 RuntimeException Classes in the java.lang Package

`RuntimeException` Class Hierarchy
class java.lang.RuntimeException
class java.lang.ArithmeticException
class java.lang.ArrayStoreException
class java.lang.ClassCastException
class java.lang.IllegalArgumentException
class java.lang.IllegalThreadStateException
class java.lang.NumberFormatException
class java.lang.IllegalMonitorStateException
class java.lang.IllegalStateException
class java.lang.IndexOutOfBoundsException
class java.lang.ArrayIndexOutOfBoundsException
class java.lang.StringIndexOutOfBoundsException
class java.lang.NegativeArraySizeException
class java.lang.NullPointerException
class java.lang.SecurityException
class java.lang.UnsupportedOperationException

RuntimeException Class

The RuntimeException class and its subclasses were described in Table 12-3. Each of these exceptions can be avoided by implementing defensive coding. For example, IndexOutOfBoundsException can be avoided by using the length of an array to process the correct index value. ArithmeticException can be avoided by ensuring that the divisor in integer division is not a 0. Well-written code and extensive testing of code can handle most run-time errors.

More Information
You can ignore only RuntimeException and its subclasses in your coding because the handling of all other exceptions is enforced carefully by the compiler. RuntimeExceptions represent programming errors, such as the following: **1** An error that you cannot catch (such as receiving a null reference handed to your method by a client programmer).   **2** An error that you, the programmer, should have checked for in your code. This involves defensive coding, such as using the length variable to ensure that the processing of an array does not extend beyond the last element resulting in a ArrayIndexOutOfBoundsException.

Fatal Errors

Errors represent conditions that programmers are not expected to do anything about. These are often fatal errors associated with machine failure or processor or memory problems. The Error class API is shown in Figure 12-7. A number of subclasses of the Error class exist, including ThreadDeath, LinkageError, and VirtualMachineError. The errors that are associated with objects of these classes represent catastrophic problems, and programmers often can do very little about the error other than note that it occurred.

Figure 12-7 Error Class API

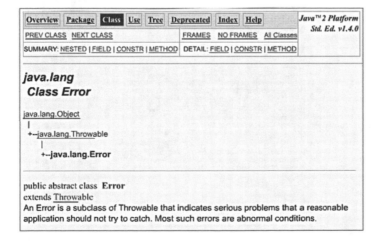

Dealing with Exceptions

A Java programmer can handle different exceptions with a number of approaches. This section consists of the following topics:

- Advertising exceptions
- Using handle and declare
- Using a **try/catch** block
- Specifying exceptions
- Catching multiple exceptions
- Using the **finally** block

Advertising Exceptions

How do programmers know that a method throws an exception that they have to catch? Just as a method must specify what type and how many arguments it accepts and what is returned, a method must specify the checked exceptions that the method can throw; this is known as *advertising or declaring exceptions*. Two common reasons that a method throws an exception are that it includes a call to another method that throws an exception, or that it creates an object of the type Throwable (usually a checked exception) and throws this object using the keyword *throw*. The API for the Exception class is shown in Figure 12-8

Figure 12-8 Exception Class API

Example 12-6 show the syntax for throwing an exception and the syntax for the declaration of a method that throws an exception.

Example 12-6 *Advertising Exceptions*

```
 1 /*
 2 The presence of the following statement requires
 3 the advertising of this action in the method signature
 4 of the method in which it appears.
 5 */
 6
 7 throw new Exception-classname();
 8
 9
10 /*
11 A method that throws an exception will have
12 the following syntax
13
14  return-type name(, ...)
15    throws Exception-classname ...
16 */
17
18 public static String getInput(String prompt)
19    throws IOException
20 {
21
22 }
```

Handle and Declare

When there are statements in the code block that can **throw** exceptions, do one of the following:

- Declare the exception—The programmer can declare that he is aware of the exception by including the clause ***throws*** *name-of-exception* (**throws** is a Java keyword). This is the "specify requirement" of the Java language. In the example shown in Example 12-7, any exception thrown is passed on to the calling method. It is up to the calling method to handle or declare and pass it on further. Although the programmer has passed on the problem and it has not been resolved, the compiler accepts that the programmer has declared knowledge of the error. You might wonder why the compiler allows this. The compiler enforces the handling of exceptions by ensuring that the exception object can be passed up the call stack until it reaches the final program. This ensures that the message gets to the user and is not buried in some level of method calls.

Example 12-7 main *Method Throws* IOException *and* ParseException

NOTE

The full version of the abbreviated code shown in this example can be viewed using the book's accompanying CD-ROM.

```
1  /**
2   * Java Program: DateConversion.java
3   * @author Cisco Teacher
4   * @version 2002
5   */
6  import java.util.*;
7  // ParseException class is in the java.text package
8  import java.text.*;
9  // IO Exception class is in the java.io package
10 import java.io.*;
11
12 public class DateConversion
13 {
14     /**
15      * @exception IOException Object can not be created
16      * @exception ParseException Date can not be parsed
17      */
18     public static void main (String[] args) throws IOException,
19     ParseException
20     {
```

For Example 12-7, you can view the explanatory text by accessing the full, interactive graphic for this example on the book's accompanying CD-ROM. The title of the activity is "main Method Throws IOException and ParseException" in e-Lab Activities.

■ Handle the exception (*handling exceptions*)—This is the "catch requirement" of the Java language. Handle the exception by enclosing the code in a **try/catch** block, as shown in Example 12-8. The **try/catch** block is described in the next section.

Example 12-8 *Handling Exceptions with* **try/catch** *Block*

NOTE

The full version of the abbreviated code shown in this example can be viewed using the book's accompanying CD-ROM.

```
 1 /**
 2  * Java Program: DateConversion.java
 3  * @author Cisco Teacher
 4  * @version 2002
 5  */
 6 import java.util.*;
 7 // ParseException class is in the java.text package
 8 import java.text.*;
 9 // IO Exception class is in the java.io package
10 import java.io.*;
11
12 public class DateConversion
13 {
14     /**
15     * @exception IOException Object can not be created
16     * @exception ParseException Date can not be parsed
17     */
18     public static void main (String[] args)
19     {
20         Date someDate;
```

For Example 12-8, you can view the explanatory text by accessing the full, interactive graphic for this example on the book's accompanying CD-ROM. The title of the activity is "Handling Exceptions with **try/catch** Block" in e-Lab Activities.

■ *Rethrow* the exception and declare this in the method signature—Use the **try/catch** block to catch the exception and rethrow the exception or another subclass of the exception. In this event, the programmer is "passing the exception" up the call stack. If an exception is rethrown, the compiler must be notified. Include the phrase **throws** *exception-name* in the method signature. The **try** block includes one or more statements that can throw an exception. In the example shown in Example 12-9, the read() method is advertised as throwing an IOException.

Example 12-9 *Handling Exceptions with a Rethrow and Declare*

```
 1 /**
 2  * Java Program: DateConversion.java
 3  * @author Cisco Teacher
```

continues

NOTE

The full version of the abbreviated code shown in this example can be viewed using the book's accompanying CD-ROM.

Example 12-9 *Handling Exceptions with a Rethrow and Declare (Continued)*

```
 4   * @version 2002
 5   */
 6  import java.util.*;
 7  // ParseException class is in the java.text package
 8  import java.text.*;
 9  // IO Exception class is in the java.io package
10  import java.io.*;
11
12  public class DateConversion
13  {
14      /**
15       * @exception IOException Object can not be created
16       * @exception ParseException Date can not be parsed
17       */
18      public static void main (String[] args) throws IOException
19      {
20          Date someDate;
```

NOTE

One of the advantages of Java exception handling is that it enables you to concentrate on the problem you are trying to solve in one place (**try** block) and then deal with errors from that code in another place (**catch** block). The section of code that might produce exceptions can be thought of as the guarded region—that is, guarded by a block labeled try { }. This section is followed by the code to handle this exception, which is labeled as the catch( ) { } block or the finally{} block.

For Example 12-9, you can view the explanatory text by accessing the full, interactive graphic for this example on the book's accompanying CD-ROM. The title of the activity is "Handling Exceptions with a Rethrow and Declare" in e-Lab Activities.

There is an exemption to these rules. An object of the type RuntimeException or Error or any of their subclasses does not need to be specified or caught. These are not checked by the compiler.

Using the try/catch Block

When a code statement is executing and results in an error, an exception object is created or thrown. The JVM unwinds the call stack searching for a code block that will handle the exception. If it finds none, the program terminates.

The Java language provides two code constructs to test code and handle exceptions when they occur. These are known as *try/catch blocks*.

Example 12-10 shows the sample code for a **try/catch** block. The **try** block always contains the code needed to execute. The **catch** block consists of an argument defining the specific type of Exception object that the **catch** block will handle. Programmers can have more than one **catch** block to catch different types of exceptions.

Example 12-10 `try`/`catch` *Block*

```
 try
{
     char x = (char)System.in.read();
}
catch (IOException  ioe)
{
     //code to handle the error
}
catch (Exception e)
{
     //code to handle other exceptions
}
```

NOTE

Each **catch** clause is like a method that takes only one argument of a particular type.

Code that can throw a known exception must be enclosed in a **try** block, or else the possibility of an exception must be advertised using the **throws** exception clause as part of the method signature. A **try** block can enclose code that can give rise to one or more exceptions. The code in the **try** block shown in Example 12-11 is known to throw the exception IOException.

Example 12-11 **try** *Block*

```
try
{
     char x = (char)System.in.read();
}
```

TIP

A number of different methods in the **try** block might generate the same exception; you need only one **catch** clause to handle this exception.

Catching the same type of error in two separate **catch** blocks associated with the same **try** block is a syntax error.

The **catch** block encloses code that is intended to handle a specific type of exception. The example shown has several **catch** blocks; each catches a different type of exception. A **try/catch** block has one **try** block and one or more **catch** blocks. If the code is expected to give rise to different errors and each error must be handled differently, be sure to code specific handlers for each error. The syntax of the **catch** block consists of the keyword **catch** and a single argument specifying the Exception class type and a variable to hold the reference to the object of that type. In Example 12-12, IOException is the Exception class type and ioe is the variable to reference the exception object that is thrown.

Example 12-12 *catch Block*

TIP

An empty **catch** block usually defeats the purpose of exceptions, which is to force you to handle exceptional conditions. Ignoring exceptions is analogous to ignoring a fire alarm, or turning off the alarm so that no one gets a chance to see if there is a real fire! If you include an empty **catch** block, insert some comments that explain why it is appropriate to ignore the exception.

```
catch (IOException  ioe)
{
     //code to handle the error
}
catch (Exception e)
{
     //code to handle other exceptions
}
```

Specifying Exceptions

When coding a method that throws exceptions, more than one exception can be defined to be thrown by the method. The two Java keywords used are **throw** and **throws**.

As shown in Example 12-13, the method signature advertises the exceptions created in the method using the clause **throws** *exception-name exception-name exception-name*. Each type of exception is listed. The order does not have any significance here.

NOTE

The full version of the abbreviated code shown in this example can be viewed using the book's accompanying CD-ROM.

Example 12-13 *Method That Throws More Than One Exception*

```
 1 /**
 2  * Java Program: DateConversion.java
 3  * @author Cisco Teacher
 4  * @version 2002
 5  */
 6 import java.util.*;
 7 // ParseException class is in the java.text package
 8 import java.text.*;
 9 // IO Exception class is in the java.io package
10 import java.io.*;
11
12 public class DateConversion
13 {
14      /**
15       * @exception IOException Object can not be created
16       * @exception ParseException Date can not be parsed
17       */
```

Example 12-13 *Method That Throws More Than One Exception (Continued)*

```
18      public static void main (String[] args) throws IOException,
19      ParseException
20      {
```

For Example 12-13, you can view the explanatory text by accessing the full, interactive graphic for this example on the book's accompanying CD-ROM. The title of the activity is "Method That Throws More Than One Exception" in e-Lab Activities.

The exceptions that are thrown could be from any of the following:

- A call to another method (which throws an exception)—A method calls the System.in.read() method, which throws an IOException. This exception is not handled by the System.in.read() method but is passed to the calling method.

- Throwing a new exception—As a result of testing a condition, a method creates and then throws a new exception object that is a user-defined exception object or an object of one of the predefined Exception subclasses. (How to create exception classes is explored in the next section.)

- Rethrowing an exception—A method may encounter an exception in a **try** block and deal with it in a corresponding **catch** block, but may also re-throw the exception.

Example 12-14 demonstrates all three possible ways to throw exceptions.

Example 12-14 *Method—Alternative Techniques for Exception Objects That Are Thrown*

```
1  /**
2   * Java Program: ExceptionExamples.java
3   * @author Cisco Teacher
4   * @version 2002
5   */
6  public class ExceptionExamples
7  {
8      // exception passed to calling method
9      public void setName() throws IOException
10     {
11         name = Console.readLine();
12     }
13
14     //exception handled and rethrown
```

NOTE

The full version of the abbreviated code shown in this example can be viewed using the book's accompanying CD-ROM.

continues

Example 12-14 *Method—Alternative Techniques for Exception Objects That Are Thrown (Continued)*

```
15    public static void setDate(int i) throws ParseException
16    {
17        try
18        {
19            DateFormate df = DateFormate.getDateInstance
20                (DateFormat.SHORT,Locale.US);
```

These three techniques can also be included in one method, as shown in Example 12-15. In this case, this method must handle all three types of exceptions. Here, the code that uses the method that throws three types of exceptions uses one **try** block and three **catch** blocks to catch each type of exception.

Example 12-15 *Source of Exceptions Thrown by a Method*

NOTE

The full version of the abbreviated code shown in this example can be viewed using the book's accompanying CD-ROM.

```
1 /**
2 * Java Program: MultipleExceptions.java
3 * @author Cisco Teacher
4 * @version 2002
5 */
6
7 import java.io.*;
8
9 public class MultipleExceptions
10 {
11     /**
12      * @exception Exception Cannot read data or do math operations
13      */
14     public static void main(String[] args) throws IOException,
15     ArithmeticException, Exception
16     {
17         try
18         {
19             // throws IOException
20             int x = Console.readInt("enter a number");
```

> **More Information**
>
> Exception handlers can be written in different ways, such as those that follow:
>
> - They can rethrow an exception.
> - They can convert one type of exception to another by throwing a different type of exception.
> - They can add to the message of the exception using the `fillStackTrace()` method.
> - They can perform any necessary recovery and resume execution after the last exception handler or after executing the code in the **finally** block, which is optional.
> - They can evaluate the situation that caused the error by querying the attributes of the exception object or its type, and then remove the cause of the error and retry by calling the original method that caused an exception.
> - They can return a status value to the environment using `System.exit(n)`, where n is some value that is defined as part of the application design standards.
> - They can ignore the exception, or log it and continue.

Catching Multiple Exceptions

It might be necessary to try and *catch multiple exceptions* because the method that is being called throws multiple exceptions, or the logic of the code could throw multiple exceptions. In this case, the use of multiple **catch** blocks is necessary. Each **catch** block should be used to catch only one type of exception. Because all exceptions that need to be caught are checked exceptions and subclasses from the Exception class, the multiple **catch** blocks should consider the possibility of polymorphic influence of the class type in the **catch** clause. Recall that polymorphism is the use of many forms of a class as an argument to a method call. Polymorphism allows the use of a general class of objects as arguments in a method, and references to objects of its subclass can be used as values in the method call. As shown in Example 12-16, as long as the object passed to the method is in the subclass hierarchy of the class defined in the method argument, it can be used by the method (*polymorphism and exceptions*).

Example 12-16 *Use of Polymorphic Arguments in Exception Handling*

```
1 /**
2  * Java Program: PolyMorphic.java
3  * @author Cisco Teacher
4  * @version 2002
5  */
6 import java.io.*;
7
8 public class PolyMorphic
```

continues

NOTE

The full version of the abbreviated code shown in this example can be viewed using the book's accompanying CD-ROM.

Example 12-16 *Use of Polymorphic Arguments in Exception Handling (Continued)*

```
 9 {
10     /**
11      * @exception Exception Cannot read data or
12      *     perform math operations
13      */
14     public static void main(String[] args) throws IOException,
15     ArithmeticException, Exception
16     {
17         try
18         {
19             // throws IOException
20             int x = Console.readInt("enter a number");
```

For Example 12-16, you can view the explanatory text by accessing the full, interactive graphic for this example on the book's accompanying CD-ROM. The title of the activity is "Use of Polymorphic Arguments in Exception Handling" in e-Lab Activities.

A **catch** clause that handles objects of the type Exception can handle any object of its subclass. A **catch** clause that handles exceptions of the type IOException can handle any object of the types FileNotFoundException, UnknownServiceException, or MalformedURLException.

In writing code blocks to catch multiple exceptions, the degree of specificity of the exception in the **catch** clause ensures that different exceptions are handled in different ways, as shown in Example 12-17. For example, to handle the exception FileNotFoundException in a different manner than the MalformedURLException, separate **catch** blocks would be coded for each of these.

Example 12-17 *Catching Different Exceptions*

NOTE

The full version of the abbreviated code shown in this example can be viewed using the book's accompanying CD-ROM.

```
1 /**
2  * Java Program: FrameworkMultipleExceptions.java
3  * @author Cisco Teacher
4  * @version 2002
5  */
6
7
8 import java.io.*;
```

continues

Example 12-17 *Catching Different Exceptions (Continued)*

```
 9
10 public class FrameworkMultipleExceptions
11 {
12     public static void main ( String args[])
13     {
14         try
15         {
16             // statements
17             // some are safe some might throw an error
18         }
19         // catches objects of FileNotFoundException and its sub-classes
20         catch (FileNotFoundException fnf)
```

For Example 12-17, you can view the highlighted code by accessing the full, interactive graphic for this example on the book's accompanying CD-ROM. The title of the activity is "Catching Different Exceptions" in e-Lab Activities.

The converse is also true. It might not be necessary to handle each of these exceptions differently and code only one **catch** block that handles any type of IOException, as shown in Example 12-18. If a MalformedURLException occurs, the **catch** block will accept this object because it is a subclass of the IOException class. Polymorphism is applied to accept any object of the subclass of the IOException class.

Example 12-18 *Use of Higher-Level Exception Classes in the* **catch** *Clause*

```
 1 /**
 2  * Java Program MultipleExceptions.java
 3  * @author Cisco Teacher
 4  * @version 2002
 5  */
 6
 7 import java.io.*;
 8
 9 public class MultipleExceptions
10 {
11     public static void main(String[] args)
12     {
13         try
```

NOTE

The full version of the abbreviated code shown in this example can be viewed using the book's accompanying CD-ROM.

Example 12-18 *Use of Higher-Level Exception Classes in the* **catch** *Clause (Continued)*

```
14              {
15                  int x = Console.readInt("enter an number");
16                   int y = Console.readInt("enter an number");
17              if (x == 9)
18                  throw new IOException("This is an IO error");
19              System.out.println("X is " + x + " and  y is " + y);
20              x /= y;
```

For Example 12-18, you can view the explanatory text by accessing the full, interactive graphic for this example on the book's accompanying CD-ROM. The title of the activity is "Use of Higher-Level Exception Classes in the **catch** Clause" in e-Lab Activities.

The sequence in which this code is placed affects whether the exceptions are caught and handled by the correct code block. The **catch** clause must be in the sequence with the most derived type first and the most basic type last. This is because if the **catch** clause for a basic class precedes the **catch** clause for a derived class, the **catch** clause with the derived class never can be executed.

In the example shown in Example 12-19, the first **catch** block handles Exception objects. Because IOException "is a" Exception object, the polymorphic behavior of the language uses this code block to handle all exceptions, including an IO exception. The **catch** block for the IOException never gets used. When using multiple **catch** blocks, arrange them in the manner of specificity. Make sure that subclasses of the Exception class are handled first.

Example 12-19 *Improper Sequencing of Multiple* **catch** *Blocks*

```
 1 try
 2 {
 3     System.in.read();
 4 }
 5 catch (Exception e)
 6 {
 7     // code to handle other error
 8 }
 9 catch ( IOException  ioe)
10 {
11     // code to handle IOExceptions
12 }
```

For Example 12-19, you can view the explanatory text by accessing the full, interactive graphic for this example on the book's accompanying CD-ROM. The title of the activity is "Improper Sequencing of Multiple **catch** Blocks" in e-Lab Activities.

The **try/catch** blocks are bonded together. Do not put any other code block between the **try/catch** blocks, as shown in Example 12-20. Variables local to the **try** block are accessible only within the **try** block. The **try** block is the scope for these variables. Trying to access the variable outside of the **try** block in any other block of code in the method, including the **catch** and **finally** blocks, results in a compiler error. Variables declared in a **try** or **catch** block exist only within the scope of the block in which they are defined.

Example 12-20 *The* **try/catch** *Blocks Are Bonded Together*

```
 1  /**
 2   * Java Program MultipleExceptions.java
 3   * @author Cisco Teacher
 4   * @version 2002
 5   */
 6
 7  import java.io.*;
 8
 9  public class MultipleExceptions
10  {
11      public static void main(String[] args)
12      {
13          try
14          {
15              int x = Console.readInt("enter an number");
16              int y = Console.readInt("enter an number");
17              if (x == 9)
18                  throw new IOException("This is an IO error");
19              System.out.println("X is " + x + " and  y is " + y);
20              x /= y;
```

NOTE

The full version of the abbreviated code shown in this example can be viewed using the book's accompanying CD-ROM.

For Example 12-20, you can view the explanatory text by accessing the full, interactive graphic for this example on the book's accompanying CD-ROM. The title of the activity is "The **try/catch** Blocks Are Bonded Together" in e-Lab Activities.

In the sample code shown in Example 12-21 for the `LoopWithTryCatch` class, the **try/catch** blocks are part of the loop. Any variables declared inside the **try** or the **catch** blocks are not available outside the block. The **int** variable `ainTry` is one such variable. The output shows that on the fourth iteration of this loop, the value of j is **0** and an `ArithmeticException` is thrown. However, after the **catch** block is executed, there will be another iteration with j having the value -1. To end the loop if the `ArithmeticException` object is thrown, insert the loop inside the **try** block.

Example 12-21 *Loop Block with* **try/catch** *Block* `LoopWithTryCatch` *Class—Code*

```
 1 /**
 2  * Java Program LoopWithTryCatch.java
 3  * @author Cisco Teacher
 4  * @version 2002
 5  */
 6 public class LoopWithTryCatch
 7 {
 8     public static void main(String [] args)
 9     {
10         int x = 10;
11         for ( int j = 4; j >= -1; j --)
12         {
13             try
14             {
15                 int ainTry = j;
16                 System.out.println
17                     ("You have entered into block count \n" +
```

NOTE

The full version of the abbreviated code shown in this example can be viewed using the book's accompanying CD-ROM.

For Example 12-21, you can view the explanatory text by accessing the full, interactive graphic for this example on the book's accompanying CD-ROM. The title of the activity is "Loop Block with **try/catch** Block `LoopWithTryCatch` Class" in e-Lab Activities.

The output shown in Figure 12-9 represents the output that would be generated if Lines 33, 34, and 41 were commented out. The compilation errors that would be generated by the print statements referencing the local **try** block variable (`ainTry`) in the **catch** block and after the **for** loop demonstrate that variables declared within the **try** block (in this case, `ainTry`) cease to exist when an exception is thrown or the program leaves the **try** block under normal execution.

Figure 12-9 Loop Block with **try/catch** Block LoopWithTryCatch Class—Output

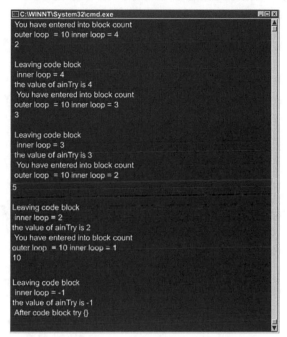

If there is a loop block that contains a **try** block, the **catch** block is also inside the loop. The **try** and **catch** blocks are part of the loop; because the **catch** is bound to the **try** block, there is an exception when the value of j is 0. As noted, after the **catch** block is executed, there is another iteration of j having the value of -1.

Even though the **try** and **catch** blocks are inside the loop, they have a different scope for the variables. This can be tested by declaring a variable inside a **try** block. This variable exists only inside the **try** block, and any attempt to reference it in the **catch** block or outside the **try** block causes a compile error. If a programmer attempts to access variables local to the **try** block from outside of it, the code will not compile.

Also, **catch** blocks can include further **try/catch** blocks. Any exceptions not caught in the nested **try** block are passed to the outer **try** block catch clauses.

The **finally** Block

Exceptions are handled as soon as they occur. The execution of the **try** block of code terminates, and the code in a **catch** block is executed. This occurs regardless of the importance of the exception or the code in the **try** block that follows the statement that caused the exception. For example, in a code block that writes data to a file, an exception in this block results in a cessation of the file-writing operations. This leaves

TIP

An exception handler cannot access variables in the scope of its **try** block because by the time the exception handler begins executing, the **try** block will have expired. Information that the handler needs normally is passed in the thrown object. Custom exception classes enable the passing of data through the exception objects.

the file that was being written to open. In this execution, any instruction in the **try** block that closes the file never is executed.

The **try/catch** block of constructs includes a construct *finally* (*finally* block), which is optional. This block of code always is executed, regardless of the exception that occurred or was caught; it executes even when there are no exceptions. The **finally** block provides a means of cleaning up at the end of executing a **try** block. This gives the programmer a way to allow the user to exit, as demonstrated in the sample code and output for the FileClosing class shown in Example 12-22 and Figure 12-10.

Example 12-22 **finally** *Block to Close a File When Exception Object Is Thrown*

NOTE

The full version of the abbreviated code shown in this example can be viewed using the book's accompanying CD-ROM.

```
1 /**
2  * Java Program: FileClosing.java
3  * @author Cisco Teacher
4  * @version 2002
5  */
6 import java.io.*;
7
8 public class FileClosing
9 {
10     public static void main(String args[]) throws IOException
11     {
12         RandomAccessFile raf = null;
13         // try block to read data
14         try
15         {
16             raf = new RandomAccessFile("myfile.txt", "r");
17             byte  b[] = new byte[1000];
18             raf.readFully(b,0,1000);
19             raf.close();
20         }
```

For Example 12-22, you can view the explanatory text by accessing the full, interactive graphic for this example on the book's accompanying CD-ROM. The title of the activity is "**finally** Block to Close a File When Exception Object Is Thrown" in e-Lab Activities.

Figure 12-10 Output of `FileClosing` Class Encountering a `FileNotFound` Exception or `IOEXception`

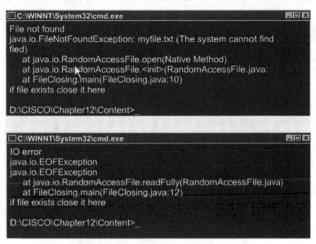

The sample code shown in Examples 12-23 and 12-24 demonstrates the use of a **finally** block within a loop.

Example 12-23 **finally** *Block Used Within a Loop—Movie*

```
1 /**
2 * Java Program: Movie.java
3 * @author Cisco Teacher
4 * @version 2002
5 */
6
7 import java.io.*;
8 import java.util.*;
9 import java.text.*;
10
11 public class Movie
12 {
13     private int dailyAttendance = 0;
14     private int showAttendance[];
15     private final Date day;
16     private final String formatShowDate = "";
17     private final int dailyShowings;
18     private final String title;
19     public static final int CAPACITY = 450;
```

NOTE

The full version of the abbreviated code shown in this example can be viewed using the book's accompanying CD-ROM.

NOTE

In languages without any destructor or garbage-collection mechanisms, a **finally** block is needed to release memory, regardless of what happens in a **try** block. Because Java does have a garbage-collection mechanism, the **finally** block is used to set something *other* than memory back to its original state. Some examples of this are objects that are used to open files and/or establish network connections, something drawn on a screen, or even devices such as switches that have been turned on and that need to be turned off.

For Example 12-23, you can view the explanatory text by accessing the full, interactive graphic for this example on the book's accompanying CD-ROM. The title of the activity is "**finally** Block Used Within a Loop" in e-Lab Activities.

Example 12-24 **finally** *Block Used Within a Loop—Custom Exception*

```
1  /**
2   * Java Program: AttendanceOutOfRangeException.java
3   * @author Cisco Teacher
4   * @version 2002
5   */
6  public class AttendanceOutOfRangeException extends Exception
7  {
8      private final String message;
9
10     public AttendanceOutOfRangeException ()
11     {
12         message = "The value you entered exceeds for the attendance" +
13             " was either negative or\ngreater than the Theater's "+
14             "capacity!";
15     }
16
17     public String getMessage()
18     (
19     return message;
20     )
```

NOTE

The full version of the abbreviated code shown in this example can be viewed using the book's accompanying CD-ROM.

NOTE

The **finally** block eliminates the need for a **goto** statement in Java.

The **finally** block is executed when any of these conditions occurs:

- When the code in the **try** block executes properly.
- When the code in the applicable **catch** block is executed after an exception occurs.
- When the code in the **try** block includes a **break** or **continue** statement.
- When the code in the **try** block includes a **return**.
- Code in **finally** does not execute when the System.exit() method is called in a **try** or **catch** block.

The sample code and output shown in Example 12-25 and Figure 12-11 for the AlwaysFinally class demonstrate the execution of the **finally** block under these different conditions.

Example 12-25 *Execution of* **finally** *Block—*AlwaysFinally*—Code*

```
1 /**
2  * Java Program: AlwaysFinally.java
3  * @author Cisco Teacher
4  * @version 2002
5  */
6 public class AlwaysFinally
7 {
8     public static void main(String[] args)
9     {
10         int x = 10;
11         for ( int y = -1; y < 10 ; y++)
12             try
13             {
14                 System.out.println("\nx = " + x + " and y = " + y);
15                 if(y == 2)
16                 {
17                     System.out.println("Leaving try code block" +
```

For Example 12-25, you can view the explanatory text by accessing the full, interactive graphic for this example on the book's accompanying CD-ROM. The title of the activity is "Execution of **finally** Block—AlwaysFinally" in e-Lab Activities.

Figure 12-11 *Execution of* **finally** *Block—*AlwaysFinally*—Output*

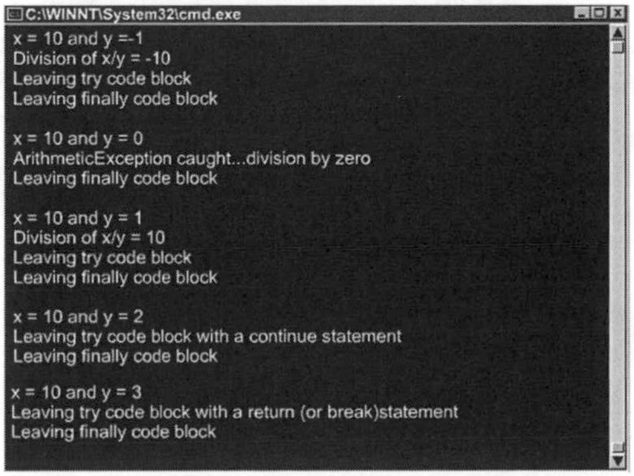

NOTE

The full version of the abbreviated code shown in this example can be viewed using the book's accompanying CD-ROM.

NOTE

When an exception is uncaught in an applet or a GUI-based application, the GUI remains displayed and the user can continue using the applet or the application even after the default exception handler runs. However, the program might be in an inconsistent state and might produce incorrect results.

Exception Objects

In addition to the extensive library of `Throwable` classes, individual exception classes can be defined. This section consists of the following topics:

- Creating an exception class
- Using user-defined exceptions
- Handling user-defined exceptions

Creating an Exception Class

These simple steps describe how to create and use customized or *user-defined exceptions*:

Step 1   Create a class that extends from `Exception`.

Step 2   In a method of another class, throw a **new** instance of the exception.

Step 3   Use the method that throws the exception in a **try/catch** block.

Customized exceptions are used in many applications to alert the user of errors that represent unexpected activity or results that are unexpected from a business point-of-view. The following are examples of such exceptions:

- A business has a policy that changes can be made to employee data during restricted times of the day and on restricted days. The programmer can implement this rule by throwing an exception if the activity of changing employee data is performed on an unauthorized day or time of the day.

- A teacher uses an assistant to grade and record test scores. The program needs to attend to unexpected events, such as a score being more than the maximum points for the test, a score being changed after a final grade has been assigned, or too many scores entered for a student.

- A bank does not permit a customer to withdraw money from an account in an amount more than the balance or funds available. Any activity attempting to withdraw more than the balance needs to be identified as an exception.

The sample code in Example 12-26 for the `ScoreExceedsMaxPointsException` class and the sample code in Example 12-27 for the `EmployeeChangedException` class demonstrate the creation of two custom exception classes.

Example 12-26 *Custom Exception Classes*—`ScoreExceedsMaxPointsException.java`

```
1  /**
2   * Java Program: ScoreExceedsMaxPointsException.java
3   * @author Cisco Teacher
```

Example 12-26 *Custom Exception Classes—*`ScoreExceedsMaxPointsException.java` *(Continued)*

```
 4  * @version 2002
 5  */
 6 public class ScoreExceedsMaxPointsException extends Exception
 7 {
 8     private final String message;
 9
10     public ScoreExceedsMaxPointsException()
11     {
12         message = "The value you entered exceeds" +
13             " the maximum points for this test.";
14     }
15
16     /**
17      * @param test The test number as an int
18      * @param points The number of points, as an int,
19      *       scored on the test
20      * @param maxpoints The total points, as an int,
```

NOTE

The full version of the abbreviated code shown in this example can be viewed using the book's accompanying CD-ROM.

You can view the highlighted code by accessing the full, interactive graphic for this example on the book's accompanying CD-ROM. The title of the activity is "Custom Exception Classes—`ScoreExceedsMaxPointsException.java`," and it is found under the e-Lab Activities.

Example 12-27 *Custom Exception Classes—*`EmployeeChangedException.java`

```
 1 /**
 2  * Java Program: EmployeeChangedException.java
 3  * @author Cisco Teacher
 4  * @version 2002
 5  */
 6 public class EmployeeChangedException extends Exception
 7 {
 8     private String message;
 9     message = "Error: Can't change employee data at this time.";
10
11     public EmployeeChangedException()
12     {
```

NOTE

The full version of the abbreviated code shown in this example can be viewed using the book's accompanying CD-ROM.

continues

Example 12-27 *Custom Exception Classes*—EmployeeChangedException.java

```
13      }
14
15      /**
16       * @param day The day as a String
17       */
18      public EmployeeChangedException(String day)
19      {
20          message += "  Unauthorized access on " + day;
```

You can view the highlighted code by accessing the full, interactive graphic for this example on the book's accompanying CD-ROM. The title of the activity is "Custom Exception Classes—EmployeeChangedException.java" in e-Lab Activities.

More Information
Like any other class, an exception class can contain instance variables and methods. A typical exception class contains only two constructors—one that takes no arguments and specifies a default exception message, and one that receives a customized exception message as a String.

You can continue to embellish the power of your exception classes by adding methods and attributes. However, these additional features might be lost on the client programmers (other programmers using your packages) because they simply might be looking for the exception to be thrown and nothing more. Most of the Java library exceptions are used in this way.

The name of the exception should represent the problem that occurred; the name should be relatively self-explanatory, as in EmployeeChangedException, ScoreExceedsMaxPointsException, and ArrayIndexOutOfBoundsException. Associating each type of serious malfunction with an appropriately named exception class improves program clarity.

Using User-Defined Exceptions

User-defined exceptions must be thrown in some method. In the example shown in Example 12-28, a definition of the setScore method advertises that the method throws ScoreExceedsMaxPointsException. In the example shown in Example 12-29, the Employee class setSalary method advertises that the method throws EmployeeChangedException. The setScore method throws the exception when the condition test (score > maximum) is **true**. The setSalary method throws the exception when the condition test (day of week is Saturday or Sunday) is **true**.

Example 12-28 *Throwing Custom Exception Classes*—Student.java

```
1  /**
2   * Student Class establishes the student id, name and grade
3   * @author Cisco Teacher
4   * @version 2002
5   */
6  public class Student
7  {
8     private final String studentName;
9     private int score[] = {0, 0, 0, 0, 0, 0};
10    private int studentID;
11    public static final int courseNumber = 12345;
12    public static final int MAXSCORE[] = {25, 25, 75, 50, 50, 100};
13
14    // null constructor
15    public Student( )
16    {
17       studentName = "Not Available";
18       studentID = 99999;
19    }
```

NOTE

The full version of the abbreviated code shown in this example can be viewed using the book's accompanying CD-ROM.

For Example 12-28, you can view the explanatory text by accessing the full, interactive graphic for this example on the book's accompanying CD-ROM. The title of the activity is "Throwing Custom Exception Classes—Student.java" in e-Lab Activities.

Example 12-29 *Throwing Custom Exception Classes*—Employee.java

```
1  /**
2   * Employee class
3   * @author Cisco Teacher
4   * @version 2002
5   */
6  import java.util.*;
7  import java.text.*;
8
9  public class Employee
10 {
11    private final String name;
```

NOTE

The full version of the abbreviated code shown in this example can be viewed using the book's accompanying CD-ROM.

continues

Example 12-29 *Throwing Custom Exception Classes*—Employee.java *(Continued)*

```
12    private int employeeID;
13    private double salary;
14    private String address;
15
16    // null constructor
17    public Employee( )
18    {
19       name = "Not Available";
20       employeeID = 99999;
```

For Example 12-29, you can view the explanatory text by accessing the full, interactive graphic for this example on the book's accompanying CD-ROM. The title of the activity is "Throwing Custom Exception Classes—Employee.java" in e-Lab Activities.

Handling User-Defined Exceptions

Handling user-defined exceptions is no different than handling any other checked exception. They can be handled as follows:

- Declare the exception and do nothing further.
- Enclose the method that throws the exception in a **try/catch** block and handle the exception
- Enclose the method that throws the exception in a **try/catch** block and rethrow the exception

In the example shown in Example 12-30, ScoreExceedsMaxPointsException is thrown when the teacher enters a score that is greater than the max points for the test. The Teacher class encloses the call to the setScore method in a **try/catch** block. In the example shown in Example 12-31 and Figure 12-12, EmployeeChangedException also is thrown when the Payroll class (using the setSalary method of the Employee class) tries to change an employee's salary on a date that falls on Sunday.

Example 12-30 *Handling Custom Exception Objects*—Teacher.java

```
1 /**
2  * Teacher Class creates students
3  * @author Cisco Teacher
4  * @version 2002
```

Example 12-30 *Handling Custom Exception Objects—*`Teacher.java` *(Continued)*

```
 5  */
 6
 7 import java.io.*;
 8
 9 public class Teacher
10 {
11     // Main method
12     public static void main(String[] args) throws IOException
13     {
14         Student s1;
15         s1 = new Student("Mary Jane", 1114);
16         try
17         {
18             //Input test scores from console
19             for(int i = 0; i <s1.MAXSCORE.length; i++)
20             {
```

NOTE

The full version of the abbreviated code shown in this example can be viewed using the book's accompanying CD-ROM.

For Example 12-30, you can view the explanatory text by accessing the full, interactive graphic for this example on the book's accompanying CD-ROM. The title of the activity is "Handling Custom Exception Objects—`Teacher.java`" in e-Lab Activities.

Example 12-31 *Handling Custom Exception Objects—*`Payroll.java`*—Code*

```
 1 /** Payroll class
 2  *  @author Cisco Teacher
 3  */
 4 public class Payroll
 5 {
 6      // Main method
 7      public static void main(String[] args)
 8      {
 9          Employee e1;
10          e1 = new Employee("Mary Smith", 1234);
11          try
12          {
13              e1.setSalary(2500);
14          }
```

continues

Example 12-31 *Handling Custom Exception Objects*—Payroll.java—*Code (Continued)*

```
15              catch(EmployeeChangedException e)
16              {
17                  System.out.println(e.getMessage());
18              }
19              finally
20              {
21                  System.out.println(e1.getName() + "'s salary is "
23                  + e1.getSalary());
24              }
25          }// end of main
26 }// end of Payroll class
```

For Example 12-31, you can view the explanatory text by accessing the full, interactive graphic for this example on the book's accompanying CD-ROM. The title of the activity is "Handling Custom Exception Objects—Payroll.java" in e-Lab Activities.

Figure 12-12 Handling Custom Exception Objects—Payroll.java—Output

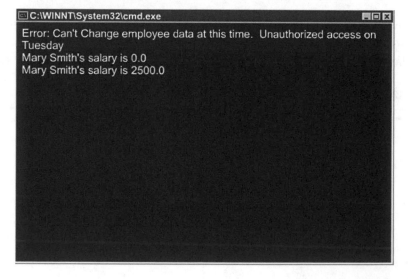

Structuring a Method and the Execution Sequence

Exceptions are essential constructs for creating good programs. This section reviews the main ideas behind the execution of exceptions. This section consists of the following topics:

- The order of exception blocks
- Execution sequence
- Execution when an exception is thrown
- Execution when an exception is not caught
- Nested **try** blocks
- Rethrowing of exceptions

The Order of Exception Blocks

As illustrated in Table 12-4, ensure that the **try**, **catch**, and **finally** blocks in the method code all are grouped together in that order: the **try** block first, the **catch** blocks next, and a single **finally** block. No other block of code can exist between these. A **try** block cannot exist without either one **catch** block or a **finally** block.

Table 12-4 Proper and Improper **try/catch** Constructs

Correct Order	
| | ```
try
{
    //code that throws exception
}
catch(SpecificException e)
{
    //code for exception
}
catch(Exception e)
{
    //code for general exception
}
finally
{
    //code to cleanup and close files
}
``` |

continues
```

Table 12-4 Proper and Improper **try/catch** Constructs (Continued)

| Unrelated Code Between Blocks | ```
try
{
    //code that throws exception
}
System.out.println(…);
catch(SpecificException e)
{
    //code for exception
}
catch(Exception e)
{
    //code for general exception
}
System.out.println(…);
finally
{
    //code to cleanup and close files
}
``` |
|---|---|
| No catch Clause | ```
try
{
    //code that throws exception
}
System.out.println(…);
``` |

Students should make it a point to include a **finally** block in the **try/catch** block of constructs.

Execution Sequence

The *execution sequence of the **try/catch**-block* begins with the first statement in a **try** block. If the statement completes without any exception, the statements in the **finally** block are executed. If there is a **return** statement in the **try** block, the **finally** block is executed before the **return** statement in the **try** block is executed. As shown in Example 12-32, any statements in the method after the **finally** block never get executed. Improper placement of a **return** in a method can result in logic errors. Always place the **return** as the last statement that needs to be executed.

The next section addresses the execution sequence of the **try/catch** block when an exception is thrown in the **try** block.

Example 12-32 *Execution Sequences*

```
1  /**
2   * Teacher Class creates students
3   * @author Cisco Teacher
4   * @version 2002
5   */
6
7  import java.io.*;
8
9  public class Teacher
10 {
11     // Main method
12     public static void main(String[] args) throws IOException
13     {
14         Student s1;
15         s1 = new Student("Mary Jane", 1114);
16         try
17         {
18             //Input test scores from console
19             for(int i = 0; i <s1.MAXSCORE.length; i++)
20             {
```

NOTE

The full version of the abbreviated code shown in this example can be viewed using the book's accompanying CD-ROM.

For Example 12-32, you can view the explanatory text by accessing the full, interactive graphic for this example on the book's accompanying CD-ROM. The title of the activity is "Execution Sequences" in e-Lab Activities.

Execution When an Exception Is Thrown

As shown in Example 12-33 and Figure 12-13, when an exception occurs, the code execution in the **try** block is terminated at the statement that caused the exception. The control of the program moves to the first **catch** clause that identifies an exception that matches the exception thrown. The statements in this **catch** block are executed. If a **catch** block has a **return** statement, the **finally** block is executed before the **return** statement.

Example 12-33 *Execution When an Exception Is Thrown—Code*

```
 1 /**
 2  * Teacher Class creates students
 3  * @author Cisco Teacher
 4  * @version 2002
 5  */
 6
 7 import java.io.*;
 8
 9 public class Teacher
10 {
11     // Main method
12     public static void main(String[] args) throws IOException
13     {
14         Student s1;
15         s1 = new Student("Mary Jane", 1114);
16         try
17         {
```

For Example 12-33, you can view the explanatory text by accessing the full, interactive graphic for this example on the book's accompanying CD-ROM. The title of the activity is "Execution When an Exception Is Thrown" in e-Lab Activities.

Figure 12-13 Execution When an Exception Is Thrown—Output

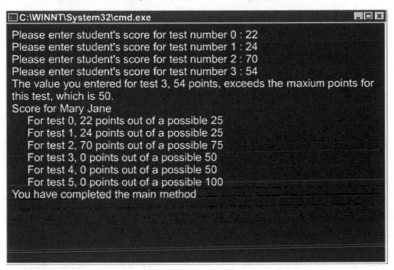

```
C:\WINNT\System32\cmd.exe                              _ □ X
Please enter student's score for test number 0 : 22
Please enter student's score for test number 1 : 24
Please enter student's score for test number 2 : 70
Please enter student's score for test number 3 : 54
The value you entered for test 3, 54 points, exceeds the maxium points for
this test, which is 50.
Score for Mary Jane
    For test 0, 22 points out of a possible 25
    For test 1, 24 points out of a possible 25
    For test 2, 70 points out of a possible 75
    For test 3, 0 points out of a possible 50
    For test 4, 0 points out of a possible 50
    For test 5, 0 points out of a possible 100
You have completed the main method
```

Execution When an Exception Is Not Caught

When an exception is not caught, the code in the **finally** block is executed. If the exception occurs in the main method, the program ends. Example 12-34 shows the sequence of searches for **catch** clauses when the exception occurs.

Example 12-34 *Execution Sequence When an Exception Is Not Caught*

```
 1 /**
 2  * Teacher Class creates students
 3  * @author Cisco Teacher3
 4  * @version 2002
 5  */
 6 public class Teacher3
 7 {
 8 // Main method
 9 /**
10  * @exception ScoreeExceedsMaxPointsException
11  * Test score is greater than the total possible points
12  */
13     public static void main(String[] args) throws
```

continues

TIP

If an exception is thrown for which no local catch is available, then when control enters the local **finally** block, the **finally** block also can throw an exception. If this happens, the first exception is lost.

Avoid trying to place code in a **finally** block that will throw an exception. If such code is required, enclose it in a **try/catch** block within the **finally** block.

NOTE

The full version of the abbreviated code shown in this example can be viewed using the book's accompanying CD-ROM.

Example 12-34 *Execution Sequence When an Exception Is Not Caught (Continued)*

```
14      ScoreExceedsMaxPointsException
15      {
16          Student s1;
17          s1 = new Student("Mary Jane", 1114);
18          try
19          {
20              //Input test scores from console
```

For Example 12-34, you can view the explanatory text by accessing the full, interactive graphic for this example on the book's accompanying CD-ROM. The title of the activity is "Execution Sequence When an Exception Is Not Caught" in e-Lab Activities.

Nested try Blocks

As shown in Example 12-35, **try/catch** blocks can be nested within **try** blocks and within **catch** blocks (*nested-**try**/**catch** blocks*). Any exception not caught in an inner block is handed to the outer block.

Example 12-35 *Nested **try**/**catch** Blocks*

NOTE

The full version of the abbreviated code shown in this example can be viewed using the book's accompanying CD-ROM.

```
1  /**
2   * TryBlockExample.java
3   * @author Cisco Teacher
4   * @version 2002
5   */
6
7  public class TryBlockExample
8  {
9      /*
10     Checking withdrawal method demonstrating nested try-catch blocks
11     This method is part of a class that holds account information for
12     both a Checking account and a Savings account and advertises
13     that it throws the custom InsufficientFundsException object.
14     */
15     public void withdrawalFromChecking(double amount) throws
```

Example 12-35 *Nested **try/catch** Blocks (Continued)*

```
16        InsufficientFundsException
17    {
18        try
19        {
20            if(balanceChecking < amount);
```

For Example 12-35, you can view the explanatory text by accessing the full, interactive graphic for this example on the book's accompanying CD-ROM. The title of the activity is "Nested **try/catch** Blocks" in e-Lab Activities.

Rethrowing Exceptions

In the sample code shown for the RethrowException2 class in Example 12-36, the fillInStackTrace() method is called before an exception is rethrown. The fillIn-StackTrace method takes no arguments; it operates on the Throwable it is called on (fills in the execution stack trace) and then returns it.

Example 12-36 *Rethrowing* Throwable *Object Reference*

```
1  /**
2   * Java Program: RethrowException2
3   * @author Cisco Teacher
4   * @version 2002
5   */
6  // rethrowing an exception
7
8  public class RethrowException2
9  {
10     public static void main(String[] args)
11     {
12         try
13         {
14             Student astudent = new Student
15                 ("Mary Post", Student.testName.length, 12345);
16             System.out.println("Student" + astudent.getName());
17             System.out.println("Tests" + Student.testName.length);
18         }
19         catch (ArrayIndexOutOfBoundsException ae)
20         {
```

NOTE

The full version of the abbreviated code shown in this example can be viewed using the book's accompanying CD-ROM.

The `fillInStackTrace` method is used primarily to hide the original location where the exception was created. This method returns a reference to a `Throwable` object. The example uses the **throw** keyword to throw a `Throwable` object reference that is returned by the `fillInStackTrace()` method. The stack information placed in the `Throwable` object that was created is replaced with the stack trace to the current location when this method is called.

In the sample code shown in Example 12-37 for the `RethrowException3` class, the `Throwable` object returned by the `fillInStackTrace()` method is cast into the same class as the original exception. The **catch** clause catches an `ArrayIndexOutOfBounds-Exception`, and the `Throwable` object returned by the `fillInStackTrace()` method is cast to the subclass `ArrayIndexOutOfBoundsException`.

Example 12-37 *Rethrowing Throwable Object Reference*

```
1 /**
2  * Java Program: RethrowException3
3  * @author Cisco Teacher
4  * @version 2002
5  */
6 // rethrowing an exception
7
8 public class RethrowException3
9 {
10     public static void main(String[] args)
11     {
12         try
13         {
14             Student astudent = new Student
15                 ("Mary Post",Student.testName.length,12345);
16             System.out.println("Student" +  astudent.getName());
17             System.out.println("Tests" +  Student.testName.length);
18         }
19         catch (ArrayIndexOutOfBoundsException ae)
20         {
```

Overriding and Exceptions

Inheritance and overriding have special implications when it comes to exceptions. This section addresses primarily the rules for *overriding methods and exception declaration.*

Rules for Overriding Methods

Example 12-38 shows the parent class and `methodA()` for the following examples on exceptions and overriding a parent method.

Example 12-38 *Overriding Methods*

```
 1 /**
 2  * TestMultiA.java
 3  * @author Cisco Teacher
 4  * @version 2002
 5  */
 6 import java.io.*;
 7 public class TestMultiA
 8 {
 9      public void methodA() throws IOException, RuntimeException
10      {
11          // do some IO stuff
12      }
13 }//end TestMultiA.java
```

1. As shown in Example 12-39, overriding a parent class method and throwing different exceptions that are a subclass of the exception thrown by the parent method is permissible.

Example 12-39 *Overriding Methods*

```
 1 /**
 2  * TestMultiB1.java
 3  * @author Cisco Teacher
 4  * @version 2002
 5  */
 6
 7 import java.io.*;
 8
```

continues

Example 12-39 *Overriding Methods (Continued)*

```
 9 public class TestMultiB1 extends TestMultiA
10 {
11     public void methodA()throws FileNotFoundException,
12     UTFDataFormatException, ArithmeticException
13     {
14         // do some IO and number crunching stuff
15     }
16 }//end TestMultiB1 class
```

For Example 12-39, you can view the explanatory text by accessing the full, interactive graphic for this example on the book's accompanying CD-ROM. The title of the activity is "Overriding Methods" in e-Lab Activities.

2. As shown in Example 12-40, overriding a parent class method and throwing different exceptions that are not a subclass of the exception thrown by the parent method is not permissible.

Example 12-40 *Overriding Methods*

```
 1 /**
 2  * TestMultiB2.java
 3  * @author Cisco Teacher
 4  * @version 2002
 5  */
 6
 7 import java.io.*;
 8
 9 public class TestMultiB2 extends TestMultiA
10 {
11     public void methodA()throws FileNotFoundException,
12     UTFDataFormatException, ArithmeticException, SQLException
13     {
14         // do some IO and number crunching stuff
15     }
16 }//end TestMultiB2 class
```

For Example 12-40, you can view the explanatory text by accessing the full, interactive graphic for this example on the book's accompanying CD-ROM. The title of the activity is "Overriding Methods" in e-Lab Activities.

3. As shown in Example 12-41, overriding a parent method and throwing fewer exceptions of the same class or subclass is permissible.

Example 12-41 *Overriding Methods*

```
1 /**
2  * TestMultiB3.java
3  * @author Cisco Teacher
4  * @version 2002
5  */
6
7 import java.io.*;
8
9 public class TestMultiB3 extends TestMultiA
10 {
11     public void methodA()throws IOException,
12     {
13         // do some IO and number crunching stuff
14     }
15 }//end TestMultiB3 class
```

For Example 12-41, you can view the explanatory text by accessing the full, interactive graphic for this example on the book's accompanying CD-ROM. The title of the activity is "Overriding Methods" in e-Lab Activities.

4. As shown in Example 12-42, overriding a parent method and throwing exceptions more general than the parent class is not permissible.

Example 12-42 *Overriding Methods*

```
1 /**
2  * TestMultiB4.java
3  * @author Cisco Teacher
4  * @version 2002
5  */
6
7 import java.io.*;
8
9 public class TestMultiB4 extends TestMultiA
```

continues

Example 12-42 *Overriding Methods (Continued)*

```
10 {
11     public void methodA()throws IOException, Exception
12     {
13         // do some IO and number crunching stuff
14     }
15 }//end TestMultiB4 class
```

For Example 12-42, you can view the explanatory text by accessing the full, interactive graphic for this example on the book's accompanying CD-ROM. The title of the activity is "Overriding Methods" in e-Lab Activities.

Case Study: JBANK Banking Application

The JBANK application introduced in Chapter 1 ("What Is Java?") provides students with an opportunity to apply the Java language concepts learned throughout this course. In the JBANK lab for Chapter 12, students enforce the business rules for withdrawal from each of the four different types of accounts by creating their own set of exception classes.

Applying Concepts to the Banking Application

In these labs, students first will create their own exceptions and then will use the exceptions in the methods of other classes. For the banking application, students will create exceptions to enforce business rules such as "amount overdrawn," "account status closed," and so on. Students will then use these classes in each of the Account classes that have methods for withdrawal and deposit. These exceptions are tested in the Teller class using the **try/catch** block. Although there are numerous prebuilt exceptions in the API, students will create many exceptions for their own needs as they program in Java. The creation and use of exception objects will help to keep the code for the method separate from the code for the errors that might arise when the method executes.

Figures 12-14 and 12-15 display what the JBANK application might look like at the end of the course.

Figure 12-14 JBANK Application

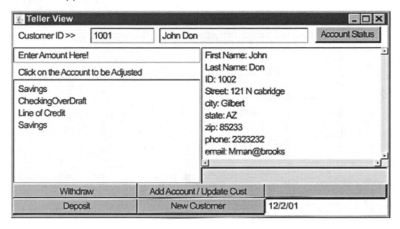

Figure 12-15 JBANK Application

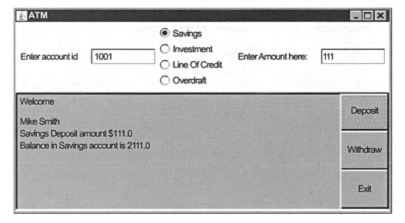

Syntax Summary

Exception:

```
public static String getInput(String prompt) throws IOException
```

try/**catch**/**finally** block:

```
try
{
    //code that throws exception
}
catch(SpecificException e)
{
```

```
    //code for exception
}
catch(Exception e)
{
    //code for general exception
}
finally
{
    //code to cleanup and close files
 }
```

Throwing an exception:

```
try
{
    if(balanceChecking < amount);
    {
        throw new InsufficientFundsException();
    }
    balanceChecking -= amount;
}
//additional code
```

Custom exception:

```
public class InsufficientFundsException extends Exception
```

Nested **try/catch** blocks:

```
try
{
    //code that throws exception
}
catch(SpecificException e)
{
    try
    {
        //code that throws exception
    }
    catch(SpecificException2 e)
    {
        //code for exception
    }
}
catch(Exception e)
{
    //code for general exception
}
finally
{
    //code to cleanup and close files
}
```

Summary

This chapter explored the concept of exceptions. Exceptions identify errors that arise in programs, representing an exception to the normal flow of processing of a program. They are objects of subclasses of the class Throwable. The Throwable class is the super-class of all Exception and Error classes. Only objects of this class or its subclasses are thrown by the JVM. Programmers can throw an exception using the **throw** statement. They can rethrow an exception or create a new exception. To handle the exception in a method, place the code that potentially can generate the exception in a **try/catch** block. A method can have several **try** blocks and several **catch** blocks for each **try** block. A **finally** block is always executed and can be used to contain code that must be executed after a **try** block or before exiting because of an exception.

Finally, the use of customized exceptions was explored as a tool used in many applications, specifically designed by the programmer to implement exceptions to normal business rules or activities.

More Information
The Java programming language also provides the ability for programmers to test assumptions about their program through the use of the assertion statement. Assertion statements provide an effective way to identify programming bugs. In addition, they improve the documentation and maintainability of the programmer's code.
To learn more about assertions refer to
http://java.sun.com/j2se/1.4.1/docs/guide/lang/assert.html
http://developer.java.sun.com/developer/Books/javaprogramming/jdk14/javapch06.PDF

Key Terms

advertising or declaring exceptions   Just as a method must specify what type and how many arguments it accepts and what is returned, a method must specify the checked exceptions that the method can throw. A method can throw an exception because it includes a call to another method that throws an exception, or because it creates an object of the type `Throwable` and throws this object using the keyword **throw**. The programmer declares these exceptions by using the keyword word **throws** and then specifying the type of exception.

call stack   The execution stack in memory that represents all the methods that were invoked and that led to the exception. The JVM unwinds the call stack searching for a code block that will handle the exception. If it finds none, the program terminates.

catching multiple exceptions   A method can throw more than one type of exception. In this case, these different types of exceptions should be named in the **throws** clause of the method, or the programmer can use multiple **catch** blocks to catch and handle the different types of exceptions.

checked exceptions   The compiler enforces exception handling by checking the code to ensure that any known `Exceptions` (but not `Errors`) have been handled or declared in the code. Except for the `RuntimeException` class and its subclasses, the compiler checks all other `Exception` subclasses. These `Exception` subclasses are known as checked exceptions.

Error and Exception classes   Two subclasses of `Throwable`. `Error` objects represent run-time and system errors. Programmers are not expected to handle these. `Exception` objects are less serious errors that represent unusual conditions that arise while a program is running; they are recoverable. These types of `Throwable` classes are to be handled by the programmer.

*execution sequence of **try/catch** block*   Execution starts with the **try** block. If successful, it proceeds to the **finally** block before the **return** statement in the **try** block is executed. Any statements after the **finally** block are not executed. If an exception occurs, the code is terminated at the statement that caused the exception. The program moves to the **catch** block matching the exception thrown, and then proceeds to the **finally** block. If the **catch** block has a **return** statement, the **finally** block is executed before the **return** statement.

finally block   Block that provides the means to clean up code at the end of executing a **try/catch** block. The **finally** block is optional.

handling exceptions   Using the **try/catch** block is a method of handling exceptions after declaration. The exception can be rethrown. This is passing the exception up the call stack.

*nested **try/catch** blocks*   Placing a **try/catch** block within another **try/catch** block. Any exception not caught in an inner **try/catch** block is handed to the outer **try/catch** block.

overriding methods and exception declaration   Overriding a parent class method and throwing different exceptions that are a subclass of the exception thrown by the parent class is allowed. It is also permissible to have fewer exceptions thrown by the overriding method. The overriding method cannot throw an exception that is not a subclass of the exception thrown by the parent class, nor one that is more general than the parent class, such as using the word Exception.

polymorphism and exceptions   Polymorphism allows the use of a general class of objects as arguments in a method, and references to objects of its subclass can be used as values in a method call. If you want to catch exceptions in a particular class, getting too specific can prevent this from happening. For example, using the IOException class, polymorphism is applied to accept any object of its subclass.

rethrow   The process of using a **try/catch** block to catch an exception and then rethrowing the exception or another subclass of the exception. In this event, the programmer is passing the exception up the call stack. If an exception is rethrown, the compiler must be notified. Include the phrase **throws** *exception-name* in the method signature.

RuntimeException   Exceptions that are handled automatically by Java. Java simply shuts down the program. These exceptions require code corrections to eliminate the exceptions.

throw   Java programming language keyword that allows the user to throw an exception or any class that implements the Throwable interface.

Throwable class   The superclass of all Exception and Error classes. Only objects of this class or its subclasses are thrown by the JVM. All member data is **private**.

throws   A Java programming language keyword used in method declarations that specifies which exceptions are not handled within the method but are passed to the next higher level of the program.

try/catch blocks The Java language provides these two code constructs to test code and handle exceptions when they occur. With the **try/catch** technique, a block of code statements is tried; if these statements cause errors, the programmer catches the error and includes code to handle the error. The programmer might need multiple **catch** blocks to catch different types of exceptions.

user-defined exceptions Exceptions specifically designed by the programmer to implement exceptions to normal business rules or activities.

Check Your Understanding

1. Which type of errors are handled in exception handling?

   A. Compiler errors

   B. Logic errors

   C. Run-time errors

   D. All types of errors

2. Which type of error does the System.in() method generate if it cannot read data from the keyboard?

   A. InputException

   B. IOException

   C. ParseException

   D. ReadException

3. Which of the following events occurs when an exception is thrown?

   A. An object is created that encapsulates data about the error.

   B. The normal execution of code is stopped.

   C. Code within a handler is executed.

   D. All of the above.

4. What is the superclass for all Exception and Error classes?

   A. Throwable

   B. Exception

   C. Error

   D. System

5. A list of all the methods that were executed leading to an error is called the

    A. Exception thread

    B. Method heap

    C. Error log

    D. Execution stack

6. What type of objects are programmers not expected to handle?

    A. `RuntimeException`

    B. `Exception`

    C. `Error`

    D. `Throwable`

7. The compiler checks for code that generates all of the following except.

    A. `IOException`

    B. `RuntimeException`

    C. `ParseException`

    D. `AWTException`

8. Which of the following is not a `RuntimeException`?

    A. `IOException`

    B. `ArrayIndexOutOfBoundsException`

    C. `NullPointerException`

    D. `ArithmeticException`

9. The keyword **throw** is used to

    A. Advertise that a method throws an exception

    B. Generate, or throw, an exception object

    C. Handle an exception object

    D. Continue normal execution of code

10. After an exception object is handled, where does execution of code resume?

    A. At the first statement in the `main` method

    B. At the point where the exception was thrown

    C. At the point immediately after the **try** block

    D. At the point immediately after the **catch** or **finally** blocks

11. If a Java statement potentially can throw a checked exception, it should be placed

   A. Within a **catch** block

   B. Within a **try** block

   C. Within a **finally** block

   D. In a **throw** statement

12. Which of the following generates a syntax error?

   A. A **try** block with more than one **catch** block, each checking a different exception

   B. A **try** block with more than one **catch** block, each checking the same exception

   C. A **try** block followed by an empty **catch** block

   D. A **try** block followed by a **catch** block and a **finally** block

13. Which of the following method declarations correctly identifies a method that throws a ParseException and IOException?

   A. `public void method1() throw ParseException, IOException {}`

   B. `public void method1() throws ParseException, throws IOException {}`

   C. `public void method1() throws ParseException, IOException {}`

   D. `public void method1() throws new ParseException, IOException {}`

14. What influence does the order of **catch** blocks have on catching multiple exceptions?

   A. The order of the **catch** blocks is unimportant.

   B. The **catch** blocks should be ordered to catch the most specific exception objects first.

   C. The **catch** blocks should be ordered to catch the most general exception objects first.

   D. The order of the **catch** blocks is important only for unchecked exceptions.

15. What is the **finally** block used for?

   A. The **finally** block is used to test code that might throw an exception.

   B. The **finally** block is used to handle an exception object.

C. The `finally` block is used to return program execution to the point where the exception was generated.

D. The `finally` block is used to execute code after a `try` block, whether or not an exception was generated.

16. Which of the following is declared in the class header to denote that the class is a user-defined exception class?

A. `throws` Exception

B. `implements` Exception

C. `extends` Exception

D. `throw new` Exception

17. Which of the following is a true statement about the order of `try`, `catch`, and `finally` blocks?

A. A `try` block can exist with no `catch` block, as long as there is a `finally` block.

B. A `try` block cannot exist without a `catch` block and a `finally` block.

C. A `try` block can be followed by multiple `catch` blocks, as long as there is a `finally` block.

D. A `try` block must be followed by a minimum of one `catch` block.

18. Given the following method declaration from the parent class, which of the following is acceptable when overriding a method in a subclass?

`public void processData(String name, int age) throws ParseException, IOException`

A. `public void processData(String name, int age)`
`throws ParseException, Exception`

B. `public void processData(String name, int age)`
`throws ParseException, EOFException`

C. `public void processData(String name, int age)`
`throws RuntimeException, IOException`

D. `public void processData(string name, int age)`
`throws Exception`

19. Which of the following lists of exceptions is in the order in which they should be caught?

    A. `Exception, IOException, FileNotFoundException`

    B. `FileNotFoundException, Exception, IOException`

    C. `IOException, FileNotFoundException, Exception`

    D. `FileNotFoundException, IOException, Exception`

20. Which of the following is a true statement about the `fillInStackTrace()` method?

    A. It returns a `Throwable` object.

    B. It hides the source of the original exception when the exception is rethrown.

    C. The method replaces the stack information of the `Throwable` object with the current location.

    D. All of the above.

Upon completion of this chapter, you will be able to

- Work with the `File` class
- Understand input and output classes
- Perform input and output operations
- Store objects in a file
- Apply the Java language concepts that you have learned in this chapter to the JBANK case study

Files, Streams, Input, and Output

Input of data into a program or *output* of data from a program is provided through the use of classes in the java.io package. In this chapter, students will explore the complex hierarchy of input/output (I/O) classes available through the application programming interface (API). Input activities represent the reading of data from a source into the program. The program methods store the data in objects or manipulate the data for immediate output. Output activities represent the writing of data from the program to a target destination. This data can be displayed on a screen, sent to a printer, or written to a file. The Java language supports input and output of data to and from files and other devices, such as network connections through streams. Streams are data structures that transfer bytes of data. Streams are built by converting objects of one input type class to another input class or from one output type class to another. Each conversion provides additional enhancement to the reading and writing of data to and from programs. This conversion results in connecting one stream object to another through the constructors for the objects. Each stream adds enhanced capabilities, enabling the programmer to send formatted data from the program and receive formatted data from a file, or to buffer data to improve the efficiency of I/O activities.

In the previous chapters, input objects and output objects were discussed in the use of System.in and System.out. In this chapter, other stream and file access technologies are explored through the I/O package of classes. Some streams store data in memory and send data to or from the program in blocks instead of 1 byte at a time. A stream that stores data in memory is said to buffer the data. The two main streams discussed here are InputStream and OutputStream.

Understanding Files

As a programmer, you need access to data from your program after the program has completed its execution. The Java language provides a number of classes to support the use of *files* to store and retrieve data. This section consists of the following topics:

- `File` class
- `RandomAccessFile` class

File Class

The data used by a program is stored in volatile memory (RAM) while the program is executing. It is no longer available after the program has completed. To make data persist beyond the life of the program, it can be stored in files. To display data, programmers send data to a monitor or a printer.

More Information
Storage of data in variables and arrays is temporary. The data is lost when the variable "goes out of scope" or when the program terminates. Programs use files for long-term retention of large amounts of data, even after the program terminates. Data that is maintained in files persists even after the program that created the data terminates. So much of our lives and world around us is codified into electronic data. Computer scientists, business professionals, and programmers are very concerned with ensuring persistence of data. Electronic storage of data can be on hard drives (disks) and CDs, also known as secondary storage devices, and each decade new technologies for storage of data emerge. A Java programmer can provide persistence of data through the use of I/O streams, file objects, and database connections. We will explore both sequential access files, in which data is stored and retrieved sequentially, and random-access files, in which data can be accessed from any location.

Java language provides several classes to send data in or out of a program. Storing data in files can occur sequentially or through random-access file techniques. To store and read data from a file in random order, the `RandomAccessFile` class and its methods are used. To store data in a file sequentially, the Java language uses software objects known as streams.

Java language provides the *File class* in which to store information about a file or directory. The `File` objects can read the contents of the underlying file system or directory of files, but not the contents of a file.

To summarize

- The `File` class provides functionality for navigating the local file system.

- The `File` class contains methods that enumerate files, directories, and access the status of these files.

- The `File` class does not create a file or add data to a file.

- Classes that implement streams or the `RandomAccessFile` objects provide the facility for reading and writing to files.

The information for a file includes a path name and a filename. The path name is the directory in which the file is located. The directory information for a file can consist of the absolute or the relative path name.

An *absolute path name* is a hierarchical listing of all the directories and subdirectories that describes the path to the file. The last item in the list is the name of the file itself. As shown in Figure 13-1, an absolute path name is complete and requires no other information to locate the file that it denotes. A *relative path name* is a hierarchical listing of the directories relative to the current working directory. A relative path name must be interpreted in terms of information taken from some other path name.

Figure 13-1 Relative Path Names

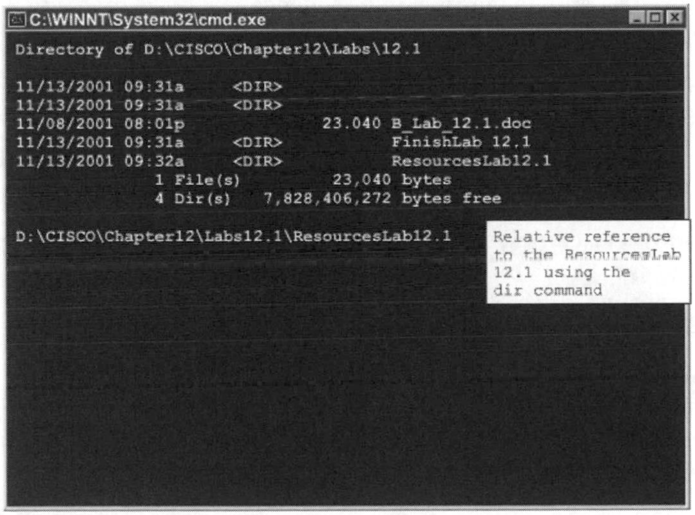

```
C:\WINNT\System32\cmd.exe                                          _ □ ×
Directory of D:\CISCO\Chapter12\Labs\12.1

11/13/2001 09:31a    <DIR>
11/13/2001 09:31a    <DIR>
11/08/2001 08:01p                23.040 B_Lab_12.1.doc
11/13/2001 09:31a    <DIR>              FinishLab 12.1
11/13/2001 09:32a    <DIR>              ResourcesLab12.1
               1 File(s)         23,040 bytes
               4 Dir(s)    7,828,406,272 bytes free

D:\CISCO\Chapter12\Labs12.1\ResourcesLab12.1    ┌─────────────────────┐
                                                │ Relative reference  │
                                                │ to the ResourcesLab │
                                                │ 12.1 using the      │
                                                │ dir command         │
                                                └─────────────────────┘
```

The constructors for the `File` class are displayed in Figure 13-2. Note the different formats for supplying the constructor with directory and filename information.

Figure 13-2 File Constructors

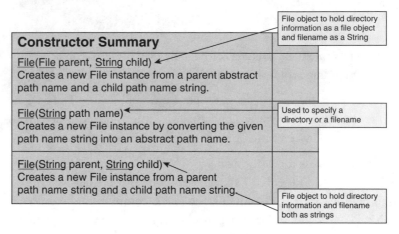

- For UNIX platforms, the prefix of an absolute path name is always /. Relative path names have no prefix. The abstract path name denoting the root directory has the prefix / and an empty name sequence.

- For Win32 platforms, the prefix of a path name that contains a drive specifier consists of the drive letter followed by :, and possibly followed by \ if the path name is absolute. The prefix of a UNC path name is \\, the host name and the share name are the first two names in the name sequence. A relative path name that does not specify a drive has no prefix.

- On Windows machines, a file path can use either forward or backward slashes as separators.

- To insert a \ in a string literal, you must use \\. This is because a single \ indicates that the \ and the next character represent an escape sequence.

- When using `String` objects that represent path information, use `File.separatorChar` to obtain the local computer's proper separator character instead of using / or \.

The code in Example 13-1 illustrates the use of the `File` class's constructors. Line 1 describes the directory for the file as a relative directory and the name of the file as `fileIO.java`. The `File` constructor that accepts two `String` objects is used in this example. Line 2 describes the filename as a `String`. Line 3 describes a directory as an absolute path, including the drive and the reference to the root directory. As for the two backslashes (\\), the first backslash serves as an escape character. An escape character is a character that signals the literal translation of the next character. Line 4 shows an alternative to Line 3, using the `File.separatorChar` static variable instead of the two backslashes. Line 5 uses the constructor that accepts a `File` object and a `String` object.

Example 13-1 *Code Using* File *Constructors*

```
1. File f1 = new File("Chapter 13", "FileIO.java");
2. File f2 = new File("FileListing.java");
3. File f3 = new File("c:\\Cisco");
4. File f3 = new File("c:" + File.separatorChar + "Cisco");
5. File f4 = new File(f3,"FileNames.java");
```

The `File` class has several useful methods to locate a file, delete files, and create directories, as described in Table 13-1.

Table 13-1 Methods of the `File` Class

File Class Method	Description
public String getName()	Returns the name of a file or directory.
public String getParent()	Returns the name of the directory that contains the file.
public String getAbsolutePath()	Returns the absolute (not relative) path to the file.
public String getCanonicalPath() **throws** IOException	Similar to the absolute path, but the symbols of . and .. are resolved. These symbols represent the current directory (.) and the parent directory (..).
public boolean canRead()	Is **true** if the file or directory can be read.
public boolean canWrite()	Is **true** if the file can be written to.
public boolean exists()	Is **true** if the file or directory exists.
public boolean isDirectory()	Is **true** if the argument references a directory; is **false** otherwise.
public boolean isFile()	Is **true** if the argument references a file.
public long length()	Gives the length of the file.

continues

Table 13-1 Methods of the `File` Class (Continued)

File Class Method	Description
`public boolean delete()`	Deletes the file and returns **true** if operation is successful.
`public String[] list()`	Returns an array with a list of files and directories within the file.
`public String[] list(FilenameFilter filter)`	Returns an array with a list of files and directories within the file that match the filter defined by the `FileNameFilter` object. An example of a filter is *.java, the filter is the `String` *.java, which represents a pattern of all files ending with the `String` .java.
`public File[] listFiles()`	Returns an array of `File` objects (not `String` objects) within the file. The file or directory names are used to construct `File` objects. Use this method when working with many files, such as when you want to zip files in a directory.
`public File[] listFiles(FilenameFilter filter)`	Returns an array of `File` objects (not `String` objects) within the file. The file or directory names are used to construct `File` objects. Use this method when working with many files, such as when you want to zip files in a directory. Uses a filter to select the files.
`public boolean mkdir()`	Makes a subdirectory in the directory referenced by the `File` object.

In general, the programmer should read and write to files using the file information provided by a `File` object. The programmer should create a `File` object to hold information about a file and then verify the file's existence before reading or writing to the file. A `File` object is immutable. Instances of the `File` class are immutable. This means that after the abstract path name represented by a `File` object is created, it will never change. The `File` object can only point to the file described in the constructor. When a `File` object is created, it cannot be changed to point to a different `File` object. It should be noted that this is in reference to the `File` object, not the variable that references the `File` object.

The program `WhichFiles`, shown in Example 13-2 and Figure 13-3, constructs four `File` objects in Lines 13 to 16 by defining the directories and filenames for each file. Lines 18 to 20 use the `System.out` object to print information about the files. The `getName()` method is called to list the name, and a conditional operator is used to test whether the file exists. The conditional operator `f1.exists()?" exists":" does not exist"`, uses the `exists()` method to print the phrase `exists` if the method returns **true** and the phrase `does not exist` if the method returns **false**.

Example 13-2 `File` *Objects and Methods—Code*

```
 1 /**
 2  * Java Program WhichFiles
 3  * @author Cisco Teacher
 4  * @version 2002
 5  */
 6
 7 import java.io.*;
 8
 9 public class WhichFiles
10 {
11     public static void main(String[] args)
12     {
13         File f1 = new File("c:\\autoexec.bat");
14         File f2 = new File("c:\\biology.101");
15         File f3 = new File("c:\\command.com");
16         File f4 = new File("c:\\windows.exe");
17
18         System.out.println("File name: " + f1.getName() +
19              (f1.exists()?" exists":" does not exist"));
20         System.out.println("File name: " + f2.getName() +
```

NOTE

The full version of the abbreviated code shown in this example can be viewed using the book's accompanying CD-ROM.

TIP

Use `File` methods to prevent errors by doing the following:

- Use a `File` object to determine whether a file exists before opening the file with a `FileInput-Stream` object.

- Use the `File` method `isFile()` to determine that a `File` object represents a file (not a directory) before attempting to open a file.

- Before attempting to open a file for reading, use the `File` method `canRead()` to determine whether the file is readable.

- Before attempting to open a file for writing, use the `File` method `canWrite()` to determine whether the file is writable.

NOTE

The full version of the abbreviated code shown in this example can be viewed using the book's accompanying CD-ROM.

Figure 13-3 File Objects and Methods—Output

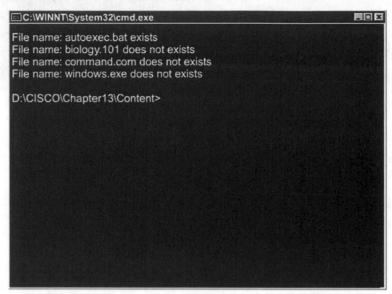

In Example 13-3 and Figure 13-4, a `File` object is used to obtain a listing of files in a directory. In Line 19, a `File` object is created to hold data about the file system for the directory provided in the constructor argument. The `listFiles()` method of the `File` class returns an array of `File` objects. In Line 23, the variable `files` is assigned to the array of `File` objects that was returned by the `listFiles()` method.

Example 13-3 *Listing Files in a Directory—Code*

```
1  /**
2   * Java Program WhichFiles
3   * @author Cisco Teacher
4   * @version 2002
5   */
6
7  import java.io.*;
8
9  public class WhichFiles
10 {
11     public static void main(String[] args)
12     {
13         File f1 = new File("c:\\autoexec.bat");
```

Example 13-3 *Listing Files in a Directory—Code (Continued)*

```
14          File f2 = new File("c:\\biology.101");

15          File f3 = new File("c:\\command.com");

16          File f4 = new File("c:\\windows.exe");

17

18          System.out.println("File name: " + f1.getName() +

19                  (f1.exists()?" exists":" does not exist"));

20          System.out.println("File name: " + f2.getName() +
```

Figure 13-4 Listing Files in a Directory—Output

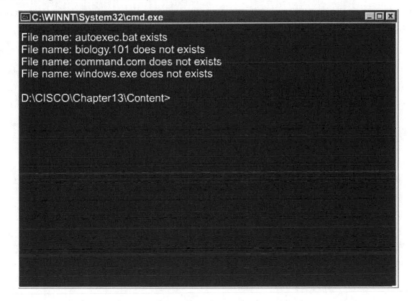

```
C:\WINNT\System32\cmd.exe

File name: autoexec.bat exists
File name: biology.101 does not exists
File name: command.com does not exists
File name: windows.exe does not exists

D:\CISCO\Chapter13\Content>
```

RandomAccessFile Class

A typical feature for input and output is the capability to randomly access data within a file (random-access file). In Java, random access to data in a file is through a RandomAccessFile object. Whereas a File object cannot read or write to a file, a RandomAccessFile object can read and write to a file. With a RandomAccessFile object, the programmer can use reading, writing, and seeking methods of the class to find a specific position within a file, read it, or write to it.

More Information

A `RandomAccessFile` is useful for direct-access applications such as transaction-processing applications, such as airline reservation systems and point-of-sales systems. With a sequential access file, each successive input/output request reads or writes to the next consecutive set of data in the file. With a random-access file, each successive input/output request can be directed to any part of the file, perhaps one widely separated from the part of the file referenced in the previous request. Direct-access applications provide rapid access to specific data items in large files. Often, such applications are used when users wait for answers, and these answers must be made available quickly or the users (often customers) will become impatient and will take their business elsewhere.

The constructors for the class accept the name of the file as a `String` or as a `File` object, as shown in Figure 13-5. The programmer should use a `File` object to hold information about the file or to verify the existence of the file before reading or writing to the file. In addition to information about the file, the constructor accepts the mode for file operations as `String` values. The values are `r` for reading and `rw` for reading and writing. The file is opened for operation in the specific mode provided in the constructor argument.

Figure 13-5 Constructors for the `RandomAccessFile` Class

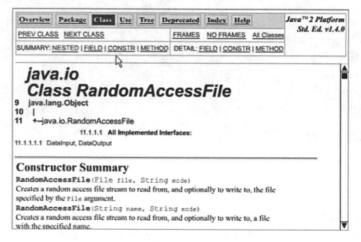

For Example 13-4, you can view the explanatory text by accessing the full, interactive graphic for this figure on the book's accompanying CD-ROM. The title of the activity is "File and Random Access" in the e-Lab Activities.

The sample code in Example 13-4 illustrates the use of a `File` object to hold information about a file, test its existence, and throw an exception if it does not exist. The file is opened for random access only if it exists.

Example 13-4 *File and Random Access*

```
 1 /**
 2  * FileDemo.java
 3  * @author Cisco Teacher
 4  * @version 2002
 5  */
 6
 7 public class FileDemo
 8 {
 9      /**
10       * @exception IOException Can not access a file
11       */
12      public static void main(String args[])
13      {
14          File  aFile = new File("C:\\Cisco","Student.dat");
15          if (!aFile.isFile() || !afile.read() || !aFile.canWrite())
16          {
17              throw new IOException();
18          }
19
20          RandomAccessFile  arandomfile = new RandomAccessFile(afile,"rw");
21
22          // some code to add data to the file.
23      }
24 }//end FileDemo
```

As long as the file exists, the file can be opened for reading and writing. The use of the short-circuit operators (|| and &&) cause the **if** statement to **throw** an exception if the file does not exist.

With random-access files, if a file does not exist and the mode is read-only (r), a `FileNotFoundException` is thrown. If the file is not found and the mode is read-write (rw), a zero-length file is created.

Table 13-2 shows the methods of the `RandomAccessFile` class. After a random-access file is created, the programmer can seek to any byte in the file and read or write a specific amount of data. In Java, the seeking of a position is relative to the start of the file.

The length of the file and the current position of the reading or writing operation can be used to seek from different positions.

Table 13-2 Methods for the `RandomAccessFile` Class

Read Methods	Write Methods
boolean readBoolean()	**void** writeBoolean(**boolean** b)
byte readbyte( )	**void** writebyte(**int** b)
short readShort()	**void** writeShort(**int** s)
char readChar()	**void** writeChar(**int** c)
int readInt()	**void** writeInt(**int** i)
long readLong()	**void** writeLong(**long** l)
float readFloat()	**void** writeFloat(**float** f)
double readDouble()	**void** writeDouble(**double** d)
int readUnsignedByte()	None
int readUnisgnedShort()	None
String readLine()	None
String readUTF	**void** writeUTF(String s)

The sample code in Example 13-5 illustrates the use of a random-access file.

Example 13-5 *File* `RandomAccessFile` *Object Use*

NOTE

The full version of the abbreviated code shown in this example can be viewed using the book's accompanying CD-ROM.

```
 1 /**
 2  * Java Program: ReadFileRandom.java
 3  * @author Cisco Teacher
 4  * @version 2002
 5  */
 6
 7 import java.io.*;
 8
 9 public class ReadFileRandom
10 {
11     /**
```

Example 13-5 *File* `RandomAccessFile` *Object Use (Continued)*

```
12        * @exception IOException Can not access a file
13        */
14       public static void main(String[] args)throws IOException
15       {
16            InputStream istream;
17            OutputStream ostream;
18            int c, pos;
19            String posString = new String();
20            char posChar;
```

The program uses two other I/O objects known as stream objects. The `System.in` and `System.out` objects are of the type `InputStream` and `OutputStream`. The next section covers the concept of streams in more detail. Line 21 opens a `RandomAccessFile` for reading. The program opens an output stream to output characters read from the file. The `System.in.read()` method is used to retrieve a value from the user that will indicate the position from which to start reading the file. In Line 35, the random-access file is read using the `inFile.read()` method. The `read()` method reads a byte of data from the file and returns it as an **int**. In Line 36, the `OutputStream` is used to output the data read to the screen. In the next example shown in Example 13-6, the `SeekAnywhereRAF` class demonstrates the use of methods to seek from either the start of the file or a current position of the file that is provided.

Example 13-6 *Using Methods of the* `RandomAccessFile` *Class*

```
 1 /**
 2  * Java Program: SeekAnywhereRAF.java
 3  * @author Cisco Student
 4  * @version 2002
 5  */
 6
 7 import java.io.*;
 8
 9 /*
10 This class will seek from end of a file or from the current
11 location of the pointer. The seek method in it's general
12 form will seek from the start of a file. The seek method
```

NOTE

The full version of the abbreviated code shown in this example can be viewed using the book's accompanying CD-ROM.

continues

Example 13-6 *Using Methods of the* RandomAccessFile *Class (Continued)*

```
13 in this class will start from an offset number. The offset
14 is a specific byte from the start of  the file.
15 */
16
17 public class SeekAnywhereRAF extends RandomAccessFile
18 {
19     //Constructor accepts a File object and the mode
20     /**
```

Input and Output Classes

This section consists of the following topics:

- Understanding the I/O class hierarchy
- Understanding streams
- Using low-level and high-level streams

I/O Class Hierarchy

The I/O classes and hierarchy are shown in Figure 13-6. The classes in the Java language that support the handling of data through streams are part of the *java.io* package.

The package java.io contains a large number of I/O–related classes. A top-level classification of these classes is as follows:

- Byte input and output streams
- Character readers and writers
- Stream reader and writer filtering
- Stream tokenization
- RandomAccessFile class

Figure 13-6 I/O Classes Hierarchy

Understanding Streams

Most input and output of data to and from a program is handled sequentially. Except in the case of RandomAccessFiles, the Java language creates software objects known as streams. These streams handle sequential input and output of data. Two stream objects that students have used are the System.out object and the System.in object. The System.out object prints data to the monitor, and the System.in object is used to read input data from the keyboard.

More Information

The term *standard I/O* refers to the UNIX concept (which is reproduced in some form in Windows and many other operating systems) of a single stream of information that is used by a program. All of the program's input can come from standard input, all of its output can go to standard output, and all of its error messages can be sent to standard error. The value of the standard I/O is that programs can be chained together easily, and one program's standard output can become the standard input for another program.

For example, a system command such as **dir** | **sort** or **ls** |**grep** 'txt' can send the output of the first command/ program (dir) as input to the second command (sort), or from the command ls to the command grep. The symbol | often is used to define the "piping" of data from one program to another.

NOTE

A stream is an abstract concept used frequently in the context of I/O programming. It represents a linear, sequential flow of bytes of input or output data. Streams can flow toward your program, in which case you have an *input stream*, or can flow away from your program, in which case you refer to it as an *output stream*. You read from input streams—that is, you read the data that the stream delivers to you; you write to output streams—that is, you transfer data to a stream.

The standard output from the program or the error message from a program can be redirected to files or printers. For example, as you develop the banking application, most of the interaction of the user will be through the GUIs. You do not want the GUIs or views to be disrupted with messages from the console window. However, you might want to capture these into a log file. As you develop professional- or commercial-level programs, be sure to create log files to document the performance of your application or collect a log of errors that occur to help you resolve problems. This will become increasingly critical. You can redirect the output of error messages (the exception messages) to a file in two ways:

1. When launching your application, using the command line
   java MyApplication 2> error.txt

2. Using the setIn(), setout(), and setErr() methods of the System class

The first, although simple, is awkward and requires that the users of your program be taught to do this. The second is more appropriate for a commercial-level program.

A *stream* can be thought of as a flow of bytes of data from a *source* to a *sink*, where the flow occurs in one direction only. For example, the source is the program and the sink could be a pipe to another program, a file, or the printer. When data flows into a program, the source is the file or a pipe, and the sink is the program itself. The term sink refers to the concept that data that has reached this destination cannot be processed by the connection to another stream. The process of data is in one direction.

A stream that initiates a flow of data is called an input stream. This is the source stream, as illustrated in Figures 13-7 and 13-8.

The different sources to an `InputStream` follow:

- An array of bytes.
- A `String` object.
- A file.
- A pipe, which works like a physical pipe: You put things in one end and they come out the other.
- A sequence of other streams so that you can collect them together into a single stream.
- Other sources, such as an Internet connection. (The `java.net` package contains the classes that are used to implement client/server connections and other Internet/intranet communications. These classes use streams to transfer data between the client and server computers.)

Figure 13-7 Simple Single-Direction Input Stream from a Keyboard to a Program

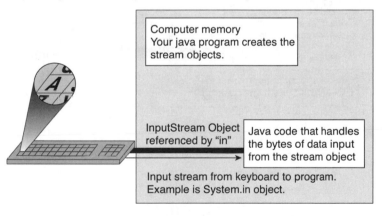

Computer memory
Your java program creates the stream objects.

InputStream Object referenced by "in"

Java code that handles the bytes of data input from the stream object

Input stream from keyboard to program.
Example is System.in object.

A stream that terminates the flow of data is called the output stream. This is the sink stream, as illustrated in Figures 13-9 and 13-10.

Figure 13-8 Simple Single-Direction Input Stream from a File to a Program

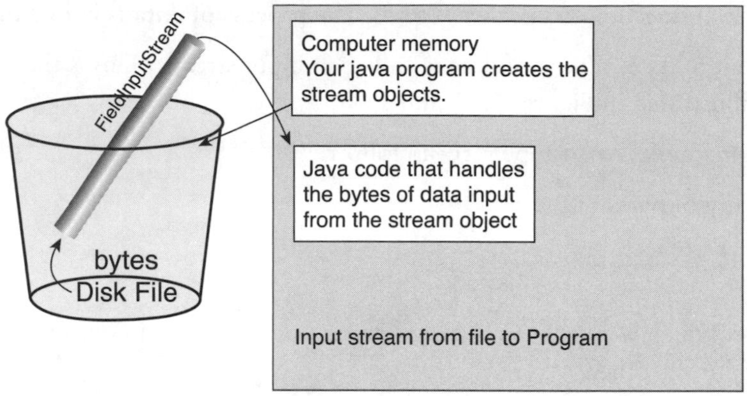

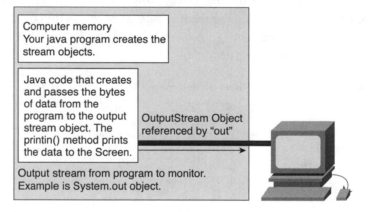

Figure 13-9 Simple Single-Direction Output Stream from a Program to a Monitor

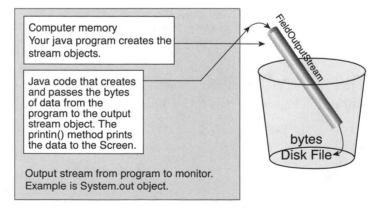

Figure 13-10 Code Using Methods of the OutputStream Class

Both input and output streams are known as *node streams*, as shown in Table 13-3. Node streams are files, memory, and pipes. Pipes and threads are special software objects that can pass data between two programs. (Threads are discussed in Chapter 15, "Threads.")

Table 13-3 Source Sink Streams Classes of I/O Stream Hierarchy Classes

Nodes	Byte Streams	Character Streams
Source streams	InputStream	Reader
Sink streams	OutputStream	Writer

Typically, the user's program is at one end of the stream. In an output stream, the program is the source of data; a file, printer, or another program is the sink. In an input stream, the source of data is a file or input from the keyboard, and the user's program is the destination for this data.

Input streams are for reading data, and output streams are for writing data. The user can read from an input stream but cannot write to it. The user can write to an output stream but cannot read from it.

Low-Level and High-Level Streams

Stream classes view input and output as a sequence of bytes. When handled as bytes, data types such as **int**, **float**, **double**, **char**, **long**, **boolean**, and **short** make programming cumbersome. The Java language uses two levels of class structure to approach reading and writing to streams.

Low-level stream classes read and write data as bytes (byte streams). In addition to reading a stream of byte data, the Java language provides classes that convert the data read to Unicode characters. These are known as reader and writer classes. The next section explains the classes used to read character data. Table 13-4 shows the low-level byte streams. These streams handle data as a sequence of bytes. These streams can read and write to devices directly (as in file streams) and or to processes (as in piped streams). The simplest of these streams is the `FileInputStream` that reads from a file and the `FileOutputStream` that writes to a file. The constructor for both classes accepts a `String` for a filename or the reference to a `File` object.

Table 13-4 Streams Table—Low-Level Byte Streams

Byte Streams			
InputStream	FileInputStream	ByteArrayInputStream	PipedInputStream
OutputStream	FileOutputStream	ByteArrayOutputStream	PipedOutputStream

NOTE

Java views each file as a sequential stream of bytes. Each file ends either with an end-of-file marker or at a specific byte number recorded in a system-maintained administrative data structure. Java abstracts this concept from the programmer. A Java program processing a stream of bytes simply receives an indication from the system when the program reaches the end of the stream; the program does not need to know how the underlying platform represents files or streams.

Readers and writers, shown in Table 13-5, are like input and output streams. These low-level varieties communicate with I/O devices. These streams are exclusively oriented to Unicode characters. The `StringReader` and `StringWriter` classes read characters from a `String` and write characters to a `StringBuffer` object.

Table 13-5 Streams Table—Low-Level Character Streams

Character Streams			
FileReader	CharacterArrayReader	PipedReader	StringReader
FileWriter	CharacterArrayWriter	PipedWriter	StringWriter

High-level stream classes, shown in Tables 13-6 and 13-7, filter the data and read or write it as Java data types, or convert between Java data types and Unicode. These also are known as filter streams. *Filter streams* can handle bytes or Unicode characters. Filter streams can be classified as byte streams or character streams. The important feature of these streams is that they filter and format the data. High-level streams cannot read and write to the I/O devices directly. These streams must be connected to an appropriate low-level stream object that actually does the reading and writing. The constructor for these classes specifies the low-level stream object that must be provided.

Table 13-6 Streams Table—High-Level Byte

Byte Streams			
Filter Streams			BufferedStreams
FilterInputStream	DataInputStream	PushbackStream	BufferedInputStream
FilterOutputStream	DataOutputStream	PrintStream	BufferedOutputStream

Table 13-7 Streams Table—High-Level Character Streams

Character Streams			
Filter Streams			BufferedStreams
InputStreamReader	LineNumberReader	PushbackReader	BufferedReader
OutputStreamWriter	PrintWriter		BufferedWriter

The stream, reader, and writer classes in the package java.io can be classified into two types according to their main concern:

1. Classes linking a stream, reader, or writer to a concrete I/O data source or destination. These also are referred to as low-level byte streams, readers, or writers. These streams connect to the source directly.

2. Classes enhancing stream, reader, or writer functionality. These include functionality such as buffering and filtering. Data that is read as bytes can be translated to Java data types or Strings, or can be reconstructed into a Java object. Data can be translated from a Java data type or an object to a sequence of bytes. Java classes that provide such functionality create high-level streams. High-level streams cannot read or write to a concrete I/O source directly. A low-level stream object, that has established a connection to a concrete source, first must exist before a high-level stream can be established.

Two of the classes that facilitate reading and writing of characters or textual data are InputStreamReader and OutputStreamWriter. These classes convert between streams of bytes and sequence of Unicode characters. The default encoding system used by these streams is the default of the machine on which the program is running, also called the platform. The programmer can construct a stream to read or use different encoding. For example, a programmer who wants to read in encoding for the Japanese alphabet can construct a stream to do this. Otherwise, the default U.S. or local language encoding is used.

The LineNumberReader class views input as a sequence of lines. The read() method of this class reads the next line of text. The programmer must keep track of each line read.

The PrintWriter class writes characters. It is similar to the PrintStream class, but it writes characters instead of bytes.

As shown in Table 13-8, the high-level *DataInputStream* has several methods to read data and convert to Java primitives. The DataOutputStream has methods to write data as Java primitives. The read methods read the bytes as Java primitives. In this table, sample code shows the use of a DataInputStream object referenced by dataInputStream, the use of the object's methods to read primitives and store in primitive variables. The table also shows the use of a DataOutputStream object referenced by dataOutputStream, the use of its methods to write primitive data. Although all data stored in a file is in binary format, the organization of bytes into primitive data simplifies reading and writing to and from files. The data that is read into the program can be processed as a Java primitive within the program.

TIP

The technique of attaching a sophisticated stream to a lower-level one is called chaining.

NOTE

The original intent of the PrintStream class was to print all the primitive data types and String objects in a viewable format. This is different from DataOutputStream, whose goal is to put data elements on a stream in a way that DataInputStream easily can reconstruct them. Whereas a DataOutputStream handles the storage of data, PrintStream handles the display of data.

Table 13-8 Methods of Filter Stream—Data Stream

DataInputStream	DataOutputStream
Examples of Read Methods	Examples of Write Methods
`byte x = dataInputStream.readByte();`	`dataOutputStream.writeByte(x);`
`char x = dataInputStream.readChar();`	`dataOutputStream.writeChar(x);`
`short x = dataInputStream.readShort();`	`dataOutputStream.writeShort(x);`
`int x = dataInputStream.readInt();`	`dataOutputStream.writeInt(x);`
`long x = dataInputStream.readLong();`	`dataOutputStream.writeLong(x);`
`float x = dataInputStream.readFloat();`	`dataOutputStream.writeFloat(x);`
`double x = dataInputStream.readDouble();`	`dataOutputStream.writeDouble(x);`
`boolean x = dataInputStream.readBoolean();`	`dataOutputStream.writeBoolean(x);`
`String x = dataInputStream.readUTF();`	`dataOutputStream.writeUTF(x);`

NOTE

The java.io package contains several piped classes that operate in pairs and in tandem. A piped input stream reads bytes that are written to a corresponding piped output stream; a piped reader reads characters from a piped writer.

Examples 13-7 and 13-8 demonstrate the use of the DataOutputStream and Random-AccessFile classes. The Student class defines the fields to store student data, methods to get student data, and methods to read and write student data to files. The StudentFile class creates the stream and RandomAccessFile objects to write student data to a file and read student data from a file. The student data includes information about the size of each student object (RecordSize). The data file is read using the RandomAccessFile object. The student information is read randomly using the student RecordSize data value to seek from the file.

Example 13-7 *Code Using Filter Streams—Student Class*

```
1      import java.util.*;
2      import java.text.*;
3      import java.io.*;
4
5      public class Student
6      {
7            private String name;
8            private int id;
9            private Date dob;
10
```

Example 13-7 *Code Using Filter Streams—Student Class (Continued)*

```
11          public static final int NAME_SIZE = 40;

12          public static final int RECORD_SIZE  = 2 * NAME_SIZE + 4 + 4 + 4 + 4;

13

14          public Student(String n, int s, Date d)

15          {

16               name = n;

17               id = s;

18               dob = d;

19          }

20

21          public void writeFixedString(String s, int size, DataOutput out)
               throws IOException

22          {

23               int i;

24               for (i = 0; i < size; i++)

25               {

26                    char ch = 0;

27                    if (i < s.length()) ch = s.charAt(i);

28                    out.writeChar(ch);

29               }

30          }

31

32          public void writeData(DataOutput out) throws IOException

33          {

34               writeFixedString(name, NAME_SIZE, out);

35               out.writeInt(id);

36               out.writeInt(dob.getYear());

37               out.writeInt(dob.getMonth());

38               out.writeInt(dob.getDay());

39          }

40

41          public String readFixedString(int size,  DataInput in)
               throws IOException

42          {

43               StringBuffer b = new StringBuffer(size);
```

continues

Example 13-7 *Code Using Filter Streams—*Student *Class (Continued)*

```
44              int i = 0;
45              boolean more = true;
46              while (more && i < size)
47              {                    char ch = in.readChar();
48              i++;                          if (ch == 0)
49              {
50                  more = false;
51              }
52              else
53              {
54                  b.append(ch);
55              }
56          }
57      in.skipBytes(2 * (size - i));
58      return b.toString();
59  }
60
61  public void readData(DataInput in) throws IOException
62  {
63      name = readFixedString(NAME_SIZE, in);
64      id = in.readInt();
65      int y = in.readInt();
66      int m = in.readInt();
67      int d = in.readInt();
68      dob = new Date(y, m, d);
69  }
70 }
```

Example 13-8 *Code Using Filter Streams—*StudentFile *Class*

```
1 import java.io.*;
2 import java.util.*;
3 import java.text.*;
4 public class StudentFile
5 {
6   public static void main(String[] args)throws ParseException
```

Example 13-8 *Code Using Filter Streams—*StudentFile *Class (Continued)*

```
 7   {
 8        Student[] students = new Student[3];
 9        SimpleDateFormat df = new SimpleDateFormat ("M/d/yy");
10        students[0] = new Student("Mary Martin", 12345,df.parse("5/20/1987"));
11        students[1] = new Student("Carl Crane", 75689,df.parse ("15/12/1987"));
12        students[2] = new Student("Tony Munoz", 38456,df.parse("15/3/1990"));
13        int i;
14        try
15        {
16              DataOutputStream out = new
17               DataOutputStream(newFileOutputStream("student.dat"));
18              for (i = 0; i < students.length; i++)
19                  students[i].writeData(out);
20              out.close();
21        }
22        catch(IOException e)
23        {
24            System.out.print("Error: " + e);
25            System.exit(1);
26        }
27        try
28        {
29            RandomAccessFile in = new RandomAccessFile("student.dat", "r");
30            int n = (int)(in.length() / Student.RECORD_SIZE);
31            Student[] newStudents = new Student[n];
32
33            for (i = n - 1; i >= 0; i--)
34            {
35                  newStudents[i] = new Student();
36                  in.seek(i * Student.RECORD_SIZE);
37                  newStudents[i].readData(in);
38            }
39            for (i = 0; i < newStudents.length; i++)
40                  newStudents[i].print();
```

continues

Example 13-8 *Code Using Filter Streams—*StudentFile *Class (Continued)*

```
41          }
42          catch(IOException e)
43          {
44              System.out.print("Error: " + e);
45              System.exit(1);
46          }
47      }
48 }
```

Writing the student data includes writing the student name as a fixed length of 40 characters, the student ID number as an **int**, and the date of birth (DOB) as separate integers to represent the day, month, and year. The date methods of getMonth(), getDay(), and getYear() are used to create the **int** values. The record size is calculated as a fixed value of twice the sum of bytes for each of the data values written. For example, 40 for the name + 4 for the ID + 4 for the year + 4 for the month + 4 for the day results in a total of 56 bytes for data and 102 bytes for record size.

Each high-level stream can be passed an object that is of the next lower stream. Figure 13-11 illustrates the connection between the streams.

Figure 13-11 Connecting Streams with Filtering and Buffering

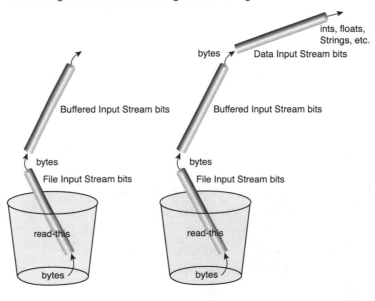

More Information
Filter streams handle conversion of bytes to specific data types, conversion of bytes to Unicode characters, or conversion of Unicode characters to other data types. In addition to filtering the stream, classes include the facility to store large blocks of data. These are the input and output classes that buffer data. Buffering of data minimizes the number of times that reading and writing to files and other devices must occur. Each of the objects is connected so that the functionality of one object is enhanced by another. This is accomplished by passing a reference to the lower-level stream object as an argument to the constructor of the next higher-level stream object. This pattern also is referred to as the decorator or translator pattern. Table 13-9 shows the relation between classes used for connecting streams.

Table 13-9 Relations Between Classes Used for Connecting Streams

Low-Level Stream Connects to the I/O Device	High-Level Buffer Stream Buffers (Stores) Data	High-Level Filter Stream Translates the Data	Your Program Code
FilterInputStream	BufferedInputStream	DataInputStream	Source-input to your program
FilterOutputStream	BufferedOutputStream	DataOutputStream	Sink-output from your program

The sequence for connecting streams is outlined here:

1. Create the low-level stream object.

```
File f=new File("c:\\cisco\chapter13","Student.dat");
InputStream fis=new FileInputStream(f);
```

2. Create the high-level buffered stream object.

```
BufferedInputStream bis=new BufferedInputStream(fis);
```

3. Create the high-level DataInputStream.

```
DataInputStream dis=new DataInputStream (bis);
```

Figure 13-12 illustrates this sequence.

TIP

The FilterInput-
Stream subclasses
can be combined with
other InputStream
classes. For example,
you could combine a
ByteArrayInput-
Stream and a Data-
InputStream or a
FileInputStream
and a Pushedback-
InputStream. To do
this, you would pass
an instance of a data
source-type Input-
Stream (Byte, File,
Piped, Sequenced, or
StringBuffer) object
as an argument to the
constructor of the fil-
ter-type InputStream
(Buffered, Data,
LineNumbered, or
Pushedback). You
could even combine
several filtering types,
such as FileInput-
Stream, Buffered-
InputStream and
DataInputStream .
These same tech-
niques are possible
with OutputStreams.

Figure 13-12 Sequence for Connecting Streams

1. Create the low-level stream object.
    File f = new File("c://cisco/Chapter 13","Student.dat");
    InputStream fis = FileInputStream(f);

FieldInputStream

bytes
Disk file

2. Create the High-level Buffered stream object.
    BufferedInputStream bis = new BufferedInputStream(fis);

3. Create the High-level DataInputStream.
    DataInputStream dis = new DataInputStream (bis);

Buffering is an I/O performance-enhancing technique. With a BufferedOutputStream or BufferedIntputStream, each output or input statement does not necessarily result in an actual physical transfer of data to the output device or from the input device. Instead, each operation is directed to a region in memory called a buffer that is large enough to hold the data of many I/O operations. Then actual transfer of the output device is performed in one large physical output operation each time the buffer fills. The output operations directed to the output buffer in memory often are called logical output operations. With a BufferedInputStream, many logical chunks of data from a file are read as one large physical input operation into a memory buffer. As a program requests new chunks of data, it is taken from the buffer, also called a logical input operation. When the buffer is empty, the next actual physical read from the input device is performed. Thus, the number of physical reads from the input operations is small compared to the number of read requests issued by the program.

Because typical physical input and output operations are extremely slow compared to the speed of accessing computer memory, buffered outputs and inputs normally yield significant performance improvements over unbuffered input or output.

Table 13-10 summarizes the stream classes, their use, and the lower-level stream object that should be passed to the constructor to create the enhanced or decorated stream.

Table 13-10 Selecting the Appropriate Stream Class

Class	Function	Constructor Arguments
		How to Use
ByteArray-InputStream	Allows a buffer in memory to be used as an InputStream	The buffer from which to extract the bytes.
		As a source of data. Connect it to a FilterInputStream object to provide a useful interface.
StringBuffer-InputStream	Converts a String into an InputStream	A String. The underlying implementation actually uses a StringBuffer.
		As a source of data. Connect it to a FilterInputStream object to provide a useful interface.
FileInputStream	For reading information from a file	A String representing the filename, or a File or File-Descriptor object.
		As a source of data. Connect it to a FilterInputStream object to provide a useful interface.
Piped-InputStream	Produces the data that's being written to the associated PipedOutputStream. Implements the piping concept.	PipedOutputStream.

continues

Table 13-10 Selecting the Appropriate Stream Class (Continued)

Class	Function	Constructor Arguments
		How to Use
		As a source of data in multi-threading. Connect it to a `FilterInputStream` object to provide a useful interface.
`Sequenced-InputStream`	Converts two or more `InputStream` objects into a single `InputStream`.	Two `InputStream` objects, or an Enumeration for a container of `InputStream` objects.
		As a source of data. Connect it to a `FilterInputStream` object to provide a useful interface.

Instruction for Input and Output Operations

Input and output operations can use different classes based upon the type of data being transferred:

- Binary
- Character or string
- Primitive

This section illustrates I/O operations for each of these types of data.

I/O Operations

The subsections that follow outline the procedures to follow in setting up input and output operations for each type of data (binary, character, and primitive).

Using a `File` object to manage information on a file, use the sequence of code shown in Example 13-9 to input or output individual bytes, otherwise known as binary data, to a file. Note that buffering improves the performance of the I/O operations. The sequence requires the programmer to use a low-level file stream object and wrap the object in a buffered stream.

Example 13-9 *Byte or Binary I/O*

```
Byte or Binary Input and Output


Input:
  1.  File f1 = new File(fileName);
  2.  FileInputStream fis = new FileInputStream(f1);
  3.  BufferedInputStream bis = new BufferedInputStream(fis);
  4.  byte[] byteArray = new byte[arrayLength];
  5.  int character = bis.read();  // read a single byte
  6.  num BytesRead = bis.read(byteArray);  //read in a byte array


Output:
  1.  File f1 = new File(fileName);
  2.  FileOutputStream fos = new FileOutputStream(f1);
  3.  BufferedOutputStream bos = new BufferedOutputStream(fos);
  4.  byte[] byteArray = new byte[arrayLength];
  5.  bos.write(character);  // write a single byte
  6.  bos.write(byteArray);  // write an array of bytes
  7.  bos.flush();
```

Character or String I/O

Using a `File` object to manage information within a file, use the sequence of code shown in Example 13-10 to input or output Unicode characters, also called text or strings, to a file. The buffering improves the performance of the I/O operations. The sequence requires the programmer to use a low-level `FileReader` object and wrap it in a `BufferedReader` object for better performance.

Example 13-10 *Character or Textual I/O*

```
Character or Textual input or output


Input:
  1.  File f1 = new File(fileName);
  2.  FileReader fr = new FileReader(f1);
  3.  BufferedReader br = new BufferedReader(fr);
```

continues

Example 13-10 *Character or Textual I/O (Continued)*

```
4.   char[] charArray = new char[arrayLength];

5.   int character = br.read();  //read a single character

6.   String line = br.readLine();  //read an entire line, line
         separator not included

7.   num CharsRead = br.read(charArray);  //read a character array


Output:

1.   File f1 = new File(fileName);

2.   FileWriter fw = new FileWriter(f1);

3.   BufferedWriter bw = new BufferedWriter(fw);

4.   PrintWriter pw = new PrintWriter(bw);

5.   pw.println(line);  //write an entire string and end it with a
         platform specific line separator

6.   pw.println(dbl);  //write a double

7.   pw.print(line);  //write an entire string, no line separator at
         end

8.   pw.checkError();  //returns boolean indicating if a problem
        occurred during the write

9.   pw.flush();  //flush the stream to ensure data is written out
```

Primitive Data Type I/O

Using a `File` object to manage information on a file, use the sequence of code shown in Example 13-11 to input or output Java primitives to a file. As with the previous examples, the buffering improves the performance of the I/O operations. Similarly, the sequence requires the programmer to use a low-level `FileInputStream` object and wrap it in a `BufferedInputStream` object for better performance.

Example 13-11 *Primitive Data Type Input and Output*

```
Primitive Data Type Input and Output


Input:

1.   File f1 = new File(fileName);

2.   FileInputStream fis = new FileInputStream(f1);

3.   BufferedInputStream bis = new BufferedInputStream(fis)

4.   DataInputStream dis = new DataInputStream(bis);

5.   byte x = dis.readByte();
```

Example 13-11 *Primitive Data Type Input and Output (Continued)*

```
6.  char x = dis.readChar();

7.  short x = dis.readShort();

8.  int x = dis.readInt();

9.  long x = dis.readLong();

10. float x = dis.readFloat();

11. double x = dis.readDouble();

12. boolean x = dis.readBoolean();

13. String x = dis.readUTF();
```

Note: These read methods throw an EOFException when they hit the end of file.

Output:

```
1.  File f1 = new File(fileName);

2.  FileOutputStream fos = new FileOutputStream(f1);

3.  BufferedOutputStream bos = new BufferedOutputStream(fos);

4.  DataOutputStream dos = new DataOutputStream(bos);

5.  dos.writeByte(x);

6.  dos.writeChar(x);

7.  dos.writeShort(x);

8.  dos.writeInt(x);

9.  dos.writeLong(x);

10. dos.writeFloat(x);

11. dos.writeDouble(x);

12. dos.writeBoolean(x);

13. dos.writeUTF(x);

14. dos.flush();
```

More Information

The StreamTokenizer class extracts identifiable substrings and punctuation from an input stream according to user-defined rules. This process is called tokenizing because the stream is reduced to tokens. Tokens are typically keywords, variable names, numerical constants, string literals, and syntactic punctuation (such as brackets, equals signs, and so on). StreamTokenizer includes various methods that affect the rules for parsing the input stream into tokens. Parsing is the procedure of breaking a stream of bytes into user-defined tokens. The StreamTokenizer class is not derived from InputStream or OutputStream classes. However, it works only with InputStream objects, so it rightfully belongs to the I/O portion of the Java packages.

NOTE

You can redirect standard I/O using the System class, as shown by the sample code in Example 13-12.

Example 13-12 *Redirecting Standard I/O*

```java
import java.io.*;


public class Redirecting {
  public static void main(String[] args) throws IOException
  {
    FileInputStream fis = new FileInputStream("Important.dat");

    BufferedInputStream in = new BufferedInputStream(fis);

    FileOutputStream fos = new FileOutputStream("Program.log");

    BufferedOutputStream bos = new BufferedOutputStream(fos);


    PrintStream out = new PrintStream(bos);


    System.setIn(in);

    System.setOut(out);

    System.setErr(out);
  }
}
```

TIP

Encoding an object as a byte stream is known as serializing the object; the reverse process is known as deserializing it. After an object has been serialized, its encoding can be transmitted from one running virtual machine to another or stored on a disk for later deserializations. Serialization provides the standard wire-level object representation for remote communication and the standard persistence format for JavaBeans architecture.

Storing Objects in a File

In each of the previous sections, the focus has been on writing bytes or characters. Programs create and use many objects that represent business data. Reading and writing object data to files needs more functionality than operating at the byte or character level. This section consists of the following topics:

- Using serialization
- Writing and reading objectives

Serialization

The Java language provides classes that can read and write an object and its data as a cohesive unit. These streams are known as *object streams*. Reading and writing objects using these streams requires understanding the concept of serialization. *Object serialization* is the process of breaking down an object and writing it out.

An object can store primitive data or references to other objects. A class can store static data (primitive or references). Serialization only sends the data. Static data is not serialized, definition of the class is not serialized, and any fields marked with the keyword

transient are not serialized. If specific data values of an object should not be saved to a file, the attribute must be marked as **transient**.

Serialization results in references to other objects, which recursively are resolved and further serialized. That is, each reference is stored as data, and the data of the object referenced also is stored as part of the first object. This recursive serialization is performed for each reference data of the first object. The serialized object stores a tree, or graph, of the data that forms the object. The JVM uses the object graph to read the serialized data and construct the object and all the objects that are referenced by it.

Not all objects can be serialized. Some objects, such as stream objects or threads, do not make sense to serialize. These objects are useful only when a program is running. The objects created to store business data all **extend** from the Object class. The Object class can be serialized. So how are objects that can be serialized marked? The interface *Serializable* is a **public** marker interface. The interface definition is the **public** interface Serializable{ }. Recall from the final labs in Chapter 10, "Creating GUIs Using AWT," and 11, "Applets and Graphics," that a marker interface was implemented to establish the Controller class identity. This was used by the handler class to accept any class that was of the type Controller. This allowed display of the GUI in a standalone application or an applet using the same handler. In the same manner, the Serializable interface is a marker interface. This enables the programmer to define instances of classes as Serializable, or capable of being written out with all the object data as one entity.

This marker interface designates a class and the objects of the class as Serializable. If the data from objects of the class need to be written out as objects, the programmer must define the class as implementing the interface Serializable. Only objects that implement the Serializable interface can be serialized. So, if the class references objects of another class that is not Serializable, sending these objects to be stored will not automatically result in the storage of data of the referenced objects.

Consider the Student object shown in Example 13-13. A Student object holds a Vector of Grade objects. A Vector is a type of array that can increase in size. Recall from Chapter 7, "Arrays," that arrays are Java built-in objects to hold information about a collection of same-type primitives, or references to objects. This collection-storage technology is available in other classes, such as the Vector class. Although the array object is fixed in size, the Vector object gives the programmer the flexibility of adding more elements or deleting elements from the Vector object. The different types of collection-storage technologies available for the Java platform are explored in greater detail in Chapter 14, "Collections."

NOTE

The full version of the abbreviated code shown in this example can be viewed using the book's accompanying CD-ROM.

Example 13-13 Student *Class*

```
1 /**
2  * Java Program Student2.java
3  * @author Cisco Teacher
4  * @version 2002
5  */
6
7 import java.util.*;
8 import java.text.*;
9 import java.io.*;
10
11 public class Student2 implements Serializable
12 {
13     private String name;
14     private int id;
15     // Grade class implements Serializable
16     Grade[] grades;
17
18     /**
19      * @param n The student's name as a String
20      * @param s The student's id as an int
```

The Grade object shown in Example 13-14 holds data about a grade, such as a score and comments from the teacher. The Student object **implements** Serializable. What would happen if the Grade object were not implemented as Serializable? The Grade objects, referenced by the Student object, would not be saved or written to a file when the Student object is written to a file. This can have very serious consequences in applications where the data is obtained from live transactions. For example, if a customer withdraws or deposits money in a bank, the banking application saves the Customer objects that reference the Account objects. If the Account object was not serializable, the bank would lose track of the activities of the customer. When storing objects to files, the programmer designing these classes must spend a significant amount of time ensuring that all objects and objects referenced by the object have implemented the Serializable interface.

Example 13-14 Grade *Class*

```
1 /**
2  * Java Program: Grade.java
3  * @author Cisco Teacher
4  * @version 2002
5  */
6
7 import java.io.*;
8
9 public class Grade implements Serializable
10 {
11     private int score;
12     private String comment;
13
14     /**
15      * @param s A score as an int
16      * @param c A comment as a String
17      */
18     public Grade(int s, String c)
19     {
20         score = s;
```

NOTE

The full version of
the abbreviated code
shown in this example
can be viewed using
the book's accompa-
nying CD-ROM.

Writing and Reading Objects

As described in the last section, objects (including objects referenced by the object) that
have implemented the Serializable interface can be stored to a file. This section
describes the classes and methods that are used to write and read these objects to a file.

Writing Objects

The output stream ObjectOutputStream provides methods for writing out object data,
as shown in Example 13-15. The operations for writing are performed through the
write(), close(), and flush() methods.

Example 13-15 *Writing* Student *Objects to a File*

```
1 /**
2  * Java Program: WriteStudentObject.java
3  * @author Cisco Teacher
```

continues

NOTE

The full version of
the abbreviated code
shown in this example
can be viewed using
the book's accompa-
nying CD-ROM.

Example 13-15 *Writing* Student *Objects to a File (Continued)*

```
4   * @version 2002

5   */

6

7  import java.io.*;

8  import java.util.*;

9

10 public class WriteStudentObject

11 {

12     /**

13      * @exception IOException Can not read the file

14      */

15     public static void main(String[] args)  throws IOException

16     {

17         /*

18         a loop could be used here to create more than one

19         student object and write each one to a file

20         */
```

Reading Objects

The object stream `ObjectInputStream` provides methods for retrieving object
data. The operations for reading are performed through the `read()` and `close()`
methods. The code in Example 13-16 reads the `Student` objects written out by
the `WriteStudentObject` class used in Example 13-15.

Example 13-16 *Reading* Student *Objects from a File*

NOTE

The full version of
the abbreviated code
shown in this example
can be viewed using
the book's accompa-
nying CD-ROM.

```
1  /**

2   * Java Program: ReadStudentObject.java

3   * @author Cisco Teacher

4   * @version 2002

5   */

6

7  import java.io.*;

8  import java.util.*;

9

10 public class ReadStudentObject

11 {
```

Example 13-16 *Reading* Student *Objects from a File (Continued)*

```
12      /**
13       * @exception IOException Can not read file
14       */
15      public static void main(String[] args) throws IOException
16      {
17          // reference for holding object retrieved from the file
18          Student2 mary = new Student2();
19
20          try
```

Case Study: Banking Application

The JBANK application introduced in Chapter 1, "What Is Java?," will provide students with an opportunity to apply the Java language concepts learned throughout this course. In the JBANK labs for Chapter 13, students will write and read Customer objects to and from a file. Students will use the Serializable interface to identify their Customer class and the Account class.

Applying Concepts to the Banking Application

The banking application stores data on customers, the bank, and customer accounts. In these labs, stream objects will be used to read and write data to files. The Customer object must be stored with all the accounts for the customer. When a Customer object is read from a file, the data for the accounts also should be read immediately. To do this, the Customer and Account classes must implement Serializable. The lab includes modifying these classes and creating a program to read and write the objects to a file.

The reading and writing of data is combined with the use of the GUI. When a teller retrieves a Customer object, the data for the accounts of the customer should be displayed on the screen. Customer objects are read from a file and stored in an array of customers.

Saving customer data includes storing Customer objects to a file. When a customer is created or when a customer withdraws or deposits money, the data needs to be stored in a file. The application lab ties the GUI actions of withdrawing and depositing to writing customer data out to a file.

Figures 13-13 and 13-14 display what the JBANK application might look like at the end of the course.

Figure 13-13 The JBANK Application

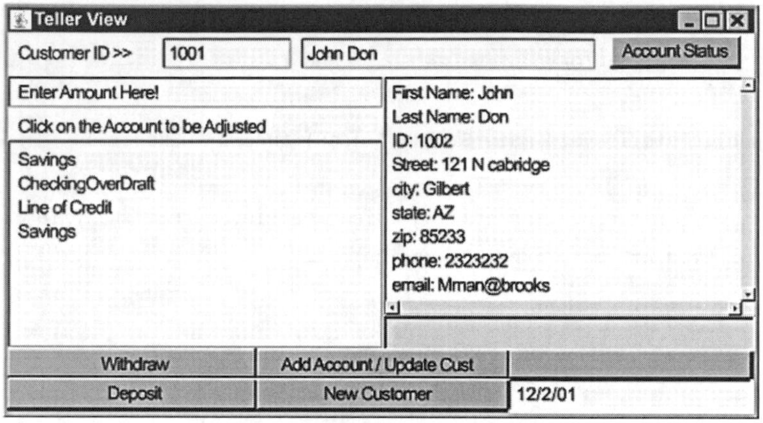

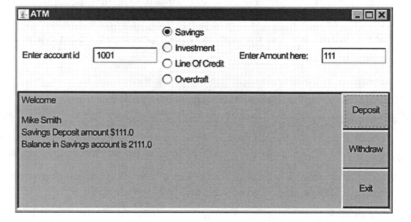

Figure 13-14 The JBANK Application

Summary

Students learned about files, streams, and input and output operations in this chapter. Most input and output operations from the JVM are stream based, regardless of whether the program is. The exception is that random-access files do not use streams. The `RandomAccessFile` class communicating with the console, files, or another program running on the network is used to read and write information at arbitrary locations within a file, without having to read or write information at preceding locations.

The classes in the java.io package provide support for input and output operations. Input and output operations are performed by constructing connected streams using high-level and low-level stream objects. High-level streams can filter the data, buffer the data, or both. The methods of the high-level stream are used to read or write data. High-level streams must connect to low-level streams. Both byte- and character-oriented streams can be low-level streams directly connecting to input or output devices. Byte streams have *InputStream and OutputStream classes* at the root of the hierarchy. Character streams have *Reader and Writer classes* at the root of the hierarchy.

Programmers can read and write objects as a whole using object serialization. Objects are written to using ObjectInputStream objects and are read from using ObjectOutput-Stream objects. Only objects that implement the Serializable interface, thus marking the object as serializable, can be written to or read using an object stream.

Syntax Summary

File object:

```
File f1 = new File("Chapter 13", "FileIO.java");
File f2 = new File("FileListing.java");
File f3 = new File("c:\\Cisco");
File f3 = new File("c:" + File.separatorChar + "Cisco");
File f4 = new File(f3,"FileNames.java");
```

RandomAccessFile object:

```
// Open for reading only.
RandomAccessFile inFile = new RandomAccessFile("data.dat", "r");

// Open for reading and writing.  If the file data.dat does not already exist,
// an attempt will be made to create the file data.dat.
RandomAccessFile outFile = new RandomAccessFile("data.dat", "rw");
```

Serializable interface:

```
public class Grade implements Serializable
{
        //body of class
}
```

Key Terms

absolute path name   Starting at the root directory, a hierarchical listing of all the directories and subdirectories that end in the location of a file or directory.

`DataInputStream`   Lets an application read primitive Java data types from an underlying input stream.

`DataOutputStream`   Lets an application write primitive Java data types to an output stream in a portable way.

files   A file is where data is stored and retrieved. Storing data in files can occur sequentially or through random-access file techniques.

`File class`   Class used to store information about a file or directory of files, but not the contents of files.

filter stream   A high-level stream that filters and formats the data. Filter streams can handle bytes or Unicode characters.

high-level stream classes   Stream that filters the data, and reads or writes it as Java data types or converts between Java data types and Unicode.

input   Reading of data from a source into the program.-Input of data into a program is provided through the use of classes in the `java.io` package.

`InputStream and OutputStream classes`   Byte streams have `InputStream` and `Output-Stream` classes at the root of the hierarchy. They are subclasses of the `Object` class.

`java.io`   The classes in the Java language that support the handling of data through streams are part of the `java.io` package. The package also contains all the classes needed for file processing. Any `File` class programming must include this package.

`java.net`   Package that provides the classes for implementing networking applications.

low-level stream classes   Stream that reads and writes data as bytes or Unicode characters.

node streams   Files, memory, and pipes. Input and output streams are known as node streams.

object serialization   The process of breaking down an object and writing it out.

object stream   The classes that can read and write an object and its data as a cohesive unit.

output   Reading of data from the program. Output of data from a program is provided through the use of classes in the `java.io` package.

random-access file   File in which records can be stored and accesses in any order.

RandomAccessFile class   Class used to read and write to a random-access file.

Reader and Writer classes   Character streams have `Reader` and `Writer` classes at the root of the hierarchy. They are subclasses of the `Object` class.

relative path name   Starting at the current working directory, a hierarchical listing of all the directories and subdirectories that end in the location of a file or directory.

Serializable interface   A marker interface that enables the programmer to define instances of classes as `Serializable`, or capable of being written out with all the object data as one entity. Only objects that implement the `Serializable` interface can be serialized. So, if the class references objects of another class that is not `Serializable`, sending these objects to be stored will not automatically result in the storage of data of the referenced objects.

sink   Data that has reached this destination cannot be processed by connection to another stream; could be a pipe to another program.

sink stream   A stream that terminates the flow of data is called the output stream, or sink stream.

source stream   A stream that initiates a flow of data is called an input stream, or source stream.

stream   A stream can be thought of as a flow of bytes of data from a source to a sink, where the flow occurs in one direction only.

Check Your Understanding

1. A group of characters that represent specific meaning is a

    A. Byte

    B. Field

    C. Record

    D. File

2. Which of the following is a false statement about the Java `File` class?

    A. The `File` class provides the functionality for navigating the local file system.

    B. A `File` object can describe the directories, files, and access status of the files.

    C. A `File` object can create a file and add additional data to the file.

    D. All of the above are false.

3. A hierarchical listing of all the directories and subdirectories that end in the location of a file is a(n)

   A. Absolute path name

   B. Relative path name

   C. CLASSPATH

   D. File path

4. Which method can be used to test whether the `File` object represents a directory?

   A. `getDirectory()`

   B. `isFile()`

   C. `returnDirectory()`

   D. `isDirectory()`

5. Which constructor correctly creates a `RandomAccessFile` object that writes to the file `MyData.dat`?

   A. `RandomAccessFile file = new RandomAccessFile("MyData", "r");`

   B. `RandomAccessFile file = new RandomAccessFile(MyData, "rw");`

   C. `RandomAccessFile file = new RandomAccessFile("MyData.dat", "rw");`

   D. `RandomAccessFile file = new RandomAccessFile("MyData.dat", "w");`

6. What is one difference between a `RandomAccessFile` object and a `File` object?

   A. A `RandomAccessFile` object can be opened for reading or reading/writing, but a `File` object can be opened only for writing.

   B. A `RandomAccessFile` object can be opened for reading or reading/writing, but a `File` object can be opened only for reading.

   C. A `RandomAccessFile` object has random access to the file, but a `File` object has sequential access to the file.

   D. A `RandomAccessFile` object can perform reading and writing, but a `File` object cannot.

7. What happens in a program when a `RandomAccessFile` constructor references a file that does not exist?

   A. A `FileNotFoundException` is always thrown.

   B. A new file is always created.

   C. It depends on which mode the `RandomAccessFile` is opened in.

   D. None of the above.

8. Which stream is the most general in the I/O hierarchy?

   A. `Stream`

   B. `OutputStream`

   C. `DataOutputStream`

   D. `PipedOutputStream`

9. Which of the following is a source for an `InputStream`?

   A. A file

   B. A `String` object

   C. A character array

   D. All of the above

10. Which method from the `System` class can be used to change the standard output from the monitor to a text file?

    A. `stdOut()`

    B. `setOut()`

    C. `setIn()`

    D. `setErr()`

11. Low-level streams read and write data as a stream of

    A. Bits

    B. Primitives

    C. Bytes

    D. Objects

12. The process of using a high-level stream along with a low-level stream is

    A. Chaining

    B. Linking

    C. Streaming

    D. Piping

13. Which class has methods such as `readInt()` and `readDouble()` to read and convert Java primitives?

    A. `DataOutputStream`

    B. `InputStreamReader`

    C. `FileInputStream`

    D. `DataInputStream`

14. Which of the following is a false statement about the buffering technique?

   A. Each output operation temporarily is written to memory before actually being written to the output device.

   B. With buffering, there are fewer I/O operations to the physical device than requested by the program.

   C. When the buffer is full, the I/O operation is performed.

   D. Buffering saves memory but slows system performance.

15. Given the following Java declaration statement, which of the following pairs of statements correctly construct a stream that can be used to extract Java primitives from a file?

```
InputStream input = new FileInputStream(new File("mydata.txt"));
```

   A.
```
BufferedOutputStream out = new BufferedOutputStream(input);
DataInputStream in = new DataInputStream(out);
```

   B.
```
BufferedInputStream inStream = new BufferedInputStream(input);
DataInputStream in = new DataInputStream(input);
```

   C.
```
BufferedInputStream inStream = new BufferedInputStream(input);
DataInputStream in = new DataInputStream(inStream);
```

   D.
```
DataInputStream inStream = new BufferedInputStream(input);
BufferedInputStream in = new BufferedInputStream(inStream);
```

16. Which class extracts user-defined identifiable substrings from a data stream?

   A. `FileStream`

   B. `StreamTokenizer`

   C. `StringTokenizer`

   D. `InputStreamTokenizer`

17. The process of encoding a Java object as a stream of bytes is known as

   A. Streaming

   B. Deserialization

   C. Serialization

   D. Persistence

18. Which keyword is used to mark data that should not be included when the object is written to a stream?

   A. `final`

   B. `volatile`

   C. `transient`

   D. `native`

19. What is the correct class header for a class, `Employee`, that can be saved to a file?

   A. `public transient class Employee{}`

   B. `public class Employee extends Serializable{}`

   C. `public class Employee extends Writeable{}`

   D. `public class Employee implements Serializable{}`

20. Which method in the `ObjectOutputStream` class can be used to write a `String` object to a file?

   A. `write();`

   B. `writeString()`

   C. `writeChar()`

   D. `writeUTF()`

Upon completion of this chapter, you will be able to

- Understand the `java.util` Package
- Understand Collections
- Understand the Collections Framework
- Apply the Java language concepts that you have learned to the JBANK case study.

Collections

This chapter introduces the many uses of utility classes. These include managing a collection of objects, manipulating date data, and obtaining information about system settings.

Managing a large number of similar objects is done with great efficiency and speed using the built-in *array* classes. The limitation of this storage technology and this data structure is the fixed size, or capacity, of the array. After an array object is created, the number of elements cannot be increased or decreased. Additionally, storing collections of data is limited to storing only those that are of the same Java type.

It might become necessary to increase or decrease the number of elements in the array or sort and access an element of the array. The array data structure does not deliver these capabilities. In addition, programmers might want to store different types of objects in the same structure. The Java platform provides the programmer with a framework for creating container type objects that can hold other objects. A framework is a formal declaration of a set of rules, procedures, and guidelines. This framework defines the behaviors of these container objects and their storage methods. The Collections API in the Java platform provides the interfaces that implement this framework and the concrete classes that can serve as containers or collections of objects. A collection is a grouping of objects. The classes that form the collections framework are part of the java.util package.

The `java.util` Package

In Chapter 6, "System, String, StringBuffer, math, and Wrapper Classes," you were introduced to the Date and Calendar classes, located in the java.util package, to support working with date information. This section expands on the prebuilt classes contained in the java.util package.

The `java.util` Package

The `java.util` package contains classes that provide the programmer with tools to perform several specialized operations:

- Classes to manage a collection of objects
- Classes to manage messaging between objects when changes occur in an object
- Classes to manipulate date information

As shown in Table 14-1, the `java.util` package contains the collections framework, legacy collection classes, event model, date and time facilities, internationalization, and miscellaneous utility classes (such as a string tokenizer, a random-number generator, and a bit array).

Table 14-1 Package `java.util` API

Class Summary	
AbstractCollection	This class provides a skeletal implementation of the Collection interface to minimize the effort required to implement this interface.
AbstractList	This class provides a skeletal implementation of the List interface to minimize the effort required to implement this interface backed by a "random access" data store (such as an array).
AbstractMap	This class provides a skeletal implementation of the Map interface to minimize the effort required to implement this interface.
AbstractSequentialList	This class provides a skeletal implementation of the List interface to minimize the effort required to implement this interface backed by a "sequential access" data store (such as a linked list).
AbstractSet	This class provides a skeletal implementation of the Set interface to minimize the effort required to implement this interface.
ArrayList	Resizable-array implementation of the List interface.
Arrays	This class contains various methods for manipulating arrays (such as sorting and searching).
BitSet	This class implements a vector of bits that grows as needed.

Table 14-1 Package java.util API (Continued)

Class Summary	
Calendar	Calendar is an abstract base class for converting between a Date object and a set of integer fields such as YEAR, MONTH, DAY, HOUR, and so on.
Collections	This class consists exclusively of static methods that operate on or return collections.
Currency	Represents a currency.
Date	The class Date represents a specific instant in time, with millisecond precision.
Dictionary	The Dictionary class is the abstract parent of any class, such as Hashtable, which maps keys to values.
EventListenerProxy	An abstract wrapper class for an EventListener class which associates a set of additional parameters with the listener.
EventObject	The root class from which all event state objects shall be derived.
GregorianCalendar	GregorianCalendar is a concrete subclass of Calendar and provides the standard calendar used by most of the world.
HashMap	Hash table based implementation of the Map interface.
HashSet	This class implements the Set interface, backed by a hash table (actually a HashMap instance).
Hashtable	This class implements a hashtable, which maps keys to values.
IdentityHashMap	This class implements the Map interface with a hash table, using reference-equality in place of object-equality when comparing keys (and values).
LinkedHashMap	Hash table and linked list implementation of the Map interface, with predictable iteration order.
LinkedHashSet	Hash table and linked list implementation of the Set interface, with predictable iteration order.
LinkedList	Linked list implementation of the List interface.

continues

Table 14-1 Package `java.util` API (Continued)

Class Summary	
ListResourceBundle	ListResourceBundle is an abstract subclass of Resource-Bundle that manages resources for a locale in a convenient and easy to use list.
Locale	A Locale object represents a specific geographical, political, or cultural region.
Observable	This class represents an observable object, or "data" in the model-view paradigm.
Properties	The Properties class represents a persistent set of properties.
PropertyPermission	This class is for property permissions.
PropertyResourceBundle	PropertyResourceBundle is a concrete subclass of ResourceBundle that manages resources for a locale using a set of static strings from a property file.
Random	An instance of this class is used to generate a stream of pseudorandom numbers.
ResourceBundle	Resource bundles contain locale-specific objects.
SimpleTimeZone	SimpleTimeZone is a concrete subclass of TimeZone that represents a time zone for use with a Gregorian calendar.
Stack	The Stack class represents a last-in-first-out (LIFO) stack of objects.
StringTokenizer	The string tokenizer class allows an application to break a string into tokens.
Timer	A facility for threads to schedule tasks for future execution in a background thread.
TimerTask	A task that can be scheduled for one-time or repeated execution by a Timer.
TimeZone	TimeZone represents a time zone offset, and also figures out daylight savings.
TreeMap	Red-Black tree based implementation of the SortedMap interface.

Table 14-1 Package `java.util` API (Continued)

Class Summary	
TreeSet	This class implements the Set interface, backed by a TreeMap instance.
Vector	The Vector class implements a growable array of objects.
WeakHashMap	A hashtable-based Map implementation with weak keys.

Collections

A *collection* is similar to an array. It is a single object that represents a group of objects. However, a collection is much more than that. This section consists of the following topics:

- Understanding collections
- Collection storage techniques
- Properties of collections
- Types of collections

Understanding Collections

The objects in the collection are called *elements*. Collections typically deal with many types of objects, all of which descend from a common parent type. In most instances, the common parent type is the `Object` class.

Collection objects represent references to other objects. Whereas array objects can represent primitives and references to other objects, collections only maintain references to objects of type `Object`. This means that any object can be stored in the collection. It also necessitates correct casting before using the object, after retrieving it from the collection. To create a collection of primitive data, the data needs to be represented as an object of the corresponding `wrapper` class. To store an **int** in a `wrapper` object, use the constructor for the `Integer` class. The collections object can store integers, doubles, and the objects of these `wrapper` classes, but not primitives. Working with primitives restricts the programmer to using the built-in array object referenced by the symbol "`[ ]`".

Collection objects provide a great deal of flexibility over array objects. Collection objects can grow dynamically, can maintain the objects in the collection in a sorted order, can move through the elements of the collection, and can add and remove elements of the structure efficiently. Methods to perform these operations are provided in most collection classes.

There are three important concepts related to understanding collections:

- Storage technologies available to store and manage a collection of objects
- Properties of collections
- Types of collection objects

Collection Storage Techniques

There are four basic storage technologies available for storing objects: array, linked list, tree, and hash table. Each of theses storage technologies is explored in the following subsections.

Array

The array storage technology provides for storage of unique values. The Java language built-in `array` object uses this technology to store data. If there are a fixed number of elements, use an array for storage. It is fast and efficient. It is very difficult to add or remove elements from an array. The array would have to be copied to create a new array. This can be memory-intensive and inefficient. In Figure 14-1, the removal of an element in the array requires copying the elements to a new array. This is so that the elements after the removed element can be moved up and the indexes can be reassigned.

Figure 14-1 Array—Removing an Element from an Array

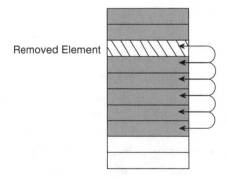

Linked-list

In this type of storage, the items are ordered and can have duplicates. Each object in the list contains a link (reference) to the object before and to the object after the object in the link. This allows objects to be added or removed very easily and efficiently. The size can grow dynamically. Accessing linked-lists can be slow, and lists do not provide a search mechanism. Linked-lists in Java are available through the `LinkedList` interface, which implements a *doubly linked* list. Some languages provide a linked-list that is singly linked. Java programmers might use a `LinkedList` that is doubly linked or implement their own singly linked collection object.

This means that programmers can move forward only to the next object in the collection. Figure 14-2 shows that links maintain a reference to the previous and the next object. This enables traversing the list using iterators (objects that can scan the list) both backward and forward.

Figure 14-2 Linked List—Doubly Linked

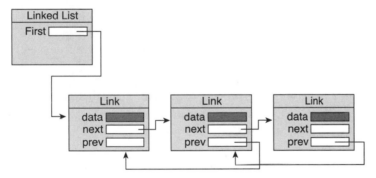

Note that the removal or addition of an element to the list results only in changes to the objects linked to this element. As shown in Figure 14-3, the entire array does not need to be recopied to reflect these changes.

Figure 14-3 Adding Elements to a List

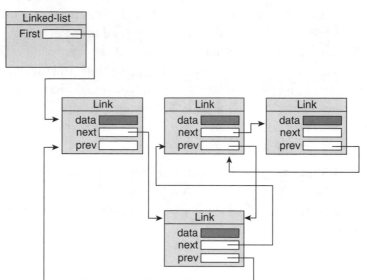

A tree is a nonlinear data structure that models a hierarchical organization. The characteristic features are that each element can have several successors (called its children) and every element except one (called the root) has a unique predecessor (called its parent). Trees are common in computer science. Computer file systems are trees, the inheritance structure for Java classes is a tree, the run-time system of method invocations during execution of a Java program is a tree, the classification of Java types is a tree, and the actual syntactical definition of the Java programming language forms a tree.

Tree

Trees, as illustrated in Figure 14-4, provide storage for items that are sorted, for example, in ascending order. If the objects are placed in a natural order that can be sorted, an index is used to search for the objects.

Figure 14-4   Tree

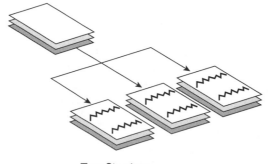

Tree Structure

Hash Table

In a *hash table*, each item in the collection consists of a key or identifier and the item. This is also called a *key-value* pair. The storage mechanism uses the key value to locate each item. Accessing items in a collection that stores items using a hash table is fast; however, additional memory is needed to maintain the key information. In Figure 14-5, the shaded area represents the key for each object. This key is stored in the object and in a table that serves as an index to the objects. Locating the key in the table and using the address of the object associated with this key retrieves the object.

Figure 14-5 Hash Table

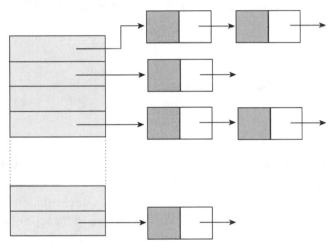

Properties of Collections

Collection objects have four properties, as displayed in Table 14-2.

Table 14-2 Properties of Collection Objects

Property	Description
Sorted	Assorted in ascending order, or sorted naturally using the `equals()` method of the object. An example is a list of courses offered or a list of teachers in a school.
Ordered/Unordered	Keeps track of determining where to place the object in the collection. A deck of cards is an ordered collection.

Table 14-2 Properties of Collection Objects (Continued)

Property	Description
Allows Duplicates	Enables duplicate orders to be added to the collection. An example is a collection of birthdays for students in a class.
Uses keys	A key object is used to reference the stored object. An example is the names of customers stored by unique customer IDs.

Types of Collections

Objects that can serve as containers for other objects can be categorized as collections, lists, sets, and maps.

Collection

A collection is a simple container. The objects in a collection can be unordered, and duplicates are permitted.

Lists

Lists are ordered collections and can have duplicates. The order can be the natural order, which is the order in which the objects were added to the list. Because the list is ordered, objects in a list can be indexed. An array is an example of a list. The collections framework includes classes that provide for dynamic lists. This type of storage is also known as a *bag* or *multiset*. Other names for this type of storage include *list* and *sequence*. Figure 14-6 shows the representation of different lists, such as array, linked-list, stack, and queue.

Figure 14-6 Lists

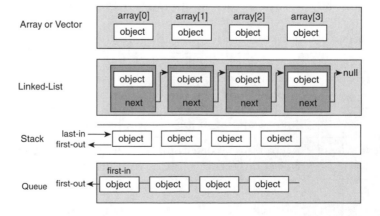

More Information

A stack is a container that implements the Last-In-First-Out (LIFO) protocol. This means that the only accessible object in the container is the last one that was inserted. A stack of books, or a stack of plates, is an example of a physical representation of a stack collection. You cannot take a plate or a book from a stack without first removing the books or plates on top.

The Stack class is an extension of the Vector class. It extends class Vector with five operations that allow a vector to be treated as a stack. The usual push (to insert an object at the top of the stack) and pop operations (to return the object at the top of the stack, after removing it) are provided, as well as a method to peek at the top item on the stack, a method to test for whether the stack is empty, and a method to search the stack for an item and discover how far it is from the top. Although most indexing in Java is 0-based indexing, the position of objects in a stack is computed using 1-based Indexing so that the top element on the stack has position 1.

A queue is a container that implements the First-In-First-Out (FIFO) protocol. This means that the only accessible object in the container is the one that was inserted first. Customers waiting in line at a bank teller's window would be an example of a queue.

There is no Queue class, similar to the Stack class, in the Java standard library.

Sets

As illustrated in Figure 14-7, a *set* is an unordered collection of objects. Duplicates are not permitted. The collection can add and remove objects.

Figure 14-7 Sets

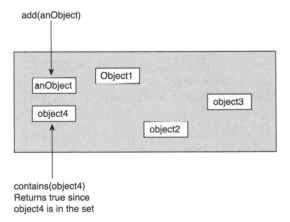

Maps

As illustrated in Figure 14-8, a *map* is a collection of arbitrary associations between a key object and a value object. In a given map, there might only be one entry for a given key. A map collection uses a set of data values to look up or index stored objects. With maps, users can search on key data. Maps are also known as *dictionaries*. For example, the student ID number in a Student object can serve as the key to the object. The student ID number can be used to retrieve Student objects. A collection of Student objects with the student ID number as key objects can be stored in a map.

Figure 14-8 illustrates that retrieving an object requires a key to be supplied. A hash-code is generated, and the key (or keys) at the location determined by the hashcode is compared with the supplied key. The key generates a hashcode, which determines where in memory the key/object pair is stored.

Figure 14-8 Maps

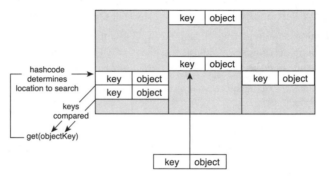

More Information
Table, Lookup table, associative array, and dictionary are other terms used to describe a map type of collection. The map is a container that allows direct access by any index type. It works like an array or vector, except that the index variable need not be an integer. An analogy is a dictionary: The index variable is the word being looked up, and the element that it indexes is its dictionary definition.
A table (map) is a sequence of pairs. The first component of the pair is called the *key*. It serves as the index into the table (not unlike the subscript integer used in arrays, as in int x[]; x[9]). The second component is the *value* of its key components. It contains the information being looked up. The table is called a map because you can think of the keys being mapped to their values. Tables are also called associated arrays, because they can be implemented using two parallel arrays: the keys in one array and the associated values in another array.

The Collections Framework

The Java platform includes the collections framework for representing and manipulating collections. This section consists of the following topics:

- Overview
- Collection interfaces
- Collection classes
- Set objects
- List objects
- Map objects
- Iterators
- Sorting and shuffling list objects

Overview

The *collections framework* represents a large number of classes and interfaces that provide the programmer with the ability to manage a large number of objects. The Collection interface extends the array storage methodology of the language. This discussion of the Collection API is a simplification of the complete API (which includes many more methods, more interfaces, and several intermediate abstract classes). For more information, read the section "Introduction to the Collections Framework" at http://developer.Java.sun.com/developer/onlineTraining/collections/.

A framework is a set of rules or guidelines. The idea behind the collections framework classes was to define a set of behaviors for objects that contain other objects. These include container behaviors for the collection objects. The collections framework consists of these features. Table 14-3 presents all the elements of the collections framework. A comprehensive coverage of the collections framework is beyond the scope of this class. This course focuses on one implementation (one class) of each type of storage method.

Table 14-3 Collections Framework

Collection Interfaces	Represent different types of collections, such as sets, lists, and maps. These interfaces form the basis of the framework.
General-purpose Implementations	Primary implementations of the collection interfaces.
Legacy Implementations	The collection classes from earlier releases, Vector and Hashtable, have been retrofitted to implement the collection interfaces.

continues

Table 14-3 Collections Framework (Continued)

Wrapper Implementations	Add functionality, such as synchronization, to other implementations.
Convenience Implementations	High-performance "mini-implementations" of the Collection interfaces.
Abstract Implementations	Partial implementations of the Collection interfaces to facilitate custom implementations.
Algorithms	Static methods that perform useful functions on collections, such as sorting a list.
Infrastructure	Interfaces that provide essential support for the Collection interfaces.
Array Utilities	Utility functions for arrays of primitives and reference objects. Strictly speaking, not a part of the collections framework, this functionality is being added to the Java platform at the same time and relies on some of the same infrastructure.

Collection Interfaces

Recall that the Java platform defines an interface as a means for implementing standards and guidelines. The collections framework defines the behaviors of collection objects using a hierarchy of interfaces. These interfaces define methods for objects that serve as containers of other objects. These interfaces represent commonly expected behaviors of collections based on type and storage technology.

The collections framework defines six interfaces. There are two root interfaces at the top of the hierarchy. These are the `Collection` and the `Map` interfaces. The chart in Figure 14-9 shows the interface hierarchy.

Figure 14-9 Collections Framework—`Map` and `Collection` Interface Hierarchy

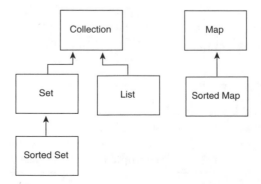

TIP

The names of most of the concrete collection classes are concatenations of the data structure/storage technologies and the interface (collection properties) implemented. For example, the *ArrayList* class uses an array storage technology to implement the `List` interface, and the `HashSet` class uses a Hash Table storage technology to implement the `Set` interface.

As shown in Table 14-4, the Collection interfaces define a variety of methods to manage the elements in the collection.

Table 14-4 Methods of the Collection Interfaces

Method	Description
Add and Remove Methods	Used to add **boolean** add(Object element) and remove **boolean** remove(Object element), individual elements. If the collection has successfully changed, the method returns **true**.
Query Methods	Used to find useful information about the collection, such as size of collection **int** size(), **boolean** isEmpty(), **boolean** contains(Object element).
Iterator Methods	Used to iterate through one element at a time. The iterator methods of the Collection, List, and Set interfaces create an Iterator object that has methods to iterate through the object. The Iterator object can access the next element using the Object next() method, check to see if there are any more objects in the collection using the **boolean** hasNext() method, and remove objects from a collection using the **void** remove() method.
Group Methods	Used to deal with the entire collection. With these, programmers can add or remove more than one element with one method call. These include **boolean** containsAll(collection collection), **boolean** addAll(Collection collection), **void** clear(), **void** removeAll(Collection collection), and **void** retainAll(Collection collection).

The Collection interface is used for any collection that is simple, that is unordered, and that can have duplicates. There are no restrictions. Any type of object can be used and can have multiple occurrences of the object. This interface supports methods for adding, removing, counting, and checking items in a collection. A collection is sometimes referred to as a bag because it does not impose any rules.

The List interface extends the Collection interface to implement an ordered set of collections. The ordered lists can be indexed and can have duplicate values.

SortedSet Extends from Set

The `Set` interface extends the `Collection` interface to implement sets that are finite. Sets do not allow duplicate values. If they permit a null value, only one null value can occur. *SortedSet*, which extends from `Set`, is an interface for sets whose values are sorted in ascending order.

The `Map` interface provides the basic methods for storing and retrieving data using key values. The key values must be unique. `Map.Entry` is an inner interface that provides for working with *key-value pairs*. *SortedMap*, which extends from `Map`, is an interface for creating a map whose elements are sorted in ascending order.

In addition to these interfaces, the collections framework defines a set of helper interfaces. These provide functionality for traversing (retrieving a collection of objects in some specific order). There are two specific interfaces that are available:

- *Iterator*—Provides a basic mechanism for iterating (looping) through the elements of a collection. Moves only forward through the list.
- *ListIterator*—Provides support of iteration through a list. Provides for scanning both forward and backward through a list.

Table 14-5 summarizes the `Collection` and `Helper` interfaces located in the `java.util` Package.

Table 14-5 `Collection` and `Helper` Interfaces

Interface	Description
Collection	A collection of elements.
List	A sequence of elements.
Set	A collection of unique elements.
SortedSet	A sorted collection of unique elements.
Map	A collection of (key,value) pairs. Keys must be unique.
SortedMap	A sorted collection of (key,value) pairs. Keys must be unique.
Iterator	An object that can traverse a collection of elements.
ListIterator	An object that can traverse a sequence of elements.

Collection Classes

The programmer can create classes that implement the collection interfaces to manage and store objects. However, an extensive group of classes are available that have implemented one or more of the collection interfaces and storage methods. Figure 14-10 shows the specific hierarchy for the set of classes that implement the Collection interfaces. Figure 14-11 shows the specific hierarchy for the legacy classes that represent older implementations of the collections framework.

Figure 14-10 Hierarchy of Collection Classes

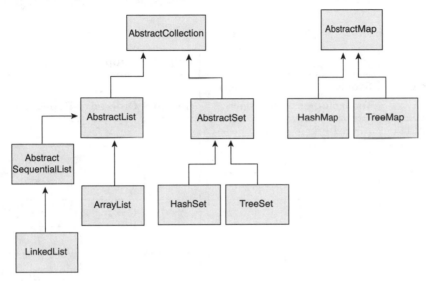

Figure 14-11 Hierarchy of Legacy Classes

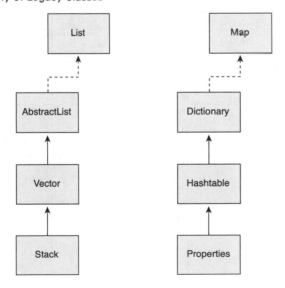

One purpose of this chapter is to help programmers select appropriate collection classes to contain their objects. In general, the name of the class includes a reference to the type of storage technology that is implemented in the class. A *TreeSet* class is therefore a collection of the type Set implementing a tree storage technology. Table 14-6 provides a summary of collection classes, properties, interfaces, and storage technologies.

Table 14-6 Collection Classes, Properties, Interfaces, and Storage Technologies

Collection Class	Storage Technologies	Collection Interface	Collection Properties			
			Sorted	Ordered	Duplicates	Key
LinkedList	Linked-List	List		x	x	
ArrayList	Array	List		x	x	
Vector	Array	List		x	x	
HashSet	Hash Table	Set				
TreeSet	Tree	SortedSet	x			
HashMap	Hash Table	Map				x
TreeMap	Tree	SortedMap	x			x
Hashtable/ Properties	Hash Table	Map				x

The next section explores the use of specific collection classes that implement a List, Set, SortedSet, Map, or SortedMap interface.

Set Objects

The two Set implementations to be discussed in this chapter are the HashSet and the TreeSet.

HashSet

The *HashSet* class implements the Set interface. In the example shown in Example 14-1 and Figure 14-12, the program declares a variable (set) of type Set and is initialized to a new HashSet object. It then adds a few elements and prints the set to standard output. A Set object does not allow duplicate objects to enter the collection. The collection is unordered and unsorted.

Example 14-1 *Code SetOfNumbers.java*

```
 1 /**
 2  * Java Program: SetOfNumber.java
 3  * @author Cisco Student
 4  * @version 2002
 5  */
 6
 7 import java.util.*;
 8
 9 // class uses wrapper class to store primitve data
10 // Collections will not store primitives, only objects
11
12 public class SetOfNumbers
13 {
14     public static void main(String[] args)
15     {
16         Set set = new HashSet();
17         /*
18         explicit cast for integer to byte
19         or short is required here. default
20         data-type for the values are
```

NOTE

The full version of the abbreviated code shown in this example can be viewed using the book's accompanying CD-ROM.

Note that the collection failed to add a duplicate value. The Double object in Line 31 is not added to the set because this is a duplicate. Note that the output is printed with commas. The HashSet class overrides the toString method and creates a sequence of the items separated by commas, delimited by the open and close brackets.

A TreeSet

The TreeSet class implements the SortedSet interface. These objects place the elements in ascending order. The elements must be nonduplicating. Because the elements are sorted, additional methods are available to take advantage of the order.

Figure 14-12 Code SetOfNumbers.java—Output

```
C:\WINNT\System32\cmd.exe
[60, 5.0, 70.0, 60.0, 4, 3, 2, 1]

D:CISCO\Chapter14\Content>
```

The TreeSet class implements the SortedSet interface directly. The example shown in Example 14-2 and Figure 14-13 demonstrates several features of the TreeSet type object.

Example 14-2 TreeSetExample—*Code*

```
1  /**
2   * Java Program: TreeSetExample.java
3   * @ author Cisco Teacher
4   * @version 2002
5   */
6
7  import java.util.*;
8
9  // A SortedSet maintains the data in an ascending order
10 public class TreeSetExample
11 {
12     public static void main (String[] args)
13     {
14         SortedSet aTree, bTree;
15         aTree = new TreeSet();
```

continues

Example 14-2 TreeSetExample—*Code (Continued)*

```
16          bTree = new TreeSet();
17          // A set of words
18          aTree.add("Xena");
19          aTree.add("Arthur");
20          aTree.add("Constance");
```

NOTE

The full version of the abbreviated code shown in this example can be viewed using the book's accompanying CD-ROM.

For Example 14-2, you can view the explanatory text by accessing the full, interactive graphic for this example on the book's accompanying CD-ROM. The title of the activity is "TreeSetExample" in e-Lab Activities.

Figure 14-13 TreeSetExample—Output

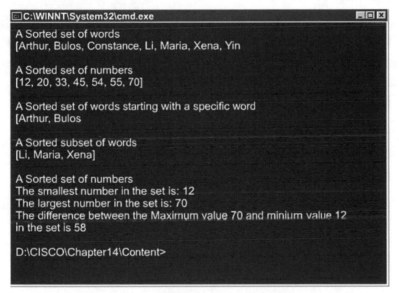

```
A Sorted set of words
[Arthur, Bulos, Constance, Li, Maria, Xena, Yin

A Sorted set of numbers
[12, 20, 33, 45, 54, 55, 70]

A Sorted set of words starting with a specific word
[Arthur, Bulos

A Sorted subset of words
[Li, Maria, Xena]

A Sorted set of numbers
The smallest number in the set is: 12
The largest number in the set is: 70
The difference between the Maximum value 70 and minium value 12
in the set is 58

D:\CISCO\Chapter14\Content>
```

More Information

Sample code using the HashSet and TreeSet classes follows:

```
Set set1, set2; // creating references of the type Set
set1 = new HashSet();
set2 = new TreeSet(); // sorted set

// use the set in some operations
set1.add(value);   //add an element to the set
boolean b = set1.contains(value); // does the set contain this element
set1.remove(value);   // remove an element from the set
```

The same operations on set2 results in the set elements being added or removed and the set being maintained in an ordered (sorted set).

List Objects

All collections store objects of the type `Object`. Retrieving an object from a collection requires explicit casting of the object to its assignable type.

More Information

The following is sample code that demonstrates creating and managing a List object:

```
List list = new LinkedList(); // this is a doubly linked list
List list2 = new ArrayList; // this is a list implemented as a growable array
list.add(value);
list.get(value);
list.remove(value);
list.subList(index, list.size()).clear();// truncating a list
```

Vector

The *Vector* class implements the `List` interface. Figure 14-14 illustrates the behavior of `Vector` objects. The dimensions of the `Vector` object include its capacity (how many elements can be added) and its initial size. The capacity of a `Vector` object can be increased after the object has been created. The `Vector` increases this to the limit set by the `capacity` attribute. The number of objects represents the length or elements of the `Vector`.

Figure 14-14 `Vector`

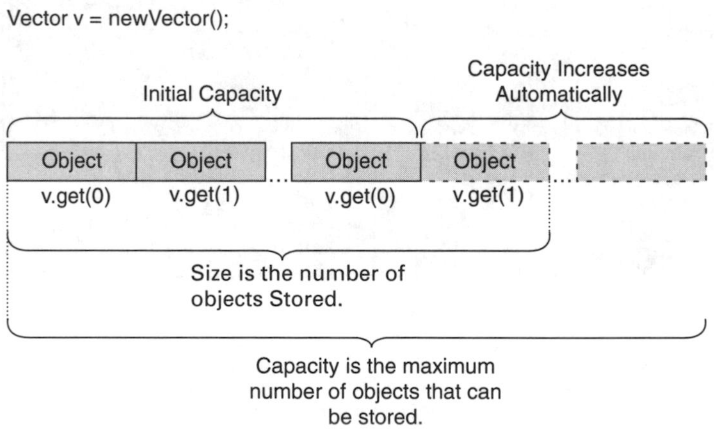

When multiple types of objects are in a `Vector`, casting an object to an assignable type might require the use of the **instanceof** operator to check the object type. An example follows:

```
String s;
Integer i;
if(v.elementAt(2)instanceof String){
    s = (String)v.get(2);
}
```

```
if(v.elementAt(2)instanceof Integer){
    i = (Integer)v.get(2);
}
```

In Example 14-3 and Figure 14-15, the code for the `SampleVector` class creates a `Vector` and adds several elements to the `Vector`. Notice that the second and fifth names include an integer to position the element in a specific order in the collection. When using an integer to position an element, the integer can position only the element relative to the number of elements currently in the list. For example, `v.add(2, "Elizabeth Taylor");` in Line 15 would result in an `ArrayIndexOutOfBoundsException`. There are only two elements in the list. The first is assigned to `0`, and the second is assigned to `1`. The integer 2 would be past the last element of the `Vector` by the time the `add` method was invoked. In this case, `v.addElement("Elizabeth Taylor")` should be used to position this object as the last element in the `Vector`. Note that to retrieve a `name`, the object returned by the `v.get(3);` method call is cast to a `String` object, using the syntax `String name = (String) v.get(3);`.

Example 14-3 *Code—A Sample* `Vector`

```
 1 /**
 2  * Java Program: SampleVector.java
 3  * @author Cisco Teacher
 4  * @version 2002
 5  */
 6
 7 import java.util.*;
 8
 9 public class SampleVector
10 {
11     public static void main(String[] args)
12     {
13         Vector v = new Vector();
14         v.add("John Wayne");
15         v.add(0, "Elizabeth Taylor");
16         v.add("Richard Harris");
17         v.add("Elizabeth Hurley");
18         v.add(1, "Richard Burton");
19         System.out.println(v);
20         String name = (String) v.get(3);
```

Example 14-3 *Code—A Sample* Vector (Continued)

```
21          System.out.println(name);
22      }
23 }// END OF CLASS
```

Figure 14-15 Code—A Sample Vector—Output

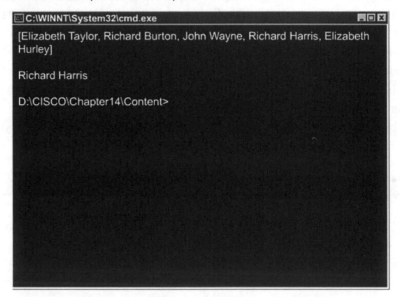

```
C:\WINNT\System32\cmd.exe
[Elizabeth Taylor, Richard Burton, John Wayne, Richard Harris, Elizabeth
Hurley]

Richard Harris

D:\CISCO\Chapter14\Content>
```

The objects in a list retain the order into which they were placed. In a set, the order is not guaranteed over time.

ArrayList

The *ArrayList* class implements the List interface. The ArrayListOfNumbers class in Example 14-20 and Figure 14-16 is a variation on the code from the SetOfNumbers class. The ArrayListOfNumbers.java program declares a variable (list) of type List and is initialized to a new ArrayList object. It then adds a few elements and prints the list to standard output. Because lists allow duplicates, all values are printed.

Example 14-4 *ArrayListOfNumbers.java—Code*

```
1 /**
2  * Java Program ArrayListOfNumber.java
3  * @author Cisco Teacher
```

continues

Example 14-4 *ArrayListOfNumbers.java—Code (Continued)*

```
 4   * @version 2002
 5   */
 6
 7 import java.util.*;
 8
 9 // class uses wrapper class to store primitve data
10 // Collections will not store primitives, only objects
11
12 public class ArrayListOfNumbers
13 {
14     public static void main(String[] args)
15     {
16         List list = new ArrayList();
17         /*
18         explicit cast for integer to byte
19         or short is required here. default
20         data-type for the values are
```

NOTE

The full version of the abbreviated code shown in this example can be viewed using the book's accompanying CD-ROM.

Figure 14-16 `ArrayListOfNumbers.java`—Output

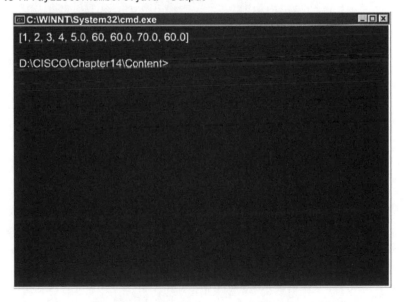

In general, the collection type should be used to declare a reference to a collection object. This makes the code flexible and modifiable to use another collection object, as shown in Example 14-5.

Example 14-5 *Declaration of Collection Type*

```
public class ArrayListOfNumbers{
    public static void main(String[] args){
        Collection list = new ArrayList();
```
```
public class SetOfNumbers{
    public static void main(String[] args){
        Collection set = new HashSet();
```

LinkedList

The *LinkedList* class implements the List interface. Removing and adding elements in the middle of arrays is time-consuming. This requires moving all the elements beyond the element. Each insertion or deletion requires copying and recopying the array because the array stores data in locations next to each other.

The LinkedList object is a better alternative. Here, the objects are stored in a separate link. Each link stores a reference to the next link, as shown in Figure 14-17.

Figure 14-17 LinkedList Objects

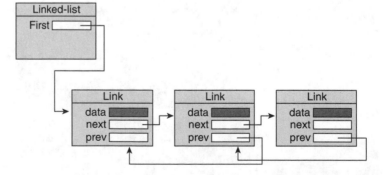

When adding an element to or removing an element from the list, only the links surrounding the element have to be updated. This saves time. In the Java platform, all lists are doubly linked. Each object has a link to the next object and a link to the previous object. The LinkedList is an ordered collection in which the position of the object matters. In general, the LinkedList adds the object to the end of the list. To add objects in the middle of the list, an `Iterator` object is responsible for locating the position. In the code (and output) shown in Example 14-6 and Figure 14-18, the names are added before the `iterator` position.

Example 14-6 *Code LinkedListExample.java*

```
1 /**
2 * Java Program: LinkedListExample.java
3 * @author Cisco Teacher
4 * @version 2002
5 */
6
7 import java.util.*;
8
9 public class LinkedListExample
10 {
11     public static void main(String[] args)
12     {
13         LinkedList actors = new LinkedList();
14         actors.add("John Wayne");
15         actors.add("Elizabeth Taylor");
16         actors.add("Richard Harris");
17         actors.add("Elizabeth Hurley");
18         actors.add("Richard Burton");
19
20         System.out.println("\n\nA list of actors");
```

NOTE

The full version of the abbreviated code shown in this example can be viewed using the book's accompanying CD-ROM.

Map Objects

The `Map` interface does not extend from the `Collection` interface. Technically, it is not a collection, but, in general terms, it is part of the collections framework. It can be used to store and manage a collection of objects using hash table storage methods.

More Information

The following code illustrates how to create a hash table using the HashMap class:

```
Map map = new HashMap(); // creates a hash table
map.put(key,value); // creates an entry for the key and an entry for the actual
value.
object = map.get(key); //returns the object(value) associated with the key.
map.remove(key); // removes the object and its key from the map/table.
```

Figure 14-18 Code LinkedListExample.java—Output

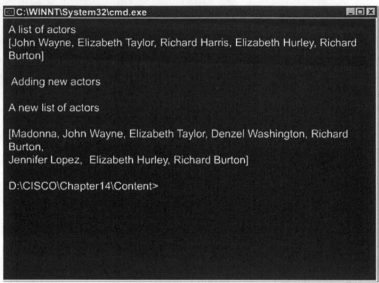

To locate an element in a set or a list, an exact copy of the element is needed. This is not a common way of looking up objects. Programmers usually have some key information, and they want to look up the associated element. A map is a collection of arbitrary associations between a key object and a value object. In a given map, there might be only one entry for a given key. A map might not store duplicate keys; it can store duplicate objects. For example, two students with the same name would represent two objects with duplicate data. However, as shown in Figure 14-19, the student ID makes each object unique.

Every object inherits the hashCode() method from the parent class Object. A hash value is an **int** that serves as an identifier for an object. If all collection objects are considered as a bucket to hold other objects, the hash value serves as the identifier to locate the object in the bucket, as shown in Figures 14-20 and 14-21. Hash values for an object are determined by the **int** hashCode() method implementation of the object. The hashCode method should be overridden in objects that will be used in collections that use the hash table storage technology.

Figure 14-19 Map Objects—Student Objects

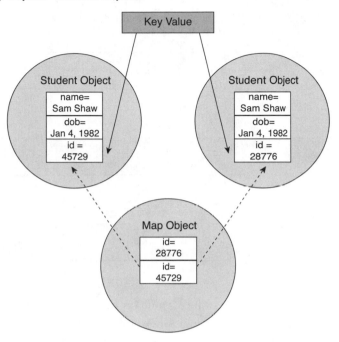

Figure 14-20 Bucket and hashvalue1

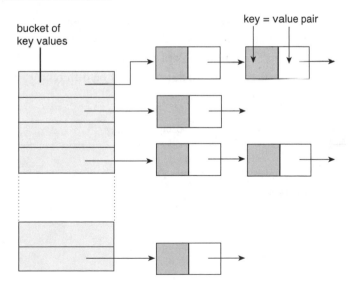

Figure 14-21 Bucket and hashvalue2

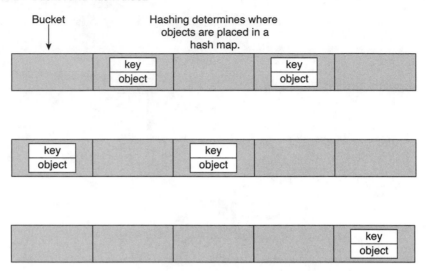

The **int** hashCode() method returns a hash value for the object. The **int** that is returned is based on any calculation that the programmer implements that will always yield a unique number for each object. In the example in Example 14-7, the programmer has implemented the hashCode method to calculate a number based on the calculation (id + (phoneNumber * 17). In the code for the StudentHasHashValue class, there are two elements in the Vector with the same data: the first and the last. Note that these two objects return the same hash value. The hash value for the third element is different because the data for the student is different in id. This can be a father and a son or older and younger siblings. The uniqueness of the id is important and serves as a key value to ensure that the hash value for each object will be different, even if all other member data (excluding the id) is the same.

Example 14-7 StudentHasHashValue.java—hashCode *Overriding*

NOTE

The full version of the abbreviated code shown in this example can be viewed using the book's accompanying CD-ROM.

```
1 /**
2  * Java Program: StudentHasHashValue.java
3  * @author Cisco Teacher
4  * @version 2002
5  */
6 import java.util.*;
7
```

continues

Example 14-7 `StudentHasHashValue.java` — hashCode *Overriding (Continued)*

```
 8 public class StudentHasHashValue
 9 {
10      private int id ;
11      private String name ;
12      private int phoneNumber;
13
14      /**
15       * @param  aId The student's id as an int
16       * @param aName The student's name as a String
17       * @param phone The student's phone number as an int
18       */
19      StudentHasHashValue(int aId, String aName, int phone)
20      {
```

This program provides two overridden methods inherited from the `Object` class: the `hashCode` and `toString` methods. The `toString` method provides the information for the `Student` in a formatted manner. Any request to print a `Student` object results in an output of information for each `Student` object in the format described in the code shown in Example 14-8.

Example 14-8 *Overriding the* `toString()` Method

```
return("hash value is: " + hashCode() + ": " + id + ":" + name
    + ":" + phoneNumber + "\n");


hash value is: 39921830: 45678:Tom Green:2345656
```

The `Vector` class also overrides the `toString` method and separates the result of the `toString` method of the `Student` objects in the `Vector`, with a comma, and also encloses the list in square brackets, as shown in Example 14-9.

Example 14-9 `Vector` *Class Overriding the* `toString()`

```
[hash value is: 39888497: 12345:Bill Wright:2345656
, hash value is: 39921830: 45678:Tom Green:2345656
, hash value is: 40568497: 12345:Bill Wright:2385656
, hash value is: 39888497: 12345:Bill Wright:2345656
]
```

> **More Information**
>
> It is recommended that you override the hashCode method whenever you override the equals method. The hashCode method returns a hash code value for the object. This method is supported for the benefit of hashtables, such as those provided by java.util.Hashtable.
>
> The general contract of hashCode follows:
>
> - Whenever it is invoked on the same object more than once during an execution of a Java application, the hashCode method must consistently return the same integer, provided no information used in the equals() comparisons on the object is modified. This integer need not remain consistent from one execution of an application to another execution of the same application.
> - If two objects are equal according to the equals(Object) method, calling the hashCode method on each of the two objects must produce the same integer result.
> - It is not required that if two objects are unequal according to the equals(Object) method, calling the hashCode method on each of the two objects must produce distinct integer results. However, the programmer should be aware that producing distinct integer results for unequal objects might improve the performance of hashtables.
>
> As much as is reasonably practical, the hashCode method defined by class Object does return distinct integers for distinct objects. (This is typically implemented by converting the internal address of the object into an integer, but this implementation technique is not required by the Java programming language.)

Map objects provide methods to add objects using key values. The put() method inserts a key and value pair into the Map. If the key already exists, the new value replaces the old value. The get() method returns the value associated with a given key or **null** if the key does not exist in the Map. The HashMap class implements the Map interface. Retrieving the set of keys, using the keySet() method, and then iterating over the key set and retrieving the values as things go along can accomplish iteration over a Map.

The program in Example 14-10 and Figure 14-22 demonstrates the use of a Map. A Map must have unique keys. In this example, the student Bill Wright with the ID number 12345 is entered three times. It is entered once in Line 24 of the program and twice when interacting with the program. Note that the code in Line 37 of Example 14-10 prints only one copy of each object.

Tom Green was entered twice (the second time his first name was entered as Thomas). Because the unique key in this case was based on the ID number, and because this key already existed, the second entry replaced the first.

Example 14-10 *MappedStudent.java—Code*

```
1 /**
2 * Java Program: MappedStudent.java
3 * @author Cisco Teacher
4 * @version 2002
5 */
6
7 import java.util.*;
8
9 public class MappedStudent
10 {
11     private int id;
12     private String name;
13     private int phoneNumber;
14
15     /**
16     * @param aId The student's id as an int
17     * @param aName The student's name as a String
18     * @param phone The student's phone number as an int
19     */
20     MappedStudent(int aId, String aName, int phone)
```

NOTE

The full version of the abbreviated code shown in this example can be viewed using the book's accompanying CD-ROM.

Figure 14-22 MappedStudent.java—Output

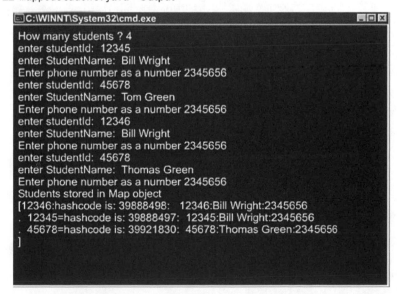

```
C:\WINNT\System32\cmd.exe

How many students ? 4
enter studentId: 12345
enter StudentName: Bill Wright
Enter phone number as a number 2345656
enter studentId: 45678
enter StudentName: Tom Green
Enter phone number as a number 2345656
enter studentId: 12346
enter StudentName: Bill Wright
Enter phone number as a number 2345656
enter studentId: 45678
enter StudentName: Thomas Green
Enter phone number as a number 2345656
Students stored in Map object
[12346:hashcode is: 39888498:   12346:Bill Wright:2345656
. 12345=hashcode is: 39888497:  12345:Bill Wright:2345656
. 45678=hashcode is: 39921830:  45678:Thomas Green:2345656
]
```

Example 14-11 *Building a Concordance for a Text File*

```java
import java.util.*;
import java.io.*;
/*
 *This class builds a concordance for a text file.
 * The concordance is output to a text file.
*/
public class Concordance
{
    private static HashMap concordance;
    private static File inputfile, outputfile;
    private static BufferedReader br;
    private static BufferedWriter bw;

    public static void main(String[] args)
    {
      try{
      inputfile = new File("Rose.txt");// use any text file you choose
      outputfile = new File("concordance.txt");
      br = new BufferedReader(new FileReader(inputfile));
      bw = new BufferedWriter(new FileWriter(outputfile));
      }
      catch (Exception e) { e.printStackTrace();}
      concordance = new HashMap();
      String line = null;
      StringTokenizer parser = null;
      int lineNumber =0;
      try{
        while ((line = br.readLine()) != null)
        {++ lineNumber;
         parser = new StringTokenizer(line,",.;:()-!?' ");
         while (parser.hasMoreTokens())
         { String word = parser.nextToken().toUpperCase();
           // find the word in the concordance list
           String listing = (String)concordance.get(word);
           // if word does not exist create a listing for it
           if (listing==null) listing = " " + lineNumber;
```

Example 14-11 *Building a Concordance for a Text File (Continued)*

```
            // if word exists append the new line number to the existing listing
            else listing += ", " + lineNumber;
            //update the concordance listing
            concordance.put(word,listing);
        }
      }
    }
    catch (Exception e) {e.printStackTrace();}
    Set set = concordance.entrySet();
    for (Iterator it = set.iterator(); it.hasNext();)
    {
        String s = it.next().toString();
        try{
        bw.write(s);
        }
        catch(Exception e)
        { e. printStackTrace();}
    }
  }
}
```

Iterators

A collection can be scanned using an iterator. Two iterator interfaces are available in the collection framework: the `Iterator` and its subclass, the `ListIterator`. Use the `ListIterator` with list objects. `Iterators` provide methods for scanning through any collection. In a set, the order is nondeterministic. This means it is not determined by the sequence in which it was added, or by some special key value. When using an `Iterator` object to move over a set, the iteration moves forward (but not backward) through the list elements, as shown in Figure 14-23.

As shown in Figure 14-23, an iterator is for one-time use. To access the objects from a collection again, you just obtain another iterator object.

TIP

An `Iterator` object traverses a data structure, visiting each element exactly once. A structure might have several `Iterator` objects traversing it simultaneously. At any moment, each `Iterator` object identifies a single element of the structure, providing access to it.

Figure 14-23 Iterator Processing

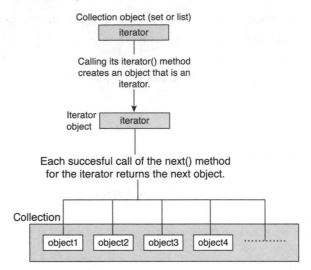

Iterator objects provide for scanning through the list and for adding and removing elements from the collection. Table 14-7 describes the methods common to Iterator objects.

Table 14-7 Common Iterator Methods

Iterator Method	Description
public boolean hasNext()	Returns **true** if a subsequent call to the next() method returns an element. Returns **true** if there is another element on the list and **false** if there is none.
public Object next()	Returns the next element in the list.
public void remove()	Removes the last element returned by the next() method.

The *ListIterator* provides additional methods for scanning forward and backward through the collection. The AbstractList class specified the listIterator and iterator methods, which return a reference to a ListIterator or an Iterator object, which can be used to scan through the collection. All subclasses of the AbstractList class, such as ArrayList, Vector, and LinkedList, can be accessed with a ListIterator. This interface includes methods for adding and removing an element from a LinkedList. The method add(Object element) adds a specific object to the LinkedList. The method remove() removes the last object accessed by the ListIterator from the LinkedList.

The method set(Object element) replaces the last object accessed by the ListIterator with a new object. The methods next() and previous() are used to change the position of the ListIterator within the LinkedList.

The remove method allows the code to remove the current item in the iteration (the item returned by the most recent next or previous method). If removal is not supported by the underlying collection, an UnsupportedOperationException is thrown.

The set method changes the element of the collection currently referenced by the Iterator cursor.

While using a ListIterator, it is common to move through the list in only one direction, that is, forward using next and backward using previous. Using previous immediately after next will not return the same element. A similar rule applies for calling next after previous.

The add method inserts the new element into the collection immediately before the Iterator cursor. Therefore, calling previous after an add returns the newly added element. However, a call to next will not be affected.

This StudentIterator class in Example 14-12 and Figure 14-24 demonstrates the use of an Iterator.

Example 14-12 *StudentIterator.java—Code*

```
 1 /**
 2  * Java Program: StudentIterator.java
 3  * @author Cisco Teacher
 4  * @version 2002
 5  */
 6
 7 import java.util.*;
 8
 9 public class StudentIterator
10 {
11     private int id;
12     private String name;
13     private int phoneNumber;
14
15     StudentIterator(int aId, String aName, int phone)
16     {
17         id = aId;
```

NOTE

The full version of the abbreviated code shown in this example can be viewed using the book's accompanying CD-ROM.

Example 14-12 *StudentIterator.java—Code (Continued)*

```
            name = aName;
            phoneNumber = phone;
        }
```

Figure 14-24 `StudentIterator.java`—Output

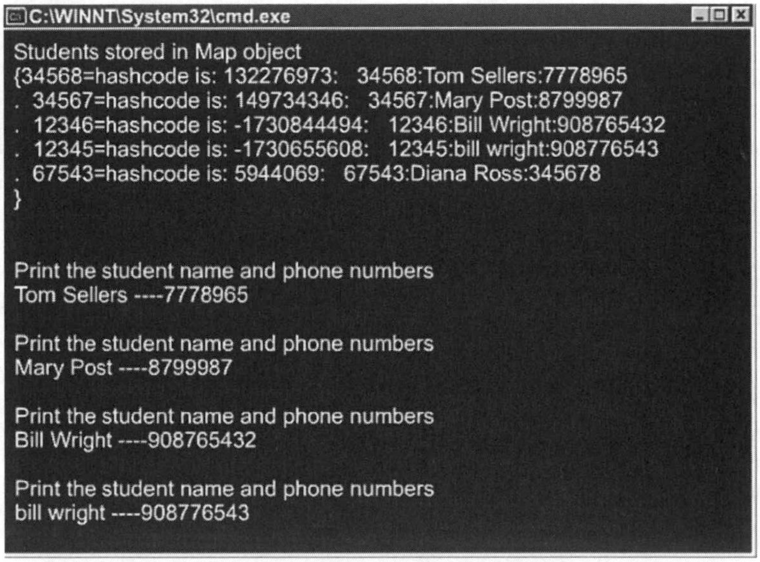

NOTE

A properties file is a simple text file that has lines of data in the format key_string=value. The key_string is the declaration of an operating system variable, or some key identifier that will be used to pass parameters from outside to the program. The value is the value assigned to the variable, or the parameter. Property files are extremely useful in setting configuration information for applications and for customizing the environment in which an application executes.

In addition to the `Iterator` interface, the Java language still allows the use of the *Enumeration* interface. The `Enumeration` interface is used most commonly to scan through a collection of key-value maps of the properties of the system. It is best to use the `Iterator` interface whenever possible because it is faster than the `Enumeration` interface.

The `MySystemProperties` class in Example 14-13 and Figure 14-25 demonstrates several important concepts. The first is the use of the `Properties` object, which is a `Map`. The properties of the system in which this program is run are maintained by the JVM as a `Map`. The structure of this collection is a key-value pair in a `String` format. The key value is a `String` representing the name of the property, and the value is also a `String` representing some specific data about the system. The `System.getProperty()` method returns an object of the type `Properties`. This is a `Map` object. Enumerate the elements of this collection using an `Enumeration` object.

Example 14-13 *MySystemProperties.java—Code*

```
1  /**
2   * Java Program MySystemProperties.java
3   * @author Cisco Teacher
4   * @version 2002
5   */
6
7  import java.util.*;
8
9  public class MySystemProperties
10 {
11     public static void main(String[] args)
12     {
13         // create a properties object. This is a Map.
14         Properties mySystem;
15
16         /*
17         load this map object with properties from
18         your system.  Use the getProperties() method
19         from the System class the Key value for this
20         map object is the form of propertyName = value
```

NOTE

The full version of the abbreviated code shown in this example can be viewed using the book's accompanying CD-ROM.

Sorting and Shuffling List Objects

It is important to know the methods of the Collections class for managing List objects. This saves valuable programming time, and the methods are very efficient. Two methods of specific use are the sort and shuffle methods.

Sorting

Sorting data or information is fundamental to any complex business application, especially when generating reports. The Collections class provides a set of static methods for sorting: Collections.sort() and Collections.reverse(). The sort() method can sort the entire List object or sort a subset. The reverse() method reverses the order of the elements in the List object.

Figure 14-25 `MySystemProperties.java`—Output

```
C:\WINNT\System32\cmd.exe                                          _ □ ×

java.specification.name=Java Platform API Specification
awt.toolkit=sun.awt.windows.WToolkit
java.version=1.2.2
java.awt.graphicsenv=sun.awt.Win32GraphicsEnvironment
user.timezone=America/Phoenix
java.specification.version=1.2
java.vm.vendor=Sun Microsystems Inc.
user.home=C:\Documents and Settings\administrator
java.vm.specification.version=1.0
os.arch=x86
java.awt.fonts=
java.vendor.url=http://java.sun.com/
user.region=US
file.encoding.pkg=sun.io
java.home=C:\Program Files\JavaSoft\JRE\1.2
java.class.path=C:\oracle\ora81\jdbc\lib\classes\12:C:\IBMVJava\eab\runti
me20:.
line.separator=

java.ext.dirs=C:\Program Files\JavaSoft\JRE\1.2\lib\ext
java.io.tmpdir=C:\DOCUME~1\ADMINI~1\LOCALS~1\Temp\
os.name=Windows NT
java.vendor=Sun Microsystems Inc.
java.awt.printerjob=sun.awt.windows.WPrinterJob
java.library.path=C:\WINNT\system32;.:C:\WINNT\System32:C:\WINNT:C:\
Program Files\WinEdit\:C:\Program Files\WinEdit\System:C:\Program
Files\WinEdit\Macros:C:\Program
Files\WinEdit\Help:C:\oracle\oradev6i2\bin:C:\oracle\ora81\bin:C:\IBMVJav
a\oab\bin:C:\oracle\oradev6i\bin:C:\oracle\ora81\Apache\Perl\5.00503\bin\
mswin32-x86:C:\Program
Files\Oracle\jre\1.1.7\bin:C:\WINNT\system32:C:\WINNT\System32\Wbem:
C:\oracle\oradev6i\jdk\bin:C:\jdk1.2.2\bin:C:\IMNnq_NT:C:\oracle\oradev6i2\
jdk\bin:C:\iracke\ora81\jdbc\lib;
java.vm.specification.vendor=Sun Microsystems Inc.
sun.io.unicode.encoding=Unicode Little
file.encoding=Cp1252
java.specification.vendor=Sun Microsystems Inc.
user.language=en
java.vendor.url.bug=http://java.sun.com\cgi-bin\bugreport.cgi
java.vm.name=Classic VM
java.class.version=46.0
java.vm.specification.name=Java Virtual Machine Specification
sun.boot.library.path=C:\Program Files\JavaSoft\JRE\1.2\bin
os.version=5.0
java.vm.info=build JDK-1.2.2-W, native threads, symcjit
java.compiler=symcjit
path.separator=:
file.separator=\
user.dir=D:\CISCO\Chapter14\Content
```

Shuffling

Shuffling rearranges the elements in a List object in some random order. The Collections.shuffle() method is overloaded. One version uses a default source for determining the random order. The second version accepts a Random object to determine the randomness for positioning the elements in the array.

In the program shown in Example 14-14 and Figure 14-26, a list of actors' names is maintained in a LinkedList. The program uses the Console class to obtain the names. It then presents them in sorted order, a reverse order (reverse of the sort), and shuffled. The sort method is called again, and then the shuffle method is called to illustrate that the shuffling is random.

Example 14-14 ActorsList.java—*Code*

```
1  /**
2   * Java Program: ActorsList
3   * @author Cisco Teacher
4   * @version 2002
5   */
6
7  import java.util.*;
8
9  public class ActorsList
10 {
11     public static void main(String[] args)
12     {
13         LinkedList actors = new LinkedList();
14         int nactors = Console.readInt("How many Actors? ");
15         for (int i = 0; i < nactors; ++i)
16         {
17             actors.add(Console.readLine("Enter an Actor's name: "));
18         }
19
20         Collections.sort(actors);
```

NOTE

The full version of the abbreviated code shown in this example can be viewed using the book's accompanying CD-ROM.

Figure 14-26 ActorsList.java—Output

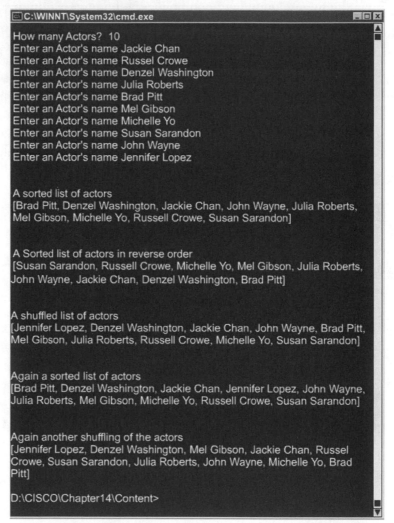

Case Study JBANK Application

The JBANK application introduced in Chapter 1 ("What Is Java?") provides students with an opportunity to apply the Java language concepts learned throughout this course. In the JBANK labs for Chapter 14, students will combine the use of I/O and collection technologies, using a Vector to retrieve Customer objects stored in a file. Students will then create a SortedSet object to hold a collection of Customer objects sorted by customer information (such as ID or name). This class will include methods to scan through the set.

The JBANK Application

The JBANK application provides several opportunities for using classes from the java.util package.

The bank maintains information on many customers. Although a Customer array could be used, the more efficient method would be to create a TreeMap. This is where a collection object is created to store a collection of Customer objects. Customer objects can be added to this as needed. Customer data can be retrieved using the Customer ID as a key. Each customer can have one or more bank accounts. A TreeSet or a SortedSet could be used to store Account objects. Additional applications make use of a Vector to extract customer data from the file and then store it in a Map.

In this lab, students work with several programming techniques to manage sets of data. This lab further stresses to the student the frequent use of the classes in the java.util package in real-world programming.

Figures 14-27 and 14-28 display what the JBANK application might look like at the end of the course.

Figure 14-27 The JBANK Application

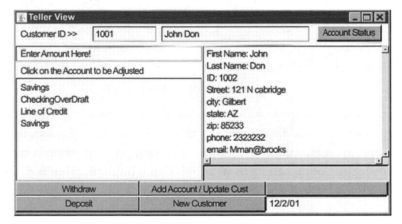

Figure 14-28 The JBANK Application

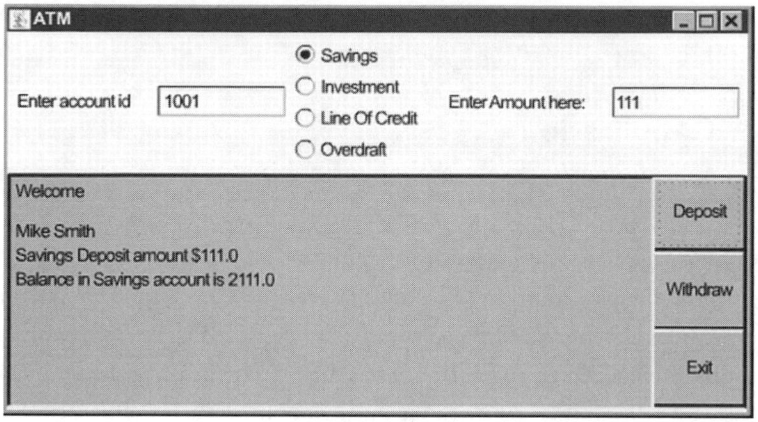

Summary

This chapter focused on utility classes of the Java API, particularly the collection classes. The collections framework represents storage methods and behaviors prescribed for collection objects. The framework is represented by six main interfaces that determine collection behavior: `Collection`, `Set`, `List`, `SortedSet`, `SortedMap`, and `Map`.

The essential differences among the types follow:

- `Collection` objects impose no rules on order or content duplication.
- `List` maintains order.
- `Set` rejects duplicate entries.
- `Map` uses unique keys to facilitate lookup of their contents.

In addition to Collection interfaces, students learned that the collections framework includes implementations of these interfaces in classes such as `ArrayList`, `LinkedList`, `Vector`, `TreeMap`, `TreeSet`, `Hashtable`, `HashMap`, and `HashSet`. Furthermore, the `Iterator` is an interface for retrieving objects from a collection. `Iterator` traverses the collection in one direction; `ListIterator` traverses the collection both backward and forward.

Syntax Summary

Set:

```
//import statement
import java.util.*;
```

```
//uses wrapper class to store primitive data
public class SetOfNumbers
{
    public static void main(String [ ] args)
    {
        Set set = new HashSet( );

            set.add(new Byte((byte) 1));
            set.add(new Short((short) 2));
            set.add(new Integer(3));
            set.add(new Integer(4));
            set.add(new Float(5.0F));
            set.add(new Long(60));
            set.add(new Double(60.00));
            set.add(new Float(70.00));
            set.add(new Double(60));
            System.out.println(set);
    }//end of main
}
//end of class
```

Vector:

```
//import statement
import java.util.*;

public class SampleVector
{
    public static void main(String [ ] args)
    {
        Vector v = new Vector( );
        v.add("John Wayne");
        v.add(0, "Elizabeth Taylor");
        v.add("Richard Harris");
        v.add("Elizabeth Hurley");
        v.add(1, "Richard Burton");
        System.out.println(v);
        String name = (String) v.get(3);
        System.out.println(name);
    }//end of main
}
//end of class
```

ArrayList:

```
//import statement
import java.util.*;

public class ArrayListOfNumbers
{
    public static void main(String [ ] args)
    {
        List list = new ArrayList( );

            list.add(new Byte((byte) 1));
            list.add(new Short((short) 2));
            list.add(new Integer(3));
            list.add(new Integer(4));
```

```
                        list.add(new Float(5.0F));
                        list.add(new Long(60));
                        list.add(new Double(60.00));
                        list.add(new Float(70.00));
                        list.add(new Double(60));
                        System.out.println(list);
                }//end of main
        }
        //end of class
```

LinkedList:

```
//import statement
import java.util.*;

public class LinkedListExample
{
    public static void main(String [ ] args)
    {
        LinkedList actors = new LinkedList( );
        actors.add("John Wayne");
        actors.add(0, "Elizabeth Taylor");
        actors.add("Richard Harris");
        actors.add("Elizabeth Hurley");
        actors.add(1, "Richard Burton");

        System.out.println("\n\nA list of actors");
        System.out.println(actors);
        System.out.println("\n\n adding new actors");

        //Iterator object to loop through List
        ListIterator actorI = actors.listIterator( );
        actorsI.add("Madonna");
        actorsI.next( );
        actorsI.next( );
        actorsI.add("Denzel Washington");
        actorsI.next( );
        actorsI.set(actors.getLast( );
        actorsI.add("Jennifer Lopez");

        System.out.println("\n\nA New list of actors");
        System.out.println(actors);
    }//end of main
}
//end of class
```

Map:

```
//import statement
import java.util.*;

public class MappedStudent
{
    private int id;
    private String name;
    private int phoneNumber;

    MappedStudent(int aId, String aName, int phone)
```

```
    {
        id = aId;
        name = aName;
        phoneNumber = phone;
    }
    public int hashCode( )
    {
        return(id + (phoneNumber * 17));
    }
    public String toString( )
    {
        return("hashcode is: " + hashCode( ) + ": " + id + ":" + name + ":" +
            phoneNumber + "\n");
    }
    public static void main(String [ ] args)
    {
        //create student object
        Map students = new HashMap( );
        MappedStudent bill = new MappedStudent(12345, "Bill Wright",
        2345656);
        Students.put(Integer.toString(bill.id), bill);
        //add student to Map
        //create loop
        int numOfstudents = Console.readInt("How many students?");
        for(int i = 0; i < numOfstudents; ++i)
        {
            MappedStudent astudent = new MappedStudent
                (Console.readInt("Enter student Id: "),
                Console.readLine("Enter StudentName: "),
                Console.readInt("Enter phone number as a number"));
            students.put(Integer.toString(astudent.id), astudent);
        }
        System.out.println("Students stored in Map object");
        System.out.println(students);  //locate student
        System.out.println("\n\n Locate astudent");
        System.out.println(students.get(Console.readLine("Enter a student
          id")));
        System.out.println("\n\n Locate a student");
        System.out.println(students.get(Console.readLine("Enter a student
          id")));
    }//end of main
}//end of class
```

Iterator:

```
//import statement
import java.util.*;

public class MappedStudent
{
    private int id;
    private String name;
    private int phoneNumber;

    MappedStudent(int aId, String aName, int phone)
    {
        id = aId;
```

```
            name = aName;
            phoneNumber = phone;
        }
        public int hashCode( )
        {
            return(id + (phoneNumber * 17));
        }
        public String toString( )
        {
            return("hashcode is: " + hashCode( ) + ": " + id + ":" + name + ":" +
                phoneNumber + "\n");
        }
        public int getPhone()
        {
            return phoneNumber;
        }
        public String getName()
        {
            return name;
        }
    }
    public static void main(String [ ] args)
    {
        Map students = new HashMap( );

        int numOfstudents = Console.readInt("How many students?");
        for(int i = 0; i < numOfstudents; ++i)
        {
            StudentIterator astudent = new StudentIterator
                (Console.readInt("Enter student Id: "),
                 Console.readLine("Enter StudentName: "),
                 Console.readInt("Enter phone number as a number"));
            students.put(Integer.toString(astudent.id), astudent);
        }
        System.out.println("Students stored in Map object");
        System.out.println(students);

        Set entries =students.entrySet();
        Iterator iter =entries.iterator();
        while (iter.hasNext())
         {
            Map.Entry entry =(Map.Entry)iter.next();
            Object Key =entry.getKey();
            StudentIterator astudent =(StudentIterator)students.get(key);
            System.out.println("\n \nPrint the student "+"name and phone numbers");
            System.out.println(astudent.getName()+"-----"+astudent.getPhone());
         }//end of while loop
        }//end of main
}
}//end of class
```

Sorting:

```
//import statement
import java.util.*;

public class ActorList
{
    public static void main(String [ ] args)
```

```
{
   LinkedList actors = new LinkedList( );
   int actors = Console.readInt("How many Actors?");
   for(int i = 0; i < actors; ++i)
   {
       actors.add(Console.readLine("Enter an Actor's name: ");
   }
    Collections.sort(actors);
    System.out.println("\n\nA sorted list of actors");
    System.out.println(actors);

   Collections.reverse(actors);
   System.out.println("\n\nA Sorted list of actors in reverse order");
   System.out.println(actors);

   Collections.shuffle(actors);
   System.out.println("\n\nA shuffled list of  actors");
   System.out.println(actors);

   Collections.sort(actors);
   System.out.println("\n\nAgain a sorted list of actors");
   System.out.println(actors);

   Collections.shuffle(actors);
   System.out.println("\n\nAgain another shuffling of the actors");
   System.out.println(actors);
   }//end of main
}
//end of class
```

Key Terms

array Represents primitives and references to other objects. It is difficult to remove or add elements to an array.

ArrayList A class that implements the `List` interface; can be thought of as a resizable-array.

bag Type of storage that provides for dynamic lists.

collection Like an array, it is a single object that represents a group of objects. Collections can grow or shrink dynamically.

collection interfaces Represent different types of collections, such as sets, lists, and maps. These interfaces (`Collection`, `List`, `Set`, `SortedSet`, `Map`, and `SortedMap`) form the basis of the collections framework.

collections framework Represents a large number of classes and interfaces that provide the programmer with the ability to manage a large number of objects. These classes and interfaces are part of the `java.util` package.

dictionaries Another name for a `Map`.

doubly linked Each object has a link to the next object and a link to the previous object.

elements The objects in a collection.

Enumeration An interface in the `java.util` package that is used to traverse through a collection of key-value maps of the properties of the system.

hash table Each item in the collection consists of a key or identifier and the item. The storage mechanism uses the key-value to locate each item.

HashSet A class that implements the `Set` interface. The collection is unordered and unsorted.

Iterator Provides a basic mechanism for looping through elements of a collection. Only moves forward through the `List`.

key-value pairs Each item in a collection consists of a key or identifier and the item.

LinkedList Each object in the list contains a link or reference to the object before and to the object after the object in the list. The size can change dynamically.

ListIterator Provides support for looping through a list. Can scan both forward and backward through a `List`.

map A collection of arbitrary associations between a key object and a value object. Uses a set of data values to lookup or index stored objects.

multiset   Type of storage that provides for dynamic lists.

ordered   Collection keeps track of determining where to place the object in the collection. A deck of cards would be an ordered collection. This is a `List`.

sequence   Type of storage that provides for dynamic lists.

set   An unordered collection of objects. Duplicates are permitted.

shuffling   Rearranges the elements in a `List` object in some random order.

sorting   The `Collections` class provides a set of static methods for sorting: `Collections.sort()` and `Collections.reverse()`. The `sort()` method can sort the entire `List` object or sort a subset. The `reverse()` method reverses the order of the elements in the `List` object.

system properties   Using `System.getProperty()` method, returns an object that is maintained by the JVM about the host system.

tree   Provides storage for items that are sorted, for example, in ascending order.

TreeSet   A class that is a collection of the type `Set` implementing a Tree storage technology. It implements the `SortedSet` interface. The objects are placed in ascending order, with no duplicates.

unordered   The order of an object is not important in a particular collection. This is a `Set`.

Vector   A class that implements the `List` interface. The dimension of a `Vector` includes its capacity and its initial size. `Vector`s can be increased after creation.

Check Your Understanding

1. What is the difference between an array and the classes in the collections framework?

   A. The collection objects can hold references to objects, but an array cannot.

   B. An array is not an object, but the collections are.

   C. The collection object can be sorted, but an array cannot.

   D. The collection objects can change their size, but an array cannot.

2. What statement must be included in the source file if the collection classes are to be used?

   A. `java.awt`

   B. `java.util`

   C. `import java.util.*;`

   D. `import java.awt.*;`

3. Which of the following is a false statement about Collection objects?

   A. A collection object can hold references to many types of objects.

   B. A collection object can hold primitive values if they are stored in a `wrapper` class.

   C. A collection object can hold a reference only to objects of type `Object`.

   D. A collection object can change its size dynamically.

4. Which of the following is not one of the four basic storage technologies available in the Java language?

   A. Array

   B. Linked tree

   C. Tree

   D. Hash table

5. Which term is not used to describe elements in a tree?

   A. Branch

   B. Parent

   C. Child

   D. Root

6. Which storage technology uses a key-value pair?

   A. Array

   B. Hash table

   C. Linked-list

   D. Tree

7. Which of these is one of the four properties of Collection Objects?

   A. Sorted

   B. Allows duplicates

   C. Uses keys

   D. All of the above

8. Which of the following is a true statement about a STACK?

   A. A stack uses a FIFO protocol.

   B. A stack uses a LIFO protocol.

   C. A `Stack` in Java is zero-indexed like an array or `Vector`.

   D. A `Stack` is an extension of the `List` class.

9. Which class can be extended to create a queue?

   A. `List`

   B. `Array`

   C. `Set`

   D. The Java framework does not support the queue structure.

10. Which of the following uses a key-value pair to store elements?

    A. `Set`

    B. `List`

    C. `Map`

    D. `Collection`

11. Which of the following is an interface?

    A. `HashMap`

    B. `Vector`

    C. `TreeMap`

    D. `SortedMap`

12. What is a difference between the `Collection` interface and the `List` interface?

    A. `Collection` supports duplicates, but `List` does not.

    B. `Collection` supports dynamic resizing, but `List` does not.

    C. `List` supports dynamic resizing, but `Collection` does not.

    D. `List` supports an ordered set, but `Collection` does not.

13. Which helper interface can scan elements both forward and backward?

   A. `ListIterator`

   B. `Iterator`

   C. Both `ListIterator` and `Iterator`

   D. Neither `ListIterator` nor `Iterator`

14. What must be included in the source file if a programmer wants to design a class that uses a `ListIterator`?

   A. The class header must include the words **implements** and `ListIterator`.

   B. The class must **import** `java.util` library.

   C. The class must implement all of the abstract methods from the `ListIterator` interface.

   D. All of the above.

15. What interface does the `HashSet` implement?

   A. `HashTable`

   B. `Set`

   C. `SortedSet`

   D. `Tree`

16. What keyword would be used to test if an `Object` is a `String`?

   A. instance

   B. volatile

   C. instanceof

   D. extends

17. Which statement correctly extracts the third element in a `Vector`, `v`, and stores it in the `String abc`?

   A. `String abc = v.get(3);`

   B. `String abc = (String)v.get(3);`

   C. `String abc = v.get(2);`

   D. `String abc = (String)v.get(2);`

18. What would occur if a `Vector` contained only four elements, but the user tried to extract the fifth element?

    A. A `VectorIndexOutOfBoundsException` would be thrown.

    B. The `Vector` returns the next closest object.

    C. An `ArrayIndexOutOfBoundsException` would be thrown.

    D. The `Vector` returns a **null** object.

19. What does the `hashvalue()` method return?

    A. The hash value as a `double`

    B. The hash value as an `int`

    C. The hash value as a `String`

    D. The hash value as a `long`

20. What is a list of words from a text document along with the line number on which they appear called?

    A. Concordance

    B. Index

    C. Hash table

    D. Linked-list

Upon completion of this chapter, you will be able to

- Understand threads and multithreading
- Understand the `Thread` class and the `Runnable` interface
- Create and run threads
- Understand the life cycle of a thread
- Manage threads

Threads

Computers can perform operations concurrently. Computers can compile a program, print a file, and receive e-mail messages concurrently. Although concurrency is important, most programming languages do not enable programmers to specify concurrent activities. Instead, programming languages generally provide only a simple set of control structures that enable programmers to perform one action at a time. The next action is performed only after the previous one is finished.

Threads are Java's way of making a single Java Virtual Machine (JVM) perform several computations at the same time. The effect is illusory. In actuality, there is only one JVM and one central processing unit (CPU), but the CPU switches among several threads of execution to give this illusion. Threads provide the programmer with a mechanism for concurrency. Although the computer seems to do several tasks with ease, the running of even the simplest programs in parallel requires that a programmer code special instructions. The Java language provides the Thread and ThreadGroup classes and the Runnable interface to accomplish concurrency.

This chapter covers the use of the Thread class and its methods, the implementation of the Runnable interface, the life cycle of threads, and the writing of thread-safe code.

Threads and Multithreading

Multithreading is a powerful concept that can improve a program's performance considerably. Not every program lends itself to multithreading, though. This section provides a general overview of multithreading and provides a foundation to further explore the specific implementation of this concept with the Java language.

This section primarily addresses threads and multithreading.

Understanding Threads and Multithreading

It is common today for desktop personal computers to be compiling a program, printing a file, and receiving electronic mail messages over a network concurrently. Most programming languages do not enable concurrent programming. Programming languages generally provide only a simple set of control structures. These control structures enable programmers to perform one action at a time and then proceed to the next action after the previous one is finished.

A simplistic view of a computer is that it has a CPU that performs computations, read-only memory (ROM) that contains the program that the CPU executes, and random-access memory (RAM) that holds the data from which the program operates. In this view, only one job is being performed; the CPU handles the data and code for a program sequentially. Only one task is performed in the CPU. The programs in the CPU run as a single set of sequential instructions, beginning with the main method. The JVM creates a single *virtual CPU* for this program. This program is running as a single thread of instructions.

Multithreaded applications deliver their potent power by running many threads concurrently within a single program. From a logical point of view, multithreading means that multiple lines of a single program can be executed at the same time; however, it is not the same as starting a program twice and saying that multiple lines of a program are being executed at the same time. In this case, the operating system is treating the programs as two separate and distinct processes. Under UNIX, forking a process creates a child process with a different address space for both code and data. However, this approach creates a lot of overhead for the operating system, making it a very CPU-intensive operation. By starting a thread instead, an efficient path of execution is created while still sharing the original data area from the parent. The idea of sharing the data area is very beneficial, but it brings up some areas of concern that are discussed later.

The simplicity of creating, configuring, and running threads lets Java programmers devise portable and powerful applets and applications that cannot be made in other third-generation languages. Threads allow any program to perform multiple tasks at once. In an Internet-aware language such as Java, this is a very important tool.

Sometimes a program must do multiple tasks concurrently. For example, a web browser displaying a sports web page runs a Java applet spinning a football in the corner. At the same time, the scrollbar is active so that the web page can be traversed. The web browser is multithreaded, allowing this flexibility. Without multithreading, the browser would be totally preoccupied with spinning the football, and you would never be able to scroll the web page. This chapter describes how to set up multiple threads in a single program so that you can do multiple tasks concurrently.

Java is unique among popular general-purpose programming languages. It makes con-current programming available to the Java applications programmer. The programmer can specify that programs should contain threads of execution. Each thread describes the code and data that will be used to create a virtual CPU. The programmer designates a portion of the program to execute concurrently with other threads. This capability is called multithreading. Multithreading gives the Java programmer powerful capabilities that are not available in most other procedural programming languages, also referred to as single-threaded languages.

If a line is drawn through the code to trace how control moves from statement to state-ment as the program runs, the tracing follows a thread of execution. All programs have at least one thread, as shown in Figure 15-1.

Figure 15-1 Program main Method

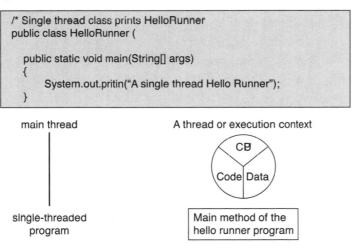

A multithread program allows more than one thread to run through the code at the same time, as shown in Figure 15-2. In a multithreaded program, control of execution is transferred among several threads, each of which is responsible for a different task.

In actuality, the JVM has been running a program in a multithreaded context. For example, the garbage-collection program runs as a separate thread. A program that includes code and data is run in another thread. One of the error messages encountered in early programs was Exception in thread "main" java.lang.NoSuchMethodError: main. This occurred when a class was sent to the interpreter without a main method.

One thread, the main thread, is launched by the JVM when the application runs or by a web browser when it starts an applet. After a single-threaded program starts, it has sole control of the process in which it runs until it ends.

Figure 15-2 Program `main` Menu

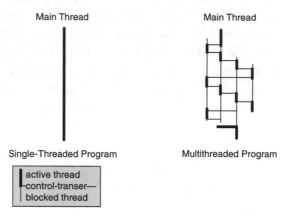

Java's garbage collector runs as a thread. When Java determines that there are no longer any references to an object, it marks the object for eventual garbage collection. The garbage-collector thread runs when processor time is available and when there are no higher-priority, runnable threads. The garbage collector runs immediately when the system is out of memory.

Writing multithreaded programs can be tricky. To see why multithreading can be difficult to program and understand, try the following experiment: Refer to Figure 15-3 and try reading the paragraphs concurrently. Read a few words from the first paragraph, then read a few words from the second paragraph, and then read a few words from the third paragraph. Now loop back and read the next few words from the first paragraph, and so on, while maintaining an understanding of each paragraph independently. After a brief time, you will rapidly appreciate the challenges of multithreading. A simulation of this experiment can be automated with multithreading as long as the programmer correctly defines the logic to drive the program.

For Figure 15-3, you can view an activity that demonstrates the challenges of trying to read three books at the same time by accessing the full, interactive graphic for this figure on the book's accompanying CD-ROM. The title of the activity is "Reading Three Books at the Same Time" in e-Lab Activities.

Figure 15-3 Reading Three Books at the Same Time

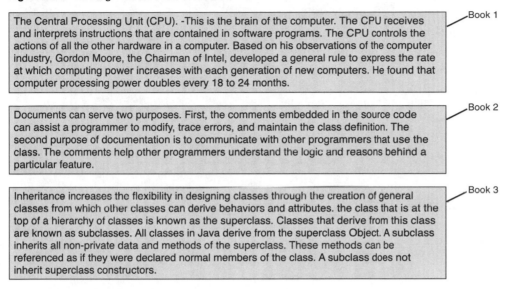

The Central Processing Unit (CPU). -This is the brain of the computer. The CPU receives and interprets instructions that are contained in software programs. The CPU controls the actions of all the other hardware in a computer. Based on his observations of the computer industry, Gordon Moore, the Chairman of Intel, developed a general rule to express the rate at which computing power increases with each generation of new computers. He found that computer processing power doubles every 18 to 24 months.

Documents can serve two purposes. First, the comments embedded in the source code can assist a programmer to modify, trace errors, and maintain the class definition. The second purpose of documentation is to communicate with other programmers that use the class. The comments help other programmers understand the logic and reasons behind a particular feature.

Inheritance increases the flexibility in designing classes through the creation of general classes from which other classes can derive behaviors and attributes. the class that is at the top of a hierarchy of classes is known as the superclass. Classes that derive from this class are known as subclasses. All classes in Java derive from the superclass Object. A subclass inherits all non-private data and methods of the superclass. These methods can be referenced as if they were declared normal members of the class. A subclass does not inherit superclass constructors.

In this module, a thread, or execution context, is considered to be the encapsulation of a virtual CPU with its own program code and data. The class java.lang.Thread enables you to create and control threads. This chapter uses the term *Thread* when referring to the class java.lang.Thread and *thread* when referring to an execution context or the virtual CPU. The three parts of a thread are shown in Figure 15-4. They are the virtual CPU, the code that the CPU is executing, and the data on which the code is working.

Figure 15-4 Three Parts of a Thread

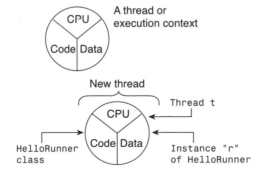

Multiple threads, independent of data, can share code. Two threads share the same code when they execute code from instances of the same class. Likewise, multiple threads, independent of code, can share data. Two threads share the same data when they share access to a common object. In Figure 15-5, thread() and thread2() contain a reference to a common object.

Figure 15-5 Threads Sharing Code and Data

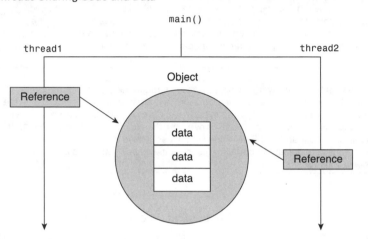

Multiprocessing

Although a virtual CPU is the execution context of a thread, the actual CPU of the computer is the hardware that makes the computer work. The computer has only one CPU. Some computer manufacturers provide more than one CPU for the computer; these are known as *multiprocessing computers*. Most desktop computers consist of a single CPU, however. A thread is the creation of a virtual CPU process, providing a separate context for executing method instructions from the main method, which launches the program. The main method is a single thread that is launched by the JVM. Thus, at the very least, a Java program has at least one thread executing. In the background, the JVM also launches the garbage-collection thread.

Regardless of whether the Java program is running on a single CPU or on a multiple-CPU computer, the computer's operating system handles allocation of time and access to the actual CPU. Although Java is the most portable programming language, certain portions of the language are platform dependent. Some of the operating systems that implement the JVM assign different priorities to threads. The methods used also are known as time-slicing and pre-emption.

The Java platform runs a thread of a given *priority* to completion or until a higher-priority thread becomes ready. At that point, pre-emption occurs. During *pre-emption*, the processor is given to the higher-priority thread while the previously running thread must wait. In the 32-bit Java implementations for Windows 95 and Windows NT, threads are time-sliced. *Time-slicing* means that each thread is given a limited amount of time (called a *time quantum*) to execute on a processor. When that time expires, the thread is made to wait while all other threads of equal priority get their chances to use their quantum in round-robin fashion. Then, the original thread resumes execution. Thus, on Windows 95 and Windows NT, a thread of equal priority can pre-empt a running thread. On the Solaris implementation, a higher-priority thread can pre-empt only a running Java thread. Solaris Java systems currently perform time-slicing and are expected to continue to do so in the future.

The `Thread` Class and the `Runnable` Interface

Now that the concept of multithreading has been explored, the next section introduces a class and an interface that are used to implement threads with Java. The `Thread` class and the `Runnable` interface both can be used to create multithreaded applications.

This section consists of the following topics:

- Thread class
- Runnable interface
- Thread class methods

Thread Class

In the Java language, the virtual CPU that is created to manage a thread is an instance of the `java.lang.Thread` class. In other words, a `Thread` object is a virtual CPU that runs code and uses data. More than one `Thread` object can share the code and data.

Example 15-1 describes the syntax for some of the constructors of the `Thread` class. When a `Thread` object is constructed, the object passed to its constructor specifies the code and the data that define its context. The argument to the first constructor is a reference to an object that **implements** the `Runnable` interface. The argument to the second constructor is a `String` that defines the name for the thread. A `Thread` object is created with that name. The null constructor for this class constructs a `Thread` whose name is `Thread-` linked sequentially with a number, such as `Thread-1`, `Thread-2`, and so on. The fourth constructor creates a `Thread` object with a name and runs the code in the `Runnable` object referenced in the first argument.

NOTE

Java's creators graciously have designed two ways of creating threads: implementing an interface and extending a class. Extending a class is the way Java inherits methods and variables from a parent class. In this case, you can extend or inherit only from a single parent class. This limitation within Java can be overcome by implementing interfaces, which is the most common way to create threads. (Note that the act of inheriting merely allows the class to be run as a thread. It is up to the class to `start()` execution and so on.)

Example 15-1 *Constructors for the* Thread *Class*

```
public Thread (Runnable target)

public Thread (String name)

public Thread ()

public Thread (Runnable target, String name)
```

Runnable Interface

Any class whose instances are intended to be executed by a thread can extend the Thread class or implement the Runnable interface. The class implementing a Runnable interface must define a method of no arguments called run. A class that **implements** Runnable can run without subclassing Thread by instantiating a Thread object and passing a reference to itself as the argument for the constructor. In most cases, the Runnable interface should be used if you are planning to override only the run() method and no other Thread methods. This is important because classes should not be subclassed unless the programmer intends to modify or enhance the fundamental behavior of the class. The documentation for the run method of the Runnable class is shown in Figure 15-6.

Figure 15-6 Runnable and Its Methods

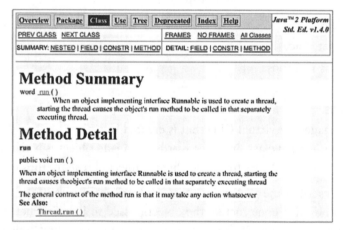

Thread Class Methods

Some of the methods of the Thread class are described in Figure 15-7. A thread starts with the start() method. This calls the run() method of the thread or the object implementing Runnable. The API docs should be referenced for a complete listing of all the Thread methods.

Figure 15-7 Thread Class and Its Methods

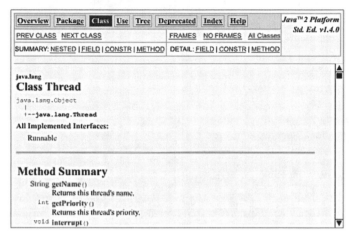

For Figure 15-7, you can view more of the methods by accessing the full, interactive graphic for this figure on the book's accompanying CD-ROM. The title of the activity is "Thread Class and Its Methods" in e-Lab Activities.

Creating and Running Threads

Programmers have much flexibility when creating threads. Using the Thread class and the Runnable interface, a programmer can choose from among several options, depending on the business rules of the application.

This section consists of the following topics:

- Using the run() method
- Running threads

The run() Method

Thread objects run code that is defined in a run() method of an object. The *run() method* can be that of an object that **implements** the Runnable interface or a Thread object that overrides the run() method. A thread can be created and executed in several ways.

One way is to create a thread in a class and pass it a reference to an object that implements Runnable, as shown in Examples 15-2 and 15-3.

Example 15-2 *Several Ways to Create a Thread*—MyThreads

```
1 /**
2 * Java Program: MyThreads.java
3 * @author Cisco Teacher
4 * @version 2002
5 */
6
7 // Thread and a Runnable object
8
9 public class MyThreads
10 {
11     public static void main(String[] args)
12     {
13         Runnable r = new RunsMyCode();
14         // creates an instance of a class that implements Runnable
15         Thread t1 = new Thread(r) ;
16         // passes the reference to the Runnable object r to Thread
17         // constructor
18         // code to start and manage the thread t1
19     }
20 } // end of class
```

Example 15-3 *Several Ways to Create a Thread*—RunsMyCode

```
1 /**
2 * Java Program: RunsMyCode.java
3 * @author Cisco Teacher
4 * @version 2002
5 */
6
7 public class RunsMyCode implements Runnable
8 {
9     public void run()    // implements the run method
10     {
11         // does something
12     }
13 } // end of class
```

A second way is to extend from Thread. The class in Example 15-4 is a subclass of Thread and overrides the run() method to implement the code that needs to be run in the thread.

Example 15-4 *Several Ways to Create a Thread*

```
 1 /**
 2  * Java Program: MyThread.java
 3  * @author Cisco Teacher
 4  * @version 2002
 5  */
 6
 7 // Thread object overrides run() method
 8
 9 public class MyThread extends Thread
10 {
11     public void run() // Implements the run method
12     {
13         // does something
14     }
15
16     public static void main(String[] args)
17     {
18         MyThread t1 = new MyThread();
19         // starts the thread and runs the code
20     }
21 } // end of class
```

A third way to create a thread is to extend from Thread and create an instance of the subclass, passing a reference to a Runnable object in the constructor. Examples 15-5 and 15-6 show this method of thread creation.

Example 15-5 *Several Ways to Create a Thread—MyThread*

```
 1 /**
 2  * Java Program: MyThread.java
 3  * @author Cisco Teacher
 4  * @version 2002
```

continues

NOTE

The full version of the abbreviated code shown in this example can be viewed using the book's accompanying CD-ROM.

Example 15-5 *Several Ways to Create a Thread—*MyThread *(Continued)*

```
5  */
6
7  // Thread and a Runnable object
8
9  public class MyThread extends Thread
10 {
11     public MyThread(Runnable r)
12     {
13         super(r);
14     }
15
16     public static void main(String[] args)
17     {
18         Runnable r = new RunsMyCode();
19         // creates an instance of a class that implements Runnable
20         MyThread t1 = new MyThread(r);
```

Example 15-6 *Several Ways to Create a Thread—*RunsMyCode

```
1  /**
2   * Java Program: RunsMyCode.java
3   * @author Cisco Teacher
4   * @version 2002
5   */
6
7  public class RunsMyCode implements Runnable
8  {
9      public void run()   // implements the run method
10     {
11         // does something
12     }
13 } // end of class
```

Running Threads

A newly created thread does not start running automatically. Its start method must be called. A program launches a thread's execution by calling the thread's start method, which, in turn, calls the run method. After the start method launches the thread, it returns to its caller immediately. The caller then executes concurrently with the launched thread. The `start` method throws an `IllegalThreadStateException` if the thread it is trying to start already has been started.

Calling the `start` method places the virtual CPU embodied in the thread into a runnable state, meaning that it becomes viable for scheduling for execution by the JVM. This does not necessarily mean that the thread runs immediately.

In Examples 15-7 and 15-8, two `Thread` classes are defined: `LovesMeThread` and `LovesMeNotThread`. The two threads are instantiated and started in the class `LoveQuestion`, shown in Example 15-9. Each thread is started using the `start()` method. When the `start()` method is called, the threads are placed in a runnable state and are ready for scheduling.

Example 15-7 *Example Thread*—LovesMeThread

```
1 /**
2  * Java Program: LovesMeThread.java
3  * @author Cisco Teacher
4  * @version 2002
5  */
6
7 public class LovesMeThread extends Thread implements Runnable
8 {
9     public void run()
10    {
11        for(int x = 0; x < 100; ++x)
12        System.out.print("Loves Me");
13    }
14 } // end of class
```

Example 15-8 *Example Thread*—LovesMeNotThread

```
1 /**
2  * Java Program: LovesMeNotThread.java
3  * @author Cisco Teacher
4  * @version 2002
5  */
6
7 public class LovesMeNotThread extends Thread
```

continues

Example 15-8 *Example Thread—*LovesMeNotThread *(Continued)*

```
 8 {
 9     public void run()
10     {
11         for(int x = 0; x < 100; ++x)
12         System.out.print("Loves Me Not");
13     }
14 } // end of class
```

Example 15-9 *Example Thread—*LoveQuestion

```
 1 /**
 2  * Java Program: LoveQuestion.java
 3  * @author Cisco Teacher
 4  * @version 2002
 5  */
 6
 7 public class LoveQuestion
 8 {
 9     public static void main(String[] args)
10     {
11         LovesMeThread a = new LovesMeThread();
12         LovesMeNotThread b = new LovesMeNotThread();
13         a.start();
14         b.start();
15     }
16 } // end of class
```

The Life Cycle of a Thread

Each thread that is created passes through several stages of a life cycle. The behavior of a thread at any given time depends on the current state of that thread. This section describes how multiple threads interact and the effects of the thread life cycle on these interactions.

This section primarily address thread states.

Thread States

At any time, a thread is said to be in one of several thread states. A thread that was just created by a constructor is in the *born state*. The thread remains in this state until the thread's start method is called. This causes the thread to enter the ready state, also known as the *runnable state*. The highest-priority ready thread enters the running state when the system assigns a processor to the thread—that is, the thread begins executing. A thread enters the *dead state* when its run method completes or terminates for any reason. The system eventually disposes of a dead thread. Although the thread becomes runnable, it does not necessarily start running immediately. Only one action at a time is performed on a machine with one CPU. All threads that are runnable are kept in temporary storage, called *pools*, according to priority.

When a thread starts running, it can enter the *blocked state* before its run method is completed. A blocked thread cannot use a processor even if one is available. One common way for a running thread to enter the blocked state is for the thread to issue an input/output (I/O) request. In this case, the blocked thread becomes ready when the I/O operation that it is waiting for is finished. Another way that a running thread can cease to be runnable is to have the thread's code execute a Thread.sleep() call, deliberately asking the thread to pause for a fixed period of time. The thread might have to wait to access a resource and cannot continue until that resource becomes available.

More Information

The blocked state is entered when one of the following events occurs:

- The thread itself or another thread calls the suspend() method.
- The thread calls an object's wait() method.
- The thread itself calls the sleep() method.
- The thread is waiting for some I/O operation to complete.
- The thread will join() with another thread.

A thread in a blocked state will not be scheduled for running. It goes back to the runnable state, competing for CPU cycles, when the counter-event for the blocking event occurs. The instances in which a thread returns to the runnable state are as follows:

- If a thread is suspended, another thread calls its resume() method.
- If the thread is blocked by calling an object's wait() method, the object's notify() or notifyAll() method is called.
- If the thread is put to sleep, the specified sleep time elapses.
- If the thread is blocked on I/O, the specified I/O operation completes.

The methods of the Thread class, including wait, sleep, notify, notifyAll, and join, are explored in a later section of this chapter.

When a thread has finished executing all the code in the run() method of the Runnable object, the thread is dead.

Figure 15-8 shows the possible states of a thread.

Figure 15-8 Thread Life Cycle

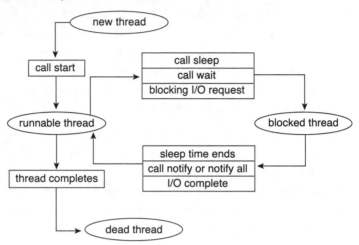

Managing Threads

The introduction of multiple threads in an application requires careful management to ensure that the highest level of integrity is maintained. Programmers must carefully monitor and understand the effects of multithreading.

This section consists of the following topics:

- Blocked state
- Thread scheduling
- How to stop threads
- Synchronization and deadlocks
- Communication between threads
- Table of Thread control methods

Blocked State

Threads can be placed in a blocked state to allow other threads to run or to wait for resources to become available. The programmer can use several methods of the Thread class to place threads in a blocked state, assign threads a priority, or notify other threads when it is done. When a blocked thread becomes runnable, it is placed back into the appropriate runnable pool. Threads from the highest-priority nonempty pool are given CPU time.

Thread sleep()

Given that Java threads are not necessarily time-sliced, a programmer must ensure that the code for the threads gives other threads a chance to execute from time to time. This can be achieved by issuing the sleep call at various intervals. A call to the *sleep()* *method* suspends the thread. The thread of the Runner class displayed in Example 15-10 appears to have executed an instruction very slowly.

Example 15-10 *Setting a Thread to Sleep*

```
1 /**
2  * Java Program: Runnable.java
3  * @author Cisco Teacher
4  * @version 2002
5  */
6
7 public class Runner implements Runnable
8 {
9     public void run()
10    {
11        while (true)
12        {
13            // do lots of interesting stuff
14
15 // Give other threads a chance
16            try
17            {
18                Thread.sleep(10);
19            } catch (InterruptedException e) {
20                // This thread's sleep was interrupted
```

NOTE

The full version of the abbreviated code shown in this example can be viewed using the book's accompanying CD-ROM.

The Thread class also contains a static method named sleep. Because this method operates on the current thread, it is referred to as Thread.sleep. When a sleep method is called in a running thread, that thread enters the sleeping state. A sleeping thread becomes ready after the designated sleep time expires, unless it is interrupted; in that case, the sleeping thread throws an InterruptedException. A sleeping thread cannot use a processor even if one is available. The static method `sleep` is called with an argument specifying how long, in milliseconds, the currently executing thread should sleep. While a thread sleeps, it does not contend for the processor, so other threads can execute. This can give lower-priority threads a chance to run.

The code in the figure shows how the **try** and **catch** blocks are used. `Thread.sleep()` and other methods that can pause a thread for periods of time are interruptible. Threads can call another thread's `interrupt` method, which signals the paused thread with an `InterruptedException`.

Thread join()

The *join method* causes the current thread to wait until the thread on which the `join` method is called terminates. The `join` method also can be called with a timeout value in milliseconds—for example, **void** `join(`**long** `timeout)`. The `join` method suspends the current thread either for `timeout` in milliseconds or until the thread it calls on terminates.

In Example 15-11, the `main` thread is joining the `timer` thread. The `join` method is invoked in a **try/catch** block. When the `join` method is called, the thread calling the `join` method (in this case, the `main` thread) is placed in a block state. If the thread it was trying to join is completed, an `InterruptedException` is thrown and the code in the exception block is executed.

Example 15-11 Thread join()

```
1 /**
2  * Java Program: JoinDemo.java
3  * @author Cisco Teacher
4  * @version 2002
5  */
6 public class JoinDemo
7 {
8     public static void main(String[] args)
9     {
10        Thread t = new Thread(new Runner(),"timer"); // timer thread
11        t.start();
12        // Do stuff in parallel with the other thread for a while
13        // Wait here for the timer thread to finish
14        try
```

Example 15-11 Thread join() *(Continued)*

```
15          {
16              t.join();
17          } catch (InterruptedException e) {
18              // t came back early and is completed
19          }
20          // Now continue in this thread
21      }
22  } // end of class
23
```

Thread interrupt()

The *interrupt method* is called to interrupt a thread. The static method interrupted returns **true** if the current thread has been interrupted and **false** otherwise. The method isInterrupted, a nonstatic method, is called to determine whether a specific thread has been interrupted. The method isAlive returns **true** if start has been called for a given thread and the thread is not dead—that is, its controlling run method has not completed execution.

Thread yield()

The *yield() method* gives other threads of the same priority a chance to execute. If other threads at the same priority are runnable, yield places the calling thread into the runnable pool and allows another thread to run. If no other threads are runnable at the same priority, yield does nothing. A sleep call gives threads of lower priority a chance to execute. The yield method gives only threads of the same priority a chance to execute.

Thread Scheduling

Within a particular piece of code, a reference to the current thread can be obtained using the static Thread method currentThread. Example 15-12 shows the use of the getName() method.

Example 15-12 *Code* Thread *Method* getName()

```
1  /**
2   * Java Program: NameRunner.java
3   * @author Cisco Teacher
```

continues

Example 15-12 *Code* `Thread` *Method* `getName()` *(Continued)*

```
 4  * @version 2002
 5  */
 6
 7 public class NameRunner implements Runnable
 8 {
 9     public void run()
10     {
11         while (true)
12         {
13             // lots of interesting stuff
14
15             // Print name of the current thread
16             System.out.println("Thread " +
17     Thread.currentThread().getName() + " completed");
18         }
19     }
20 } // end of class
```

A thread can be in an unknown state. Use the method `isAlive` to determine whether a thread is still viable. Alive does not imply that the thread is running. The `isAlive` method returns **true** for a thread that has been started but has not completed its task.

A programmer cannot control the schedule for a thread, but can assign a priority to a thread. The JVM schedules threads of the same priority. Other method calls can be used to yield to a thread of the same or higher priority. Use the `getPriority` method to determine the current priority of the thread. Use the `setPriority` method to set the priority of the thread. The priority is an integer value. The `Thread` class includes the following constants:

- `Thread.MIN_PRIORITY`
- `Thread.NORM_PRIORITY`
- `Thread.MAX_PRIORITY`

Figure 15-9 shows the `Thread` class's field summary for each of these constants. Note that the integer values for `MIN_PRIORITY`, `NORM_PRIORITY`, and `MAX_PRIORITY` are `1`, `5`, and `10`, respectively.

Figure 15-9 Thread Priorities

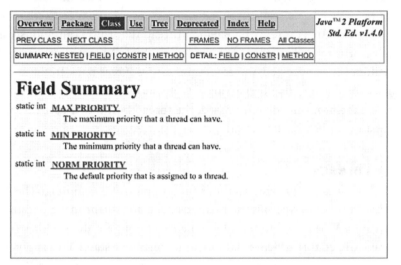

The scheduler can be of two flavors, pre-emptive or non–pre-emptive. Pre-emptive schedulers give a certain time-slice to all threads running on the system. The scheduler decides which thread is next to run and resumes that thread for some constant period of time. When the thread has executed for that time period, it is suspended and the next thread scheduled is resumed. Non–pre-emptive schedulers decide which thread should run and then run it until the thread is complete. The thread has full control of the system for as long as it likes. The `yield()` method is a way for a thread to force the scheduler to start executing another waiting thread. Depending on the system that Java is running on, the scheduler can be either pre-emptive or non–pre-emptive.

Daemon threads sometimes are called "service" threads that normally run at a low priority and provide a basic service to a program or programs when activity on a machine is reduced. An example of a daemon thread that runs continuously is the garbage-collector thread. This thread, provided by the JVM, scans programs for variables that will never be accessed and frees up their resources back to the system. A thread can set the daemon flag by passing a **true boolean** value to the setDaemon() method. If a **false boolean** value is passed, the thread becomes a user thread. However, this must occur before the thread has been started.

Stopping Threads

The Thread class does not provide methods for stopping and resuming. These methods were available in older JVMs, but the methods *stop* and *suspend* were found to be inherently unsafe. When used to terminate the execution of a thread, these methods can make the stopped thread leave data in an inconsistent state. This is potentially problematic if that data is accessed concurrently by more than one thread. The resume method is deprecated because, without suspend, there is never a need to call it.

When a thread completes execution and terminates, it cannot run again. Stop a thread by using a flag that indicates that the run method should exit. The code shown in Examples 15-13 and 15-14 illustrates the use of flags to stop a thread. Flags are created using a **boolean** variable that is set to **true** when the thread should run and **false** when it should be stopped. Here a stopRunning() method in the Runnable class is used to set a flag variable to **false**. The stopRunning() method is called specifically in the stopThread() method of the ThreadController class.

Example 15-13 *Stopping a Thread*—StopThread

```
 1 public class StopThread implements Runnable {
 2
 3   private boolean timeToQuit=false;
 4
 5   public void run() {
 6     while ( ! timeToQuit ) {
 7
 8     }
 9     // clean up before run() ends
10   }
11
```

Example 15-13 *Stopping a Thread*—StopThread

```
12    public void stopRunning() {
13       timeToQuit=true;
14    }
15 }
16
```

Example 15-14 *Stopping a Thread*—ThreadController

```
 1 /** * Java Program: ThreadController.java
 2 * @author Cisco Teacher
 3 * @version 2002
 4 */
 5
 6 public class ThreadController
 7 {
 8    private StopThread r = new StopThread();
 9    private Thread t = new Thread(r);
10
11    public void startThread()
12    {
13    t.start();
14    }
15
16    public void stopThread()
17    {
18       // use specific instance of Runner
19       r.stopRunning();
20    }
21 } // end of class
```

The following steps illustrate the recommended way to make all threads stop:

Step 1   Define an instance variable in the thread's class that acts as a flag indicating whether it is time to stop.

Step 2   Make sure that the variable itself is not affected by concurrent access from other threads.

Step 3   In the thread, check the value of the variable frequently.

Step 4   Return from the run method as soon as possible when the flag indicates that the thread should stop.

Synchronization and Deadlocks

Threads can be created to share the same data and code. When several threads share the same code, data, or both, the programmer must be sure that the data being used by one thread is not being modified by another thread, before completing the task. For example, consider a checking account shared by two customers, Mary and John. The beginning balance is $500. Mary makes a withdrawal of $100 at the same moment that John deposits $200. The balance shown to John is $600 instead of $700. Although having the two customers share an account is ideal, when one customer is using the account, the other has to wait or be locked out of it. Java provides a mechanism to synchronize code and data. Using this mechanism, the programmer can ensure that the class runs in thread-safe context.

More Information

An important OS-level concept to understand is atomicity. An atomic operation cannot be interrupted by another thread. Java does define at least a few atomic operations. In particular, assignment to variables of any type except **long** or **double** is guaranteed to be atomic, but on a given platform, **long** and **double** assignments might be atomic as well. You don't have to worry about a thread pre-empting a method in the middle of the assignment. In practice, this means that you never have to synchronize a method that does nothing but return the value of (or assign a value to) a **boolean** or **int** instance variable. Similarly, a method that does a lot of computation using only local variables and arguments, and which assigned the results of that computation to an instance variable as the last thing it did, would not have to be **synchronized**, as illustrated in Example 15-15.

Example 15-15 *Atomicity and the Need to Use* **synchronized**

```
class some_class
{
    int some_field;

    void f( some_class arg ) // deliberately not synchronized
    {
        // Do lots of stuff here that uses local variables
        // and method arguments, but does not access
        // any fields of the class (or call any methods
        // that access any fields of the class).
```

Example 15-15 *Atomicity and the Need to Use* **synchronized** *(Continued)*

```
        // ...

        some_field = new_value; // do this last.
    }
}
```

In Java, every object has an object lock associated with it, as shown in Figure 15-10. The keyword **synchronized** enables interaction with this lock and allows exclusive access to code that affects shared data.

Figure 15-10 Lock on an Object

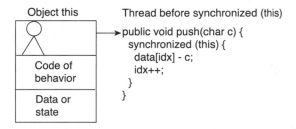

When the thread reaches the **synchronized** statement, it examines the object passed as the argument and tries to obtain the lock flag from that object before continuing. This behavior is shown in Figure 15-11.

What happens if the **synchronized** statement protects an object and another thread tries to execute the method of the object while the original thread holds the lock flag of the **synchronized** object? This scenario is displayed in Figure 15-12. When the thread tries to execute the **synchronized**(this) statement, it tries to take the lock flag from the object referenced by this. Because the flag is not present, the thread cannot continue execution. The thread then joins a pool of waiting threads that are associated with that object's lock flag. When the flag is returned to the object, a thread that was waiting for the flag is given it, and the thread continues to run.

Figure 15-11 Obtaining a Lock

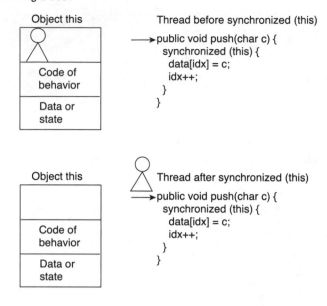

Figure 15-12 Blocked State Waiting for a Lock

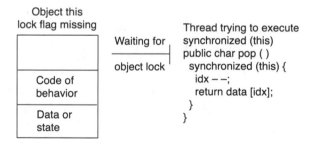

A thread waiting for the lock flag of an object cannot resume running until the flag is available. Therefore, it is important for the holding thread to return the flag when it no longer is needed. The lock flag is given back to its object automatically. When the thread that holds the lock passes the end of the **synchronized** code block for which the lock was obtained, the lock is released. Java technology ensures that the lock always is returned automatically, even if an encountered exception or **break** statement transfers code execution out of a **synchronized** block. Also, if a thread executes nested blocks of code that are **synchronized** on the same object, the object's flag is released correctly upon exit from the outermost block, and the innermost block is ignored. These rules make using **synchronized** blocks much simpler to manage than using equivalent facilities in some other systems.

Two kinds of locks exist. Object locks apply to instance methods. Class locks apply to all the class methods. The locks do not have to be operated on explicitly. The **synchronized** keyword tells the JVM that the method requires a lock to run.

The **synchronized** mechanism works only if all access to delicate data occurs within the **synchronized** blocks. Mark delicate data protected by **synchronized** blocks as **private**. Consider the accessibility of the data items that form the delicate parts of the object. If these are not marked as **private**, they can be accessed from code outside the class definition. Therefore, other programmers must not omit the protections that are required.

Synchronization is a special thread state. Figure 15-13 shows the state of a thread when synchronization is used.

Figure 15-13 Thread State When Locks Are Used

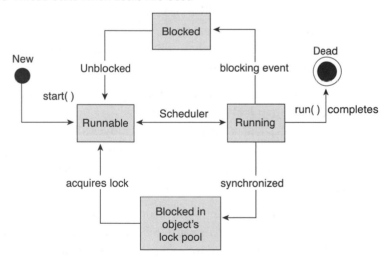

Deadlock can occur when all threads are in a blocked state. Java provides no automatic way of detecting and resolving deadlock. Java technology neither detects nor attempts to avoid this condition. It is the programmer's responsibility to ensure that a deadlock cannot arise. Programmers should remember a general rule for avoiding deadlock: If a programmer needs **synchronized** access to multiple objects, a global decision must be made regarding the order in which the programmer will obtain those locks; that order then must be adhered to throughout the program. Release the locks in the reverse order that you obtained them.

Communication Between Threads

The `java.lang.Object` class provides the *wait method* and the `notify` method for thread communication. If a thread issues a `wait` call on rendezvous object x, that thread pauses its execution until another thread issues a `notify` call on the same rendezvous object x. For a thread to call either `wait` or `notify` on an object, the thread must have the lock for that particular object. In other words, `wait` and `notify` are called only from within a **synchronized** block on the instance on which they are being called.

When a thread executes **synchronized** code that contains a `wait` call on a particular object, that thread is placed in the wait pool for that object. Additionally, the thread that calls `wait` automatically releases the lock flag. Although the thread running the synchronized code releases the lock on the object, it is possible that the call to `wait()` in the code did not include a call to `notify()` or `notifyAll()`. This situation could cause a deadlock. Deadlock occurs when two threads are waiting for a lock, the lock has been dropped, and the threads have not been explicitly notified that the lock is available. Threads in the waiting state for a lock must be awakened explicitly with a `notify()` or `interrupt()`, or a thread will wait forever. There are versions of the `wait()` method that receive arguments indicating maximum wait time. Using these methods results in a thread becoming ready to execute if it is not notified in the specified amount of time, thus avoiding deadlocks.

When a `notify` call is executed on a particular object, an arbitrary thread is moved from that object's wait pool to a lock pool where threads stay until the lock flag for that object becomes available. The `notifyAll` method moves all threads waiting on that object out of the wait pool and into the lock pool. Only from the lock pool can a thread obtain the lock flag for that object, which allows the thread to continue running where it left off when it called `wait`.

In many systems that implement the `wait`/`notify` mechanism, the thread that wakes up is the one that has been waiting the longest. However, Java does not guarantee this. The `notify` call can be issued without regard to whether any threads are waiting. If the `notify` method is called on an object when no threads are blocked in the wait pool, the call has no effect. The wait pool, shown in Figure 15-14, is also a special thread state. Furthermore, calls to `notify` are not stored.

Figure 15-14 Wait Pool

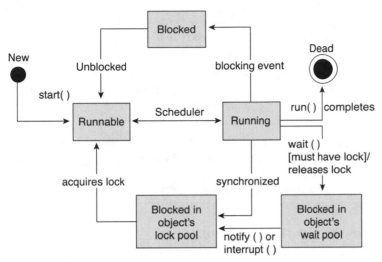

Example 15-16 illustrates the state of thread using wait and notify.

Example 15-16 *Code for Proper Thread Control*

```
1 /**
2  * Java Program: ControlledThread.java
3  * @author Cisco Teacher
4  * @version 2002
5  */
6
7 public class ControlledThread extends Thread
8 {
9     static final int SUSP = 1;
10    static final int STOP = 2;
11    static final int RUN = 0;
12    private int state = RUN;
13
14    /**
15     * @param s An integer
16     */
17    public synchronized void setState(int s)
18    {
19        state = s;
20        if (s == RUN)
```

NOTE

The full version of
the abbreviated code
shown in this example
can be viewed using
the book's accompa-
nying CD-ROM.

> **More Information**
>
> Every Java object instance and class potentially has a monitor associated with it. I say *potentially* because if you don't use any of the synchronization functions, the monitor never actually is allocated; it's waiting there just in case.
>
> A *monitor* is simply a lock that serializes access to an object or a class. To gain access, a thread first acquires the necessary monitor and then proceeds. This happens automatically every time you enter a **synchronized** method. You create a **synchronized** method by specifying the keyword **synchronized** in the method's declaration.
>
> During the execution of a **synchronized** method, the thread holds the monitor for that method's object; if the method is static, it holds the monitor for that method's class. If another thread is executing the **synchronized** method, your thread is blocked until that thread releases the monitor (either by exiting the method or by calling wait()).

Table of Thread Control Methods

Several methods of the Thread class are used to manage and control threads and their interactions. The following list identifies and summarizes some of these methods and describes how they are used with thread management.

- **void** start() **throws** IllegalThreadStateException—Used to start the execution of the thread body defined in the run() method. Program control immediately is returned to the caller, and a new thread is scheduled to execute the run() method concurrently with the caller's thread.

- **void** stop()—Deprecated. Used to stop the execution of the thread, no matter what the thread is doing. The thread then is considered dead, the internal states of the thread are cleared, and the resources allocated are reclaimed. Using this method has the potential to leave data in an inconsistent state and should be avoided.

- **void** suspend()—Deprecated. Used to temporarily stop the execution of the thread. All the states and resources of the thread are retained. The thread later can be restarted by another thread calling the resume() method. Using this method has a strong potential for deadlocks and should be avoided; you should use the Object.wait() method instead.

- **void** resume()—Deprecated. Used to resume the execution of a suspended thread. The suspended thread is to run. If it has higher priority than the running thread, the running thread is pre-empted; otherwise, the thread just resumed waits in queue for its turn to run. Using this method has a strong potential for deadlocks and should be avoided; you should use the Object.notify method instead.

- **static void** sleep(**long** sleepTimeInMilliseconds) **throws** Interrupted-Exception—A class method that causes the caller thread to suspend execution for at least the number of milliseconds provided as the argument. The InterruptedException can be thrown while a thread is sleeping or anytime if you do an interrupt() on it. Either a **try/catch** statement needs to be defined to handle this exception, or it should be declared in the method signature using the **throws** keyword.

- **static void** yield()—This class method temporarily stops the caller's thread and puts it at the end of the queue to wait for another turn to be executed. It is used to make sure that other threads of the same priority have a chance to run.

Summary

Multithreading is a powerful concept that can improve a program's performance considerably. However, not every program lends itself to multithreading. This chapter taught students how to create threads. Techniques for synchronizing threads and communicating between them also were discussed. A class can run as a separate thread if it **extends** the Thread class or **implements** the Runnable interface. Each thread that is created passes through several stages of a life cycle. The behavior of a thread at any given time depends on the current state of that thread. Programming for multithreading ensures that the threads do not interfere with each other or go into deadlock by entering a wait state. Finally, use the methods wait, notify, and notifyAll to provide a way of communicating between threads.

Syntax Summary

Threads:

```
public class MyThreads
{
    public static void main(String [ ] args)
    {
        Runnable r = new RunsMyCode( );
        //create instance which implements Runnable
        Thread t1 = new Thread(r);
        //pass reference to object "r"
        //constructor
        //code for Thread
    }//end of main
}//end of class



public class MyThread extends Thread
{
    public void run( )
    {
        //starts the run() method
        //statements
    }
    public static void main(String [ ] args)
    {
        MyThread t1 = new MyThread( );
        //starts Thread and runs code
    }//end of main
}//end of class



public class MyThread extends Thread
{
    public MyThread (Runnable r)
    {
        super (r);
    }
    public static void main(String [ ] args)
    {
        Runnable r = new RunsMyCode( );
        //create instance
        MyThread t1 = new MyThread(r);
        //pass reference to object "r"
        //constructor
        //code for Thread
    }//end of main
}//end of class
```

Putting a thread to bed:

The following class illustrates how a thread would be in the blocked state indefinitely because the `sleep()` method is called within an infinite loop:

```
public class Runner implements Runnable
{
   public void run( )
   {
      while(true)
      {
         try
         {
            Thread.sleep(10);
         }
         catch (InterruptedException e)
         {

         }//end of try-catch block
      }//end of while loop
   }//end of run()method
}//end of class



Thread join( ):

public class JoinDemo
{
   public static void main(String [ ] args)
   {
      Thread t = new Thread(new Runner( ), "Timer");
      t.start( );

      //statements


      try
      {
         t.join( );
      }
      catch (InterruptedException e)
      {

      }//end of try-catch block
   }//end of main
}
//end of class
```

Key Terms

blocked state A life-cycle state of a thread. A thread in a blocked state is not eligible for processor time.

born state A life-cycle state of a thread. A thread in the born state is one for which the run method has just been called.

daemon thread A low-priority service thread. The JVM will not terminate if any threads are executing unless the thread(s) are daemon threads.

dead state A life-cycle state of a thread. A thread in the dead state has ceased to execute and will be removed by garbage collection.

deadlock A scenario in which all active threads enter the blocked state at the same time.

interrupt() Method of the Thread class that is used to interrupt the execution of a thread. It is useful in preventing deadlocks.

join() Method of the Thread class that is used to cause the current thread to wait until the thread on which the join method is called terminates. The join method also can be called with a timeout value in milliseconds, in which case the join method suspends the current thread either for a time specified in milliseconds or until the thread that it calls on terminates.

monitor A lock that serializes access to an object.

multiprocessing computer Computer with more than one central processing unit.

multithreaded application An application through which there is more than one path of execution.

notify() Method of the Object class that is used in conjunction with the wait method to facilitate communication between threads. When a notify call is executed on a particular object, an arbitrary thread is moved from that object's wait pool to a lock pool, where threads stay until the lock flag for that object becomes available.

pool A collection of runnable threads, organized by priority and kept in temporary storage until CPU time is available.

pre-emption Method used by a CPU to allow multiple threads access. Higher-priority threads are given CPU time as it is available.

priority The classification unit of threads used in determining processing sequence.

resume() Method of the Thread class that is used to move a thread from the blocked state to the runnable state.

run()   Method of the Thread class that contains the code that is executed by a thread.

Runnable   Interface that is provided in the Java language to create thread objects.

runnable state   A life cycle of a thread. A thread in the runnable state is ready for execution.

sleep()   Static method of the Thread class that causes the current thread to enter the blocked state and gives other threads an opportunity to execute.

start()   Method of the Thread class that is used to allow a thread to begin execution. The start method prompts the JVM to call the run method of the thread.

stop()   Deprecated method of the Thread class. Using the stop method to terminate execution of a thread is unsafe because objects can be left in inconsistent states.

suspend()   Deprecated method of the Thread class. Using the suspend method to pause thread execution temporarily is unsafe because its use is prone to deadlocks.

synchronized   A keyword in the Java programming language that, when applied to a method or code block, guarantees that at most one thread at a time executes that code.

Thread   Class provided in the Java language to create multithreaded applications.

time quantum   The amount of time that the current thread is given to execute on the CPU.

time-slicing   Method used by the CPU to allocate time to multiple threads. Each thread is given a certain amount of time to execute.

virtual CPU   Consists of the code and data to be executed by each thread.

wait()   Method of the Object class that is used in conjunction with the notify method to facilitate thread communication. If a thread issues a wait call on rendezvous object x, that thread pauses its execution until another thread issues a notify call on the same rendezvous object x.

yield()   Method of the Thread class that is used to cause a thread to allow another thread access to the CPU.

Check Your Understanding

1. The purpose of threads on a nonmultiprocessing computer is to

    A. Perform a single task on multiple CPUs

    B. Perform a single task on a single CPU

    C. Perform multiple tasks on multiple CPUs

    D. Perform multiple tasks on a single CPU

2. Which of the following is not one of the three parts of a thread?

    A. The virtual CPU

    B. The actual CPU

    C. The code being processed

    D. The data on which the code is working

3. Can multiple threads share code?

    A. Yes, if they execute code from multiple instances of the same class.

    B. Yes, if they execute code from multiple instances of different classes.

    C. Yes, if they execute code from a single instance of a single class.

    D. No, multiple threads cannot share code.

4. What is the difference between two threads running parallel and two threads running concurrently?

    A. Parallel threads run on the same CPU.

    B. Parallel and concurrent threads are the same things.

    C. Parallel threads run on different CPUs

    D. Concurrent threads run on different CPUs.

5. What is the process of giving threads of equal priority the same amount of CPU time before switching to another thread?

    A. Pre-emption

    B. Prioritizing

    C. Time-slicing

    D. Quantum execution

6. How can a thread class be created?

   A. Extend `Runnable`

   B. Implement `Thread`

   C. Override the `start()` method

   D. Implement `Runnable`

7. Which method begins the execution of a thread?

   A. `start()`

   B. `run()`

   C. `main()`

   D. `init()`

8. What happens when the `start()` method of a thread is called?

   A. The thread begins executing immediately.

   B. The thread begins executing only if it is the lowest-priority thread.

   C. The thread is put into a blocked state.

   D. The thread is put into a runnable state.

9. Which of the following is not one of the thread states?

   A. Born state

   B. Determined state

   C. Dead state

   D. Running state

10. What happens to a blocked thread when another thread calls the blocked thread's `resume()` method?

   A. The blocked thread enters the born state.

   B. The blocked thread enters the ready state.

   C. The blocked thread enters the running state.

   D. The blocked thread enters the dead state.

11. Using the following declaration, how would myThread be suspended for 10 seconds? Assume that Runner **extends** the Thread class.

```
Runner myThread = new Runner();
myThread.start();
```

   A. myThread.sleep(10);

   B. myThread.sleep(10000);

   C. Thread.sleep(10000);

   D. Runner.sleep(10000);

12. Which method causes the current thread to complete only when another thread has completed?

   A. wait()

   B. sleep()

   C. notify()

   D. join()

13. Is there a difference between sleep() and yield()?

   A. Yes. sleep() gives threads of the same priority a chance to execute.

   B. No. sleep() and yield() both give threads of the same priority a chance to execute.

   C. Yes. yield() gives threads of a lower priority a chance to execute.

   D. Yes. yield() gives threads of the same priority a chance to execute.

14. Which of the following is not one of the thread priorities?

   A. Thread.MIN_PRIORITY

   B. Thread.MAX_PRIORITY

   C. Thread.SAME_PRIORITY

   D. Thread.NORM_PRIORITY

15. To ensure that an operation is atomic, which keyword should be used?

   A. **native**

   B. **synchronized**

   C. **transient**

   D. **protected**

16. What happens when all threads enter a blocked state at the same time?

    A. Deadlock occurs.

    B. The JVM returns the thread with the highest priority to a runnable state.

    C. The JVM moves the thread with the lowest priority to a dead state.

    D. The JVM kills all blocked threads and then calls the `start()` method of each thread.

17. What two properties of a thread are used to determine an execution schedule?

    A. The priority and the runnable state

    B. The runnable state and the daemon flag

    C. The priority and the daemon flag

    D. The priority and the pre-emption

18. How can a running thread be stopped?

    A. Using the static `stop()` method of the `Thread` class

    B. Using a custom method such as `stopThread()`

    C. Using the overridden `suspend()` method

    D. Using the overridden `stop()` method

19. Which of the following is a true statement about locks?

    A. Three types of locks exist: object locks, class locks, and method locks.

    B. A method declared **transient** tells the JVM that a lock is required to run the method.

    C. A thread waiting for the lock flag runs only after the `releaseLock()` method is called.

    D. A lock is obtained when a **synchronized** method is called.

20. Which two methods are used for thread communication?

    A. `wait()` and `notify()`

    B. `wait()` and `resume()`

    C. `resume()` and `notify()`

    D. `start()` and `run()`

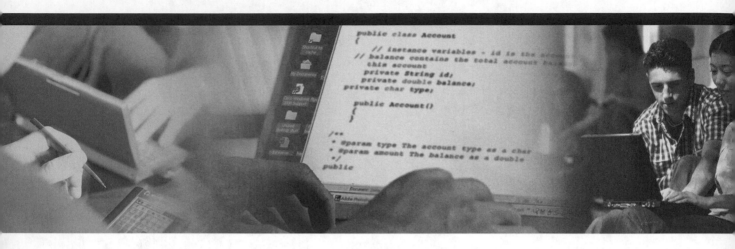

Glossary of Key Terms

<APPLET> </APPLET>   To embed applets in an HTML document, the two sets of tags used are <HTML> </HTML> and <APPLET> </APPLET>. Place the attributes CODE, WIDTH, and HEIGHT inside the applet tag. CODE is the attribute that points to the name of the Java class file. WIDTH is the width of the applet on the screen. HEIGHT is the height of the applet on the screen.

<HTML> </HTML>   To embed applets in an HTML document, the two sets of tags used are <HTML> </HTML> and <APPLET> </APPLET>. The <HTML> tag is always the beginning of an HTML program. The </HTML> tag is the closing tag of an HTML document.

absolute path name   Starting at the root directory, a hierarchical listing of all the directories and subdirectories that end in the location of a file or directory.

abstract   A keyword used in a class definition to specify that a class is not to be instantiated, but rather inherited by other classes. An abstract class can have abstract methods that are not implemented in the abstract class, but in subclasses.

Abstract Window Toolkit (AWT)   The Java platform provides extensive support for programming GUIs through the classes found in the java.awt package.

abstraction   When designing classes, common fields, and behaviors lead to generalizations about the classes. These generalizations can be implemented through the design of parent classes that also are known as superclasses. Superclasses then can be designed to describe required and optional fields and behaviors. A superclass can be an abstract representation of common behaviors and data.

access modifiers   Defines the level of access to the class, data, or method.

access modifiers   Identify different levels of encapsulation. They define the level of access to the class, data, or method.

> *private*   Only methods of the object have access. Access to private data by a method of another class may be available by using one of the class's non-private accessor (getter) methods.
>
> *public*   All classes and objects of the class have access.
>
> *default*   Objects of the class and classes in the same directory or package have access.
>
> *protected*   Subclasses and objects of the class have access.

accessor methods   Are methods to retrieve data for an object.

adapter classes   Abstract classes that implement the methods for a specific listener interface.

add() method   Method that adds other components or containers to each container object.

addXXXListener() method—Method that implements the listener of a particular event. The XXX represents the name of a specific listener.

advertising or declaring exceptions   Just as a method must specify what type and how many arguments it accepts and what is returned, a method must specify the checked exceptions that the method can throw. A method can throw an exception because it includes a call to another method that throws an exception, or because it creates an object of the type Throwable and throws this object using the keyword **throw**. The programmer declares these exceptions by using the keyword word **throws** and then specifying the type of exception.

anonymous inner classes   Using an entire class definition within the scope of an expression.

API Documentation (Application Programming Interface)   The specification of how a programmer writing an application accesses the behavior and state of classes and objects.

API packages   Packages that contain all the classes included with the Java language.

applet   A Java program that typically executes and displays in a web browser but can execute in a variety of other applications or devices that support the applet programming model.

applet security   The following list shows the security actions prevented (by default) for applets accessed over the Internet:

File I/O

Calls to any native methods

Attempts to open a socket to any system except the host that provided the applet

A remotely loaded applet that attempts to perform any of these actions causes exceptions to be thrown, and the applet will fail to load.

`appletviewer`   The Java 2 SDK provides the `appletviewer` utility to test applets.

array length   The fixed number of storage locations (for either primitive values or object references) that the array object will reference. This information is stored in a **final int** variable of the array object labeled `length`.

array of objects   The data in the array object is a sequence of object references, all of which are of the same data type. The array object is referenced through a single variable.

array of primitives   The data in the array object is a sequence of primitive values, all of which are of the same data type. The array object is referenced through a single variable.

array   Represents primitives and references to other objects. It is difficult to remove or add elements to an array.

`ArrayList`   A class that implements the `List` interface; can be thought of as a resizable array.

associative property   Determines whether the operation of the operator is performed left to right or right to left. Arithmetic expressions are performed left to right. Assignment operators are performed right to left.

attributes or data of a class   Describe the state of objects. Attributes are also called data.

attributes   The data that describes an object.

AWT classes   Classes found in the `java.awt` package that enable a programmer to construct graphical user interfaces.

bag   Type of storage that provides for dynamic lists.

behaviors or operations or methods of a class   Describe what objects can do. Behaviors are also called operations or methods.

BigDecimal `class`   Class that implements arbitrary precision floating-point arithmetic.

BigInteger `class`   Class that implements arbitrary precision integer arithmetic.

blocked state   A life-cycle state of a thread. A thread in a blocked state is not eligible for processor time.

BlueJ   Integrated Java environment specifically designed for introductory teaching.

boolean *data type*   A primitive data type that stores a single-bit representation of the values **true** or **false**.

born state   A life-cycle state of a thread. A thread in the born state is one for which the run method has just been called.

bubble sort   Method of comparing two values. If the values are out of order, they are swapped to place them in order.

button   A rounded polygon-shaped figure that a user clicks to initiate an action.

bytecode   Computer object code that is processed by a program, usually referred to as a virtual machine, instead of by the "real" computer machine, the hardware processor. The virtual machine converts each generalized machine instruction into a specific machine instruction or instructions that this computer's processor will understand. A bytecode is the result of compiling source code written in a language that supports this approach.

Calendar class   Class that sets or changes the date for a `Date` object. Part of the `java.util` package.

call stack   The execution stack in memory that represents all the methods that were invoked and that led to the exception. The JVM unwinds the call stack searching for a code block that will handle the exception. If it finds none, the program terminates.

casting and conversion   Process that assigns a value of one data type to a variable of another data type. If the two types are compatible, Java converts it automatically.

catching multiple exceptions   A method can throw more than one type of exception. In this case, these different types of exceptions should be named in the **throws** clause of the method, or the programmer can use multiple **catch** blocks to catch and handle the different types of exceptions.

char *data type*   A primitive data type that stores a single 16-bit Unicode character.

character   A symbol that represents items such as letters and numbers in a particular writing system. For example, lowercase g is a character.

checked exceptions   The compiler enforces exception handling by checking the code to ensure that any known `Exceptions` (but not `Errors`) have been handled or declared in the code. Except for the `RuntimeException` class and its subclasses, the compiler checks all other `Exception` subclasses. These `Exception` subclasses are known as checked exceptions.

class   A blueprint for an object. A class contains the attributes and behaviors of the object it defines.

class data   Also known as static variables. Stored in the class and are available to all objects of a class or objects of other classes if access is permitted.

class definition   Defines the object's behavior and its attributes.

class loading   Process in which the Java interpreter loads a Java class and any class referenced by the class by searching directories specified on the CLASSPATH for the `.class` files.

CLASSPATH variable   An environmental variable that tells the Java Virtual Machine where to find the class libraries, including user-defined class libraries.

collection interfaces   Represent different types of collections, such as sets, lists, and maps. These interfaces (`Collection`, `List`, `Set`, `SortedSet`, `Map`, and `SortedMap`) form the basis of the collections framework.

collection   Like an array, it is a single object that represents a group of objects. Collections can grow or shrink dynamically.

collections framework   Represents a large number of classes and interfaces that provide the programmer with the ability to manage a large number of objects. These classes and interfaces are part of the `java.util` package.

Color   Class within the AWT package. An integer value represents the various colors within the class. The constant colors are red, green, and blue. The integer range is `0` through `255`.

compilation unit   A source file for a java class named with the `.java` extension.

compiler   Program to translate source code into code to be executed by a computer. The Java compiler translates source code written in the Java programming language into bytecode for the Java Virtual Machine.

Component   The abstract class that is at the root of all the classes that create GUI components objects.

components   Objects that display a graphic image and can monitor user interactions with the image.

concatenation   Process of putting together two values (where at least one of the values is a `String`) into a new `String`. When a `String` is concatenated (using the overloaded + operator) with a value that is not a `String`, the latter value is converted to a `String`.

concatenation   Process of using the overloaded + operator, which is also used in adding numeric data, to combine `String` objects.

constructor method   Is a method that defines procedures for how to create an object. It possesses the same name as the class.

constructors   Are methods to construct an object; they define the specifics of object creation.

> *default*   If a constructor is not defined for a class, the Java compiler inserts a constructor in the class definition. This constructor will have the same name as the class, requires no arguments, and will not have any specialized instructions. This type of a constructor is also referred to as the null constructor. All member data are initialized to their default values or to the initialization values that explicitly are assigned in the declaration section of the class or an initializer block.

> *defined*   When a class definition includes an explicit constructor, the compiler will use the constructor. The compiler will not insert a null constructor in the class definition. Member data can be defined in the constructor method.

Container   A subclass of the `Component` class. A `Container` object can hold other components; a group of components can be treated as a single entity.

container   Component that holds other components so that a group of components can be treated as a single entity.

control structure   A standard progression of logical steps to control the execution sequence of statements.

> *sequence*   Actions are performed in sequence or in order until successfully completed.

> *selection*   A program is told which action to perform based upon a certain condition. Two types of selection control are used in Java:
> — *if*-then-**else** structures
> — *case-control* or ***switch*** structures

repetition   Instructs the computer to repeatedly perform a set of actions. This structure is also called looping or iteration (which means "to repeat"). Three repetition structures are available in Java:

— *for* loop

— *while* loop

— *do* loop

current working directory   The location, specified by a period (.), where the compiler will search for .class files to be loaded.

custom methods   Are user-defined methods for performing a particular task.

daemon thread   A low-priority service thread. The JVM will not terminate if any threads are executing unless the thread(s) are daemon threads.

data type   Describes what kind of information a certain attribute is.

DataInputStream   Lets an application read primitive Java data types from an underlying input stream.

DataOutputStream   Lets an application write primitive Java data types to an output stream in a portable way.

Date class   Class that creates a Date object. Part of the java.util package.

DateFormat class   Class that displays the date in different formats. Part of the java.text package. The parse() method of the DateFormat class can be used to convert a date represented in a String object into a Date object. This method requires the declaration of a **throws** ParseException. The format() method of the DateFormat class can be used to convert a Date object into a String object.

dead state   A life-cycle state of a thread. A thread in the dead state has ceased to execute and will be removed by garbage collection.

deadlock   A scenario in which all active threads enter the blocked state at the same time.

Declarations:

> *Variable:*

```
<modifiers> datatype identifier;
```

> *Class:*

```
<modifiers> class Classname
{
// definition
}
```

> *Method:*

```
<modifiers> return-type methodname (<modifier data-type
identifier>, <modifier data-type identifier>, …)
{
// method instructions
}
```

> *Constructor:*

```
<modifiers> Classname (<modifier data-type identifier>,
<modifier data-type identifier>, …)
{
// constructor instructions
}
```

default directory   Location where a source file without an explicit package declaration is saved.

derived methods   Methods inherited from the parent class.

destruction of an object   An object is considered available for garbage collection when the object is out of scope, or all reference variables to the object are reset to **null**. The reference variable(s) still exists within the block of code.

dictionaries   Another name for a Map.

directory   A unit of the file-management structure that specifies a location to store files.

doubly linked   Each object has a link to the next object and a link to the previous object.

dynamic binding or virtual method invocation   A technique of resolving the behaviors of an object at runtime. Also resolves the handling of the arguments being passed to a method.

elements   The objects in a collection.

encapsulation   Packaging an object's attributes into a cohesive unit that can be used as a complete entity. In Java this has a special meaning of hiding information, such that an object's attributes cannot be changed directly by another object.

encapsulation   The process of combining data and methods together in one class.

Enumeration   An interface in the `java.util` package that is used to traverse through a collection of key-value maps of the properties of the system.

err field of the System class   A reference to a `PrintStream` object used to display error messages.

Error and Exception classes   Two subclasses of `Throwable`. `Error` objects represent run-time and system errors. Programmers are not expected to handle these. `Exception` objects are less serious errors that represent unusual conditions that arise while a program is running; they are recoverable. These types of `Throwable` classes are to be handled by the programmer.

event listener   Object that is interested in a particular event.

event-delegation model   Model that Java uses to handle events. It is composed of event source, event objects, and event handlers.

> *event source*   Object that generates an event object.
>
> *event object*   Object describes what action has happened; derived from the `java.awt.AWTEvent` class.
>
> *event handler*   Object that handles the event, performing some task.

event delegation model   Model that Java uses to handle events. It is composed of event source, event objects, and event handlers.

*execution sequence of **try/catch** block*   Execution starts with the **try** block. If successful, it proceeds to the **finally** block before the **return** statement in the **try** block is executed. Any statements after the **finally** block are not executed. If an exception occurs, the code is terminated at the statement that caused the exception. The program moves to the **catch** block matching the exception thrown, and then proceeds to the **finally** block. If the **catch** block has a **return** statement, the **finally** block is executed before the **return** statement.

explicit package declaration   The process of specifying a package to which the class will belong, using a **package** statement as the first statement in the definition.

extends   A keyword used to signify that one class is a subclass of a parent class.

File class   Class used to store information about a file or directory of files, but not the contents of files.

files A file is where data is stored and retrieved. Storing data in files can occur sequentially or through random-access file techniques.

filter stream A high-level stream that filters and formats the data. Filter streams can handle bytes or Unicode characters.

final A keyword used to define an entity once. In inheritance models, when **final** is applied to the methods of a class, it prevents the method from being overridden by any subclass. When applied to a class definition, **final** prevents a class from being used as a superclass.

finalize Method A programmer can insert a custom definition of the `finalize` method to provide a mechanism for cleanup activities, such as closing files or saving certain data to a file, to occur before the relevant object is garbage-collected.

finalizers Methods that perform actions to be completed before objects are discarded by the JVM's garbage collector.

finally block Block that provides the means to clean up code at the end of executing a **try/catch** block. The **finally** block is optional.

fixed size After the array object is created, its length is fixed, or **final**.

font The technology for displaying symbols of the spoken language in different shapes, sizes, and styles.

Frame A subclass of the `Window` class. `Frames` are created so that other objects can be placed in them for display.

Garbage Collection The JVM uses an algorithm to clear memory. Objects that no longer are used and no longer have any references or reference variables storing the addresses are marked for destruction. When the JVM needs memory for new objects, the garbage collector releases the marked objects and cleans them out of memory.

glyph When a particular character has been rendered, a shape now represents this character (glyph).

graphical user interface (GUI) Provides a means for the program to display data and to obtain input from the user.

graphics Text, pictures, images, buttons, and so on.

Graphics The abstract base class for all graphics contexts that allow an application to draw onto components. The method `getGraphics()` of the `Component` class creates a graphics context for a component.

GUI   Graphical user interface. Refers to the techniques involved in using graphics, along with a keyboard and a mouse, to provide an easy-to-use interface to some program.

handling exceptions   Using the **try/catch** block is a method of handling exceptions after declaration. The exception can be rethrown. This is passing the exception up the call stack.

hardware   Physical aspect of computers, telecommunications, and other information technology devices.

hash table   Each item in the collection consists of a key or identifier and the item. The storage mechanism uses the key-value to locate each item.

HashSet   A class that implements the Set interface. The collection is unordered and unsorted.

high-level stream classes   Stream that filters the data, and reads or writes it as Java data types or converts between Java data types and Unicode.

Hypertext Markup Language (HTML)   A special markup language for hypertext documents on the Internet.

Identifiers   Labels assigned to data or storage addresses about an object.

immutability   In the Java language, **final** is used to qualify a class attribute or method as immutable (unchangeable). Data that is fixed or **final** also is referred to as constant data or as constants.

implements   The keyword optionally included in the class declaration to specify any interfaces that are implemented by the current class.

import statement   A statement used at the beginning of a source file that can specify classes or entire packages to be referred to later without including their package names in the reference.

in field of the System class   A reference to an InputStream object, typically used to stream in data from keyboard input or another input source specified by the host environment or user. The read() method of the InputStream object referenced by the in variable can be used to read one character at a time. The data returned from the read() method has an **int** data type; it must be converted to a **char**. The (**char**) cast explicitly requests the conversion of the **int** to the Unicode **char**. The read() method can be used to flush out keystrokes, such as carriage return or new line.

index   The value inside the square brackets, used to access a specific array element. The index value is an **int**.

IndexOutOfBoundsException   Error that occurs when the code references an element of an array for which there is no index. The program then ends.

information hiding   Is achieved by instituting the keyword **private** to enable limited access to data or methods.

inheritance hierarchies   Shows the relationship between classes (superclasses and subclasses).

inheritance   Is when some objects derive attributes and behaviors from other objects.

inheritance   The process of deriving new class definitions from an existing class definition. Defines "is a" relationships among classes and objects.

initialization of the array object   Process done with the **new** operator. The number in the square brackets creates storage for the amount of a particular data type.

initialization block   Two types of initialization blocks exist:

> *static initialization block*   is used to initialize static variables. This block is executed only once at runtime. The other type of initialization is the nonstatic block that is executed for each object created and that initializes instance variables in a class. Nonstatic blocks can initialize both static and nonstatic instance variables.

> *nonstatic initialization block*   is executed for each object created and initializes both static and instance variables.

inner or enclosed classes   Defining a class within another class, either inside or outside a method.

input   Reading of data from a source into the program.-Input of data into a program is provided through the use of classes in the `java.io` package.

InputStream and OutputStream classes   Byte streams have `InputStream` and `Output-Stream` classes at the root of the hierarchy. They are subclasses of the `Object` class.

instance   An object of a particular class. An instance of a class is created using the new operator followed by the class name.

Instance of a Class   An object of a particular class. In programs written in the Java programming language, an instance of a class is created using the new operator followed by the class name.

instance of a class   An object of a particular class. The object is a specific instance of a general class.

integrated development environment (IDE)   Programming environment that has been packaged as an application program, typically consisting of a code editor, a compiler, a debugger, and a graphical user interface (GUI) build.

interfaces   The Java language provides interface classes for implementing inheritance from two unrelated sources. Interface classes contain only constants and abstract methods.

interpreter   Module that alternately decodes and executes every statement in some body of code. The Java interpreter decodes and executes bytecode for the Java Virtual Machine.

`interrupt()`   Method of the `Thread` class that is used to interrupt the execution of a thread. It is useful in preventing deadlocks.

`invalidate()`   Method that marks an applet as outdated when changes have occurred on the applet.

`Iterator`   Provides a basic mechanism for looping through elements of a collection. Only moves forward through the `List`.

jar   Utility included with the Java Development Kit deployment, used to pack several classes into one archive.

Java 2 Software Development Toolkit (Java 2 SDK)   Software Developer's Kit (SDK) is a set of programs used by a computer programmer to write application programs.

Java Data Types   A data type of Java is a classification of a particular form of information. It tells the computer how to interpret and store the data:

> *Primitive*   Data types used to store simple data. Eight types of Java primitives exist: **boolean**, **char**, **byte**, **short**, **int**, **long**, **float**, and **double**. With primitive data types, this means that each variable has a defined amount of storage allocated.

> *Reference*   The complex data types that are not primitive. Variables that store references to object addresses are considered to hold reference data types.

Java programming language   Object-oriented programming language developed at Sun Microsystems, Inc.

Java Syntax Rules   Programming rules established to allow a program to execute properly.

Java Virtual Machine (JVM)   Software "execution engine" that safely and compatibly executes the bytecode in Java class files on a microprocessor (whether in a computer or in another electronic device).

java.io   The classes in the Java language that support the handling of data through streams are part of the java.io package. The package also contains all the classes needed for file processing. Any File class programming must include this package.

java.net   Package that provides the classes for implementing networking applications.

javac   Command used in the Java language to compile a program.

javadoc comments   Start with /** on one line and, after several lines of comments, terminate with */. These comments are designed to be extracted automatically by a program called javadoc, to create HTML (web page–like) documentation for the program. This is an excellent innovation that speeds up the documentation process for Java projects.

join()   Method of the Thread class that is used to cause the current thread to wait until the thread on which the join method is called terminates. The join method also can be called with a timeout value in milliseconds, in which case the join method suspends the current thread either for a time specified in milliseconds or until the thread that it calls on terminates.

key-value pairs   Each item in a collection consists of a key or identifier and the item.

Keywords and Symbols   Elements of a language that represents data and operations of that language. Symbols are used to communicate rules and syntax.

Label   Noncontainer object of the Component class that holds text that can be displayed.

layout manager   Sets the position for displaying each component.

> *BorderLayout*   Breaks up the area into five regions: North, South, East, West, and Center. The layout manager controls the size of each region.
>
> *FlowLayout*   Places components from left to right, top to bottom.
>
> *GridLayout*   Uses a grid of rows and columns. It fills each grid with one component from left to right and top to bottom.

life cycle methods   The painting and repainting of an applet. The life cycle methods are `init()`, `start()`, `stop()`, and `destroy()`. These methods do not have to be written in a program; Java automatically creates them:

> *init()*   The first method used to create an applet. The code for presenting the components is included in this method.

> *start()*   Method that starts the applet program.

> *stop()*   Method that stops the program when completed.

> *paint()*   Method called by the start() method. This method is running when Java displays the applet. It is generated automatically by Java or can be overridden by the programmer.

`LinkedList`   Each object in the list contains a link or reference to the object before and to the object after the object in the list. The size can change dynamically.

`ListIterator`   Provides support for looping through a list. Can scan both forward and backward through a `List`.

low-level stream classes   Stream that reads and writes data as bytes or Unicode characters.

map   A collection of arbitrary associations between a key object and a value object. Uses a set of data values to lookup or index stored objects.

`Math class`   Class that contains static methods to perform mathematical operations.

math package   Package that contains the `BigDecimal` and `BigInteger` classes that are useful for maintaining a high level of precision and manipulating a long sequence of numbers, such as scientific calculations or security codes.

message sending   Objects interact with each other by sending messages. These actions occur in methods. A message is sent to an object using the method signature, which identifies the name of the method and the data defined in the method.

method   A set of instructions that are executed by an object.

method arguments   Is the information that a method requires to perform its task.

method signature   Identifies the name of the method and provides the method with the data.

method syntax   Can be understood in terms of three sections or parts:

- The method identifier elements, which include modifiers, qualifiers, return-type, and name.
- The method arguments, which include data types received by the method defined inside the parentheses ( ).
- The method body defined inside opening and closing braces { }.

When no arguments are used in a method, the syntax is ( ). When defining arguments, the qualifiers for each argument are defined within the ( ).

methods:

instance   Can be accessed only through an object of a class

`main`   The entry point in an application

overloading   Two or more methods defined in the same class and given the same name.

`static`   Require that no objects of the class be created to use these methods. Instance variables and nonstatic methods cannot be directly accessed by static methods of the same class (an instance of the class must be created within the static method to access instance variables and nonstatic methods).

Model View Controller pattern   An object-oriented concept in which the code to display a graphical user interface, the code to respond to user interaction, and the code to define the nature of the program are created separately.

Modifiers   A class, method, or variable definition can include modifiers. Two categories of modifiers exist:

Accessors   Access specifiers define the level of access to the method, variable, or class. The keywords are `private`, `public`, and `protected`. If the access specifier is left blank, the access is defined to be default.

Qualifiers   Qualifiers define the state of the object, variable, or method. The keywords are `static`, `final`, `native`, and `transient`.

monitor   A lock that serializes access to an object.

multidimensional array   An array of arrays. The first set of brackets holds the index reference to the elements of the first dimension of the array. The second set of brackets holds the index reference to the elements of the second dimension.

multiple inheritance   The ability to inherit from more than one class. In the Java language, a capability provided through the use of interfaces.

multiprocessing computer   Computer with more than one central processing unit.

multiset   Type of storage that provides for dynamic lists.

multithreaded application   An application through which there is more than one path of execution.

Mutability   Determines whether an object can or cannot be changed during its lifetime.

mutability of an object   Objects can be defined as immutable, and classes can be defined as immutable. When a class is defined as immutable using the keyword **final**, the class cannot be inherited (or derived) as a subclass or child class. The objects of a class can also be defined as immutable by declaring all of the attributes (data, fields) of the class as **final**.

mutator methods   Are methods that change or manipulate data for an object.

`NegativeArraySizeException`   Exception thrown when you try to create an array with a negative size. The JVM ends the program and issues an error message.

*nested **try/catch** blocks*   Placing a **try/catch** block within another **try/catch** block. Any exception not caught in an inner **try/catch** block is handed to the outer **try/catch** block.

new   Keyword used to define and reserve memory for the creation of a new object.

node streams   Files, memory, and pipes. Input and output streams are known as node streams.

nonstatic initialization block   Used to initialize nonstatic data and update static data.

`notify()`   Method of the `Object` class that is used in conjunction with the `wait` method to facilitate communication between threads. When a `notify` call is executed on a particular object, an arbitrary thread is moved from that object's wait pool to a lock pool, where threads stay until the lock flag for that object becomes available.

null method definition   An implementation of a method definition without any procedural code.

Object class   The superclass from which all objects inherit data and methods. In general, class design should include overriding of the `equals()`, `hashCode()`, and `toString()` methods:

> *equals() method*   Compares its reference value with that of another object. This is a comparison of addresses, not data.

> *hashCode() method*   Returns a hash code value in the form of an **int** for the object.

> *toString() method*   Converts the reference value of an object to a `String`.

object   Contains data and instructions for processing the data. An object is a representation of something.

object data (or instance variables)   Stored in each object of a class.

object destruction   The JVM implements the garbage collector program, which cleans up objects destroyed by the programmer.

object mutability   Is whether the object data can be changed. The keyword **final** makes data unchangeable.

object relationships and associations   Is based on the associations of objects in a context. An object knows about another object.

object serialization   The process of breaking down an object and writing it out.

object stream   The classes that can read and write an object and its data as a cohesive unit.

object-oriented programming languages   Object-oriented programming is a method of programming based on a hierarchy of classes and well-defined and cooperating objects.

operator precedence grouping   A set of rules or priorities that Java imposes on the use of operators.

operators:

> *arithmetic operators*   Operators needed to execute a computation, such as a plus sign. The arithmetic operators include +, -, *, /, and %.

> *Assignment operators*   These operators include =, +=, -=, *=, /=, %=, &=, |=, ^=, <<=, >>=, and >>>=.

> *bitwise shift operators*   Perform bit shifts of the binary representation of the left operand. The bitwise shift operators include <<, >>, and >>>.

bitwise logical operators—Provide multiple comparisons of binary representations and return a binary representation:

— *& (AND)*—For a given bit comparison, 1 and 1 produces 1, and all others produce 0.

— *| (OR)*—For a given bit comparison, 0 and 0 produces 0, and all others produce 1.

— *^ (XOR)*—For a given bit comparison, 1 and 0 produces 1, as does 0 and 1. All others produce 0.

boolean *logical operators*—Provide multiple **boolean** comparisons, and return a **boolean** result:

— *& (AND)*—All expressions must be true for a true result.

— *| (OR)*—If one expression is true, the result is true.

— *^ (XOR)*—The result is true when one expression is true and the other expression is false. The result is false when both expressions are true or both expressions are false.

— *|| (short-circuit OR)*—If the first expression is true, the result is true without regard for the second expression.

casting and conversion of data types   Operation with primitive data types that assigns a value of one data type to a variable of another data type. If the two types are compatible, Java does the conversion automatically.

comparison operators   Operators that test the relative values of two operands and return a **boolean** result:

— *ordinal*   Tests the relative values of two numeric values: < (less than), > (greater than), >= (greater than or equal to), or <= (less than or equal to)

— *equality*   Uses the symbols == (equal to) and != (not equal to) for comparing two values.

— *object-type*   Uses the keyword **instanceof** to determine whether the runtime type of an object is of a particular class or subclass.

— *&& (short-circuit AND)*—If the first expression is false, the result is false without regard for the second expression.

conditional operator (?:)—Used to assign one of two different values to a variable based upon a condition.

object operators:

— The **new** operator is used to create a new object (instance) of a class.

— The *dot operator* is used to access methods or member data of an object.

unary operators   Requires only one operand. The unary operators include +, -, ++ (prefix), ++ (postfix), --(prefix), --(postfix), ~, !, and (cast operator).

ordered   Collection keeps track of determining where to place the object in the collection. A deck of cards would be an ordered collection. This is a `List`.

out field of the `System` class   A reference to a `PrintStream` object used to stream out data for printing output. Two commonly used methods of the `PrintSteam` object referenced by the out variable include:

`println()`   Adds a line separator to produce a complete line of output

`print()`   Does not add the line separator, so one line of output can be built up with several calls to the `print` method

output   Reading of data from the program. Output of data from a program is provided through the use of classes in the `java.io` package.

overloading   When an operator or method can perform more than the same action with different types of data. The + operator, which is used in adding numeric data, also can be used to combine `String` objects. This often is referred to as concatenation.

overriding methods and exception declaration   Overriding a parent class method and throwing different exceptions that are a subclass of the exception thrown by the parent class is allowed. It is also permissible to have fewer exceptions thrown by the overriding method. The overriding method cannot throw an exception that is not a subclass of the exception thrown by the parent class, nor one that is more general than the parent class, such as using the word `Exception`.

overriding   The capability of a programmer to redefine or customize the definition of a parent-class method.

packages   A collection of classes.

`Panel`   A free-floating container that must be displayed on another container such as a `Window`, `Frame`, or `Dialog` (or inside a web browser's window in an applet).

`Panel`   A subclass of the `Container` class, it is a free-floating `Container` that cannot be displayed by itself. It usually is displayed in a `Window` or `Frame`.

parallel array   The value in one element of the array has corresponding meaning for the value of the same element in another array.

PATH variable   An operating system variable that specifies the directories that contain many executable files, including the Java compiler and interpreter.

polymorphism   A mechanism in Java that allows the same code to have different effects at runtime, depending on the context.

polymorphism and exceptions   Polymorphism allows the use of a general class of objects as arguments in a method, and references to objects of its subclass can be used as values in a method call. If you want to catch exceptions in a particular class, getting too specific can prevent this from happening. For example, using the IOException class, polymorphism is applied to accept any object of its subclass.

pool   A collection of runnable threads, organized by priority and kept in temporary storage until CPU time is available.

pre-emption   Method used by a CPU to allow multiple threads access. Higher-priority threads are given CPU time as it is available.

priority   The classification unit of threads used in determining processing sequence.

procedural programming languages   Procedural program is written as a list of instructions, telling the computer step by step what to do: Open a file, read a number, multiply by 4, display something. Program units include the main or program block, subroutines, functions, procedures; file scoping; includes/modules; and libraries.

protected   A keyword used in a method or variable declaration. It signifies that the method or variable can be accessed only by elements residing in its class, subclasses, or classes in the same package.

qualifier modifiers for methods   Define special limitations or capabilities of the method. The keywords used include the following:

> **final**   The method definition cannot be changed. This qualifier is used primarily while implementing inheritance or subclasses.
>
> **static**   An object of this class does not need to exist, and the method can be called by referencing class-name.method().

RAM (random-access memory)   A computer's main or primary memory.

> *Stack*   Storage location in RAM for methods and variables.
>
> *Heap*   Storage location in RAM for objects.
>
> *Static*   Storage location in RAM for shared methods or variables.
>
> *Constant*   Storage location in RAM for nonchanging variables.

random-access file   File in which records can be stored and accesses in any order.

RandomAccessFile class   Class used to read and write to a random-access file.

Reader and Writer classes   Character streams have Reader and Writer classes at the root of the hierarchy. They are subclasses of the Object class.

relative path name   Starting at the current working directory, a hierarchical listing of all the directories and subdirectories that end in the location of a file or directory.

repaint()   Method used when it is necessary to update a window. This method calls another method named update(), which calls paint().

resume()   Method of the Thread class that is used to move a thread from the blocked state to the runnable state.

rethrow   The process of using a **try/catch** block to catch an exception and then rethrowing the exception or another subclass of the exception. In this event, the programmer is passing the exception up the call stack. If an exception is rethrown, the compiler must be notified. Include the phrase **throws** *exception-name* in the method signature.

return values for methods   Value required by the method's definition to be sent back to any method that calls that particular method.

reuse   Or overloading methods, is the reuse of the same method name (in the same program) to handle multiple types of input.

run()   Method of the Thread class that contains the code that is executed by a thread.

Runnable   Interface that is provided in the Java language to create thread objects.

runnable state   A life cycle of a thread. A thread in the runnable state is ready for execution.

runtime   The process of executing the .class byte code. The runtime system includes all the code necessary to load programs written in the Java programming language, dynamically link native methods, manage memory, handle exceptions, and implement the Java Virtual Machine.

RuntimeException   Exceptions that are handled automatically by Java. Java simply shuts down the program. These exceptions require code corrections to eliminate the exceptions.

scope and lifetime   Class variables are available for as long as the class is in memory. The scope of an object variable or method variable is for the duration of the code block. When the block has finish executing, the variables inside the block are said to be out of scope. When an instance variable references an object as part of a class definition, the lifetime of the referenced object is tied to the lifetime of the object of the enclosing class.

sequence   Type of storage that provides for dynamic lists.

Serializable interface   A marker interface that enables the programmer to define instances of classes as `Serializable`, or capable of being written out with all the object data as one entity. Only objects that implement the `Serializable` interface can be serialized. So, if the class references objects of another class that is not `Serializable`, sending these objects to be stored will not automatically result in the storage of data of the referenced objects.

set   An unordered collection of objects. Duplicates are permitted.

setLayout() method   Method used to change the default layout manager for each container.

   setSize()method   Method to set the physical size of a component.

   setVisible() method   Method used to display components.

shuffling   Rearranges the elements in a `List` object in some random order.

sink   Data that has reached this destination cannot be processed by connection to another stream; could be a pipe to another program.

sink stream   A stream that terminates the flow of data is called the output stream, or sink stream.

sleep()   Static method of the `Thread` class that causes the current thread to enter the blocked state and gives other threads an opportunity to execute.

software, programs, applications   General terms for the various kinds of programs used to operate computers and related devices.

sorting   The `Collections` class provides a set of static methods for sorting: `Collections.sort()` and `Collections.reverse()`. The `sort()` method can sort the entire `List` object or sort a subset. The `reverse()` method reverses the order of the elements in the `List` object.

sorting   The process of arranging a series of objects in some logical order.

source code   Programming statements that are created by a programmer with a text editor or an IDE and then saved in a file.

source stream   A stream that initiates a flow of data is called an input stream, or source stream.

standard classes   The core classes that belong to the Java language, located automatically and unaffected by the CLASSPATH variable.

start()   Method of the Thread class that is used to allow a thread to begin execution. The start method prompts the JVM to call the run method of the thread.

static initialization block   Used to initialize static data.

static methods   Methods that require that no objects of the class be created to use these methods.

stop()   Deprecated method of the Thread class. Using the stop method to terminate execution of a thread is unsafe because objects can be left in inconsistent states.

Storage Size   Defined as the number of bits that are required to store a representation of the number, character symbol, or Boolean status:

> *Bit*   Each bit can be represented as a place value in the binary number system—that is, a number system using two digits: 1 or 0.

> *Byte*   Eight (8) bits equals one (1) byte.

stream   A stream can be thought of as a flow of bytes of data from a source to a sink, where the flow occurs in one direction only.

String   A collection of one or more Unicode characters stored in an object. String objects are immutable. After a String object is created, its value cannot change.

String class   Class used to create and store a sequence of immutable character (text) data. The String class is defined as **final**, so any objects created of this class are considered immutable or unchangeable. The individual characters of the String class cannot be changed.

StringBuffer class   Class that holds mutable character (text) data.

StringBuffer   Class that provides for the storage of string data that will change.

subclass or *child class*   A class that is derived from a parent class and that shares common attributes and behaviors with the parent class.

subscript   An integer contained within square brackets that indicates one of an array's elements.

super   A keyword used within a subclass to refer to data and methods from the parent class.

superclass   A class from which a particular class is derived, perhaps with one or more classes in between. A superclass can be either a concrete or an abstract class.

suspend()   Deprecated method of the `Thread` class. Using the `suspend` method to pause thread execution temporarily is unsafe because its use is prone to deadlocks.

synchronized   A keyword in the Java programming language that, when applied to a method or code block, guarantees that at most one thread at a time executes that code.

System class   A Java core class, used for many operations that require data about the underlying operation system settings. The `System` class has three **public static final** fields, in, out, and err. These fields are designed to connect to the underlying system's stdin, stdout, and stderr devices. The `System` class also has a method to request garbage collection using the static method `gc()`.

System class objects   Objects used to access properties of the underlying operating system devices to stream data in and out of the program.

   in   Accepts data from the keyboard buffer.

   out   Sends output to the display or redirects to a designated file.

   err   Sends output to the monitor. Used for prompts and error messages.

system fonts   A collection of shapes for representing characters in a host software.

system properties   Using `System.getProperty()` method, returns an object that is maintained by the JVM about the host system.

TextArea   Multiline textbox with scrollbars, which accepts input from the user.

TextComponent   Parent class for `TextArea` and `TextField`.

TextField   Single-line textbox that accepts input from the user.

this   A keyword used to represent an instance of the class in which it appears. The **this** variable can be used to access class variables and methods.

this variable   Java programming language keyword that can be used to represent an instance of the class in which it appears. The keyword **this** can be used to access class variables and methods.

Thread   Class provided in the Java language to create multithreaded applications.

throw   Java programming language keyword that allows the user to throw an exception or any class that implements the `Throwable` interface.

Throwable class   The superclass of all `Exception` and `Error` classes. Only objects of this class or its subclasses are thrown by the JVM. All member data is **private**.

throws A Java programming language keyword used in method declarations that specifies which exceptions are not handled within the method but are passed to the next higher level of the program.

time quantum The amount of time that the current thread is given to execute on the CPU.

time-slicing Method used by the CPU to allocate time to multiple threads. Each thread is given a certain amount of time to execute.

toString method Method inherited from the `Object` class that renders an object as a `String`. Unless the method is overridden, it will return a `String` consisting of the name of the class of which the object is an instance, the at-sign character '@', and the unsigned hexadecimal representation of the hash code of the object.

tree Provides storage for items that are sorted, for example, in ascending order.

TreeSet A class that is a collection of the type `Set` implementing a Tree storage technology. It implements the `SortedSet` interface. The objects are placed in ascending order, with no duplicates.

try/catch *blocks* The Java language provides these two code constructs to test code and handle exceptions when they occur. With the **try/catch** technique, a block of code statements is tried; if these statements cause errors, the programmer catches the error and includes code to handle the error. The programmer might need multiple **catch** blocks to catch different types of exceptions.

Unified Modeling Language (UML) A uniform system of symbols and terms to communicate the design of classes and applications and their relationships.

unique domain Using packages to create a unique namespace for classes prevents name collisions when these classes are shared.

unordered The order of an object is not important in a particular collection. This is a `Set`.

update() Method called by `repaint()`. The `update()` method clears the current display and calls `paint()` to produce another image.

URL (uniform resource locator) A standard for writing a text reference to an arbitrary piece of data on the World Wide Web. A specific address for HTML documents.

user-defined exceptions Exceptions specifically designed by the programmer to implement exceptions to normal business rules or activities.

validate() Method that redraws any invalid window when changes to the applet are made.

Variables   A variable is a storage location in memory that a programmer can use to store data. A variable has five facets. Data types are declared when a variable is created. The data or value in a variable can be a primitive or can be a reference data type.

Vector   A class that implements the List interface. The dimension of a Vector includes its capacity and its initial size. Vectors can be increased after creation.

virtual CPU   Consists of the code and data to be executed by each thread.

wait()   Method of the Object class that is used in conjunction with the notify method to facilitate thread communication. If a thread issues a wait call on rendezvous object x, that thread pauses its execution until another thread issues a notify call on the same rendezvous object x.

Window   A freestanding native window on the display that is independent of other containers. Two important types of Window exist: Frame and Dialog.

wrapper classes   Classes that manipulate primitive data elements as objects. After the primitive value is initialized in the wrapper object, it cannot be changed. Wrapper classes are useful because of the many wrapper class methods available; however, wrapper classes cannot be used with arithmetic operators or conditions.

Wrapper Classes   Each primitive type has a wrapper class defined in the core classes. Wrapper classes wrap object features and capabilities around a single primitive data type value. This enables a programmer to operate on these types of data as objects.

yield()   Method of the Thread class that is used to cause a thread to allow another thread access to the CPU.

zero-based indexing   All arrays start with an index of 0 for the first element.

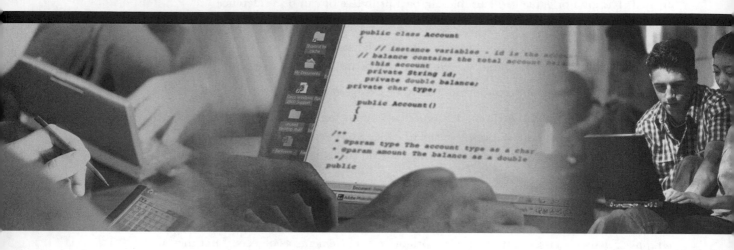

Check Your Understanding Answer Key

Chapter 1

1. B
2. C
3. B
4. C
5. C
6. D
7. D
8. B
9. B
10. D
11. B
12. D
13. C
14. A
15. D
16. B
17. A
18. C
19. B

Chapter 2

1. B
2. C
3. D
4. A
5. D
6. C
7. B
8. D
9. B
10. A
11. C
12. A
13. B
14. D
15. D
16. B
17. D
18. C
19. B
20. D

Chapter 3

1. B
2. C
3. C
4. B
5. B
6. D
7. D

8. C
9. A
10. C
11. B
12. D
13. D
14. B
15. C
16. A
17. D
18. B
19. A
20. D

Chapter 4

1. D
2. B
3. C
4. B
5. B
6. B
7. D
8. A
9. B
10. A
11. D
12. B
13. D
14. C
15. D

16. B

17. D

18. C

19. A

20. A

Chapter 5

1. B

2. C

3. D

4. C

5. D

6. C

7. D

8. A

9. C

10. D

11. C

12. A

13. C

14. D

15. B

16. A

17. D

18. C

19. D

20. C

Chapter 6

1. B
2. D
3. C
4. B
5. A
6. B
7. D
8. B
9. C
10. B
11. D
12. B
13. D
14. C
15. A
16. A
17. B
18. C
19. B
20. B

Chapter 7

1. D
2. B
3. B
4. D
5. B
6. C
7. D

   8. A

   9. B

  10. B

  11. A

  12. C

  13. D

  14. B

  15. C

  16. D

  17. B

  18. D

  19. D

  20. C

Chapter 8

  1. B

  2. A

  3. C

  4. D

  5. B

  6. D

  7. B

  8. C

  9. C

  10. B

  11. A

  12. C

  13. D

  14. C

  15. D

16. C
17. D
18. D
19. B
20. C

Chapter 9

1. B
2. D
3. B
4. B
5. A
6. B
7. C
8. A
9. D
10. B
11. D
12. C
13. B
14. B
15. B
16. D
17. C
18. A
19. D
20. C

Chapter 10

1. D
2. B
3. B
4. A
5. D
6. B
7. C
8. B
9. C
10. D
11. B
12. A
13. D
14. D
15. B
16. A
17. C
18. D
19. C
20. D

Chapter 11

1. C
2. D
3. B
4. D
5. A
6. D
7. B

8. C

9. D

10. B

11. C

12. D

13. C

14. B or C

15. B

16. C

17. B

18. D

19. A

20. D

Chapter 12

1. C

2. B

3. D

4. A

5. D

6. C

7. B

8. A

9. B

10. D

11. B

12. B

13. C

14. B

15. D

16. C
17. A
18. B
19. D
20. D

Chapter 13

1. B
2. C
3. A
4. D
5. C
6. D
7. D
8. B
9. D
10. B
11. C
12. A
13. D
14. D
15. C
16. B
17. C
18. C
19. D
20. D

Chapter 14

1. D
2. C
3. A
4. B
5. A
6. B
7. D
8. B
9. D
10. C
11. D
12. D
13. A
14. D
15. B
16. C
17. D
18. C
19. B
20. A

Chapter 15

1. D
2. B
3. A
4. C
5. C
6. D
7. A

8. D

9. B

10. B

11. C

12. D

13. D

14. C

15. B

16. A

17. C

18. B

19. D

20. A

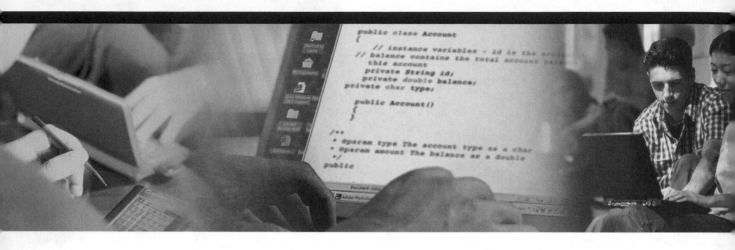

Fundamentals of Java Programming and the College Board

Overview

The Advanced Placement (AP) Computer Science curriculum, sponsored by the College Board (www.collegeboard.com/), is an accelerated program consisting of two tracks, A and AB. The goal of this program is to prepare students for introductory college-level computer science programming courses. The A track is a subset of AB; the two together are equivalent to a first-year computer science programming course.

The Java subsets are available from the College Board at the following addresses:

www.collegeboard.com/ap/students/compsci/java_subsetA.html

www.collegeboard.com/ap/students/compsci/java_subsetAB.html

The AP Computer Science curriculum provides a broader coverage of programming objectives than an introduction to programming course might have. The curriculum includes comprehensive coverage of problem solving, project specifications, data and algorithm design, and solution testing methodologies. Students also learn about computer hardware and software and their correct usage. The core topics of the curriculum include intrinsic programming constructs, such as data types, data structures, language, and syntax.

Programming is the primary skill used in practicing the fundamental concepts of computer science. More specifically, an introduction to object-oriented programming is widely accepted by universities as the first exposure to such skills for computer science students. Object-oriented programming and design principles provide a solid foundation of knowledge and skills necessary for student success in a computer science discipline.

The AP Computer Science curriculum consists of a programming language subset and a case study to teach the introductory concepts of programming. It is not practical to cover every feature of the programming language on the exams, so a subset of features has been identified to guide students and teachers in preparation for the exams. The case study that has been developed is a tool for students to practice and enhance their skills. A thorough understanding of the language subset and case study is required for the AP Computer Science exams. The AP Computer Science exams consist of 40 multiple-choice questions and 4 free-response questions. Students are given three hours to complete the exams.

The Academy Program's Fundamentals of Java Programming course, along with the *Cisco Press Companion Guide* and other related titles, prepares students for the concepts covered in the AP Computer Science A and AB exams. The course explores the introductory principles of object-oriented programming, focusing on intrinsic programming concepts of language syntax, data types, data structures, and program libraries, with Java as the programming language. In addition to Java, this course includes discussions on other topics related to computer science programming, such as documentation, project management, and creation of reusable libraries. The course included a threaded case study in which students gain practical experience applying the skills learned.

The Switch to Java

Beginning with the academic year of 2003–2004, the College Board replaced C++ with Java as the required programming language for the AP Computer Science courses. This move comes as a result of the decision to analyze the AP Computer Science program and ensure its alignment with changing trends in university programs and to reflect changes in the computer industry. In addition to exploring modifications to the content of the curriculum, the College Board examined whether C++ effectively supported the objectives of the program.

The College Board requires a safe and portable language for AP Computer Science. A safe language is one in which programming errors are identified with well-defined explanations, and a portable language gives students the opportunity to develop programming skills independent of hardware commitments and reliance. Perhaps one of the strongest learning tools for students is resolving identified errors in the code they have just written. Java is a safe language. The compiler and run-time environment identify many errors. And unlike C++, limitations of the Java language prevent students from creating hazardous situations in the first place. Furthermore, the portability of Java appeals to students who program on multiple platforms. Because Java is hardware independent, it can be written on one platform and delivered on another. Java enables students to learn the fundamental skills of programming without having to worry about platform specific idiosyncrasies.

Java is also a simple language. The language used to express the fundamentals of object-oriented programming should not prevent the student from learning it. The language constructs are familiar to English speakers, and Java's syntax is easy to learn. Java can be used to create simple classes and programs, or complex enterprise application implementations.

And Java is an object-oriented language. Object-oriented programming closely models the problem-solving methodology that people use in everyday life. When the basics of the paradigm are learned, its implementation is more intuitive than procedural solutions.

Because Java is a safe, simple, and object-oriented language, it is the ideal candidate to support the AP Computer Science curriculum. Additionally, many universities are changing their courses to use Java. With the change from C++ to Java, the College Board needed to redefine the language subset and create a case study implemented in Java.

The Java Subsets

To expressly declare the features of Java that could appear in AP exam questions, the College Board has published Java subsets for the Computer Science A and AB courses. These features are a subset of those that should be included in an introductory course. Many of the features of the subsets rely upon other excluded features to be fully understood. For example, only some of the primitive data types are included in the subset, but to be fully versed in the Java language, an understanding of all the primitive data types is required.

The subsets also identify standard classes and interfaces of the Java language that are tested on each exam. The number of classes is small in comparison to what might be encountered in an introductory course, but the decision to keep the subset manageable allows students to better prepare for the exams.

In addition, the College Board has identified several topics of potential relevance to first-year computer science courses. These topics are not included in the AP course and are not tested on the exam.

The Academy Program's Fundamentals of Java Programming course offers complete and thorough coverage of the Java subsets for both the A and AB exams; every language feature and class in each subset is included in this course. The course includes both conceptual discussion and syntax and implementation information for the language features of each subset. Additionally, the course includes those language features identified as potentially relevant to first-year computer science courses. These features are explored in depth in the course and accompanying Cisco Press materials, including many interactive exercises to practice and understand the language features more fully.

Beyond the requirements of the College Board, this course adequately prepares students with a solid foundation of Java skills. The scope of this course is much wider than the subsets and provides the guidance and resources necessary to understand and apply introductory computer science principles and object-oriented programming skills using the Java language.

The JBANK Case Study

To prepare students with the experience of working through a case study, the Academy Program's Fundamentals of Java Programming course includes the threaded JBANK case study. This case study is introduced in the first chapter and is continually modified and enhanced throughout the remaining chapters. The JBANK case study guides students through five phases of development to implement a functional, object-oriented graphical application.

The JBANK application closely models a virtual bank. Customers interact with a teller or ATM to deposit and withdraw money. The project includes functions for customer actions and account management of several types of accounts.

The JBANK consists of five phases. The general topics of each phase are as follows.

Phase 1: Creating a Class and Object

Students create a simple, functional banking application to become familiar with the basic features of the Java language.

Phase 2: Using the Java Standard Classes

The application is modified to incorporate Java standard classes, some of which are included in the Java subsets.

Phase 3: Using Inheritance, Encapsulation, and Polymorphism

Students apply the principles of object-oriented programming to improve the application design and give enhanced flexibility and functionality to the banking application.

Phase 4: Using the GUI, the AWT, and the Model View Controller Pattern

Students create a graphical application that can be executed across the Internet as an applet.

Phase Five: Using Exceptions, I/O, and Collections

In the final phase of the JBANK case study, students implement exception handling to create a robust application and examine alternative data structures.

JBANK Labs Matrix

The following table is a detailed outline of the JBANK labs and their objectives.

Phase Objectives	Chapter	Lab Title	Classes Introduced
Phase 1: Build the business classes for the JBANK application (Customer, Bank, Account, and Teller)	2, "Object-Oriented Programming"	"Designing and Describing Classes Using UML"	Bank Teller Customer Account
		"Develop the Bank Classes for Phase 1"	
	3, "Java Language Elements"	"Inserting Documentation for the Classes in the Banking Application"	
		"Generating API Docs for JBANK Classes Using the javadoc Tool"	
		"Creating the Classes for Phase 1 of the JBANK Application"	

continues

Phase Objectives	Chapter	Lab Title	Classes Introduced
	5, "Basics of Defining and Using Classes"	"Constructors and Methods"	
		"Completing the JBANK Phase 1 Application"	
Phase 2: Implement core API classes in the JBANK application.	6, "System, String, String-Buffer, Math, and Wrapper Classes"	"System, String, StringBuffer, and Use of Console Class"	
Implement array objects to reference multiple instances of objects (Customer and Account).		"Wrapper Classes, Math Class, and Date Class"	
	7, "Arrays"	"Implementing Arrays in the JBANK Application"	
Phase 3: Build the inheritance relationship for the business classes in the JBANK application.	8, "Classes and Inheritance"	"Implement Abstraction in Phase 2 of the Banking Application"	
		"Implement Inheritance, Extending from Abstract and Concrete Classes"	Savings Investment
		"Abstraction at Several Levels— Checking Account"	Checking LineOfCredit OverDraft-Protection

Phase Objectives	Chapter	Lab Title	Classes Introduced
		"Polymorphism in the Banking Application"	
Phase 4: Build the view and controller classes for a Model View Controller design pattern implementation.	9, "Understanding Packages"	"Build a Banking Package"	
		"Designing a GUI to Represent an ATM for Customers"	
		"Designing the GUI Interfaces"	
	10, "Creating GUI Applications Using AWT"	"Creating the Components (`TellerView` Class)"	
		"Creating the Components (`ATMGUI` Class)"	`ATMGUI`
		"Selecting Containers (`TellerGUI` Class)"	
		"Selecting Containers (`ATMGUI` Class)"	
		"Layout Managers (`TellerGUI` Class)"	
		"Layout Managers and Adding Components (`ATMGUI` Class)"	

continues

Phase Objectives	Chapter	Lab Title	Classes Introduced
		"Identifying Event-Handler Features in the `TellerGUI` Class"	
		"Implement Event Handling for the `ATMGUI` Class"	`ATMControl`
		"Implement the Model for the `ATMGUI` Class"	
		"Finalizing the Model View Controller Pattern for the `ATMGUI` Class"	
	11, "Applets and Graphics"	"Creating an ATM Applet"	`ATMApplet`

Phase 5: Complete the JBANK application by implementing:
 	
1. Exception handling
	12, "Exceptions"	"Exceptions for the JBANK Application"	`AmountOverDrawn-Exception`
			`AccountType-AlreadyExists-Exception`
			`AccountTypeNot-FoundException`

2. Persistence solutions for the business data	13, "Streams, Files, and Stream Output"	"Writing Customer Objects to a File"	`WriteToCustomer-File`
		"Reading Customer Objects from a File"	`ReadFrom-CustomerFile`
3. The more efficient Collection framework to replace array objects	14, "Collections"	"File I/O Using Collection Classes"	
		"Sets and Iterators"	

The Marine Biology Simulation and JBANK case studies are comprehensive Java projects designed to supplement an introductory object-oriented programming curriculum. The major difference between the projects is that the JBANK case study involves the threaded creation of a comprehensive project, while the MBS is a deconstruction of a completed project.

Also, in contrast to the Marine Biology Simulation case study, the JBANK case study provides students with hands-on experience in all stages of the project, including initial specifications, development and testing, documentation, and final implementation. The JBANK case study is designed as a tool to more fully understand and directly practice the application of Java language elements.

The Marine Biology Simulation Case Study

A major component of the AP Computer Science courses is the inclusion of a case study. The case study consists of a problem statement, a solution, and exploration of the solution, including implementation, design alternatives, and testing. It provides the unique opportunity to examine a complete project solution and apply concepts to a practical situation. The case study generally sets the example of best practices for a given topic—in this case, object-oriented programming with Java.

The Marine Biology Simulation case study, published by the College Board, is a comprehensive project implemented with the Java programming language. It includes Java code, documentation for the classes, and an extensive narrative, as well as problem sets and exercises.

The project for this case study is a graphical application used to simulate an environment for fish. The program emulates fish behavior, such as movement and breeding. The application is used by marine biologists to study the behavior of different types of fish in different environments. The narrative is written from the perspective of a student analyzing, testing, and improving the simulation program with the guidance of a master programmer.

The narrative is composed of five chapters. Chapters 1–4 are required for Computer Science A, and the entire narrative is required for Computer Science AB. The general topics of each chapter and their coverage by the Academy Program's Fundamentals of Java course are detailed next.

Chapter 1: Experimenting with the Marine Biology Simulation Program

This is a general introduction to the case study. No Java skills are required for the majority of this chapter.

Java Language Feature	Corresponding Fundamentals of Java Programming Chapter	Corresponding *Cisco Press Companion Guide* Chapter	Coverage in JBANK Case Study or Lab Activity
Execution of a Java program	Chapter 1	Chapter 1	Yes
Object instantiation	Chapters 2, 3, 5, and 8	Chapters 2, 3, 5, and 8	Yes
Class constants	Chapters 2, 3, and 5	Chapters 2, 3, and 5	Yes
The main Method	Chapters 2 and 5	Chapters 2 and 5	Yes
Loop structures	Chapter 4	Chapter 4	Yes

Chapter 2: A Guided Tour of the Marine Biology Simulation Implementation

The Java classes of the simulation program are explored thoroughly in this section. The narrative explains the purpose of the classes and how they work.

Java Language Feature	Corresponding Fundamentals of Java Programming Chapter	Corresponding *Cisco Press Companion Guide* Chapter	Coverage in JBANK Case Study or Lab Activity
Object interaction	Chapters 2, 3, and 5	Chapters 2, 3, and 5	Yes
Class documentation	Chapter 3	Chapter 3	Yes
Class implementation	Chapters 2, 3, 5, and 8	Chapters 2, 3, 5, and 8	Yes
Instance variables	Chapters 2, 3, and 5	Chapters 2, 3, and 5	Yes

Java Language Feature	Corresponding Fundamentals of Java Programming Chapter	Corresponding *Cisco Press Companion Guide* Chapter	Coverage in JBANK Case Study or Lab Activity
Class variables	Chapters 2, 3, and 5	Chapters 2, 3, and 5	Yes
Interfaces	Chapter 8	Chapter 8	Yes
Random numbers	Chapter 6	Chapter 6	Yes
Keyword this	Chapters 5 and 8	Chapters 5 and 8	Yes
equals vs. ==	Chapters 4 and 8	Chapters 4 and 8	Yes
Constructor methods	Chapters 2, 3, 5, and 8	Chapters 2, 3, 5, and 8	Yes

Chapter 3: Creating a Dynamic Population

The project specifications have been changed so that the student can practice modifying classes and accurately testing them.

Java Language Feature	Corresponding Fundamentals of Java Programming Chapter	Corresponding *Cisco Press Companion Guide* Chapter	Coverage in JBANK Case Study or Lab Activity
Conditional operators	Chapter 4	Chapter 4	Yes
Casting	Chapters 4 and 6	Chapter 4 and 6	Yes
Modifying classes	Chapters 2, 3, 5, and 8	Chapters 2, 3, 5, and 8	Yes
Access modifiers	Chapters 2, 3, 5, and 8	Chapters 2, 3, 5, and 8	Yes

Chapter 4: Implementation of Inheritance Concepts

Subclasses have been added to the project to show inheritance concepts of object-oriented programming.

Java Language Feature	Corresponding Fundamentals of Java Programming Chapter	Corresponding *Cisco Press Companion Guide* Chapter	Coverage in JBANK Case Study or Lab Activity
Inheritance	Chapter 8	Chapter 8	Yes
Keyword extends	Chapter 8	Chapter 8	Yes
Method overriding	Chapter 8	Chapter 8	Yes
Polymorphism	Chapter 8	Chapter 8	Yes
Abstract classes	Chapter 8	Chapter 8	Yes
Keyword super	Chapter 8	Chapter 8	Yes
Random class	Chapter 6	Chapter 6	Yes
toString method	Chapter 6	Chapter 6	Yes

Chapter 5: Environment Implementations

The project has been changed to incorporate various data structures, such as two-dimensional arrays, hashmaps, trees, and others.

Java Language Feature	Corresponding Fundamentals of Java Programming Chapter	Corresponding *Cisco Press Companion Guide* Chapter	Coverage in JBANK Case Study or Lab Activity
Interfaces	Chapter 8	Chapter 8	Yes
Multidimensional array	Chapter 7	Chapter 7	Yes
Data structures	Chapter 14	Chapter 14	Yes
Abstract class	Chapter 8	Chapter 8	Yes
Exceptions	Chapter 12	Chapter 12	Yes

Java Language Feature	Corresponding Fundamentals of Java Programming Chapter	Corresponding *Cisco Press Companion Guide* Chapter	Coverage in JBANK Case Study or Lab Activity
ArrayList class	Chapter 14	Chapter 14	Yes
Color class	Chapters 10 and 11	Chapters 10 and 11	Yes

The Java classes used to create the Marine Biology Simulation are extensive. Students can explore and modify ten source files. Additionally, there are two Java archives of more than 60 class files. In this way, students have access to only a small portion of the code. Students have client access to some of the classes through the documentation interface. Much of the inner workings of the project are completely abstracted. The source files employ good design and thorough documentation, giving students an example to follow.

The Marine Biology Simulation case study is not meant for instruction by itself, but it serves as a supplement to teach the fundamentals of the Java programming language, and to more fully understand and explore the general concepts of object-oriented programming and develop students' fundamental programming skills. The case study also involves soft programming skills, such as code efficiency, design alternatives, testing methodologies, and others that are related not specifically to Java, but to object-oriented programming in general.

The case study also provides detailed explanations of the project specifications and code to implement them. Many of the discussions are pseudocode versions of methods and classes. Much of the text is devoted to explaining how the lines of code accomplish the tasks for which they are designed. Additionally, the narrative focuses on explaining concepts instead of language elements. For example, the case study offers a thorough conceptual explanation of interfaces and discusses why programmers use interfaces and how they are different from classes without covering all the syntax rules to implement them with Java.

Java Subset Coverage by Case Studies

Although many of the features of the Java subsets are incorporated into the Marine Biology Simulation case study, their syntax rules, usage, and general concepts are not fully explored in the context of the narrative. Students using this case study are expected to have learned these already. The Academy Program's Java course and case study offer complete coverage of the Java subsets. The course provides all the necessary resources to learn the Java skills needed to understand and complete this case study.

No Java language elements are covered by the Marine Biology Simulation case study that are not covered in the Academy Program's Fundamentals of Java Programming course. The JBANK case study thoroughly incorporates Java usage into the project and is modified continually with almost every topic introduced throughout the course. The JBANK case study enables students to concretely apply the language concepts covered by the Marine Biology Simulation case study.

Marine Biology Simulation and the AP Exams

The Marine Biology Simulation case study is included in both AP Computer Science exams. At least one free-response question and five multiple-choice questions relate specifically to the case study. Students are provided with copies of the case study classes for use during the exam. Students might be asked to explain the relationships among classes or to modify the classes to provide increased functionality. Students also might be asked to write an additional class or method that will work in tandem with the existing case study classes.

Not only are the concepts of the case study covered in the AP exams, but the actual classes from the case study are required as well. Therefore, it is recommended that students gain a familiarity with the classes and how they are related before taking the AP exam. The entire case study, including the narrative, classes, and deployment instructions, can be downloaded from the College Board website: www.collegeboard.com/ap/students/compsci/download.html.

Academy Program's Fundamentals of Java Programming Resources and Simulation Case Study

e-Lab Activities

The Academy Program's Fundamentals of Java Programming course includes more than 95 interactive exercises that enable students to practice with context-sensitive feedback the fundamental Java concepts emphasized in the Marine Biology case study.

These activities are spread throughout each chapter to reinforce the learning objectives in a real-time environment. The formats for these interactive exercises include the following:

- Drag and drop
- Fill in the blank
- Check box activity
- BlueJ rollover, with additional topic-related text
- BlueJ toggle between code and resulting output

Hands-On labs

The course contains more than 90 hands-on lab activities that enable students to apply concepts from the curriculum to practical problems. These lab activities cover all the language features of the Java subsets. Each lab exercise identifies learning objectives for the activity and includes questions to test students' knowledge about main concepts covered in the labs. Lab exercises require 15 to 90 minutes to complete. The JBANK case study is composed of more than 25 lab activities. The other lab activities give students additional opportunities to gain familiarity with language features before applying them to the case study.

The lab activity by chapter includes the following:

- **Chapter 1, "What Is Java?"**—This chapter presents lab exercises that cover the location of resources, managing editors, and interfacing with the console window. It includes lab activities on creating and running your first Java class, accepting input from the user at runtime, debugging and correcting errors in predefined classes, and exploring the BlueJ IDE, as well as an introduction to the JBANK threaded case study application.
- **Chapter 2, "Object-Oriented Programming,"**—This chapter presents lab exercises that cover the definition of a Java class and the creation of an object of that class. Students will identify the attributes of a Student class and use a main method to create and operate on Student objects. This chapter also includes lab activities on designing and describing classes using the Unified Modeling Language (UML), and designing the initial banking classes for Phase 1 of the JBANK case study.
- **Chapter 3, "Java Language Elements"**—This chapter presents lab exercises that cover the documentation of classes and the Core API, including the use of javadoc parameters for creating documentation. It also includes lab activities on defining variables, applying access modifiers, using constructors, and creating the classes for Phase 1 of the JBANK case study.

- **Chapter 4, "Java Language Operators and Control Structures"**—This chapter presents lab exercises that cover the use and precedence of operators, and the implementation of control structures. It includes lab activities on arithmetic operators, use of operators, String concatenation, the `if` statement, `switch` statements, loops (`do while`, `while`, `for`), the `java.lang.System` class, and the `Console` class.

- **Chapter 5, "Basics of Defining and Using Classes"**—This chapter presents lab exercises that cover the steps, processes, and syntax necessary to define a class and then create an object of that class. It includes lab activities on the four steps to creating objects, encapsulation concepts, attributes, constructors, methods, overloaded methods and constructors, scope of variables, and the completion of Phase 1 of the JBANK case study.

- **Chapter 6, "`System`, `String`, `StringBuffer`, `Math`, and Wrapper Classes"**—This chapter presents lab exercises that cover the use of the API documentation to implement the methods and attributes of Java core classes. It includes lab activities on reading input using `System.in`, using the `String` and `StringBuffer` methods, performing casting and conversion, using wrapper classes, using the `Math` class, using the math package, working with dates and the `Date` class, and using the `Console` class.

- **Chapter 7, "Arrays"**—This chapter presents lab exercises that cover the creation, initialization, and use of arrays. It includes lab activities on creating and traversing arrays, passing an array to a method, searching and sorting an array, traversing a multidimensional array, and implementing arrays in the JBANK case study.

- **Chapter 8, "Classes and Inheritance"**—This chapter presents lab exercises that cover the design and implementation of classes using inheritance. It includes lab activities on extending classes from abstract and concrete classes, implementing interfaces, using polymorphism, and implementing abstraction and polymorphism in the JBANK case study.

- **Chapter 9, "Understanding Packages"**—This chapter presents lab exercises that cover the organization of classes into packages, including how to access classes in a package. In addition, this chapter provides an introduction to the Abstract Window Toolkit (AWT). It includes lab activities on exploring the API packages, building a banking package for the JBANK case study, and identifying graphic components to build an ATM GUI and Teller GUI for the JBANK case study.

- **Chapter 10, "Creating GUIs Using AWT"**—This chapter presents lab exercises that cover the implementation of GUIs in the JBANK case study using AWT. It includes lab activities on creating components, selecting containers, using layout managers to add components, implementing event handling, and utilizing the Model View Controller pattern for the JBANK case study.

- **Chapter 11, "Applets and Graphics"**—This chapter presents lab exercises that cover the design and launch of applets that display and run in a web browser. It includes lab activities on creating an applet, using GUI components in applets, changing the location of the components in an applet, and creating an ATM applet for the JBANK case study.

- **Chapter 12, "Exceptions"**—This chapter presents lab exercises that cover the use of the `Throwable` class, for handling errors. This includes the use of the keywords `try`, `catch`, `finally`, `throw`, and `throws` to manage exceptions. It includes lab activities on testing for run-time exceptions, using the `finally` block, creating user-defined exceptions, and implementing exceptions in the JBANK case study.

- **Chapter 13, "Files, Streams, Input, and Output"**—This chapter presents lab exercises that cover the input and output of data (into and from a program), provided through the use of classes in the `java.io` package. It includes lab activities on displaying file statistics, using the `RandomAccessFile` class to seek positions within a file, and writing or reading `Customer` objects to or from a file for the JBANK case study.

- **Chapter 14, "Collections"**—This chapter presents lab exercises that cover the classes in the `java.util` package that provide the programmer with prebuilt classes to manage a collection of objects. It includes lab activities on using the `ArrayList` class, using the `ListIterator` class, creating a collection to store `Integer` objects, implementing file I/O using collection classes in the JBANK case study, and implementing a `SortedSet` (to hold a collection of Customer objects) and an `Iterator` in the JBANK case study.

- **Chapter 15, "Threads"**—This chapter presents lab exercises that cover the use of the `Thread` and `ThreadGroup` classes and the `Runnable` interface to perform operations concurrently. It includes lab activities on assigning thread priorities, controlling threads using methods of the `Thread` class, and creating a digital clock.

The Engineering Journal

The companion Cisco Press materials include an Engineering Journal. The 15 chapters of this title correspond to the *Fundamentals of Java Programming* chapters. The Engineering Journal chapters contain several sections:

- **Introduction**—A summary of the learning objectives for each chapter
- **Concept Questions**—Free-response questions focusing on the major topics of the chapter
- **Vocabulary Exercises**—Keywords defined for each chapter

- **Focus Questions**—Free-response questions targeting specific language features
- **Review Questions**—Multiple-choice, multiple-answer questions

The Engineering Journal is designed to provide opportunities to further develop programming skills beyond what is expected from the labs and chapter exercises. The exercise sets are difficult and will challenge the students.

BlueJ and the Marine Biology Simulation Case Study

BlueJ is an integrated development environment (IDE) created by Monash University (Australia) and the Mærsk Institute at the University of Southern Denmark, and it is supported by Sun Microsystems. It is an IDE application written in Java that was developed specifically as a tool to teach object-oriented programming. BlueJ has a powerful set of tools behind its simple, user-friendly interface. Novice students respond positively to a user interface that is not cluttered with complex options that they might not yet understand. Learning to navigate this IDE does not interfere with learning to program in Java. The quasi-UML look and feel also helps students see how their classes are related. The IDE provides an excellent visualization of object-oriented programming concepts.

BlueJ is freely available to students and can be downloaded from www.bluej.org. The BlueJ site contains an extensive tutorial for students to learn how to use the IDE, as well as other resources that relate to Java and object-oriented programming.

BlueJ is used extensively in the Academy Program's Fundamentals of Java course. The Lab Manual contains a lab on exploring the BlueJ environment. All the lab instructions are written for students using this IDE, and many of the illustration and interactive activities in the course show the BlueJ interface and functionality for code examples. Students who use this course will gain an intimate familiarity with BlueJ and might feel more comfortable using it to analyze the Marine Biology Simulation case study than using the command line.

The developers of BlueJ have also created a resource on their site to specifically address the use of this IDE for the Marine Biology Simulation Case Study and AP preparation: See www.bluej.org/help/ap.html.

A modified version of the case study code can be downloaded to be used with BlueJ. The BlueJ download consists of five separate code folders; each code folder is a BlueJ project. These BlueJ projects are used individually as students progress through the case study. For example, there is a BlueJ project called SimpleMBSDemo1 that is used in the first chapter only. Each BlueJ project contains only those classes relevant for the chapter in which it is used. In this way, the BlueJ set is a manageable implementation of the Marine Biology Simulation.

Tips and Tricks for the Marine Biology Simulation Case Study

The Marine Biology Simulation is an important inclusion to the AP Computer Science curriculum. The narrative contains valuable discussions and information directly related to fundamental computer science principles, as well as the AP exams. To use it most effectively, general guidelines for its use are presented here.

The case study should be referred to regularly and often throughout the course. The narrative is not something that can be digested in one sitting. It is rich with content, exercises, and challenging problem sets. Students who revisit previous sections might understand or absorb something new with recently acquired knowledge.

Students should thoroughly address each of the Exercise Sets and Analysis Questions. Many of these can be completed individually, but some require collaboration. Students working in small groups or one on one with an instructor will be able to discuss those questions.

The companion Cisco Press Lab Manual and Engineering Journal contain numerous activities that help students understand and apply concepts encountered in this case study. Students should complete these exercises to become more proficient with the Java language elements that appear on the Java subsets.

Students are encouraged to experiment with the classes in ways that might not be explicitly stated in the case. If some aspect of the project seems interesting, students should explore alternative approaches to implementing design changes. Individual exploration is a powerful learning tool.

For exam preparation, students should become quite familiar with the classes and their relationships with each other. The comments within the classes should not be overlooked. Students should understand the fields and methods of each class and should be ready to defend implemented design choices. Although students are supplied with copies of the case classes during the exam, having familiarity with them before the exam is a great advantage.

Additional Information on the Marine Biology Simulation Case Study

The College Board website (www.collegeboard.com/ap/students/compsci/index.html) is the official website for all the Advance Placement courses. It contains extensive, up-to-date information concerning the AP Computer Science curriculum. The Java subsets, as well as background information and exam questions for the exams, are published on this website. Information about the Marine Biology Simulation case study, download instructions, and tips for getting started can also be found on the College Board website.

Alyce Brady, the primary author of the Marine Biology Simulation case study, maintains a website with pertinent information for the case study and the AP program: http://max.cs.kzoo.edu/AP/. She provides several additional projects that can be used with the case study. Brady's site also includes the source code for all the classes of the case study. The source code for the classes can be examined to gain a full understanding of the application.

Additionally, this site has several object diagrams that are useful to visualize the classes of this project and how they are related. The methods of these classes are shown as pseudocode.

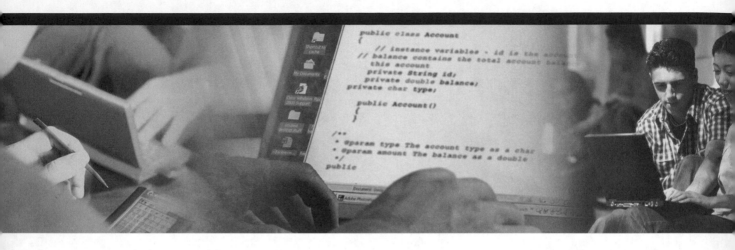

Operator Precedence Chart

From *Java How to Program*, Fourth Edition; Harvey M. Deitel, Paul J. Deitel, Prentice Hall, 8-8-2001.

Operators are shown in decreasing order of precedence from top to bottom.

Operator	Type	Associativity
() [] .	parentheses array subscript member selection	left to right
++ --	unary postincrement unary postdecrement	right to left
++ - - + - ! ~ (type)	unary preincrement unary predecrement unary plus unary minus unary logical negation unary bitwise complement unary cast	right to left
* / %	multiplication division modulus	left to right
+ -	addition subtraction	left to right
<< >> >>>	bitwise left shift bitwise right shift with sign extension bitwise right shift with zero extension	left to right

continues

Operator	Type	Associativity
 <= > >= instanceof	relational less than relational less than or equal to relational greater than relational greater than or equal to type comparison	left to right
== !=	relational is equal to relational is not equal to	left to right
&	bitwise AND	left to right
^	bitwise exclusive OR boolean logical exclusive OR	left to right
|	bitwise inclusive OR boolean logical inclusive OR	left to right
&&	logical AND	left to right
||	logical OR	left to right
?:	ternary conditional	right to left
= += -= *= /= %= &= ^= |= <<= >>= >>>=	assignment addition assignment subtraction assignment multiplication assignment division assignment modulus assignment bitwise AND assignment bitwise exclusive OR assignment bitwise inclusive OR assignment bitwise left shift assignment bitwise right shift with sign extension assignment bitwise right shift with zero extension assignment	right to left

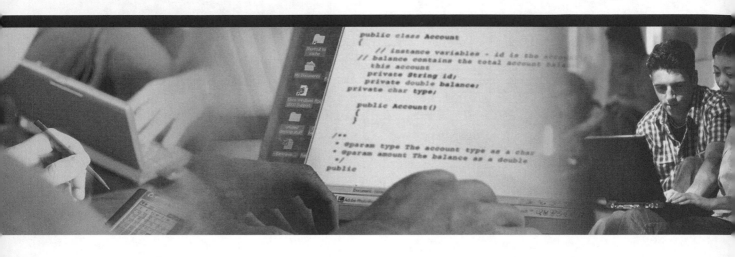

ASCII Character Set

From *Java How to Program*, Fourth Edition; Harvey M. Deitel, Paul J. Deitel, Prentice Hall, 8-8-2001.

	0	1	2	3	4	5	6	7	8	9
0	nul	soh	stx	etx	eot	enq	ack	bel	bs	ht
1	nl	vt	ff	cr	so	si	dle	dc1	dc2	dc3
2	dc4	nak	syn	etb	can	em	sub	esc	fs	gs
3	rs	us	sp	!	"	#	$	%	&	`
4	(	)	*	+	,	-	.	/	0	1
5	2	3	4	5	6	7	8	9	:	;
6	<	=	>	?	@	A	B	C	D	E
7	F	G	H	I	J	K	L	M	N	O
8	P	Q	R	S	T	U	V	W	X	Y
9	Z	[	\	]	^	_	'	a	b	c
10	d	e	f	g	h	i	j	k	l	m
11	n	o	p	q	r	s	t	u	v	w
12	x	y	z	{	|	}	~	del		

The digits at the left of the table are the left digits of the decimal equivalent (0-127) of the character code, and the digits at the top of the table are the right digits of the character code. For example, the character code for 'F' is 70, and the character code for '&' is 38.

More Information
Most users of this book are interested in the ASCII character set used to represent English characters on many computers. The ASCII character set is a subset of the Unicode character set used by Java to represent characters from most of the world's languages. For more information on the Unicode character set, visit the World Wide Web site **http://unicode.org**

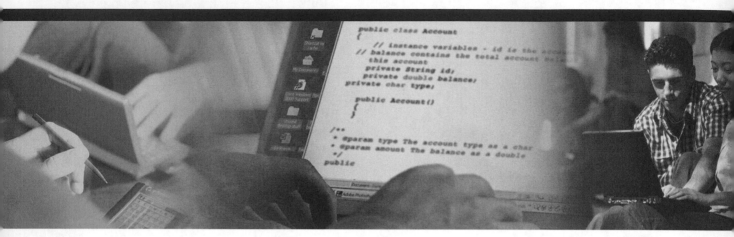

INDEX

Q-R